P9-EDM-605

THE
ANCESTRY FAMILY HISTORIAN'S
ADDRESS BOOK

THE ANCESTRY FAMILY HISTORIAN'S ADDRESS BOOK

A COMPREHENSIVE LIST OF
LOCAL, STATE, AND FEDERAL AGENCIES AND INSTITUTIONS,
AND ETHNIC AND GENEALOGICAL ORGANIZATIONS

by
Juliana Szucs Smith

Ancestry®

© 1997 Ancestry Incorporated
All rights reserved
Printed in the United States

No portion of this book may be reproduced in any form
without written permission from the publisher,
Ancestry Incorporated, P.O. Box 476, Salt Lake City, UT 84110-0476

Library of Congress Cataloging-in-Publication Data

Smith, Juliana Szucs, 1962-
The Ancestry family historian's address book: a comprehensive list of local, state, and federal agencies, and institutions, and ethnic, and genealogical organizations/by Juliana Szucs Smith.
p. cm.
ISBN 0-916489-74-4 (softcover)
I. Title
CS44.S65 1997
929'.1'02573—dc21 97-42618
CIP

ISBN 0-916489-74-4

10 9 8 7 6 5 4 3 2 1

www.ancestry.com

CONTENTS

GENERAL RESOURCES

STATE ADDRESSES

PREFACE

Information in this work has been gathered directly from the archives, libraries, government offices, genealogical societies, and other agencies listed wherever possible. In an attempt to make this the most complete collection possible of addresses for family and local historians, and in order to include even the more obscure addresses, a number of credible reference sources were consulted. Over a period of eight months, many sources were verified with individual sites on the Internet as well. Time-consuming as this process was, it was worthwhile and an education in itself. In many instances there were conflicting addresses. Occasionally, addresses listed in literature published by the institutions themselves were not the same as the addresses that were posted on their Web pages; this was definitely the most frustrating part of the project. Hopefully, the result will make your work easier. Full street addresses, telephone and fax numbers, and Internet addresses (where applicable) should make it easy for you to contact Federal, state, and local sources, as well as large and small genealogical societies.

Despite every effort to enter addresses correctly, changes will occur. Offices and societies move, and area codes and ZIP codes change. Inadvertent omission is a possibility as well; we sincerely hope that we have not left out your society or favorite place to do research. Please contact Ancestry with any changes or corrections so that they can be included in future editions of this work. Meanwhile, for your convenience, some blank pages have been added at the back of this book so that you can make notes and corrections, and add newly discovered sources.

While many of the organizations and agencies listed here can be found through their Websites, the need still exists for a conventional, easy-to-use-everywhere address book with postal addresses and telephone numbers; not everyone wants to rely on a computer to look up an address.

When I started this project, I thought it would be useful to include the operating hours of the resources listed. After consulting with various organizations, libraries, and archives, and after visiting site after site on the Internet, however, I realized that hours of operation are often seasonal and are subject to change. I reasoned that it is far better to include telephone numbers, postal addresses, and Web addresses so that you can call or write or visit the Website before you make a trip. A word of advice: always find out what your options are before you plan a trip to any of these places. Sometimes local holidays, renovations, or other temporary problems cause unexpected closures, schedule adjustments, or affect the availability of collections. It is also wise to find out what the collections include and to make sure that the collection is relevant to your research.

The Internet is an especially useful tool for planning research. Websites usually provide a description of the particular source of interest and of the access policy, up-to-date news about the collection, and notices about exhibits, conferences, and meetings. Some of these sites even have searchable databases that provide details and enable researchers to work from the comfort of their own homes. In some cases, you can obtain specific information by submitting an e-mail request; some states allow you to get vital records that way. If you have a computer and a modem, mailing lists are a great way to find other people with similar research interests. (In the section titled "Helpful Websites for the Genealogist," I have included several Websites which contain lists of mailing lists and instructions on how to subscribe to them.) The people I have communicated with in the course of this project have been very generous. The chances are good that you will be able to find someone who can provide the missing pieces to your research problem.

If you don't have a computer of your own, you can still enjoy this new technology. Many libraries have computers available for public use and some even offer classes in the use of these valuable tools.

The information in this book is divided into chapters by state. A separate chapter for "General Resources" contains some ethnic and religious societies and libraries. The individual state chapters include the following sections:

- State and National Archives
- Genealogical Societies
- Historical Societies
- Family History Centers of The Church of Jesus Christ of Latter-day Saints
- Archives/Libraries/Museums
- Major Newspaper Repositories
- Vital Records
- [State] on the Web (a list of particularly helpful or interesting Websites for each state)

The chapter on General Resources contains the following sections:

- National Societies
- National Archives/Libraries/Museums
- Military/Federal Government Agencies (includes National Archives)
- Ethnic /Ecclesiastical Societies, Resources, and Websites (both international and domestic in some cases)
- Helpful Websites for the Genealogist (includes some Search Engines and Directories)

I hope this book will prove to be a useful tool in your genealogical pursuits and that, if you are not already "online," it will inspire you to take a look at the wonderful things that are happening out there thanks to some very generous and dedicated people. I want to take this opportunity to thank those individuals; without their contributions, I would not have been able to compile this book.

Juliana Szucs Smith

ACKNOWLEDGMENTS

There are many people who made great contributions to this project. I sincerely appreciate all their help. I especially want to thank my family. My wonderful husband, Mark, introduced me to the Web and taught me how to make it work for me. He helped me with the research and encouraged me throughout a seemingly endless project. Mark also took on many extra household jobs, so that I could stay at the computer. He even put up with the astronomical phone bills that I incurred in doing research for this publication. Our beautiful one-and-a-half-year-old daughter, Madelon, helped me by playing alongside me at her own desk. She made me laugh and smile when I was discouraged during long days and nights of research and typing.

I am also eternally grateful to my mother, who suggested the project and put up with my phone calls and questions. Her expertise has been invaluable. My sister, Laura Pfeiffer, helped research several large states. My dad, my brother-in-law, John Sullivan, and our good friend Chris Hinson were my always-important "technical support and encouragement team." They upgraded, fixed, rehabilitated, and basically kept my computer up and running throughout this project and deserve special thanks. I also got a lot of moral support from my sisters and their families, and from my mother-in-law, Anne McWilliams. Last, but not least, I would like to thank Ancestry for giving me the opportunity to fulfill my dream of having a book published.

My thanks again to all.

National Societies

American Antiquarian Society
185 Salisbury Street
Worcester, MA 01609-1634
Tel: 508-755-5221
URL: gopher://mark.mwa.org/

American Association for State and Local History
530 Church Street, Suite 600
Nashville, TN 37219
Tel: 615-255-2971
Fax: 615-255-2979
URL: http://www.nashville.net/~aaslh/

American Genealogical Lending Library
Genealogical Services
P.O. Box 244
Bountiful, UT 84011
Tel: 801-298-5358
800-760-AGLL
Fax: 801-298-5468
URL: http://www.agll.com/

American Genealogical Society (AGS)
Depository and Headquarters
Samford University Library
Box 2296
800 Lakeshore Drive
Birmingham, AL 35229
Tel: 205-870-2749

American Historical Association (AHA)
400 A Street, SE
Washington, DC 20003-3889
Tel: 202-544-2422
Fax: 202-544-8307
Email: aha@theaha.org
URL: http://chnm.gmu.edu/chnm/aha//

Association for Professional Genealogists
P.O. Box 40393
Denver, CO 80204-0393
Email: apg-editor@apgen.org
URL: http://www.apgen.org/~apg/

Augustan Society, Inc.
1510 Cravens Avenue
Torrance, CA 90501

Board for Certification of Genealogists
P.O. Box 14291
Washington, DC 20044
URL: http://www.genealogy.org/~bcg/

Colonial Dames of America
Dumbarton Oaks Museum
2715 Q Street, NW
Washington, DC 20007
Tel: 202-337-2288

Daughters of American Colonists-National Society
2205 Massachusetts Avenue, NW
Washington, DC 20008

Daughters of the American Revolution, National Society
1776 D Street, NW
Washington, DC 20006-5303
Tel: 202-628-1776
Email: dar@chesapeake.net
URL: http://www.chesapeake.net/DAR/

Daughters of Union Veterans of the Civil War (DUV)
National Headquarters, DUV Registrar's Office
503 South Walnut Street
Springfield, IL 62704
Tel: 217-544-0616
Email: DUVCW@aol.com
URL: http://suvcw.org/duv/

Descendants of the Signers of the Constitution, Society of
325 Chestnut Street
Philadelphia, PA 19106

Federation of Genealogical Societies
P.O. Box 830220
Richardson, TX 75083-0220
Tel/Fax: 972-907-9727
Email: fgs-office@fgs.org
URL: http://www.fgs.org/~fgs/

GENTECH
P.O. Box 28021
Dallas, TX 75228-0021
Tel/Fax: 972-495-1569
URL: http://www.genealogy.org/~gentech/welcome.html

Genealogical Society of Mayflower Descendants
P.O. Box 3297
Plymouth, MA 02361
URL (Unofficial Site):
http://members.aol.com/calebj/mayflower.html

General Society of the War of 1812
P.O. Box 106
Mendenhall, PA 19357
Tel: 215-388-6015

Grand Army of the Republic
Grand Army of the Republic Memorial Museum
78 East Washington Street
Chicago, IL 60602
Tel: 312-269-2926
URL: http://suvcw.org/gar.htm

Huguenot Society of America/Library
122 East 58th Street
New York, NY 10022
Tel: 212-755-0592

Immigrant Genealogical Society
1310-B Magnolia Blvd.
P.O. Box 7369
Burbank, CA 91510
Tel: 818-848-3122
Fax: 818-716-6300
Email: ted.hanft@panasia.com
URL: http://feefhs.org/igs/frg-igs.html

Immigration History Society
University of Cincinnati
3410 Bishop Street
Cincinnati, OH 45220
Tel: 513-861-7462
Fax: 513-556-7901
Email: alexanje@ucbeh.san.uc.edu

Ladies of the Grand Army of the Republic
c/o Elizabeth Koch, National Secretary
119 N. Swarthmore Avenue, Apt. 1-H
Ridley Park, PA 19078
URL: http://suvcw.org/lgar.htm

National Genealogical Society/Library
4527 Seventeenth Street, North
Arlington, VA 22207-2363
Tel: 703-525-0050
703-841-9065 (Library)
Fax: 703-525-0052
Email: 76702.2417@compuserve.com
Library Email: ngslibe@wizard.net
URL: http://www.genealogy.org/~ngs/

National Historical Society
6405 Flank Drive
Harrisburg, PA 17112
Tel: 717-657-9555

National Huguenot Society
9033 Lyndale Avenue, S. - Suite 18
Bloomington, MN 55420
Tel: 612-893-9747

National Institute on Genealogical Research
Drawer HP, P.O. Box 14274
Washington, DC 20044-4274
URL: http://www.genealogy.org/~nigr

National Maritime Historical Society
5 John Walsh Blvd.
Peekskill, NY 10566
Tel: 914-737-7878
Email: nmhs@marineart.com
URL: http://www.marineart.com/nmhs/

National Railway Historical Society
100 N. 17th Street
Philadelphia, PA 19102
Tel: 215-557-6606

New England Historical and Genealogical Society (NEHGS)
7101 Newbury Street
Boston, MA 02116-3007
Tel: 617-836-5740
888-AT-NEHGS (Membership & Education)
888-BY-NEHGS (Sales)
888-90-NEHGS (Library Circulation)
Fax: 617-536-7307
Email: nehgs@nehgs.org
URL: http://www.nehgs.org/

Order of Descendants of Ancient Planters
http://tyner.simplenet.com/PLANTERS.HTM

Oregon-California Trails Association
P.O. Box 1019
Independence, MO 64051-0519
Tel: 816-252-2276
Fax: 816-836-0919
URL: http://bobcat.etsu.edu/octa/octahome.htm

Pilgrim Society
Pilgrim Hall Museum
75 Court Street
Plymouth, MA 02360
Tel: 508-746-1620

Society of American Archivists
600 S. Federal, Suite 504
Chicago, IL 60605
Tel: 312-922-0140
Email: sfox@archivists.org
URL: http://www.archivists.org

Sons and Daughters of the Pilgrims, National Society
c/o Arthur Louis Finnell
3917 Heritage Hills Drive, #104
Bloomington, MN 55437
Tel: 612-893-9747
Email: ALFINNELL@compuserve.com
URL: http://members.tripod.com/~NSSDP/

Sons of the American Revolution, National Society
1000 South Fourth Street
Louisville, KY 40203
Tel: 502-589-1776
URL: http://www.sar.org/

Sons of Confederate Veterans
URL: http://scv.org

Sons of Union Veterans of the Civil War
411 Bartlett Street
Lansing, MI 48915
URL: http://sucvcw.org/

United Daughters of the Confederacy (UDC)
UDC Memorial Building
328 North Boulevard
Richmond, VA 23220-4057
Tel: 804-355-1636
Fax: 804-355-1396
Email: hqudc@aol.com
URL: http://www.hsv.tis.net/~maxs/UDC/

ARCHIVES, LIBRARIES & MUSEUMS

Allen County Public Library
900 Webster Street
Fort Wayne, IN 46802
Tel: 219-424-7241
URL: http://www.acpl.lib.in.us/

American Genealogical Lending Library
P.O. Box 244
Bountiful, UT 84011
Tel: 801-298-5358
800-760-AGLL
Fax: 801-298-5468
URL: http://www.agll.com/

Balch Institute for Ethnic Studies
Center for Immigrant Research
18 South 7th Street
Philadelphia, PA 19106-3794
Tel: 215-925-8090
Email: BALCHLIB@HSLC.ORG
URL: http://www.libertynet.org/~balch/

Civil War Library and Museum
1805 Pine Street
Philadelphia, PA 19103
Tel: 215-735-8196
URL: http://www.libertynet.org/~cwlm/

Cleveland Public Library
325 Superior Avenue
Cleveland, OH 44114-1271
Tel: 216-623-2800
Fax: 216-623-7015
Email: info@library.cpl.org
URL: http://www.cpl.org/

Daughters of the American Revolution, National Society
1776 D Street, NW
Washington, DC 20006-5303
Tel: 202-628-1776
Email: dar@chesapeake.net
URL: http://www.chesapeake.net/DAR/

David Library of the American Revolution
1201 River Road
P.O. Box 748
Washington Crossing, PA 18977
Tel: 215-493-6776
Fax: 215-493-9276
Email: dlar@libertynet.org
URL: http://www.libertynet.org/~dlar/dlar.html

Denver Public Library
Genealogy Division
1357 Broadway
Denver, CO 80203-2165
Tel: 303-571-2190
303-571-2171
303-571-2009

Detroit Public Library
Burton Historical Collection
5201 Woodward Avenue
Detroit, MI 48202
Tel: 313-833-1480
Fax: 313-832-0877
Email: nvangor@cms.cc.wayne.edu
URL: http://www.detroit.lib.mi.us/special_collections.htm

Ellis Island Immigration Museum
American Family Immigration History Center
Liberty Island
New York, NY 10004
Tel: 212-363-3200
212-269-5755 (Circle Line Ferry for schedules/rates)
URL: http://www.ellisisland.org/

Family History Library
Church of Jesus Christ of Latter-Day Saints
35 North West Temple
Salt Lake City, UT 84150
Tel: 801-240-2331
Some Unofficial Sites:
URL: http://bobcat.etsu.edu/ftpdir/genealogy/LDStext/ut08456.txt
http://www.genealogy.org/~uvpafug/fhlslc.html
http://www.aros.net/~drwaff/slcfhl.htm
http://http.tamu.edu:8000/~mbg5500/genealogy/lds_gen_info.html

Genealogical Center Library (operates by mail)
P.O. Box 71343
Marietta, GA 30007-1343

Grand Army of the Republic War Museum/Ruan House Library
4278 Griscom Street
Philadelphia, PA 19124-3954
Tel: 215-289-6484
Email: GARMUSLIB@aol.com
URL: http://suvcw.org/garmus.htm

Historical Trails Library
Route 1, Box 373
Philadelphia, MS 39350
Tel: 601-656-3506

Immigration History Research Center
University of Minnesota
826 Berry Street
Saint Paul, MN 55114
Tel: 612-627-4208
Fax: 612-627-4190
Email: ihrc@gold.tc.umn.edu
URL: http://www.umn.edu/ihrc/

Leo Baeck Institute
German-Jewish Families
129 East 73rd Street
New York, NY 10021
Tel: 212-744-6400
URL: http://www.users.interport.net/~lbi1/

Library of Congress
Local History & Genealogy Divison
101 Independence Avenue, SE
Washington, DC 20540
Email: lcweb@loc.gov
URL: http://lcweb.loc.gov/

Los Angeles Public Library
History & Genealogy Department
630 West 5th Street, LL4
Los Angeles, CA 90071
Tel: 213-228-7400
Fax: 213-228-7409
Email: history@lapl.org
URL: http://www.lapl.org/central/hihp.html

Mid-Continent Public Library
Genealogy and Local History Department
317 West 24 Highway
Independence, MO 64050
Tel: 816-252-0950
Email: ge@mcpl.lib.mo.us
URL: http://www.mcpl.lib.mo.us/gen.htm

National Genealogical Society/Library
4527 Seventeenth Street, North
Arlington, VA 22207-2363
Tel: 703-525-0050
703-841-9065 (Library)
Fax: 703-525-0052
Email: 76702.2417@compuserve.com
Library Email: ngslibe@wizard.net
URL: http://www.genealogy.org/~ngs/

New England Historical and Genealogical Society (NEHGS)
101 Newbury Street
Boston, MA 02116-3007
Tel: 617-836-5740
888-AT-NEHGS (Membership & Education)
888-BY-NEHGS (Sales)
888-90-NEHGS (Library Circulation)
Fax: 617-536-7307
Email: nehgs@nehgs.org
URL: http://www.nehgs.org/

New York Public Library
U.S. History, Local History, and Genealogy Resources
5th Avenue and 42nd Street, Room 315S
New York, NY 10016
Tel: 212-340-0849
URL: http://www.nypl.org/research/chss/lhg/genea.html

Newberry Library
60 West Walton Street
Chicago, IL 60610-3305
Tel: 312-943-9090 (Main)
312-255-3506 (Reference)
312-255-3512 (Genealogy)
Email: furmans@newberry.org
URL: http://www.newberry.org/

St. Louis Public Library
1301 Olive Street
St. Louis, MO 63103
Tel: 314-241-2288
Fax: 314-539-0393
TDD: 314-539-0364
Email: webmaster@slpl.lib.mo.us
URL: http://www.slpl.lib.mo.us/

Seattle Public Library
Humanities Department
1000 4th Avenue
Seattle, WA 98104
Tel: 206-386-4625
206-386-4640
URL: http://www.spl.lib.wa.us/contents.html

Smithsonian Institute
1000 Jefferson Drive
Washington, DC 20560
Tel: 202-357-2700
TTY: 202-357-1729
URL: http://www.si.edu/

Sutro Library
480 Winston Drive
San Francisco, CA 94132
Tel: 415-731-4477
URL: http://sfpl.lib.ca.us/gencoll/gencolsu.htm
MELVYL Catalog URL: http://www.dla.ucop.edu/

United States Civil War Center
Louisiana State University
Baton Rouge, LA 70803
Tel: 504-388-3151
Fax: 504-388-4876
URL: http://www.cwc.lsu.edu/

United States Holocaust Memorial Museum
100 Rauol Wallenberg Place, SW
Washington, DC 20024-2150
Tel: 202-488-0400
Email: research@ushmm.org
archive@ushmm.org
UEL: http://www.ushmm.org/

Western Reserve Historical Society
Case Western Reserve University
History Library
10825 East Boulevard
Cleveland, OH 44106
Tel: 216-721-5722
URL: http://www.cwru.edu/CWRU/buildings/cultural/historical_society_annex.html

Wisconsin, State Historical Society of
816 State Street
Madison, WI 53706
Tel: 608-264-6534
608-264-6535 (Reference)
608-264-6525 (Government Publications Reference)
URL: http://www.shsw.wisc.edu/

ETHNIC & ECCLESIASTICAL RESOURCES AND WEBSITES

ACADIAN/CAJUN/CREOLE

Acadian Cultural Society Page de la Maison
P.O. Box 2304
Fitchburg, MA 01460-8804
Email: r-m-s-frazier@worldnet.att.net
URL: http://www.angelfire.com/ma/1755/index.html

Action Cadienne (Cajun Action)
P.O. Box 30104
Lafayette, LA 70593
URL: http://www.rbmulti.nb.ca/cadienne/cadienne.htm

Creole-American Genealogical Society, Inc.
P.O. Box 2666, Church Street Station
New York, NY 10008

WEBSITES:

Acadian Genealogy Homepage
http://www.freespace.net/~cajun/genealogy/

Genealogy of Acadia
http://www.cam.org/~beaur/gen/acadie-e.html

AFRICAN AMERICAN

African-American Cultural & Genealogical Society
314 North Main Street
P.O. Box 25251
Decatur, IL 62525
Tel: 217-429-7458
URL: http://www.decaturnet.org/afrigenes.html

African-American Genealogy Group (AAGG)
P.O. Box 1798
Philadelphia, PA 19105-1798
Tel: 215-572-6063
Fax: 215-885-7244
URL: http://www.libertynet.org/~gencap/aagg.html

Afro American Historical & Cultural Museum
7th and Arch Streets
Philadelphia, PA 19106
Tel: 215-574-0380
URL: http://www.fieldtrip.com/pa/55740380.htm

Afro-American Historical and Genealogical Society
P.O. Box 73086
Washington, DC 20056

Association for the Study of Afro-American Life and History
1407 14th Street, NW
Washington, DC 20005
Tel: 202-667-2822
Fax: 202-387-9802

WEBSITES:

Afrigeneas Homepage
http://www.msstate.edu/Archives/History/afrigen/index.html

Afrikaans-English Online Dictionary
http://dictionaries.travlang.org/AfrikaansEnglish/

Christine's Genealogy Website
http://ccharity.com/

ASIAN

Chinese Historical Society of America
650 Commercial Street
San Francisco, CA 94111
Tel: 415-391-1188

Filipino-American Historical Society
5462 S. Dorchester Avenue
Chicago, IL 60615-5309
Tel: 773-752-2156

Japanese American History Archives
1840 Sutter Street
San Francisco, CA 94115
Tel: 415-776-0661
URL: http://www.e-media.com/fillmore/museum/jt/jaha/jaha.html

Morikami Museum and Japanese Gardens
4000 Morikami Park Rd.
Delray Beach, FL 33446
Tel: 407-495-0233

Pacific Asia Museum
46 North Los Robles Avenue
Pasadena, CA 91101
Tel: 818-449-2742

AUSTRALIAN

Australian Institute of Genealogical Studies
P.O. Box 339
Blackburn, Victoria, 3130
Australia
Tel: (61 3) 9887 3789
Fax: (61 3) 9887 9066
URL: http://www.cohsoft.com.au/afhc/aigs.html

Military Historical Society of Australia
P.O. Box 30
Garran, ACT 2605
Australia
Email: astaunto@pcug.org.au
URL: http://www.pcug.org.au/~astaunto/mhsa.htm

WEBSITES:

Australian Archives
http://www.aa.gov.au/

Australian Family History Compendium
http://www.cohsoft.com.au/afhc/

Genealogy in Australia
(Sponsored by the Canberra Dead Persons Society)
http://www.pcug.org.au/~mpahlow/welcome.html

BAPTIST

American Baptist Historical Society
Samuel Colgate Historical Library
1106 South Goodman Street
Rochester, NY 14620-2532
Tel: 716-473-1740

North American Baptists Archives
1605 Euclid Avenue
Sioux Falls, SD 57105
Tel: 605-336-6588

BELGIAN/DUTCH

Belgian American Heritage Association (BAHA)
62073 Fruitdale Lane
LaGrande, OR 97850

Holland Library
Market Street
Alexandria Bay, NY 13607
Tel: 315-482-2241

Holland Society of New York
122 E. 58th Street
New York, NY 10022
Tel: 212-758-1875

WEBSITES:

Dutch-English Online Dictionary
http://dictionaries.travlang.org/DutchEnglish/

Genealogy in Belgium (Flanders)
http://win-www.uia.ac.be/u/pavp/index.html

Genealogy in Belgium (French)
http://www.cam.org/~beaur/gen/belgiq-f.html

Yvette's Dutch Genealogy Homepage
http://wwwedu.cs.utwente.nl/~hoitink/genealogy.html

CANADIAN

American-Canadian Genealogical Society (ACGS)
4 Elm Street
P.O. Box 6478
Manchester, NH 03108
Email: 102475.2260@compuserve.com
URL: http://ourworld.compuserve.com/homepages/ACGS/homepage.htm

National Archives of Canada
Genealogy Reference Services
395 Wellington Street
Ottawa, Ontario KLA ON3
Tel: 613-996-7458
Fax: 613-996-6274
URL: http://www.archives.ca/

WEBSITES:

Canadian Genealogy Resources
http://www.iosphere.net/~jholwell/cangene/gene.html

Sources in Canada by National Archives of Canada,
Genealogical Reference Services
http://www.archives.ca/www/GenealogicalSources.html

CATHOLIC

American Catholic Historical Association
Catholic University of America
Mullen Library, Room 318
Washington, DC 20064
Tel: 202-319-5079

Archdiocese for the Military Services
924 Wayne Avenue
Silver Springs, MD 20910
Tel: 301-495-4100

U.S. Roman Catholic Historical Society
The Catholic Center
1011 First Avenue
New York, NY 10022
Tel: 800-225-7999
Email: UPTA57A@prodigy.com
URL: http://www.catholic.org/uschs/

CHRISTIAN

Congregational Christian Historical Society
14 Beacon Street
Boston, MA 02108

CHURCH OF JESUS CHRIST OF LATTER-DAY SAINTS

Family History Library
Church of Jesus Christ of Latter-Day Saints
35 North West Temple
Salt Lake City, UT 84150
Tel: 801-240-2331
Some Unofficial Sites:
URL: http://bobcat.etsu.edu/ftpdir/genealogy/LDStext/ut-08456.txt
http://www.genealogy.org/~uvpafug/fhlslc.html
http://www.aros.net/~drwaff/slcfhl.htm
http://http.tamu.edu:8000/~mbg5500/genealogy/lds_gen_info.html
(See State Listings for Family History Centers)

Mormon History Association
2470 North 1000 West
Layton, UT 84041
Tel: 801-773-4620
Fax: 801-779-1348
Email: valh15a@prodigy.com

EASTERN EUROPEAN

(See Also German)

American Hungarian Historical Society/Library
215 East 82nd Street
New York, NY 10028
Tel: 212-744-5298

Archives of the Moravian Church
41 W. Locust Street
Bethlehem, PA 18018
Tel: 610-866-3255

Carpatho/Rusyn Society
125 Westland Drive
Pittsburgh, PA 15217
Email: ggressa@carpatho-rusyn.org
URL: http://www.carpatho-rusyn.org/

Croatian Ethnic Institute
4851 South Drexel Blvd.
Chicago, IL 60615
Tel: 773-373-2248

Croatian Heritage Museum & Library
34900 Lake Shore Blvd.
Willoughby, OH 44095-2043
Tel: 216-946-2044

Czech Heritage Preservation Society
P.O. Box 3
Tabor, SD 57063

Czechoslovak Genealogical Society Intl., Inc.
P.O. Box 16225
St. Paul, MN 55116-0225
Email: cgsi@aol.com
URL: http://members.aol.com/cgsi/index.html

Federation of East European Family History Societies (FEEFHS)
P.O. Box 510898
Salt Lake City, UT 94151-0898
Email: feefhs@feefhs.org
URL: http://feefhs.org/masteri.html

Hungarian-American Friendship Society
2701 Corabel Lane #34
Sacramento, CA 95821-5233
Tel: 916-489-9599
Email: HAFS@dholmes.com
URL: http://www.dholmes.com/hafs.html

Hungarian Genealogical Society
124 Esther Street
Toledo, OH 43605-1435

Lithuanian American Genealogical Society
c/o Balzekas Museum of Lithuanian Culture
6500 South Pulaski Road
Chicago, IL 60629-5136
Tel: 773-582-6500

Moravian Historical Society
214 E. Center Street
Nazareth, PA 18064
Tel: 610-759-5070

Polish American Cultural Center
308 Walnut Street
Philadelphia, PA 19106
Tel: 215-922-1700

Polish American Museum
16 Bellview Avenue
Port Washington, NY 11050
Tel: 516-883-6542
URL: http://www.liglobal.com/t_i/attractions/museums/polish/

Polish Genealogical Society of America
Polish Museum of America
984 North Milwaukee Avenue
Chicago, IL 60622
Tel: 773-384-3352
URL: http://www.pgsa.org/

Polish Museum of America
984 North Milwaukee Avenue
Chicago, IL 60622-4101
Tel: 312-384-3352

Slovenian Genealogy Society
c/o Al Peterlin, Pres.
52 Old Farm Road
Harrisburg, PA 17011-2604
Tel: 717-731-8804
URL: http://feefhs.org/slovenia/frg-sgsi.html

Ukrainian Fraternal Association
440 Wyoming Avenue
Scranton, PA 18503
Tel: 717-342-0937

Ukrainian Museum/Archives
1202 Kenilworth Avenue
Cleveland, OH 44113-4417
Tel: 216-781-4329

Ukrainian National Museum
2453 West Chicago Avenue
Chicago, IL 60622-4633
Tel: 773-276-6565

WEBSITES:

Alex Glendinning's Hungarian Pages
http://user.itl.net/~glen/Hungarianintro.html

Eastern Slovakia, Slovak, and Carpatho-Rusyn Genealogy Resources
http://www.iarelative.com/slovakia.htm

Hungarian-English Online Dictionary
http://www.sztaki.hu/services/dictionary/index.html

Radio Prague History Online
http://www.radio.cz/history/

Slovakia Home Page
http://www.tuzvo.sk/homepage.html

EPISCOPAL

Episcopal Church Home Archives
505 Mount Hope Avenue
Rochester, NY 14620
Tel: 716-546-8400
Fax: 716-325-6553

WEBSITES:

Dioceses of the Episcopal Church
http://www.aescon.com/episcopal/diocese.htm

FRENCH

(See also Acadian)

American-French Genealogical Society
(Library at the First Universalist Church
78 Earle Street
Woonsocket, RI 02895
P.O. Box 2113
Pawtucket, RI 02861
Tel/Fax: 401-765-6141
Email: afgs@ids.net
URL: http://users.ids.net/~afgs/afgshome.html

WEBSITES:

French-English Online Dictionary
http://dictionaries.travlang.com/FrenchEnglish/

GERMAN

American Historical Society of Germans from Russia
631 D Street
Lincoln, NE 68502-1199
Tel: 402-474-3363
Fax: 402-474-7229
Email: ahsgr@aol.com
URL: http://www.teleport.com/nonprofit/ahsgr/

Anglo-German Family History Society
14 River Reach
Teddington, Middlesex
England, UK TW11 9QL
URL: http://feefhs.org/uk/frgagfhs.html

Bukovina Society of the Americas/Museum
722 Washington
P.O. Box 81
Ellis, KS 67637
Tel: 913-625-9492
913-726-4568

Email: owindholz@juno.com
URL: http://members.aol.com/LJensen/bukovina.html

Federation of East European Family History Societies (FEEFHS)
P.O. Box 510898
Salt Lake City, UT 94151-0898
Email: feefhs@feefhs.org
URL: http://feefhs.org/masteri.html

German-American Heritage Institute
7824 West Madison Street
Forest Park, IL 60130-1485
Tel: 708-366-0017

German-Bohemian Heritage Society
P.O. Box 822
New Ulm, MN 56073
Email: lalgbhs.@newulmtel.net
URL: http://www.qrz.com/gene/reg/SUD/sudet_GBHS.html

Germans from Russia Heritage Society
1008 East Central Avenue
Bismarck, ND 58501
Tel: 701-223-6167
Email: grhs@btigate.com
URL: http://www.teleport.com/nonprofit/grhs

Gluckstal Colonies Research Association
611 Esplanade
Redondo Beach, CA 90277-4130
Tel: 310-540-1872
Email: gcra31@aol.com
URL: http://www.dcn.davis.ca.us/feefhs/FRGGCRA/gcra.html

Palatines to America Society
Capital University, Box 101
Columbus, OH 43209-2394
Email: pal-am@juno.com
URL: http://genealogy.org/~palam/

WEBSITES:

Archives in Germany
http://www.bawue.de/~hanacek/info/earchive.htm

German and American Sources for German Emigration to America
by Michael P. Palmer
http://www.genealogy.com/gene/www/emig/emigrati.htm

German-English Online Dictionary
http://dictionaries.travlang.com/GermanEnglish/

German Genealogy Home Page
URL: http://www.genealogy.com/gene/

Internet Sources of German Genealogy
http://www.bawue.de/~hanacek/info/edatbase.htm

ODESSA...A German-Russian Genealogical Library
http://pixel.cs.vt.edu/library/odessa.html

Palatines to America: Immigrant Ancestor Register Index
http://genealogy.org/~palam/ia_index.htm

GREEK

Greek Family Heritage Committee
75-21 177th Street
Flushing, NY 11366
Tel: 718-591-9342

HISPANIC

American Portugese Genealogical & Historical Society, Inc.
P.O. Box 644
Taunton, MA 02780-0644

Hispanic Genealogical Research Center-New Mexico
1331 Juan Tabo, NE
Suite P, No. 18
Albuquerque, NM 87112
Tel: 505-836-5438
Email: HGRC@HGRC-NM.ORG
URL: http://www.hgrc-nm.org/

Portugese Genealogical Society of Hawaii
810 North Vineyard Blvd., Room 11
Honolulu, HI 96817
Tel: 808-841-5044
Email: chism@hi.net
URL: http://www.lusaweb.com/pgsh.htm

Puerto Rican/Hispanic Genealogical Society
25 Ralph Avenue
Brentwood, NY 11717-2421
Tel: 516-834-2511
Email: prgen@aol.com
URL: http://www.linkdirect.com/hispsoc/

Society of Hispanic Historical and Ancestral Research
P.O. Box 490
Midway City, CA 92655-0490
Email: shharnet@webcom.com
URL: http://www.webcom.com/shharnet/

WEBSITES:

Basque Genealogy Homepage
http://www.concentric.net/~Fybarra/

Compuserve's Hispanic Genealogy
http://ourworld.compuserve.com/hompages/Alfred_Sosa/

Cuban Genealogy Resources
http://ourworld.compuserve.com/homepages/ee/
Hispanic Heraldry
http://www.ctv.es/artes/home.htm/home.html

Spanish-English Online Dictionary
http://dictionary.travlang.org/SpanishEnglish/

HUGUENOT

Huguenot Historical Society
P.O. Box 339
New Paltz, NY 12561
Tel: 914-255-1660
Email: Huguenothistoricalsociety@worldnet.att.net
URL: http://home.earthlink.net/~rctwig/hhs1.htm

Huguenot Society of America/Library
122 East 58th Street
New York, NY 10022
Tel: 212-755-0592

National Huguenot Society
9033 Lyndale Avenue, S. - Suite 18
Bloomington, MN 55420
Tel: 612-893-9747

WEBSITES:

Huguenots
http://www.geocities.com/SoHo/3809/Huguen.htm

HUNGARIAN
(See Eastern European)

IRISH
(See United Kingdom)

ITALIAN

Italian Cultural Center
1621 North 39th Avenue
Stone Park, IL 60165-1105
Tel: 630-345-3842

Italian Genealogical Group, Inc.
7 Grayon Drive
Dix Hills, NY 11746
Fax: 516-499-5524
Email: jdelalio@aol.com
URL: http://www.fgs.org/~fgs/soc0091.htm

Italian Genealogy Society of America
P.O. Box 8571
Cranston, RI 02920-8571

Italian Historical Society of America
111 Columbia Hts
Brooklyn, NY 11201
Tel: 718-852-2929

WEBSITES:

Italian Genealogy Homepage
http://www.italgen.com/

Italian Surname Database
http://www.italgen.com/surnames.htm

JEWISH

American Jewish Archives
Hebrew Union College/Jewish Institute of Religion
3101 Clifton Avenue
Cincinnati, OH 45220-2488
Tel: 513-221-7444 ext. 403
Fax: 513-221-7812
Email: AJA@fuse.net
URL: http://home.fuse.net/aja/

American Jewish Historical Society
2 Thornton Road
Waltham, MA 02154
Tel: 617-891-8110
Fax: 617-899-9208
URL: http://www.ajhs.org/

Annenberg Research Institute
420 Walnut Street
Philadelphia, PA 19106
Tel: 215-238-1290
Fax: 215-238-1540
URL: http://libertynet.org/~gencap/ari.html

Association of Jewish Genealogical Society (AJGS)
P.O. Box 50245
Palo Alto, CA 94303
Tel: 415-424-1622
Email: RWeissJGS@aol.com
URL: http://www1.jewishgen.org/ajgs/index.html

Holocaust Library & Research Center
557 Bedford Avenue
Brooklyn, NY 11211
Tel: 718-599-5833

Jewish Genealogical Society, Inc.
P.O. Box 6398
New York, NY 10128
Tel: 212-330-8257
URL: http://www.fgs.org/~fgs/soc0096.htm

Institute for Jewish Research
1048 Fifth Avenue
New York, NY 10028

Leo Baeck Institute
German-Jewish Families
129 East 73rd Street
New York, NY 10021
Tel: 212-744-6400

National Museum of American Jewish History
55 North 5th Street
Philadelphia, PA 19123
Tel: 215-923-3811

Philadelphia Jewish Archives Center
Balch Institute for Ethnic Studies
18 South 7th Street
Philadelphia, PA 19106-3794
Tel: 215-925-8090
Email: BALCHLIB@HSLC.ORG
URL: http://www.libertynet.org/~balch/

Schomburg Center for Research/Branch New York Public Library
515 Malcolm X Blvd.
New York, NY 10037-1801
Tel: 212-491-2200
URL: http://www.nypl.org/research/sc/sc.html

Yivo Institute for Jewish Research
555 West 57th Street (Temporary Location)
New York, NY 10019
or
15 West 16th Street (Sometime in 1997)
New York, NY 10011
URL: http://spanky.osc.cuny.edu/~rich/yivo/

WEBSITES:

Jewish Resources on the Internet
http://www.opus1.com/emol/tucson/directory/jewish.html

JewishGen
http://www.jewishgen.org

LUTHERAN AND EVANGELICAL

Archdiocese of the Evangelical Lutheran Church in America
5400 Milton Parkway
Rosemont, IL
Mail:
8765 W. Higgins Road
Chicago, IL 60631
Tel: 800-638-3522
773-380-2818
Fax: 773-380-2977
Email: archives@elca.org
URL: http://www.elca.org/os/archives/intro.html

Evangelical Covenant Church of America
Archives & Historical Library
125 N. Spaulding Avenue, Rm. 25
Chicago, IL 60637
Tel: 773-583-2700 ext. 287

Evangelical & Reformed Church, Historical Society of
Archives
West James Street and College Avenue
Lancaster, PA 17604
Tel: 717-393-0654

Lutheran Church in American Archives
1100 East 55th Street
Chicago, IL 60615
Tel: 773-667-3500

MENNONITE

Mennonite Family History Library
10 W. Main Street
Elverson, PA 19520-0171
Tel: 610-286-0258
Fax: 610-286-6860
URL: http://feefhs.org/men/frg-mfh.html

Mennonite Heritage Center
565 Yoder Road
P.O. Box 82
Harleysville, PA 19438
Tel: 215-256-3020
Fax: 215-256-3023
Email: mennhist@pond.com
URL: http://www.pond.com/~mennhist/

METHODIST

Methodist Historical Center
326 New Street
Philadelphia, PA 19106

United Methodist Archives Center
Drew University
GCAH
P.O. Box 127
Madison, NJ 07940
Tel: 201-408-3189
Email: dpatters@drew.edu
URL: http://www.drew.edu/infosys/library/uma.html

NATIVE AMERICAN

Anchorage Museum of History & Art
121 West 7th Avenue
P.O. Box 196650
Anchorage, AK 99519-6650
Tel: 907-343-4326
Fax: 907-343-6149
URL: http://www.ci.anchorage.ak.us/Services/Departments/Culture/Museum/index.html

Baranov Museum
Kodiak Historical Society
101 Marine Way
Kodiak, AK 99615
Tel: 907-486-5920
Fax: 907-486-3166

Bishop Museum and Library/Archives
1525 Bernice Street
P.O. Box 19000-A
Honolulu, HI 96817-0916
Tel: 808-848-4147/8
808-848-4182/3
Fax: 808-841-8968
URL: http://www.bishop.hawaii.org/bishop/library/library.html
http://www.bishop.hawaii.org/bishop/archives/arch.html

Bureau of Indian Affairs
U.S. Department of the Interior
Office of Public Affairs
1849 C Street, NW
Washington, DC 20240-0001
Tel: 202-208-3711
Fax: 202-501-1516
URL: http://www.doi.gov/bureau-indian-affairs.html
Genealogy Resources
URL: http://www.doi.gov/bia/ancestry/genealog.html

Dacotah Prairie Museum
21 S. Main
Aberdeen, SD 57401
Tel: 605-626-7117
Fax: 605-626-4010

Daughters of Hawaii
Queen Emma's Summer Palace
2913 Pali Highway
Honolulu, HI 96817
Tel: 808-595-6291
808-595-3167
Fax: 808-595-4395

Mescalero Apache Cultural Center
P.O. Box 176
Mescalero, NM 88340
Tel: 505-671-4494

Native American Heritage Museum at Highland Mission
Route 1
P.O. Box 152C
Highland, KS 66035
Tel: 913-442-3304
URL: http://kuhttp.cc.ukans.edu/heritage/kshs/places/highland.htm

Pueblo Cultural Center
2401 12th Street, NW
Albuquerque, NM 87192
Tel: 505-843-7270
800-766-4406
Fax: 505-842-6959
URL: http://hanksville.phast.umass.edu/defs/independent/PCC/PCC.html

Siouxland Heritage Museum
200 W. 6th Street
Sioux Falls, SD 57104-6001
Tel: 605-367-4210
Fax: 605-367-6004

Tanana-Yukon Historical Society
Wickersham House Museum
Alaskaland Park, Airport Way
P.O. Box 71336
Fairbanks, AK 99707
Tel: 907-474-4013
Email: tyhs@polarnet.com
URL: http://www2.polarnet.com/~tyhs/

Totem Heritage Center
601 Deermont Street
(Mailing Address: 629 Dock St.)
Ketchikan, AK 99901
Tel: 907-225-5900
Fax: 907-225-5602

Trading Post Historical Society/Museum
Trading Post, KS (mile post 96)
Route 2
P.O. Box 145A
Pleasanton, KS 66075
Tel: 913-352-6441

UCLA American Indian Studies Center
3220 Campbell Hall
Box 951548
Los Angeles, CA 90095-1548
Tel: 310-825-7315
Fax: 310-206-7060
Email: aisc@ucla.edu
URL: http://www.sscnet.ucla.edu/indian/CntrHome.html

Ute Mountain Ute Tribal Research Archives Library
Tribal Compound
Box CC
Towaoc, CO 81334
Tel: 303-565-3751 x257
Fax: 303-565-7412
URL: http://www.swcolo.org/Tourism/IndianCulture.html

Yupiit Piciryarait Cultural Center and Museum
420 Chief Eddie Hoffman State Highway
Mailing address:
AVCP, Inc.
P.O. Box 219
Bethel, AK 99559
Tel: 907-520-5312
Fax: 907-543-3596

WEBSITES:

Index of Native American Resources on the Internet
http://hanksville.phast.umass.edu/misc/NAresources.html

Native American Genealogy
http://members.aol.com/bbbenge/front.html

Native American Who's Hot
http://www.cris.com/~misterg/award/whoshot.shtml

NativeWeb
http://web.maxwell.syr.edu/nativeweb/index.html

POLISH
(See Eastern European)

POLYNESIAN

Polynesian Voyaging Society
1250 Lauhala Street, Apt. 314
Honolulu, HI 96813
Tel: 808-547-4172
Email: dennisk@hawaii.edu
URL: http://leahi.kcc.hawaii.edu/org/pvs/

PRESBYTERIAN

Presbyterian Historical Society
425 Lombard Street
Philadelphia, PA 19147
Tel: 215-627-1852
Fax: 215-627-0509
URL: http://www.libertynet.org/~gencap/presbyhs.html

QUAKER

National Society of Descendants of Early Quakers
c/o Richard Harley Calendine
111 Webster Park Avenue
Columbus, OH 43214

WEBSITES:

Quaker Corner
http://www.rootsweb.com/~quakers/

RUSSIAN

American Historical Society of Germans from Russia
631 D Street
Lincoln, NE 68502-1199
Tel: 402-474-3363
Fax: 402-474-7229
Email: ahsgr@aol.com
URL: http://www.teleport.com/nonprofit/ahsgr/

Russian Baltic Information Center - BLITZ
907 Mission Avenue
San Rafael, CA 94901
Tel: 415-453-3579
Fax: 415-453-0343
Email: enute@igc.apc.org
URL: http://dcn.davis.ca.us/go/feefhs/blitz/frgblitz.html

Germans from Russia Heritage Society
1008 East Central Avenue
Bismarck, ND 58501
Tel: 701-223-6167
Email: grhs@btigate.com
URL: http://www.teleport.com/nonprofit/grhs

WEBSITES:

Russian Heraldry
http://sunsite.cs.msu.su/heraldry/

SCANDINAVIAN

American-Swedish Historical Museum
(in Franklin Delano Roosevelt Park)
1900 Patterson Avenue
Philadelphia, PA 19145
Tel: 215-389-1776
Email: ashm@libertynet.org
URL: http://www.libertynet.org/~ashm/

Concordia College
Carl B. Ylvisaker Library
Moorhead, MN 56562
Tel: 218-299-4239
Email: library@cord.edu
URL: http://home.cord.edu/dept/library/

Finnish-American Heritage Center
Suomi College
Hancock, MI 49930
Tel: 906-487-7367
Fax: 906-487-7383
URL: http://www.suomi.edu/Ink/FHC.html

Finnish-American Historical Archives
Suomi College
601 Quincy Street
Hancock, MI 49930
Tel: 906-487-7273

Finnish-American Historical Society, Minnesota
P.O. Box 34
Wolf Lake, MN 56593

Norwegian American Bygdelagenes Fellesraad
c/o Marilyn Somdahl, Pres.
10129 Goodrich Circle
Bloomington, MN 55437
Tel: 612-831-4409
Email: rsylte@ix.netcom.com
URL: http://www.lexiaintl.org/sylte/bygdelag.html

Norwegian-American Historical Association (NAHA)
1510 St. Olaf Avenue
Northfield, MN 55057
Fax: 507-646-3734
Email: naha@stolaf.edu
URL: http://www.stolaf.edu/stolaf/other/naha/naha.html

Norwegian Emigrant Museum
Akershagan
2312 Ottestad
Norway
Tel: +47 62 57 85 77
Fax: +47 62 57 84 59
Email: knut.djupedal@emigrant.museum.no
URL: http://www.hamarnett.no/emigrantmuseum/

Norwegian Emigration Center
Bergjelandsgt. 30
N-4012 Stavenger
Norway
Tel: +47 5150 1274
Fax: +47 5150 1290
Email: detnu@telepost.no
URL: http://home.sn.no/home/henningh/utvasent.htm
Scandinavian American Genealogical Society (SAGS)
P.O. Box 16069
St. Paul, MN 55116-0069
URL: http://www.mtn.org/mgs/branches/sags.html

Swedish-American Historical Society/Library
5125 North Spaulding Avenue
Chicago, IL 60625-4816
Tel: 773-583-2700 ext. 5267

Swedish-American Museum Center
5211 N. Clark Street
Chicago, IL 60640-2101
Tel: 773-728-8111

Swedish Colonial Society
c/o Wallace Richter, Registrar
336 South Devon Avenue
Wayne, PA 19087
Tel: 610-688-1766
URL: http://libertynet.org/~gencap/scs.html

Swenson Swedish Immigration Research Center
Augustana College
639 38th Street
Rock Island, IL 61201-2273
Tel: 309-794-7204
Fax: 309-794-7443
Email: swsa@augustana.edu
URL: http://www2.augustana.edu/admin/swenson/

Vesterheim Genealogical Center and Naeseth Library
415 W. Main Street
Madison, WI 53703-3116
Fax: 608-258-6842
Email: vesterheim@juno.com
URL: http://fjordinfo.vestdata.no/offentleg/sffarkiv/sffutvgc.htm

WEBSITES:

Danish-English Online Dictionary
http://dictionaries.travlang.org/DanishEnglish/

Finnish-English Online Dictionary
http://dictionaries.travlang.org/FinnishEnglish/

Genealogy Finland
http://www.mediabase.fi/suku/genealog.htm

Norwegian Historical Data Centre
http://isv.uit.no/seksjon/rhd/

SCOTTISH
(See United Kingdom)

SOUTH AFRICAN

Albany Museum: Ancestry Research-Genealogy
Somerset Street
GRAHAMSTOWN, 6139
South Africa
Intl. Tel: +27 461 22312
Intl. Fax: +27 461 22398
Email: amwj@giraffe.ru.ac.za
URL: http://www.ru.ac.za/departments/am/geneal.html

WEBSITES:

Afrikaans-English Online Dictionary
http://dictionaries.travlang.org/AfrikaansEnglish/

SWISS

Swiss Mennonite Cultural and Historical Association
109 East Hirschler
Moundridge, KS 67107
Tel: 316-345-2844

Swiss Society of Genealogy Studies
Email: nickj@3dplus.ch
URL: http://www.3dplus.ch/~nickj/Engl_SSEG.html

WEBSITES:

Swiss Genealogy
http://www.mindspring.com/~philipp/che.html

Swiss Genealogy on the Internet
http://www.kssg.ch/chgene/welcome-e.htm

UNITED KINGDOM/IRELAND/SCOTLAND

British Heritage Society
4177 Garrick Avenue
Warren, MI 48091
Tel: 810-757-4177
Email: Anton_The_Lord_Hartforth@msn.com

Clan MacDuff Society of America
Barabara Huff-Duff, Society Genealogist
237 Madeline Drive
Monrovia, CA 91016-2431
Email: huffduff@cco.caltech.edu
URL: http://www.crimson.com/scots_austin/macduff.htm

Irish-American Cultural Institute
683 Osceola Avenue
St. Paul, MN 55105

Irish-American Heritage Center Museum and Art Gallery
4626 North Knox Avenue
Chicago, IL 60630-4030
Tel: 773-282-7035

Irish American Heritage Museum
19 Clinton Avenue
Albany, NY 12207
Tel: 518-432-6598

The Irish Ancestral Research Association (TIARA
Dept. W
P.O. Box 619
Sudbury, MA 01776
URL: http://world.std.com/~ahern/TIARA.html

Irish Family History Forum, Inc.
P.O. Box 351
Rockville Center, NY 11571-0351
URL: http://www.fgs.org/~fgs/soc0090.htm

Irish Genealogical Society, Intl. (IGSI)
P.O. Box 13585
St. Paul, MN 55116-0585
Email: raymarsh@minn.net
URL: http://www.rootsweb.com/~irish/

Jersey Archives Service
The Weighbridge
St. Helier, Jersey
Channel Islands JE2 3NF
Tel: 01534-617441
Fax: 01534-66085
URL: http://www.jersey.gov.uk/heritage/archives/jasweb.html

National Library of Scotland
George IV Bridge
Edinburgh, EH1 1EW
Scotland
URL: http://www.nls.uk/

Office for National Statistics
1 Myddelton Street
London
EC1R 1UW
Tel: 0181 392 5300
Fax: 0181 392 5307

Public Record Office (PRO)
Ruskin Avenue
Kew
Surrey
TW9 4DU
Tel: 0181 392 5200
Fax: 0181 878 8905
Email: enquiry.pro.rsd.kew@gtnet.gov.uk
URL: http://www.open.gov.uk/pro/prohome.htm

Scotch-Irish Society of the U.S.A.
3 Parkway, 20th Floor
Philadelphia, PA 19102

Scottish Genealogy Society
15 Victoria Terrace
Edinburgh, EH1 2JL
Scotland
Tel: +44 0131 220 3677
Email: scotgensoc@sol.co.uk
URL: http://www.taynet.co.uk/users/scotgensoc/

Society of Genealogists
14 Charterhouse Buildings
Goswell Road
London EC1M 7BA
Tel: 0171-251-8799
URL: http://www.cs.ncl.ac.uk/genuki/SoG/

WEBSITES:

A Little Bit of Ireland
http://members.aol.com/LABATH/irish.htm

Channel Islands Genealogy
http://users.aol.com/johnf14246/ci.html

Electric Scotland; Scottish Clans
http://www.electricscotland.com/webclans/index.html

Genealogical Guide to Ireland
http://www.bess.tcd.ie/roots/prototype/genweb2.htm

GENUKI
http://cs6400.mcc.ac.uk/genuki/
or
http://midas.ac.uk/genuki/

Irish Emigrants
http://genealogy.org/~ajmorris/ireland/ireemg1.htm

Irish Family History Foundation
http://www.mayo-ireland.ie/ireland.htm

Irish Genealogy
http://genealogy.org/~ajmorris/ireland/ireland.htm

IRLGEN: Tracing Your Irish Ancestors
http://www.bess.tcd.ie/roots_ie.htm

National Archives of Ireland
http://www.kst.dit.ie/nat-arch/

Scotland Genealogy: Tracing Your Scottish Ancestry
http://www.geo.edu.ac.uk/home/Scotland/genealogy.html
Scottish Reference Information (Database)
http://www.ktb.net/~dwills/13300-scottishreference.htm

MILITARY & FEDERAL GOVERNMENT AGENCIES

MILITARY

American Battle Monuments Commission
5119-5120 Pulaski Building
20 Massachusetts Avenue, NW
Washington, DC 20314-0001
Tel: 202-475-1329

American Merchant Marine Museum
U.S.M.M.A.
Kings Point, NY 11024
Tel: 516-773-5515

American Veterans Historical Museum
P.O. Box 115
Pleasantville, NY 10570
Tel: 914-769-5297

Archdiocese for the Military Services
924 Wayne Avenue
Silver Springs, MD 20910
Tel: 301-495-4100

Center for Military History
1099 14th Street, NW
Washington, DC 20005-3402
Tel: 202-761-5413
Email: cmhweb@cmh-smtp.army.mil
URL: http://www.army.mil/cmh-pg/default.htm

Citadel
Daniel Library
171 Moultrie Street
Charleston, SC 29409
Tel: 803-953-2569 (Reference)
Fax: 803-953-5190
Email: reichardtk@citadel.edu
URL: http://www.citadel.edu/citadel/otherserv/library/index.htm

Dept. of Veterans Affairs
810 Vermont Avenue, NW
Washington, DC 20420
Tel: 202-233-4000
800-827-1000
URL: http://www.va.gov/foia/index.htm

Marine Corps Historical Center
Washington Navy Yard, Building 58
Ninth and M Streets, SE
Washington, DC 20374-0580
Tel: 202-433-3483
URL: http://www.usmc.mil/usmcfaq/usmcfaq.htm

Military Heritage Museum
195 Washington Avenue
Albany, NY 12205
Tel: 518-436-0103

Military Order of the Loyal Legion of the United States
1805 Pine Street
Philadelphia, PA 19103
Tel: 215-546-2425
Email: YJNW42A@prodigy.com
URL: http://suvcw.org/mollus.htm

National Guard Association of the United States Library
One Massachusetts Avenue, NW
Washington, DC 20001
Tel: 202-789-0031

National Museum of Health and Medicine/Archives
Building 54
Armed Forces Institute of Pathology
Walter Reed Army Medical Center
Georgia Avenue, NW
Washington, DC 20306-6000
Tel: 202-576-2334

Naval Historical Center
Washington Navy Yard
901 M Street, SE
Washington, DC 20374-5060
Library:
Tel: 202-433-4132
Fax: 202-433-9553
Museum:
Tel: 202-433-4882
Fax: 202-433-8200
Operational Archives:
Fax: 202-433-2833
Ships History Branch:
Tel: 202-433-3643
Fax: 202-433-6677
URL: http://www.history.navy.mil/

U.S. Air Force Historical Research Agency
Mail:
HQ AFHRA/RSA
600 Chennault Circle
Maxwell AFB, AL 36112-6424
Email: AFHRANEWS1%RS%AFHRA@MAX1.au.af.mil
URL: http://www.au.af.mil/au/afhra/

U.S. Army Institute of Heraldry
9235 Gunston Road, Room S-112
Fort Belvoir, VA 22060-5579
Tel: 703-806-4968
703-806-4969

U.S. Army Military History Institute
22 Ashburn Drive, Carlisle Barracks
Carlisle, PA 17013
Tel: 717-245-3611
Email: MHI-SC@carlisle-emh2.army.mil (Special Collections)
MHI-AR@carlisle-emh2.army.mil (Archives Collection)
MHI-HR@carlisle-emh2.army.mil (Historical Reference)
URL: http://carlisle-www.army.mil/usamhi/

U.S. Army Publications Center
2800 Eastern Boulevard
Baltimore, MD 21220-2896
Tel: 410-671-2272

U.S. Coast Guard Academy
Fifteen Mohegan Avenue
New London, CT 06320-4195
Tel: 203-444-8501

U.S. Coast Guard Historian's Office (G-CP-4)
2100 2nd Street, SW
Washington, DC 20593
Tel: 202-267-0948
Email: rbrowning@comdt.uscg.mil
sprice@comdt.uscg.mil
URL: http://www.dot.gov/dotinfo/uscg/hq/g-cp/history/collect.html

U.S. Military Academy/Museum and Archives
Building 2107
Pershing Center
West Point, NY 10996-2099
Tel: 914-938-7052
Email: museum@www.usma.edu
URL: http://www.usma.edu/Museum

U.S. Naval Academy
Nimitz Library
589 McNair Road
Annapolis, MD 21402-5029
Tel: 410-293-2220 (Special Collections)
410-293-2178 (Archives)
Email: cummings@nadn.navy.mil
URL: http://www.nadn.navy.mil/Library

U.S. Naval Institute
U.S. Naval Academy Campus
118 Maryland Avenue
Annapolis, MD 21402-5035
Tel: 410-268-6110
URL: http://www.usni.org/

U.S. Naval War College/Library
Code 1E3
686 Cushing Road
Newport, RI 02841-1207
Tel: 401-841-1435
401-841-3397
401-841-4345 (Government Documents)
Email: LIBREF@USNWC.EDU
URL: http://users.ids.net/~nwcird/

WEBSITES:

Americal Division Veterans' Administration;
Army Awards and Decorations
http://www3.servtech.com/americal/awards/

American Civil War-Resources on the Internet
http://www.dsu.edu/~jankej/civilwar.html

Master Index of Army Records
http://www.army.mil/cmh-pg/records.html

Medals of Honor Index
(List of Medal of Honor recipient by conflict with information about each honoree)
http://www.army.mil/cmh-pg/moh1.htm

New York Public Library's Military History Collection
http://web.nypl.org/research/chss/subguides/milhist/home.html

U.S. Civil War Center
http://www.cwc.lsu.edu/

FEDERAL GOVERNMENT AGENCIES

Bureau of Indian Affairs
U.S. Department of the Interior
Office of Public Affairs
1849 C Street, NW
Washington, DC 20240-0001
Tel: 202-208-3711
Fax: 202-501-1516
URL: http://www.doi.gov/bureau-indian-affairs.html
Genealogy Resources
URL: http://www.doi.gov/bia/ancestry/genealog.html

Bureau of Land Management (Headquarters)
1849 C Street
Washington, DC 20240
URL: http://www.blm.gov/

Dept. of Veterans Affairs
810 Vermont Avenue, NW
Washington, DC 20420
Tel: 202-233-4000
800-827-1000
URL: http://www.va.gov/foia/index.htm

Office of Information and Privacy
SAIS-IDP-F/P, Suite 201
1725 Jefferson Davis Highway
Arlington, VA 22202-4102
Tel: 703-607-3377
URL: http://www.usdoj.gov/oip/oip.html

Government Printing Office (GPO)
Washington, DC 20401
Tel: 888-293-6498
202-512-1530
Fax: 202-512-1262
Email: gpoaccess@gpo.gov
URL: http://www.access.gpo.gov/
GPO Access Databases
URL: http://www.access.gpo.gov/su_docs/aces/aaces003.html

Immigration and Naturalization Service (INS)
425 I Street, NW
Room 5304
Washington, DC 20536
Tel: 800-755-0777
800-870-3676 (To request forms)
http://www.ins.usdoj.gov/
Forms Download
http://www.ins.usdoj.gov/forms/index.html
Request Forms by Mail
http://www.ins.usdoj.gov/exec/forms/formsbymail.asp

INS Regional Offices

Alaska
620 East 10th Avenue
Anchorage, AK 99501-7581

Arizona
2035 N. Central Avenue
Phoenix, AZ 85004

California
865 Fulton Mall
Fresno, CA 93721-2816

California
Chet Holifield Federal Building
24000 Avila Road
P.O. Box 30080
Laguna Niguel, CA 92607-0080

California
300 North Los Angeles Street
Los Angeles, CA 90012

California
711 J Street
Sacramento, CA 95814

California
880 Front Street
San Diego, CA 92188

California
630 Sansome Street
San Francisco, CA 94111-2280

California
280 South First Street, Room 1150
San Jose, CA 95113

Colorado
Albrook Center
4730 Paris Street
Denver, CO 80239-2804

Connecticut
Ribicoff Federal Building
450 Main Street
Hartford, CT 06103-3060

Florida
400 West Bay Street, Room G-18
P.O. Box 35029
Jacksonville, FL 32202

Florida
7880 Biscayne Blvd.
Miami, FL 33138

Florida
5509 W. Gray Street, Suite 113
Tampa, FL 33609

Georgia
77 Forsyth Street, SW
Room 284
Atlanta, GA 30303

Guam
801 Pacific News Building
238 O'Hara Street
Agana, Guam 96910

Hawaii
595 Ala Moana Blvd.
Honolulu, HI 96813

Illinois
10 West Jackson Blvd., 2nd Floor
Chicago, IL 60604

Indiana
Gateway Plaza
950 North Meridian, Suite 400
Indianapolis, IN 46204

Kentucky
Gene Snyder Courthouse
West 6th and Broadway, Room 601
Louisville, KY 40202

Louisiana
Postal Service Building
701 Loyola Avenue, Room T-8005
New Orleans, LA 70113

Maine
739 Warren Avenue
Portland, ME 04103

Maryland
Equitable Bank Center
100 South Charles Street, 12th Floor Tower
Baltimore, MD 21201

Massachusetts
JFK Federal Building
Government Center
Boston, MA 02203

Michigan
Federal Building
333 Mt. Elliott Street
Detroit, MI 48207-4381

Minnesota
2901 Metro Drive, Suite 100
Bloomington, MN 55425

Minnesota
Bishop Henry Whipple Federal Building
One Federal Drive
Fort Snelling, MN 55111-4007

Missouri
9747 North Conant Avenue
Kansas City, MO 64153

Missouri
Robert A. Young Federal Building
1222 Spruce Street, Room 1100
St. Louis, MO 63101-2815

Montana
2800 Skyway Drive
Helena, MT 59601

Nebraska
3736 South 132nd Street
Omaha, NE 68144

Nebraska
Northern Service Center
850 S. Street
Lincoln, NE 68508

Nevada
300 Las Vegas Blvd., Room 1430
Las Vegas, NV 89101

Nevada
3373 Pepper Lane
Las Vegas, NV 89120

Nevada
712 Mill Street
Reno, NV 89502

New Jersey
Federal Building
970 Broad Street
Newark, NJ 07102

New Mexico
517 Gold Avenue, SW
Room 1010
P.O. Box 567
Albuquerque, NM 87103

New York
James T. Foley Federal Courthouse
445 Broadway, Room 220
Albany, NY 12207

New York
130 Delaware Avenue
Buffalo, NY 14202

New York
26 Federal Plaza
New York, NY 10278

North Carolina
6 Woodlawn Green, Room 138
Charlotte, NC 28217

Ohio
J.W. Peck Federal Building
550 Main Street, Room 8525
Cincinnati, OH 45202

Ohio
Anthony Celebreeze
Federal Building
1240 East 9th Street, Room 1917
Cleveland, OH 44199

Oklahoma
149 Highline Blvd., Suite 300
Oklahoma City, OK 73108

Oregon
Federal Office Building
511 NW Broadway
Portland, OR 97209

Pennsylvania
1600 Callowhill Street
Philadelphia, PA 19130

Pennsylvania
Federal Building, Room 2130
1000 Liberty Avenue
Pittsburgh, PA 15222

Puerto Rico
P.O. Box 365068
San Juan, PR 00936

Rhode Island
Federal Building
203 John O. Pastore
Providence, RI 02903

Tennessee
245 Wagner Place, Suite 250
Memphis, TN 38103-3815

Texas
7701 North Stemmons Freeway
Dallas, TX 75247-9998

Texas
8101 North Stemmons Freeway
Dallas, TX 75247

Texas
700 E. San Antonio Street
P.O. Box 9398
El Paso, TX 79984

Texas
1545 Hawkins Blvd., Suite 170
El Paso, TX 79925

Texas
P.O. Box 152122
Irving, TX 75105-0212

Texas
2102 Teege Road
Harlingen, TX 78550

Texas
509 North Belt
Houston, TX 77060

Texas
8940 Fourwinds Drive
San Antonio, TX 78239

Utah
5272 South College Drive
Salt Lake City, UT 84123

Vermont
Eastern Service Center
75 Lower Welden Street
St. Albans, VT 05479-0001

Vermont
70 Kimball Avenue
South Burlington, VT 05403-6813

Virginia
Norfolk Federal Building
Norfolk, VA 23510

Virginia
4420 North Fairfax Drive
Arlington, VA 22203

Washington
815 Airport Way, South
Seattle, WA 98134

Washington
691 U.S. Courthouse Building
Spokane, WA 99201

Wisconsin
517 E. Wisconsin Avenue
Milwaukee, WI 53202

Passport Office
Dept. of State
1111 19th Street, NW
Suite 200
Washington, DC 20522
Tel: 202-955-0291

Social Security Administration
Office of Disclosure Policy
3-A-6 Operations Building
6401 Security Boulevard
Baltimore, MD 21235
http://www.ssa.gov/

U.S. Census Bureau
1201 E. Tenth Street
P.O. Box 1545
Jeffersonville, IN 47131
http://www.census.gov/
Census records after 1920

U.S. Geological Survey
Tel: 800-USA-MAPS
Fax on Demand: 703-648-4888
URL: http://www.usgs.gov/

USGS Regional Libraries

U.S. Geological Survey Library
950 National Center
12201 Sunrise Valley
Reston, VA 20192
Tel: 703-648-4302 (Reference)
703-648-6080 (History Project)
Fax: 703-648-6373
TDD: 703-648-4105
Email: library@usgs.gov
URL: http://library.usgs.gov/reslib.html

U.S. Geological Survey Library
345 Middlefield Road, MS 955
Menlo Park, CA 94025-3591
Tel: 415-329-5009
Fax: 415-329-5132
TDD: 415-329-5094
Email: men_lib@usgs.gov
URL: http://library.usgs.gov/menlib.html

U.S. Geological Survey Library
2255 N. Gemini Drive
Flagstaff, AZ 86001
Tel: 520-556-7272
Fax: 520-556-7156
Email: flag_lib@usgs.gov
URL: http://library.usgs.gov/flaglib.html

U.S. Geological Survey Library
Denver Federal Center, Building 20
Box 25046, MS 914
Denver, CO 80225-0046
Tel: 303-236-1010
Fax: 303-236-0015
TDD: 303-236-0998
Email: den_lib@usgs.gov
URL: http://library.usgs.gov/denlib.html

USGS Mapping Information: Geographic Names Information System
Online Data Base Query Form
URL: http://mapping.usgs.gov/www/gnis/gnisform.html

U.S. Patent and Trademark Office Library
Crystal Park 3, Suite 481
Washington, DC 20231
Tel: 703-308-5558
Fax: 703-306-2654
URL; http://www.uspto.gov/web/offices/ac/ido/cpti/ptdlhm3.htm
Searchable Patent Database 1976-1997
URL: http://patents.uspto.gov/patbib_index.html

National Archives and Records Administration

URL: http://www.nara.gov/

National Archives and Records Administration (NARA)
Archives I
8th & Pennsylvania Avenues
Washington, DC 20408
Tel: 202-501-5410 (Genealogical Staff)
202-501-5400 (Record Availability)
Fax: 301-713-6905 (Fax-on-Demand Information)
Email: inquire@arch1.nara.gov
URL: http://www.nara.gov/nara/dc/Archives1_info.html

National Archives and Records Administration (NARA)
Archives II
8601 Adelphi Road
College Park, MD 20740
Tel: 202-501-5400 (Record Availability)
301-713-6800 (General Reference)
301-713-7040 (Cartographic Reference)
Fax: 301-713-6905 (Fax-on-Demand Information)
Email: inquire@arch2.nara.gov
URL: http://www.nara.gov/nara/dc/Archives1_info.html

National Records Centers

National Personnel Records Centers, NARA
http://www.nara.gov/nara/frc/nprc.html

Civilian Records Facility
111 Winnebago Street
St. Louis, MO 63118-4199
Tel: 314-425-5761
Fax: 314-425-5719
Email: center@cpr.nara.gov
URL: http://www.nara.gov/nara/frc/cpr.html

Military Records Facility
9700 Page Avenue
St. Louis, MO 63132-5100
Recorded Information Lines
314-538-4243 Air Force
314-538-4261 Army
314-538-4141 Navy/Marine/Coast Guard
Fax: 314-538-4175
Email: center@stlouis.nara.gov
URL: http://www.nara.gov/nara/frc/mpr.html

Pittsfield Federal Records Center, NARA
100 Dan Fox Drive
Pittsfield, MA 01201-8230
Tel: 413-445-6885
Fax: 413-445-7305
Email: center@pittsfield.nara.gov
URL: http://www.nara.gov/nara/frc/1ncloc.html

Washington National Records Center, NARA
Shipping Address:
4205 Suitland Road
Suitland, MD 20746-2042
Mailing Address:
4205 Suitland Road
Washington, DC 20409-0002
Tel: 301-457-7000
Fax: 301-457-7117
Email: center@suitland.nara.gov
URL: http://www.nara.gov/nara/frc/newbloc.html

REGIONAL ARCHIVES

National Archives-Alaska Region
654 W. 3rd Avenue
Anchorage, AK 99501-2145
Tel: 907-271-2441
Fax: 907-271-2442
Email: archives@alaska.nara.gov
URL: http://www.nara.gov/nara/regional/11nsgil.html
(Alaska)

National Archives-Central Plains Region
2312 East Bannister Road
Kansas City, MO 64131
Tel: 816-926-6272
Fax: 816-926-6982
Email: archives@kansascity.nara.gov
URL: http://www.nara.gov/nara/regional/06nsgil.html
(Iowa, Kansas, Minnesota, Missouri, Nebraska, North Dakota, and South Dakota)

National Archives-Great Lakes Region
7358 Pulaski Road
Chicago, IL 60629
Tel: 773-581-7816
Fax: 312-353-1294
Email: archives@chicago.nara.gov
URL: http://www.nara.gov/nara/regional/05nsgil.htm
(Illinois, Indiana, Michigan, Minnesota, Ohio, and Wisconsin)

National Archives-Mid Atlantic Region
Ninth and Market Streets
Philadelphia, PA 19107
Tel: 215-597-3000
Fax: 215-597-2303
Email: archives@philarch.nara.gov
URL: http://www.nara.gov/nara/regional/03nsgil.html
(Delaware, Maryland, Pennsylvania, Virginia, and West Virginia)

National Archives-New England Region
380 Trapelo Road
Waltham, MA 02154-8104
Tel: 617-647-8100
Fax: 617-647-8460
Email: archives@waltham.nara.gov
URL: http://www.nara.gov/nara/regional/01nsbgil.html
(Connecticut, Maine, Massachusetts, New Hampshire, Rhode Island, and Vermont)

National Archives-Northeast Region
201 Varick Street
New York, NY 10014
Tel: 212-337-1300
Fax: 212-337-1306
Email: archives@newyork.nara.gov
URL: http://www.nara.gov/nara/regional/02nsgil.html
(New Jersey, New York, Puerto Rico, and U.S. Virgin Islands)

National Archives-Pacific Northwest Region
6125 Sand Point Way, NE
Seattle, WA 98115
Tel: 206-526-6507
Fax: 206-526-4344
Email: archives@seattle.nara.gov
URL: http://www.nara.gov/nara/regional/10nsgil.html
(Idaho, Oregon, and Washington)

National Archives-Pacific Sierra Region
1000 Commodore Drive
San Bruno, CA 94066
Tel: 415-876-9009
Fax: 415-876-9233
Email: archives@sanbruno.nara.gov
URL: http://www.nara.gov/nara/regional/09nssgil.html
(Northern California, Hawaii, Nevada (except Clark County), Guam, American Samoa, and the Trust Territory of the Pacific Islands)

National Archives-Pacific Southwest Region
24000 Avila Rd., First Floor-East Entrance
P.O. Box 6719
Laguna Niguel, CA 92607-6719
Tel: 714-360-2641
Fax: 714-360-2644
Email: archives@laguna.nara.gov
URL: http://www.nara.gov/nara/regional/09nslgil.html
(Arizona, Southern California, and Clark County, NV)

National Archives-Rocky Mountain Region
Denver Federal Center, Building 48
P.O. Box 25307
Denver, CO 80225-0307
Tel: 303-236-0817
Fax: 303-236-9354
Email: archives@denver.nara.gov
URL: http://www.nara.gov/nara/regional/08nsgil.html
(Colorado, Montana, New Mexico, North Dakota, South Dakota, Utah, and Wyoming)

National Archives-Southeast Region
1557 St. Joseph Avenue
East Point, GA 30344-2593
Tel: 404-763-7477
Fax: 404-763-7033

Email: archives@atlanta.nara.gov
URL: http://www.nara.gov/nara/regional/04nsgil.html
(Alabama, Florida, Georgia, Kentucky, Mississippi, North Carlina, South Carolina, and Tennessee)

National Archives-Southwest Region
501 W. Felix Street, Building 1
P.O. Box 6216
Fort Worth, TX 76115-0216
Tel: 817-334-5525
Fax: 817-334-5621
Email: archives@ftworth.nara.gov
URL: http://www.nara.gov/nara/regional/07nsgil.html
(Arkansas, Oklahoma, Louisiana, and Texas)

HELPFUL NARA WEBSITES

American Indians
http://www.nara.gov/publications/microfilm/amerindians/indians.html

Black Studies
http://www.nara.gov/publications/microfilm/blackstudies/blackstd.html

Census Records
http://www.nara.gov/publications/microfilm/census.html

Federal Court Records-A Select Catalog of NARA Microfilm Publ.
http://www.nara.gov/publications/microfilm/courts/fedcourt.html

Genealogical and Biographical Research
http://www.nara.gov/publications/microfilm/biographical/genbio.html

Genealogical Searchable Database-NAIL
http://www.nara.gov/nara/nail/nailgen.html

Genealogy Page
http://www.nara.gov/genealogy/genindex.html

Immigrant and Passenger Arrivals
http://www.nara.gov/publications/microfilm/immigrant/immpass.html

Microfilm Resources for Research
http://www.nara.gov/publications/microfilm/comprehensive/compcat.html

Military Service Records
http://www.nara.gov/publications/microfilm/military/service.html

Naturalization Records
http://www.nara.gov/genealogy/natural.html

Post Office Records
http://www.nara.gov/genealogy/postal.html

HELPFUL WEBSITES

Ancestry's Hometown
http://www.ancestry.com/

The Attic-Genealogy Resources
http://www.geocities.com/TheTropics/1127/attic.html

Barrel of Genealogical Links
http://cpcug.org/user/jlacombe/mark.html

Cemetery Internment Lists on the Internet
http://users.deltanet.com/~steven/cemetery.html

Charlotte's Web Genealogical Gleanings
http://www.charweb.org/gen/gleanings/

Charts for Reference in Genealogy Research
http://members.tripod.com/~Silvie/charts.html

Christine's Genealogy Website
http://ccharity.com/

Cyndi's List of Genealogical Sites
http://www.oz.net/~cyndihow/sites.htm

Directory of Underground Railroad Operators
http://www.ugrr.org//ur-names.html

Emigration/Ships Lists and Resources
http://www.geocities.com/Heartland/5978/Emigration

Genealogical Resources on the Internet
http://www.tc.umn.edu/~pmg/genealogy.html

Genealogical Websites of Societies and CIGs
http://genealogy.org/PAF/www/gwsc/

Genealogy
http://pibweb.it.nwu.edu/~pib/genealo.htm

Genealogy Home Page
http://genhomepage.com/

Genealogy Online
http://genealogy.emcee.com/

Genealogy's Most Wanted
http://www.citynet.net/mostwanted/

Geneanet (Surname Database)
http://www.geneanet.org/

Helms Genealogy Toolbox
http://genealogy.tbox.com/

IMC's Genealogical Listings
http://www.memphismemphis.com/genealogy/states/main.htm

Land Records
http://www.ultranet.com/~deeds/

Lineages, Inc.
http://www.lineagesnet.com/

Mailing Lists, from Genealogy Resources on the Internet
http://users.aol.com/johnf14246/gen_mail.html

Mapquest
http://www.mapquest.com/

Maritime History on the Internet
http://ils.unc.edu/maritime/home.html

Maritime History Virtual Archives
http://pc-78-129.udac.se:8001/WWW/Nautica/Nautica.html

Olive Tree
http://www.rootsweb.com/~ote/

Online Genealogical Databases
http://www.gentree.com/

Oregon-California Trails Association
http://calcite.rocky.edu/octa/octahome.htm

Political Graveyard
http://www.potifos.com/tpg/index.html

Railroad Historical
http://www.rrhistorical.com/index.html

Rand Genealogical Group
http://www.rand.org/personal/Genea

Rootsweb
http://www.rootsweb.com/

Roots-L Resources (State by state listings for resources)
http://www.rootsweb.com/roots-l/usa.html

Travlang's Translating Dictionaries
http://dictionaries.travlang.com/

U.S. GenWeb Project
http://www.usgenweb.org/

Directories and Search Engines

Alta Vista
http://altavista.digital.com/

Big Yellow Directory
http://s11.bigyellow.com/t_how_to_advertise/t_whybigyellow.html

DejaNews
http://www.dejanews.com/

Excite
http://www.excite.com/

Lycos
http://www.lycos.com

Metacrawler (Search Engine)
http://www.metacrawler.com/

NAIS Private Investigator's Link List (Lots of directories, search engines, and other goodies)
http://www.pimall.com/nais/links.html

Switchboard (Directory)
http://www.switchboard.com/

Webcrawler
http://webcrawler.com

Yahoo
http://www.yahoo.com/

Zip+4 Code Lookup from the US Postal Service
http://www.usps.gov/ncsc/lookups/lookup_zip+4.html

555-1212's Fast Area Code Lookup
http://www.555-1212.com/aclookup.html

ALABAMA

ARCHIVES, STATE & NATIONAL

Alabama Deptartment of Archives & History
624 Washington Avenue
Montgomery, AL 36130-0100
Tel: 334-242-4452
Fax: 334-242-4452
URL: http://www.asc.edu/archives/agis.html

National Archives—Southeast Region
1557 St. Joseph Avenue
East Point, GA 30344-2593
Tel: 404-763-7477
Fax: 404-763-7033
Email: archives@atlanta.nara.gov
URL: http://www.nara.gov/nara/regional/04nsgil.html

GENEALOGICAL SOCIETIES

Alabama Genealogical Society
AGS Depository and Headquarters
Samford University Library
Box 2296
800 Lakeshore Drive
Birmingham, AL 35229

Alabama Society, Sons of the American Revolution
507 Bonnett Hill Circle
Mobile, AL 36609

AlaBenton Genealogical Society
c/o Anniston-Calhoun Public Library, The Alabama Room
P.O. Box 308
Anniston, AL 36202
URL: http://pages.prodigy.net/tracks/ABENINQ.HTM

Autauga Genealogical Society
P.O. Box 680668
Prattville, AL 36067-0668

Baldwin County Genealogical Society
P.O. Box 501
Lillian, AL 36549

Birmingham Genealogical Society
P.O. Box 2432
Birmingham, AL 35201

Butler County Historical and Genealogical Society
309 Fort Dale
Greenville, AL 36037

Central Alabama Genealogical Society
P.O. Box 125
Selma, AL 36701

Civil War Descendants Society
P.O. Box 233
Athens, AL 35611

Coosa River Valley Historical & Genealogical Society
P.O. Box 295
Centre, AL 35960

Genealogical Society of East Alabama
P.O. Drawer 1351
Auburn, AL 36830

Genealogical Society of Washington County
P.O. Box 399
Chatom, AL 36518
Tel: 334-847-3156
or 334-847-2286
http://members.aol.com/JORDANJM2/WCGS.html

Lamar County Genealogical Society
P.O. Box 357
Vernon, AL 35592

Limestone County Genealogical Society
c/o Limestone County Historical Society
The Donnell House
601 South Clinton Street
P.O. Box 82
Athens, AL 35611

Lowndes County Historical and Genealogical Society
Route 1, P.O. Box 408
Fort Deposit, AL 36032

Marion County Genealogical Society
P.O. Drawer O
Winfield, AL 35594

Mobile Genealogical Society
P.O. Box 6224
Mobile, AL 36606

Montgomery Genealogical Society
P.O. Box 230194
Montgomery, AL 36123-0194

Natchez Trace Genealogical Society
P.O. Box 420
Florence, AL 35631-0420

North Alabama Genealogical Society
3327 Danville Road, SW
Decatur, AL 35603-9027

North Central Alabama Genealogical Society
P.O. Box 13
Cullman, AL 35056-0013

Northeast Alabama Genealogical Society
P.O. Box 8268
Gadsden, AL 35902
Email: AlwaysPS@aol.com
URL: http://www.bham.mindspring.com/~awillcut/alwaysps.htm

Pea River Historical and Genealogical Society
Box 628
Enterprise, AL 36330

Pickens County Genealogical Society
P.O. Box 336
Gordo, AL 35466

Piedmont Historical and Genealogical Society
P.O. Box 47
Spring Garden, AL 36275

Pike County Historical & Genealogical Society
Route 2, Box 272
Goshen, AL 36035

Southeast Alabama Genealogical Society (SEAGS)
P.O. Box 143
Dothan, AL 36302

Southern Society of Genealogists
P.O. Box 295
Centre, AL 35960

Tennessee Valley Genealogical Society
P.O. Box 1568
Huntsville, AL 35807
URL: http://iquest.com/~rwhite/TVGS/tvgs.htm

Tuscaloosa Genealogical Society
2020 Third Court East
Tuscaloosa, AL 35401

Walker County Genealogical Society
P.O. Box 3408
Jasper, AL 35502

Historical Societies

Alabama Historical Association
P.O. Box 2877
Tuscaloosa, AL 35486

Arab Historical Society
Rt. 4, Box 418C
Arab, AL 35016

Auburn Heritage Association
P.O. Box 2248
Auburn, AL 36830

Autauga County Heritage Association
102 E. Main Street
Prattville, AL 36067

Baldwin County Historical Society
P.O. Box 69
Stockton, AL 36579

Bibb County Heritage Association
Route 1, Box 147
Brierfield, AL 35035

Birmingham Historical Society
1 Sloss Quarter
Birmingham, AL 35203

Blount County Historical Society
P.O. Box 45
Oneonta, AL 35121

Blount County Memorial Museum
204 2nd Street N.
Oneonta, AL 35121-1740
Tel: 205-625-6905

Bullock County Historical Society
P.O. Box 663
Union Springs, AL 36089

Butler County Historical and Genealogical Society/Library
309 Fort Dale Street
Greenville, AL 36037

Chilton County Historical Society and Archives, Inc.
Chilton/Clanton Public Library
P.O. Box 644
Clanton, AL 35045

Citronelle Historical Preservation Society
18990-19000 South Center Street
P.O. Box 384
Citronelle, AL 36522

Clarke County Historical Society
P.O. Box 131
Jackson, AL 36545

Coosa County Historical Society
P.O. Box 5
Rockford, AL 35136

Coosa River Valley Historical & Genealogical Society
P.O. Box 295
Centre, AL 35960

Covington County Historical Society
P.O. Box 1582
Andalusia, AL 36420

Cullman County Historical Society
1505 Pinecrest NW
Cullman, AL 35055

Dale County Historical Society
P.O. Box 196
Ariton, AL 36311

Escambia County Historical Society
P.O. Box 276
Brewton, AL 36427

Eufaula Heritage Association, Inc.
340 North Eufaula Avenue
Eufaula, AL 36027

Fayette County Historical Society
P.O. Box 309
Fayette, AL 35555-0309

Greene County Historical Society
P.O. Box 746
Eutaw, AL 35462

Henry County Historical Society
c/o Abbeville Memorial Library, History Room
P.O. Box 222
Abbeville, AL 36310

Historic Mobile Preservation Society, Inc.
300 Oakleigh Place
Mobile, AL 36604

Historic Chattahoochee Commission
P.O. Box 33
Eufaula, AL 36027

Jackson County Historical Association
P.O. Box 1494
Scottsboro, AL 35768

Lee County Historical Society
P.O. Box 206
Loachapoka, AL 36865

Limestone County Historical Society
The Donnell House
601 South Clinton Street
P.O. Box 82
Athens, AL 35611

Lowndes County Historical and Genealogical Society
Route 1, P.O. Box 408
Fort Deposit, AL 36032

Pea River Historical and Genealogical Society
Box 628
Enterprise, AL 36331

Piedmont Historical and Genealogical Society
P.O. Box 47
Spring Garden, AL 36275

Pike County Historical & Genealogical Society
Route 2, Box 272
Goshen, AL 36035

Saint Clair Historical Society
Route 1, Box 241
Springville, AL 35146

Shelby County Historical Society
P.O. Box 457
Columbiana, AL 35051
Tel: 205-669-3912

Society of Pioneers of Montgomery, Inc.
P.O. Box 413
Montgomery, AL 36101

Southern Society of Genealogists, Inc.
Stewart University
P.O. Box 295
Centre, AL 35960

Talladega County Historical Association
106 Broome Street
Talladega, AL 35160

Tennessee Valley Historical Society
P.O. Box 149
Sheffield, AL 35660

LDS Family History Centers

Birmingham Family History Center
2768 Altadena Road
Birmingham, AL 35243-4507
Tel: 205-967-7279

Byrd Springs and Weatherly Wards Family History Center
2110 Byrd Springs Road
Huntsville, AL 35802-2146
Tel: 205-881-4461
URl: http://members.aol.com/r3morgan/byrd.html

Huntsville Stake Family History Center
1804 Sparkman Drive
Huntsville, AL 35243
Tel: 205-721-0905
URL: http://members.aol.com/terryann2/fhcinal.htm

Madison and Harvest Wards Family History Center
1297 Slaughter Road
Madison, AL 35758-8685
Tel: 205-722-9450
URL: http://members.aol.com/terryann/madison.htm

Montgomery Family History Center
3460 Carter Hill Rd.
Montgomery, AL 36111-1808
Tel: 334-264-6181

ARCHIVES/LIBRARIES/MUSEUMS

Abbeville Memorial Library
301 Kirkland Street
Abbeville, AL 36310

Aliceville Public Library
416 3rd Avenue North
Aliceville, AL 35442
Tel: 205-373-6691
Email: apl@pickens.net
URL: http://ns1.tusc.net/~apl/

Andalusia Public Library
212 S. Three Notch Street
Andalusia, AL 36420-3799
Tel: 334-222-6612

Anniston Calhoun County Public Library
(Liles Memorial Library)
The Alabama Room
108 E. 10th Street
P.O. Box 308
Anniston, AL 36202-0308
Tel: 205-237-8501
Email: tracks@prodigy.net
URL: http://pages.prodigy.net/tracks/ABENINQ.HTM

Auburn University Library
Special Collections Department
231 Mell Street
Auburn, AL 36830
Tel: 334-844-1755
Email: fostecd@lib.auburn.edu
URL: http://www.lib.auburn.edu/special/

Baldwin Heritage Museum Association
P.O. Box 1117
Foley, AL 36536

Birmingham Public Library
2100 Park Place
Birmingham, AL 35203
Tel: 205-226-3610
URL: http://www.bham.lib.al.us/

Black Heritage Museum of West Alabama
Stillman College
P.O. Box 1430
Tuscaloosa, AL 35403
Tel: 205-349-4240

Blount County Memorial Museum
Courthouse Square
Oneonta, AL 35121

Brent-Centreville Public Library
153 Walnut Street
Centreville, AL 35042

Butler County Historical Society/Library
309 Fort Dale Street
Greenville, AL 36037

Carrollton Public Library
P.O. Box 92
Carrollton, AL 35447
Tel: 205-367-2142

Cullman County Library
200 Clarke Street NE
Cullman, AL 35055

Escambia County Library
700 E. Church Street
P.O. Box 1026
Atmore, AL 36504

Evergreen Conecuh Public Library
201 Park Street
Evergreen, AL 36401-2903
Tel: 334-578-2670

Florence-Lauderdale Public Library
218 N. Wood Avenue
Florence, AL 35630-4707
Tel: 205-764-6563

Foley Public Library
319 East Laurel Avenue
Foley, AL 36535

Gadsden Etowah County Library
254 College Street
Gadsden, AL 35999-3100
Tel: 205-549-4699

Gordo Public Library
Main Street
P.O. Box 336
Gordo, AL 35466
Tel: 205-364-7148

Historic Mobile Preservation Society, Inc.
300 Oakleigh Place
Mobile, AL 36604

Horseshoe Bend Regional Library
207 N. West Street
Dadeville, AL 36853
Tel: 205-825-9232

Huntsville-Madison County Public Library
Huntsville Heritage Room
915 Monroe Street, SW
P.O. Box 443
Huntsville, AL 35804

Tel: 205-532-5940
205-532-5969 (Huntsville Heritage Room)
URL: http://www.hsvchamber.org/guide/amenities/hsvlibrary.html

Interstate Library Contract
6030 Monticello Drive
Montgomery, AL 36130
Tel/Fax: 334-213-3900

Limestone County Department of History and Archives
310 West Washington Street
Athens, AL 35611

Mobile Public Library
704 Government Street
Mobile, AL 36602-1402
Tel: 334-434-7073

Monroe County Heritage Museum
P.O. Box 1637
Monroeville, AL 36461

Museums of the City of Mobile
355 Government Street
Mobile, AL 36602-2315
Tel: 334-434-7569

Pickens County Cooperative Library
P.O. Box 489
Carrollton, AL 35447
Tel: 205-367-8407

Reform Public Library
Main Street
P.O. Box 819
Reform, AL 35481
Tel: 205-375-6240

Samford University Institute of Genealogy and Historical Research
Samford University Library
800 Lakeshore Drive
Birmingham, AL 35229-7008
Tel: 205-870-2780
Fax: 205-870-2483
URL: http://www.samford.edu/schools/ighr/ighr.html

Scottsboro/Jackson County Heritage Center
Tel: 205-259-2122

Scottsboro Public Library
1002 S. Broad Street
Scottsboro, AL 35768-2512
Tel: 205-574-4335

Shelby County Museum and Archives
P.O. Box 457
Columbiana, AL 35051

Troy Public Library
500 East Elm Street
Troy, AL 36081

Tuscaloosa Public Library
1801 River Road
Tuscaloosa, AL 35401
Tel: 205-345-5820

University of Alabama Library
William Stanley Hoole Special Collections Library
P.O. Box 870266
Tuscaloosa, AL 35487-0266
Tel: 205-348-0500
URL: http://www.lib.ua.edu/hoole.htm

University of Southern Alabama
History Department
Humanities Building 344
Mobile, AL 36688

Wallace State Community College Library
Family & Regional History Program
Wallace State Community College
801 Main Street
P.O. Box 2000
Hanceville, AL 35077-2000

NEWSPAPER REPOSITORIES

Alabama Deptartment of Archives & History
Newspaper Program
624 Washington Avenue
Montgomery, AL 36130-0100
Tel: 334-242-4441
Fax: 334-242-4452
Email: ebridges@dsmd.dsmd.state.al.us
URL: http://www.asc.edu/archives/referenc/form.html

VITAL RECORDS

Alabama Department of Archives & History
Government Records Division
P.O. Box 300100
Montgomery, AL 36130-0100
Tel/Fax: 334-242-4452
URL: http://www.asc.edu/archives/agis.html

Center for Health Statistics
State Dept. of Public Health
P.O. Box 5625
Montgomery, AL 36103-5625
Tel: 202-242-5033

ALABAMA ON THE WEB

Alabama Ancestral Database
http://www.bham.mindspring.com/~awillcut/alwaysps.htm

Alabama Department of Archives & History
http://www.asc.edu/archives/agis.html

Alabama GenWeb Project
http://www.rootsweb.com/~algenweb/index.html

Birmingham Public Library by A.C. Alexander
http://www.bham.lib.al.us/

Old Huntsville Magazine
http://www.cntnet.com/oldhvill/

Tracking Your Roots by Lisa R. Franklin, RN
http://members.aol.com/GenWebLisa/index.html

Travellers Southern Families
http://genealogy.traveller.com/genealogy/

ALASKA

ARCHIVES, STATE & NATIONAL

Alaska State Archives & Records Management Services
141 Willoughby Avenue
Juneau, AK 99801-1720
Tel: 907-465-2276
907-465-2317
Fax: 907-465-2465
Email: archives@educ.state.ak.us
URL: http://ccl.alaska.edu/local/archives/table.html

National Archives—Alaska Region
654 W. 3rd Avenue
Anchorage, AK 99501-2145
Tel: 907-271-2441
Fax: 907-271-2442
Email: archives@alaska.nara.gov
URL: http://www.nara.gov/nara/regional/11nsgil.html

GENEALOGICAL SOCIETIES

Alaska Genealogical Society
7030 Dickerson Dr.
Anchorage, AK 99504

Anchorage Genealogical Society
P.O. Box 212265
Anchorage, AK 99521

Fairbanks Genealogical Society
P.O. Box 60534
Fairbanks, AK 99706-0534
URL: http://www.polarnet.com/users/fgs/

Gastineau Genealogical Society
3270 Nowell Avenue
Juneau, AK 99801
Tel: 907-586-3695

Kenai Totem Tracers
c/o Kenai Community Library
63 Main Street Loop
Kenai, AK 99611

Sons of the American Revolution
Alaska Society
1925 North Salem Drive
Anchorage, AK 99504

Wrangell Genealogical Society
P.O. Box 928EP
Wrangell, AK 99929

Historical Societies

Alaska Historical Society
524 West Fourth Avenue, Suite 208
P.O. Box 100299
Anchorage, AK 99510-0299

Cook Inlet Historical Society
Anchorage Museum of History & Art
121 West 7th Avenue
P.O. Box 196650
Anchorage, AK 99519-6650
Tel: 907-343-4326
Fax: 907-343-6149
URL: http://www.ci.anchorage.ak.us/Services/Departments/Culture/ Museum/index.html

Copper Valley Historical Society
Mile 101 Old Richardson Highway
Copper Center Loop Road
P.O. Box 84
Copper Center, AK 99573
Tel: 907-822-5285

Cordova Historical Society
Cordova Historical Museum
Centennial Building
622 First Street
Box 391
Cordova, AK 99574
Tel: 907-424-6665
Fax: 907-424-6000 (City Hall)

Eagle Historical Society & Museum
Box 23
Eagle City, AK 99738
Tel: 907-547-2325

Gastineau Channel Historical Society
P.O. Box 21264
Juneau, AK 99802
Tel: 907-586-5235

Resurrection Bay Historical Society
336 3rd Avenue
P.O. Box 55
Seward, AK 99664-0055
Tel/Fax: 907-224-3902

Sealaska Heritage Foundation
One Sealaska Plaza, Suite 201
Juneau, AK 99801
Tel: 907-463-4844

Sitka Historical Society
Isabel Miller Museum
330 Harbor Drive
Sitka, AK 99835
Tel: 907-747-6455
Fax: 907-747-3739

Soldotna Historical Society & Museum, Inc.
Centennial Park Road
P.O. Box 1986
Soldotna, AK 99669
Tel: 907-262-3756
Fax: 907-262-8466

Talkeetna Historical Society
P.O. Box 76
Talkeetna, AK 99676
Tel/Fax: 907-733-2487

Tanana-Yukon Historical Society
Wickersham House Museum
Alaskaland Park, Airport Way
P.O. Box 71336
Fairbanks, AK 99707
Tel: 907-474-4013
Email: tyhs@polarnet.com
URL: http://www2.polarnet.com/~tyhs/

Wasilla-Knik-Willow Creek Historical Society
Dorothy Page Museum & Old Wasilla Townsite Park
323 Main Street
Wasilla, AK 99654
Tel: 907-376-2005
Fax: 907-373-9072

LDS Family History Centers

Fairbanks Family History Center
1500 Cowles
P.O. Box 73263
Fairbanks, AK 99701
Tel: 907-456-1095
Email: 74077.122@compuserv.com

Juneau Family History Center
5100 Glacier Highway
P.O. Box 32599
Juneau, AK 99803-2599
Tel: 907-586-3518
or 907-780-4281

Wasilla Family History Center
Bogart Road
P.O. Box 0974
Wasilla, AK 99645
Tel: 907-376-9774

Archives/Libraries/Museums

Adak Community Museum
PSC 486, Box 1313
FPO AP 96506-1271
Tel/Fax: 907-592-8064

Alaska Historical Collections
Alaska State Library
8th Floor, State Office Building
333 Willoughby Avenue
P.O. Box 110571
Juneau, AK 99811-0571
Phone: 907-465-2925
Fax: 907-465-2990
Email: asl@muskox.alaska.edu
URL: http://www.edu.state.ak.us/lam/library.html

Alaska State Museum
395 Whittier Street
Juneau, AK 99801-1718
Tel: 907-465-2901
Fax: 907-465-2976
URL: http://ccl.alaska.edu/local/museum/home.htm

Alpine Historical Park
Mile 61.5 Glenn Highway
General Delivery
Sutton, AK 99674
Tel: 907-745-7000

Alutiiq Museum and Archaelogical Repository
215 Mission Road, Suite 101
Kodiak, AK 99615
Tel/Fax: 907-486-7004/7048
Email: 75203.1432@Compuserv.com

Anchorage Museum of History & Art
121 West 7th Avenue
P.O. Box 196650
Anchorage, AK 99519-6650
Tel: 907-343-4326
Fax: 907-343-6149
URL: http://www.ci.anchorage.ak.us/Services/
Departments/Culture/ Museum/index.html

Baranov Museum
Kodiak Historical Society
101 Marine Way
Kodiak, AK 99615
Tel: 907-486-5920
Fax: 907-486-3166

Carrie McLain Memorial Museum
200 E. Front Street
Box 53
Nome, AK 99762
Tel: 907-443-2566
Fax: 907-443-5349

Circle Historical Museum
Mile 128 Steese Highway
P.O. Box 1893
Central, AK 99730
Tel/Fax: 907-520-5312

Consortium Archives
University of Alaska, Anchorage
4101 University Drive
Anchorage, AK 99508

Cordova Historical Museum
622 First Street
Box 391
Cordova, AK 99574
Tel: 907-424-6665
Fax: 907-424-6000 (City Hall)

Dorothy Page Museum & Old Wasilla Townsite Park
Wasilla-Knik-Willow Creek Historical Society
323 Main Street
Wasilla, AK 99654
Tel: 907-376-2005
Fax: 907-373-9072

Duncan Cottage Museum
Duncan Street
P.O. Box 8
Metlakatla, AK 99926
Tel/Fax: 907-886-7363

Elmer E. Rasmuson Library
Rare Books, Archives and Manuscripts
University of Alaska, Fairbanks
Fairbanks, AK 99701
URL: http://www.uaf.alaska.edu/library/libweb/

Eagle Historical Society & Museum
Box 23
Eagle City, AK 99738
Tel: 907-547-2325

George Ashby Memorial Museum
Copper Valley Historical Society
Mile 101 Old Richardson Highway
Copper Center Loop Road
P.O. Box 84
Copper Center, AK 99573
Tel: 907-822-5285

Heritage Library and Museum
National Bank of Alaska
301 W. Northern Lights Blvd.
P.O. Box 100600
Anchorage, AK 99510-0600
Tel: 907-265-2834
Fax: 907-265-2002

House of Wickersham Museum
213 Seventh Street
Juneau, AK 99801
Tel: 907-465-4563

Isabel Miller Museum
Sitka Historical Society
330 Harbor Drive

Sitka, AK 99835
Tel: 907-747-6455
Fax: 907-747-3739

Juneau/Douglas City Museum
155 South Seward Street
Juneau, AK 99801
Tel: 907-586-3572
Fax: 907-586-3203
URL: http://www.ptialaska.net/~cbjhelp/museum.htm

Kake Tribal Heritage Foundation
93009 Glacier Hwy.
P.O. Box 263
Juneau, AK 99801
Juneau Tel: 907-790-2214
Kake Tel: 907-785-3221
Fax: 907-785-6407

Kenitzee Indian Tribe, IRA
2255 Ames Street
P.O. Box 988
Kenai, AK 99611
Tel: 907-283-3633
Fax: 907-283-3052

Klondike Gold Rush National Historical Park
Second & Broadway
P.O. Box 517
Skagway, AK 99840
Tel: 907-983-2921
Fax: 907-983-2046

Museums Alaska
(Statewide Organization)
P.O. Box 242323
Anchorage, AK 99524
Tel/Fax: 907-243-4714

NANA Museum of the Artic
100 Shore Avenue
P.O. Box 49
Kotzebue, AK 99752
Tel: 907-442-3304
Fax: 907-442-2866

Pratt Museum
3779 Bartlett Street
Homer, AK 99603
Tel: 907-235-8635
Fax: 907-235-2764
Email: pratt@alaska.net

Resurrection Bay Historical Society
336 3rd Avenue
P.O. Box 55
Seward, AK 99664-0055
Tel/Fax: 907-224-3902

Sheldon Jackson Museum
104 College Drive
Sitka, AK 99835-7657
Tel: 907-747-8981
Fax: 907-747-3004
http://ccl.alaska.edu/local/museum/home.html

Sheldon Museum & Cultural Center
Main & First Street
Box 269
Haines, AK 99827
Tel: 907-766-2366
Fax: 907-766-2368

Sitka National Historical Park
106 Metlakatla Street; Lincoln St.
P.O. Box 738
Sitka, AK 99835
Tel: 907-747-6281
Fax: 907-747-5938

Soldotna Historical Society & Museum, Inc.
Centennial Park Road
P.O. Box 1986
Soldotna, AK 99669
Tel: 907-262-3756
Fax: 907-262-8466

Talkeetna Historical Society
P.O. Box 76
Talkeetna, AK 99676
Tel/Fax: 907-733-2487

Tongass Historical Museum
629 Dock Street
Ketchikan, AK 99901
Tel: 907-225-5600
Fax: 907-225-5602

Totem Heritage Center
601 Deermont Street
(Mailing Address: 629 Dock St.)
Ketchikan, AK 99901
Tel: 907-225-5900
Fax: 907-225-5602

Trail of '98 City Museum
7th & Spring Streets
Box 415
Skagway, AK 99840
Tel: 907-983-2420
Fax: 907-983-2151

University of Alaska, Anchorage
Library System
Archives and Manuscripts Department
3211 Providence Drive
Anchorage, AK 99508
Tel: 907-786-1825
Fax: 907-786-6050
Email: AYLIB@orion.alaska.edu

University of Alaska Fairbanks Museum
907 Yukon Drive
P.O. Box 756960
Fairbanks, AK 99775-6960
Tel: 907-474-7505
Fax: 907-474-5469
URL: http://www.uaf.alaska.edu/museum/

Valdez Museum & Historical Archive
217 Egan Drive
Box 8
Valdez, AK 99686-0008
Tel: 907-835-2764
Fax: 907-835-4597 or 5800
Email: vldzmuse@alaska.net
URL: http://www.alaska.net/~vldzmuse/index.html

Wickersham House Museum
Tanana-Yukon Historical Society
Alaskaland Park, Airport Way
P.O. Box 71336
Fairbanks, AK 99707
Tel: 907-474-4013
Email: tyhs@polarnet.com
URL: http://www2.polarnet.com/~tyhs/

Wrangell Museum
318 Church Street
P.O. Box 1050
Wrangell, AK 99929
Tel/Fax: 907-874-3770

Yupiit Piciryarait Cultural Center and Museum
420 Chief Eddie Hoffman State Highway
Mailing address:
AVCP, Inc.
P.O. Box 219
Bethel, AK 99559
Tel: 907-520-5312
Fax: 907-543-3596

Newspaper Repositories

Alaska Newspaper Project
Alaska State Library
8th Floor, State Office Building
333 Willoughby Avenue
P.O. Box 110571
Juneau, AK 99811-0571
Phone: 907-465-2919
Fax: 907-465-2990
Email: maryn@muskox.alaska.edu
URL: http://www.edu.state.ak.us/lam/library/hist/newspaper.html

Elmer E. Rasmuson Library
Rare Books, Archives and Manuscripts
University of Alaska, Fairbanks
Fairbanks, AK 99701
URL: http://www.uaf.alaska.edu/library/libweb/

Fairbanks Genealogical Society
P.O. Box 60534
Fairbanks, AK 99706-0534
URL: http://www.polarnet.com/users/fgs/

Vital Records

Department of Health & Social Services
Bureau of Vital Statistics
P.O. Box 110675
Juneau, AK 99811-0675
Tel: 907-465-3392
Fax: 907-465-3618
URL: http://health.hss.state.ak.us/htmlstuf/dph/vitals/vitalst.htm
(includes request forms)

Alaska on the Web

Alaska GenWeb Project
http://www.rootsweb.com/~akgenweb/

Alaska State Library
http://www.educ.state.ak.us/lam/library.html

Fairbanks Genealogical Society
http://www.polarnet.com/users/fgs/

Library of Congress exhibit on "The Russian Church and Native Alaskan Cultures"
http://lcweb.loc.gov/exhibits/russian/s1a.html

ARIZONA

ARCHIVES, STATE & NATIONAL

Arizona Department of Library,
Archives and Public Records
Archives Division
State Capitol, Suite 442
1700 W. Washington St.
Phoenix, AZ 85007
Tel: 602-542-4159
Fax: 602-542-4402
Email: archive@dlapr.lib.az.us
URL: http://www.lib.az.us/archives/archdiv.html

National Archives—Pacific Southwest Region
24000 Avila Rd., First Floor-East Entrance
P.O. Box 6719
Laguna Niguel, CA 92607-6719
Tel: 714-360-2641
Fax: 714-360-2644
Email: archives@laguna.nara.gov
URL: http://www.nara.gov/nara/regional/09nslgil.html

GENEALOGICAL SOCIETIES

Afro-American Historical & Genealogical Society
7739 East Broadway, Suite 195
Tucson, AZ 85710

Apache Genealogy Society
P.O. Box 1084
Sierra Vista, AZ 85636-1084

Arizona Genealogical Advisory Board
P.O. Box 5641
Mesa, AZ 85211-5641
Fax: 602-256-6372

Arizona Genealogical Computer Interest Group
4411 S. Rural Road, Suite 104
Tempe, AZ 85282
URL: http://www.getnet.com/non-profit/agcig/

Arizona Society of Genealogists
6565 East Grant Road
Tucson, AZ 85715

Arizona State Genealogical Society
P.O. Box 42075
Tucson, AZ 85733-2075

Black Family History Society
P.O. Box 1515
Gilbert, AZ 85299-1515

Cherokee Family Ties
516 North 38th Street
Mesa, AZ 85208

Cochise Genealogical Society
P.O. Box 68
Pirtleville, AZ 85626

Coconino County Genealogical Society
649 E. Edison
Williams, AZ 86046

Daughters of the American Revolution
Arizona Society
2622 Papago Trail
Sierra Vista, AZ 85635

Family History Society of Arizona
P.O. Box 63094
Phoenix, AZ 85082-3094
URL: http://www.getnet.com/charity/fhs
Christown Chapter
Tel: 602-468-9573
East Valley Chapter
Tel: 602-892-1778
Maryvale Chapter
Tel: 602-934-5854
Paradise Valley Chapter
Tel: 602-971-2068
Tempe Chapter
Tel: 602-893-0469
Glendale Chapter
Tel: 602-841-7037
Scottsdale Chapter
Tel: 602-990-7914
Fountain Chapter
Tel: 602-837-6678

Genealogical Society of Arizona
P.O. Box 27237
Tempe, AZ 85282

Genealogical Society of Yuma Arizona
P.O. Box 2905
Yuma, AZ 85366-2905

Genealogical Workshop of Mesa
P.O. Box 6052
Mesa, AZ 85216-6052

Genealogy Society of Pinal County
1128 North Kaduta Avenue
Casa Grande, AZ 85222

Green Valley Genealogical Society
P.O. Box 1009
Green Valley, AZ 85622-1009

Hispanic Family History Society
3607 S. Kenneth Place
Tempe, AZ 85282

Lake Havasu Genealogical Society
P.O. Box 953
Lake Havasu City, AZ 86405-0953

Mohave County Genealogical Society
400 West Beale Street
Kingman, AZ 86401

Monte Vista Genies
Monte Vista Village Resort
Pueblo Room
8865 E. Baseline Rd.
Mesa, AZ 85208-5309

Northern Arizona Genealogical Society
P.O. Box 695
Prescott, AZ 86302
Email: dixon@aztec.asu.edu

Northern Gila County Genealogical Society
P.O. Box 952
Payson, AZ 85547

Ohio Genealogical Society
Arizona Chapter
P.O. Box 677
Gilbert, AZ 85299-0677

Phoenix Genealogical Society
1117 W. Northview Avenue
Phoenix, AZ 85021-8066

Sedona Genealogy Club
60 Sierra Road
Sedona, AZ 86336

Sons of the American Revolution
Arizona Society
7000 E. Berneil Dr.
Paradise Valley, AZ 85253

Sun Cities Genealogical Society
P.O. Box 1448
Sun City, AZ 85372-1448

Tri-States Genealogical Society
P.O. Box 6045
Mohave Valley, AZ 86440

Historical Societies

Arizona Historical Foundation
Hayden Library, ASU
P.O. Box 871006
Tempe, AZ 85287-1006
Tel: 602-965-3283
URL: http://www.public.asu.edu/~wabbit/ahf.htm

Arizona Historical Society
Central Arizona Division
1300 North College Avenue
Tempe, AZ 85281
Tel: 602-929-0292
Fax: 602-967-5450
URL: http://www.tempe.gov/ahs/

Arizona Historical Society
Southern Arizona Division
949 E. Second Street
Tucson, AZ 85719
Tel: 520-628-5774
Fax: 520-628-5695
Email: azhist@azstarnet.com
URL: http://www.azstarnet.com/~azhist/index.html

Arizona Historical Society
Rio Colorado Division
Century House Museum
240 Madison Avenue
Yuma, AZ 85364
Phone: 520-782-1841
UL: http://www.tempe.gov/ahs/yuma.htm

Arizona Jewish Historical Society
720 West Edgewood Avenue
Mesa, AZ 85210-3513

Arizona Pioneers Historical Society
949 East Second Street
Tucson, AZ 85719

Graham County Historical Society
Box 127
Safford, AZ 85548
Tel: 520-348-3212 (at museum)
URL: http://www.zekes.com/~dspidell/histsoc.html

Prescott Historical Society
West Gurley Street
Prescott, AZ 86301

Southern Arizona Jewish Historical Society
4181 E. Pontatoc Canyon Dr.
Tucson, AZ 85718

LDS Family History Centers

St. David Arizona Family History Center
Pomerene Road
Benson, AZ 85602
Tel: 520-586-7040

Mesa Family History Center
41 S. Hobson
Mesa, AZ 85204-1021
Tel: 602-964-1200

Phoenix Arizona West Stake
Family History Center
3102 North 18th Avenue
Phoenix, AZ 85015
Tel: 602-265-7762

Show Low Family History Center
1401 W. Deuce of Clubs Avenue
Show Low, AZ 85901
Tel: 520-537-2331

Sierra Vista Family History Center
115 North Highway 90 Bypass
Sierra Vista, AZ 85635
Tel: 520-459-1284

Tucson Family History Center
500 S. Langley Avenue
Tucson, AZ 85710
Tel: 520-298-0905

Winslow Arizona Stake
Family History Center
Corner of Lee St. & Warren Avenue
Winslow, AZ 86047
Tel: 520-298-0905

ARCHIVES/LIBRARIES/MUSEUMS

Arizona State Library
Department of Library, Archives & Public Records
State Capitol
1700 West Washington
Phoenix, AZ 85007
Tel: 602-542-3942
URL: http://www.dlapr.lib.az.us/dindex.html
Archives Division:
Tel: 602-542-4159
Fax: 602-542-4402
Email: archive@dlapr.lib.az.us
Research Division:
Email: rerefde@dlapr.lib.az.us
Federal Documents:
Email: feddocs@dlapr.lib.az.us

Arizona State University
Hayden Library
Cady Mall
Tempe, AZ 85287-1006
Tel: 602-965-6164
URL: http://www.lib.asu.edu/top-menus/hayden.html

Bisbee Historical Society Museum
37 Main Street
Old Bisbee, AZ 85603

Bisbee Mining Historical Museum
5 Copper Queen Plaza
Old Bisbee, AZ 85603
Tel: 520-432-7071
URL: http://www.amdest.com/az/Bisbee/bmining.html

Bloom Southwest Jewish Archives
1052 N. Highland Avenue
Tucson, AZ 85721
Tel: 520-621-5774
URL: http://dizzy.library.arizona.edu/images/swja/swjal-ist.html

Graham County Historical Museum
808 Eighth Street
Safford, AZ 85546
Tel: 520-348-3212

Heard Museum Library & Archives
22 East Monte Vista Road
Phoenix, AZ 84004-1480
Tel: 602-252-8840
Fax: 602-252-9757
URL: http://www.heard.org/library

University of Arizona Library
1510 E. University Blvd.
P.O. Box 210055
Tucson, AZ 85721-0055
Tel: 520-621-6441
URL: http://dizzy.library.arizona.edu/

NEWSPAPER REPOSITORIES

Research Division
Department of Library, Archives & Public Records
State Capitol
1700 West Washington
Phoenix, AZ 85007
Tel: 602-542-3701
Email: ratevis@dlapr.lib.az.us
URL: http://www.dlapr.lib.az.us/research/newspapr.html

Arizona Historical Society
949 E. Second Street
Tucson, AZ 85719
Tel: 520-628-5774
Fax: 520-628-5695
Email: azhist@azstarnet.com
URL: http://www.opus1.com/emol/tucson/ahs/ahsindex.html

University of Arizona Library
1510 E. University Blvd.
P.O. Box 210055
Tucson, AZ 85721-0055
Tel: 520-621-6441
URL: http://dizzy.library.arizona.edu/

VITAL RECORDS

Arizona Department of Health Services
Vital Records Section
2727 W. Glendale Avenue
P.O. Box 3887
Phoenix, AZ 85030-3887
Tel: 602-255-3260

State Historic Preservation Office (SHPO)
Arizona State Parks
1300 W. Washington
Phoenix, AZ 85007
Tel: 602-542-7115
URL: http://www.pr.state.az.us/partnerships/shpo/shpo.html\

Arizona on the Web

Arizona Genealogy Computer Interest Group
http://www.getnet.com/non-profit/agcig/

Arizona Genweb
http://www.u.arizona.edu/~mjarvis/azgenweb/

Arizona Historical Society
http://www.opus1.com/emol/tucson/ahs/ahsindex.html

Arizona Internet Yellow Pages
http://www.amdest.com/az/yellow_pages.html

Arizona State Archives
http://www.lib.az.us/archives/archdiv.html

Family History Society of Arizona
http://www.getnet.com/charity/fhs

Arkansas

Archives, State & National

Arkansas History Commission & State Archives
One Capitol Mall
Little Rock, AR 72201
Tel: 501-682-6900
URL: http://www.state.ar.us/ahc/index.htm

National Archives—Southwest Region
501 W. Felix Street, Building 1
P.O. Box 6216
Fort Worth, TX 76115-0216
Tel: 817-334-5525
Fax: 817-334-5621
Email: archives@ftworth.nara.gov
URL: http://www.nara.gov/nara/regional/07nsgil.html

Southwest Arkanasa Regional Archives
Old Washington Historic State Park
Hempstead County Courthouse
P.O. Box 98
Washington, AR 71862
Tel: 501-983-2684 (Mon-Fri)
501-983-2733 (Sat-Sun)
URL: http://www.gorp.com/gorp/location/ar/parks/old.htm

Genealogical Societies

Ancestors Unknown
404 Angus
Conway, AR 72032

Ark-La-Tex Genealogical Association, Inc.
P.O. Box 4462
Shreveport, LA 71104

Arkansas Genealogical Research
805 East 5th Street
Russellville, AR 72801

Arkansas Genealogical Society
P.O. Box 908
Hot Springs, AR 71902-0908
Tel: 501-262-4513
http://www.uark.edu/ALADDIN/agsinfo/

Arkansas Genealogical Society
4200 A Street
Little Rock, AR 72205

Ashley County Genealogical Society
P.O. Drawer R
Crossett, AR 71635-1819

Batesville Genealogical Society
P.O. Box 3883
Batesville, AR 72503-3883

Baxter County Historical & Genealogical Society
P.O. Box 1508
Mountain Home, AR 72653
URL: http://www.geocities.com/Athens/2101/bchgs.html

Bradley County Genealogical Society
P.O. Box 837
Warren, AR 71671-0837

Clay County Genealogy Society
c/o Piggott Public Library
361 West Main
Piggott, AR 72454-2099

Corbin Genealogical Society
RR 3, Box 86
Paris, AR 72855-9517

Crawford County Genealogical Society
P.O. Box 276
Alma, AR 72921

Crowley's Ridge Genealogical Society
P.O. Box 2091
State University, AR 72467

Dallas County Genealogical & Historical Society
c/o Dallas County Library
Fordyce, AR 71742

Daughters of the American Revolution
Enoch Ashley Chapter
2613 Dauphine Drive
Rogers, AR 72756

Frontier Researchers Genealogical Society
P.O. Box 2123
Fort Smith, AR 72902

Greene County Historical & Genealogical Society
c/o Greene County Library
120 N. 12th Street
Paragould, AR 72450
URL: http://www.cswnet.com/~michael/gcghs.html

Hempstead County Genealogical Society
P.O. Box 1158
Hope, AR 71801

Heritage Club
218 Howard
Nashville, AR 71852

Heritage Seekers Genealogy Club
P.O. Box 532
North Little Rock, AR 72115-0532

Hot Springs County Historical & Genealogical Society
P.O. Box 674
Malvern, AR 72104

Jefferson County Genealogical Society
P.O. Box 2215
Pine Bluff, AR 71613

Madison County Genealogical & Historical Society
P.O. Box 427
Huntsville, AR 72740
Tel: 501-738-6408
URL: http://home.sprynet.com/sprynet/progers/mcghsinf.htm

Marion County, Arkansas Historic & Genealogical Society
c/o Marion County Library
P.O. Box 554
Yellville, AR 72687

Melting Pot Genealogical Society
400 Winans Avenue
Hot Springs, AR 71901

Newton County Historical & Genealogical Society
P.O. Box 360
Jasper, AR 72641
Tel: 501-434-5931

Northwest Arkansas Genealogical Society
P.O. Box 796
Rogers, AR 72757-0796
Tel: 501-273-3890

Ouachita-Calhoun Genealogical Society
P.O. Box 2092
Camden, AR 71701-2092

Polk County Genealogical Society
P.O. Box 12
Hatfield, AR 71945-0012

Professional Genealogists of Arkansas, Inc.
P.O. Box 1807
Conway, AR 72033-1807

Pulaski County Historical Society
P.O. Box 653
Little Rock, AR 72203

Saline County Historical & Heritage Society
P.O. Box 221
Alexander, AR 72022-0221

Sons of the American Revolution
Arkansas Society
1119 Scenic Way
Benton, AR 72015

Southwest Arkansas Genealogical Society
1022 Lawton Circle
Magnolia, AR 71753

Stone County Genealogical Society
P.O. Box 557
Mountain View, AR 72560

Texarkana USA Genealogical Society
Rte. 7, Box 466, BA7
Texarkana, AR 75501

Tri-County Genealogical Society
(Monroe, Phillips, & Lee Co.)
P.O. Box 580
Marvell, AR 72366

Union County Genealogical Society
Barton Library
200 East 5th Street
El Dorado, AR 71730

Village Genealogical Society
6 Aguila Way
Hot Springs Village, AR 71909

Yell County Historical & Genealogical Society
108 West 18th
P.O. Box 356
Russellville, AR 72801-7119

HISTORICAL SOCIETIES

Arkansas Historical Association
History Department
Ozark Hall, 12, University of Arkansas
Fayetteville, AR 72701
Phone: (501)575-5884

Arkansas Historical Society
422 South Sixth Street
Van Buren, AR 72956

Arkansas History Commission
One Capitol Mall
Little Rock, AR 72201
Phone: (501)682-6900
URL: http://www.state.ar.us/ahc/index.htm

Baxter County Historical & Genealogical Society
P.O. Box 1508
Mountain Home, AR 72653
URL: http://www.geocities.com/Athens/2101/bchgs.html

Benton County Historical Society
302 Northeast 2nd Street
P.O. Box 1034
Bentonville, AR 72712

Carroll County Historical Society
Berryville, AR 72616

Clark County Historical Association
Box 516
Arkadelphia, AR 71923

Cleburne County Historical Society
P.O. Box 794
Heber Springs, AR 72543

Craighead County Historical Society
P.O. Box 1011
Jonesboro, AR 72403-1011
URL: http://www.couchgenweb.com/society/

Crawford County Historical Society
929 East Main Street
Van Buren, AR 72956

Dallas County Genealogical & Historical Society
c/o Dallas County Library
Fordyce, AR 71742

Desha County Historical Society
P.O. Box 432
McGehee, AR 71654

Drew County Historical Society
404 South Main Street
Monticello, AR 71655

Faulkner County Historical Society
P.O. Box 731
Conway, AR 72032
URL: http://www.users.intellinet.com/~wmeriwet/faulkner.htm

Fort Smith Historical Society
61 South 8th Street
Fort Smith, AR 72901

Grand Prairie Historical Society
P.O. Box 122
Gilette, AR 72055

Greene County Historical & Genealogical Society
c/o Greene County Library
120 N. 12th Street
Paragould, AR 72450
URL: http://www.cswnet.com/~michael/gcghs.html

Hempstead County Historical Society
P.O. Box 1257
Hope, AR 71801

Hot Springs County Historical & Genealogical Society
P.O. Box 674
Malvern, AR 72104

Independence County Historical Society
P.O. Box 1412
Batesville, AR 72501

Izard County Arkansas Historical Society
c/o Izard County Historian
P.O. Box 84
Dolph, AR 72528

Johnson County Historical Society
P.O. Box 505
Clarksville, AR 72830

Lafayette County Historical Society
P.O. Box 180
Bradley, AR 71826

Lawrence County Historical Society
Powhatan Courthouse State Park
P.O. Box 93
Powhatan, AR 72458

Logan County Historical Society
P.O. Box 40
Magazine, AR 72943-0040

Madison County Genealogical & Historical Society
P.O. Box 427
Huntsville, AR 72740
Tel: 501-738-6408

Marion County, Arkansas Historical & Genealogical Society
c/o Marion County Library
P.O. Box 554
Yellville, AR 72687

Monroe County Historical & Cemetery Association
804 Walker Street
Clarendon, AR 72029-2438

Montgomery County Historical Society
P.O. Box 520
Mount Ida, AR 71957-0520
Tel: 501-867-3121

Newton County Historical & Genealogical Society
P.O. Box 360
Jasper, AR 72641
Tel: 501-434-5931

Orphan Train Heritage Society of America
614 E. Emma Avenue, #115
Springdale, AR 72764
Tel: 501-756-2780
Fax: 501-756-0769
Email: mjohjnson@jcf.jonesnet.org

Ouachita County Historical Society
926 Washington NW
Camden,AR 71701

Poinsett County Historical Society
P.O. Box 424
Harrisburg, AR 72432

Pope County Historical Society
1120 North Detroit
Russellville, AR 72801

Pulaski County Historical Society
P.O. Box 653
Little Rock, AR 72203

Saline County History & Heritage Society
P.O. Box 221
Bryant, AR 72022-0221

Saline County Historical Commission
c/o Gunn Museum Saline County
218 South Market Street
Benton, AR 72015

Scott County Historical & Genealogical Society
P.O. Box 1560
Waldron, AR 72958

Sevier County Historical Society
509 West Heynecker
DeQueen, AR 71832

Van Buren County Historical Society/Museum
3rd & Poplar
P.O. Box 1023
Clinton, AR 72031
Tel: 501-745-4066
URL: http://www.ntanet.net/nta/historical.html

Washington County Arkansas Historical Society
118 East Dickson Street
Fayetteville, AR 72701
http://home.sprynet.com/sprynet/progers/wchs.htm

Yell County Historical & Genealogical Society
108 West 18th
P.O. Box 356
Russellville, AR 72801-7119

LDS Family History Centers

Fort Smith Family History Center
8012 Horan Drive
Ft. Smith, AR 72903-5159
Tel: 501-484-5373

Hot Springs Family History Center
2765 Malvern Road
Hot Springs, AR 71901-8177
Tel: 501-262-5640

Jacksonville Family History Center
6110 T.P. White Drive
Jacksonville, AR
Tel: 501-985-2501

Little Rock Family History Center
13901 Quail Run Drive
Little Rock, AR 72209-6915
Tel: 501-455-4998

Rogers Family History Center
2805 N. Dixieland Road
Rogers, AR 72756-2146
Tel: 501-636-0740

Russellville Family History Center
200 South Cumberland
Russellville, AR 72801-4663
Tel: 501-968-3114

Springdale Family History Center
922 East Emma, Room 138
Springdale, AR 72756
Tel: 501-756-8090 ext. 138

Archives/Libraries/Museums

Arkansas Records Center
314 Vine Street
Newport, AR 72112

Arkansas State Library
One Capitol Mall
Little Rock, AR 72201-1081
Tel: 501-682-1527
URL: http://www.state.ar.us/html/statelibrary.html

Arkansas Territorial Restoration
200 East Third Street
Little Rock, AR 72201-1608
Tel: 501-324-9351
Voice: 501-324-9345
Fax: 501-324-9811 TDD
Email: info@dah.state.ar.us
URL: http://www.heritage.state.ar.us/atr/her_atr.html

Central Arkansas Library System
Downtown Branch
700 South Louisiana
Little Rock, AR 72203

Corning Library
613 Pine St.
Corning, AR 72422
Tel: 501-857-3453

Dean B. Ellis Library
Arkansas State University
108 Cooley Dr.
Jonesboro, AR 72467
Tel: 870-972-3078
URL: http://www.astate.edu/docs/library

Delta Cultural Center
95 Missouri Street
Helena, AR 72342
Tel: 501-338-4350
Fax: 501-338-4358
Email: INFO@DAH.STATE.AR.US
URL: http://wwwheritage.state.ar.us/her_dcc.html

Fayetteville Public Library/Ozarks Regional Library System
217 E. Dickson St.
Fayetteville, AR 72701
Tel: 501-442-2242
Fax: 501-442-5723
Email: publib@www.uark.edu
URL: http://www.uark.edu/ALADDIN/publib/index.html

Greene County Library
120 N. 12th Street
Paragould, AR 72450
Tel: 501-236-8711

Hot Spring County Public Library
Ash & E Streets
Malvern, AR 72104
Tel: 501-332-5441
Lipscomb Room Greene County Library
120 North 12th Street
Paragould, AR 72450-4155

Little Rock Public Library
700 Louisiana Street
Little Rock, AR 72201
Tel: 501-370-5950

Morrilton-Conway County Library
101 W. Church
Morrilton, AR 72110
Tel: 501-354-5204

Northwest Arkansas Genealogical Library
400 S. Walton Boulevard
Bentonville, AR 72712

Orphan Train Riders Research Center
614 E. Emma Avenue, #115
Springdale, AR 72764
Tel: 501-756-2780
Fax: 501-756-0769
Email: mjohjnson@jcf.jonesnet.org

Piggott Library
361 West Main St.
Piggott, AR 72454-2016
Tel: 501-598-3666

Pike County Archives
DeWayne Gray, President
c/o Happy Valley Grocery
Murfreesboro, AR 71958

Powhatan Courthouse State Park
P.O. Box 93
Powhatan, AR 72458
Tel: 501-878-6794

Prescott-Nevada County Depot Museum
400 W. 1st Street South
P.O. Box 10
Prescott, AR 71857
Tel: 870-887-5821
URL: http://wolfden.swsc.k12.ar.us/depot_museum/

Rector Library
Box 252
212 South Main
Rector, AR 72461
Tel: 501-595-2410

Shiloh Museum of Ozark History
118 West Johnson Avenue
Springdale, AR 72764
Tel: 501-750-8165
Fax: 501-750-8171
URL: http://www.uark.edu/ALADDIN/shiloh/

University of Arkansas Libraries
Special Collections Dept.
Fayetteville, AR 72701
Tel: 501-575-5417
Email: mdabrish@saturn.uark.edu
URL: http://cavern.uark.edu/libinfo/speccoll/

Newspaper Repositories

Arkansas History Commission
One Capitol Mall
Little Rock, AR 72201
Phone: (501)682-6900
URL: http://www.state.ar.us/ahc/index.htm

University of Arkansas Libraries
Special Collections Dept.
Fayetteville, AR 72701
Tel: 501-575-5417
Email: mdabrish@saturn.uark.edu
URL: http://cavern.uark.edu/libinfo/speccoll/

Vital Records

Department of Arkansas Heritage
1500 Tower Building
323 Center Street
Little Rock, AR 72201
Voice: 501-324-9150
Fax: 501-324-9154
TDD: 501-324-9811
URL: http://wwwheritage.state.ar.us/dahhome.html

Division of Vital Records
Arkansas Department of Health
4815 West Markham Street, Slot 44
Little Rock, AR 72205-3867
Tel: 501-661-2336

Arkansas on the Web

Arkansas Genweb Project
http://www.rootsweb.com/~argenweb/

Arkansas History Commission & State Archives
http://www.state.ar.us/ahc/index.htm

Original Arkansas Genealogy
http://www.compnetar.com/~billc/

Persistence of the Spirit
African-American Experience in Arkansas
URL: http://www.aristotle.net/persistence/

Travellers Southern Families
http://genealogy.traveller.com/genealogy/

University of Arkansas, Fayetteville
http://cavern.uark.edu/libinfo/speccoll/index.html

CALIFORNIA

ARCHIVES, STATE & NATIONAL

California State Archives
1020 O Street
Sacramento, CA 95814
Tel: 916-653-2246
Fax: 916-653-7363
Email: ArchivesWeb@ss.ca.gov
URL: http://www.ss.ca.gov/archives/archives_home.htm

National Archives—Pacific Southwest Region
24000 Avila Road, First Floor-East Entrance
Laguna Niguel, CA 92607-6719
Tel: 714-360-2641
Fax: 714-360-2644
Email: archives@laguna.nara.gov
URL: http://www.nara.gov/nara/regional/09nslgil.html

National Archives—Pacific Sierra Region
1000 Commodore Drive
San Bruno, CA 94066
Tel: 415-876-9009
Fax: 415-876-9233
Email: archives@sanbruno.nara.gov
URL: http://www.nara.gov/nara/regional/09nssgil.html

GENEALOGICAL SOCIETIES

Afro-American Genealogical Society
California Afro-American Museum
600 State Drive, Exposition Park
Los Angeles, CA 90037

Amador County Genealogical Society
322 Via Verde, Sutter Terrace
Sutter Creek, CA 95685

Antelope Valley Genealogical Society
P.O. Box 1049
Lancaster, CA 93534-1049
Tel: 805-942-4676
URL: http://www.hughes-ec.com/org/avgs/

Association of Jewish Genealogical Societies
P.O. Box 50245
Palo Alto, CA 94303

Association of Professional Genealogists
Southern California Chapter (SCC-APG)
P.O. Box 9486
Brea, CA 92822-9486
URL: http://www.compuology.com/sccapg/

Basin Research Associates, Inc.
14731 Catalina Street
San Leandro, CA 94577

Calaveras Genealogical Society
753 Main Street
P.O. Box 184
Angels Camp, CA 95222-0184

California African-American Genealogical Society
P.O. Box 8442
Los Angeles, CA 90008-0442

California Genealogical Society
300 Brennan Street
P.O. Box 77105
San Francisco, CA 94107-0105
Tel: 415-777-9936
URL: http://pw2.netcom.com/~dwilma/cgs.html

California Pioneers of Santa Clara County
P.O. Box 8208
San Jose, CA 95155

California Society of Colonial Pioneers
456 McAlister Street
San Francisco, CA 94102

California State Genealogical Alliance
c/o Wendy Elliott
4808 E. Garland St.
Anaheim, CA 92807-1005
Tel: 714-777-0483
URL: http://feefhs.org/csga/frg-csga.html

California State Society
Daughters of the American Revolution
URL: http://granite.koan.com/~nnnwade/index.html

Chester Genealogy Club
P.O. Box 107
Chester, CA 96020

Chula Vista Genealogical Society
c/o Chula Vista City Library
4th & F Streets
Chula Vista, CA, 91910

Clan Diggers Genealogical Society
(Kern River Valley, Kern County)
P.O. Box 531
Lake Isabella, CA 93240
Tel: 619-376-6210

Coachella Valley Genealogical Society
P.O. Box 124
Indio, CA 92202

Colorado River-Blythe Quartsite Genealogical Society
P.O. Box 404
Blythe, CA 92226

Colusa County Genealogical Society
P.O. Box 973
Williams, CA 95987

Computer Rooters
P.O. Box 161693
Sacramento, CA 95816

Computer Genealogy Society of San Diego (CGSSD)
P.O. Box 370357
San Diego, CA 92137-0357
Tel: 619-670-0960
Email: cgssd-board@ucsd.edu.
URL: http://www-irps.ucsd.edu/cgssd/

Conejo Valley Genealogical Society
2331 Borchard Rd
Newbury Park, CA 91230
Mail:
P.O. Box 1228
Thousand Oaks, CA 91358-1228
Tel: 805-497-8293
URL: http://www.tol.lib.ca.us/1cvgshis.html

Contra Costa Genealogical Society
P.O. Box 910
Concord, CA 94522
URL: http://www.geocities.com/Heartland/Plains/4335/cccgs.html

Daughters of the American Revolution (DAR)
Covina California Chapter
2441 Cameron Avenue
Covina, CA 91724

Davis Genealogical Club/Library
Davis Senior Center
646 A Street
Davis, CA 95616
Tel: 916-753-2672

Delta Genealogical Interest Group
P.O. Box 157
Knightsen, CA 94548

East Bay Genealogical Society
405 14th St., Terrace Level (library)
P.O. Box 20417
Oakland, CA 94620-0417
Tel: 415-451-9599

East Kern Genealogical Society
9716 Irene Avenue
California, CA 93505-1329
Tel: 619-373-4728

El Dorado Research Society
P.O. Box 56
El Dorado, CA 95623

Escondido Genealogical Society
P.O. Box 2190
Escondido, CA 92025-2190
Tel: 619-743-6049

Fresno Genealogical Society
P.O. Box 1429
Fresno, CA 93716-1429
Tel: 209-488-3195

Genealogical Society of Hispanic America
Southern California Branch (GSHA-SC)
P.O. Box 2472
Santa Fe Springs, CA 90670-0472
URL: http://home.earthlink.net/~ririgoyen/

German Research Association, Inc. (GRA)
P.O. Box 711600
San Diego, CA 92171-1600
URL: http://www.feefhs.org/gra/frg-gra.html

German Genealogical Society
2125 Wright Avenue, C9
LaVerne, CA 91750

Glendora Genealogical Group
P.O. Box 1141
Glendora, CA 91740

Glenn Genealogy Group
1121 Marin
Orland, CA 95963

Grass Roots Genealogical Group
11350 McCourtney Road
Grass Valley, CA 95949-9759
URL: http://www.nccn.net/leisure/crafthby/genealog.htm

Hadley Genealogical Society of Southern California
33210 Baily Park Dr.
Menifee, CA 92584

Hayward Area Genealogical Society
P.O. Box 754
Hayward, CA 94543

Hemet-San Jacinto Genealogical Society
1779 East Florida Ave, Unit C-1
Hemet, CA 92544
Mail:
P.O. Box 2516
Hemet, CA 92546-2516
Tel: 909-658-6153

Heritage Genealogical Society
12056 Lomica Dr.
San Diego, CA 92128
Tel: 619-485-6009

Hi Desert Genealogical Society
P.O. Box 1271
Victorville, CA 92393
Tel: 619-247-8835
URL: http://vvo.com/comm/hdgs.htm

Humboldt County Genealogical Society
2336 G Street
P.O. Box 882
Eureka, CA 95502

Immigrant Genealogical Society
1310-B Magnolia Blvd.
P.O. Box 7369
Burbank, CA 91510
Tel: 818-848-3122
Fax: 818-716-6300
Email: ted.hanft@panasia.com
URL: http://feefhs.org/igs/frg-igs.html

Imperial County Genealogical Society
1573 Elam Street
El Centro, CA 92243-3133

Indian Wells Valley Genealogical Society
131 Los Flores
P.O. Box 2047
Ridgecrest, CA 93555

Intermountain Genealogical Society
P.O. Box 399
Burney, CA 96013

Jewish Genealogical Society of Los Angeles
4530 Woodley Avenue
Encino, CA 91436

Jewish Genealogical Society of Orange County
11751 Cherry Street
Los Alamitos, CA 90720

Jewish Genealogical Society of Sacramento
2351 Wyda Way
Sacramento, CA 95825

Jewish Genealogical Society of San Diego
255 South Rios Avenue
Solana Beach, CA 92075

Kern County Genealogical Society
P.O. Box 2214
Bakersfield, CA 93303
Tel: 805-831-7527

Lake Elsinore Genealogical Society
Box 807
Lake Elsinore, CA 92330

Lake County Genealogical Society/Museum
255 North Forbes Street
P.O. Box 1323
Lakeport, CA 95453
Tel: 707-263-4555

Lake Elsinore Genealogical Society (LEGS)
P.O. Box 807
Lake Elsinore, CA 92531-0808
Tel: 909-674-5776

Leisure World Genealogical Workshop/Library
2300 Beverly Manor Road
Seal Beach, CA 90740

Livermore-Amador Genealogical Society (L-AGS)
P.O. Box 901
Livermore, CA 94551
Tel: 510-846-4265
510-447-9386
Email: lags@california.com
URL: http://www.l-ags.org/index.html

Los Angeles Westside Genealogical Society
P.O. Box 10447
Marina del Rey, CA 90295

Los Banos California Genealogical Society
16778 South Place
P.O. Box 1106
Los Banos, CA 93635
Tel: 209-826-4882

Los Californianos
P.O. Box 5155
San Francisco, CA 94101

Lucerne Valley Genealogy Association, Root Diggers
c/o Lucerne Valley Library
P.O. Box 408
Lucerne Valley, CA 92356

Madera Genealogical Society
P.O. Box 495
Madera, CA 93639-0495
Tel: 209-661-1219

Maidu Genealogical Society
Maidu Committee Center
1550 Maidu Drive
Roseville, CA 95661
Tel: 916-786-0186

Marin County Genealogical Society
P.O. Box 1511
Novato, CA 94948-1511
Tel: 415-435-2310
Email: stst@uclink4.berkeley.edu
URL: http://trimble.reshall.berkeley.edu/mcgs/

Mayflower Descendants Society of the State of California
405 Fourteenth Street, Terrace Level
Oakland, CA 94612

Mendocino Coast Genealogical Society
P.O. Box 762
Fort Bragg, CA 95437

Merced County Genealogical Society
P.O. Box 3061
Merced, CA 95340
Tel: 209-723-9019

Mission Oaks Genealogical Club
Mission Oaks Community Center
4701 Gibbons Dr.
Carmichael, CA 95609
Mail:
P.O. Box 216
Carmichael, CA 95609-0216
Tel: 916-482-8531

Mojave Desert Genealogical Society
P.O. Box 1320
Barstow, CA 92311

Monterey County Genealogical Society
P.O. Box 8144
Salinas, CA 93912-9144

Morongo Basin Genealogical Society
P.O. Box 234
Yucca Valley, CA 92284

Mt. Diablo Genealogical Society
1938 Tice Blvd.
P.O. Box 4654
Walnut Creek, CA 94596
Tel: 415-932-4423

Napa Valley Genealogical & Biographical Society
1701 Menlo Avenue
P.O. Box 385
Napa, CA 94558
Tel: 707-252-2252

Nevada County Genealogical Society
Dept. I
P.O. Box 176
Cedar Ridge, CA 95924
Tel: 619-257-3780
URL: http://www.nccn.net/leisure/crafthby/genealog.htm1

North San Diego County Genealogical Society
P.O. Box 581
Carlsbad, CA 92018-0581
URL: http://www.compuology.com/nsdcgs/

Norwegian Genealogy Group
c/o Sons of Norway Lodge
2006 East Vista Way
Vista, CA 92084-3321

Ohio Genealogical Society
Southern California Chapter
P.O. Box 5057
Los Alamitos, CA 90721-5057

Orange County California Genealogical Society (OCCGS)
7111 Talbert
Huntington Beach, CA
Mail:
P.O. Box 1587
Orange, CA 92668
URL: http://www/conentusa.com/occgs.html

Pajaro Valley Genealogical Society
53 North Drive
Freedom, CA 95019

Palm Springs Genealogical Society
P.O. Box 2093
Palm Springs, CA 92263-2093
Email: editor1@earthlink.net
URL: http://www.ci.palm-springs.ca.us/Library/lgen.html

Paradise Genealogical Society
P.O. Box 460
Paradise, CA 95967-0460
Tel: 916-877-2330

Pasadena Genealogy Society
P.O. Box 94774
Pasadena, CA 91109-4774
Tel: 818-794-7973

Patterson Genies
525 Clover Avenue
Patterson, CA 95363

Placer County Genealogical Society
P.O. Box 7385
Auburn, CA 95604-7385
Tel: 916-885-2695
Email: gunruh@pcgenes.com
URL: http://www.webcom.com/gunruh/pcgs.html

Pocahontas Trail Genealogical Society
6015 Robin Hill Drive
Lakeport, CA 95453
Tel: 707-263-5829

Pocahontas Trail Genealogical Society
3628 Cherokee Lane
Modesto, CA 95356

Polish Genealogical Society of California (PGS CA)
P.O. Box 713
Midway City, CA 92655-0713
URL: http://www.feefhs.org/pol/frgpgsca.html

Pomona Valley Genealogical Society
P.O. Box 286
Pomona, CA 91768-0286
Tel: 909-599-2166

Questing Heirs Genealogical Society
P.O. Box 15102
Long Beach, CA 90815-0102
Tel: 310-596-8736

Rancho Bernardo Genealogy Group
c/o RB Branch
San Diego Public Library
16840 Bernardo Center
San Diego, CA 92128
Tel: 619-485-6977

Redwood Genealogical Society
P.O. Box 645
Fortuna, CA 95540-0645
Tel: 707-725-3791
URL: http://www.humboldt1.com/~fortuna/genealgy.htm

Renegade Root Diggers
9171 Fargo Avenue
Hanford, CA 93230

Riverside Genealogical Society
P.O. Box 2557
Riverside, CA 92516

Root Cellar Sacramento Genealogical Society
P.O. Box 265
Citrus Heights, CA 95611
Tel: 916-481-4930

Sacramento Genealogical Association
P.O. Box 28297
Sacramento, Ca 95828

Sacramento German Genealogy Society
P.O. Box 660061
Sacramento, CA 95866-0061
URL: http://www.dcn.davis.ca.us/go/feefhs/sggs/frg-sggs.html

Sacramento Valley, Genealogical and Historical Council of the
P.O. Box 214749
Sacramento, CA 95821-0749
Tel: 916-331-4349
URL: http://feefhs.org/ghcsv/frgghcsv.html

San Bernardino Valley Genealogical Society
P.O. Box 26020
San Bernardino, CA 92406
Tel: 909-883-7468

San Diego African-American Genealogy Research Group
c/o Milton Hines
9026 Three Seasons Road
San Diego, CA 92126
Email: fmtw38a@prodigy.com

San Diego Genealogical Association
P.O. Box 422
Ramona, CA 92065

San Diego Genealogical Society
1050 Pioneer Way, Suite E
El Cajon, CA 92020-1943
Tel: 619-588-0065
Email: sdgs@genealogy.org
URL: http://www.genealogy.org/~sdgs/

San Diego Jewish Genealogical Society
c/o Lawrence Family Jewish Community Center
4126 Executive Dr.
La Jolla, CA 92037

San Fernando Valley Genealogical Society
2042 Socrates Avenue
Simi, CA 93065

San Francisco Bay Area Jewish Genealogical Society
921 S. El Camino Real
San Mateo, CA 94402

San Gorgonio Genealogical Society
1050 Brinton Avenue
Banning, CA 92220

San Joaquin Genealogical Society
P.O. Box 4817
Stockton, CA 95104

San Luis Obispo County Genealogical Society
P.O. Box 4
Atascadero, CA 93423-0004
Tel: 805-927-8172

San Mateo County Genealogical Society (SMCGS)
25 Tower Road
P.O. Box 5083
San Mateo, CA 94402
Email: smcgs@genealogy.org
URL: http://www.genealogy.org/~smcgs/

San Ramon Valley Genealogical Society
P.O. Box 305
Diablo, CA 94528
Tel: 510-837-8858

Santa Barbara County Genealogical Society
711 Santa Barbara St.
P.O. Box 1303
Goleta, CA 93116-1303
Tel: 805-967-8954

Santa Clara Historical & Genealogical Society
2635 Homestead Road
Santa Clara, CA 95051-5387
Tel: 408-984-3236

Santa Cruz County, Genealogical Society of
P.O. Box 72
Santa Cruz, CA 95063
Tel: 408-429-3530

Santa Maria Valley Genealogical Society
P.O. Box 1215
Santa Maria, CA 93456

Sequoia Genealogical Society
Tulare Public Library
113 North F Street
Tulare, CA 93274-3803

Shasta Genealogical Society
P.O. Box 994652
Redding, CA 96099-4652

Siskiyou County Genealogical Society
P.O. Box 225
Yreka, CA 96097
Tel: 916-842-8175

Sloughhouse Area Genealogical Society
Rancho Murietta, CA 95683
Tel: 916-354-2807

Society of California Pioneers
P.O. Box 191850
San Francisco, CA 94119-1850

Society of Hispanic Historical & Ancestral Research
P.O. Box 5294
Fullerton, CA 92635
Email: SHHARPres@AOL.com
http://www.webcom.com/shharnet/welcome.html

Solano County Genealogical Society
Old Town Hall
620 E. Main St.
Vacaville, CA
Mail:
P.O. Box 2494
Fairfield, CA 94533
Tel: 707-446-6869

Sonoma County Genealogical Society
P.O. Box 2273
Santa Rosa, CA 95405-0273

Email: hwmiller@wco.com
URL: http://web.wco.com/~hwmiller/genealogy/scgs.htm

South Bay Cities Genealogical Society
P.O. Box 6071
Torrance, CA 90504

South Humboldt Historical & Genealogical Society
P.O. Box 656
Garberville, CA 95440

South Orange County California Genealogy Society (SOCCGS)
P.O. Box 4513
Mission Viejo, CA 92690-4513
Email: Soccgs@emcee.com
URL: http://genealogy.emcee.com/~soccgs/

Southern California Genealogical Society (SCGS)
122 S. San Fernando Blvd.
P.O. Box 4377
Burbank, CA 91503-4377
Tel: 818-843-7247
URL: http://netvoyage.net/~leda/scgs.htm

Southern California Genealogical Society, Inc.
600 South Central Avenue
Glendale, CA 91204

Stanislaus County Genealogical Society
P.O. Box 4735
Modesto, CA 95352-4735
Tel: 209-522-2880

Sutter-Yuba Genealogical Society
P.O. Box 1274
Yuba City, CA 95991

TRW Genealogical Society
One Space Park S-1420
Redondo Beach, CA 90278

Taft Area Genealogical Society
P.O. Box 1411
Taft, CA 93268

Tehama Genealogical & Historical Society
P.O. Box 415
Red Bluff, CA 96080

Tule Tree Tracers
Porterville Public Library
41 West Thurman Avenue
Porterville, CA 93257
Tel: 209-784-0177

Tuolumne County Genealogical Society
158 West Bradford Avenue
P.O. Box 3956
Sonora, CA 95370
Tel: 209-532-1317

Ukiah Tree Tracers Genealogical Society
P.O. Box 72
Ukiah, CA 95482

Universal Genealogical Society of Bellflower
8251 Cedar Street
Bellflower, CA 90706

Vandenberg Genealogical Society
P.O. Box 814
Lompoc, CA 93438-0814
Tel: 805-736-9637
805-736-4778

Ventura County Genealogical Society
P.O. Box 24608
Ventura, CA 93002
Tel: 805-648-2715
805-642-1242

Whittier Area Genealogical Society (WAGS)
P.O. Box 4367
Whittier, CA 90607-4367
Tel: 310-946-1758
URL: http://www.compuology.com/wags/

Yorba Linda Genealogical Society
4751 Libra Place
Yorba Linda, CA 92686

Yucaipa Valley Genealogical Society
P.O. Box 32
Yucaipa, CA 92399

Historical Societies

Alamedo County Historical Society
5461 Fernhoff Road
Oakland, CA 94619-3111
Tel: 510-531-0222

Alamedo Historical Society
2264 Santa Clara Avenue
Alameda, CA 94501

Alpine County Historical Society
P.O. Box 24
Markleeville, CA 96120

Alvarado Adobe
#1 Alvarado Square
San Pablo, CA 94806

Amador-Livermore Valley Historical Society
603 Main Street
P.O. Box 573
Pleasanton, CA 94566
Tel: 510-462-2766

Amador County Historical Society
P.O. Box 761
Jackson, CA 95642

Amador County Historical Society
P.O. Box 147
Pine Grove, CA 95665

American Historical Association
Loyola Marymount-Dept. of History
Los Angeles, CA 90045

American Historical Society of Germans from Russia
3233 North West
Fresno, CA 93705

Anaheim Historical Society
Anaheim Blvd. at Broadway
P.O. Box 927
Anaheim, CA 92815
Tel: 714-778-3301

Anderson Valley Historical Society
P.O. Box 676
Boonville, CA 95415
Tel: 707-895-3207

Association for Northern California Records & Research
P.O. Box 3024
Chico, CA 95927
Tel: 916-898-62137

Atascadero History Society
6500 Palma
P.O. Box 1047
Atascadero, CA 93423
Tel: 805-466-8341

Augustan Society, Inc.
1510 Cravens Avenue
Torrance, CA 90501

Azusa Historical Society, Inc.
City Hall Complex
213 E. Foothill Blvd.
Azusa, CA 91702

Belmont Historical Society
Historical Room
1225 Ralston Avenue
Belmont, CA 94002
URL: http://www.belmont.gov/hist/index.html

Belvedere-Tiburon Landmark Society
1600 Juanita Lane
P.O. Box 134
Tiburon, CA 94920

Berkeley Historical Society
1931 Center Street
P.O. Box 1190
Berkeley, CA 94701-1190
Tel: 510-848-0181
Email: berkhist@ix.netcom.com
URL: http://www.ci.berkeley.ca.us/histsoc/

Big Bear Valley Historical Society
Big Bear City Park
P.O. Box 513
Big Bear City, CA 92314
Tel: 714-585-8100

Bishop Museum/Historical Society
P.O. Box 363
Bishop, CA 93514
Tel: 619-873-5950

Black Historical Society of Santa Clara
468 North 11th Street
San Jose, CA 95112
Tel: 408-295-9183

Boulder Creek Historical Society
Highway 9 & Flat Street
Boulder Creek, CA 95006
Tel: 408-338-6617

British Family Historical Society of Los Angeles
22941 Felbar Avenue
Torrance, CA 90505

Buena Vista Historical Society
7843 Whitaker Street
Buena Park, CA 90621

Butte County Historical Society
P.O. Box 2195
Oroville, CA 95965
Tel: 916-533-5316

Cabrillo Historical Association
P.O. Box 6670
San Diego, CA 92106

Calaveras County Historical Society, Museum, & Archives
30 North Main Street
P.O. Box 723
San Andreas, CA 95249
Tel: 209-754-1058

California Committee for the Promotion of History
6000 J Street
Sacramento, CA 95819

California Historical Society
678 Mission Street
San Francisco, CA 94105
Tel: 415-357-1848
Fax: 415-357-1850
URL: http://www.calhist.org

California Historical Society
1120 Old Mill Road
San Marino, CA 91108

California History Center Foundation
21250 Stevens Creek Blvd.
Cupertino, CA 95014

California Mennonite Historical Society
4824 E. Butler
Fresno, CA 93727
URL: http://www.fresno.edu/cmhs

California Pioneers of Santa Clara County
661 Empey Way
P.O. Box 8208
San Jose, CA 95155
Tel: 408-998-1174

Californian Southern Division,
U.S. Mormon Battalion, Inc.
6477 Elmhurst Dr.
San Diego, CA 92120
Tel: 619-582-7243

Chinese Historical Society of America
650 Commercial Street
San Francisco, CA 94111
Tel: 415-391-1188

Chino Valley Historical Society
P.O. Box 972
Chino, CA 91708

Chula Vista Historical Society
P.O. Box 1222
Chula Vista, CA 92012
Tel: 619-426-1222

City of San Bernardino Historical & Pioneer Society
P.O. Box 875
San Bernardino, CA 92402

Coachella Valley Historical Society
P.O. Box 505
Indio, CA 92202-0505
Tel: 619-342-6651

Colusa County Historical Records Commission
c/o Colusa County Free Library
738 Market Street
Colusa, CA 95932
Tel: 916-458-7671

Colusa County Historical Society
P.O. Box 510
Glenn, CA 95943

Commission for the Preservation
of Pioneer Jewish Cemeteries and Landmarks
2911 Russell Street
Berkeley, CA 94705
Tel: 510-849-2710

Concord Historical Society
P.O. Box 404
Concord, CA 94122

Conejo Valley Historical Society
P.O. Box 1692
Thousand Oaks, CA 91360

Conference of California Historical Societies
University of the Pacific
Stockton, CA 95211
Tel: 209-946-2169

Contra Costa County Historical Society
1700 Oak Park Boulevard-CS
P.O. Box 821
Pleasant Hill, CA 94522
Tel: 510-939-9180
Email: cchistry@ix.netcom.com
URL: http://www.ecis.com/~oakhrst/history.html

Coronado Historical Association
P.O. Box 393
Corona Del Mar, CA 92625
Tel: 619-435-7242

Costa Mesa Historical Society
1870 Anaheim Avenue
P.O. Box 1764
Costa Mesa, CA 92628
Tel: 714-631-5918

Covina Valley Historical Society
125 East College Street
Covina, CA 91723

Cupertino Committee for the Promotion of History
21250 Stevens Creek Blvd.
Cupertino, CA 95014

Cypress College Local History Association
Cypress College
Cypress, CA 90630

De Anza Trek Lancer Society
20739 Sunrise Drive
Cupertino, CA 95014

Del Mar Historical Society
1442 Camino del Mar
Del Mar, CA 92014
Tel: 619-259-0421

Del Norte Historical Society
577 H Street
Crescent City, CA 95531
Tel: 707-464-3922

Delano Historical Society & Heritage Park
330 Lexington Street
Delano, CA 93215
Tel: 805-725-6730

Desert Hot Springs Historical Society
P.O. Box 1267
Desert Hot Springs, CA 92240

Downey Historical Society
P.O. Box 554
Downey, CA 90241

Duarte Historical Society
P.O. Box 263
Duarte, CA 91010

Eagle Rock Valley Historical Society
2035 Colorado Blvd.
Eagle Rock, CA 90041

East Contra Costa Historical Society
2nd & Dainty
Brentwood, CA 94513

El Cajon Historical Society
P.O. Box 1973
El Cajon, CA 92020
Tel: 619-444-3800

El Monte Historical Society
3150 North Tyler Avenue
El Monte, CA 91731

Encino Historical Society
16756 Moorpark Street
Encino, CA 91436

Escondido Historical Society
321 N. Broadway
P.O. Box 263
Escondido, CA 92025
Tel: 619-743-8207

Fallbrook Historical Society
P.O. Box 1375
Fallbrook, CA 92028

Federation of Orange County Historical Organizations
P.O. Box 4048
Santa Ana, CA 92702
Tel: 714-834-5560

Fillmore Historical Society
P.O. Box 314
Fillmore, CA 93015

Folsom Historical Society
823 Sutter Street
Folsom, CA 95630
Tel: 916-983-4157

Fontana Historical Society/Library
8459 Wheeler Avenue
P.O. Box 426
Fontana, CA 92334
Tel: 714-823-1733

Fort Crook Historical Society
P.O. Box 397
Fall River Mills, CA 96028

Fort Point National Historic Site
Funsten Avenue and Lincoln Blvd.
P.O. Box 29163
San Francisco, CA 94129
Tel: 415-921-8193

Fortuna Historical Commission
621 11th Street
Fortuna, CA 95540

Fresno City & County Historical Society
7160 W. Kearney Blvd.
P.O. Box 2029
Fresno, CA 93706
Tel: 209-441-0862

Friends of the Adobes, Inc.
South Mission Street
San Miguel, CA 93451

Friends of the Carrillo Adobe
P.O. Box 2843
Santa Rosa, CA 95405

Garden Grove Historical Society
12174 Euclid Street
Garden Grove, CA 92640
Tel: 714-530-8871

Genealogical and Historical Council of the Sacramento Valley
P.O. Box 214749
Sacramento, CA 95821-0749
Tel: 916-331-4349
URL: http://feefhs.org/ghcsv/frgghcsv.html

Gilroy Historical Society
P.O. Box 2190
Gilroy, CA 95021

Glendora Historical Society
P.O. Box 532
Glendora, CA 91740

Goleta Valley Historical Society
304 North Los Carneros
Goleta, CA 93117
Tel: 805-964-4407

Hayward Area Historical Society/Museum
22701 Main Street
Hayward, CA 94541
Tel: 510-581-0223

Healdsburg Historical Society
221 Matheson
Healdsburg, CA 95448

Heritage Association of El Dorado County
P.O. Box 62
Placerville, CA 95667
Historic Preservation Committee
501 Poli
Ventura, CA 93001

Historical Society of Long Beach
428 Pine Avenue
P.O. Box 1869
Long Beach, CA 90801

Historical Society of Southern California
200 East Avenue
Los Angeles, CA 90031

Historical Society of the Upper Mojave Desert
c/o Maturango Museum
100 E. Las Flores Avenue
Ridgecrest, CA 93555
Tel: 619-375-6900
URL: http://www.ridgecrest.ca.us/~matmus/Hist.html

Humboldt County Historical Society
P.O. Box 8000
Eureka, CA 95502
Tel: 707-443-3515

Huntington Beach Historical Society
19820 Beach Blvd.
Huntington Beach, CA 92648
Tel: 714-962-5777

Irvine Historical Society & Museum
5 Rancho San Joaquin
Irvine, CA 92717
Tel: 714-786-4112

Julian Historical Society
P.O. Box 513
Julian, CA 92036
Tel: 619-765-2184

Kern-Antelope Historical Society
P.O. Box 325
Rosamond, CA 93560
Tel: 805-943-3221

Kern County Historical Organizations & Museums
Kern County Historical Records Commission
3801 Chester
Bakersfield, CA 93301
Tel: 805-861-2132

Kern River Valley Historical Society
P.O. Box 651
Kernville, CA 93238
Tel: 619-379-5895

Kern County Historical Society
P.O. Box 141
Bakersfield, CA 93302

La Habra Old Settlers Historical Society
600 Linden Lane
La Habra, CA 90631
Tel: 213-697-1271

La Jolla Historical Society
7846 Eads Avenue
P.O. Box 2085
La Jolla, CA 92038
Tel: 619-459-5335
Email: features@iaco.com
URL: http://www.iaco.com/features/lajolla/lifeinlj/history/ljhs.html

La Mesa Historical Society
8369 University Avenue
P.O. Box 882
La Mesa, CA 91944-0882
Tel: 619-466-0197

La Puente Valley Historical Society
P.O. Box 522
La Puente, CA 91744

Lafayette Historical Society
P.O. Box 133
Lafayette, CA 94549
Tel: 510-283-6822

Lake County Historical Society
P.O. Box 1011
Lakeport, CA 95453

Lake Tahoe Historical Society
P.O. Box 404
South Lake Tahoe, CA 95705

Las Virgines Historical Society
P.O. Box 124
Agoura, CA 91301

Lakeside Historical Society
9906 Maine Avenue
P.O. Box 1423
Lakeside, CA 92040
Tel: 619-561-1886

Lassen County Historical Society
William H. Pratt Museum
105 North Weatherlow St.
P.O. Box 321
Susanville, CA 96130
Tel: 916-257-6551

Leisure World Historical Society of Laguna Hills
23522 Paseo de Valencia
P.O. Box 2220
Laguna Hills, CA 92654
Tel: 714-951-2330

Lemon Grove Historical
P.O. Box 624
Lemon Grove, CA 91945
Tel: 619-465-9925

Little Landers Historical Society
10110 Commerce Avenue
Tujunga, CA 91042

Livermore Heritage Guild
P.O. Box 961
Livermore, CA 94550

Lomita Historical Society
24016 Benhill Avenue
Lomita, CA 90717

Lompoc Valley Historical Society
P.O. Box 88
Lompoc, CA 93438

Los Angeles City Historical Society
P.O. Box 41046
Los Angeles, CA 90041

Los Altos Hills Historical Society
27200 Elena Road
Los Altos Hills, CA 94022

Los Altos Historical Commission
1 North San Antonio Road
Los Altos Hills, CA 94022

Madera County Historical Society
210 West Yosemite Avenue
P.O. Box 478
Madera, CA 93639
Tel: 209-673-0291

Marin County Historical Society
1125 D Street
San Rafael, CA 94901
Tel: 415-454-8538

Marin Heritage
P.O. Box 1432
San Rafael, CA 94902

Maritime Research Society of San Diego
2427 Howard Avenue
San Diego, CA 92104

Mendocino County Historical Society
603 W. Perkins St.
Ukiah, CA 95482-4726
Tel: 707-462-6969

Mendocino County Heritage Network
400 East Commercial
Willits, CA 95490

Mendocino Historical Research
Kelley House Museum
45007 Albion St.
P.O. Box 922
Mendocino, CA 95460
Tel: 707-937-5791

Menlo Park Historical Association
Menlo Park Library
800 Alma Street
Menlo Park, CA 94025

Merced County Historical Society
Old County Courthouse
21st and N Streets
Merced, CA 95340
Tel: 209-385-7426

Millbrae Historical Society
P.O. Box 511
Millbrae, CA 94030
Tel: 415-692-5786
415-692-3720

Mission San Miguel
P.O. Box 69
San Miguel, CA 93451

Modoc County Historical Society and Museum
600 S. Main Street
Alturas, CA 96101

Mohahve Historical Society
P.O. Box 21
Victorville, CA 92392
URL: http://vvo.com/comm/mhs.htm

Mokelumne Hill Historical Society
8367 Center Street
Mokelumne Hill, CA 95245
Tel: 209-286-1770

Montecito History Committee
1469 East Valley Road
Montecito, CA 93108

Monterey County Historical Society
333 Boronda Rd.
P.O. Box 3576
Salinas, CA 93912
Tel: 408-757-8085

Monterey History & Art Association
P.O. Box 805
Monterey, CA 93942
Tel: 408-372-2608

Monterey Park Historical Society
P.O. Box 272
Monterey Park, CA 91754

Moraga Historical Society and Archives
1500 St. Mary's Road
P.O. Box 103
Moraga, CA 94556
Tel: 510-376-6952

Morgan Hill Historical Society
P.O. Box 1258
Morgan Hill, CA 95037

Mount Lassen Historical Society
P.O. Box 291
Shingletown, CA 96088

Mountain Empire Historical Society
P.O. Box 394
Campo, CA 92006
Tel: 619-478-5707

Mountain View Pioneer & Historical Association
P.O. Box 252
Mountain View, CA 94041

Napa County Historical Society
1219 First Street
Napa, CA 94559
Tel: 707-224-1739

National Trust for Historic Preservation
Western Regional Office
802 Montgomery Street
San Francisco, CA 94133

Native American Heritage Commission
915 Capitol Room 288
Sacramento Mall, CA 95814
Tel: 916-445-7370

Nevada County Historical Society
P.O. Box 1300
Nevada City, CA 95959
Tel: 916-265-5468
URL: http://www.ncen.net/orgsclbs/history/histsoc/welcome.htm

Newport Beach Historical Society
c/o Sherman Library
614 Dahlia Avenue
Corona Del Mar, CA 92625
Tel: 714-673-1880

North Lake Tahoe Historical Society
130 West Lake Blvd.
Tahoe City, CA 95730

Ojai Valley Museum & Historical Society
P.O. Box 204
Ojai, CA 93023

Olompali State Historical Park
P.O. Box 510
Novato, CA 94948
Tel: 707-892-3383

Orange County Historical Commission
2002 North Main
Santa Ana, CA 92706

Orange County Historical Society
101 N. Center
P.O. Box 5484
Orange, CA 92613-5484
Tel: 714-532-0361

Orange County Historical Society
3101 Harvard
P.O. Box 10984
Santa Ana, CA 92711-0984
Tel: 714-557-7074

Orange County Pioneer Council
2320 N. Towner St.
Santa Ana, CA 92706

Orland Historical & Cultural Society
P.O. Box 183
Orland, CA 95963
Tel: 916-865-1444

Pacific Beach Historical Society
P.O. Box 9200
San Diego, CA 92169
Tel: 619-272-6655

Pacific Grove Heritage Society
Laurel and 17th Streets
P.O. Box 1007
Pacific Grove, CA 93950
Tel: 408-372-2898

Pacific Palisades Historical Society
P.O. Box 1299
Los Angeles, CA 90272

Pajaro Valley Historical Association
261 East Beach Street
Watsonville, CA 95076
Tel: 408-722-0305

Palm Springs Historical Society
221 South Palm Canyon Drive
P.O. Box 1498
Palm Springs, CA 92263
Tel: 619-323-8297

Palo Alto Historical Association
P.O. Box 193
Palo Alto, CA 94302
URL: http://www.commerce.digital.com/palo-alto/historical-assoc/home.html

Paradise Fact and Folklore, Inc.
P.O. Box 1696
Paradise, CA 95969
Tel: 916-877-3699

Pasadena Historical Society
470 West Walnut St.
Pasadena, CA 91103

Patterson Township Historical Society
P.O. Box 15
Patterson, CA 95363

Pioneer Historical Society of Riverside
P.O. Box 246
Riverside, CA 92502

Placentia Historical Committee
401 East Chapman Avenue
Placentia, CA 92670

Plumas County Historical Society
P.O. Box 695
Quincy, CA 95971

Pomona Valley Historical Society
1569 North Park
Pomona, CA 91768

Portugese Historical & Cultural Society
P.O. Box 161990
Sacramento, CA 95816
Tel: 916-454-4144

Ramona Pioneer Historical Society, Inc.
645 Main Street
P.O. Box 625
Ramona, CA 92065
Tel: 619-789-7644

Rancho Santa Fe Historical Society
P.O. Box 2414
Rancho Santa Fe, CA 92067-2414
Tel: 619-756-3464

Redlands Area Historical Society
P.O. Box 1024
Redlands, CA 92373
Tel: 714-792-4026

Redondo Beach Historical Society
P.O. Box 978
Redondo Beach, CA 90277

Reedley Historical Society
P.O. Box 877
Reedley, CA 93654
Tel: 209-638-1913

Reina del Mar Parlor 126
Native Daughter of the Golden West
P.O. Box 404
Santa Barbara, CA 93102

Rialto Historical Society
205 North Riverside Avenue
P.O. Box 413
Rialto, CA 92377
Tel: 714-875-1750

Ridge Route Communities Museum/Historical Society
P.O. Box 1463
Lebec, CA 93243
Tel: 805-248-6091

Riverside County Historical Association
4600 Crestmore Rd.
P.O. Box 3507
Riverside, CA 92519
Tel: 714-275-4310

Sacramento County Historical Society
P.O. Box 1175
Sacramento, CA 95806

Sacramento Historical Museum
101 I Street
Sacramento, CA 95814
Tel: 916-449-2057

Sacramento Museum & History Commission
1930 J Street
Sacramento, CA 95814

Sacramento River Delta Historical Society
P.O. Box 293
Walnut Grove, CA 95690

Saddleback Area Historical Society
25151 Seranno Road
P.O. Box 156
El Toro, CA 92630
Tel: 714-586-8485

San Antonio Valley Historical Association
216 Grove Place
King City, CA 93930
Tel: 408-385-3587

San Antonio Valley Historical Society/Museum
P.O. Box 21
Lodi, CA 95241

San Benito County Historical Society
P.O. Box 357
Hollister, CA 95023

San Clemente Historical Society
2501 S. El Camino Real
P.O. Box 283
San Clemente, CA 92672
Tel: 714-492-3142

San Diego Historical Society
P.O. Box 81825
San Diego, CA 92138-1825
Tel: 619-232-6203 ext. 105
URL: http://edweb.sdsu.edu/SDHS/HistSoc.html

San Diego Military Heritage Society
P.O. Box 33672
San Diego, CA 92163

San Fernando Valley Historical Society
10940 Sepulveda Blvd.
Mission Hills, CA 91345

San Francisco African American Historical & Cultural Society
Fort Mason Center, Bldg. C, Room 165
San Francisco, CA 94123
Tel: 415-441-0640

San Francisco Historical Society
P.O. Box 569
San Francisco, CA 94101
Tel: 415-567-2725

San Gabriel Historical Association
318 South Mission Drive
San Gabriel, CA 91776

San Gabriel Historical Society
Los Compadrinos Museum
807 Montecito Drive
San Gabriel, CA 91776

San Joaquin County Historical Society/Museum
11793 N. Micke Grove Road
Lodi, CA 95240
Tel: 209-331-2055
Fax: 209-331-2057
Email: sjmuseum@inreach.com
URL: http://www.imon.com/sjmuseum

San Joaquin Pioneer & Historical Society
The Haggin Museum
1201 North Pershing Avenue
Stockton, CA 95203

San Juan Bautista Historical Society
P.O. Box 1
San Juan Bautista, CA 95045

San Juan Capistrano Historical Society
31831 Los Rios Street
P.O. Box 81
San Juan Capistrano, CA 92675
Tel: 714-493-8444

San Leandro Library & Historical Commission
300 Estudillo Avenue
San Leandro, CA 94577

San Luis Obispo Historical Society
696 Monterey Street
San Luis Obispo, CA 93401

San Marcos Historical Society
105 Richmar
San Marcos, CA
Tel: 619-744-9025

San Marino Historical Society
P.O. Box 80222
San Marino, CA 91108

San Mateo Co. Historical Assn. & Museum
1700 West Hillside Blvd.
San Mateo, CA 94402
Tel: 415-574-6441

San Pablo Historical Society and Museum
#1 Alvarado Square
San Pablo, CA 91806
Tel: 510-215-3080
510-222-3519

San Ramon Valley Historical Society
P.O. Box 521
Danville, CA 94526

Santa Ana Mountain Historical Society
28192 Silverado Canyon Rd.
P.O. Box 301
Silverado, CA 92676
Tel: 714-649-2216

Santa Barbara Historical Society
136 E. De la Guerra Street
P.O. Box 578
Santa Barbara, CA 93102
Tel: 805-966-1601

Santa Clara Historical & Genealogical Society
2635 Homestead Road
Santa Clara, CA 95051-5387
Tel: 408-984-3236
408-248-8205

Santa Clara Historical Heritage Commission
70 West Hedding Street
San Jose, CA 95110

Santa Clarita Valley Historical Society
24107 San Fernando Road
P.O. Box 221925
Newhall, CA 91322
Tel: 805-254-1275
URL: http://www.scvnet.com/~highlites/scvhs/index.html

Santa Cruz County Society of Historical Preservation, Inc.
118 Cooper Street
Santa Cruz, CA 95060

Santa Cruz Historical Society
P.O. Box 246
Santa Cruz, CA 95061

Santa Fe Springs Historical Committee
11710 Telegraph Road
Santa Fe Springs, CA 90670

Santa Maria Valley Historical Society
616 South Broadway
P.O. Box 584
Santa Maria, CA 93454
Tel: 805-922-3130

Santa Monica Historical Society
Will Rogers Station
P.O. Box 3059
Santa Monica, CA 90403

Santa Ynez Valley Historical Society
Faraday and Sagunto Streets
P.O. Box 181
Santa Ynez, CA 93460
Tel: 805-688-7889

Saratoga Historical Foundation
P.O. Box 172
Saratoga, CA 95070

Sausalito Historical Society
P.O. Box 352
Sausalito, CA 94966

Selma Museum Historical Society
1880 Art Gonzales Pkwy.
Selma, CA 93662
Tel: 209-896-8871

Shafter Historical Society
150 Central Valley Highway
P.O. Box 1088
Shafter, CA 93263
Tel: 805-746-1557

Shasta Historical Society
at Redding Museum of Art & History
56 Quartz Hill Road
Caldwell Park
Redding, CA
Mail:
P.O. Box 990277
Redding, CA 96099-0277
Tel: 916-243-3720
URL: http://www.shastalink.k12.ca.us/rmah/SHS.html

Shrine Foundation Historical Society
2482 San Diego Avenue
San Diego, CA 92110

Sierra County Historical Society
P.O. Box 260
Sierra City, CA 96125

Sierra Madre Historical Society
P.O. Box 202
Sierra Madre, CA 91024

Simi Valley Historical Society
Strathearn Historical Park
137 Strathearn Place
Simi Valley, CA 93065

Siskiyou County Historical Society & Museum
910 South Main
Yreka, CA 96097

Society of California Pioneers
P.O. Box 19850
San Francisco, CA 94119

Society of Hispanic Historical & Ancestral Research
P.O. Box 5294
Fullerton, CA 92635
Email: SHHARPres@AOL.com
http://www.webcom.com/shharnet/welcome.html

Solano County Historic Records Commission
c/o Central Services
1745 Enterprise Drive
Building 2, Suite A
Fairfield, CA 94533

Solano County Historical Society
P.O. Box 922
Vallejo, CA 94590

Sonoma County Historical Society
P.O. Box 1373
Santa Rosa, CA 95402

Sonoma Valley Historical Society
P.O. Box 861
Sonoma, CA 95476

South San Francisco History Room
306 Walnut Avenue
South San Francisco, CA 94080

Spanishtown Historical Society
505 Johnson Street
P.O. Box 62
Half Moon Bay, CA 94019
Tel: 415-726-7084

Sunnyvale Historical Society
and Museum Association
P.O. Box 61301
Sunnyvale, CA 98086

Surveyors' Historical Society
P.O. Box 2820
Dublin, CA 94568-0820

Surveyors' Historical Society
31457 Hugh Way
Hayward, CA 94544

Surveyors' Historical Society
P.O. Box 160502
Sacramento, CA 95816

Sutter County Historical Society
57117 Twenty-nine Palms Highway
Yucca Valley, CA 92284

Tehama Genealogical & Historical Society
P.O. Box 415
Red Bluff, CA 96080

Tomales Elementary Local History Center
13755 Bodega Highway
Sebastopol, CA 94972
Tel: 707-878-2398

Torrance Historical Society
1345 Post Avenue
Torrance, CA 90501

Trinity County Historical Society
P.O. Box 333
Weaverville, CA 96093

Truckee-Donner Historical Society
P.O. Box 893
Truckee, CA 96160
URL: http://www.tahoenet.com/tdhs/tpnewslt.html#intro

Tulare County Historical Society
P.O. Box 295
Visalia, CA 93279

Tuolumne County Historical Society
P.O. Box 695
Sonora, CA 95370

Tustin Area Historical Society
395 El Camino Real
P.O. Box 185
Tustin, CA 92681
Tel: 714-731-5701

Twenty-Nine Palms Historical Society
City Building,
6136 Adobe Road
P.O. Box 1926
Twenty-Nine Palms, CA 92277

Villa Park Historical Society
City Hall of Villa Park
Villa Park, CA 92667

Vista Ranchos Historic Society, Inc.
651 E. Vista Way, Suite A
P.O. Box 1032
Vista, CA 92085-1032

Walnut Creek Historical Society
P.O. Box 4562
Walnut Creek, CA 94596

Washington Township Historical Society
P.O. Box 3045
Fremont, CA 94539
Tel: 510-656-3761

Western Sonoma County Historical Society
P.O. Box 816
Sebastopol, CA 95472

Willow Creek/China Flat Museum
P.O. Box 102
Willow Creek, CA 95573

Whittier Historical Society
6755 Newlin Avenue
Whittier, CA 90601

Windsor Square-Hancock Park Historical Society
542 1/2 North Larchmont Blvd.
Los Angeles, CA 90004

Yolo County Historical Society
P.O. Box 1447
Woodland, CA 95695

LDS FAMILY HISTORY CENTERS

Anaheim Family History Center
440 North Loara
Anaheim, CA 9 2801-5525
Tel: 714-533-2772

Anderson Family History Center
4075 Riverside Avenue
Anderson, CA 96007-3125
Tel: 916-347-3240

Antioch Family History Center
2350 Jeffrey Way
Antioch, CA
Tel: 510-634-9004

Auburn Family History Center
1255 Bell Road
Auburn, CA 95603-9519
Tel: 916-888-9702

Bakersfield Family History Center
5600 Pamorama Drive
Bakersfield, CA 93306-2473
Tel: 805-872-5683

Bakersfield Family History Center
316 A Street
Bakersfield, CA 93304-1968
Tel: 805-393-6403

Bakersfield Family History Center
2801 South Real Rd.
Bakersfield, CA 93309-6040
Tel: 805-831-2036

Barstow Family History Center
2571 Barstow Road
Barstow, CA 92311-6650
Tel: 619-252-4117

Blythe Family History Center
Third and Barnard
Blythe, CA
Tel: 619-922-4019

Buena Park Family History Center
7600 Crescent Avenue
Buena Park, CA 90620-3946
Tel: 714-527-2448

Burbank Family History Center
136 North Sunset Canyon Drive
Burbank, CA 91501-1101
Tel: 818-843-5362

Camarillo Family History Center
1201 Paseo Camarillo
Camarillo, CA 93010
Tel: 805-388-7215

Carlsbad Family History Center
1981 Chestnut
Carlsbad, CA 92008-2714

Carlsbad Family History Center
2725 Jefferson, Suite 4A
Carlsbad, CA 92008-1705
Tel: 619-434-4941

Carson Family History Center
22731 Main Street
Carson, CA 90745-4516
Tel: 310-835-6733

Cerritos Family History Center
17909 Bloomfield Avenue
Cerritos, CA 90703-8516
Tel: 213-924-3676

Chatsworth Family History Center
10123 Oakdale Avenue
Chatsworth, CA 91311-3532
Tel: 818-885-1303

Chico Family History Center
2430 Mariposa Avenue
Chico, CA 95926-7330
Tel: 916-343-6641

Chino Family History Center
3354 Eucalyptus Ave.
Chino, CA 91709-1814
Tel: 909-393-1936

Chula Vista/Sweetwater Family History Center
3737 Valley Vista Way
Bonita, CA 91902
Tel: 619-472-1506

Clovis Family History Center
220 N. Peach
Clovis, CA 93612-0217
Tel: 209-298-8768

Clovis Family History Center
1880 Gettysburg Ave.
Clovis, CA 93611-5219
Tel: 209-291-2448

Concord/Walnut Creek Family History Center
3700 Concord Blvd.
Concord, CA 94517
Tel: 510-686-1766

Corona Family History Center
1501 Taber Rd.
Corona, CA 91719-4113
Tel: 714-735-2619

Covina Family History Center
656 S. Grand Avenue
Covina, CA 91724-3638
Tel: 818-331-7117

El Cajon Stake Family History Center
1270 S. Orange Ave.
El Cajon, CA 92020-7522
Tel: 805-588-1426

El Centro Family History Center
1280 South Eighth St.
El Centro, CA 92243-3903
Tel: 619-353-3019

Escondido Stake Family History Center
1917 E. Washington Ave
Escondido, CA 92027-2114
Tel: 619-741-8441

Escondido Family History Center
3260 Bear Valley Pkwy.
Escondido, CA

Eureka Family History Center
2806 Dolbeer St.
Eureka, CA 95501-4763
Tel: 707-443-7411

Fairfield Family History Center
2700 Camrose Drive
Fairfield, CA 94533-1226
Tel: 707-425-2027

Fontana Family History Center
7526 Alder Avenue
Fontana, CA 92336-2304
Tel: 909-355-1006

Fremont Family History Center
48950 Green Valley Road
Fremont, CA 94539-8001
Tel: 510-623-7496

Fremont Family History Center
3551 Decoto Road
Fremont, CA 94555-3109
Tel: 510-790-1800

Fresno Family History Center
5685 North Cedar
Fresno, CA 93710-6603
Tel: 209-431-3759

Fresno Family History Center
3375 West Sierra Ave.
Fresno, CA 93711-0952
Tel: 209-431-4759

Glendale Family History Center
1130 East Wilson Avenue
Glendale, CA 91206-4537
Tel: 818-241-8763

Goleta Family History Center
2107 Santa Barbara Street
Goleta, CA 93105-3543
Tel: 805-682-2092

Grass Valley Family History Center
Litton Building
1300 E. Main
Grass Valley, CA 95945-5208

Gridley Family History Center
400 Spruce Street
Gridley, CA 95948-2262
Tel: 916-846-3921

Hacienda Heights Family History Center
16750 Colima Road
Hacienda Heights, CA 91745-5640
Tel: 818-961-8765

Hanford Family History Center
2400 North 11th Avenue
Hanford, CA 93230-7060
Tel: 209-582-8960

Hemet Family History Center
425 N. Kirby Avenue
Hemet, CA 92545-3633
Tel: 714-658-8104

Huntington Beach Family History Center
8702 Altanta Avenue
Huntington Beach, CA 92646-7111
Tel: 714-536-4736

Huntington Park Family History Center (Spanish)
6531 Middleton Street
Huntington Park, CA 90255-3820
Tel: 213-585-7767

La Crescenta Family History Center
4550 Raymond Avenue
La Crescenta, CA 91214-2917
Tel: 818-957-0925

Lake Elsinore Family History Center
18220 Dexter Street
Lake Elsinore, CA
Tel: 909-245-4063

Lancaster Family History Center
3150 West Avenue K Street
Lancaster, CA 93536-5403
Tel: 805-943-1670

Lancaster Family History Center
750 East Avenue J
Lancaster, CA 93535-3844
Tel: 805-942-3993

Lemon Grove Family History Center
8472 Blossom Lane
Lemon Grove, CA 91945-4229
Tel: 619-463-7236

Livermore Family History Center
950 Mocho Street
Livermore, CA 94550

Lompoc Family History Center
212 East Central Avenue
Lompoc, CA 93436
Tel: 805-735-4939

Los Alamitos Family History Center
4142 Cerritos Avenue
Los Alamitos, CA 90720-2521
Tel: 714-821-6914

Los Altos California Stake Family History Center
1300 Grant Road
Los Altos, CA 94024-5729
Tel: 415-964-3001
415-968-1019

Los Angeles Family History Center
Basement of Temple Visitors Center
10741 Santa Monica Blvd.
West Los Angeles, CA 90025
Tel: 213-474-2202
310-474-2202

Manteca Family History Center
6060 E. Northland Road
Manteca, CA 95336
Tel: 209-239-5516

Menlo Park Family History Center
1105 Valparaiso Avenue
Menlo Park, CA 94025
Tel: 415-325-9711

Merced Family History Center
980 East Yosemite Avenue
Merced, CA 95340-9115
Tel: 209-722-1307

Miranda Family History Center
250 School Rd
Miranda, CA
Tel: 707-943-3071

Mission Viejo Family History Center
27976 Marguerite Parkway
Mission Viejo, CA 92692-3609
Tel: 714-364-2742

Modesto Family History Center
731 El Vista Avenue
Modesto, CA 95354-1844
Tel: 209-571-0370

Modesto Family History Center
4300 Dale Road
Modesto, CA 95356-9767
Tel: 209-545-4814

Monterey Park Family History Center (Spanish)
2316 Hillview Avenue
Monterey Park, CA 91754-6818
Tel: 213-726-8145

Moreno Valley Family History Center
23300 Old Lake Drive
Moreno Valley, CA 92557-2709
Tel: 909-247-8839

Mt. Shasta Family History Center
Mormon Way
Mt. Shasta, CA
Tel: 916-926-6671

Napa Family History Center
2590 Trower Avenue
Napa, CA 94558-2532
Tel: 707-257-2887

Needles Family History Center
Coronado & Lilly Hill Drive
Needles, CA
Tel: 609-326-3363

Nevada City Family History Center
615 Hollow Way
Nevada City, CA 95959
Tel: 916-265-5892
916-885-2167

Newbury Park Family History Center
35 South Wendy Drive
Newbury Park, CA 91320-4353
Tel: 805-499-1258

North Edwards Family History Center
16509 Frank Street
North Edwards, CA
Tel: 619-769-4345

Northridge Family History Center
17101 Plummer St.
Northridge, CA
Tel: 818-886-5953

Norwalk Family History Center
15311 S. Pioneer Blvd.
Norwalk, CA 90650-6402
Tel: 213-868-8727

Oakland Family History Center
4766 Lincoln Avenue
Oakland, CA 94602-2535
Tel: 415-531-3905

Orange Family History Center
674 S. Yorba Street
P.O. Box 6471
Orange, CA 92613-7710
Tel: 714-997-7710

Pacifica Family History Center
730 Sharp Park Road
Pacifica, CA 94044
Tel: 415-355-4986

Palm Desert Family History Center
72-960 Park View
Palm Desert, CA 92260-9357
Tel: 619-340-6094

Palmdale Family History Center
2120 East Avenue R
Palmdale, CA 93550
Tel: 805-947-1694

Pasadena Family History Center
770 N. Sierra Madre Villa
Pasadena, CA 91107-2042
Tel: 818-351-8517

Placerville Family History Center
3275 Cedar Ravine Road
Placerville, CA 95667-6555
Tel: 916-621-1378

Porterville Family History Center
837 E. Morton Avenue
Porterville, CA 93257
Tel: 209-784-2311

Poway Family History Center
15750 Bernardo Heights Pkwy.
San Diego, CA 92128-3180

Quincy Family History Center
55 Bellamy Lane
Quincy, CA 95971-9346
Tel: 916-283-3112

Rancho Palos Verdes Family History Center
5845 Crestridge Road
Rancho Palos Verdes, CA 90275-4955
Tel: 213-541-5644

Redding Family History Center
3410 Churn Creek Road
Redding, CA 96001
Mail: 1555 Pleasant St.
Redding, CA 96001
Tel: 916-222-4949

Redlands Family History Center
350 S. Wabash Avenue
Redlands, CA 92374-4296
Tel: 714-794-3844

Ridgecrest Family History Center
1031 South Norma St.
Ridgecrest, CA 93555-3109
Tel: 619-375-6998

Riverside Family History Center
5900 Grand Avenue
Riverside, CA 92504-1328
Tel: 714-784-1918

Riverside Family History Center
5950 Serendipity Road
Riverside, CA 92509-4775
Tel: 714-360-8547

Riverside Family History Center
4375 Jackson St.
Riverside, CA 92503-3322
Tel: 714-687-5542

Sacramento Family History Center
2745 Eastern Avenue
Sacramento, CA 95821-6638
Tel: 916-487-2090

Sacramento Family History Center
8925 Vintage Park Drive
Sacramento, CA 95829-1612
Tel: 916-688-7670

San Bernardino Family History Center
3860 N. Waterman Avenue
San Bernardino, CA 92404-1739
Tel: 714-881-5355

San Bruno Family History Center
975 Sneath Lane
San Bruno, CA 94066
Tel: 415-873-1928

San Diego East Stake Family History Center
6767 51st St. (north of Zion)
San Diego, CA 92120-1262

San Diego Family History Center
15750 Bernardo Heights
San Diego, CA 92128-3180
Tel: 619-487-2304

San Diego Family History Center
3705 Tenth Avenue
San Diego, CA 92103-4416
Tel: 619-295-9808

San Diego Multi-Stake Family History Center
4195 Camino del Rio South
San Diego, CA 92108
Tel: 619-584-ROOT

San Jose Family History Center
4977 San Felipe Road
San Jose, CA 95135-1219
Tel: 408-274-8592

San Jose Family History Center
3110 Cropley Avenue
San Jose, CA 95132-3546
Tel: 408-259-5501
408-274-8592

San Luis Obispo Family History Center
55 Casa Street
San Luis Obispo, CA 93405-1801
Tel: 805-543-6328

Santa Barbara Family History Center
2107 Santa Barbara St.
Santa Barbara, CA 93105-3543
Tel: 805-682-2092

Santa Clara Family History Center
875 Quince Avenue
Santa Clara, CA 95051-5292
Tel: 408-241-1449

Santa Cruz Family History Center
220 Elk Street
Santa Cruz, CA 95065-1309
Tel: 408-426-1078

Santa Maria Family History Center
908 E. Sierra Madre Avenue
Santa Maria, CA 93454-6335
Tel: 805-928-4722

Santa Rosa Family History Center
1725 Peterson Lane
Santa Rosa, CA 95403-2304
Tel: 707-525-0399

Seaside Family History Center
1024 Noche Buena
Seaside, CA 93955-6221
Tel: 408-394-1124

Simi Valley Family History Center
3979 Township
Simi Valley, CA 93063-1067
Tel: 805-581-2456

Sonora Family History Center
19481 Hillsdale Drive
Sonora, CA 95370-9219
Tel: 209-536-9206

Stockton Family History Center
820 West Brookside Rd.
Stockton, CA 95207-7019
Tel: 209-951-7060

Susanville Family History Center
905 Richmond Road
Susanville, CA
Tel: 916-257-4411

Sutter Creek Family History Center
12924 Ridge Road
Sutter Creek, CA 95685-9651
Tel: 209-267-1139

Thousand Oaks Family History Center
1600 Erbes Road
Thousand Oaks, CA 91362-1927
Tel: 805-495-2362

Torrance Family History Center
22605 Kent Avenue
Torrance, CA 90505-2343
Tel: 310-791-6526

Upland Family History Center
785 N. San Antonio Avenue
Upland, CA 91786
Tel: 909-985-8821

Ukiah Family History Center
1337 South Dora Street
Ukiah, CA 95482-6512
Tel: 707-468-5746

Vacaville Family History Center
480 Wrentham Dr.
Vacaville, CA 95688-1050
Tel: 707-451-8394

Valencia Family History Center
24443 McBean Parkway
Valencia, CA 91355-1945
Tel: 805-259-9535

Ventura Family History Center
3501 Loma Vista Road
Ventura, CA 93003
Tel: 805-643-5607

Victorville Stake Family History Center
12100 Ridgecrest Rd.
Victorville, CA
Tel: 619-243-5632

Visalia Family History Center
825 West Tulare Avenue
Visalia, CA 93277-2554
Tel: 209-932-3712

Vista Family History Center
1310 Foothill
Vista, CA 92084
Tel: 619-945-6053

Weaverville Family History Center
Mormon Lane
Weaverville, CA
Tel: 916-623-5227

Westminster Family History Center
10332 Bolsa Avenue
Westminster, CA 92683-6718
Tel: 714-554-0592

Whittier Family History Center
15265 Mulberry Drive
Whittier, CA 90604-1531
Tel: 310-946-1880

Woodland Family History Center
County Road 97 (1/2 mile S. of Highway 16)
Woodland, CA
Tel: 916-662-1538

Yuba City Family History Center
1470 Butte House Rd.
Yuba City, CA 95993-2702
Tel: 916-673-0113

ARCHIVES/LIBRARIES/MUSEUMS

Alpine County Museum
School Street
P.O. Box 24
Markleeville, CA 96120
Tel: 916-694-2317

Amador County Museum
225 Church Street
Jackson, CA 95642
Tel: 209-223-6386

American Victorian Museum
325 Spring Street
Nevada City, CA 95959

Anderson Valley Historical Museum
P.O. Box 676
Boonville, CA 95415

Angel Island State Park
P.O. Box 318
San Francisco, CA 94920

Archival Center
15151 San Fernando Mission Blvd
Mission Hills, CA 91345

Association for Northern California Records & Research
P.O. Box 3024
Chico, CA 95927
Tel: 916-898-62137

Atherton Heritage Association
Atherton Town Hall
91 Ashfield Road
Atherton, CA 94027
Tel: 415-688-6540

Bancroft Library
University of California-Berkeley
Berkeley, CA 94720
Tel: 510-642-6481

Belmont Historical Society
Historical Room
1225 Ralston Avenue
Belmont, CA 94002
URL: http://www.belmont.gov/hist/index.html

Benicia Capitol State Historic Park
P.O. Box 5
Benicia, CA 94510

Berkeley Historical Society Museum
Veterans Memorial Building
1931 Center Street
Berkeley, CA
Tel: 510-848-0181

Bidwell Mansion Association
525 Esplanade
Chico, CA 95926

Bishop Museum-Historical Society
P.O. Box 363
Bishop, CA 93514
Tel: 619-873-5950

Boulder Creek Historical Society
Highway 9 & Flat Street
Boulder Creek, CA 95006
Tel: 408-338-6617

Burlingame Historical Society
Washington Park
P.O. Box 144
Burlingame, CA 94011
Tel: 415-340-9960
URL: http://www.best.com/~spectrum/history/history.html

Butte County Historical Society
Ehmann Home
1480 Lincoln Street
Oroville, CA 95965
Tel: 916-533-5316

Cabrillo National Monument
1800 Cabrillo Memorial Drive
San Diego, CA 92106
Tel: 619-557-5450

Calaveras County Historical Society, Museum, & Archives
30 North Main Street
P.O. Box 723
San Andreas, CA 95249
Tel: 209-754-1058

California Afro-American Museum
Afro-American Genealogical Society
600 State Drive, Exposition Park
Los Angeles, CA 90037

California Ethnic and Multicultural Archives (CEMA)
Davidson Library
University of California
Santa Barbara, CA 93106
Tel: 805-893-8563
805-893-3062
Fax: 805-893-4676
URL: http://www.library.ucsb.edu//speccoll/cemabro.html

California Genealogical Society Library
300 Brannan Street, Suite 409
P.O. Box 77105
San Francisco, CA 94107-0105
Tel: 415-777-9936
URL: http://pw2.netcom.com/~dwilma/cgs.html

California Historical Society Library
2099 Pacific Avenue
San Francisco, CA 94109
Tel: 415-357-1848
Email: info@calhist.org
URL: http://www.calhist.org/

California History Center Foundation
21250 Stevens Creek Blvd.
Cupertino, CA 95014
Tel: 408-864-8712

California State Capitol Museum
State Capitol Room 124
Sacramento, CA 95814

California State Indian Museum
2618 K Street
Sacramento, CA 95816

California State Library
California History Room
900 N Street, Room 200
Sacramento, CA 95814

Tel: 916-654-0176
Email: csl-adm@library.ca.gov
URL: http://library.ca.gov/california/State_Library/

California State Univ. L.A. History
5151 State University Drive
Los Angeles, CA 90032

Campbell Historical Museum
51 N. Central Avenue
Campbell, CA 95008
Tel: 408-866-2119

Capitola Historical Museum
410 Capitola Avenue
Capitola, CA 950101-3318
Tel: 408-464-0322

Carlsbad City Library
1250 Carlsbad Village Dr.
Carlsbad, CA 92008-1991

Carnegie History and Cultural Arts Center
424 South C Street
Oxnard, CA 93030

Casa de Rancho Cucamonga/Rains' House
8810 Hemlock
Rancho Cucamonga, CA 91730
Tel: 909-989-4970

Catalina Island Museum Society, Inc.
Casino Bldg.
1 Casino Way
Avalon, CA 90704

Center for Museum Studies
John F. Kennedy University
1717 17th Street
San Francisco, CA 94103

Center for San Diego Studies
Department of History
2900 Lomaland Drive
San Diego, CA 92106

Chaffey Communities Cultural Center
P.O. Box 772
Upland, CA 91785-0772
Tel: 909-982-8010
Email: mavb@worldnet.att.net
URL: http://www.culturalcenter.org/

Chaffey-Garcia House
7150 Etiwanda Avenue
Rancho Cucamonga, CA 91739
Tel: 909-899-1209

Charles W. Bowers Museum
2002 North Main
Santa Ana, CA 92706

Cherokee Heritage and Museum Association
Route 7, Box 297
Cherokee, CA 95965

Cherokee Museum Association
4227 Cherokee Road
Oroville, CA 95965
Tel: 916-533-1849

Chico Museum
141 Salem Street
Chico, CA 95928
Tel: 916-891-4336

Chula Vista City Library
4th & F Streets
Chula Vista, CA 91910

Clarke Memorial Museum
240 East Street
Eureka, CA 95501

Colton Hall Museum & Old MOnterey
Pacific & Jefferson
Monterey, CA 93940

Colusa County Historical Records Commission
c/o Colusa County Free Library
738 Market Street
Colusa, CA 95932
Tel: 916-458-7671

Community Memorial Museum of Sutter County
P.O. Box 1555
Yuba City, CA 95991

Cooper Regional History History Museum
217 East A Street
P.O. Box 772
Upland, CA 91785-0722
Tel: 909-982-8010

Delano Historical Society & Heritage Park
330 Lexington Street
Delano, CA 93215
Tel: 805-725-6730

Depot Park Museum
P.O. Box 861
Sonoma, CA 95476

Discovery Museum of Orange County
3101 West Harvard Street
Santa Ana, CA 92704

East Bay Genealogical Society
405 14th St., Terrace Level (library)
P.O. Box 20417
Oakland, CA 94620-0417
Tel: 415-451-9599

El Pueblo de Los Angeles Historic Park
845 North Alameda
Los Angeles, CA 90012

El Dorado County Historical Museum
100 Placerville Drive
Placerville, CA 95667
Tel: 916-621-5865

Escondido Public Library
Pioneer Room
2245 E. Valley Parkway
Escondido, CA 92027-2713

Ferndale Museum
P.O. Box 431
Ferndale, CA 95536
Tel: 707-786-4466

Fontana Historical Society/Library
8459 Wheeler Avenue
P.O. Box 426
Fontana, CA 92334
Tel: 714-823-1733

Fort Crook Historical Society/Museum
Fort Crook Avenue and Highway 299
P.O. Box 397
Fall River Mills, CA 96028
Tel: 916-336-5110

Fort Point & Army Museum Association
P.O. Box 29163
San Francisco, CA 94129

Fort Ross State Historic Park
19005 Coast Highway 1
Jenner, CA 95450

Fresno Metropolitan Museum
1515 Van Ness
Fresno, CA 93721
Tel: 209-441-1444

Gilroy Historical Museum
195 Fifth Street
Gilroy, CA 95020

Harrison Memorial Library
P.O. Box 800
Carmel-by-the-Sea, CA 93921

Hayward Area Historical Society/Museum
22701 Main Street
Hayward, CA 94541
Tel: 510-581-0223

Healdsburg Museum
221 Matheson
Healdsburg, CA 95448

Held-Poage Library
Mendocino County Historical Society
603 West Perkins
Ukiah, CA 95482-4726
Tel: 707-462-6969
707-462-2039

Hemet-San Jacinto Genealogical Society Library
1779 E. Florida, C1
Hemet, CA 92544
Mail:
P.O. Box 2516
Hemet, CA 92546-2516
Tel: 909-658-6153

Heritage Association of El Dorado County
P.O. Box 62
Placerville, CA 95667
Tel: 916-622-8388
916-621-5793

Heritage Park
12100 Mora Drive
Santa Fe Springs, CA 90670

Holt-Atherton Pacific Center
University of the Pacific
Stockton, CA 95211

Honnold/Mudd Library of The Claremont Colleges
Special Collections
800 North Dartmouth
Claremont, CA 91711
Tel: 909-621-8000
URL: http://voxlibris.claremont.edu/speccoll.html

Huntington Beach Public Library
7111 Talbert Avenue
Huntington Beach, CA 92648-1296
Tel: 714-960-8836

Indian Grinding Rock State Historic Park
14881 Pine Grove-Volcano Road
Pine Grove, CA 95665
Tel: 209-269-7488

Irish Cultural Center Library
2700 45th Street
San Francisco, CA 94116-2696
Tel: 415-661-2700

Irvine Historical Society & Museum
5 Rancho San Joaquin
Irvine, CA 92717

Japanese American History Archives
1840 Sutter Street
San Francisco, CA 94115
Tel: 415-776-0661
URL: http://www.e-media.com/fillmore/museum/jt/jaha/jaha.html

Judah L. Magnes Memorial Museum/Blumenthal Library
2911 Russell Street
Berkeley, CA 94705
Tel: 510-849-2710
510-549-6950

Julian Pioneer Museum
2811 Washington St.
Julian, CA 92036
Tel: 619-765-0227

Kern County Museum
3801 Chester Avenue
Bakersfield, CA 93301
Tel: 805-861-2132

Kern River Valley Historical Society & Museum
P.O. Box 651
Kernville, CA 93238
Tel: 619-379-5895

Lake County Genealogical Society/Museum
255 North Forbes Street
P.O. Box 1323
Lakeport, CA 95453
Tel: 707-263-4555

Lake Oroville State Historic Site
400 Glen Drive
Oroville, CA 95965

Lake Tahoe Museum
3058 South Highway 50
P.O. Box 404
South Lake Tahoe, CA 95705
Tel: 916-541-5458

Leisure World Genealogical Workshop/Library
2300 Beverly Manor Road
Seal Beach, CA 90740-2599
Tel: 310-598-2431

Los Angeles Public Library
History & Genealogy Department
630 West 5th Street, LL4
Los Angeles, CA 90071
Tel: 213-228-7400
Fax: 213-228-7409
Email: history@lapl.org
URL: http://www.lapl.org/central/hihp.html

Malki Museum
Morongo Indian Reservation
11-795 Fields Road
Banning, CA 92220
Tel: 714-849-7289
714-849-8304

Marin Museum of the American Indian
2200 Novato Blvd.
Novato, CA 94948
Tel: 415-897-4064

Mariposa Museum and History Center
5119 Jessie Street
P.O. Box 606
Mariposa, CA 95338
Tel: 209-966-2924

Maturango Museum
100 E. Las Flores Avenue
Ridgecrest, CA 93555
Tel: 619-375-6900
Fax: 619-375-0479
Email: matmus@ridgecrest.ca.us
URL: http://www.ridgecrest.ca.us/~matmus/Hist.html

Mayflower Society Library
405 14th Street
Oakland, CA 94612
Tel: 510-451-9599

McHenry Museum
1402 I Street
Modesto, CA 95354

McPherson Center for Art & History
705 Front Street
Santa Cruz, CA 95062
Tel: 408-425-7278
Fax: 408-429-1954
URL: http://www.cruzio.com/~scva/mcpherson.html

Menlo Park Library
Menlo Park Historical Association
800 Alma Street
Menlo Park, CA 94025

Meriam Library Special Collections at
California State University, Chico
Chico, CA 95929-0295
Tel: 916-898-6342
URL: http://www.csuchico.edu/lbib/spc/spbrochr.html

Mill Valley Public Library
Historical Records Section
375 Throckmorton Avenue
Mill Valley, CA 94941

Mission Inn Museum
3739 Sixth Street
Riverside, CA 92501
Tel: 714-781-8241

Mission Santa Cruz
126 High Street
Santa Cruz, CA 95060
Tel: 408-426-5686

Modoc County Historical Society and Museum
600 S. Main Street
Alturas, CA 96101
Tel: 910-233-2944

Mojave River Valley Museum Association
270 E. Virginia Way
P.O. Box 1282
Barstow, CA 92312-1282
Tel: 619-256-5452

Montclair Library
5111 Benito
Montclair, CA 91750
Tel: 909-624-4671

Moraga Historical Society and Archives
1500 St. Mary's Road
P.O. Box 103
Moraga, CA 94556
Tel: 510-376-6952

Morgan Hill Museum
40 El Toro Avenue
Morgan Hill, CA 95037

Museum of Cultural History
University of California
405 Hilgard Avenue
Los Angeles, CA 90024

Museum of History & Art
225 South Euclid Avenue
Ontario, CA 91762
Tel: 909-983-3198

Museum of the City of San Diego
Historical & Research Archives
Casa de Balboa
1649 El Prado
P.O. Box 81825
San Diego, CA 92138
Tel: 619-232-6203

Museum of the City of San Francisco
2801 Leavenworth St. (at Jefferson)
San Francisco, CA 94133
Tel: 415-928-0289
URL: http://www.sfmuseum.org/

Museum of Russian Culture
2450 Sutter Street
San Francisco, CA 94115
Tel: 415-911-4082

National City Public Library
Hollingsworth Local History Room
200 E. 12th Street
San Diego, CA 92101-7414
Tel: 619-336-4280

National Maritime Museum & Library
Fort Mason Center, Building E
860 Beach Street
San Francisco, CA 94123
Tel: 415-556-9870 Library
415-556-3002
415-556-8177 Museum
Email: SAFR_Administration@nps.gov
URL: http://www.apl.com/nmma/safrpg.html

Newbury Park Branch Library
2331 Borchard Road
Newbury Park, CA 91320
Tel: 805-498-2139
URL: http://www.tol.lib.ca.us/1newbury.html

Northern California Center for Afro-American History
5606 San Pablo Avenue
Oakland, CA 94608
Tel: 510-658-3158

Novato History Museum and Archives
815 Delong Avenue
Novato, CA 94945
Mail:
901 Sherman Avenue
Novato, CA 94945
Tel: 415-897-4320

Oakland Museum-History Dept.
1000 Oak Street
Oakland, CA 94607
Tel: 510-273-3401

Ojai Valley Museum & Historical Society
P.O. Box 204
Ojai, CA 93023

Old Mission San Jose Museum
43300 Mission Boulevard
P.O. Box 3159
Fremont, CA 94539
Tel: 510-657-1797

Old Mission San Luis Obispo de Tolosa
P.O. Box 1483
San Luis Obispo, CA 93406

Ontario City Library
Model Colony Room
215 East C Street
Ontario, CA 91764
Tel: 909-988-8481

Orange County Library
Cypress Branch
5331 Orange Avenue
Cypress, CA 90630-2985
Tel: 714-826-0350

Orange County Library
El Toro Branch
24672 Raymond Way
Lake Forest, CA 92630-4489
Tel: 714-855-8173

Orange County Library
Garden Grove Regional Library
11200 Stanford Avenue
Garden Grove, CA 92640-5398
Tel: 714-530-0711

Orange County Library
Tustin Branch Library
345 E. Main Street
Tustin, CA 92680-4491
Tel: 714-544-7725

Pacific Asia Museum
46 North Los Robles Avenue
Pasadena, CA 91101

Pajaro Valley Historical Association
261 East Beach Street
Watsonville, CA 95076-4830
Tel: 408-722-0305

Palm Springs Public Library
300 S. Sunrise Way
Palm Springs, CA 92262
Email: 74111.3302@compuserve.com

Palmdale City Library
700 E. Palmdale Blvd.
Palmdale, CA 93550-4742
Tel: 805-267-5600

Palo Alto Main Library
1213 Newell Road
Palo Alto, CA 94303
Tel: 415-329-2436
415-329-2664
URL: http://www.city.palo-alto.ca.us/palo/city/library.html.cgi

Paradise Fact & Folklore
P.O. Box 1696
Paradise, CA 95967
Tel: 916-877-3699

Pardee Home Museum
672 11th Street
Oakland, CA 94607
Tel: 510-444-2187

Pasadena Public Library
Centennial Room
285 E. Walnut St.
Pasadena, CA 91101

Petaluma Museum & Historical Library
20 4th Street
Petaluma, CA 94952

Petaluma State Historic Park
3325 Adobe Road
Petaluma, CA 94952

Pleasanton Library
400 Old Bernal Avenue
Pleasanton, CA 94566

Porterville Public Library
41 West Thurman Avenue
Porterville, CA 93257
Tel: 209-784-0177

Presidio of Monterey Museum
Bldg. 1113 Ewing Road
Monterey, CA 93940

Presidio Army Museum
Bldg. 2, Presidio of San Francisco
San Francisco, CA 94129

Ramona Museum of California History
4580 North Figueroa St.
Los Angeles, CA 90065

Rancho Los Cerritos Historic Site
4600 Virginia Road
Long Beach, CA 90807

Redding Museum of Art & History
56 Quartz Hill Road
Caldwell Park
P.O. Box 990427
Redding, CA 96099-0427
Tel: 916-243-8801
Fax: 916-243-8929
Email: redmuse@shastalink.k12.ca.us
URL: http://www.shastalink.k12.ca.us/rmah/RMAHmain.html

Redwood City Public Library
Archives & Local History Collection
1044 Middlefield Road
Redwood City, CA 94063
Tel: 415-780-7030

Richmond Museum
400 Nevin Avenue
P.O. Box 1267
Richmond, CA 94802
Tel: 510-235-7387

Ridge Route Communities Museum/Historical Society
P.O. Box 1463
Lebec, CA 93243
Tel: 805-248-6091

Riverside City/County Library
Local History Office
P.O. Box 468
Riverside, CA 92502

Riverside Municipal Museum
3720 Orange Street
Riverside, CA 92501

Roman Catholic Church Archives
320 Middlefield Road
Menlo Park, CA 94025
Tel: 415-328-6502

Rosemead Library
8800 Valley Blvd.
Rosemead, CA 91770

Ruben Salazar Library
Sonoma State University
1801 East Cotati Avenue
Rohnert Park, CA 94928
URL: http://libweb.sonoma.edu/default.html

Sacramento Museum & History Commission
1930 J Street
Sacramento, CA 95814

Sacramento Valley Museum Association
1491 E Street
P.O. Box 53
Williams, CA 95987
Tel: 916-473-2978

San Bernardino County Archives
777 E. Rialto
San Bernardino, CA 92415-0795
Tel: 909-387-2030

San Bernardino County Historical Archives
104 West Fourth Street
San Bernardino, CA 92415

San Bernardino County Museum
2024 Orange Tree Lane
Redlands, CA 92374
Tel: 909-798-8570
URL: http://www.co.san-bernardino.ca.us/ccr/museum/museums.htm

San Bruno Local History Room
701 West Angus Avenue
San Bruno, CA 94066

San Carlos Historical Museum
533 Laurel Street
San Carlos, CA 94070
Tel: 415-595-5842

Santa Cruz County Historical Museum
118 Cooper Street
Santa Cruz, CA 95060
Tel: 408-425-2540

San Diego Historical Society Library
Casa de Balboa, LL
1649 El Prado
San Diego, CA 92101-1621
Tel: 619-232-6203 ext. 105
URL: http://edweb.sdsu.edu/SDHS/Archive.html

San Diego Maritime Museum
1492 North Harbor Drive
San Diego, CA 92101

San Diego Public Library
820 E Street
San Diego, CA 92101
Tel: 619-236-5800
URL: http://www.sannet.gov/public-library/

San Francisco Maritime Natl. Historic Park
Building 204, Fort Mason
San Francisco, CA 94123

San Francisco Public Library-Main Branch
San Francisco Archives
Larkin and Grove Streets
San Francisco, CA 94102
Tel: 415-557-4400

San Jacinto Valley Museum Associaton
P.O. Box 922
San Jacinto, CA 92383

San Joaquin County Historical Society/Museum
11793 N. Micke Grove Road
P.O. Box 21
Lodi, CA 95241
Tel: 209-331-2055
Fax: 209-331-2057

San Jose Historical Museum/Archives
Chinese Historical & Cultural Project
Kelley Park
1600 Senter Road
San Jose, CA 95112-2599
Tel: 408-287-2290
408-277-4017
URL: http://www.dnai.com/~rutledge/CHCP_museum.html

San Jose Public Library
160 W. San Carlos Street
San Jose, CA 95113-2005
Tel: 408-277-4846

San Leandro Library & Historical Commission
300 Estudillo Avenue
San Leandro, CA 94577

San Luis Obispo Historical Society Museum
696 Monterey Street
P.O. Box 1391
San Luis Obispo, CA 93401
Tel: 805-548-0638

San Mateo County Historical Museum
1700 West Hillside
San Mateo, CA 94403
Tel: 415-877-5344

San Mateo County Library-San Carlos
San Mateo County Genealogical Collection
655 Chestnut Street
San Carlos, CA 94070
Tel: 415-591-0341

San Mateo County Genealogical Society Library
25 Tower Road
San Mateo, CA 94402-4000

San Pablo Historical Society and Museum
#1 Alvarado Square
San Pablo, CA 91806
Tel: 510-215-3080
510-222-3519

Santa Ana Public Library
26 Civic Center Plaza
Santa Ana, CA 92701-4010
Tel: 714-647-5250

Santa Clara Central Library
Santa Clara County Historical & Genealogical Society
2635 Homestead Road
Santa Clara, CA 95051-5387
Tel: 408-984-3236
408-984-3097

Santa Cruz Mission State Historic Park
144 School Street
Santa Cruz, CA 95060-3726
Tel: 408-425-5849

Santa Cruz Public Library
Central Branch
224 Church Street
Santa Cruz, CA 95060

Santa Monica Heritage Square Museum
2612 Main Street
Santa Monica, CA 90405

Searls Historical Library
214 Church Street
Nevada City, CA 95959
Tel: 916-265-5468

Seaver Center of Western History Research
900 Exposition Blvd.
Los Angeles, CA 90007

Sharpsteen Museum
1311 Washington
Calistoga, CA 94515

Shasta State Historic Park
P.O. Box 2430
Shasta, CA 96087

Silverado Museum
1490 Library Lane
Saint Helena, CA 94574

Simi Valley Historical Society
Strathearn Historical Park
137 Strathearn Place
Simi Valley, CA 93065

Siskiyou County Historical Society & Museum
910 South Main
Yreka, CA 96097
URL: http://www.snowcrest.net/fueston/museum.html

Siskiyou Public Library
719 Fourth Street
Yreka, CA 96097
URL: http://www.snowcrest.net/fueston/special.html#Genealogy

Society of California Archivists
ASUC Store, Box 605
Bancroft Way and Telegraph Ave.
Berkeley, CA 94720-1111
Tel: 714-643-4241

Sonoma County Museum
425 7th Street
Santa Rosa, CA 95401

Sonoma State Historic Park
20 East Spain Street
Sonoma, CA 95476

Sourisseau Academy for State & Local History
San Jose State University, WLN 606
San Jose, CA 95192
Tel: 408-924-6510

South San Francisco Public Library
South San Francisco History Room
306 Walnut Street
San Francisco, CA 94080

Spanishtown Historical Society
505 Johnson Street
Half Moon Bay, CA 94019
Tel: 415-726-7084

Stanford House State Historic Park
802 N Street
Sacramento, CA 95814

Stanford University
Green Library
(behind Hoover Tower)
Stanford, CA 94035-6004
Tel: 415-725-1064
URL: http://www-sul.stanford.edu/depts/green/index.html

Sutro Library
480 Winston Drive
San Francisco, CA 94132
Tel: 415-731-4477
URL: http://sfpl.lib.ca.us/gencoll/gencolsu.htm
MELVYL Catalog URL: http://www.dla.ucop.edu/

Sutter's Fort State Historic Park
2701 L Street
Sacramento, CA 95814

Tehama County Museum Foundation
P.O. Box 275
Tehama, CA 96090

Thousand Oaks Library
Janss Road
Thousand Oaks, CA 91361
Tel: 805-497-6282
URL: http://www.tol.lib.ca.us/1library.html

Tomales Elementary Local History Center
P.O. Box 6
Tomales, CA 94971

Tulare Public Library
113 North F Street
Tulare, CA 93274-3803

University of California
Riverside, CA 92521-0154
Tel: 909-787-5841
Email: bm.ehs@rlg.org
URL: http://lib-www.ucr.edu/

Upland Public Library
450 North Euclid Avenue
Upland, CA 91786
Tel: 909-931-4200

Vacaville Museum
213 Buck Avenue
Vacaville, CA 95688

Vallejo Naval & Historical Museum
734 Marin Street
Vallejo, CA 94590

Ventura County Museum of History & Art
100 East Main Street
Ventura, CA 93001

Victorville Branch Library
15011 Circle Drive
Victorville, CA 92392
Tel: 619-245-4222
Fax: 619-245-2273
URL: http://vvo.com/comm/sbclvv.htm

Walter W. Stiern Library at
California State University-Bakersfield
Special Collections, Room 102
9001 Stockdale Hwy.
Bakersfield, CA 93311-1099
Tel: 805-664-3372
Fax: 805-664-3339
URL: http://www.lib.csubak.edu/html/Special_collections.html

Weaverville Joss House State Historic Park
P.O. Box 1217
Weaverville, CA 96093

Wells Fargo Bank History Dept.
475 Sansome Street
San Francisco, CA 94111

Western Jewish History Center
2911 Russell Street
Berkeley, CA 94705
Tel: 510-849-2710

William H. Pratt Museum
Lassen County Historical Society
105 North Weatherlow St.
P.O. Box 321
Susanville, CA 96130
Tel: 916-257-6551

William S. Hart Museum
24151 San Fernando Road
Newhall, CA 91321

Yolo County Historical Museum
512 Gibson Road
Woodland, CA 95695

Newspaper Repositories

California State Library
California History Room
900 N Street, Room 200
Sacramento, CA 95814
Tel: 916-654-0176
Email: csl-adm@library.ca.gov
URL: http://library.ca.gov/california/State_Library/

Sutro Library
480 Winston Drive
San Francisco, CA 94132
Tel: 415-731-4477
URL: http://sfpl.lib.ca.us/gencoll/gencolsu.htm

University of California
Riverside, CA 92521-0154
Tel: 909-787-5841
Email: bm.ehs@rlg.org
URL: http://lib-www.ucr.edu/cb_s/cnphome.html

Vital Records

Department of Health Services
Vital Statistics Section
P.O. Box 730241
Sacramento, CA 94244-0241
Tel: 916-445-2684

California on the Web

California Genealogical Resources by James Stevenson Publ.
http://www.jspub.com/~jsp/genresor.html

California Genealogical Society
http://pw2.netcom.com/~dwilma/cgs.html

California Genweb Project
http://www.compuology.com/cagenweb/

California Historical Society
http://www.calhist.org/
California Pioneer Project
http://www.compuology.com/cagenweb/cpl_main.htm

Computer Genealogical Society of San Diego
http://www-irps.ucsd.edu/cgssd

NORCAL
http://www.best.com/~bearbr/genealogy/caindexes/index.html

San Francisco Genealogy by Pamela Storm Wolfskill
http://www.sfo.com/timandpamwolf/sfrancty.htm

Southern California Chapter-Association of Professional Genealogists
http://www.compuology.com/sccapg/

Southern California Libraries
http://home.earthlink.net/~jsmog/library.html

Colorado

Archives, State & National

Colorado State Archives
1313 Sherman Street, Rm. 1B-20
Denver, CO 80203
Tel: 303-866-2358
Fax: 303-866-2257
Email: comments@www.state.co.us
URL: http://www.state.co.us/gov_dir/gss/archives/index.html

National Archives—Rocky Mountain Region
Denver Federal Center, Building 48
P.O. Box 25307
Denver, CO 80225-0307
Tel: 303-236-0817
Fax: 303-236-9354
Email: archives@denver.nara.gov
URL: http://www.nara.gov/nara/regional/08nsgil.html

Genealogical Societies

Ancestor Seekers Genealogy Society
P.O. Box 693
Castle Rock, CO 80104
Tel: 303-688-3388
303-688-4316

Archuleta County Genealogical Society
P.O. Box 1611
Pagosa Springs, CO 81147

Aurora Genealogical Society of Colorado
1298 Peoria Street
P.O. Box 31732
Aurora, CO 80041-0732

Black Genealogy Search Group
P.O. Box 40674
Denver, CO 80204-0674

Boulder Genealogical Society
P.O. Box 3246
Boulder, CO 80307-3246

Brighton Genealogy Society
343 S. 21st Street
Brighton, CO 80602-2525

Colorado Association of Professional Genealogists
P.O. Box 740637
Arvada, CO 80006-0637

Colorado Cornish Cousins
7945 S. Gaylord Way
Littleton, CO 80122

Colorado Council of Genealogical Societies
P.O. Box 24379
Denver, CO 80224-0379

Colorado Genealogical Society
P.O. Box 9218
Denver, CO 80209-0218
Tel: 303-571-1535
Email: mafinlay@cogensoc.org
URL: http://www.cogensoc.org/cgs/cgs-home.htm

Colorado Genealogical Society
Computer Interest Group
6437 Arbor Dr.
Littleton, CO 80123-3827

Columbine Genealogical and Historical Society
P.O. Box 2074
Littleton, CO 80161-2074

Czech and Slovak Search Group
209 S. Ogden
Denver, CO 80209-2321

Estes Park Genealogical Society
1281 High Drive MR
Estes Park, CO 80517

Foothills Genealogical Society
P.O. Box 150382
Lakewood, CO 80215-0382

Four Corners Genealogy Society
P.O. Box 2636
Durango, CO 81302

Fore-Kin Trails Genealogical Society
8508 High Mesa Road
Olathe, CO 81425

Fremont County Genealogical Society
1836 Flora Court
Canon City, CO 81212

Genealogical Research Society of Durango
2720 Delwood
Durango, CO 81301

Genealogical Society of Hispanic America
P.O. Box 9606
Denver, CO 80209-0606

High County Genealogical Society
304 South Colorado Street
Gunnison, CO 81230

Jewish Genealogical Society of Colorado
1982 S. Oneida Street
Denver, CO 80224

Larimer County Genealogical Society
P.O. Box 9502
Fort Collins, CO 80525-9502
Tel: 970-226-6146
URL: http://jymis.com/~lcgs/lcgs.shtml

Logan County Genealogical Society
c/o Leona Patton
Route 1
Sterling, CO 80751

Longmont Genealogical Society
P.O. Box 6081
Longmont, CO 80501-2077

Mesa County Genealogical Society
P.O. Box 1506
Grand Junction, CO 81502-1506

Mountain Genealogists
19637 Hill Drive
Morrison, CO 80465

Ohio Genealogical Society
Colorado Chapter
P.O. Box 1106
Longmont, CO 80502-1106
Email: WJSN81A@prodigy.com
Tel: 303-499-1925

Palatines to America
Colorado Chapter
7079 South Marshall St.
Littleton, CO 80123-4607
Tel: 303-979-5968
URL: http://www.dcn.davis.ca.us/~feefhs/frgpalco.html

Pikes Peak Genealogical Society, Inc.
P.O. Box 1262
Colorado Springs, CO 80901

Prowers County Genealogical Society
P.O. Box 928
Lamar, CO 81052-0928

San Luis Valley Genealogical Society
P.O. Box 1541
Alamosa, CA CO 81101

Sedgewick County Genealogical Society
P.O. Box 89
Julesburg, CO 80737

Slovenian Genealogy Society
Colorado Chapter
837 Swiggler Road

Jefferson, CO 90456-9732
URL: http://www.feefhs.org/~feefhs/slovenia/frgsgsco.html

Southeastern Colorado Genealogy Society, Inc.
P.O. Box 4207
Pueblo, CO 81003-0207
Email: PD1881@aol.com
URL: http://members.aol.com/annray5543/private/Local.html

Weld County Genealogical Society
P.O. Box 278
Greeley, CO 80632
URL: http://www.rootsweb.com/~coweld/society.htm

Western Trails Genealogical Society
1570 S. Knox Court
Denver, CO 80219

WISE Search Group (Wales, Ireland, Scotland, England)
1840 S. Wolcott Court
Denver, CO 80219-4309

Yuma County Genealogical Society
P.O. Box 24
Yuma, CO 80759

Historical Societies

American Historical Society of Germans from Russia
Denver Metro Chapter
3900 Garrison Street
Wheat Ridge, CO 80211
Tel: 303-422-4201
URL: http://www.teleport.com/nonprofit/ahsgr/codenver.html

American Historical Society of Germans from Russia
Northern Colorado Chapter
1476 43rd Avenue
Greeley, CO 80634
Tel: 970-353-3612
URL: http://www.teleport.com/nonprofit/ahsgr/conorthe.html

Colorado Historical Society
Stephen H. Hart Library
1300 Broadway
Denver, CO 80202
Tel: 303-866-3395
303-866-2305
303-866-4605
URL: http://www.aclin.org/other/historic/chs/

Douglas County Historical Society
620 Lewis
Castle Rock, CO 80104

Eagle County Historical Society
P.O. Box 357
Eagle, CO 81631

Fort Collins Historical Society
121 North Grant Avenue
Fort Collins, CO 80521

Frontier Historical Society
1001 Colorado Avenue
Glenwood Springs, CO 81601

Larimer County Historic Alliance
3711 N. Taft Hill Road
Fort Collins, CO 80524

Mesa County Historical Society
P.O. Box 841
Grand Junction, CO 81502

Museum of Western Colorado
Research Center and Special Library
Fifth and Ute
P.O. Box 2000
Grand Junction, CO 81502-5020

Negro Historical Association of Colorado Springs (NHACS)
P.O. Box 16123
Colorado Springs, CO 80935
Tel: 719-596-6796

Park County Historical Society
P.O. Box 43
Bailey, CO 80421
Tel: 303-838-9511

Phillip S. Miller Branch Library
961 South Plum Creek Boulevard
Castle Rock, CO 80104

Pioneer Association/Pioneer Women
Donath Lake Farm
8420 South Co. Road 13
Fort Collins, CO 80525

Pueblo County Historical Society
217 South Grand
Pueblo, CO 81003
Tel: 719-543-6772
URL: http://griffon.mwsc.edu/~edtech/pueblo.html

Scottish Society of Northern Colorado
3200 Silverthorn Dr.
Fort Collins, CO 80526

South Park Historical Foundation
South Park City Museum
100 Fourth Street
P.O. Box 634
Fairplay, CO 80440
Tel: 303-836-2387

Summit County Historical Society
309 North Main
Breckenridge, CO 97045-9022

LDS Family History Centers

Alamosa Family History Center
Third and Richardson
Alamosa, CO 81101
Tel: 719-589-5511

Arvada Family History Center
7080 Independence
Arvada, CO 80004
Tel: 303-421-0920

Aurora Family History Center
950 Laredo
Aurora, CO 80011-7441
Tel: 303-367-0570

Colorado Springs Family History Center
150 Pine Avenue
Colorado Springs, CO 80906
Tel: 719-634-0572

Cortez Family History Center
1800 East Empire Street
Cortez, CO 81321
Tel: 970-565-7400

Craig Family History Center
1295 West 9th Street
Craig, CO 81625
Tel: 303-824-2763

Denver Family History Center
2710 S. Monaco Parkway
Denver, CO 80237
Tel: 303-758-6460
URL: http://pw1.netcom.com/~rossmi/denfhc.html

Durango Family History Center
2 Hilltop Circle
Durango, CO 81301
Tel: 303-259-1061

Fort Collins Family History Center
600 E. Swallow Drive
Fort Collins, CO 80525
Tel: 970-226-5999

Frisco Family History Center
400 Forest Drive
Frisco, CO 80443
Tel: 970-668-5633

Grand Junction
543 Melody Lane
Grand Junction, CO 81501
Tel: 970-243-2782

Greeley Family History Center
501 Fourth Avenue
Greeley, CO 80631
Tel: 970-356-1904

La Jara Family History Center
718 Broadway
La Jara, CO 81140
Tel: 719-274-4032

Lakewood Family History Center
6465 W. Jewell
Lakewood, CO 80232
Tel: 303-935-3003
URL: http://pw1.netcom.com/~rossmi/lwfhc.html

Littleton Stake Family History Center
1939 East Easter Avenue
Littleton, CO 80122
Tel: 303-798-6461

Littleton Family History Center
6705 S. Webster
Littleton, CO 80123
Tel: 303-973-4771
303-973-3727

Longmont Family History Center
1721 Red Cloud Road
Longmont, CO 80501-2083
Tel: 303-772-4373

Louisville Family History Center
701 South Boulder Rd.
Louisville, CO 80027
Tel: 303-665-4685

Montrose Family History Center
2030 Stratford
Montrose, CO 81401-5530
Tel: 970-249-4739

Northglenn Family History Center
100 East Malley Drive
Northglenn, CO 80233
Tel: 303-451-7177

Pagosa Springs Family History Center
Piedra Estates
Pagosa Springs, CO 81147
Tel: 970-731-2623

Paonia Family History Center
5th and Oak Street
Paonia, CO 81428
Tel: 303-527-4084

Pueblo Family History Center
4720 Surfwood
Pueblo, CO 81005-2667
Tel: 719-564-0793

Sterling Family History Center
513 North 7th Avenue
Sterling, CO 80757
Tel: 970-522-6407

ARCHIVES/LIBRARIES/MUSEUMS

Aurora History Museum/Library
15001 E. Alameda Drive
Aurora, CO 80012
Tel: 303-739-6660
Email: jwlikes@aol.com
URL: http://www.artstozoo.org/Homestead_City/page8000.htm

Berthod Public Library
328 Massachusetts Avenue
Berthod, CO 80513
Tel: 970-532-2757

Boulder Museum of History
1206 Euclid Avenue
Boulder, CO 80302
Tel: 303-449-3464
URL: http://bcn.boulder.co.us/arts/bmh/

Boulder Public Library
1000 Canyon Blvd.
Boulder, CO 80302
Tel: 303-441-3100
URL: http://bcn.boulder.co.us/library/bpl/home.html

Buena Vista Heritage Museum
P.O. Box 1414
Buena Vista, CO 81211
Tel: 719-395-8458

Buena Vista Public Library
131 Linderman Avenue
Buena Vista, CO 81211
Tel: 719-395-8700

Carnegie Branch Library
1125 Pine Street
P.O. Drawer H
Boulder, CO 80306
Tel: 303-441-3110
URL: http://bcn.boulder.co.us/library/bpl/general/carn.html

Chautauqua Association
Archive and History Room
Administration Building
900 Baseline Road
Boulder, CO 80302
Tel: 303-442-3282
303-545-6924

Colorado College
Tutt Library
1021 N. Cascade Avenue
Colorado Springs, CO 80903-2165

Colorado Historical Society
Stephen H. Hart Library
1300 Broadway
Denver, CO 80203
Phone: (303)866-2305

Colorado Springs Public Library
21 West Kiowa Street
Colorado Springs, CO 80902

Colorado State Library
201 E. Colfax Avenue
Denver, CO 80203
Tel: 303-866-6728
Fax: 303-830-0793

Colorado State University
Special Collections
Fort Collins, CO 80523
Tel: 970-491-3977 Information
970-491-1841 Social Sciences/Humanities
970-491-1882 Government Documents
970-491-1844 Archives-Voice
Fax: 970-491-1195
URL: http://www.colostate.edu/Depts/LTS/libhome2.html

Cortez Center
25 North Market Street
Cortez, CO 81321
Tel: 303-565-1151
URL: http://www.swcolo.org/Tourism/IndianCulture.html

Denver Public Library
10 West 14th Avenue Pkwy.
Denver, CO 80204
Tel: 303-640-6200
303-640-6291
URL: http://www.dp120.denver.lib.co.us

Denver Public Library
Genealogy Division
1357 Broadway
Denver, CO 80203-2165
Tel: 303-571-2190
303-571-2171
303-571-2009

Edwin A. Bemis Library
6014 S. Datura Street
Littleton, CO 80120
Tel: 303-795-3961

Estes Park Area Historical Museum
200 Fourth Street
Estes Park, CO 80517
Tel: 970-586-6256
URL: http://estes.on-line.com/epmuseum/

Estes Park Public Library
335 East Elkhorn Avenue
Estes Park, CO 80517
Tel: 970-586-8116
URL: http://estes.on-line.com/evpld/

Fort Collins Museum
200 Mathews
Fort Collins, CO 80524
Tel: 970-221-6738

Fort Collins Public Library
201 Peterson Street
Fort Collins, CO 80524
Tel: 970-221-6380 Reference
970-221-6688 Local History
URL: http://www.ci.fort-collins.co.us/C_LIBRARY/index.htm

Friend Genealogy Library
1448 Que Street
Penrose, CO 81240

Golden Library
1019 Tenth Street
Golden, CO 80401
Tel: 303-279-4585
URL: http://jefferson.lib.co.us/

Greeley Public Library
City Complex Building
919 7th Street
Greeley, CO 80631

Gunnison County Public Library
307 North Wisconsin
Gunnison, CO 81230

Historical Society Library
14th & Sherman
Denver, CO 80203

Lakewood Library
10200 W. 20th Avenue
Lakewood, CO 80215
Tel: 303-232-9507
URL: http://jefferson.lib.co.us/

Loveland Museum and Gallery
503 N. Lincoln Avenue
Loveland, CO 80537
Tel: 970-962-2410

Loveland Public Library
300 N. Adams Avenue
Loveland, CO 80537
Tel: 970-962-2665

Montrose Public Library
434 S. 1st Street
Montrose, CO 81401
Tel: 970-249-9656

Norlin Library
Government Publications
University of Colorado at Boulder
Boulder, CO 80309
Tel: 303-492-8834

Penrose Public Library
20 N. Cascade
Colorado Springs, CO 80903
Tel: 719-531-6333
Fax: 719-528-5289

Pueblo Regional Library
100 Abriendo Avenue
Pueblo, CO 81004
Tel: 719-543-9600

Salida Museum
Salida Chamber of Commerce
406 W. Rainbow Blvd.
Salida, CO 81201
Tel: 719-539-2068

Salida Regional Library
405 E Street
Salida, CO 81201
Tel: 719-539-4826

Sisson Memorial Library
811 San Juan
P.O. Box 849
Pagosa Springs, CO 81147
Tel: 970-264-2208

Southern Peaks Public Library
423 Fourth Street
Alamosa, CO 81101
Tel: 719-589-6592

Southern Ute Community Library
330 Burns Avenue
P.O. Box 989
Ignacio, CO 81137-0348
Tel: 970-563-0235
Fax: 970-563-0396

Stagecoach Library
1840 S. Wolcott Ct.
Denver, CO 80219

Standley Lake Library
8485 Kipling Street
Arvada, CO 80004
Tel: 303-456-0806
URL: http://jefferson.lib.co.us/

University of Colorado at Boulder Archives
Campus Box 184
Basement, Norlin Library
Boulder, CO 80309

Ute Mountain Ute Tribal Research Archives Library
Tribal Compound
Box CC
Towaoc, CO 81334
Tel: 303-565-3751 x257
Fax: 303-565-7412
URL: http://www.swcolo.org/Tourism/IndianCulture.html

Weld County Library
2227 23rd Avenue
Greeley, CO 80631
Tel: 303-330-7691

Wellington Public Library
3800 Wilson Avenue
Wellington, CO 80549
Tel: 970-568-3040

NEWSPAPER REPOSITORIES

Colorado Historical Society
Stephen H. Hart Library
1300 Broadway
Denver, CO 80203
Tel: (303)866-4680

Denver Public Library
Genealogy Division
1357 Broadway
Denver, CO 80203-2165
Tel: 303-571-2190
303-571-2171
303-571-2009

University of Colorado at Boulder
Norlin Library
Government Publications
Boulder, CO 80309
Tel: 303-492-8834

VITAL RECORDS

Colorado Department of Public Health and Environment
Vital Records
4300 Cherry Creek Drive South
Denver, CO 80222-1530
Tel: 303-756-4464
Fax: 303-782-5576
URL: http://www.state.co.us/gov_dir/cdphe_dir/hs/cshom.html

COLORADO ON THE WEB

Census Schedules and Black Genealogical Research:
One Family's Experience
http://www.aclin.org/other/society_culture/african_american/blgen/cover.htm
Colorado Archives Genealogy Resources and Databases
http://www.state.co.us/gov_dir/gss/archives/geneal.html

Colorado GenWeb Project
http://www.rootsweb.com/~cogenweb/comain.html

Denver Public Library-Genealogy Resources-Colorado Resources
gopher://dpl20.denver.lib.co.us

CONNECTICUT

ARCHIVES, STATE & NATIONAL

Connecticut State Archives
Connecticut State Library
231 Capitol Avenue
Hartford, CT 06106
Tel: 860-566-5650
Fax: 860-566-2133
Email: markj@cslnet.ctstateu.edu
URL: http://www.cslnet.ctstateu.edu/archives.htm

National Archives—New England Region
380 Trapelo Road
Waltham, MA 02154
Tel: 617-647-8100
Fax: 617-647-8460
Email: archives@waltham.nara.gov
URL: http://www.nara.gov/nara/regional/01nsbgil.html

GENEALOGICAL SOCIETIES

Connecticut Ancestry Society, Inc.
P.O. Box 249
Stamford, CT 06904-0249

Connecticut Professional Genealogists Council
P.O. Box 4273
Hartford, CT 06147-4273

Connecticut Society of Genealogists
175 Maple Street
East Hartford, CT 06118
Mail:
P.O. Box 435
Glastonbury, CT 06033-0435
Tel: 860-569-0435
203-569-0002

Descendants of the Founders of Ancient Windsor
P.O. Box 39
Windsor, CT 06095-0039

French Canadian Genealogical Society of Connecticut
P.O. Box 928
Tolland, CT 06084-0928
URL: http://ourworld.compuserve.com//homepages/RLCarpenter/frenchca.htm

Jewish Genealogical Society of Connecticut
17 Salem Walk
Milford, CT 06430

Killingly Historical and Genealogical Society, Inc.
196 Main Street
P.O. Box 6000
Danielson, CT 06239
Tel: 860-774-2758
URL: http://ourworld.compuserve.com/homepages/RLCarpenter/killingl.htm

Middlesex Genealogical Society
25 Old King's Highway, North
P.O. Box 1111
Darien, CT 06820-1111
Tel: 203-655-9233
URL: http://www.darien.lib.ct.us/mgs/default.htm

New England Historic Genealogical Society
101 Newbury Street
Boston, MA 02116-3007
Tel: 617-536-5740
1-800-AT-NEHGS
Fax: 617-536-7307
Email: nehgs@nehgs.org
URL: http://www.nehgs.org/

Polish Genealogical Society of Connecticut
c/o Jonathan Shea
8 Lyle Road
New Britain, CT 06053

Society of Mayflower Descendants in Connecticut
36 Arundel Avenue
Hartford, CT 06107

Sons of the American Revolution
Connecticut Society (CTSSAR)
P.O. Box 270275
West Hartford, CT 06127-0275
URL: http://www.ctssar.org/

Southington Genealogical Society
Southington Historical Center
239 Main Street
Southington, CT 06489
Tel: 203-628-7831

HISTORICAL SOCIETIES

Amity and Woodbridge Historical Society
Thomas Darling House
Litchfield Turnpike
Woodbridge, CT 06525

Andover Historical Society
Bunker Hill Road
Andover, CT 06232
Tel: 860-742-6796

Aspincok Historical Society of Putnam
P.O. Box 465
Putnam, CT 06260
Tel: 860-928-6128

Bantam Historical Society
P.O. Box 436
Bantam, CT 06750-0436

Barkhamsted Historical Society
P.O. Box 94
Pleasant Valley, CT 06063

Beacon Falls Historical Commissions
10 Maple Avenue
Beacon Falls, CT 06403
Tel: 203-729-4340

Branford Historical Society
124 Main Street
P.O. Box 504
Branford, CT 06405
Tel: 203-488-4828

Bridgewater Historical Society
Main Street
Bridgewater, CT 06752

Brookfield Historical Society
Whisconier Road
P.O. Box 5231
Brookfield, CT 06804
Tel: 203-740-8140
URL: http://www.danbury.org/org/brookhc/index.htm

Brooklyn Historical Society
P.O. Box 90
Brooklyn, CT 06234
Tel: 860-774-7728

Canton Historical Society
11 Front Street
Collinsville, CT 06022
Tel: 860-693-2793

Chatham Historical Society of East Hampton
Bevin Boulevard
East Hampton, CT 06424

Chester Historical Society
P.O. Box 204
Chester, CT 06412

Colchester Historical Society
P.O. Box 13
Colchester, CT 06415

Colebrook Historical Society
Colebrook Center
558 Colebrook Road
P.O. Box 85
Colebrook, CT 06021
Tel: 860-738-3142

Columbia Historical Society
486 Route 66
Columbia, CT 06237
Tel: 860-228-9385

Connecticut Historical Commission
59 South Prospect Street
Hartford, CT 06106
Tel: 203-566-3005
Email: archnet@spirit.lib.uconn.edu
URL: http://spirit.lib.uconn.edu/ArchNet/Topical/CRM/Conn/ctshpo.html

Connecticut Historical Society
1 Elizabeth Street at Asylum Avenue
Hartford, CT 06105
Tel: 860-236-5621
Fax: 860-236-2664
Email: cthist@ix.netcom.com (library)
ctmus@ix.netcom.com (museum)
URL: http://www.hartnet.org/chs/

Connecticut League of Historical Societies
2105 Chester Village West
Chester, CT 06412
Mail:
P.O. Box 906
Darien, CT 06820

Cornwall Historical Society
Pine Street
P.O. Box 115
Cornwall, CT 06753

Coventry Historical Society
South Street
P.O. Box 307
Coventry, CT 06238

Danbury Scott-Fanton Museum/Historical Society
43 Main Street
Danbury, CT 06810
Tel: 203-743-5200

Darien Historical Society
Bates-Scofield Homestead
45 Old King's Highway, North
Darien, CT 06820
Tel: 203-655-9233

Denison Society
P.O. Box 42
Mystic, CT 06355

Derby Historical Society
37 Elm Street
Ansonia, CT 06401
Mail:
P.O. Box 331
Derby, CT 06418
Tel: 203-735-1908

Durham Historical Society
Main Street
P.O. Box 345
Durham, CT 06422

East Haddam Historical Society
P.O. Box 27
East Haddam, CT 06423

East Hartford Historical Society
52 Pitkin Street
East Hartford, CT 06108

East Haven Historical Society
133 Main Street
P.O. Box 120052
East Haven, CT 06512
Tel: 203-467-1766

East Windsor Historical Society
Scantic Road
P.O. Box 232
East Windsor, CT 06088

Easton Historical Society
P.O. Box 121
Easton, CT 06612
Tel: 203-452-8372

Enfield Historical Society
1294 Enfield Street
Enfield, CT 06082
Tel: 860-745-1729

Essex Historical Society
Hills Academy
Prospect Street
P.O. Box 123
Essex, CT 06426
Tel: 860-767-0681

Fairfield Historical Society
636 Old Post Road
Fairfield, CT 06430-6647
Tel: 203-259-1598

Falls Village-Canaan Historical Society
Main Street
P.O. Box 206
Falls Village, CT 06031
860-824-0707

Farmington Historical Society
P.O. Box 1645
Farmington, CT 06034

Franklin Historical Society
Route 32
North Franklin, CT 06254

Gaylordsville Historical Society
P.O. Box 25
Gaylordsville, CT 06755
http://www.eci.com/Gaylordsville/

Glastonbury Historical Society
1944 Main Street
P.O. Box 46
Glastonbury, CT 06033
Tel: 203-633-6890

Goshen Historical Society
21 Old Middle Road (Rte. 63)
Goshen, CT 06756-2001
Tel: 860-491-2665

Greater Bristol Historical Society
54 Middle Street
P.O. Box 1393
Bristol, CT 06010
Tel: 203-583-6309

Greenwich Historical Society
39 Strickland Road
Cos Cob, CT 06807
Tel: 203-869-6899

Griswold Historical Society
P.O. Box 261
Jewett City, CT 06351

Groton Bank Historical Association
49 Soundview Road
Groton, CT 06340

Guilford Keeping Society
171 Boston Street
P.O. Box 363
Guilford, CT 06437

Haddam Historical Society
P.O. Box 97
Haddam, CT 06438-0097

Hamden Historical Society
P.O. Box 5512
Hamden, CT 06518-0512
Tel: 203-248-8001
203-562-1483

Hampton Antiquarian & Historical Society
Main Street
P.O. Box 12
Hampton, CT 06247

Hartland Historical Society
East Hartland, CT 06027
Tel: 860-653-3055

Harwinton Historical Society
P.O. Box 84
Harwinton, CT 06791
Tel: 860-485-1202

Huntington Historical Society
P.O. Box 2155
Shelton, CT 06484
Tel: 203-925-1803

Killingly Historical and Genealogical Society, Inc.
196 Main Street
P.O. Box 6000
Danielson, CT 06239
Tel: 860-774-2758
URL: http://ourworld.compuserve.com/homepages/RLCarpenter/killingl.htm

Lebanon Historical Society
P.O. Box 151
Lebanon, CT 06249

Litchfield Historical Society
7 South Street
Litchfield, CT 06759
Tel: 860-567-4501

Lyme Historical Society/Archives
96 Lyme Street
Old Lyme, CT 06371-1426
Tel: 860-434-5542

Madison Historical Society
853 Boston Post Road
Madison, CT 06443

Manchester Historical Society
106 Hartford Road
Manchester, CT 06040
Tel: 860-643-5588

Mansfield Historical Society
954 Storrs Road, Route 195
P.O. Box 145
Storrs, CT 06268
Tel: 860-429-6575

Marlborough Historical Society
P.O. Box 281
Marlborough, CT 06447
Tel: 860-295-8106

Mattatuck Historical Society/Museum
144 West Street
Waterbury, CT 06702
Tel: 203-753-0381

Middlebury Historical Society
26 Wheeler Road
Middlebury, CT 06762

Middlesex County Historical Society
151 Main Street
Middletown, CT 06457
Tel: 860-346-0746

Milford Historical Society
34 High Street
Milford, CT 06460
Tel: 203-874-2664

Monroe Historical Society
Wheeler and Old Tannery Road
Monroe, CT 06468

Morris Historical Society
South Street
P.O. Box 234
Morris, CT 06763

Mystic River Historical Society
Old New London Rd. and High Street
P.O. Box 245
Mystic, CT 06355
Tel: 860-536-4779

Naugatuck Historical Society
144 Meadow Street
P.O. Box 317
Naugatuck, CT 06770

New Canaan Historical Society
13 Oenoke Ridge
New Canaan, CT 06840
Tel: 203-966-1776

New England Historic Genealogical Society
101 Newbury Street
Boston, MA 02116-3007
Tel: 617-536-5740
1-800-AT-NEHGS
Fax: 617-536-7307
Email: nehgs@nehgs.org
URL: http://www.nehgs.org/

New Fairfield Historical Society
Fairfield Public Library
Route 39
P.O. Box 8156
New Fairfield, CT 06812
Tel: 203-746-3289
203-775-3223

New Hartford Historical Museum/Library
Route 44
New Hartford, CT 06057
Tel: 860-379-6626

New Haven Colony Historical Society
Whitney Library
114 Whitney Avenue
New Haven, CT 06510
Tel: 203-562-4183
URL: http://statelab.stat.yale.edu/cityroom/test/hist/loc_srcs/colony/index.html

New London County Historical Society
11 Blinman Street
New London, CT 06320
Tel: 860-443-1209

New Milford Historical Society
6 Aspetuck Avenue
P.O. Box 566
New Milford, CT 06776
Tel: 860-354-3069

Newington Historical Society & Trust
679 Willard Avenue
Newington, CT 06111
Tel: 860-666-7118

Newtown Historical Society
44 Main Street
P.O. Box 189
Newtown, CT 06470

Noank Historical Society/Museum
17 Sylvan St.
P.O. Box 9454
Groton, CT 06340
Tel: 860-536-5021
860-536-7026

Norfolk Historical Society
Village Green
Norfolk, CT 06058
Tel: 860-542-5761

North Haven Historical Society
27 Broadway
North Haven, CT 06473
Tel: 203-239-7722

North Stonington Historical Society
Main Street
P.O. Box 134
North Stonington, CT 06359

Norwalk Historical Commission
141 East Avenue
Norwalk, CT 06851
Tel: 203-866-0202

Norwalk Historical Society
P.O. Box 355
Norwalk, CT 06852
Tel: 203-853-4228

Old Bethlehem Historical Society
North Main St.
Bethlehem, CT 06751
Tel: 203-266-5188

Old Post Road Association
P.O. Box 581
Fairfield, CT 06430

Old Saybrook Historical Society
Archival Section
Gen. William Hart House
350 Main Street
P.O. Box 4
Old Saybrook, CT 06475
Tel: 860-388-1874
860-388-2622

Old Woodbury Historical Society
P.O. Box 705
Woodbury, CT 06798

Orange Historical Society
615 Orange Center Road
P.O. Box 784
Orange, CT 06477
Tel: 203-795-3106
203-795-9466

Oxford Historical Society
154 Bowers Hill Road
Oxford, CT 06478
Tel: 203-888-0363

Plainville Historical Society
Plainville Historical Center
Farmington Canal Room
29 Pierce Street
P.O. Box 464
Plainville, CT 06062

Plymouth Historical Society
7 West Main
Plymouth, CT 06781

Pomfret Historical Society
P.O. Box 152
Pomfret, CT 06259

Portland Historical Society
P.O. Box 98
Portland, CT 06480

Prospect Historical Society
Center Street
Mail:
31 Summit Road
Prospect, CT 06712

Ridgefield Library and Historical Assn.
Historical Collection
472 Main Street
Ridgefield, CT 06877
Tel: 203-438-2282

Rocky Hill Historical Society/Academy Hall Museum
785 Old Main Street
Rocky Hill, CT 06067
Tel: 860-563-8710
860-563-6704 (museum)

Rowayton Historical Society
177 Rowayton Avenue
P.O. Box 106
Rowayton, CT 06853

Roxbury Historical Society
Blue Stone Ridge
Roxbury, CT 06783

Salisbury Association
Scoville Library, History Room
38 Main Street
P.O. Box 516
Salisbury, CT 06068-0516
Tel: 203-435-9440

Salmon Brook Historical Society
208 Salmon Brook Street
Granby, CT 06035
Tel: 860-653-3965

Seymour Historical Society
59 West Street
Seymour, CT 06483
Tel: 203-888-7471
203-888-0037

Sherman Historical Society
Sherman Center
10 Route 37
Sherman, CT 06784
Tel: 203-354-3083

Simsbury Historical Society
Massacoh Plantation
800 Hopmeadow Street
P.O. Box 2
Simsbury, CT 06070
Tel: 860-628-2500

South Windsor Historical Society
P.O. Box 216
South Windsor, CT 06074

Southbury Historical Society
P.O. Box 124
Southbury, CT 06488
Tel: 203-264-2993

Southington Historical Society
Southington Historical Center
239 Main Street
Southington, CT 06489
Tel: 860-621-4811

Sprague Historical Society
1 Main Street
Baltic, CT 06330

Stafford Historical Society
11 Murphy Road
P.O. Box 56
Stafford Springs, CT 06075
Tel: 860-684-9189

Stamford Historical Society/Library/Museum
1508 High Ridge Road
Stamford, CT 06903
Tel: 203-329-1183
Fax: 203-322-1607
URL: http://www.cslnet.ctstateu.edu/stamford/

Stonington Historical Society
Wadawanuck Square
P.O. Box 103
Stonington, CT 06378-0103
Tel: 860-535-1131
860-535-0888

Stratford Historical Society
Judson House & Catherine B. Mitchell Museum
967 Academy Hill
P.O. Box 382
Stratford, CT 06497
Tel: 203-378-0630

Suffield Historical Society
232 South Main Street
Suffield, CT 06078
Tel: 203-668-5256

Thomaston Historical Society
158 Main Street
Thomaston, CT 06787
Tel: 860-283-2159
860-283-9474

Thompson Historical Society
Thompson Hill Road and Chase
P.O. Box 47
Thompson, CT 06277

Tolland Historical Society
P.O. Box 107
Tolland, CT 06084

Torrington Historical Society
192 Main Street
Torrington, CT 06790
Tel: 860-482-8260

Totoket Historical Society
1605 Foxon Road
P.O. Box 563
North Branford, CT 06471
Tel: 203-488-0423

Trumbull Historical Society
65 Woolsley Avenue
Trumbull, CT 06611
Tel: 203-268-3545

Union Historical Society
Town Hall Road
Mail:
655 Buckley Highway
Union, CT 06076
Tel: 860-684-7078

Voluntown Historical Society
448H Tanglewood Lane
Voluntown, CT 06384
Tel: 860-376-9563

Wallingford Historical Society
180 South Main Street
Wallingford, CT 06492

Warren Historical Society
The Academy
Sackett Hill Road
Mail:
100 Town Hill Road
Warren, CT 06754

Waterford Historical Society
Jordan Green
Rope Ferry Road
P.O. Box 117
Waterford, CT 06385

Watertown Historical Society
22 DeForest Street
Watertown, CT 06795
Tel: 860-274-1634

West Hartford Historical Society/Noah Webster Foundation
227 South Main Street
West Hartford, CT 06107
Tel: 860-521-5362

Weston Historical Society
104 Weston Road
P.O. Box 1092
Weston, CT 06883

Westport Historical Society
Wheeler House
25 Avery Place
Westport, CT 06880
Tel: 203-226-2694

Wethersfield Historical Society
150 Main Street
Wethersfield, CT 06109
Tel: 860-529-7656

Willington Historical Society
48 Red Oak Hill
West Willington, CT 06279
Tel: 860-429-2656

Wilton Historical Society
Wilton Library, History Room
137 Old Ridgefield Road
Mail:
249 Danbury Road
Wilton, CT 06897
Tel: 203-762-3950
203-762-7257

Windsor Historical Society/Library
96 Palisado Avenue
Windsor, CT 06095
Tel: 860-688-3813

Windsor Locks Historical Society
Noden-Reed Park
58 West Street
Windsor Locks, CT 06096
Tel: 860-623-4143

Wintonbury Historical Society
21 Westbrook Road
Bloomfield, CT 06002

Woodstock Historical Society
P.O. Box 65
Woodstock, CT 06281

LDS Family History Centers

Bloomfield Family History Center
1000 Mountain Road
Bloomfield, CT 06002
Tel: 860-242-1607

Madison Family History Center
275 Warpas Road
Madison, CT 06443
Tel: 203-245-8267

Manchester Family History Center
Woodside Street
Manchester, CT 06040
Tel: 860-643-4003

Mystic Family History Center
1230 Flanders Rd.
Mystic, CT 06355
Tel: 860-536-5102

New Canaan Family History Center
682 South Avenue
New Canaan, CT 06840-6324
Tel: 203-966-1305

Woodbridge Family History Center
990 Racebrook Rd.
Woodbridge, CT 06525-2543
Tel: 203-387-2012

ARCHIVES/LIBRARIES/MUSEUMS

Abington Social Library
536 Hampton Road
Abington, CT 06230
Tel: 860-974-0415

Academy Hall Museum
Rocky Hill Historical Society
785 Old Main Street
Rocky Hill, CT 06067
Tel: 860-563-8710
860-563-6704 (museum)

Beardsley Memorial Library
40 Munroe Street
Winsted, CT 06098-1423
Tel: 860-379-6043

Bridgeport Public Library
Burroughs Library Building
Historical Collection, 3rd Floor
925 Broad Street
Bridgeport, CT 06604
Tel: 203-576-7417
URL: http://kiwi.futuris.net/bpl/

Bristol Public Library
5 High Street
Bristol, CT 06010
Tel: 860-584-7787

Canton Historical Museum
11 Front Street
Collinsville, CT 06022
Tel: 860-693-2793

Connecticut College Library
Mohegan Avenue
New London, CT 06320
URL: http://shain.lib.conncoll.edu/

Litchfield Historical Society
7 South Street
Litchfield, CT 06759
Tel: 860-567-4501

Connecticut Historical Society
1 Elizabeth Street at Asylum Avenue
Hartford, CT 06105
Tel: 860-236-5621
Fax: 860-236-2664
Email: cthist@ix.netcom.com (library)
ctmus@ix.netcom.com (museum)
URL: http://www.hartnet.org/chs/

Connecticut Polish American Archive
Ellen Burritt Library
Central Connecticut State University
1615 Stanley Street
New Britain, CT 06050
Tel: 860-832-2086
860-832-2085
Fax: 860-832-2118
860-832-3409
Email: wolynska@ccsu.ctstateu.edu
vickreyr@ccsu.ctstateu.edu
URL: http://library.ccsu.ctstateu.edu/~wolynska/
home.htm

Connecticut State Library
History & Genealogy Unit
231 Capitol Avenue
Hartford, CT 06106
Tel: 860-566-3692
Fax: 860-566-2133
Email: richardr@cslnet.ctstateu.edu
URL: http://www.cslnet.ctstateu.edu/

Cyrenius H. Booth Library
25 Main Street
Newtown, CT 06470

Danbury Public Library
170 Main Street
Danbury, CT 06810-7835
Tel: 203-797-4505

Danbury Scott-Fanton Museum/Historical Society
43 Main Street
Danbury, CT 06810-8011
Tel: 203-743-5200

Darien Historical Society
Bates-Scofield Homestead
45 Old King's Highway, North
Darien, CT 06820
Tel: 203-655-9233

Darien Library
35 Leroy Avenue
Darien, CT 06820-4497
Tel: 203-655-2568

Dodd Research Center
University of Connecticut
405 Babbidge Rd., Box U-205
Storrs, CT 06269-1205
Email: doddref@lib.uconn.edu
URL: http://www.lib.uconn.edu/DoddCenter/index.html

East Hartford Public Library
840 Main Street
East Hartford, CT 06108

Fairfield Historical Society Library
636 Old Post Road
Fairfield, CT 06430-6647
Tel: 203-259-1598

Fairfield Public Library
Old Post Road
Fairfield, CT 06430
Tel: 203-256-3155

Fairfield Public Library
Route 39
P.O. Box 8156
New Fairfield, CT 06812
Tel: 203-746-3289
203-775-3223

Farmington Museum
37 High Street
Farmington, CT 06032

Ferguson Library
One Public Library Plaza
Stamford, CT 06904
Tel: 203-964-1000
URL: http://kiwi.futuris.net/ferg/

Godfrey Memorial Library
134 Newfield Street
Middletown, CT 06457
Tel: 860-346-4375
Fax: 860-347-9874
Email: godfrey@connix.com
URL: http://www.godfrey.org/

Greenwich Library
101 West Putnam Avenue
Greenwich, CT 06830
Tel: 203-622-7900

Groton Public Library
Groton, CT 06340
Tel: 860-441-6750

Gunn Memorial Library
Wykeham Road
Washington, CT 06793
Tel: 860-868-7586

Hartford Public Library
500 Main Street
Hartford, CT 06103
Tel: 860-293-6000

Indian and Colonial Research Center
Main Street (Route 27)
Old Mystic, CT 06372
Tel: 860-536-9771

Kent Memorial Library
50 North Main Street
Suffield, CT 06078-2117
Tel: 860-668-3896

Killingly Historical and Genealogical Center
196 Main Street
P.O. Box 6000
Danielson, CT 06239
Tel: 860-774-2758
URL: http://ourworld.compuserve.com/homepages/RLCarpenter/killingl.htm

Litchfield Historical Society Museum
7 South Street
Litchfield, CT 06759
Tel: 860-567-4501
860-567-5769

Living Museum of Avon
8 East Main Street
Avon, CT 06001
Tel: 860-678-7621

Lyme Historical Society Archives
96 Lyme Street
Old Lyme, CT 06371-1426
Tel: 860-434-5542

Mattatuck Historical Society/Museum
144 West Street
Waterbury, CT 06702
Tel: 203-753-0381

Morris Historical Society Museum
Old Town Hall
1772 Mill School
Morris, CT 06763

Museum of Connecticut History
Connecticut State Library
231 Capitol Avenue
Hartford, CT 06106
Tel: 860-566-3056
Fax: 860-566-2133
Email: deann@cslnet.ctstateu.edu
URL: http://www.cslnet.ctstateu.edu/museum.htm

Museum on the Green
1944 Main Street
Glastonbury, CT 06033
Tel: 860-633-6890

Mystic and Noank Library
40 Library Street
Mystic, CT 06355-2418
Tel: 860-536-7721
860-536-3019
Fax: 860-536-2350
URL: http://www.localnews.com/Library/index.htm

Mystic Seaport
P.O. Box 6000
75 Greenmanville Avenue
Mystic, CT 06355
Tel: 860-572-0711
860-572-5315
URL: http://www.mystic.org/

New Britain Public Library
20 High Street
P.O. Box 1291
New Britain, CT 06050

New Canaan Historical Society/Library
13 Oenoke Ridge
New Canaan, CT 06840
Tel: 203-966-1776

New England Historic Genealogical Society
101 Newbury Street
Boston, MA 02116-3007
Tel: 617-536-5740
1-800-AT-NEHGS
Fax: 617-536-7307
Email: nehgs@nehgs.org
URL: http://www.nehgs.org/

New Hartford Historical Museum
New Hartford Library
Route 44
P.O. Box 247
New Hartford, CT 06057-0247
Tel: 860-379-6626 (museum)
860-379-7235 (library)

New Haven Colony Historical Society
Whitney Library
114 Whitney Avenue
New Haven, CT 06510
Tel: 203-562-4183
URL: http://statelab.stat.yale.edu/cityroom/test/hist/loc_srcs/colony/index.html

New Haven Free Public Library
Local History Room
133 Elm Street
New Haven, CT 06510
Tel: 203-946-8130
URL: http://statlab.stat.yale.edu/cityroom/test/city/elm/NHpublib.html

New London Public Library
63 Huntington Street
New London, CT 06320-6194
Tel: 860-447-1411

Noah Webster Memorial Library
20 S. Main Street
West Hartford, CT 06107
Tel: 860-523-3277
URL: http://www.crlc.org/westhartford/whplpage.htm

Noank Historical Society/Museum
17 Sylvan St.
P.O. Box 9454
Groton, CT 06340
Tel: 860-536-5021
860-536-7026

Old Saybrook Historical Society
Archival Section
Gen. William Hart House
350 Main Street
P.O. Box 4
Old Saybrook, CT 06475
Tel: 860-388-1874
860-388-2622

Oliver Wolcott Library
160 South Street
P.O. Box 187
Litchfield, CT 06778
Tel: 860-567-8030

Otis Library
261 Main Street
Norwich, CT 06360

Pequot Library
720 Pequot Avenue
Southport, CT 06490

Phoebe Griffin Noyes Library
Old Lyme, CT 06371
Tel: 860-434-1684

Ridgefield Library and Historical Assn.
Historical Collection
472 Main Street
Ridgefield, CT 06877
Tel: 203-438-2282

Russell Library
123 Broad Street
Middletown, CT 06459
Tel: 860-347-2528
860-347-2520
Fax: 860-347-4048
URL: http://www.state.ct.us/MUNIC/MIDDLETOWN/middletown~library.htm

Salmon Brook Settlement
208 Salmon Brook Street (Rtes. 10 & 202)
Granby, CT 06035
Tel: 860-653-3965

Scoville Library, History Room
38 Main Street
P.O. Box 516
Salisbury, CT 06068-0516
Tel: 203-435-9440

Seymour Public Library
46 Church Street
Seymour, CT 06483-2612
Tel: 203-888-3903

Simsbury Genealogical & Historical Research Library
749 Hopmeadow Street
P.O. Box 484
Simsbury, CT 06070

Southington Public Library
255 Main Street
Southington, CT 06489-2509
Tel: 860-628-0947

Stamford Historical Society/Library/Museum
1508 High Ridge Road
Stamford, CT 06903
Tel: 203-329-1183
Fax: 203-322-1607
URL: http://www.cslnet.ctstateu.edu/stamford/

Sterling Memorial Library
Yale University
120 High Street
New Haven, CT 06511
URL: http://www.library.yale.edu/sml.html

Stratford Historical Society
Judson House & Museum
967 Academy Hill
P.O. Box 382
Stratford, CT 06497
Tel: 203-378-0630

Trinity College
Watkinson Library
300 Summit Street
Hartford, CT 06106

U.S. Coast Guard Academy
Fifteen Mohegan Avenue
New London, CT 06320-4195
Tel: 203-444-8501

Wadsworth Atheneum Auerbach
600 Main Street
Hartford, CT 06103-2990
Tel: 860-278-2670

Wesleyan University
Olin Memorial Library
Special Collection & Archives
Church Street
Middletown, CT 06459
Tel: 203-685-3863
Email: eswaim@wesleyan.edu
dperron@wesleyan.edu
URL: http://www.wesleyan.edu/libr/olinhome/olinhome.htm

West Hartford Public Library
20 South Main Street
West Hartford, CT 06107

Westport Historical Society
Wheeler House
25 Avery Place
Westport, CT 06880
Tel: 203-226-2694

Wilton Library, History Room
137 Old Ridgefield Road
Mail:
249 Danbury Road
Wilton, CT 06897
Tel: 203-762-3950
203-762-7257

Windsor Historical Society/Library
96 Palisado Avenue
Windsor, CT 06095
Tel: 860-688-3813

Wood Memorial Library
783 Main Street
South Windsor, CT 06074
Tel: 860-289-1783

Yale University Library
Manuscripts & Archives
P.O. Box 208240
New Haven, CT 06520-8240
Email: mssa.assist@yale.edu
URL: http://www.library.yale.edu/mssa/home1.htm

Newspaper Repositories

Connecticut Historical Society
1 Elizabeth Street at Asylum Avenue
Hartford, CT 06105
Tel: 860-236-5621
Fax: 860-236-2664
Email: cthist@ix.netcom.com (library)
ctmus@ix.netcom.com (museum)
URL: http://www.hartnet.org/chs/

Connecticut State Library
History & Genealogy Unit
231 Capitol Avenue
Hartford, CT 06106
Tel: 860-566-3560
Fax: 860-566-2133
Email: jcullinane@cslnet.ctstateu.edu
URL: http://www.cslnet.ctstateu.edu/cnp.html

Vital Records

Connecticut Department of Public Health
Vital Records
150 Washington Street
Hartford, CT 06106
Tel: 860-566-2334
860-566-1124
URL: http://www.ctstateu.edu/~dph/vr-birth.html

Connecticut State Library
History & Genealogy Unit
231 Capitol Avenue
Hartford, CT 06106
Tel: 860-566-3692
Fax: 860-566-2133
Email: richardr@cslnet.ctstateu.edu
URL: http://www.cslnet.ctstateu.edu/

Connecticut on the Web

Ancestry's Marriage Records On-line
http://www.ancestry.com/marriage/

Barbour Collection of Connecticut Vital Records
http://www.cslnet.ctstateu.edu/barbour.htm

Charles R. Hale Collection
http://www.cslnet.ctstateu.edu/halecol2.htm

Connecticut Genweb Project
http://q.continuum.net/~jrothgeb/ctgenweb.htm

Connecticut Vital Records
http://www.ctstateu.edu/~dph/vr-birth.html

Delaware

Archives, State & National

Delaware State Archives
Hall of Records
Bureau of Archives and Records Management
Duke of York St. & Legislative Avenue
Dover, DE 19901
Tel: 302-674-5680
302-739-5318
Fax: 302-739-6710
URL: http://www.ravenet.com/dsa/

National Archives—Mid Atlantic Region
Ninth and Market Streets
Philadelphia, PA 19107-4292
Tel: 215-597-3000
FAx: 215-597-2303
Email: archives@philarch.nara.gov
URL: http://www.nara.gov/nara/regional/03nsgil.html

Genealogical Societies

Delaware Genealogical Society
505 Market Street Mall
Wilmington, DE 19801-3091
URL: http://delgensoc.org/

Lower Delmarva Genealogical Society (LDGS)
Salisbury State College Library
P.O. Box 3602
Salisbury, MD 21802-3602
Tel: 410-742-3501
410-546-0314
URL: http://bay.intercom.net/ldgs/index.html

Sons of the American Revolution
Delaware Society
P.O. Box 2169
Wilmington, DE 19899

Historical Societies

Afro-American Historical Society of Delaware
512 East 4th Street
Wilmington, DE 19801
Tel: 302-571-9300
Fax: 302-571-9300 (please call first)

Bethel Historical Society
P.O. Box 55
Bethel, DE 19931
Tel: 302-875-5425

Bridgeville Historical Society
P.O. Box 306
Bridgeville, DE 19933
Tel: 302-337-7823
302-327-7125

Chester County Historical Society
225 North High Street
West Chester, PA 19380
Tel: 215-692-4800
URL: http://chesco.com/~cchs

Delaware, Historical Society of
Old Town Hall
505 Market Street
Wilmington, DE 19801
Tel: 302-655-7161
Fax: 302-655-7844
Email: hsd@dca.net
URL: http://www.hsd.org/

Fort Delaware Society
(Ferry Dock in Delaware City off route 1)
P.O. Box 553
Delaware City, DE 19706
Tel: 302-834-1630
URL: http://204.183.92.8/org/fort/

Frederica Historical Society
R.D. 2, Box 161AA
Lewes, DE 19958
Tel: 302-945-0680

Georgetown Historical Society
Georgetown Chamber of Commerce
Old Town Hall
114 E. Market Street
P.O. Box 1
Georgetown, DE 19947
Tel: 302-855-9660
302-856-1544
Fax: 302-856-6348

Greater Harrington Historical Society
108 Fleming Street
P.O. Box 64
Harrington, DE 19952
Tel: 302-398-3698

Historical Society of Pennsylvania
1300 Locust Street
Philadelphia, PA 19107
Tel: 215-732-6201

Jewish Historical Society of Delaware
c/o Historical Society of Delaware
505 Market Street
Wilmington, DE 19801
Tel: 302-655-7161
Fax: 302-655-7844

Laurel Historical Society
P.O. Box 92
Laurel, DE 19956
Tel: 302-875-7015

Lewes Historical Society
110 Shipcarpenter Street
Lewes, DE 19958-1210
Tel: 302-645-7670

Milford Historical Society
P.O. Box 352
Milford, DE 19963
Tel: 302-422-3115

Milton Historical Society
210-212 Union Street
Milton, DE 19968
Tel: 302-684-8851
302-684-8676

Nanticoke Indian Association
R.D. 4, Box 107A
Millsboro, DE 19966
Tel: 302-945-3400
302-947-9137

Newark Historical Society
Box 711
Newark, DE 19711
Tel: 302-731-0955

Port Penn Historical Society
P.O. Box 120
Port Penn, DE 19731
Tel: 302-834-2464
302-834-2421

Presbyterian Historical Society
425 Lombard Street
Philadelphia, PA 19147-1516
Tel: 215-627-1852

Rehoboth Beach Historical Society
Anna Hazzard Museum
P.O. Box 42
Rehoboth Beach, DE 19971
Tel: 302-227-6111
302-226-1119

Seaford Historical Society
Ross Plantation
Route 1, Box 393
Seaford, DE 19973
Tel: 302-628-9500
Fax: 302-628-9501

LDS FAMILY HISTORY CENTERS

Dover Family History Center
Route 10 (near Old Mill Road)
Dover, DE 19711
Tel: 302-697-2700

Wilmington Family History Center
143 Dickinson Lane
Wilmington, DE 19807
Tel: 302-654-1911

ARCHIVES/LIBRARIES/MUSEUMS

Barratt's Chapel and Museum/Research Library
6362 Bay Road
Frederica, DE 19946
Tel: 302-335-5544
Email: Barratts@aol.com
URL: http://users.aol.com/Barratts/home.html

Corbit-Calloway Memorial Library
115 High Street
P.O. Box 128
Odessa, DE 19730
Tel: 302-378-8838
Fax: 302-378-7803

Delaware Division of Libraries
Department of Community Affairs
43 South Dupont Highway
Dover, DE 19901

Delaware State University
William C. Jason Library-Learning Center
Dover, DE 19901
Tel: 302-736-5111
Fax: 302-739-3560
URL: http://www.dsc.edu/

Dover Public Library
45 South State Street
Dover, DE 19901
Tel: 302-736-7030

Hagley Museum/Library
Route 141 & Brandywine River
Wilmington, DE 19807
Tel: 302-658-2400 (weekdays)
302-658-4674 (weekends)
Fax: 302-658-0568
URL: http://www.hagley.lib.de.us/

Hendrickson House Museum & Old Swedes Church
606 North Church Street
Wilmington, DE 19801-4421
Tel: 302-652-5629

Historical Society of Delaware Library/Museum
Old Town Hall
505 Market Street
Wilmington, DE 19801
Tel: 302-655-7161
302-656-0637 (museum)
Fax: 302-655-7844
Email: hsd@dca.net
URL: http://www.hsd.org/

Holy Trinity (Old Swedes) Episcopal Church
606 Church Street
Wilmington, DE 19801
Tel: 302-652-5629
Email: OldSwedes@aol.com

Laurel Public Library
6 East Fourth Street
Laurel, DE 19956
Tel: 302-875-3184
Fax: 302-875-4519

Lewes Chamber of Commerce
Fisher Martin House
120 Kings Highway
P.O. Box 1
Lewes, DE 19958
Tel: 302-645-8073
Fax: 302-645-8412
URL: http://www.leweschamber.com/

Lewes Public Library
111 Adams Avenue
Lewes, DE 19958

Meetinghouse Galleries
316 S. Governors Avenue
Dover, DE 19904-6706

Milford Public Library
11 S.E. Front Street
Milford, DE 19963-1941
Tel: 302-422-8996

New Castle County Library
Concord Pike & Whitby Road, Sharpley
Wilmington, DE 19803

New Castle Public Library
424 Delaware Street
New Castle, DE 19720
Tel: 302-328-1995
Fax: 302-328-4412

Redmen Nanticoke Tribe
Route 113
Georgetown, DE 19947
Tel: 302-856-2405

Rockwood Museum
610 Shipley Road
Wilmington, DE 19809-3609
Tel: 302-761-4340
Email: info@rockwood.org
URL: http://www.rockford.org/index.html

Roman Catholic Archives
Diocese of Wilmington
P.O. Box 4019
Greenville, DE 19807
Tel: 302-655-0597

Episcopal Church
Diocese of Delaware
400 Burnt Mill Road
Centerville, DE 19807
Tel: 302-654-4148
Fax: 302-654-7615

Salisbury State College Library
Research Center for DelMarVa History & Culture
Wayne Street
Salisbury, MD 21801
Tel: 410-742-3501
410-546-0314
URL: http://bay.intercom.net/ldgs/ldgs_rc.htm

Seaford District Library
402 North Porter Street
Seaford, DE 19973
Tel: 302-629-2524
Fax: 302-629-9181

Smyrna Public Library
107 South Main Street
Smyrna, DE 19977
Tel: 302-653-4579

University of Delaware
Morris Library
Special Collections Department
South College Avenue
Newark, DE 19717-5267
Tel: 302-831-2229
302-831-2231
Fax: 302-831-1046
URL: http://www.lib.udel.edu/
or gopher://gopher.lib.udel.edu/11/ud/spec

Wesley College
Parker Library
College Square
Dover, DE 19901
Tel: 302-736-2413
Fax: 302-736-2301
URL: http://www.wesley.edu/geninfo.htm

Wicomico County Free Library
122 South Division Street
Salisbury, MD 21801-4929
Tel: 410-749-5171
410-749-3612
URL: http://www.co.wicomico.md.us/library.html

Widener University School of Law
Legal Information Center
Brandywine Valley Historical Collection
4601 Concord Pike
P.O. Box 7475
Wilmington, DE 19803
Tel: 302-477-2063
Fax: 302-477-2240
URL: http://www.widener.edu/law/lic/dir.htm

Wilmington Institute Free Library
10 S. Market Street
P.O. Box 2303
Wilmington, DE 19899-2303
Tel: 302-571-7416
Fax: 302-654-9132

Winterthur Museum, Gardens, and Library
Winterthur Museum Archives
Winterthur, DE 19735
Tel: 302-888-4701
302-888-4699
Fax: 302-888-4870
URL: http://www.libertynet.org/~pacscl/winterthur/index.html

NEWSPAPER REPOSITORIES

Delaware, Historical Society of Old Town Hall
505 Market Street
Wilmington, DE 19801
Tel: 302-655-7161
Fax: 302-655-7844
Email: hsd@dca.net
URL: http://www.hsd.org/

Delaware State Archives
Hall of Records
Bureau of Archives and Records Management
Duke of York St. & Legislative Avenue
Dover, DE 19901
Tel: 302-674-5680
302-739-5318
Fax: 302-739-6710
URL: http://www.ravenet.com/dsa/

University of Delaware Libraries
South College Avenue
Newark, DE 19716
Tel: 302-831-2231
Fax: 302-831-1046
Email: craig.wilson@mvs.udel.edu
URL: http://www.lib.udel.edu/

VITAL RECORDS

Delaware State Archives
Hall of Records
Bureau of Archives and Records Management
Duke of York St. & Legislative Avenue
Dover, DE 19901
Tel: 302-674-5680
302-739-5318
Fax: 302-739-6710
URL: http://www.ravenet.com/dsa/

DELAWARE ON THE WEB

Delaware Family Forest
http://www.familyforest.com/whois.html

Delaware Genealogical Society
http://delgensoc.org/

Delaware Genweb Project
http://www.geocities.com/Heartland/8074/state_de.htm

Delaware State Library
http://www.lib.de.us/

Historical Society of Delaware
http://www.hsd.org/

Lower DelMarVa Genealogical Society
http://bay.intercom.net/ldgs/index.html

DISTRICT OF COLUMBIA

ARCHIVES, STATE & NATIONAL

District of Columbia Archives
1300 Naylor Court, NW
Washington, DC 20001-4225
Tel: 202-727-2054

National Archives and Records Administration (NARA)
Archives I
8th & Pennsylvania Avenues
Washington, DC 20408
Tel: 202-501-5410 (Genealogical Staff)
202-501-5400 (Record Availability)
Fax: 301-713-6905 (Fax-on-Demand Information)
Email: inquire@arch1.nara.gov
URL: http://www.nara.gov/nara/dc/Archives1_info.html

National Archives and Records Administration (NARA)
Archives II
8601 Adelphi Road
College Park, MD 20740
Tel: 202-501-5400 (Record Availability)
301-713-6800 (General Reference)
301-713-7040 (Cartographic Reference)
Fax: 301-713-6905 (Fax-on-Demand Information)
Email: inquire@arch2.nara.gov
URL: http://www.nara.gov/nara/dc/Archives1_info.html

National Archives and Records Administration (NARA)
Washington National Records Center
Shipping Address:
4205 Suitland Road
Suitland, MD 20746-2042
Mail:
4205 Suitland Road
Washington, DC 20409-0002
Tel: 301-457-7000
Fax: 301-457-7117
Email: center@suitland.nara.gov
URL: http://www.nara.gov/nara/frc/newbloc.html

GENEALOGICAL SOCIETIES

African-American Historical & Genealogical Society
P.O. Box 73086
Washington, DC 20056-3086

African-American National Capital Area Historical Genealogical Society
P.O. Box 34683
Washington, DC 20043

Jewish Genealogy Society of Greater Washington
P.O. Box 412
Vienna, VA 22183-0412

National Genealogical Society
4527 Seventeenth Street North
Arlington, VA 22207-2399
URL: http://www.genealogy.org/~ngs/

National Society-Daughters of American Colonists
2205 Massachusetts Avenue, NW
Washington, DC 20008

National Society, Daughters of the American Revolution
Memorial Continental Hall
1776 D Street NW
Washington, DC 20006-5303
Tel: 202-628-1776
Email: dar@chesapeake.net
URL: http://www.chesapeake.net/DAR/

Historical Societies

Historical Society of Washington, DC
1307 New Hampshire Avenue, NW
Washington, DC 20036
Tel: 202-785-2068

U.S. Capitol Historical Society
200 Maryland Avenue, NE
Washington, DC 20002
Tel: 202-543-8919

White House Historical Association
740 Jackson Place, NW
Washington, DC 20506

LDS Family History Centers

(See Maryland)

Archives/Libraries/Museums

Anderson House Library & Museum
2118 Massachusetts Avenue, NW
Washington, DC 20008

Catholic University of America
Department of Archives, Manuscripts, and Museum Collections
5 Mullen Library
Washington, DC 20064
Tel: 202-319-5065
Email: meagher@cua.edu
URL: http://www.cua.edu/www/mullen/archcoll.html

Georgetown University
Lauinger Library
Special Collections
Box 571174
Washington, DC 20057-1174
URL: http://gulib.lausun.georgetown.edu/

Library of Congress
Local History & Genealogy Divison
1st-2nd Streets, SE
Washington, DC 20540
Email: lcweb@loc.gov
URL: http://lcweb.loc.gov

Martin Luther King Memorial Library
901 G Street, NW
Washington, DC 20001
Tel: 202-727-1199
Email: rdeane1110@aol.com

National Society, Daughters of the American Revolution
Memorial Continental Hall
1776 D Street NW
Washington, DC 20006-5303
Tel: 202-628-1776
Email: dar@chesapeake.net
URL: http://www.chesapeake.net/DAR/

Smithsonian Institute
1000 Jefferson Drive
Washington, DC 20560
Tel: 202-357-2700
TTY: 202-357-1729
URL: http://www.si.edu/

United States Holocaust Memorial Museum
100 Rauol Wallenberg Place, SW
Washington, DC 20024-2150
Tel: 202-488-0400
Email: research@ushmm.org
archive@ushmm.org
URL: http://www.ushmm.org/

Newspaper Repositories

Library of Congress
Local History & Genealogy Divison
1st-2nd Streets, SE
Washington, DC 20540
Email: lcweb@loc.gov
URL: http://lcweb.loc.gov

Martin Luther King Memorial Library
901 G Street, NW
Washington, DC 20001
Tel: 202-727-1199
Email: rdeane1110@aol.com

Vital Records

District of Columbia Dept. of Human Services
Vital Records Branch
613 G Street, NW
Washington, DC 20001
Tel: 202-727-9281
202-727-5314

National Archives and Records Administration (NARA)
Archives I
8th & Pennsylvania Avenues
Washington, DC 20408
Tel: 202-501-5410 (Genealogical Staff)
202-501-5400 (Record Availability)
Fax: 301-713-6905 (Fax-on-Demand Information)
Email: inquire@arch1.nara.gov
URL: http://www.nara.gov/nara/dc/Archives1_info.html

D.C. on the Web

District of Columbia GenWeb Project
http://members.aol.com/georgia62/dc/index.html

Florida

Archives, State & National

Florida State Archives
Bureau of Archives Management
Division of Library & Information Services
Public Services Section
R.A. Gray Building
500 South Bronough Street
Tallahassee, FL 32399-0250
Tel: 904-487-2073
URL: http://stafla.dlis.state.fl.us/

National Archives—Southeast Region
1557 St. Joseph Avenue
East Point, GA 30344
Tel: 404-763-7477
Fax: 404-763-7033
Email: archives@atlanta.nara.gov
URL: http://www.nara.gov/nara/regional/04nsgil.html

Genealogical Societies

AAHGS Central Florida
P.O. Box 5742
Deltona, FL 32728

Alachua County Genealogical Society
P.O. Box 12078
Gainesville, FL 32604-0078

Amelia Island Genealogical Society
P.O. Box 6005
Fernandina Beach, FL 32035-6005

Bay County Genealogical Society
P.O. Box 662
Panama City, FL 32401

Bonita Springs Genealogical Club
27312 Shriver Avenue, SE
Bonita Springs, FL 33923

Brevard Genealogical Society
P.O. Box 1123
Cocoa, FL 32922

Broward County Genealogical Society
P.O. Box 485
Fort Lauderdale, FL 33302
Email: thalassa@bcfreenet.seflin.lib.fl.us
URL: http://www.seflin.org/gsbc/index.html

Central Florida Genealogy Society
P.O. Box 177
Orlando, FL 32802-0177
URL: http://www.magicnet.net/~paulench/cfgs.html

Charlotte County Genealogical Society
P.O. Box 2682
Port Charlotte, FL 33952

Citrus County Genealogical Society
1511 Druid Road
P.O. Box 2211
Inverness, FL 34451-2211

Clay County Genealogical Society
P.O. Box 1071
Green Cove Springs, FL 32043

Collier County, Genealogical Society of
P.O. Box 7933
Naples, FL 33941-7933
URL: http://www.naples.net/clubs/geneosoc.htm

Florida Genealogical Society
P.O. Box 18624
Tampa, FL 33679-8624

Florida Society of Genealogical Research
8415 122nd Street, North
Seminole, FL 34642

Florida State Genealogical Society
P.O. Box 10249
Tallahassee, FL 32302

Geneva Historical & Genealogical Society
P.O. Box 145
Geneva, FL 32732

Golden Gate-Naples Genealogical Society
1689 Bonita Court
Naples, FL 33962

Greater Miami, Genealogical Society of
P.O. Box 162905
Miami, FL 33116-2905

Halifax Genealogical Society
30 Beach Street
Ormond, FL 32174

Hernando County, Genealogy Society of
P.O. Box 1793
Brooksville, FL 34605-1793

Highlands County Genealogical Society
110 North Museum Avenue
Avon Park, FL 33825

Huxford Genealogical Society
P.O. Box 595
Homerville, GA 31634
Tel: 912-487-2310
Email: clineberger@mail.datasys.net
URL: http://www.datasys.net/users/stu/clineberger/homepage.htm

Imperial Polk Genealogical Society
P.O. Box 10
Kathleen, FL 33849-0010

Indian River Genealogical Society, Inc.
P.O. Box 1850
Vero Beach, FL 32961-1850

International Fellowship of Rotarians Genealogy
5721 Antietam Drive
Sarasota, FL 34231

Jacksonville Genealogical Society
P.O. Box 60756
Jacksonville, FL 32236-0756

Jewish Genealogical Society of Broward County
P.O. Box 17251
Fort Lauderdale, FL 33318

Jewish Genealogical Society of Central Florida
P.O. Box 520583
Longwood, FL 32752

Jewish Genealogical Society of Greater Miami
8340 Southwest 151st Street
Miami, FL 33158

Jewish Genealogical Society of Greater Orlando
P.O. Box 941332
Maitland, FL 32784-1332
Fax: 407-671-7485

Jewish Genealogical Society of Palm Beach County
6037 Point Regal Circle #205
Delray Beach, FL 33484-1814

Keystone Genealogical Society
695 E. Washington Street (library)
P.O. Box 50
Monticello, FL 32344
Tel: 904-997-3304
Email: canesyrup@aol.com

Lake County Kinseekers Genealogical Society
P.O. Box 492711
Leesburg, FL 32749-2711

Lee County Genealogical Society
P.O. Box 150153
Cape Coral, FL 33915-0153

Lehigh Acres Genealogical Society
P.O. Box 965
Lehigh Acres, FL 33970-0965

Lemon Bay Historical & Genealogical Society
P.O. Box 236
Englewood, FL 33533

Manasota Genealogical Society
1405 4th Avenue, W
Bradenton, FL 34205-7507

Martin County Genealogical Society
1395 NE Waveland
Jensen Beach, FL 33457

Mayflower Society of Florida
Governor William Bradford Colony
19601 Lake Osceola Lane
Odessa, FL 33556-1710

Monroe County Genealogical Society
21 Ventana Lane
Big Coppitt Key, FL 33040

North Brevard, Genealogical Society of (GSNB)
P.O. Box 897
Titusville, FL 32781-0897

Ocala/Marion County Genealogical Society
P.O. Box 1206
Ocala, FL 34478-1206

Ohio Genealogical Society
Florida Chapter
P.O. Box 232
Madison, FL 32340-0232

Okaloosa County, Genealogical Society of
P.O. Box 1175
Fort Walton Beach, FL 32549

Okeechobee, Genealogical Society of
P.O. Box 371
Okeechobee, FL 33472

Osceola County Dept. of Genealogical Research
326 Eastern Avenue
St. Cloud, FL 32769

Palm Beach County Genealogical Society
P.O. Box 1746
West Palm Beach, FL 33402-1746

Pinellas Genealogy Society, Inc.
@ Largo Public Library
351 East Bay Drive
P.O. Box 1614
Largo, FL 33779-1614
URL: http://www.geocities.com/Heartland/Plains/8283/

Putnam County Genealogical Society
P.O. Box 2354
Palatka, FL 32178-2354

Ridge Genealogical Society
P.O. Box 477
Babson Park, FL 33827

Roots & Branches Genealogical Society
P.O. Box 612
DeLand, FL 32721-0612

St. Augustine Genealogical Society
c/o St. Johns County Public Library
1960 N. Ponce de Leon Blvd.
St. Augustine, FL 32084

Sarasota Genealogical Society
P.O. Box 1917
Sarasota, FL 34230-1917

Seminole County, Genealogical Group of
P.O. Box 2148
Casselberry, FL 32707

Sons of the American Revolution, Florida Society
URL: http://www.flssar.org/index.html

South Bay Genealogy Club
P.O. Box 5202
Sun City Ctr., FL 33571

South Brevard County, Genealogical Society of
P.O. Box 786
Melbourne, FL 32902-0786

South Hillsborough Genealogists
Route 1, Box 400
Palmetto, FL 33561

Southeast Volusia County, Genealogical Society of
105 South Riverside Drive
New Smyrna, FL 32168-7197

Southern Genealogists Exchange Society, Inc.
P.O. Box 2801
Jacksonville, FL 32203-2801
Tel: 904-387-9142

Suncoast Genealogy Society
P.O. Box 1294
Palm Harbor, FL 34682-1294
Fax: 813-799-2281

Suwannee Valley Genealogical Society, Inc.
c/o Historical Museum
208 N. Ohio Avenue
Live Oak, FL 32060

Tallahassee Genealogical Society
P.O. Box 4371
Tallahassee, FL 32315

Treasure Coast Genealogical Society
P.O. Box 3401
Fort Pierce, FL 34948-3401

Volusia Genealogical & Historical Society
P.O. Box 2039
Daytona Beach, FL 32015

West Florida Genealogical Society
P.O. Box 947
Pensacola, FL 32594-0947

West Pasco Genealogical Society
5636 Club House Drive
New Port Richey, FL 34653-4405

Historical Societies

Baker County Historical Society
P.O. Box 856
Macclenny, FL 32063

Clearwater Historical Society
P.O. Box 175
Clearwater, FL 34617
URL: http://public.lib.ci.clearwater.fl.us/cpl/chs/chs.html

Dunedin Historical Society/Museum
349 Main Street
P.O. Box 2393
Dunedin, FL 34697-2393
Tel: 813-736-1176
813-529-3307

East Hillsborough Historical Society
Quintilla Geer Bruton Archives Center
605 North Collins Street
Plant City, FL 33566

Florida Baptist Historical Society
Stetson University
P.O. Box 8353
DeLand, FL 32720

Florida Historical Society
1320 Highland Avenue
Melbourne, FL 32935
Tel: 407-259-0947
URL: http://www.lib.usf.edu/spcoll/fhs/fhs.html

Geneva Historical & Genealogical Society
P.O. Box 145
Geneva, FL 32732

Halifax Historical Society
252 S. Beach St.
Daytona Beach, FL 32114-4407
Tel: 904-255-6976

Hillsborough County Historical Commission
Museum, Historical & Genealogical Library
County Courthouse
Tampa, FL 33602

Indian River County Historical Society
Vero Beach Railroad Station
2336 14th Avenue
Vero Beach, FL
Mail:
P.O. Box 6535
Vero Beach, FL 32961

Jacksonville Historical Society
100-B Wharfside Way
Jacksonville, FL 32207
Tel: 904-396-6307
Fax: 904-398-4647
Email: ldormad@junix.ju.edu

Lake County Historical Society
315 West Main Street
Tavares, FL 32778

Loxahatchee Historical Society/Museum
805 N. U.S. Highway 1
Jupiter Beach, FL 33477
Tel: 407-747-6639

Maitland Historical Society
840 Lake Lily Drive
Maitland, FL 32751-5613
Tel: 407-644-2451

Martin County, Historical Society of
825 NE Ocean Boulevard
Hutchinson Island
Stuart, FL 34996-1696
Tel: 407-225-1961
URL: http://www.classicar.com/museums/histmart/histmart.htm

Micanopy Historical Society/Museum
706 NE Cholokka Blvd.
P.O. Box 462
Micanopy, FL 32667
Email: micanopy@afn.org
URL: http://www.afn.org/~micanopy

North Brevard Historical Society
801 S. Washington Avenue
P.O. Box 6199
Titusville, FL 32782-6199
Tel: 407-269-3658

Orange County Historical Society/Museum
812 E. Rollins Street
Orlando, FL 32803
Tel: 407-897-6350
Fax: 407-897-6409
Email: 75620.2455@compuserve.com

Palm Beach County Historical Society
105 S. Narcissus Avenue
West Palm Beach, FL 33401
Tel: 407-832-4164

Pensacola Historical Society/Museum
117 East Government Street
Pensacola, FL 32501
Tel: 904-433-1559

Polk County Historical Association
P.O. Box 2749
Bartow, FL 33830-2749

St. Augustine Historical Society
271 Charlotte Street
St. Augustine, FL 32084-5033
Tel: 904-824-2872
Email: oldhouse@aug.com
URL: http://www.oldcity.com/oldhouse/historical.htm

Sebastian Area Historical Society
P.O. Box 781348
Sebastian, FL 32978-1348

South Brevard Historical Society
615 N. Riverside
Indialantic, FL 32903
Tel: 407-723-6835 (also fax)

Tampa Historical Society
245 S. Hyde Park Avenue
Tampa, FL 33606
Tel: 813-259-1111

LDS Family History Centers

Arcadia Family History Center
East Gibson Street
Arcadia, FL 34266
Tel: 941-993-0996

Belle Glade Family History Center
601 North East Avenue A
Belle Glade, FL 33430-3129
Tel: 407-996-6355

Boca Raton Family History Center (Spanish)
1530 West Camino Real
Boca Raton, FL 33486-8455
Tel: 407-395-6644

Bradenton Family History Center
2400 Cortez Road, W
Bradenton, FL 34207-1248
Tel: 941-755-6909

Dayton Beach Family History Center
6th Street
Daytona Beach, FL 32114
Tel: 904-253-9223

Fort Myers Family History Center
3105 Broadway
Fort Myers, FL 33901-7260
Tel: 941-275-0001

Gainesville Family History Center
10600 SW 24th Avenue
Gainesville, FL 32607-4618
Tel: 352-331-8542

Homestead Family History Center
29600 SW 167th Avenue
Homestead, FL 33030-3421
Tel: 954-246-2486

Jacksonville East Stake Family History Center
7665 Fort Carolina Road
Jacksonville, FL 32277-2214
Tel: 904-743-0527

Key West Family History Center
3424 Northside Drive
Key West, FL 33040-4254
Tel: 305-294-9400

Lake City Family History Center
706 Country Club Road
Lake City, FL 32025-6413
Tel: 904-755-9423

Lake Mary Family History Center
2255 Lake Emma Drive
Lake Mary, FL 32746-4963
Tel: 407-333-0137

Lakeland Family History Center
1839 Gib-Galloway Road
Lakeland, FL 33809
Tel: 941-853-1582

Largo Family History Center
9001 106th Avenue, N
Largo, FL 33777-1148
Tel: 813-399-8018

Lecanto Family History Center
3474 West Southern Street
Lecanto, FL 34461-8613
Tel: 352-746-5943

Leesburg Family History Center
1875 Mt. Vernon Rd.
Leesburg, FL 34748-7026
Tel: 904-787-5633

Miami Family History Center
8500 SW 8th Street, #248
Miami, FL 33144-4002
Tel: 305-265-1045

New Port Richey Family History Center
10606 Hilltop Drive
New Port Richey, FL 34654-2530
Tel: 813-863-2076
813-868-8225

Orange Park Family History Center
461 Blanding Blvd.
Orange Park, FL 32073-5002
Tel: 904-272-1150

Orlando Family History Center
45 East Par Avenue
Orlando, FL 32804-3928
Tel: 407-895-4832

Palm Beach Gardens Family History Center
4311 Hood Road
Palm Beach Gardens, FL 33410-2177
Tel: 407-626-7989
561-626-7989

Palm City Family History Center
2401 SW Matheson Avenue
Palm City, FL 34990
Tel: 561-287-0167

Panama City Family History Center
3140 State Avenue
Panama City, FL 32405-2216
Tel: 904-785-9290

Pensacola Family History Center
940 Foxrun
Pensacola, FL 32514
Tel: 904-478-5211

Plantation Family History Center (Spanish)
851 North Hiatus Road
Plantation, FL 33325-1503
Tel: 941-472-0524

Port Charlotte Family History Center
1303 Forest Nelson Blvd.
Port Charlotte, FL 33952-2127
Tel: 941-627-6446

Rockledge Family History Center
1801 Fiske Boulevard
Rockledge, FL 32955-3003
Tel: 407-636-2431

Tallahassee Family History Center
312 Stadium Drive
Tallahassee, FL 32304-3450
Tel: 904-222-8870

Tampa Family History Center
4106 East Fletcher Avenue
Tampa, FL 33613-4834
Tel: 813-971-2869

Vero Beach Family History Center
3980 12th Street
Vero Beach, FL 32960-3816
Tel: 561-569-5122

Winter Haven Family History Center
1958 9th Street, SE
Winter Haven, FL 33880-4732
Tel: 941-299-1691

ARCHIVES/LIBRARIES/MUSEUMS

Amelia Island Museum of History
223 South Third Street
Fernandina Beach, FL 32034
Tel: 904-261-7378
URL: http://www.ameliaisland.com/pix/mosiac/museum.htm

Bay County Public Library
25 West Government St.
Caller Box 2625
Panama City, FL 32402

Black Archives
Florida A&M University
Tallahassee, FL 32307
Tel: 904-599-3020
URL: http://www.famu.edu/dev/Dblackarchives.html

Black Archives History Foundation
5400 NW 22nd Avenue
Miami, FL 33142
Tel: 305-636-2390
Fax: 305-636-2391

Bonita Springs Public Library
26876 Pine Avenue
Bonita Springs, FL 33923

Brevard Community College
Learning Resource Centers
Tel: 407-632-1111 ext. 62963 (Genealogy)
Cocoa Campus
BCC/UCF Joint Use Library
1519 Clearlake Rd.
Cocoa, FL 32922-6597
URL: http://www.brevard.cc.fl.us/lrc/libc.htm

Palm Bay Campus
Florida Advanced Technology Center
250 Grassland Road, SE
Palm Bay, FL 32909-2299
URL: http://www.brevard.cc.fl.us/lrc/libp.htm
Melbourne Campus
Philip F. Nohrr Learning Resources Center
3865 North Wickham Road
Melbourne, FL 32935-2399
URL: http://www.brevard.cc.fl.us/lrc/libm.htm
Titusville Campus
Dr. Frank Elbert Williams Learning Resources Center
1311 North U.S. 1
Titusville, FL 32796-2192
URL: http://www.brevard.cc.fl.us/lrc/libt.htm

Brevard County Public Library-Melbourne
540 Fee Avenue
Melbourne, FL 32901
Tel: 407-952-4514

Cape Coral Public Library
921 SW 39th Terrace
Cape Coral, FL 33914-5721
Tel: 941-542-3953

Cedar Key Historical Society Museum
2nd Street at SR 24
P.O. Box 222
Cedar Key, FL 32625
Tel: 904-543-5549

Central Brevard Library & Reference Center
308 Forrest Avenue
Cocoa, FL 32922
Tel: 407-633-1792
URL: http://www.brev.lib.fl.us/library/locations/cla.html

Clearwater Public Library
100 North Osceola Avenue
Clearwater, FL 34615-4083
Tel: 813-462-6800
Fax: 813-462-6420
Email: library@public.lib.ci.clearwater.fl.us
URL: http://public.lib.ci.clearwater.fl.us/cpl/cpl.htm

Cocoa Public Library
430 Delannoy Avenue
Cocoa, FL 32922

Collier County Museum/Margaret T. Scott Library
3301 Tamiami Trail, East
Naples, FL 34112
Tel: 941-774-8476
Fax: 941-774-8580

Collier County Public Library
650 Central Avenue
Naples, FL 33940-6027
Tel: 941-261-8208

Cooper Memorial Library
620 Montrose Street
Clermont, FL 34711
Tel: 904-394-4265

Cornell Museum
Delray Beach Historical Society Archives
51 N. Swinton Avenue
Delray Beach, FL 33444
Tel: 407-243-7922

DeLand Public Library
130 E. Howry Avenue
DeLand, FL 32724-5517
Tel: 904-734-2424
904-822-6430

Florida Division of Historical Resources
500 S. Bronough Street
Tallassee, FL 32399
Tel: 904-488-1480
URL: http://www.dos.state.fl.us/dhr/

Florida State University Library
Special Collections
Tallahassee, FL 32306-2047
Tel: 904-644-3271
URL: http://www.fsu.edu/~speccoll/index.html

Fort Myers-Lee County Public Library
2050 Lee Street
Fort Myers, FL 33901
Tel: 941-338-3150

Gainesville Public Library
222 East University Avenue
Gainesville, FL 32601

Genealogical Society of Broward County Library
c/o Helen B. Hoffman Library
501 N. Fig Tree Lane
Plantation, FL 33317

Halifax Historical Society/Museum
252 S. Beach St.
Daytona Beach, FL 32114-4407
Tel: 904-255-6976

Haydon Burns Library
122 N. Ocean Street
Jacksonville, FL 32203

Hillsborough County Historical Commission
Museum, Historical & Genealogical Library
County Courthouse, Room 250
Tampa, FL 33602
Tel: 813-272-5919

Historical Museum of South Florida
101 West Flagler Street
Miami, FL 33130
Tel: 305-375-1492
Email: hasf@ix.netcom.com
URL: http://www.historical-museum.org/index.htm

Holocaust Memorial & Resource Center of Central Florida
851 N. Maitland Avenue
Maitland, FL 32751

Homestead Branch Library
700 N. Homestead Blvd.
Homestead, FL 33030
Tel: 305-246-0168
URL: http://cga.mdpls.lib.fl.us/branches/homestea.htm

Indian River County Main Library
Florida History & Genealogy Dept.
1600 21st Street
Vero Beach, FL 32960
Tel: 561-770-5060
Fax: 561-770-5066

Jackson County Florida Library
413 North Green Street
Maryanna, FL 32446

Jacksonville Public Library
122 North Ocean Street
Jacksonville, FL 32202-3314
Tel: 904-630-2409
http://jpl.itd.ci.jax.fl.us/

Largo Library
351 East Bay Drive
Largo, FL 33770
Tel: 813-586-7410
Email: bpotters@largo.com
URL: http://www.largo.com/library.html

Loxahatchee Historical Society/Museum
805 N. U.S. Highway 1
Jupiter Beach, FL 33477
Tel: 407-747-6639

Maitland Historical Museum
221 Packwood Avenue
P.O. Box 941001
Maitland, FL 32794
Tel: 407-644-2451
URL: http://sundial.net/~bayston/Maitland/histsoc.html

Manatee County Central Library
1301 Barcarrota Blvd., W
Bradenton, FL 34205-7599
Tel: 941-748-5555
Fax: 941-749-7191

Melbourne Public Library
540 East Fee Avenue
Melbourne, FL 32901
Tel: 407-952-4514
URL: http://www.brev.lib.fl.us/library/locations/mla.htm

Metro-Dade Cultural Resource Center
111 NW 1st Street
Miami, FL 33128-1902
Tel: 305-375-4635

Miami-Dade Public Library
Main Library
101 West Flagler St.
Miami, FL 33130
Tel: 305-375-2665
URL: http://cga.mdpls.lib.fl.us/branches/main.htm

Micanopy Historical Society/Museum
706 NE Cholokka Blvd.
P.O. Box 462
Micanopy, FL 32667
Email: micanopy@afn.org
URL: http://www.afn.org/~micanopy

Mission San Luis de Apalachee
Division of Historical Resources
2020 Mission Road
Tallahassee, FL 32304-1624
Tel: 904-487-3655
URL: http://www.dos.state.fl.us/dhr/bar/san_luis/index.html

Morikami Museum and Japanese Gardens
4000 Morikami Park Rd.
Delray Beach, FL 33446
Tel: 407-495-0233

Museum of Florida History
Division of Historical Resources
500 S. Bronough Street
Tallahassee, FL 32399
Tel: 904-488-1484
URL: http://www.dos.state.fl.us/dhr/museum/c_r.html

North Brevard Historical Society
801 S. Washington Avenue
P.O. Box 6199
Titusville, FL 32782-6199
Tel: 407-269-3658

North Brevard Public Library
2121 Hopkins Avenue
Titusville, FL 32780
Tel: 407-264-5026
Fax: 407-264-5030
URL: http://www.brev.lib.fl.us/library/locations/nba.htm

North Indian River County Library
1001 Country Road 512
Sebastian, FL 32958
Tel: 561-589-1355

Orange County Historical Society/Museum
812 E. Rollins Street
Orlando, FL 32803
Tel: 407-897-6350
Fax: 407-897-6409
URL: http://www.inusa.com/tour/fl/orlando/orange.htm

Orlando Public Library
101 East Central Blvd.
Orlando, FL 32801
Tel: 407-425-4694
URL: http://www.ocls.lib.fl.us/ge.htm

Ormond Beach Public Library
30 S. Beach Street
Ormond Beach, FL 32174-6380
Tel: 904-673-0163

Palm Beach County Historical Society
105 S. Narcissus Avenue
West Palm Beach, FL 33401
Tel: 407-832-4164

Palm Harbor Library
2330 Nebraska Avenue
Palm Harbor, FL 34683
Tel: 813-784-3332
Fax: 813-785-6534
813-787-8388 (reference fax)
URL: http://snoopy.tblc.lib.fl.us/phlib/

Pensacola Historical Society/Museum
117 East Government Street
Pensacola, FL 32501
Tel: 904-433-1559

Polk County Historical & Genealogical Library
Old Courthouse Building
100 East Main Street
Bartow, FL 33830

Safety Harbor Public Library
101 Second Street, N
Safety Harbor, FL 34695
Tel: 813-724-1525
Email: reed@scfn.thpl.lib.fl.us
URL: http://snoopy.tblc.lib.fl.us/shpl/homepg.htm

St. Augustine Historical Society/Research Library
271 Charlotte Street
St. Augustine, FL 32084-5033
Tel: 904-824-2872
Email: oldhouse@aug.com
URL: http://www.oldcity.com/oldhouse/historical.htm

St. Johns County Public Library
1960 Ponce de Leon Blvd.
St. Augustine, FL 32084-2620
Tel: 904-823-2650

St. Petersburg Public Library
3745 9th Avenue North
St. Petersburg, FL 33713
Tel: 813-893-7724
813-893-7928
URL: http://snoopy.tblc.lib.fl.us/sppl/SPPLS.html

Sanibel Public Library
770 Dunlop Road
Sanibel, FL 33957
Tel: 941-472-2483
Fax: 941-472-9524
URL: http://www.usa-chamber.com/spl/splhome.html

Selby Public Library
1001 Boulevard of the Arts
Sarasota, FL 34236-4807
Tel: 941-316-1181/3
941-951-5501/2

Southern Genealogists Exchange Society
1580 Blanding Blvd.
Jacksonville, Fl 32203

State Library of Florida
Florida Collection
Division of Library & Information Services
R.A. Gray Building
500 South Bronough Street
Tallahassee, FL 32399-0250
Tel: 904-487-2651
URL: http://stafla.dlis.state.fl.us/

Tampa Bay Historical Center
225 S. Franklin Street
P.O. Box 948
Tampa, FL 33601-0948
Tel: 813-228-0097
Fax: 813-223-7021
URL: http://www.wlwdesign.com/tbhcopen.html

Tampa Bay Library Consortium
10002 Princess Palm Avenue, Suite 124
Tampa, FL 33619
Tel: 813-622-8252
Fax: 813-628-4425
Email: helpdesk@snoopy.tblc.lib.fl.us
URL: http://snoopy.tblc.lib.fl.us/

Tampa-Hillsborough Public Library System
Main Library
Special Collections-Genealogy Collection
900 North Ashley Drive
Tampa, FL 33602
Tel: 813-273-3652
URL: http://scfn.thpl.lib.fl.us/thpl/main/spc/geneal.htm

University of Central Florida Library
P.O. Box 160000
Orlando, FL 32816
URL: http://pegasus.cc.ucf.edu/~library/special.htm

University of Florida
P.K. Yonge Library of Florida History
Room 404, Library West
Gainesville, FL 32611
URL: http://www.uflib.ufl.edu/

University of Miami
Otto G. Richter Library
Coral Gables, FL 33124
URL: http://www.ir.miami.edu/

University of South Florida Library, LIB 407
Special Collections Department
4202 East Fowler Avenue
Tampa, FL 33620
Tel: 813-974-2731
Fax: 813-974-5153
URL: http://www.lib.usf.edu/spccoll/genea.html

University of West Florida
John Chandler Pace Library
11000 University Parkway
Pensacola, FL 32514-5750
URL: http://www.uwf.edu/treasure/chapters/chaptr28.html

Volusia County Public Library
City Island
Daytona Beach, FL 32114
Tel: 904-255-3765

NEWSPAPER REPOSITORIES

Amelia Island Museum of History
223 South Third Street
Fernandina Beach, FL 32034
Tel: 904-261-7378
URL: http://www.ameliaisland.com/pix/mosiac/museum.htm

Palm Beach County Historical Society
105 S. Narcissus Avenue
West Palm Beach, FL 33401
Tel: 407-832-4164

St. Augustine Historical Society/Research Library
271 Charlotte Street
St. Augustine, FL 32084-5033
Tel: 904-824-2872
Email: oldhouse@aug.com
URL: http://www.oldcity.com/oldhouse/historical.htm

State Library of Florida
Florida Collection
Division of Library & Information Services
R.A. Gray Building
500 South Bronough Street
Tallahassee, FL 32399-0250
Tel: 904-487-2651
URL: http://stafla.dlis.state.fl.us/

University of Florida
P.K. Yonge Library of Florida History
Room 204, Library West
Gainesville, FL 32611-7001
Tel: 352-392-0342
Email: marhrus@nervm.nerdc.ufl.edu
URL: http://www.uflib.ufl.edu/flnews/

VITAL RECORDS

State of Florida Dept. of Health & Rehabilitative Services
Vital Statistics
1217 Pearl Street
P.O. Box 210
Jacksonville, FL 32231
Tel: 904-359-6900
904-359-6911

FLORIDA ON THE WEB

Dayna's Southern Genealogy Page
http://home.texoma.net/~mmcmullen/welcome.html

Florida GenWeb Project
http://www.mindspring.com/~mmundy/flindex.htm

Traveller Southern Families
http://genealogy.traveller.com/genealogy/

GEORGIA

ARCHIVES, STATE & NATIONAL

Georgia Department of Archives and History
Office of Secretary of State
330 Capitol Avenue, SE
Atlanta, GA 30334
Tel: 404-656-2358
Fax: 404-657-8427
Email: director@archives.sos.state.ga.us
URL: http://www.sos.state.ga.us/archives

National Archives—Southeast Region
1557 St. Joseph Avenue
East Point, GA 30344-2593
Tel: 404-763-7477
Fax: 404-763-7033
Email: archives@atlanta.nara.gov
URL: http://www.nara.gov/nara/regional/04nsgil.html

GENEALOGICAL SOCIETIES

African-American Family History Association
P.O. Box 115268
Atlanta, GA 30310

Ancestors Unlimited, Inc.
P.O. Box 1507
Jonesboro, GA 30336

Augusta Genealogical Society/Library
1109 Broad Street
P.O. Box 3743
Augusta, GA 30914-3743
Tel: 706-722-4073
URL: http://interoz.com/ags/index.htm

Bartow County Genealogical Society/Research Library
425 W. Main Street
P.O. Box 993
Cartersville, GA 30120-0993
Tel: 770-606-0706

Butts County Genealogical Society
P.O. Box 1297
Jackson, GA 30233
Email: VSHarrison@aol.com
URL: http://www.lofthouse.com/USA/ga/butts/#society

Carroll County Genealogical Society
P.O. Box 576
Carrollton, GA 30117
Tel: 770-832-7746
Email: mfword@aol.com
URL: http://members.aol.com/carrollgen/index.htm

Central Georgia Genealogical Society
P.O. Box 2024
Warner Robbins, GA 31099-2024

Clarke-Oconee Genealogical Society
P.O. Box 6403
Athens, GA 30604

Coastal Georgia Genealogical Society
201 Palmetto Court, W
St. Simons Island, GA 31522

Cobb County Georgia Genealogical Society
P.O. Box 1413
Marietta, GA 30061-1413

Colonial Dames of America in the State of Georgia
329 Abercorn Street
Savannah, GA 31401
Tel: 912-233-6854
Fax: 912-338-1828

Colonial Dames of XVII Century
Georgia Society
P.O. Box 249
Eastman, GA 31023-0249

Coweta County Genealogical Society
32 Clark Street
P.O. Box 1014
Newnan, GA 30264
Tel: 770-251-2877

Daughters of the American Revolution
Georgia State Society
600 Woodhaven Road
Eastman, GA 31023-2600

Dawson County Historical and Genealogical Society
P.O. Box 1074
Dawsonville, GA 30534

DeKalb County, Genealogy Study Group of
c/o Life Enrichment Center
1340 McConnell Drive
Decatur, GA 30033

Delta Genealogical Society
504 McFarland Avenue
Rossville, GA 30741
Tel: 706-866-1368
Fax: 706-858-0251
Email: rossvill@voyageronline.com

Etowah Valley Family Tree Climbers
c/o Gold Dome Courthouse
West Cherokee Avenue
P.O. Box 1886
Cartersville, GA 30120
Tel: 770-606-8862
Email: Lulu23285@aol.com

First Families of Georgia, 1733-1797
15 Watson Drive
Newnan, GA 30263

Genealogy Unlimited Society
2511 Churchill Drive
Valdosta, GA 31602-2547
Tel: 912-244-0464

Georgia Genealogical Society
P.O. Box 54575
Atlanta, GA 30308-0575
Tel: 404-475-4404
Email: Georgiagen@gnn.com
URL: http://members.gnn.com/georgiagen/index.htm

Georgia Salzburger Society
2980 Ebenezer Road
Rincon, GA 31326
Tel: 912-754-7001
URL: http://www.msstate.edu/Archives/History/salzb/index.html

Henry and Clayton Counties, Genealogical Society of
P.O. Box 1296
McDonough, GA 30253

Henry County Georgia Genealogical Society
71 Macon Street
P.O. Box 1296
McDonough, GA 30253

Huguenot Society of Virginia
Founders of Manakin
Georgia Branch
206 Bolling Road, NE
Atlanta, GA 30305-3107
Tel/Fax: 404-233-1920

Huxford Genealogical Society
P.O. Box 595
Homerville, GA 31634
Tel: 912-487-2310
Email: clineberger@mail.datasys.net
URL: http://www.datasys.net/users/stu/clineberger/homepage.htm

Jamestowne Society
First Georgia Company
494 Hickory Hills Trail
Stone Mountain, GA 30083-4372
Tel: 770-469-5224
URL: http://www.jamestowne.org/company/gal.htm

Mayflower Descendants
Georgia Society
2423 Lively Trail, NE
Atlanta, GA 30345-3836
Tel: 404-877-1741

Muscogee Genealogical Society
P.O. Box 761
Columbus, GA 31902
Tel/Fax: 706-561-5831

Northeast Georgia Historical and Genealogical Society
5845 Norton Circle
Flowery Branch, GA 30542
Mail:
P.O. Box 907643 NLS
Gainesville, GA 30501
Tel: 770-967-3808

Northwest Georgia Historical and Genealogical Society
P.O. Box 5063
Rome, GA 30162
Tel: 706-236-4607
Fax: 706-236-4605
Email: kinzerj@mail.floyd.public.lib.ga.us

Original Muscogee County, Genealogical Society of
W.C. Bradley Memorial Library
120 Bradley Drive
Columbus, GA 31906

Piedmont Regional Genealogy Society
Athens Street
P.O. Box 65
Auburn, GA 30203
Tel: 770-963-5877
Email: krainey@interramp.com

Quitman-Brooks County Genealogical Society
121 N. Culpepper Street
Quitman, GA 31643

Rockdale County Genealogical Society
c/o Nancy Guinn Memorial Library
864 Green Street
Conyers, GA 30207
Tel: 770-388-5040
Fax: 770-388-5043
URL for newsletter:
http://www.atl.mindspring.com/~bevr/html/newsletters.html

Savannah Area Genealogical Association
P.O. Box 15385
Savannah, GA 31416

Savannah River Valley Genealogical Society
c/o Hart County Library
150 Benson Street
Hartwell, GA 30643

Smyrna Historical and Genealogical Society
2865 King Street
Smyrna, GA 30080
Tel: 770-435-7549
Fax: 770-431-2858

Sons of the American Revolution
116 Ridley Circle
Decatur, GA 30030-1117
Tel: 404-378-9590
Email: TC7@prism.gatech.edu
URL: http://lynx.avana.net/douglass/gassar/index.html

Sons of Confederate Veterans
Georgia Division
P.O. Box 763
Kennesaw, GA 30144
Tel: 770-436-9600
Fax: 770-436-0607

South Georgia Genealogical Society
P.O. Box 246
Ochlocknee, GA 31773

Southwest Georgia Genealogical Society
P.O. Box 4672
Albany, GA 31706

Taylor County Historical-Genealogical Society
P.O. Box 1925
Butler, GA 31006
Tel: 912-862-3410
Email: nodlu2@aol.com

United Daughters of the Confederacy
Georgia Division
1604 Executive Park Lane, NE
Atlanta, GA 30329-3115
Tel/Fax: 404-634-9866

U.S. Daughters of 1812
Georgia State Society
P.O. Box 160
Kingston, GA 30145-0160

Warren County Genealogical Society
103 Memorial Drive
P.O. Box 47
Warrenton, GA 30828

West Central Georgia Genealogical Society
P.O. Box 2291
LaGrange, GA 30241

Historical Societies

Alma-Bacon County Historical Society
201 N. Pierce Street
P.O. Box 2026
Alma, GA 31510
Tel: 912-632-8450
Fax: 912-632-4512

Alpharetta Historical Society
P.O. Box 1386
Alpharetta, GA 30239
Tel: 770-475-4663
Fax: 770-475-0091

Athens Historical Society
P.O. Box 7745
Athens, GA 30604-7745

Atlanta Historical Society
3099 Andrews Drive
P.O. Box 12423
Atlanta, GA 30355

Banks County Historical Society
P.O. Box 473
Homer, GA 30547
Tel: 706-335-3786

Barnesville-Lamar County Historical Society
P.O. Box 805
Barnesville, GA 30204
Tel: 770-358-7905
770-358-0150 (museum)

Barrow County Historical Society
Athens Street
P.O. Box 277
Winder, GA 30680
Tel: 770-307-1183

Bonaventure Historical Society
1317 East 55th Street
Savannah, GA 31404-4615

Brantley County Historical & Preservation Society
P.O. Box 1096
Nahunta, GA 31553

Brooks County Historical Society
P.O. Box 676
Quitman, GA 31643

Bulloch County Historical Society
P.O. Box 42
Statesboro, GA 30459
Tel: 912-681-1956

Butts County Historical Society
Highway 42, Indian Spring
P.O. Box 215
Jackson, GA 30233
Tel: 770-775-6734

Byron Area Historical Society
P.O. Box 755
Byron, GA 31008
Tel: 912-956-3600
Fax: 912-956-5299
URL: http://www.hom.net/Byron/

Candler County Historical Society
P.O. Box 325
Metter, GA 30439

Carroll County Historical Society
West Avenue
P.O. Box 1308
Carrollton, GA 30117
Tel: 770-836-6494
Fax: 770-836-6626
Email: ruskell@westga.edu
URL: http://www.westga.edu/cgi-bin/libhome.cgi

Catoosa County Historical Society
P.O. Box 113
Ringgold, GA 30736

Cave Spring Historical Society
13 Cedartown Road
P.O. Box 715
Cave Spring, GA 30124
Tel: 706-777-8865

Charlton County Historical Society
P.O. Box 575
Folkston, GA 31537-0575

Chattahoochee Valley Historical Society
1213 Fifth Avenue
West Point, GA 31833

Chattooga County Historical Society
119 E. Washington Street
Summerville, GA 30747
Tel: 404-651-2707
Tel: 404-651-2804

Cherokee County Historical Society
P.O. Box 1287
Canton, GA 30114
Tel: 770-345-6663
Fax: 770-345-6743
URL: http://www.tib.com/cchm/cchmpict.htm

Coastal Georgia Historical Society
101 12th Street
P.O. Box 21136
St. Simons Island, GA 31522-0636
Tel: 912-638-4666
Fax: 912-638-6609

Cobb Landmarks and Historical Society
145 Denmeade Street
Marietta, GA 30060
Tel: 770-426-4982

College Park Historical Society
P.O. Box F
College Park, GA 30337
Tel: 404-767-6202

Colquitt County Historical Society
214 16th Avenue, SE
Moultrie, GA 31778
Tel: 912-985-3413

Columbia County Historical Society
P.O. Box 203
Appling, GA 30802

Cook County Historical Society
P.O. Box 497
Adel, GA 31647

Crawford County Historical Society
Crawford County Business Development Center
Roberta, GA 31078
Tel: 912-836-3158
Fax: 912-836-2355

Dawson County Historical and Genealogical Society
P.O. Box 1074
Dawsonville, GA 30534

Decatur County Historical Society
P.O. Box 682
Bainbridge, GA 31717

DeKalb Historical Society
Old Courthouse on the Square
101 East Court Square
Decatur, GA 30030
Tel: 404-373-1088
Fax: 404-378-8287
URL: http://atlantagames.com/atl/attdekl.htm

Douglas County Historical Society
8562 Campbellton Street
P.O. Box 2018
Douglasville, GA 30133

Early County Historical Society
P.O. Box 564
Blakely, GA 31723

East Point Historical Society
1685 Norman Berry Drive
P.O. Box 90675
East Point, GA 30364-0675

Eatonton-Putnam County Historical Society
104 Church Street
Eatonton, GA 31024
Tel: 706-485-6442

Elbert County Historical Society
One Deadwyler Street
P.O. Box 1033
Elberton, GA 30635

Eleventh Circuit Historical Society
P.O. Box 1556
Atlanta, GA 30301

Etowah Valley Historical Society
P.O. Box 1886
Cartersville, GA 30120
Tel: 770-606-8862

Fayette County Historical Society
195 Lee Street
P.O. Box 421
Fayetteville, GA 30214
Tel: 770-461-7152

Forsyth County Heritage Foundation
P.O. Box 3121
Cumming, GA 30128

Fort Gaines Historical Society
P.O. Box 6
Fort Gaines, GA 31751

Foxfire Fund/Museum
P.O. Box 541
Mountain City, GA 30562
Tel: 706-746-5828
Fax: 706-746-5829

Franklin County Historical Society
310 McFarlin Bridge Road
Carnesville, GA 30521

Georgia Historical Society
Hodgson Hall Archives and Library
501 Whittaker Street
Savannah, GA 31499
Tel: 912-651-2125
912-651-2128
Fax: 912-651-2831
Email: gahist@ix.netcom.com
URL: http://www.savga.com/ghs/
http://savga.com/orgs/ghs/ghshp.htm

Gordon County Historical Society
P.O. Box 342
Calhoun, GA 30701
Tel: 706-629-1515
Fax: 706-629-4510

Grady County Historical Society
P.O. Box 586
Cairo, GA 31728

Greene County Historical Society
201 Green Street
P.O. Box 238
Greensboro, GA 30642
Tel: 706-453-2588
Fax: 706-453-4970

Griffin-Spalding Historical Society
P.O. Box 196
Griffin, GA 30224
Tel: 770-229-2432
Fax: 770-227-5586

Guale Historical Society
P.O. Box 398
St. Marys, GA 31558

Guyton Historical Society
205 Lynn Bonds Avenue
P.O. Box 99
Guyton, GA 31312
Tel: 912-772-3353
Fax: 912-772-3152

Gwinnett Historical Society
P.O. Box 261
Lawrenceville, GA 30245
Tel: 770-822-5174
URL: http://www.adsd.com/ghs/

Habersham County Historical Society
P.O. Box 1552
Clarkesville, GA 30523

Hahira Historical Society
202 E. Lawson Street
Hahira, GA 31632
Tel: 912-794-2274

Hall County Historical Society
892 Chattahoochee Drive, NW
Gainesville, GA 30506
Tel: 770-532-2242
Fax: 770-536-7072

Hapeville Historical Society
P.O. Box 82055
Hapeville, GA 30354

Haralson County Historical Society
Old Haralson County Courthouse
P.O. Box 585
Buchanan, GA 30113

Hart County Historical Society
31 East Howell Street
P.O. Box 96
Hartwell, GA 30643
Tel: 706-376-6330
Fax: 706-376-1456

Heard County Historical Society
161 Shady Street
P.O. Box 990
Franklin, GA 30217
Tel: 706-675-6507

Historic Oglethorpe County, Inc.
P.O. Box 1793
Lexington, GA 30648

Historical Effingham Society
Pine and Early Streets
P.O. Box 665
Springfield, GA 31329
Tel: 912-826-4976

Jackson County Historical Society
c/o Crawford W. Long Museum
28 College Street
Jefferson, GA 30549
Tel: 706-367-5307

Jefferson County Historical Society
P.O. Box 491
Louisville, GA 30434-0491

Jenkins County Historical Society
Chamber of Commerce
548 Cotton Street
Millen, GA 30442
Tel: 912-982-5595
Fax: 912-982-5112

Johnson County Historical Society
Route 1, Box 795
Wrightsville, GA 31096

Kennesaw Historical Society
2829 Cherokee Street
Kennesaw, GA 30144
Tel: 770-975-0887

Laurens County Historical Society
Dublin-Laurens Museum
Academy and Bellevue Streets
P.O. Box 1461
Dublin, GA 31040
Tel: 912-272-9242

Lee County Historical Society
245 Walnut Street
P.O. Box 49
Leesburg, GA 31763-0049
Tel: 912-759-9090

Liberty County Historical Society
P.O. Box 982
Hinesville, GA 31310

Lincoln County Historical Society
147 Lumber Street
P.O. Box 869
Lincolnton, GA 30817
Tel: 706-359-1031

Louisville Historical Society
P.O. Box 491
Louisville, GA 30434-0491

Lower Altamaha Historical Society
P.O. Box 1405
Darien, GA 31305
Tel: 912-485-2251
Fax: 912-485-2141
Email: bsullivan@ocean.nos.noa.gov

Lowndes County Historical Society/Museum
305 W. Central Avenue
P.O. Box 434
Valdosta, GA 31603
Tel: 912-247-4780
Fax: 912-247-2840

Lumpkin County Historical Society
P.O. Box 894
Dahlonega, GA 30533
Tel: 706-864-3668
URL: http://www.ngeorgia.com/cgi-bin/county/Lumpkin/

Macon County Historical Society
North Dooly Street
P.O. Box 571
Montezuma, GA 31063

Madison County Heritage Association
P.O. Box 74
Danielsville, GA 30633
Tel: 706-795-2017

Marble Valley Historical Society
Main Street
P.O. Box 815
Jasper, GA 30143
Tel: 706-692-6327

McDuffie County Historical Society
633 Hemlock Drive
P.O. Box 1816
Thomson, GA 30824
Tel: 706-595-5584
Fax: 706-595-4710

Meriwether Historical Society
P.O. Box 741
Greenville, GA 30222

Middle Georgia Historical Society
935 High Street
P.O. Box 13358
Macon, GA 31208-3358
Tel: 912-743-3851

Monroe County Historical Society
East Johnston Street
P.O. Box 401

Forsyth, GA 31029
Tel: 912-994-5070

Moreland Community Historical Society
P.O. Box 128
Moreland, GA 30259

Morgan Cunty Historical Society
277 South Madison Street
Madison, GA 30650
Tel: 706-342-9627

National Society of Andersonville
P.O. Box 65
Andersonville, GA 31711

Newnan-Coweta Historical Society
Male Academy Museum
30 Temple Avenue
P.O. Box 1001
Newnan, GA 30264
Tel/Fax: 770-251-0207
URL: http://www.newnan.com/nchs/index.html

Newton County Historical Society
Chamber of Commerce Building
2100 Washington Street
P.O. Box 2415
Covington, GA 30210
Tel: 770-786-7310
Fax: 770-786-1294

North Georgia Methodist Historical Society
1015 Ruckersville Road
Elberton, GA 30635
Tel: 706-283-8426
Email: RevAnn@juno.com

Northeast Georgia Historical and Genealogical Society
5845 Norton Circle
Flowery Branch, GA 30542
Mail:
P.O. Box 907643 NLS
Gainesville, GA 30501
Tel: 770-967-3808

Northwest Georgia Historical and Genealogical Society
P.O. Box 5063
Rome, GA 30162
Tel: 706-236-4607
Fax: 706-236-4605
Email: kinzerj@mail.floyd.public.lib.ga.us

Old Campbell County Historical Society
P.O. Box 342
Fairburn, GA 30213-0342
Tel: 770-997-3385
Fax: 770-996-6796

Old Capitol History Society
P.O. Box 4
Milledgeville, GA 31061
Tel: 912-453-9049
912-452-4637

Old Clinton Historical Society
RFD 5-Clinton-Box 143
Gray, GA 31032

Paulding County Historical Society
P.O. Box 333
Dallas, GA 30132

Perry Area Historical Society
P.O. Drawer D
Perry, GA 31069

Pioneer Historical Society
c/o Ruby White
Highway 280
McRae, GA 31055

Polk County Historical Society
205 N. College Avenue
P.O. Box 203
Cedartown, GA 30125
Tel: 770-749-0073

Rabun County Historical Society
P.O. Box 921
Clayton, GA 30525

Randolph Historical Society
Route 1, Box 1005
Shellman, GA 31786
Mail:
P.O. Box 456
Cuthbert, GA 31740
Tel: 912-679-5165

Richmond County Historical Society
c/o Reese Library, Augusta College
2500 Walton Way
Augusta, GA 30904-2200
Tel: 706-737-1532
Fax: 706-667-4415

Rockdale County Historical Society
967 Milstead Avenue
P.O. Box 351
Conyers, GA 30207
Tel: 770-483-4398

Rome Area History Museum
303-305 Broad Street
Rome, GA 30161
Tel: 706-235-8051

Roswell Historical Society
P.O. Box 1636
Roswell, GA 30077
URL: http://www.ethom.com/roswell/histmone.htm

Schley County Historical Society
P.O. Box 326
Ellaville, GA 31806

Seminole County Historical Society
P.O. Box 713
Donalsonville, GA 31759

Senoia Area Historical Society
P.O. Box 301
Senoia, GA 30276

Seven Springs Historical Society
3901 Brownsville Road
P.O. Box 4
Powder Springs, GA 30073
Tel: 770-943-7949

Smyrna Historical and Genealogical Society
2865 King Street
Smyrna, GA 30080
Tel: 770-435-7549
Fax: 770-431-2858

Society of Georgia Archivists
P.O. Box 80631
Athens, GA 30608
URL: http://peacock.gac.peachnet.edu/~sga/

Southeastern Cherokee Confederacy
P.O. Box 367
Ochlockee, GA 31733
Tel: 912-547-5497
Fax: 912-365-6017

Sparta-Hancock County Historical Society
353 E. Broad Street
Sparta, GA 31087
Tel: 706-444-6411

Stephens County Historical Society
313 S. Pond Street
P.O. Box 125
Toccoa, GA 30577
Tel: 706-282-5055

Suwanee Historical Association
P.O. Box 815
Suwanee, GA 30174

Taliaferro County Historical Society
P.O. Box 32
Crawfordville, GA 30631

Taylor County Historical-Genealogical Society
P.O. Box 1925
Butler, GA 31006
Tel: 912-862-3410
Email: nodlu2@aol.com

Terrell County Restoration Society
P.O. Box 63
Dawson, GA 31742
Tel: 912-995-2125
Fax: 912-995-4000
Email: eduskin@surfsouth.com

Thomas County Historical Society
725 N. Dawson Street
P.O. Box 1922
Thomasville, GA 31799
Tel: 912-226-7664

Toombs County Historical Society
P.O. Box 2825
Vidalia, GA 30474
Tel: 912-537-4383

Towns County Historical and Genealogical Society
P.O. Box 101
Young Harris, GA 30582-0101
Tel: 706-379-3150
Email: jerrytaylor@juno.com

Treutlen County Historical Society
Treutlen County Courthouse
Soperton, GA 30457
Tel: 912-529-6711
Fax: 912-529-6062

Troup County Historical Society and Archives
136 Main Street
P.O. Box 1051
LaGrange, GA 30241
Tel: 706-884-1828
Fax: 706-884-1838
Email: kaye@mentor.lgc.peachnet.edu
URL: http://www.lgc.peachnet.edu/archives/tcarchiv.htm

Turner County Historical Society
233 East College Avenue
P.O. Box 766
Ashburn, GA 31714
Tel: 912-567-3431
Fax: 912-567-9284

Tybee Island Historical Society
30 Meddin Drive, Fort Screven
Tybee Island, Ga 31328
Tel: 912-786-5801
Fax: 912-786-6538
URL: http://zuma.lib.utk.edu/lights/tybee.html

Union County Historical Society
Courthouse Square
P.O. Box 35
Blairsville, GA 30514-0035
Tel: 706-745-5493
URL: http://www.ngeorgia.com/uchs.html

Upson Historical Society
P.O. Box 363
Thomaston, GA 30286
Tel: 706-647-6839
Fax: 706-646-3524

Walker County Historical Society
P.O. Box 707
LaFayette, GA 30728

Washington County Historical Society
129 Jones Street
P.O. Box 6088
Sandersville, GA 31082
Tel: 912-552-6965
Fax: 912-552-1449

Wayne County Historical Society
125 NE Broad Street
Jesup, GA 31545-5516
Tel: 912-427-3233

White County Historical Society
Courthouse Square
P.O. Box 1139
Cleveland, GA 30528
Tel: 706-865-3225
URL: http://georgiamagazine.com/chamber/white_ch.htm

Whitfield-Murray Historical Society
Crown Garden and Archives
715 Chattanooga Avenue
Dalton, GA 30720
Tel: 706-278-0217

Worth County Historical Society
P.O. Box 5040
Sylvester, GA 31791

LDS Family History Centers

Albany Family History Center
2700 Westgate Blvd.
Albany, GA 31707
Tel: 912-436-8637

Brunswick Family History Center
2911 Community Road
Brunswick, GA 31520
Tel: 912-265-5912

Columbus Family History Center
4400 Reese Road
Columbus, GA 31907
Tel: 706-563-7216

Douglas Family History Center
200 Chester Avenue
Douglas, GA 31533
Tel: 912-384-0607

Evans Family History Center
835 North Belair Road
Evans, GA 30809
Tel: 706-860-1024

Gainesville Family History Center
1234 Riverside Drive
Gainesville, GA 30501
Tel: 770-536-4391

Jonesboro Family History Center
2100 Jodeco Road
Jonesboro, GA 30236
Tel: 770-477-5985

Macon Family History Center
1624 Williamson Road
Macon, GA 31206
Tel: 912-788-5885

Marietta Family History Center
3195 Trickum Road
Marietta, GA 30066
Tel: 770-578-8758

Powder Springs Family History Center
2595 New Macland Road
Powder Springs, GA 30073
Tel: 404-943-1983

Rome Family History Center
3300 Garden Lakes
Rome, GA 30165
Tel: 706-235-2281

Roswell Family History Center
500 Norcross Street
Roswell, GA 30077
Tel: 770-594-1706
URL: http://www.mindspring.com/~noahsark/lds-fhc.html

Savannah Family History Center
1234 King George Blvd.
Savannah, GA 31419
Tel: 912-927-6543

Suwanee Family History Center
4833 Suwanee Dam Road
Suwanee, GA 30174
Tel: 770-271-3450

Tucker Family History Center
1947 Brockett Road
Tucker, GA 30084
Tel: 770-723-9941

ARCHIVES/LIBRARIES/MUSEUMS

Andersonville National Historic Site
Route 1, Box 800
Andersonville, GA 31711
Tel: 912-924-0343
Fax: 912-928-9640
URL: http://www.nps.gov/ande/

Andrew College Archives
Pitts Library
413 College Street
Cuthbert, GA 31740
Tel: 912-732-2171
Fax: 912-732-2176
Email: karan.berryman@bbs.serve.org

Appling County Heritage Center
Thomas & Harvey Streets
P.O. Box 87
Baxley, GA 31513
Tel: 912-367-7791
Fax: 912-367-8104

Athens Regional Library
Heritage Room
2025 Baxter Street
Athens, GA 30606
Tel: 706-613-3650
Fax: 706-613-3660
Email: kames@mail.clarke.public.lib.ga.us

Atlanta-Fulton Public Library
Georgia History & Genealogy Department
1 Margaret Mitchell Square
Atlanta, GA 30303-1089
Tel: 404-730-1940
Fax: 404-730-1989

Atlanta History Center
130 West Paces Ferry Road, NW
Atlanta, GA 30305-1366
Tel: 404-814-4000
Fax: 404-814-4186
URL: http://www.atlhist.org/html/ahslibr.htm

Atlanta University Center
Robert W. Woodruff Library
Emory University
Atlanta, GA 30322-2870
URL: http://galaxy.cau.edu/CAU/library

Auburn Avenue Research Library
101 Auburn Avenue, NE
Atlanta, GA 30303
Tel: 404-659-4008
Email: jhunter@cel.af.public.lib.ga.us
URL: http://atlantagames.com/atl/aublibr.htm

Augusta Genealogical Society/Library
1109 Broad Street
P.O. Box 3743
Augusta, GA 30914-3743
Tel: 706-722-4073
URL: http://interoz.com/ags/index.htm

Augusta-Richmond County Public Library
East Central Georgia Regional Library
902 Greene Street
Augusta, GA 30901-2294
Tel: 706-821-2600
Fax: 706-724-6762
Email: leachr@mail.richmond.public.lib.ga.us
URL: http://204.71.8.24:80/publib/

Augusta State University
Reese Library
Special Collections
2500 Walton Way
Augusta, GA 30904-2200
Tel: 706-737-1745

Austell City Museum
2716 Broad Street
Austell, GA 30001
Tel: 770-944-4309

Barnesville-Lamar County Historical Society
P.O. Box 805
Barnesville, GA 30204
Tel: 770-358-7905
770-358-0150 (museum)

Bartow County Genealogical Society/Research Library
425 W. Main Street
Cartersville, GA 30120
Tel: 770-606-0706

Bartow County Public Library
429 W. Main Street
Cartersville, GA 30120
Tel: 770-382-4203
Fax: 770-386-3056
URL: http://www.innerx.net/non-profit/lib

Bartram Trail Regional Library
204 E. Liberty Street
Washington, GA 30673
Tel: 706-678-7736
Fax: 706-678-1474
Email: stoverc@mail.wilkes.public.lib.ga.us

Bradley Memorial Library
Chattahoochee Valley Regional Library
120 Bradley Drive

Columbus, GA 31906-2800
Tel: 706-649-0780
Fax: 706-649-1914
Email: holdenm@mail.muscogee.public.lib.ga.us

Brooks County Public Library
404 Tallokas Road
Quitman, GA 31643
Tel: 912-263-4412
Fax: 912-263-8002

Brunswick Regional Library
208 Gloucester Street
Brunswick, GA 31521

Bryan Lang Historical Library
P.O. Box 725
Woodbine, GA 31569
Tel: 912-576-5601

Carter-Coile Country Doctors Museum
111 Marigold Lane
P.O. Box 306
Winterville, GA 30683
Tel: 706-742-8600
Fax: 706-742-5476

Catholic Archdiocese of Atlanta Archives
680 Peachtree Street, NW
Atlanta, GA 30308-1984
Tel: 404-888-7802
Fax: 404-885-7494
URL: http://www.archatl.com/archives.htm

Catholic Diocese of Savannah Archives
601 E. Liberty Street
Savannah, GA 31401-5196
Tel: 912-238-2320
Fax: 912-238-2335
URL: http://www.interpath.net/~mdoyle/svhhom.html

Chatham-Effingham-Liberty Regional Library
2002 Bull Street
Savannah, GA 31499-4301
Tel: 912-652-3600
Fax: 912-652-3638
Email: lond@cel.co.chatham.ga.us
URL: http://www.co.chatham.ga.us/

Chattahoochee Valley State Community College
Learning Resource Center
2602 College Drive
Phenix City, AL 36869

Chattooga County Library System
201 Ferrar Drive
Summerville, GA 30747-2016
Tel: 706-857-2553
Fax: 706-857-7841
Email: sstewart@mail.chattooga.public.lib.ga.us

Cherokee Regional Library
Lafayette-Walker County Library
Georgia History & Genealogy Room
305 S. Duke Street
P.O. Box 707
LaFayette, GA 30728
Tel: 706-638-2992
Fax: 706-638-4028
Email: brian@www.walker.public.lib.ga.us
URL: http://www.walker.public.lib.ga.us

Chestatee Regional Library
127 Main Street
Gainesville, GA 30505-2399
Tel: 770-532-3311
Fax: 770-532-4305
Email: dbronson@crls.hall.public.lib.ga.us
URL: http://www.hall.public.lib.ga.us/

Chieftains Museum
800 Riverside Parkway
P.O. Box 373
Rome, GA 30162
Tel/Fax: 706-291-9494
URL: http://www.romegeorgia.com/chiefmus.html

Chipley Historical Center of Pine Mountain
P.O. Box 1055
Pine Mountain, GA 31822
Tel: 770-663-4044

Clayton County Library System
Genealogy & Local History Room
865 Battlecreek Road
Jonesboro, Ga 30236
Tel: 770-473-3850
Fax: 770-473-3858
Email: stewartc@mail.clayton.public.lib.ga.us

Coastal Plain Regional Library
214 Chestnut Street
P.O. Box 7606
Tifton, GA 31793-7606
Tel: 912-386-3400
Fax: 912-386-7007
Email: frizellg@mail.tift.public.lib.ga.us

Cobb County Public Library
The Georgia Room
266 Roswell Street
Marietta, GA 30060-2004
Tel: 770-528-2333
Fax: 770-528-2367

Cobb Memorial Archives
3419 Twentieth Avenue
Valley, AL 36854
Tel: 334-768-2161
Fax: 334-768-7272

Columbia Theological Seminary
John Bulow Campbell Library
701 Columbia Drive
Decatur, GA 30030
Tel: 404-687-4549
Fax: 404-377-9696

Commerce Public Library
Heritage Room
1344 S. Broad Street
Commerce, GA 30529
Tel: 706-335-5946

Confederate P.O.W. Museum
115 Church Street
P.O. Box 6
Andersonville, GA 31711
Tel: 912-924-2558

Confederate Research Center
P.O. Box 619
Hillsboro, TX 76645

Cordele-Crisp Carnegie Library
115 East 11th Avenue
Cordele, GA 31015
Tel: 912-276-2644

Crawford W. Long Museum
Jackson County Historical Society
28 College Street
Jefferson, GA 30549
Tel: 706-367-5307
URL: http://www.amdatel.com/cyberplaza/dcrwford

Crescent Farm Historical Center
Cherokee County Historical Society
P.O. Box 1287
Canton, GA 30114

Crown Garden and Archives
Whitfield-Murray Historical Society
715 Chattanooga Avenue
Dalton, GA 30720
Tel: 706-278-0217

Dahlonega Courthouse Gold Museum
Public Square
P.O. Box 2042
Dahlonega, GA 30533
Tel: 706-864-2257
URL: http://georgiamagazine.com/tosee/goldmus.htm

DeKalb County Public Library System
Decatur Library
215 Sycamore Street
Decatur, GA 30030
Tel: 404-370-3070
Fax: 404-370-8469
Email: willeyd@mail.dekalb.public.lib.ga.us
URL: http://www.dekalb.public.lib.ga.us

DeSoto Trail Regional Library
145 E. Broad Street
Camilla, GA 31730
Tel: 912-336-8372
Fax: 912-336-9353
Email: 73512.2711@compuserve.com

Dougherty County Public Library
Genealogy Room
300 Pine Avenue
Albany, GA 31701
Tel: 912-431-2900
Fax: 912-431-2915
Email: duganm@mail.dougherty.public.lib.ga.us

Dublin-Laurens Museum
Laurens County Historical Society
Academy and Bellevue Streets
P.O. Box 1461
Dublin, GA 31040
Tel: 912-272-9242

Elbert County Public Library
345 Heard Street
Elberton, GA 30635
Tel: 706-283-5375
Fax: 706-283-5456
Email: suddethp@mail.elbert.public.lib.ga.us

Ellen Payne Odom Genealogy Library
Moultrie-Colquitt County Library
204 Fifth Street, SE
P.O. Box 1110
Moultrie, GA 31776-1110
Tel: 912-985-6540
Fax: 912-985-0936
Email: jenkinsm@mail.colquitt.public.lib.ga.us
URL: http://www.firstct.com/fv/EPO.html

Emory University
Pitts Theology Library
Archives and Manuscripts
Atlanta, GA 30322
Tel: 404-727-4166
Fax: 404-727-1219
Email: archivist@sys1.pitts.emory.edu
URL: http://sys1.pitts.emory.edu

Emory University
R.W. Woodruff Library
Special Collections and Archives Department
111 James P. Brawley Drive, SW
Atlanta, GA 30322-2870
Tel: 404-727-6887
Fax: 404-727-0053
Email: libbdb@emory.edu
URL: http://www.emory.edu/LIB/schome.htm

Factor's Walk Military Museum
P.O. Box 10041
Savannah, GA 31412
Tel: 912-232-8003
Fax: 912-232-5457

Fayette County Library
155 S. Jeff Davis Dr.
Fayetteville, GA 30214-2131
Tel: 770-461-8841

First African Baptist Church Museum
23 Montgomery Street
Savannah, GA 31401
Tel: 912-233-2244
Fax: 912-234-7950

Fitzgerald-Ben Hill County Library
123 N. Main Street
Fitzgerald, GA 31750
Tel: 912-423-3642
Fax: 912-423-4493

Flint River Regional Library
800 Memorial Drive
Griffin, GA 30223-4499
Tel: 770-412-4770
Fax: 770-412-4773
Email: murphyw@mail.spalding.public.lib.ga.us

Forsyth County Public Library
585 Dahlonega Road
Cummings, GA 30130
Tel: 770-781-9840
Email: mcdanielj@mail.forsyth.public.lib.ga.us

Fort Frederica National Monument
Route 9, Box 286-C
St. Simons Island, GA 31522-9710
Tel/Fax: 912-638-3639
Email: fofr_superintendent@nps.gov
URL: http://www.nps.gov/fofr/

Fort McAllister Historic Park
3894 Fort McAllister Road
Richmond Hill, GA 31324
Tel: 912-727-2339
URL: http://www.us-travel.com/ga/parks/fortmcal.htm

Foxfire Fund/Museum
P.O. Box 541
Mountain City, GA 30562
Tel: 706-746-5828
Fax: 706-746-5829

Genealogical Center Library (operates by mail)
P.O. Box 71343
Marietta, GA 30007-1343

Georgia Agrirama Development Authority
P.O. Box Q
Tifton, GA 31793
Tel: 912-386-3344
Fax: 912-386-3386
URL: http://www.ajc.com/atl/attagri.htm

Georgia Baptist Historical Society Archives
Mercer University, Main Library
1300 Edgewood Avenue
Macon, GA 31207
Tel: 912-752-2968
Fax: 912-752-2111
URL: http://www.mercer.edu/www/main/mainhome.html

Georgia College
Ina Dillard Russell Library
Milledgeville, GA 31061
Tel: 912-454-0988
Fax: 912-453-6847
Email: scinfo@mail.gax.peachnet.edu
URL: http://library.gac.peachnet.edu

Georgia State Library
Capitol Hill Station
301 State Judicial Building
Atlanta, GA 30334

Georgia State University
Pullen Library
Special Collections Dept.
100 Decatur Street, SE
Atlanta, GA 30303-3202
Tel: 404-651-2477
Fax: 404-651-2476
Email: LIBSC@LANGATE.GSU.EDU
URL: http://wwwlib.gsu.edu/spcoll/

Gwinnett County Public Library
1001 Lawrenceville Highway
Lawrenceville, GA 30245
Tel: 770-822-4522
Fax: 770-822-5379
Email: jpinder@mial.gwinnett.public.lib.ga.us
URL: http://www.gcpl.public.lib.ga.us/

Gwinnett History Museum
455 Perry Street
Lawrenceville, GA 30245
Tel: 770-822-5178
Fax: 770-822-8835

Hart County Library
150 Benson Street
Hartwell, GA 30643-1392
Tel: 706-376-4655
Fax: 706-376-1157
Email: bissoa@mail.hart.public.lib.ga.us

Houston County Public Libraries
1201 Washington Avenue
Perry, GA 31069-2599
Tel: 912-987-3050
Fax: 912-987-4572
Email: goldenj@mail.houston.public.lib.ga.us

Huxford Genealogical Society Library
Municipal Complex
P.O. Box 595
Homerville, GA 31634
Tel: 912-487-2310

Jarrell Plantation State Historic Site
Route 2, Box 220
Juliette, GA 31046

Jefferson County Library
306 E. Broad Street
Louisville, GA 30434-1624
Tel: 912-625-3751
Fax: 912-625-7683
Email: rogersc@mail.jefferson.public.lib.ga.us

Kennesaw Civil War Museum
2829 Cherokee Street
Kennesaw, GA 30144
Tel: 770-427-2117
Fax: 770-429-4559
URL: http://www.ngeorgia.com/history/kcwm.html

Kennesaw Mountain National Battlefield Park
Kennesaw Mountain Historical Association
905 Kennesaw Mountain Dr.
Kennesaw, GA 30152
Tel: 770-427-4686
Fax: 770-528-8399
URL: http://www.nps.gov/kemo/

Kennesaw State University
Horace W. Sturgis Library
1000 Chastain Road
Kennesaw, GA 30144
Tel: 770-423-6186
Fax: 770-499-3376
Email: rwilliam@ksumail.kennesaw.edu

Kinchafoonee Regional Library
334 N. Main Street
Dawson, GA 31742
Tel: 912-995-2902
Fax: 912-928-3383
Email: russells@mail.terrell.public.lib.ga.us

Ladson Genealogical & Historical Foundation Library
119 Church Street
Vidalia, GA 30474
Mail:
c/o Ohoopee Regional Library System
610 Jackson Street
Vidalia, GA 30474
Tel/Fax: 912-537-8186
Email: ladsonl@mail.toombs.public.lib.ga.us

Lake Blackshear Regional Library
307 E. Lamar Street
Americus, GA 31709
Tel: 912-924-8091
Fax: 912-928-4445
Email: hendrixj@mail.sumter.public.lib.ga.us

Lake Lanier Regional Library
Pike Street
Lawrenceville, GA 30245

Lower Muskogee Creek Tribe
Tama Tribal Town
107 Long Pine Drive
Whigham, GA 31797
Tel/Fax: 912-762-3165

Lowndes County Historical Society/Museum
305 W. Central Avenue
P.O. Box 434
Valdosta, GA 31603
Tel: 912-247-4780
Fax: 912-247-2840

Lumpkin County Library
125 Hill Street
Dahlonega, GA 30533
Tel: 706-864-3668
Fax: 706-864-3937

Mercer University
Main Library
1300 Edgewood Avenue
Macon, GA 31207
Tel: 912-752-2960
URL: http://atl1.mercer.edu/~mainlib/

Methodist Museum
Epworth-by-the-Sea
P.O. Box 20407
St. Simons Island, GA 31522
Tel: 912-638-4050

Midway Museum
U.S. Highway 17
P.O. Box 195
Midway, GA 31320
Tel: 912-884-5837

Morgan County African-American Museum
156 Academy Street
P.O. Box 482
Madison, GA 30650
Tel: 706-342-9191
Fax: 706-342-9197

Morgan County Records Archives
Hancock Street
P.O. Box 130
Madison, GA 30650
Tel: 706-342-3605
Fax: 706-342-7806

Mountain Regional Library
698 Miller Street
P.O. Box 159
Young Harris, GA 30582
Tel: 706-379-3732
Fax: 706-379-2047
Email: haymoret@mail.towns.public.lib.ga.us

Nancy Guinn Memorial Library
Conyers-Rockdale Library System
864 Green Street
Conyers, GA 30207
Tel: 770-388-5041
Fax: 770-388-5043
Email: mangetd@mail.rockdale.public.lib.ga.us

Neva Lomason Memorial Library
West Georgia Regional Library
710 Rome Street
Carrollton, GA 30117-3046
Tel: 770-836-6711

Newnan-Coweta Historical Society
Male Academy Museum
30 Temple Avenue
P.O. Box 1001
Newnan, Ga 30264
Tel/Fax: 770-251-0207
URL: http://www.newnan.com/mam/index.html

Newton County Library System
1174 Monticello Street
Covington, GA 30209
Tel: 770-784-2090
Fax: 770-784-2092
Email: soltisl@mail.newton.public.lib.ga.us

Northeast Georgia Regional Library
P.O. Box 2020
Clarksville, GA 30523
Tel: 706-754-4413
Fax: 706-754-3479
Email: e_murphy@cyberhighway.net

Northwest Georgia Regional Library
310 Cappes Street
Dalton, GA 30720-4123
Tel: 706-278-4507
Fax: 706-278-7519
Email: forseej@mail.whitfield.public.lib.ga.us

Ocmulgee Regional Library System
505 Second Avenue
P.O. Box 4369
Eastman, GA 31203
Tel: 912-374-4711
Fax: 912-374-5646
Email: dwilson@mail.dodge.public.lib.ga.us

Oconee Regional Library
801 Bellevue Avenue
P.O. Box 100
Dublin, GA 31021
Tel: 912-272-5710
Fax: 912-272-5381
Email: williams@mail.laurens.public.lib.ga.us
URL: http://www.laurens.public.lib.ga.us/geneal.htm

Ohoopee Regional Library System
610 Jackson Street
Vidalia, GA 30474-2835
Tel: 912-537-9283
Fax: 912-537-3735
Email: gres@mail.toombs.public.lib.ga.us

Okefenokee Regional Library System
401 Lee Avenue
P.O. Box 1669
Waycross, GA 31501
Tel: 912-287-4978
Fax: 912-287-4981
Email: robertss@mail.ware.public.lib.ga.us

Peach Public Libraries
213 Persons Street
Fort Valley, GA 31030-4196
Tel: 912-825-6992
Fax: 912-825-6996
Email: stanberg@mail.peach.public.lib.ga.us
URL: http://www.peach.public.lib.ga.us/

Piedmont Regional Library
189 Bell View Street
Winder, GA 30680
Tel: 770-867-2762
Fax: 770-867-7483

Pine Mountain Regional Library
218 Perry Street
P.O. Box 508
Manchester, GA 31816

Roddenbery Memorial Library
320 North Broad Street
Cairo, GA 31728-2199
Tel: 912-377-3632
Fax: 912-377-7204
Email: akaye@mail.grady.public.lib.ga.us

Rossville Public Library
504 McFarland Avenue
Rossville, GA 30741
Tel: 706-866-1368
Fax: 706-858-0251
Email: rossvill@voyageronline.net
URL: http://www.walker.public.lib.ga.us/branches/rossvill.xtm

Roswell Research Library and Archives
Roswell Historical Society
Roswell Municipal Auditorium, 2nd Floor
Roswell, GA 30075
Tel: 770-594-6405

Sara Hightower Regional Library
Rome-Floyd County Library
205 Riverside Parkway
Rome, GA 30161-2913
Tel: 706-236-4609
Fax: 706-236-4631
Email: kinzerj@mail.floyd.public.lib.ga.us

Satilla Regional Library
201 S. Coffee Avenue
Douglas, GA 31533
Tel: 912-384-4667
Fax: 912-389-4365
Email: schildb@mail.coffee.public.lib.ga.us

Savannah Jewish Archives
@ Georgia Historical Society
501 Whitaker Street
Savannah, GA 31401

Screven-Jenkins Regional Library
106 South Community Drive
Sylvania, GA 30467-2055
Tel: 912-564-7526
Fax: 912-564-7080
Email: slively@mail.screven.public.lib.ga.us

R.T. Jones Memorial Library
Sequoyah Regional Library
116 Brown Industrial Parkway
Canton, GA 30114
Tel: 770-479-3090
Fax: 770-479-3069
Email: 73324-265@compuserve.com
URL: http://www.mindspring.com/~tede/cherokee_ga/library1.html

Signal Archives
Command Historian
U.S. Army Signal Center and Fort Gordon
Attn: ATZH-MH, Fort Gordon
Fort Gordon, GA 30905
Tel: 706-791-5212
Fax: 706-791-5777

Sixth Cavalry Museum
#2 Barnhardt Circle
Fort Oglethorpe, GA 30742
Tel: 706-861-2860

Smyrna Museum
Smyrna Historical and Genealogical Society
2865 King Street
Smyrna, GA 30080
Tel: 770-435-7549
Fax: 770-431-2858

South Georgia Regional Library
300 Woodrow Wilson Drive
Valdosta, GA 31602-2592
Tel: 912-333-5285
Fax: 912-245-6483
Email: lizan@mail.lowndes.public.lib.ga.us
URL: http://www.valdosta.peachnet.edu/~dpeeeples/sgrl.html

Southwest Georgia Regional Library
Genealogy Room
301 South Monroe Street
Bainbridge, GA 31717
Tel: 912-248-2665
Fax: 912-248-2670
Email: whittles@mail.decatur.public.lib.ga.us
URL: http://www.decatur.public.lib.ga.us/openpage.htm

State University of West Georgia
Ingram Library
Carrollton, GA 30118
Tel: 770-830-2350
URL: http://www.westga.edu/library/

Statesboro Regional Library
124 S. Main Street
Statesboro, GA 30458
Tel: 912-764-7573
Fax: 912-764-2861

Thomas College Library Archives
1501 Millpond Road
Thomasville, GA 31792
Tel: 912-226-1621

Thomas County Public Library System
201 North Madison Street
Thomasville, GA 31792
Tel: 912-225-5252
Fax: 912-225-5258
Email: edend@mail.thomas.public.lib.ga.us

Thomaston-Upson Archives
301 S. Carter Street
P.O. Box 1137
Thomaston, GA 30286
Tel: 706-647-2437
Fax: 706-646-3524

Thomasville Genealogical, History, and Fine Arts Library
600 East Washington Street
P.O. Box 1597
Thomasville, GA 31799
Tel: 912-226-9640
Fax: 912-226-3199
URL: http://www.rose.net/culture.htm

Thomasville Landmarks
312 N. Broad Street
P.O. Box 1285
Thomasville, GA 31799
Tel: 912-226-6016
Fax: 912-226-6672
Email: tli@rose.net

Troup County Historical Society and Archives
136 Main Street
P.O. Box 1051
LaGrange, GA 30241
Tel: 706-884-1828
Fax: 706-884-1838
Email: kaye@mentor.lgc.peachnet.edu
URL: http://www.lgc.peachnet.edu/archives/tcarchiv.htm

Troup-Harris-Coweta Regional Library
115 Alford Street
LaGrange, GA 30240
Tel: 706-882-7784
Fax: 706-882-7342
Email: bechamg@mailbox.troup.public.lib.ga.us

Uncle Remus Regional Library
1131 East Avenue
Madison, GA 30650
Tel: 706-342-4974
Fax: 706-342-4510
Email: schaefer@mail.morgan.public.lib.ga.us

Union County Historical Society
P.O. Box 35
Blairsville, GA 30514-0035
Tel: 706-745-5493
URL: http://www.ngeorgia.com/uchs.html

U.S. Navy Supply Corps Museum
1425 Prince Avenue
Athens, GA 30606-2205
Tel: 706-354-7349
Fax: 706-354-7239

University of Georgia
Department of Archives
Main Library
Athens, GA 30602
Tel: 706-542-8151
Fax: 706-542-4144
Email: eghead@uga.cc.ega.edu
URL: http://www.libs.uga.edu/darchive/

University of Georgia
Hargrett Library
Athens, GA 30602-1641
Tel: 706-542-7123
706-542-7131
Fax: 706-542-4144
URL: http://www.libs.uga.edu/darchive/hargrett.html

University of Georgia
Richard B. Russell Library
Athens, GA 30606-1641
Tel: 706-542-5788
Fax: 706-542-4144
Email: sbvogt@uga.cc.uga.edu
pdean@uga.cc.uga.edu
URL: http://www.libs.uga.edu/russell/russell.html

Vann House State Historical Park
Georgia Highways 52 and 225, N
Chatsworth, GA 30705
Tel: 706-695-2598
URL: http://www.ngeorgia.com/cgi-bin/park/Chief

Washington Memorial Library
Middle Georgia Regional Library/Archives
Genealogical & Historical Room
1180 Washington Avenue
Macon, GA 31208-6334
Tel: 912-744-0820 (library)
912-744-0851 (archives)
Fax: 912-744-0893

West Georgia Museum of Tallapoosa
21 West Lyon Street
Tallapoosa, GA 30176
Tel: 770-574-3125

West Georgia Regional Library
710 Rome Street
Carrollton, GA 30117
Tel: 770-836-6711
Fax: 770-836-4787
Email: cooper@mail.carroll.public.lib.ga.us

William Breman Jewish Heritage Museum
Ida Pearle & Joseph Cuba Jewish Archives & Genealogical Center
1440 Spring Street
Atlanta, GA 30309
Tel: 404-873-1661
Fax: 404-874-7043
Email: darby@mail.glynn.public.lib.ga.us

Young Harris College
Duckworth Libraries
Young Harris, GA 30582
Tel: 706-379-4313
Fax: 706-379-4314
Email: bobrich@yhc.edu
URL: http://www.yhc.edu

NEWSPAPER REPOSITORIES

Chatham-Effingham-Liberty Regional Library
2002 Bull Street
Savannah, GA 31499-4301
Tel: 912-652-3600
Fax: 912-652-3638
Email: lond@cel.co.chatham.ga.us
URL: http://www.co.chatham.ga.us/

Commerce Public Library
Heritage Room
1344 S. Broad Street
Commerce, GA 30529
Tel: 706-335-5946

Etowah Valley Historical Society
P.O. Box 1886
Cartersville, GA 30120

Oconee Regional Library
801 Bellevue Avenue
P.O. Box 100
Dublin, GA 31021
Tel: 912-272-5710
Fax: 912-272-5381
Email: williams@mail.laurens.public.lib.ga.us
URL: http://www.laurens.public.lib.ga.us/geneal.htm

Rossville Public Library
504 McFarland Avenue
Rossville, GA 30741
Tel: 706-866-1368
Fax: 706-858-0251
Email: rossvill@voyageronline.net
URL: http://www.walker.public.lib.ga.us/branches rossvill.xtm

University of Georgia
Department of Archives
Photographic Services
Athens, GA 30602
Tel: 706-542-2131
Email: bhennebe@uga.cc.uga.edu
URL: http://www.libs.uga.edu/darchive/aboutgnp.html

VITAL RECORDS

Georgia Department of Human Resources
Vital Records Unit, Room 217-H
47 Trinity Avenue, SW
Atlanta, GA 30334
Tel: 404-656-4900

GEORGIA ON THE WEB

Genealogical Computer Society of Georgia
http://www.mindspring.com/~noahsark/gcsga

Georgia Genealogical Information by Beverly S. Roden
http://www.mindspring.com/~bevr/index.html

Georgia GenWeb Project
http://www.rootsweb.com/~gagenweb/gaindex.htm

Paul Hickey's Genealogy Corner
http://www1.surfsouth.com/~phickey/

State of Georgia, Office of Secretary of State
Georgia Department of Archives and History
http://www.sos.state.ga.us/archives

Travellers Southern Families
http://genealogy.traveller.com/genealogy/

HAWAII

ARCHIVES, STATE & NATIONAL

Hawaii State Archives
Iolani Palace Grounds
Kekauluohi Building
King & Richards Streets
Honolulu, HI 96813
Tel: 808-586-0313
808-586-0329
Fax: 808-586-0330
URL: http://www.htdc.org/~hsa/

National Archives—Pacific Sierra Region
1000 Commodore Drive
San Bruno, CA 94066-2350
Tel: 415-876-9009
Fax: 415-876-9233
Email: archives@sanbruno.nara.gov
URL: http://www.nara.gov/nara/regional/09nssgil.html

GENEALOGICAL SOCIETIES

Daughters of Hawaii
Queen Emma's Summer Palace
2913 Pali Highway
Honolulu, HI 96817
Tel: 808-595-6291
808-595-3167
Fax: 808-595-4395

Hawaii County Genealogical Society
P.O. Box 831
Keaau, HI 96749

Portugese Genealogical Society of Hawaii
810 North Vineyard Blvd., Room 11
Honolulu, HI 96817
Tel: 808-841-5044
Email: chism@hi.net
URL: http://www.lusaweb.com/pgsh.htm

Sandwich Islands Genealogical Society
Manoa Gardens Community Center
2790 Kahaloa Drive
Manoa Gardens, HI 96822
URL: http://www.hpcug.org/sandils.htm

HISTORICAL SOCIETIES

Hawaiian Historical Society/Library
560 Kawaiahao Street
Honolulu, HI 96813
Tel: 808-537-6271
URL: http://www.aloha.com/~mem/hhshome.html

Kauai Historical Society
4428 Rui Street
Lihue, HI 96766
Tel: 808-245-6931

Kona Historical Society/Museum
Highway 11
Kealakekua, HI
Mail:
P.O. Box 398
Captain Cook, HI 96704
Tel: 808-323-3222

Maui Historical Society/Library
2375 A Main Street
P.O. Box 1018
Wailuku, HI 96793
Tel: 808-244-3326
Fax: 808-242-4878

Polynesian Voyaging Society
1250 Lauhala Street, Apt. 314
Honolulu, HI 96813
Tel: 808-547-4172
Email: dennisk@hawaii.edu
URL: http://leahi.kcc.hawaii.edu/org/pvs/

LDS FAMILY HISTORY CENTERS

Hilo Stake Family History Center
1373 Kilauea Avenue
Hilo, HI 96720
Tel: 808-935-0711

Honolulu Family History Center
1723 Beckley Street
Honolulu, HI 96819
Tel: 808-841-4118

Honolulu Stake Family History Center
1560 South Beretania Street
Honolulu, HI 96814
Tel: 808-955-8910

Honolulu West Stake (Kalihi) Family History Center
2203-A Makanani Drive
Honolulu, HI 96817
Tel: 808-845-9701

Kahului Family History Center
25 West Kamahaneha Avenue
Kahului, HI 96732
Tel: 808-871-8841

Kailua-Kona Family History Center
75-234 Nani Kailua Drive #48
Kailua-Kona, HI 96740
Tel: 808-329-4469

Kaneohe Stake Family History Center
46-117 Halaulani Street
Kaneohe, HI 96744
Tel: 808-247-3134

Laie & Laie North Stake Family History Center
55-600A Naniloa Loop
Laie, HI 96762
Tel: 808-293-2133

Lihue Family History Center
4568 Ehiku Street
Lihue, HI 96766
Tel: 808-246-9119

Mililani Stake Family History Center
95-1039 Meheula Parkway
Mililani, HI 96789
Tel: 808-623-1712

Waipahu Stake Family History Center
94-210 Kahualii
Waipahu, HI 96797
Tel: 808-678-0752

Archives/Libraries/Museums

Bishop Museum and Library/Archives
1525 Bernice Street
P.O. Box 19000-A
Honolulu, HI 96817-0916
Tel: 808-848-4147/8
808-848-4182/3
Fax: 808-841-8968
URL: http://www.bishop.hawaii.org/bishop/library/library.html
http://www.bishop.hawaii.org/bishop/archives/arch.html

Brigham Young University Hawaii Campus Archives
Joseph F. Smith Library
55-220 Kulanui Street
Laie, HI 96762-1266
Tel: 808-293-3868
Fax: 808-293-3877
URL: http://websider.byuh.edu/lrc/

Cooke Library
Punahou School
1601 Punahou Street
Honolulu, HI 96822
Tel: 808-944-5711
URL: http://www.punahou.edu/eg.agci/facilities.html

DAR/SAR Memorial Library
1914 Makiki Heights Drive
Honolulu, HI 96822
Tel: 808-949-7256

Daughters of Hawaii
Queen Emma's Summer Palace
2913 Pali Highway
Honolulu, HI 96817
Tel: 808-595-6291
808-595-3167
Fax: 808-595-4395

Episcopal Church in Hawaii
Queen Emma Square
Honolulu, HI 96813
Tel: 808-536-7776

Ethnic Records and Resource Center
4945 Kiluea Avenue
Box 17827
Honolulu, HI 96817

Hana Cultural Center & Museum
4974 Uakea Road
P.O. Box 27
Hana, HI 96713-0027
Tel: 808-248-8622
Fax: 808-248-8620
Email: hccm@aloha.net
URL: http://www.planet-hawaii.com/hana/

Hawaii Chinese History Center
111 North King Street, Room 410
Honolulu, HI 96817
Tel: 808-521-5948

Hawaii Maritime Center Library & Photo Archives
Pier 7
Honolulu, HI 96813
Tel: 808-523-6151
808-536-6373
Fax: 808-536-1519

Hawaii State Library
478 South King Street
Honolulu, HI 96813
Tel: 808-586-3535 (Hawaii & Pacific Section)
URL: http://www.hcc.hawaii.edu/hspls/hpov.html
Tel: 808-586-3499 (Language, Literature, & History Section)
URL: http://www.hcc.hawaii.edu/hspls/llhov.html

Hawaiian Historical Society/Library
560 Kawaiahao Street
Honolulu, HI 96813
Tel/Fax: 808-537-6271
URL: http://www.aloha.com/~mem/hhshome.html

Hawaiian Mission Children's Society Library
553 South King Street
Honolulu, HI 96813-3002
Tel: 808-531-0481
Fax: 808-545-2280
URL: http://www.hcc.hawaii.edu/artweb/mission/mission.html
http://www.aloha.com/~mem/mhmlib.html

Honolulu City and County,
Municipal Reference and Records Center
City Hall Annex
538 S. King Street
Honolulu, HI 96813
Tel: 808-527-5662
Fax: 808-523-4985

Kauai Museum
4428 Rice Street
P.O. Box 248
Lihue, HI 96766
Tel: 808-245-6931
Fax: 808-245-6864

Kona Historical Society/Museum
Highway 11
Kealakekua, HI
Mail:
P.O. Box 398
Captain Cook, HI 96704
Tel: 808-323-3222

Lahaina Restoration Foundation
Hale Pa'i Reading Room
1022 Front Street
P.O. Box 338
Lahaina, HI 96767-0338
Tel: 808-661-3262
Fax: 808-661-9309
URL: http://www.cfws.org/WHALES/lahaina.htm\

Lyman House Memorial Museum
276 Haili Street
Hilo, HI 96720
Tel: 808-935-5021
Fax: 808-244-3920
URL: http://www.lei.net:8080/lei/DigitalHI/hiltonwaikoloa/bigisland/museums/lyman.html

Maui Historical Society/Library
2375 A Main Street
P.O. Box 1018
Wailuku, HI 96793
Tel: 808-244-3326
Fax: 808-242-4878

Roman Catholic Diocese of Honolulu
1184 Bishop Street
Honolulu, HI 96813
Tel: 808-533-1791

University of Hawaii at Hilo
Edwin Mookini Library
200 West Kawili Street
Hilo, HI 96720
Tel: 808-974-7346
URL: http://www2.hawaii.edu/~mookini/mookinihome.html

University of Hawaii at Manoa
Sinclair and Hamilton Libraries
2550 The Mall
Honolulu, HI 96822
Tel: 808-956-8264
Fax: 808-956-5968
Email: libweb@hawaii.edu
URL: http://nic2.hawaii.net/uhlib2/external/library_research_colls.html

NEWSPAPER REPOSITORIES

Bishop Museum and Library/Archives
1525 Bernice Street
P.O. Box 19000-A
Honolulu, HI 96817-0916
Tel: 808-848-4147/8
808-848-4182/3
Fax: 808-841-8968
URL: http://www.bishop.hawaii.org/bishop/library/library.html
http://www.bishop.hawaii.org/bishop/archives/arch.html

Hawaii State Archives
Iolani Palace Grounds
Kekauluohi Building
King & Richards Streets
Honolulu, HI 96813
Tel: 808-586-0313
808-586-0329
Fax: 808-586-0330
URL: http://www.htdc.org/~hsa/

Hawaiian Historical Society/Library
560 Kawaiahao Street
Honolulu, HI 96813
Tel/Fax: 808-537-6271
URL: http://www.aloha.com/~mem/hhshome.html

University of Hawaii at Manoa
Sinclair and Hamilton Libraries
2550 The Mall
Honolulu, HI 96822
Tel: 808-956-8264
Fax: 808-956-5968
Email: libweb@hawaii.edu
URL: http://nic2.hawaii.net/uhlib2/external/library_research_colls.html

NEWSPAPER REPOSITORIES

University of Hawaii/Manoa
Sinclair and Hamilton Libraries
2550 The Mall
Honolulu, HI 96822
Tel: 808-956-7205
Fax: 808-956-5968
Email: haak@hawaii.edu
URL: http://nic2.hawaii.net/~speccoll/habout.html#hanchor2

VITAL RECORDS

Hawaii Department of Health
Vital Records Section
P.O. Box 3378
Honolulu, HI 96801-9984
Tel: 808-586-4535
URL: http://www.hawaii.gov/health/vr_gene.htm

HAWAII ON THE WEB

Hawaii GenWeb Project
http://www.rootsweb.com/~higenweb/

Hawaiian Genealogy
http://hawaii-shopping.com/~sammonet/genealogy.html

Hawaiian History
http://www.outrigger.com/destguide/h_time.html

Pearl Harbor Casualty List
ftp://ftp.rootsweb.com/pub/usgenweb/hi/military/pearl.txt

IDAHO

ARCHIVES, STATE & NATIONAL

Idaho State Historical Library & Archives
325 W. State Street
Boise, ID 83702
Tel: 208-334-2150
Fax: 208-334-4016
URL: http://www.state.id.us/isl/hp.htm

National Archives—Pacific Northwest Region
6125 Sand Point Way, NE
Seattle, WA 98115
Tel: 206-526-6507
Fax: 206-526-4344
Email: archives@seattle.nara.gov
URL: http://www.nara.gov/nara/regional/10nsgil.html

GENEALOGICAL SOCIETIES

Bonner County Genealogical Society
P.O. Box 27
Dover, ID 83825

Caldwell Genealogical Group
3504 S. Illinois Street
Caldwell, ID 83605

Friends of the Idaho Genealogical Library
9846 Westview Drive
Boise, ID 83704
Email: dyingst@rmci.net
URL: http://www.rmci.net/idaho/genidaho/

Idaho Genealogical Society
4620 Overland Road, #204
Boise, ID 83705-2867
Tel: 208-384-0542
Email: dyingst@rmci.net
URL: http://www.rmci.net/idaho/genidaho/igs.htm

Kamiah Genealogical Society
P.O. Box 322
Kamiah, ID 83536

Kootenai County Genealogical Society
8385 N. Government Way
Hayden Lake, ID 83835

Latah County Genealogical Society
327 E. Second Street
Moscow, ID 83843
Tel: 208-882-5943

Pocatello Branch Genealogical Society
156 South 6th Avenue
P.O. Box 4272
Pocatello, ID 83201

Shoshone County Genealogical Society
P.O. Box 183
Kellogg, ID 83837

Snake River Genealogical Society of Southeastern Idaho
122 North Front Street
P.O. Box 30
Sugar City, ID 83448-0030
Tel: 208-356-7072

Twin Rivers Genealogical Society
P.O. Box 386
Lewiston, ID 83501

Valley County Genealogical Society
c/o Cascade Library
105 Front Street
P.O. Box 606
Cascade, ID 83611
Tel: 208-382-4757
Email: casclib@mailhost.cyberhighway.net

HISTORICAL SOCIETIES

Adams County Historical Society
P.O. Box 352
New Meadows, ID 83654

Bannock Historical Society/Museum
Upper Level of Ross Park
3000 Alvord Loop
Pocatello, ID 83204
URL: http://www.ohwy.com/id/b/bannochm.htm

Bonner County Historical Society/Museum
609 S. Ella Avenue
P.O. Box 1063
Sandpoint, ID 83864
Tel: 208-263-2344

Bonneville County Historical Society
P.O. Box 1784
Idaho Falls, ID 83401

Boundary County Historical Society/Free Museum
7229 Main Street
P.O. Box 808
Bonners Ferry, ID 83805
Tel: 208-267-7720

Camas County Historical Society
General Delivery
Fairfield, ID 83327

Canyon County Historical Society
P.O. Box 595
Nampa, ID 83651

Caribou County Historical Society
c/o County Courthouse
Soda Springs, ID 83276

Cassia County Historical Society/Museum
E. Main Street & Highland
P.O. Box 331
Burley, ID 83318
Tel: 208-678-7172

Clearwater County Historical Society
P.O. Box 1454
Orofino, ID 83544

Crane Historical Society
Crane House
Main Street
P.O. Box 152
Harrison, ID 83833
Tel: 208-689-3519

Elmore County Historical Foundation
P.O. Box 204
Mountain Home, ID 83647

Fremont County Historical Society
St. Anthony, ID 83445

Gooding County Historical Society/Museum
134 Seventh Avenue, W
Gooding, ID 83330-1228

Idaho State Historical Society
1109 Main Street, Suite 250
Boise, ID 83702-5642
Tel: 208-334-2682
Fax: 208-334-2774
URL: http://www.state.is.us/ishs/index.htm

Latah County Historical Society
McConnell Mansion
110 Adams Street
Moscow, ID 83843
Tel: 208-882-1004

Lewis County Historical Society
Route 2 - Box 10
Kamiah, ID 83536

Minidoka County Historical Society
100 East Baseline
Rupert, ID 83350

Nez Perce Historical Society
P.O. Box 86
Nez Perce, ID 83542

Nez Perce Historical Society
Luna House Museum
Third and C Streets
Lewiston, ID 83501
Tel: 208-743-2535

Old Fort Boise Historical Society
Parma, ID 83660

Payette County Historical Society
90 South Ninth Street
P.O. Box 476
Payette, ID 83661
Tel: 208-642-4883

South Bannock County Historical Society/Museum
110 East Main Street
Lava Hot Springs, ID 83246
URL: http://www.ohwy.com/id/s/sbchcm.htm

South Custer County Historical Society
P.O. Box 355
MacKay, ID 83251

Spirit Lake Historical Society
Spirit Lake, ID 83869

Upper Snake River Valley Historical Society/Library
P.O. Box 244
Rexburg, ID 83440

Wood River Historical Society
P.O. Box 552
Ketchum, ID 83340

LDS Family History Centers

Arimo Family History Center
286 Henderson Avenue
Arimo, ID 83214
Tel: 208-254-3888

Basalt Family History Center
133 South Main
Basalt, ID 83218
Tel: 208-346-6011

Blackfoot Family History Center
815 North Fisher
Blackfoot, ID 83221
Tel: 208-785-5022

Blackfoot Family History Center
101 North, 900 West
Blackfoot, ID 83221
Tel: 208-684-3784

Boise Family History Center
McMillan & Shamrock
Boise, ID 83713
Tel: 208-376-0452

Boise Family History Center
3676 Dorian St.
Boise, ID 83705
Tel: 208-338-3811

Boise Family History Center
12040 West Amity Road
Boise, ID 83709
Tel: 208-362-2638

Burley Family History Center
224 East 14th Street
Burley, ID 83318
Tel: 208-678-7286

Caldwell Family History Center
3015 South Kimball
Caldwell, ID 83605
Tel: 208-454-8324

Coeur d'Alene Family History Center
2801 North Fourth
Coeur d'Alene, ID 83814
Tel: 208-765-0150

Driggs Family History Center
221 North First, East
Driggs, ID 83422
Tel: 208-354-2253

Eagle Family History Center
2090 N. Eagle Road
Eagle, ID 83616
Tel: 208-939-4738

Emmett Family History Center
980 West Central Rd.
Emmett, ID 83617
Tel: 208-365-4112

Fruitland Family History Center
325 N. Pennsylvania Avenue
Fruitland, ID 83619
Tel: 208-452-4345

Grangeville Family History Center
402 North Myrtle St.
Grangeville, ID 83530
Tel: 208-983-2110

Hailey Family History Center
Broadford & Main
Hailey, ID 83333
Tel: 208-788-4250

Idaho Falls Family History Center
750 West Elva Street
Idaho Falls, ID 83402
Tel: 208-524-5291

Idaho Falls Family History Center
1860 Kearney
Idaho Fall, ID 83401
Tel: 208-529-9805

Idaho Falls Family History Center
3000 Central Avenue
Idaho Falls, ID 83406
Tel: 208-529-4087

Lewiston Family History Center
Ninth & Preston
Lewiston, ID 83501
Tel: 208-746-6910

Malad Family History Center
20 South, 100 West
Malad, ID 83252
Tel: 208-766-2332

McCall Family History Center
Church on Elo Raod
McCall, ID 83250
Tel: 208-634-2300

McCammon Family History Center
403 West 16th
McCammon, ID 83252
Tel: 208-254-3259

Montpelier Family History Center
138 North Sixth Street
Montpelier, ID 83254
Tel: 208-847-0340

Moore Family History Center
3100 North, 3350 West
Moore, ID 83255
Tel: 208-554-2121

Moscow Family History Center
657 South Blaine
Moscow, ID 83843
Tel: 208-882-1769

Mountain Home Family History Center
1150 North, Eighth East
Mountain Home, ID 83647
Tel: 208-587-5249

Nampa Family History Center
143 Central Canyon
Nampa, ID 83657
Tel: 208-467-5827

Pocatello Family History Center
156-1/2 South Sixth Avenue
Pocatello, ID 83202
Tel: 208-232-9262

Preston Family History Center
55 East, 1st South
Preston, ID 83263
Tel: 208-852-0710

Ricks College Family History Center
McKay Library
Rexburg, ID 83440
Tel: 208-356-2377

Rigby Family History Center
4021 East, 300 North
Rigby, ID 83442
Tel: 208-745-8789

Rigby Family History Center
258 West, 1st North
Rigby, ID 83442
Tel: 208-745-8660

Salmon Family History Center
400 South Daisy
Salmon, ID 83467
Tel: 208-756-3514

Sandpoint Family History Center
433 South Boyer
Sandpoint, ID 83864
Tel: 208-263-8721

Shelley Family History Center
544 Seminary Street
Shelley, ID 83274
Tel: 208-357-3128

Soda Springs Family History Center
290 South, 3rd West
Soda Springs, ID 83276
Tel: 208-547-3232

Terreton Family History Center
Highway 33
Terreton, ID 83450
Tel: 208-663-4389

Twin Falls Family History Center
401 Maurice Street, North
Twin Falls, ID 83301
Tel: 208-733-8073

Weiser Family History Center
300 East Main Street
Weiser, ID 83672
Tel: 208-549-1575

ARCHIVES/LIBRARIES/MUSEUMS

Aberdeen Public Library
76 E. Central Avenue
Aberdeen, ID 83210
Tel: 208-397-4427

Ada Community Library
10664 West Victory Road
Boise, ID 83709
Tel: 208-362-0181
Fax: 208-362-0303

Albertson College of Idaho
Terteling Library
College Campus
Caldwell, ID 83605
Tel: 208-459-5505
Fax: 208-459-5299
URL: http://www.acofi.edu/~library/

Appaloosa Museum & Heritage Center
5070 Highway 8 West
Moscow, ID 83843-4000
Tel: 208-882-5578
Fax: 208-882-8150

Bannock County Historical Museum
3000 Alvord Loop
P.O. Box 253
Pocatello, ID 83204
Tel: 208-233-0434

Bicentennial Historical Museum
305 N. College Street
Grangeville, ID 83530
Tel: 208-983-2573

Bingham County Historical Museum
190 N. Shilling Avenue
Blackfoot, ID 83221
Tel: 208-785-8065
208-785-8040

Blackfoot Library
129 N. Broadway
Blackfoot, ID 83221
Tel: 208-785-8628

Blaine County Historical Museum
N. Main Street
P.O. Box 124
Hailey, ID 83333-0124
Tel: 208-788-2809
208-788-4185

Boise Basin District Library
411 Montgomery Street
Idaho City, ID 83631
Tel: 208-392-4558
Email: dree@boisebasin.lib.id.us
URL: http://boisebasin.lib.us.id/

Boise Basque Museum and Cultural Center
611 Grove Street
Boise, ID 83702
Tel: 208-343-2671

Boise Public Library
715 S. Capitol Blvd.
Boise, ID 83702
Tel: 208-384-4171

Boise State University
Albertsons Library
1910 University Drive
Boise, ID 83725
Tel: 208-385-1235
URL: http://library.idbsu.edu/

Bonner County Historical Society/Museum
609 S. Ella Avenue
P.O. Box 1063
Sandpoint, ID 83864
Tel: 208-263-2344

Boundary County Historical Society/Free Museum
7229 Main Street
P.O. Box 808
Bonners Ferry, ID 83805
Tel: 208-267-7720

Boundary County Public Library
6370 Kootenai
P.O. Box Y
Bonners Ferry, ID 83805-1276
Tel: 208-267-3750

Bureau of Land Management
Public Service Section
3380 Americana Terrace
Boise, ID 83706
Tel: 208-384-3000
URL: http://www3.primenet.com/~blmida/

Caldwell Public Library
1010 Dearborn
Caldwell, ID 83605
Tel: 208-459-3242

Canyon County Historical Museum
1200 Front Street
Nampa, ID 83651
Tel: 208-467-7611

Cascade Public Library
105 Front Street
P.O. Box 697
Cascade, ID 83611
Tel: 208-382-4757
Email: casclib@cyberhighway.com
URL: http://www.eils.lib.id.us/cascade/cascade.html

Cassia County Historical Society/Museum
E. Main Street & Highland
P.O. Box 331
Burley, ID 83318
Tel: 208-678-7172

Centennial Library
215 W. North Street
Grangeville, ID 83530
Tel: 208-983-0951

Clearwater County Museum
P.O. Box 1454
Orofino, ID 83544
Tel: 208-476-5033

Coeur d'Alene Public Library
201 Harrison Avenue
Coeur d'Alene, ID 83814
Tel: 208-769-2315
Fax: 208-769-2381
Email: cdapl@dmi.net
URL: http://www.dmi.net/cdalibrary/

Craigmont City Library
112 W. Main St.
Craigmont, ID 83523
Tel: 208-924-5510

Crane Historical Society
Crane House
Main Street
P.O. Box 152
Harrison, ID 83833
Tel: 208-689-3519

Eagle Public Library
67 E. State Street
P.O. Box 908
Eagle, ID 83616
Tel: 208-939-6814

Elmore County Historical Museum
180 South, 3 East Mountain
Home, ID 83647
Tel: 208-587-6847

Garden City Library
201 East 50
Boise, ID 83714
Tel: 208-377-2180

Garden Valley Library
Hc 76, Box 2199
Garden Valley, ID 83622-9703
Tel: 208-462-3317
Email: grdnvaly@micron.net

Glenns Ferry Historical Museum
211 West Cleveland Glenns
Ferry, ID 83623
Tel: 208-366-2760

Hayden Branch, Kootenai-Shoshone Area Library
8385 N. Government Way
Hayden, ID 83835
Tel: 208-772-5612
Fax: 208-772-2498
Email: hay@cin.kcl.org
URL: http://spidaweb.eils.lib.id.us/K-S/index.htm

Horseshoe Bend Library
Route 1, Box 10A
Horseshoe Bend, ID 83629-9701
Tel: 208-793-2460

Idaho City Historical Museum
402 Montgomery
P.O. Box 325
Idaho City, ID 83631
Tel: 208-392-4550

Idaho State Historical Society
Historic Sites Office
Old Idaho Penitentiary
2445 Old Penitentiary Road
Boise, ID 83712-8254
Tel: 208-334-2844
Fax: 208-334-3225
URL: http://www.state.id.us/ishs/index.htm

Idaho State Historical Library
325 West State Street
Boise, ID 83702
Tel: 208-334-2150
Fax: 208-334-4016
URL: http://www.state.id.us/isl/hp.htm

Idaho State Historical Museum
610 North Julia Davis Drive
Boise, ID 83702-7695
Tel: 208-334-2120
Fax: 208-334-4059
URL: http://www.state.id.us/ishs/museum.htm

Idaho State Historical Society
Library & Archives
450 North Fourth Street
Boise, ID 83702-6027
Tel: 208-334-3356
Fax: 208-334-3198
URL: http://www.state.id.us/ishs/library.htm

Idaho State Historical Society
Oral History Center
450 N. Fourth St.
Boise, ID 83702
Tel: 208-334-3863
Fax: 208-334-3198
URL: http://www.state.id.us/ishs/oralhist.htm

Idaho State University
E.M. Oboler Library
850 S. Ninth Street
P.O. Box 8089
Pocatello, ID 83209-0009
Tel: 208-236-2997
Fax: 208-236-4295
URL: http://www.isu.edu/departments/library/home.htm

Kamiah Library
507 Main
Kamiah, ID 83536
Tel: 208-935-0428

Kuna Public Library
1360 W. Boise
Kuna, ID 83634
Tel: 208-922-1002

Latah County Historical Society
McConnell Mansion
110 Adams Street
Moscow, ID 83843
Tel: 208-882-1004

Lewis-Clark State College Library
500 8th Avenue
Lewiston, ID 83501
Tel: 208-799-2397 (Collections)
208-799-2395 (Reference)
208-799-2394 (Periodicals)
Fax: 208-799-2831
URL: http://www.lcsc.edu/~library/

Lewiston-Nez Perce County Library
428 Thain Road
Lewiston, ID 83501-5399
Tel: 208-743-6519

Massacre Rocks State Park
3592 N. Park Lane
American Falls, ID 83211
Tel: 208-548-2672

McCall City Library
218 Park Street
P.O. Box 848
McCall, ID 83638-0848
Tel: 208-634-5522
Email: mccint@cyberhighway.net

Middleton Public Library
307 E. Main
Middleton, ID 83644
Tel: 208-585-3931

Mountain Home Public Library
790 North, 10 East
Mountain Home, ID 83647
Tel: 208-587-4716

Nampa Public Library
11 Avenue South
Nampa, ID 83651
Tel: 208-465-2263

Nez Perce Historical Society
Luna House Museum
Third and C Streets
Lewiston, ID 83501
Tel: 208-743-2535

Nez Perce National Historical Park
P.O. Box 93
Spalding, ID 83551
Tel: 208-843-2261
URL: http://www.nps.gov/nepe/

North Bingham County District Library
136 S. State
Shelley, ID 83274
Tel: 208-357-7801
Email: nbcdl@ida.net

North Idaho College Library
1000 West Garden Avenue
Coeur d'Alene, ID 83814
Tel: 208-769-3355
Fax: 208-769-3428
URL: http://www.nic.edu/learning.res/lib/index.html

Our Memories Museum
1122 Main Street
Caldwell, ID 83605
Tel: 208-459-1413

Owyhee County Historical Museum
Bassey Street
P.O. Box 67
Murphy, ID 83650
Tel: 208-495-2319

Payette Public Library
24 South Tenth
Payette, ID 83661-2861
Tel: 208-642-6029
Email: payetlib@primenet.com

Prairie Community Library
508 King Street
Cottonwood, ID 83522
Tel: 208-962-3714

Rails and Trails Museum
914 Washington St.
Montpelier, ID 83254

Ricks College Library
David O. McKay Library
Rexburg, ID 83440
URL: http://www.ricks.edu/Ricks/Ricks/Admissions/McKay.html

St. Gertrude's Library/Museum
Hc 3 Box 121
Cottonwood, ID 83522
Tel: 208-962-7123
208-962-3224
Fax: 208-962-7212

Shoshone-Bannock Indian Tribes
P.O. Box 306
Fort Hall, ID 83203
Tel: 208-238-3700
208-237-9791
Fax: 208-237-0797
URL: http://www.eerc.und.nodak.edu/cert/shosh.htm

South Bannock County Historical Center/Museum
110 East Main Street
P.O. Box 387
Lava Hot Springs, ID 83246
Tel: 208-776-5254

Three Island Crossing State Park
P.O. Box 609
Glenns Ferry, ID 83623
URL: http://www.wvi.com/users/TIC/tic.htm

University of Idaho Library
Special Collections and Archives
Moscow, ID 83844-2351
Tel: 208-885-7951
URL: http://www.lib.uidaho.edu/special-collections/

Upper Snake River Valley Historical Society/Library
P.O. Box 244
Rexburg, ID 83440

Valley County Museum, Roseberry
13131 Farm to Market Road
Donnelley, ID 83615
Tel: 208-325-8628
208-325-8383

Wilder Public Library
207 A Avenue
Wilder, ID 83678
Tel: 208-482-7880

Newspaper Repositories

Boundary County Public Library
6370 Kootenai
P.O. Box Y
Bonners Ferry, ID 83805

Idaho Historical Society
Idaho State Historical Library & Archives Bldg.
325 W. State Street
Boise, ID
Mail:
Idaho State Historical Library & Archives
450 North 4th Street
Boise, ID 83702
Tel: 208-334-3356/7
URL: http://www.rmci.net/idaho/genidaho/contents.htm

Idaho State Historical Library & Archives
325 W. State Street
Boise, ID 83702
Tel: 208-334-2150
Fax: 208-334-4016
Email: kford@isl.state.id.us
URL: http://www.state.id.us/isl/hp.htm

Lewis-Clark State College Library
500 8th Avenue
Lewiston, ID 83501
Tel: 208-799-2397 (Collections)
208-799-2395 (Reference)
208-799-2394 (Periodicals)
URL: http://www.lcsc.edu/~library/

Payette Public Library
24 South Tenth
Payette, ID 83661-2861
Tel: 208-642-6029
Email: payetlib@primenet.com

Vital Records

Vital Statistics Unit
Department of Health & Welfare
Statehouse Mall
450 West State Street
Boise, ID 83720-9990
Tel: 208-334-5988

Idaho on the Web

Genealogical Records in Idaho
http://www.lib.uidaho.edu/special-collections/genealgl.htm

Genealogy Idaho
http://www.rmci.net/idaho/genidaho/contents.htm

Historical Archive Collection of Nez Perce People
http://www.nezperce.com/archive2.html

Idaho GenWeb Project
http://www.rootsweb.com/~idgenweb/

ILLINOIS

ARCHIVES, STATE & NATIONAL

Illinois State Archives
Reference Unit
Margaret Cross Norton Building
Capitol Complex
Springfield, IL 62756
Tel: 217-782-3556
Fax: 217-524-3930
URL: http://www.sos.state.il.us/depts/archives/serv_sta.html

National Archives—Great Lakes Region
7358 Pulaski Road
Chicago, IL 60629
Tel: 773-581-7816
Fax: 312-353-1294
Email: archives@chicago.nara.gov
URL: http://www.nara.gov/nara/regional/05nsgil.htm

Illinois Regional Archives Depository (IRAD)
Illinois State Archives
Reference Unit
Margaret Cross Norton Building
Capitol Complex
Springfield, IL 62756
Tel: 217-785-1266
URL: http://www.sos.state.il.us/depts/archives/serv_loc.html

Eastern Illinois University (IRAD)
Booth Library
Charleston, IL 61920
Tel: 217-581-6093
217-581-6061
Fax: 217-581-6066
URL: http://www.eiu.edu/~booth/
Serves the following counties: Clark, Clay, Coles, Crawford, Cumberland, Douglas, Edgar, Edwards, Effingham, Jasper, Lawrence, Moultrie, Richland, Shelby, Wabash, Wayne.

Illinois State University (IRAD)
Williams Hall
Normal, IL 61761-5500
Tel: 309-452-6027
Serves the following counties: Champaign, DeWitt, Ford, Grundy, Iroquois, Kankakee, Livingston, Logan, Marshall, McLean, Piatt, Tazewell, Vermilion, Woodford.

Northeastern Illinois University (IRAD)
Ronald Williams Library
5500 N. St. Louis Avenue
Chicago, IL 60625-4699
Tel: 312-794-6279
Serves Cook County.

Northern Illinois University (IRAD)
Swen Parson Hall, Room 155
DeKalb, IL 60115
Tel: 815-753-1779
URL: http://www.niu.edu/depts/library/rhc.html
Serves the following counties: Boone, Bureau, Carroll, DeKalb, DuPage, Jo Daviess, Kane, Kendall, Lake, LaSalle, Lee, McHenry,Ogle, Putnam, Stephenson, Whiteside, Will, Winnebago.

Southern Illinois University (IRAD)
Morris Library
Special Collections
Carbondale, IL 62901-6632
Tel: 618-453-3040
URL: http://www.lib.siu.edu/
Serves the following counties: Alexander, Clinton, Franklin, Gallatin, Hamilton, Hardin, Jackson, Jefferson, Johnson, Madison, Marion, Massac, Monroe, Perry, Pope, Pulaski, Randolph, St. Clair, Saline, Union, Washington, White, Williamson.

University of Illinois at Springfield (IRAD)
Brookens Library
P.O. Box 19243
Springfield, IL 62794
Tel: 217-786-6520
Fax: 217-786-6633
URL: gopher://eagle.uis.edu/11/.libdir/
Serves the following counties: Bond, Cass, Christian, Fayette, Greene, Jersey, Macon, Macoupin, Mason, Menard, Montgomery, Morgan, Sangamon, Scott.

Western Illinois University (IRAD)
University Library
Archives & Special Collections
1 University Circle
Macomb, IL 61455
Tel: 309-298-2717/8
Email: mfgrl@WIU.edu
URL: http://www.wiu.edu/users/milibo/index.htm
Serves the following counties: Adams, Brown, Calhoun, Fulton, Hancock, Henderson, Henry, Knox, McDonough, Mercer, Peoria, Pike, Rock Island, Schuyler, Stark, Warren.

GENEALOGICAL SOCIETIES

African-American Cultural & Genealogical Society
314 North Main Street
P.O. Box 25251
Decatur, IL 62525
Tel: 217-429-7458
URL: http://www.decaturnet.org/afrigenes.html

African-American Genealogical and Historical Society (AAHGS)
P.O. Box 377651
Chicago, IL 60637-7651

African-American Genealogical and Historical Society (AAHGS)
Little Egypt
703 South Wall Street #5
Carbondale, IL 62901

African-American Genealogical and Historical Society (AAHGS)
Patricia Liddell Researchers
P.O. Box 438652
Chicago, IL 60643

Bishop Hill Old Settlers Association
Descendants of the Bishop Hill Colonists
Box 68
Bishop Hill, IL 61419

Blackhawk Genealogical Society
P.O. Box 3912
Rock Island, IL 61204-3912
URL: http://www.geocities.com/Heartland/Plains/1507/bhgs.htm

Bond County Genealogical Society
P.O. Box 172
Greenville, IL 62246

Bureau County Genealogical Society
P.O. Box 402
Princeton, IL 61356-0402
URL: http://www.anet-chi.com/~jeffb/bureau/bcgs.htm

Carroll County Genealogical Society
P.O. Box 347
Savanna, IL 61074

Cass County Historical & Genealogical Society
P.O. Box 11
Virginia, IL 62691

Champaign County Genealogical Society
c/o Champaign County Historical Archives
201 South Race Street
Urbana, IL 61801-3235

Chicago Genealogical Society
P.O. Box 1160
Chicago, IL 60690-1160
Tel: 773-725-1306
773-834-7491 (library)

Christian County Genealogical Society
P.O. Box 174
Taylorville, IL 62568

Clark County Genealogical Society
309 Maple Street
P.O. Box 153
Marshall, IL 62441

Clay County Genealogical Society
P.O. Box 94
Louisville, Il 62858

Coles County Genealogical Society
P.O. Box 592
Charleston, IL 61920

Council of Northeastern Illinois Genealogical Societies
820 Lisdowney Dr.
Lockport, IL 60441

Crawford County Genealogical Society
P.O. Box 120
Robinson, IL 62454

Cumberland County Genealogical Society
P.O. Box 393
Greenup, IL 62428

Czech & Slovak American Genealogy Society of Illinois
P.O. Box 313
Sugar Grove, IL 60554
URL: http://members.aol.com/chrismik/csagsi/csagsi.htm

Decatur Genealogical Society/Library
356 North Main Street
P.O. Box 1548
Decatur, IL 62525-1548
Tel: 217-429-0135
URL: http://www.decaturnet.org/genesociety.html

DeKalb County Historical-Genealogical Society
DeKalb County Courthouse
P.O. Box 295
Sycamore, IL 60178-0295
Tel: 815-756-1048

Des Plaines Genealogical Questors
Des Plaines Historical Society
789 Pearson
Des Plaines, IL 60016-4506
Tel: 847-391-5399

DeWitt County Genealogical Society
P.O. Box 632
Clinton, IL 61727

Douglas County Genealogical Society
P.O. Box 113
Tuscola, IL 61953

Dunton Genealogical Society
Arlington Hieghts Memorial Library
500 North Dunton
Arlington Heights, IL 60004-5966
Tel: 847-392-0100

DuPage County, Illinois, Genealogical Society
P.O. Box 133
Lombard, IL 60148-0133
URL: http://www.dcgs.org/

Edgar County Genealogical Society
408 N. Main
P.O. Box 304
Paris, IL 61944-0304
Tel: 217-463-4209
URL: http://www.fgs.org/~fgs/soc0048.htm

Effingham County Genealogical Society
P.O. Box 1166
Effingham, IL 62401

Elgin Genealogical Society
P.O. Box 1418
Elgin, IL 60121-1418
Email: egs@listserv.nslsilus
URL: http://nsn.nslsilus.org/elghome/egs/index.html

Elmhurst, Genealogical Forum of
120 East Park Avenue
Elmhurst, IL 60126-3420
Tel: 630-832-2600

Farmer City Genealogical & Historical Society
P.O. Box 173
Farmer City, IL 61842

Fayette County Genealogical Society
P.O. Box 177
Vandalia, IL 62471

Fox Valley Genealogical Society
705 North Brainerd St.
P.O. Box 5435
Naperville, IL 60567-5435
Tel: 630-355-4370
Email: fvgs1@aol.com
URL: http://members.aol.com/fvgs1/index.html

Frankfort Area Genealogical Society
P.O. Box 427
West Frankfort, IL 62896-0427

Franklin County Genealogical Society
P.O. Box 524
West Frankfort, IL 62896

Freeburg Genealogical & Historical Society
P.O. Box 69
Freeburg, IL 62243

Fulton County Historical & Genealogical Society
45 North Park Drive
P.O. Box 583
Canton, IL 61520
URL: http://www.outfitters.com/illinois/history/family/fulton/fulton.html

Grayslake Genealogical Society
c/o Grayslake Historical Municipal Museum
164 Hauley Street
P.O. Box 185
Grayslake, IL 60030-0185
Tel: 708-223-4978

Great River Genealogical Society
c/o Quincy Public Library
526 Jersey Street
Quincy, IL 62301-3996
Email: jeankay@bcl.net
URL: http://www.outfitters.com/~grgs/

Green Hills Genealogical Society
c/o Green Hills Library
8611 West 103rd Street
Palos Hills, IL 60465

Greene County Genealogical & Historical Society
P.O. Box 137
Carrollton, IL 62016

Griggsville Area Genealogical & Historical Society
P.O. Box 75
Griggsville, IL 62340

Hancock County Genealogical & Historical Society
P.O. Box 68
Carthage, IL 62321

Hardin County Historical & Genealogical Society
P.O. Box 72
Elizabethtown, IL 62931

Henry County Genealogical Society
P.O. Box 346
Kewanee, IL 61443

Henry Historical & Genealogical Society
610 North Street
Henry, IL 61537

Illiana Genealogical & Historical Society
19 E. North Street
P.O. Box 207
Danville, IL 61834-0207

Illinois Mennonite Historical & Genealogical Society
P.O. Box 819
Metamora, IL 61548

Illinois State Genealogical Society
P.O. Box 10195
Springfield, IL 62791-0195
URL: http://smtp.tbox.com/isgs/

Iroquois County Genealogical Society
Old Courthouse
103 West Cherry Street
Watseka, IL 60970
Tel: 815-432-3730

Jacksonville Area Genealogical & Historical Society
P.O. Box 21
Jacksonville, IL 62650

Jasper County Genealogical & Historical Society
c/o Newton Public Library
100 South Van Buren
Newton, IL 62448

Jefferson County Genealogical Society
c/o C.E. Brehm Memorial Library
101 South Seventh Street
Mt. Vernon, IL 62864-4187

Jersey County Genealogical Society
P.O. Box 12
Jerseyville, IL 62052

Jewish Genealogical Society of Illinois
P.O. Box 515
Northbrook, IL 60065-0515

Jewish Genealogical Society, South Suburban Branch
c/o Ellen Kahn
3416 Ithaca
Olympia Fields, IL 60461

Kane County Genealogical Society
P.O. Box 504
Geneva, IL 60134-0504
Tel: 630-695-5893
Email: ederd@mail.jostens.com
URL: http://users.ilnk.com/ejcornell/Kane_co.htm

Kankakee Valley Genealogical Society
P.O. Box 442
Bourbonnais, Il 60914-0442
Tel: 815-933-5529
URL: http://www.keynet.net/~lee/k3gensoc.html

Kendall County Genealogical Society
P.O. Box 123
Yorkville, IL 60560-0123

Knox County Genealogical Society
P.O. Box 13
Galesburg, IL 61401-0013

LaHarpe Historical & Genealogical Society
P.O. Box 289
LaHarpe, IL 61450

Lake County, Illinois, Genealogical Society
P.O. Box 721
Libertyville, IL 60048-0721
URL: http://www.fgs.org/~fgs/soc0108.htm

LaSalle County Genealogical Guild
115 West Glover Street
Ottawa, IL 61350
Tel: 815-433-5261
Email: dpc@mtco.com
URL: http://genealogy.org/~dpc/welcome1.html

Lawrence County Genealogical Society
RR 1, Box 44
Bridgeport, IL 62417

Lee County Genealogical Society
310 1/2 Cedar Street (library)
P.O. Box 63
Dixon, IL 61021-0063
Tel: 815-288-6702
Email: dave.needham@pegasoft-dixon.org
URL: http://www.rootsweb.com/~illee/lcgs.htm

Lexington Genealogical & Historical Society
318 W. Main Street
Lexington, IL 61753

Lithuanian American Genealogical Society
c/o Balzekas Museum of Lithuanian Culture
6500 South Pulaski Road
Chicago, IL 60629-5136
Tel: 773-582-6500

Logan County Genealogical & Historical Society
P.O. Box 283
Lincoln, IL 62656

Macoupin County Genealogical Society
P.O. Box 95
Staunton, IL 62088-0095
Email: smckenzi@midwest.net
URL: http://www.rootsweb.com/~ilmacoup/m_gensoc.htm

Madison County Genealogical Society
P.O. Box 631
Edwardsville, IL 62025
Tel: 618-692-7556
URL: http://library.wustl.edu/~spec/archives/aslaa/madison-genealogy.html

Marion County Genealogical & Historical Society
P.O. Box 342
Salem, IL 62881

Marissa Genealogical & Historical Society
P.O. Box 47
Marissa, IL 62257-0047
Tel: 618-295-2562
URL: http://library.wustl.edu/~spec/archives/aslaa/marissa.html

Mason County Genealogical & Historical Society
P.O. Box 246
Havana, IL 62644

Massac County Genealogical Society
P.O. Box 1043
Metropolis, IL 62960

McDonough County Genealogical Society
P.O. Box 202
Macomb, IL 61455
URL: http://www.macomb.com/mcgs/

McHenry County, Illinois, Genealogical Society
P.O. Box 184
Crystal Lake, IL 60039-0184
Tel: 815-385-0686
URL: http://www.fgs.org/~fgs/soc0116.htm

McLean County Genealogical Society
Old Courthouse Museum/Library
200 N. Main Street
Bloomington, IL
Mail:
P.O. Box 488
Normal, IL 61761-0488
URL: http://www.ice.net/public/courthouse/muse.html

Mercer County Genealogical & Historical Society
RR 2
Aledo, IL 61231

Meredosia Area Historical & Genealogical Society
P.O. Box 304
Meredosia, IL 62665

Montgomery County Genealogical Society
P.O. Box 212
Litchfield, IL 62056

Morgan Area Genealogical Association
P.O. Box 84
Jacksonville, IL 62651-0084

Moultrie County Genealogical & Historical Society
P.O. Box MM
Sullivan, IL 61951

Mt. Vernon Genealogical Society
c/o Mt. Vernon Public Library
101 South Seventh Street
Mt. Vernon, IL 62864

North Central Illinois Genealogical Society
P.O. Box 4635
Rockford, IL 61110-4635

North Suburban Genealogical Society
c/o Winnetka Public Library
768 Oak Street
Winnetka, IL 60093-2583
Tel: 847-446-7220
URL: http://www.fgs.org/~fgs/soc0139.htm

Northern Will County Genealogical Society
603 Derbyshire Lane
Bolingbrook, IL 60439

Northwest Suburban Council of Genealogists
P.O. Box AC
Mt. Prospect, IL 60056-9019
Tel: 847-394-3897

Odell Prairie Trails Historical & Genealogical Society
P.O. Box 82
Odell, IL 60460

Ogle County Genealogical Society
P.O. Box 251
Oregon, IL 61061

Peoria Genealogical Society
P.O. Box 1489
Peoria, IL 61655

Piatt County Genealogical & Historical Society
P.O. Box 111
Monticello, IL 61856

Pike/Calhoun Counties Genealogical Society
P.O. Box 104
Pleasant Hill, IL 62366

Polish Genealogical Society of America
Polish Museum of America
984 North Milwaukee Avenue
Chicago, IL 60622
Tel: 773-384-3352
URL: http://www.fgs.org/~fgs/soc0151.htm

Poplar Creek Genealogical Society
200 Kosan Circle
Streamwood, IL 60103

Randolph County Genealogical Society/Library
600 State Street, Suite 306
Chester, IL 62233

Richland County Genealogical & Historical Society
P.O. Box 202
Olney, IL 62450

St. Clair County Genealogical Society
P.O. Box 431
Belleville, IL 62222
Tel: 815-233-3000

Saline County Genealogical Society
P.O. Box 4
Harrisburg, IL 62946

Sangamon County Genealogical Society
P.O. Box 1829
Springfield, IL 62705

Schaumburg Genealogical Society
c/o Schaumburg Public Library
32 West Library Lane
Schaumburg, IL 60194

Schuyler-Brown Genealogical & Historical Society
Schuyler Jail Museum
200 South Congress
Rushville, IL 62681

Shelby County Genealogical & Historical Society
P.O. Box 286
Shelbyville, IL 62565

Sons of the American Revolution
State of Illinois
http://www.execpc.com/~drg/sril.html

South Suburban Genealogical and Historical Society
320 East 161st Place
Mail:
P.O. Box 96
South Holland, IL 60473-0096
Tel: 708-333-9474
URL: http://www.fgs.org/~fgs/soc0174.htm
or http://www.rootsweb.com/~ssghs/ssghs.htm

Southern Illinois, Genealogy Society of
c/o John A. Logan College
700 Logan College Road
Carterville, IL 62918
URL: http://jal.cc.il.us/gssi.html

Stark County Genealogical Society
P.O. Box 83
Toulon, IL 61483

Stephenson County Genealogical Society
P.O. Box 514
Freeport, IL 61032-0514
URL: http://www.fgs.org/~fgs/soc0180.htm

Tazewell County Genealogical Society
P.O. Box 312
Pekin, IL 61555-0312

Tinley Moraine Genealogical Society
P.O. Box 521
Tinley Park, IL 60477-0521

Tri-State Genealogical Society
c/o Willard Library
21 First Avenue
Evansville, IN 47710
Tel: 812-425-4309
Email: tsgs@evansville.net
URL: http://www.evansville.net/~tsgs/tsgs.html

Union County Genealogical & Historical Society
101 East Spring Street
Anna, IL 62906

Versailles Area Genealogical & Historical Society
P.O. Box 92
Versailles, IL 62378

Warren County Genealogy Society
Genealogy Room
58 Public Square
Monmouth, IL
Mail:
P.O. Box 761
Monmouth, IL 61462-0761
URL: http://www.misslink.net/warrenlibrary/genhome.htm

Waverly Genealogical & Historical Society
157 E. Tremont
Waverly, IL 62692

Western Springs Genealogical Society
c/o Western Springs Historical Society
Grand Avenue School
4211 Grand Avenue
P.O. Box 139
Western Springs, IL 60558-0139
Tel: 708-246-7073

Whiteside County Genealogists
P.O. Box 145
Sterling, IL 61081

Will/Grundy Counties Genealogical Society
P.O. Box 24
Wilmington, IL 60481-0024
URL: http://www.fgs.org/~fgs/soc0201.htm

Winnebago/Boone Counties Genealogical Society
P.O. Box 10166
Rockford, IL 61131-0166

Zion Genealogical Society
c/o Zion Benton Public Library
2400 Gabriel Avenue
Zion, IL 60099-2296
Tel: 847-623-3501

HISTORICAL SOCIETIES

Adams and Quincy County Historical Society
425 South 12th
Quincy, IL 62301
Tel: 217-222-1835
URL: http://library.wustl.edu/~spec/archives/aslaa/quincy.html

African-American Genealogical and Historical Society (AAHGS)
P.O. Box 377651
Chicago, IL 60637-7651

African-American Genealogical and Historical Society (AAHGS)
Little Egypt
703 South Wall Street #5
Carbondale, IL 62901

African-American Genealogical and Historical Society (AAHGS)
Patricia Liddell Researchers
P.O. Box 438652
Chicago, IL 60643

American Historical Society of Germans from Russia (AHSGR)
Northern Illinois Chapter
961 E. 166th Place
South Holland, IL 60473
Tel: 708-333-4506
URL: http://www.teleport.com/nonprofit/ahsgr/ilnorthe.html

Arlington Heights, Historical Society of
110 West Fremont
Arlington Heights, IL 60004-5912
Tel: 847-255-1225

Barrington Area Historical Society
212-218 West Main Street
Barrington, IL 60010
Tel: 847-381-1730

Bartlett Historical Society
P.O. Box 8257
Bartlett, IL 60103-8257
Tel: 630-837-0800

Berwyn Historical Society
P.O. Box 479
Berwyn, IL 60402-0479
Tel: 708-484-0020

Blue Island Historical Society
c/o Blue Island Public Library
2433 York Street
Blue Island, IL 60406-2094
Tel: 708-371-8546

Bureau County Historical Society/Library & Museum
109 Park Avenue West
Princeton, IL 61356
Tel: 815-875-2184

Calumet City Historical Society
P.O. Box 1917
Calumet City, IL 60409-3515
Tel: 708-862-8662

Chicago & East Illinois Railroad Historical Society
P.O. Box 606
Crestwood, IL 60445-0606
Tel: 708-385-8182
URL: http://www.justnet.com/cei/index.html

Chicago & Northwestern Railroad Historical Society/Archives
1812 Hood Avenue
Chicago, IL 60660
Tel: 773-743-1159

Chicago & Northwestern Railroad Historical Society
8703 North Olcott Avenue
Niles, IL 60648-2023
Tel: 773-794-5633

Chicago Heights Historical Society
15th Street & Chicago Road
Chicago Heights, IL 60411
Tel: 708-754-0323

Chicago Historical Society
Clark Street at North Avenue
Chicago, IL 60614-6099
Tel: 312-642-5035 ext. 356
Fax: 312-266-2077
URL: http://www.chicagohs.org/

Chicago Jewish Historical Society
618 South Michigan Avenue
Chicago, IL 60605
Tel: 312-580-2020

Chicago Lawn Historical Society
4043 West 63rd Street
Chicago, IL 60629-4638
Tel: 773-582-8778

Cicero, Historical Society of
2423 South Austin Boulevard
Cicero, IL 60650-2695
Tel: 708-652-8305

Clinton County Historical Society
1091 Franklin Street
Carlyle, IL 62231

Croatian Ethnic Institute
4851 South Drexel Blvd.
Chicago, IL 60615
Tel: 773-373-2248

Cumberland County Historical Society
RR 2, Box 39
Greenup, IL 62428

DeKalb County Historical-Genealogical Society
DeKalb County Courthouse
P.O. Box 295
Sycamore, IL 60178-0295
Tel: 815-756-1048

Des Plaines Historical Society/Museum/Library
789 Pearson
Des Plaines, IL 60016-4506
Tel: 847-391-5399

East Side Historical Society
3658 East 106th Street
Chicago, IL 60617-6611
Tel: 773-721-7948

Edgewater Historical Society
1112 West Bryn Mawr
Chicago, IL 60660-4410
Tel: 773-334-5609

Elk Grove Historical Society
399 Biesterfield Road
Elk Grove, IL 60007-3625
Tel: 847-439-3994

Elmwood Park, Historical Society of
c/o Elmwood Park Library
2823 North 77th Avenue
Elmwood Park, IL 60635-1408
Tel: 630-453-1133

Evanston Historical Society/Museum & Library
225 Greenwood Street
Evanston, IL 60201-4713
Tel: 847-475-3410
URL: http://www.adena.com/ehs/res.htm

Evergreen Park Historical Society
3538 West 98th Street
Evergreen Park, IL 60642

Farmer City Genealogical & Historical Society
P.O. Box 173
Farmer City, IL 61842

Filipino-American Historical Society
5462 S. Dorchester Avenue
Chicago, IL 60615-5309
Tel: 773-752-2156

Flagg Creek Historical Society
P.O. Box 227
Western Springs, IL 60558
Tel: 708-246-4142

Forest Park, Historical Society of
519 Jackson Blvd.
Forest Park, Il 60130-1896
Tel: 708-771-7716

Freeburg Genealogical & Historical Society
P.O. Box 69
Freeburg, IL 62243

Fulton County Historical & Genealogical Society
45 North Park Drive
P.O. Box 583
Canton, IL 61520
URL: http://www.outfitters.com/illinois/history/family/fulton/fulton.html

Glencoe Historical Society
999 Green Bay Road
Glencoe, IL 60022-1263
Tel: 847-835-4935

Glenview Area Historical Society
1121 Waukegan Road
Glenview, IL 60025-3036
Tel: 847-724-2235

Greene County Genealogical & Historical Society
P.O. Box 137
Carrollton, IL 62016

Griggsville Area Genealogical & Historical Society
P.O. Box 75
Griggsville, IL 62340

Grove Heritage Association
P.O. Box 484
Glenview, IL 60025-0484
Tel: 847-299-6096

Hancock County Genealogical & Historical Society
P.O. Box 68
Carthage, IL 62321

Hardin County Historical & Genealogical Society
P.O. Box 72
Elizabethtown, IL 62931

Hazel Crest Historical Trust Fund
3102 West 175th Street
Hazel Crest, IL 60429-1623
Tel: 708-335-0929

Henry Historical & Genealogical Society
610 North Street
Henry, IL 61537

Historic Pullman Foundation, Inc.
11111 S. Forrestville Avenue
Chicago, IL 60628-4649
Tel: 773-785-8181

Homewood Historical Society
2035 West 183rd Street
P.O. Box 1144
Homewood, IL 60430
Tel: 708-799-1896

Hyde Park Historical Society
5529 South Lake Park
Chicago, IL 60637-1916
Tel: 773-493-1893

Illiana Genealogical & Historical Society/Library
19 E. North Street
P.O. Box 207
Danville, IL 61834-0207

Illinois Heritage Association
602 1/2 East Green Street
Champaign, IL 61820
Tel: 217-359-5600
Email: plmxiha@prairienet.org
URL: http://www.prairienet.org/iha/

Illinois Mennonite Historical & Genealogical Society
P.O. Box 819
Metamora, IL 61548

Illinois State Historical Society
210 South Sixth Street, Suite 210
Springfield, IL
Mail/Library:
1 Old State Capitol Plaza
Springfield, IL 62701-1507
Tel: 217-782-2635
217-782-4286
Fax: 217-524-8042
Email: ishs@eosinc.com
URL: http://www.prairienet.org/ishs/

Illinois Labor History Society
28 East Jackson Blvd.
Chicago, IL 60604-2215
Tel: 312-663-4107

Illinois Postal History Society
P.O. Box 1513
Des Plaines, IL 60017-1513
Tel: 847-443-4442

Irving Park Historical Society
4122 North Kedvale
Chicago, IL 60641-2245
Tel: 773-736-2143

Jackson County Historical Society
P.O. Box 7
Murphysboro, IL 62956

Jacksonville Area Genealogical & Historical Society
P.O. Box 21
Jacksonville, IL 62650

Jasper County Genealogical & Historical Society
c/o Newton Public Library
100 South Van Buren
Newton, IL 62448

LaGrange Area Historical Society
444 South LaGrange Road
LaGrange, IL 60525-2448
Tel: 847-482-4248

LaHarpe Historical & Genealogical Society
P.O. Box 289
LaHarpe, IL 61450

Lansing Historical Society
P.O. Box 1776
Lansing, IL 60438-0633
Tel: 708-474-6160

Lemont Area Historical Society/Museum
306 Lemont Street
P.O. Box 126
Lemont, IL 60439-0126
Tel: 630-257-2972

Lexington Genealogical & Historical Society
318 W. Main Street
Lexington, IL 61753

Leyden Historical Society
P.O. Box 506
Franklin Park, IL 60131
Tel: 847-678-1929

Logan County Genealogical & Historical Society
P.O. Box 283
Lincoln, IL 62656

Lyons Historical Commission
P.O. Box 392
Lyons, IL 60534-0392
Tel: 630-447-7907

Macoupin County Historical Society/Library & Museum
Breckenridge Street
P.O. Box 432
Carlinville, IL 62626
Tel: 217-854-8916
or 217-854-8500
URL: http://www.rootsweb.com/~ilmacoup/m_hstsoc.htm

Maine West Historical Society
Maine West High School
1755 S. Wolf Road
Des Plaines, IL 60018-1994
Tel: 847-827-6176

Marissa Genealogical & Historical Society
P.O. Box 47
Marissa, IL 62257-0047
Tel: 618-295-2562
URL: http://library.wustl.edu/~spec/archives/aslaa/marissa.html

Marshall County Historical Society
314 Fifth Street
P.O. Box 123
Lacon, IL 61540-0123
URL: http://www.rootsweb.com/~ilmarsha/mphs.htm

Mason County Genealogical & Historical Society
P.O. Box 246
Havana, IL 62644

Matteson Historical Society/Museum
813 School Avenue
Matteson, IL 60443
Tel: 708-748-3033

Maywood Historical Society
202 South 2nd Avenue
Maywood, IL 60153-2304
Tel: 630-344-4282

McLean County Historical Society
Old Courthouse Museum
200 N. Main Street
Bloomington, IL 61701
Tel: 309-827-0428
URL: http://www.ice.net/public/courthouse/muse.html or http://www.dave-world.net/community/mchs/mchs.html

Melrose Park Historical Society
P.O. Box 1453
Melrose Park, IL 60160

Mercer County Genealogical & Historical Society
RR 2
Aledo, IL 61231

Meredosia Area Historical & Genealogical Society
P.O. Box 304
Meredosia, IL 62665

Midlothian Historical Society
14609 Springfield
Midlothian, IL 60445
Tel: 708-389-5066

Morton Grove Historical Society/Museum
Haupt-Yehl House
Harrer Park
6240 Dempster Street
P.O. Box 542
Morton Grove, IL 60053-2946
Tel: 847-965-7185

Moultrie County Genealogical & Historical Society
P.O. Box MM
Sullivan, IL 61951

Mt. Greenwood Historical Society
c/o Mt. Greenwood Public Library
11010 South Kedzie Avenue
Chicago, IL 60655-2222
Tel: 773-239-2805

Mt. Prospect Historical Society/Museum
1100 South Linneman Road & 101 S. Maple
P.O. Box 81
Mt. Prospect, IL 60056-0081
Tel: 847-392-9006

National Baha'i Archives
Wilmette, IL 60091
Tel: 847-869-9039

National Railway Historical Society
Chicago Chapter
P.O. Box 53
Oak Park, IL 60303-0053
Tel: 708-386-2809

Neponset Township Historical Society/Museum
Neponset, IL 61345
Tel: 309-594-2197

North Eastern Illinois Historical Council
7007 Fargo Avenue
Niles, IL 60714-3719
Tel: 847-647-0185

Northbrook Historical Society
1776 Walters Avenue
P.O. Box 2021
Northbrook, IL 60065
Tel: 847-998-1322

Norwood Park Historical Society
5624 North Newark Avenue
Chicago, IL 60631-3137
Tel: 773-631-1496

Oak Forest Historical Society
15440 South Central Avenue
Oak Forest, IL 60452-2104
Tel: 708-687-4050

Oak Lawn Historical Society
9526 South Cook Avenue
Oak Lawn, IL 60453
Tel: 708-425-3424

Oak Park and River Forest, Historical Society/Museum of
217 Home
P.O. Box 771
Oak Park, IL 60303-0771
Tel: 708-848-6755

Odell Prairie Trails Historical & Genealogical Society
P.O. Box 82
Odell, IL 60460

O'Fallon Historical Society/Museum
101 West State Street
P.O. Box 344
O'Fallon, IL 62269
URL: http://www.ofallon.com/museum/index.shtml

Old Edgebrook Historical Society
6173 North McClellan
Chicago, IL 60646-4013
Tel: 773-631-2854

Orland Historical Society
P.O. Box 324
Orland Park, IL 60462-0324
Tel: 708-349-3216

Palatine Historical Society
P.O. Box 134
Palatine, IL 60078-0134
Tel: 847-991-6460

Palos Heights Historical Society
7607 College Drive
Palos Heights, IL 60463

Palos Historical Society
12332 Forest Glen Boulevard
Palos Park, IL 60464-1707
Tel: 708-448-1410

Park Forest Historical Society
400 Lakewood Blvd.
Park Forest, IL 60466-1684
Tel: 708-748-3731

Park Ridge Historical Society
41 West Prairie Avenue
Park Ridge, IL 60068

Perry County Historical Society
Perry County Jail Museum
108 W. Jackson Street
Pinckneyville, IL 62274
Tel: 618-357-2225
URL: http://www.fnbpville.com/perrycounty.html

Piatt County Genealogical & Historical Society
P.O. Box 111
Monticello, IL 61856

Putnam County Historical Society
P.O. Box 74
Hennepin, IL 61327

Ravenswood-Lakeview Historical Society
4455 N. Lincoln Avenue
Chicago, IL 60625-2192
Tel: 773-442-7616

Richland County Genealogical & Historical Society
P.O. Box 202
Olney, IL 62450

Rock Island County Historical Society
P.O. Box 632
Moline, IL 61265

Ridge Historical Society
10621 South Seely Avenue
Chicago, IL 60643-2618
Tel: 773-445-5806

Riverdale Historical Society
c/o Riverdale Library
208 West 144th Street
Riverdale, IL 60627-2788
Tel: 630-841-3311

Robbins Historical Society
P.O. Box 1561
Robbins, IL 60472-1561
Tel: 708-389-5393

Rogers Park Historical Society
2555 West Farwell
Chicago, IL 60645-4617
Tel: 773-764-2401

St. Clair County Historical Society
701 East Washington Street
Belleville, IL 62220
Tel: 618-234-0600
URL: http://library.wustl.edu/~spec/archives/aslaa/stclair_historical.html

Schiller Park Historical Society
4501 North 25th Avenue
Schiller Park, IL 60176
Tel: 847-678-2550

Sheffield Historical Society/Museum
Corner of Cook and Washington
Sheffield, IL 61361
Tel: 815-454-2788

Shelby County Genealogical & Historical Society
P.O. Box 286
Shelbyville, IL 62565

Skokie Historical Society
8031 Floral
Skokie, IL 60077
Tel: 847-675-3674

Society of American Archivists
600 South Federal, Suite 504
Chicago, IL 60605-1898
Tel: 312-922-0140

South Holland Historical Society/Museum
South Holland Public Library
16250 Wausau Avenue, Lower Level
P.O. Box 48
South Holland, IL 60473-0048
Tel: 708-596-2722

South Shore Historical Society
7566 South Shore Drive
Chicago, IL 60649
Tel: 773-375-1699

South Side Irish Archives Project
South Side Irish Parade and Heritage Foundation
10926 South Western Avenue

Chicago, IL 60643
Tel: 773-238-1969

South Suburban Genealogical and Historical Society
Roosevelt Center
320 East 161st Place
Mail:
P.O. Box 96
South Holland, IL 60473-0096
Tel: 708-333-9474
URL: http://www.fgs.org/~fgs/soc0174.htm
or http://www.rootsweb.com/~ssghs/ssghs.htm

South Suburban Heritage Association
P.O. Box 716
Tinley Park, IL 60477-3450
Tel: 708-614-8713

Stone Park Historical Association
Village Hall
1629 N. Mannheim Road
Stone Park, IL 60165-1118
Tel: 630-345-2272

Streamwood Historical Society/Museum
777 West Bartlett Road
Streamwood, IL 60107-1394
Tel: 630-289-3276

Swedish-American Historical Society/Library
5125 North Spaulding Avenue
Chicago, IL 60625-4816
Tel: 773-583-2700 ext. 5267

Thornton Historical Society/Library and Museum
208 Schwab Street
P.O. Box 34
Thornton, IL 60476-0034
Tel: 708-877-9394

Thornton Township Historical Society
154 East 154th
Harvey, IL 60426-3326
Tel: 708-331-4247

Tinley Park Historical Society/Museum
6727 West 174th Street
P.O. Box 325
Tinley Park, IL 60477-0325
Tel: 708-429-4210
Email: lrtphist@lincolnnet.net

Triton Community History Organization
Triton College
2000 5th Avenue
River Grove, IL 60171-1995
Tel: 708-456-0300 ext. 245

Union County Genealogical & Historical Society
101 East Spring Street
Anna, IL 62906

Versailles Area Genealogical & Historical Society
P.O. Box 92
Versailles, IL 62378

Washington County Historical Society
326 S. Kaskaskia St.
Nashville, IL 62263

Waverly Genealogical & Historical Society
157 E. Tremont
Waverly, IL 62692

West Side Historical Society
115 S. Pulaski Rd.
Chicago, IL 60624

Westchester Historical Society
10332 Bond Street
Westchester, IL 60154-4361
Tel: 630-865-1972

Western Springs Historical Society/Museum
Grand Avenue School
4211 Grand Avenue
P.O. Box 139
Western Springs, IL 60558-0139
Tel: 708-246-7073

Wheeling Historical Society
P.O. Box 3
Wheeling, IL 60090-0003
Tel: 847-537-0327

White County Historical Society
Ratcliff Inn (library)
P.O. Box 121
Carmi, IL 62821
Email: cbconly@midwest.net
URL: http://www.midwest.net/scribers/cbconly/wchs.htm

Williamson County Historical Society
105 S. Van Buren
Marion, IL 62959
Tel: 618-997-5863

Wilmette Historical Society
565 Hunter Road
Wilmette, IL 60091-2209
Tel: 847-251-8092

Winnetka Historical Society
P.O. Box 142
Winnetka, IL 60093-0142
Tel: 847-501-6025

LDS Family History Centers

Buffalo Grove Family History Center
15 East Port Clinton
Buffalo Grove, IL 60089
Tel: 847-913-5387

Champaign Family History Center
604 West Windsor Road
Champaign, IL 61820
Tel: 217-352-8063

Chicago Heights Family History Center
402 Longwood Drive
Chicago Heights, IL 60411
Tel: 708-754-2525

Naperville Family History Center
1320 Ridgeland Road
Naperville, IL 60563
Tel: 630-505-0233

Nauvoo Family History Center
Corner of Hibbard and Durphy
Nauvoo, IL 62354
Tel: 217-453-6347

O'Fallon Family History Center
255 Fairwood Hills Road
O'Fallon, IL 62269
Tel: 618-632-0210

Peoria Family History Center
3700 West Reservoir Blvd.
Peoria, IL 61615
Tel: 309-682-4073

Rockford Family History Center
620 North Alpine Road
Rockford, IL 61107
Tel: 815-399-2660

Schaumburg Family History Center
1320 West Schaumburg Road
Schaumburg, IL 60194
Tel: 312-885-4130

Springfield Family History Center
3601 Buckeye Drive
Springfield, IL 62707
Tel: 217-529-7930

Wilmette Family History Center
2701 Lake Avenue
Wilmette, IL 60091
Tel: 847-251-9818

Archives/Libraries/Museums

AASR Valley of Chicago
915 North Dearborn Street
Chicago, IL 60610
Tel: 312-787-7605 ext. 9

Algonquin Area Public Library
115 Eastgate Drive
Algonquin, IL 60102
Tel: 847-658-4343
Fax: 847-658-0179
URL: http://www.nslsilus.org/~reference/alkhome.html

American Police Center and Museum
1717 South State Street
Chicago, IL 60616-1215
Tel: 312-431-0005

Arlington Heights Historical Museum
110 W. Fremont
Arlington Heights, IL 60004-5912
Tel: 847-255-1225

Arlington Heights Memorial Library
500 North Dunton
Arlington Heights, IL 60004-5966
Tel: 847-392-0100
Fax: 847-392-0136

Assumption Public Library
131 North Chestnut
P.O. Box 227
Assumption, IL 62510-0227

Augustana College Library
3435 9-1/2 Avenue
Rock Island, IL 61201
Tel: 309-794-7317
Fax: 309-794-7230
Email: libraryinfo@augustana.edu
URL: http://www.augustana.edu/library/

Avalon Branch of the Chicago Public Library
8828 South Stony Island
Chicago, IL 60617
Tel: 312-747-5234

Balzekas Museum of Lithuanian Culture
6500 South Pulaski Road
Chicago, IL 60629-5136
Tel: 773-582-6500
Fax: 773-582-5133

Belleville Public Library
Genealogy Section
121 E. Washington St., #4114
Belleville, Il 62220-2205
Tel: 618-234-0441

Fax: 618-234-9474
URL: http://library.wustl.edu/~spec/archives/aslaa//belleville-public-library.html

Blue Island Public Library
2433 York Street
Blue Island, IL 60406-2094
Tel: 708-388-1078
708-371-8546 (Hist. Soc.)
Fax: 708-388-1143

Bourbonnais Public Libary
250 W. Casey Drive
Bourbonnais, IL 60914
Tel: 815-933-1727
Fax: 815-933-1961

Brehm Memorial Library
101 South Seventh Street
Mount Vernon, IL 62864
Tel: 618-242-6322
Fax: 618-242-0810

Bryan-Bennett Library
217 West Main Street
Salem, IL 62881
Tel: 618-548-7784
Fax: 618-548-9593

Bureau County Historical Society/Library & Museum
109 Park Avenue West
Princeton, IL 61356
Tel: 815-875-2184

Calumet City Historical Society Museum
760 Wentworth Avenue
Calumet City, IL 60409-3515
Tel: 708-862-8662

Carnegie Public Library
712 6th Street
Charleston, IL 61920
Tel: 217-345-4913
Fax: 217-348-5616

Champaign County Historical Archives
201 South Race Street
Urbana, IL 61801-3235

Chicago & Northwestern Railroad Historical Society/Archives
1812 Hood Avenue
Chicago, IL 60660
Tel: 773-743-1159

Chicago Heights Public Library
25 West 15th Street
Chicago, IL 60411
Tel: 773-754-0323
Fax: 773-754-0325

Chicago Historical Society
Clark Street at North Avenue
Chicago, IL 60614-6099
Tel: 312-642-5035 ext. 356
Fax: 312-266-2077
URL: http://www.chicagohs.org/

Chicago Lawn Library
6120 Kedzie Avenue
Chicago, IL 60629-4638
Tel: 312-747-0639
Fax: 312-747-6182

Chicago Municipal Reference Library
City Hall, Room 1004
121 North LaSalle Street
Chicago, IL 60602

Chicago Public Library
Harold Washington Center
Special Collections Department
400 South State Street, 9th Floor
Chicago, IL 60605
Tel: 312-747-4875/6
TDD: 312-747-4969
URL: http://cpl.lib.uic.edu/001hwlc/hwspe.html

Chicago Tribune Archives
Tribune Tower
435 North Michigan Avenue, Rm. 1231
Chicago, IL 60611
Tel: 312-222-3026

Collinsville Memorial Public Library
Collinsville Historical Museum
408 West Main Street
Collinsville, IL 62234
Tel: 618-344-1112
Fax: 618-345-6401
URL: http://www.ezl.com/~cmpl/

Cook Memorial Library
413 N. Milwaukee Avenue
Libertyville, IL 60048
Tel: 847-362-2330
Fax: 847-362-2354
Email: jules@cooklib.org
URL: http://www.cooklib.org/

Crystal Lake Public Library
126 W. Paddock Street
Crystal Lake, IL 60014
Tel: 815-459-1687

Czechoslovak Heritage Museum, Library and Archives
CSA Fraternal Life
122 W. 22nd Street
Oak Brook, IL 60521
Tel: 630-795-5800

Danville Public Library
307 N. Vermilion Street
Danville, IL 61832
Tel: 217-477-5220
Fax: 217-477-5230

Decatur Genealogical Society/Library
356 North Main Street
P.O. Box 1548
Decatur, IL 62525-1548
Tel: -429-0135
URL: http://www.decaturnet.org/genesociety.html

DePaul University Archives
2323 North Seminary
Chicago, IL 60614
Tel: 773-341-8088

Des Plaines Historical Society/Museum/Library
789 Pearson
Des Plaines, IL 60016-4506
Tel: 847-391-5399

Des Plaines Public Library
841 Graceland Avenue
Des Plaines, IL 60016
Tel: 847-827-8551
Email: dppl@nsn.nslsilus.org
URL: http://nsn.nslsilus.org/dpkhome/dppl/index.html

DuPage County Historical Museum
103 East Wesley Street
Wheaton, IL 60187

DuQuoin Public Library
28 S. Washington Street
DuQuoin, IL 62832-1396
Tel: 618-542-5045

DuSable Museum of African-American History/Archives
740 East 56th Place
Chicago, IL 60637-1408
Tel: 773-947-0600

East Side Historical Society Museum
Calumet Park Fieldhouse
9801 Avenue G.
Calumet Park, IL 60617
Tel: 708-721-7948

Edwardsville Public Library
Madison County Genealogical Society Library
112 S. Kansas Street
Edwardsville, IL 62025
Tel: 618-692-7556
Fax: 618-692-9566

Elmhurst Historical Museum
120 East Park Avenue
Elmhurst, IL 60126-3420
Tel: 630-833-1457

Elkwood House Museum
509 N. First Street
DeKalb, IL 60115

Elmwood Park Library
4 Conti Parkway
Elmwood Park, IL 60707
Tel: 630-453-7645
Fax: 630-453-4671

Episcopal Diocese of Chicago
Archives & Historical Collections
St. James Cathedral
65 East Huron
Chicago, IL 60611
Tel: 312-787-6410

Evangelical Covenant Church of America
Archives & Historical Library
125 N. Spaulding Avenue, Rm. 25
Chicago, IL 60637
Tel: 773-583-2700 ext. 287

Evans Public Library
215 S. 5th Street
Vandalia, IL 62471
Tel: 618-283-2824
Fax: 618-283-2705

Evanston Historical Society/Museum & Library
225 Greenwood Street
Evanston, IL 60201-4713
Tel: 773-475-3410

Flagg Creek Historical Museum
Pleasantdale Park District
7425 South Wolf Road
Burr Ridge, IL 60525
Tel: 630-246-4142

Fossil Ridge Library
386 Kennedy Road
Braidwood, IL 60408
Tel: 815-458-2187
Fax: 815-458-2042

Franklin Park Historical Museum
Franklin Park Public Library
9545 West Belmont
Franklin Park, IL 60131-2706
Tel: 847-455-6016

Freeport Public Library
314 W. Stephenson Street
Freeport, IL 61031
Tel: 815-233-3000

Gale Borden Public Library
200 N. Grove Avenue
Elgin, IL 60120

Tel: 847-742-2411
Fax: 847-742-0485
URL: http://nsls1.nslsilus.org/GailB/

Galena Historical Museum
211 South Bench Street
Galena, IL 61036

Galena Public Library
601 S. Bench Street
Galena, IL 61036
Tel: 815-777-0200
Fax: 815-777-0219

Galesburg Public Library
40 East Simmons Street
Galesburg, IL 61401
Tel: 309-343-6118
Fax: 309-343-4877
URL: http://wwwlib.knox.edu/WEB/general/gburglib.htm

Glenview Public Library
1930 Glenview Road
Glenview, IL 60025
Tel: 847-729-7500
Fax: 847-729-7682

German-American Heritage Institute
7824 West Madison Street
Forest Park, IL 60130-1485
Tel: 708-366-0017

Glencoe Historical Museum
999 Green Bay Road
Glencoe, IL 60022-1263
Tel: 847-835-4935

Glenview Area Historical Museum and Library
1121 Waukegan Road
Glenview, IL 60025-3036
Tel: 847-724-2235

Grayslake Historical Municipal Museum
164 Hauley Street
P.O. Box 185
Grayslake, IL 60030-0185
Tel: 708-223-4978

Green Hills Library
8611 West 103rd Street
Palos Hills, IL 60465
Tel: 708-598-8446
Fax: 708-598-0856

Grove National Historic Landmark
1421 Milwaukee Avenue
Glenview, IL 60025-1436
Tel: 847-299-6096

Hellenic Museum and Cultural Center
400 North Franklin Street
Chicago, IL 60610-4403

Homewood Historical Museum
2035 West 183rd Street
Homewood, IL 60430-1044
Tel: 708-799-1896

Illiana Genealogical & Historical Society/Library
19 E. North Street
P.O. Box 207
Danville, IL 61834-0207

Illinois Association for the Preservation of
Historic Arms and Armaments, Inc.
1800 Western Avenue
Flossmoor, IL 60422-0339
Tel: 708-798-1109

Illinois State Historical Society
210 South Sixth Street, Suite 210
Springfield, IL
Mail/Library:
1 Old State Capitol Plaza
Springfield, IL 62701-1507
Tel: 217-782-2635
217-782-4286
Fax: 217-524-8042
Email: ishs@eosinc.com
URL: http://www.prairienet.org/ishs/

Illinois State Library
300 South Second Street
Springfield, IL 62701-1796
Tel: 217-785-5600
800-665-5576 (in Illinois only)
TDD: 217-524-1137 (Circulation desk)
URL: http://www.sos.state.il.us/depts/library/isl_home.html

Illinois Veteran's Home Library
1707 North 12th Street
Quincy, IL 62301
Tel: 217-222-8641 ext. 248
Fax: 217-222-0139

Irish-American Heritage Center Museum and Art Gallery
4626 North Knox Avenue
Chicago, IL 60630-4030
Tel: 773-282-7035

Italian Cultural Center
1621 North 39th Avenue
Stone Park, IL 60165-1105
Tel: 630-345-3842

Jacob & Bernard Hostert Log Cabins
West Avenue and 147th Street
Mail:
14228 Union Avenue
Orland Park, IL 60462-2011
Tel: 708-349-0046

James P. Fitzgibbons Historical Museum
Calumet Park Fieldhouse
9800 Avenue G
Chicago, IL
Mail:
3558 E. 106th Street
Chicago, IL 60617
Tel: 708-721-7948

John Crerar Library
35 West 33rd Street
Chicago, IL 60616
Tel: 312-225-2526

John Mosser Public Library
106 West Meek Street
Abingdon, IL 61410-1450
Tel/Fax: 309-462-3129

Joliet Public Library
150 N. Ottawa Street
Joliet, IL 60431
Tel: 815-740-2660
Fax: 815-740-6161
URL: http://www.htls.lib.il.us/JPB/

Kankakee County Historical Museum
801 South 8th Avenue
Kankakee, IL 60901
Tel: 815-932-5279
URL: http://www.artcom.com/museums/nv/gl/60901-47.htm

Kankakee Public Library
304 S. Indiana Avenue
Kankakee, IL 60901
Tel: 815-939-4564
Fax: 815-939-9057
URL: http://www.keynet.net/~lee/k3libgen.html

Kenilworth Historical Museum and Library
415 Kenilworth Avenue
P.O. Box 181
Kenilworth, IL 60043-1134
Tel: 847-251-2565

Knox College
Seymour Library
2 Cedar Street
P.O. Box 500x
Galesburg, IL 61401-0500
Tel: 309-341-7246 ext. 491
Fax: 309-343-9292
URL: http://wwwlib.knox.edu/

LaGrange Area Historical Museum and Library
444 South LaGrange Road
LaGrange, IL 60525-2448
Tel: 847-482-4248

LaGrange Public Library
10 West Cossitt
LaGrange, IL 60525
Tel: 847-352-0576 ext.10
Fax: 847-352-1620

Lansing Historical Museum
2750 Indiana Avenue
Lansing, IL 60438-0633
Tel: 708-474-6160

Lemont Area Historical Society/Museum
306 Lemont Street
P.O. Box 126
Lemont, IL 60439-0126
Tel: 630-257-2972

Lincoln Library
Sangamon Valley Collection
326 South Seventh Street
Springfield, IL 62701
Tel: 217-753-4900/10
Fax: 217-753-5329

Litchfield Carnegie Library
400 N. State Street
P.O. Box 212
Litchfield, IL 62056-0212
Tel: 217-324-3866
Fax: 217-324-3884

Little Rock Township Public Library
North Center Street
Plano, IL 60545

Loyola University Archives
6525 Sheridan Road
Chicago, IL 60626
Tel: 773-274-3000 ext. 791

Lutheran Church in American Archives
1100 East 55th Street
Chicago, IL 60615
Tel: 773-667-3500

Lyons Public Library
4209 Joliet Avenue
Lyons, IL 60534
Tel: 630-447-3577
Fax: 630-447-3589

Macomb Public Library
Local History/Genealogy Room
235 South Lafayette
P.O. Box 220
Macomb, IL 61455
Tel/Fax: 309-833-2714

Madison County Historical Museum and Library
715 North Main Street
Edwardsville, IL 62025
Tel: 618-656-7562
URL: http://library.wustl.edu/~spec/archives/aslaa madison-historical.html

Malcolm X College
1900 West Van Buren Street
Chicago, IL 60612-3145
Tel: 312-738-5845

Matson Public Library
Bureau County Genealogical Society Collection
15 Park Avenue, West
2nd Floor
Princeton, IL 61356
Tel: 815-875-1331
Fax: 815-875-1376

Matteson Historical Society/Museum
813 School Avenue
Matteson, IL 60443
Tel: 708-748-3033

Mattoon Public Library
1600 Charleston Avenue
P.O. Box 809
Mattoon, IL 61938-0809
Tel: 217-234-2621
Fax: 217-234-2660

McHenry Public Library
809 N. Front St.
McHenry, IL 60050
Tel: 815-385-0036
Fax: 815-385-7035

McLean County Genealogical Society
Old Courthouse Museum/Library
200 N. Main Street
Bloomington, IL
Mail:
P.O. Box 488
Normal, IL 61761-0488
URL: http://www.ice.net/public/courthouse/muse.html

Midwest Archives Conference (MAC) Archives
Northwestern University Library Archives
Evanston, IL 60201
Tel: 847-491-3136

Mitchell Indian Museum at Kendall College
2408 Orrington Avenue
Evanston, IL 60201-2899
Tel: 847-866-1395

Moody Bible Institute Library
820 North LaSalle
Chicago, IL 60610
Tel: 312-329-4140

Morton B. Weiss Museum of Judaica
K.A.M. Isaiah Israel Congregation
100 East Hyde Park Boulevard
Chicago, IL 60615-2899
Tel: 773-924-1234

Morton Grove Historical Society/Museum
Haupt-Yehl House
Harrer Park
6240 Dempster Street
P.O. Box 542
Morton Grove, IL 60053-2946
Tel: 847-965-7185

Morton Grove Public Library
6140 Lincoln Avenue
Morton Grove, IL 60053
Tel: 847-965-4220
TDD: 847-965-4236
Fax: 847-965-7903
Email: refdesk@mgk.nslsilus.org
URL: http://www.nslsilus.org/mgkhome/mgpl/mgpldoc.html

Mt. Greenwood Public Library
11010 South Kedzie Avenue
Chicago, IL 60655-2222
Tel: 773-747-0148

Mt. Prospect Historical Society/Museum
1100 South Linneman Road & 101 S. Maple
P.O. Box 81
Mt. Prospect, IL 60056-0081
Tel: 847-392-9006

Mt. Prospect Public Library
10 South Emerson Street
Mt. Prospect, IL 60056-3251
Tel: 847-253-5675
Fax: 847-253-0642
URL: http://nsls1.nslsilus.org/~mppl/

Mt. Vernon Public Library
101 South Seventh Street
Mt. Vernon, IL 62864

Mundelein College Archives-Chicago
6363 Sheridan Road
Chicago, IL 60660
Tel: 773-262-8100

Newberry Library
60 West Walton Street
Chicago, IL 60610-3305
Tel: 312-943-9090 (Main)
312-255-3506 (Reference)
312-255-3512 (Genealogy)
Email: furmans@newberry.org
URL: http://www.newberry.org/

Niles Historical Society/Museum
8970 Milwaukee Avenue
Niles, IL 60714-1737
Tel: 847-390-0160

Northeastern Illinois University Library
Ronald Williams Library
5500 North St. Louis
Chicago, IL 60625
Tel: 773-583-4050 ext. 479
773-794-6279

Northwestern University Library
Special Collections-Archives
Evanston, IL 60201
Tel: 847-492-3635

Oak Lawn Public Library
9427 South Raymond Avenue
Oak Lawn, IL 60453
Tel: 708-422-2990
Fax: 708-422-5061

Oak Park and River Forest, Historical Society/Museum of
217 Home
P.O. Box 771
Oak Park, IL 60303-0771
Tel: 708-848-6755

Oak Park Public Library
834 Lake Street
Oak Park, IL 60301
Tel: 708-383-8200
Fax: 708-383-6384

O'Fallon Historical Society/Museum
101 West State Street
P.O. Box 344
O'Fallon, IL 62269
URL: http://www.ofallon.com/museum/index.shtml

Paarlberg Farmstead Homestead
172nd Place and Paxton Avenue
P.O. Box 48
South Holland, IL 60473-0048
Tel: 708-596-2722

Palatine Park District
Clayson House Museum
224 East Palatine Road
P.O. Box 134
Palatine, IL 60078-0134
Tel: 847-991-6460

Parlin-Ingersoll Library
205 West Chestnut
Canton, IL 61520-2499
Tel: 309-647-0328
Fax: 309-647-8117
Email: kbunner@darkstar.rsa.lib.il.us
URL: http://www.rsa.lib.il.us/~kbunner/parlin.htm

Peoria Public Library
107 NE Monroe Street
Peoria, IL 61602
Tel: 309-672-8858
Fax: 309-674-0116

Plainfield Public Library
705 N. Illinois Street
Plainfield, IL 60544
Tel: 815-436-6639
Fax: 815-439-2878
URL: http://www.htls.lib.il.us/PLB/

Polish Museum of America
984 North Milwaukee Avenue
Chicago, IL 60622-4101
Tel: 312-384-3352

Poplar Creek Public Library District
1405 South Park Avenue
Streamwood, IL 60107-2997
Tel: 630-837-6800

Quincy Public Library
526 Jersey Street
Quincy, IL 62301-3996
Tel: 217-223-1309
Fax: 217-222-3052

Randolph County Genealogical Society/Library
600 State Street, Suite 306
Chester, IL 62233

Reddick Library
1010 Canal Street
Ottawa, IL 61350
Tel: 815-434-0509
Fax: 815-434-2634

Riverdale Library
208 West 144th Street
Riverdale, IL 60627-2788
Tel: 630-841-3311

Riverside Historical Museum
Longommon and Pine Roads
27 Riverside Road
Riverside, IL 60546-2264
Tel: 630-442-0711

Rock Island Public Library
401 19th Street
Rock Island, IL 61201
Tel: 309-788-7627
Fax: 309-788-6591

Rockford Public Library
215 N. Wyman Street
Rockford, IL 61101
Tel: 815-965-6731
TDD: 815-965-3007
Fax: 815-965-0866

Romanian Folk Art Museum
2526 Ridgeway
Evanston, IL 60201-1160
Tel: 847-328-9099

Saint Peter Lutheran Church Museum
208 East Schaumburg Rd.
Schaumburg, IL 60194
Tel: 847-843-0799

Schaumburg Public Library
32 West Library Lane
Schaumburg, IL 60194
Tel: 847-885-3373
Fax: 847-885-7348
URL: http://www.stdl.org/

Schuyler Jail Museum
200 South Congress
P.O. Box 96
Rushville, IL 62681

Sheffield Historical Society/Museum
Sheffield, IL 61361
Tel: 815-454-2788

South Holland Historical Society/Museum
South Holland Public Library
16250 Wausau Avenue, Lower Level
P.O. Box 48
South Holland, IL 60473-0048
Tel: 708-596-2722

South Suburban Genealogical and Historical Society Library
320 East 161st Place
Mail:
P.O. Box 96
South Holland, IL 60473-0096
Tel: 708-333-9474
URL: http://www.fgs.org/~fgs/soc0174.htm

Spertus Museum
618 South Michigan Avenue
Chicago, IL 60605-1901
Tel: 312-922-9012
Fax: 312-922-6406

Staunton Public Library
George and Santina Sawyer Genealogy Room
306 West Main
Staunton, IL 62088
Mail:
Macoupin County Genealogical Society
P.O. Box 95
Staunton, IL 62088-0095
Email: smckenzi@midwest.net
URL: http://www.rootsweb.com/~ilmacoup/m_gensoc.htm

Streamwood Historical Society/Museum
777 West Bartlett Road
Streamwood, IL 60107-1394
Tel: 630-289-3276

Swedish-American Historical Society/Library
5125 North Spaulding Avenue
Chicago, IL 60625-4816
Tel: 773-583-2700 ext. 5267

Swedish-American Museum Center
5211 N. Clark Street
Chicago, IL 60640-2101
Tel: 773-728-8111

Swenson Swedish Immigration Research Center
Augustana College
639 38th Street
Rock Island, IL 61201-2273
Tel: 309-794-7204
Fax: 309-794-7443
Email: swsa@augustana.edu
URL: http://www2.augustana.edu/admin/swenson/

Thornton Historical Society/Library and Museum
208 Schwab Street
P.O. Box 34
Thornton, IL 60476-0034
Tel: 708-877-9394

Three Rivers Public Library
25207 W. Channon Dr.
P.O. Box 300
Channahon, IL 60410-0300
Tel: 815-467-6200
Fax: 815-467-4012

Tinley Park Historical Society/Museum
6727 West 174th Street
P.O. Box 325
Tinley Park, IL 60477-0325
Tel: 708-429-4210

Trailside Museum
738 Thatcher Avenue
River Forest, IL 60305
Tel: 708-366-6530

Ukrainian National Museum
2453 West Chicago Avenue
Chicago, IL 60622-4633
Tel: 773-276-6565

University of Chicago
Joseph Regenstein Library
1100 East 57th Street
Chicago, IL 60637
Tel: 773-753-2887
773-962-8705

University of Illinois at Urbana-Champaign
University Archives
1408 W. Gregory Drive
Urbana, IL 61801
Tel: 217-333-0798 (Archives)
217-333-8400 (General Information)
Fax: 217-333-2214
Email: illiarch@uiuc.edu
URL: http://www.staff.uiuc.edu/~jstraw/ahx/default.html
or http://www.library.uiuc.edu/

University of Illinois at Chicago
801 S. Morgan, Room 220
P.O. Box 8198
Chicago, IL 60607
Tel: 312-996-2756

Urbana Free Library
201 South Race Street
Urbana, IL 61801
Tel: 217-367-4057
Fax: 217-367-4061

Vogel Genealogical Research Library
305 1st Street, Box 132
Holcomb, IL 64043

Warren County Library
60-62 Public Square
Monmouth, IL 61462
Tel: 309-734-3166
Fax: 309-734-5955
Email: warren.library@misslink.net
URL: http://www.misslink.net/warrenlibrary/

Western Springs Historical Society/Museum
Grand Avenue School
4211 Grand Avenue
P.O. Box 139
Western Springs, IL 60558-0139
Tel: 708-246-7073

Wheaton Public Library
225 N. Cross Street
Wheaton, IL 60187
Tel: 630-668-1374
Fax: 630-668-1465
URL: http://www.wheaton.lib.il.us/library/wpl.html

Wheeling Historical Museum
251 North Wolf Road
P.O. Box 3
Wheeling, IL 60090-0003
Tel: 847-537-0327

Wilmette Historical Museum
565 Hunter Road
Wilmette, IL 60091-2209
Tel: 847-256-5838

Winnetka Historical Museum and Library
1140 Elm Street
Mail:
510 Green Bay Road
Winnetka, IL 60093-2563
Tel: 847-501-6025

Winnetka Public Library
768 Oak Street
Winnetka, IL 60093-2583
Tel: 847-446-7220
Fax: 847-446-5085

Withers Public Library
202 East Washington
Bloomington, IL 61701

Woodlands Native American Indian Museum/Art Gallery
6384 West Willow Wood Drive
Palos Heights, IL 60463-1847
Tel: 708-614-0334

Woodson Regional Library
9525 South Halsted
Chicago, IL 60628
Tel: 312-747-6900
TDD: 312-747-0121
Fax: 312-747-3396
URL: http://cpl.lib.uic.edu/002branches/woodson/
woodson.html

Wyanet Historical Society
Main Street
Wyanet, IL 61379
Tel: 815-699-2531

Zion Benton Public Library
2400 Gabriel Avenue
Zion, IL 60099-2296
Tel: 847-623-3501
847-872-4680

NEWSPAPER REPOSITORIES

Belleville Public Library
Genealogy Section
121 E. Washington St., #4114
Belleville, Il 62220-2205
Tel: 618-234-0441
Fax: 618-234-9474
URL: http://library.wustl.edu/~spec/archives/aslaa/
/belleville-public-library.html

Chicago Historical Society
Clark Street at North Avenue
Chicago, IL 60614-6099
Tel: 312-642-5035 ext. 350
Fax: 312-266-2077
Email: mcneill@chicagohs.org
URL: http://www.chicagohs.org/USNP.html

Illinois State Archives
Archives Building
Springfield, IL 62756-0001
Tel: 217-782-4682

Illinois State Historical Library
Newspaper Library
Old State Capitol
Springfield, IL 62701
Tel: 217-785-7941

Joliet Public Library
150 N. Ottawa Street
Joliet, IL 60431
Tel: 815-740-2660
Fax: 815-740-6161
URL: http://www.htls.lib.il.us/JPB/

Plainfield Public Library
705 N. Illinois Street
Plainfield, IL 60544
Tel: 815-436-6639
Fax: 815-439-2878
URL: http://www.htls.lib.il.us/PLB/

University of Illinois at Urbana-Champaign
University Archives
1408 W. Gregory Drive
Urbana, IL 61801
Tel: 217-333-2579
Email: s-clark3@uiuc.edu
URL: http://www.library.uiuc.edu/nex/default.htm

VITAL RECORDS

Illinois State Vital Records Office
Division of Vital Records
605 West Jefferson Street
Springfield, IL 62702-5097
Tel: 217-782-6553
800-545-2200

ILLINOIS ON THE WEB

Genealogy-Family History Research in Illinois
http://www.outfitters.com/illinois/history/family/

IlGenWeb Project
http://www.starnetinc.com/ilgenweb/

Illinois Ancestor Exchange
http://www.outfitters.com/illinois/history/family/IAE/

Illinois Gateway - Genealogy Feature
http://www.sos.state.il.us/special/genealog/genealog.html

Illinois in the Civil War
http://www.outfitters.com/illinois/history/civil/civil.html

Illinois Public Domain Land Sales Search
gopher://gopher.uic.edu/11/library/libdb/landsale

INDIANA

ARCHIVES, STATE & NATIONAL

Indiana State Archives
Commission on Public Records
State Library Building, Room 117
140 N. Senate Avenue
Indianapolis, IN 46204
Tel: 317-232-3660
Fax: 317-233-1085
URL: http://www.state.in.us/acin/icpr/index.html

National Archives—Great Lakes Region
7358 Pulaski Road
Chicago, IL 60629-5898
Tel: 773-581-7816
Fax: 312-353-1294
Email: archives@chicago.nara.gov
URL: http://www.nara.gov/nara/regional/05nsgil.htm

GENEALOGICAL SOCIETIES

African-American Historical & Genealogical Society (AAHGS)
502 Clover Terrace
Bloomington, IN 47404-1809

Alexandria/Monroe Township Genealogy Society
302 West Tyler Street
Alexandria, IN 46001

Allen County Genealogical Society (ACGSI)
P.O. Box 12003
Fort Wayne, IN 46802
Email: violetta@ipfw.indiana.edu
URL: http://cvax.ipfw.indiana.edu/www/depts/history/ftwayne/acgsi.html

Bartholomew County Genealogical Society
P.O. Box 2455
Columbus, IN 47202-2455

Blackford-Wells Genealogy Society
P.O. Box 54
Bluffton, IN 46714-0054

Brown County Genealogical Society
P.O. Box 1202
Nashville, IN 47448

Cass County Genealogical Society
P.O. Box 373
Logansport, IN 46947

Clay County Genealogical Society/Library
P.O. Box 56
Center Point, IN 47840-0056
Tel: 812-835-5005
Email: fred@indiana.net
URL: http://indiana.net/clay/ccgs.htm

Clinton County Genealogical Society
609 N. Columbia Street
Frankfort, IN 46041

County Seat Genealogy Society
310 Urban Street
Danville, IN 46122

Crawford County Historical & Genealogical Society
P.O. Box 133
Leavenworth, IN 47137
Tel: 812-739-2358

Daviess County Genealogical Society
703 Front Street
Washington, IN 47501

Dubois County Genealogical Society
P.O. Box 84
Ferdinand, IN 47532-0084

Elkhart County Genealogical Society
1812 Jeanwood Drive
Elkhart, IN 46514

Fountain County Genealogical Society
2855 S. Kingman Road
Kingman, IN 47952
Email: emoyhbo@glenmar.com
URL: http://glenmar.com/~emoyhbo/fcgs.html

Grant County Genealogical Society
1419 West 11th Street
Marion, IN 46952

Grant County Genealogy Club
Grant County Courthouse
24 Herbal Drive
Marion, IN 46952

Hendricks County Genealogical Society
101 South Indiana Street
Danville, IN 46122

Howard County Genealogical Society
P.O. Box 2
Oakford, IN 46965
Email: morris@netusa1.net
URL: http://www.rootsweb.com/~inhoward/gensoc.html

Illiana Genealogical & Historical Society
P.O. Box 207
Danville, IN 61832

Indiana Genealogical Society
P.O. Box 10507
Fort Wayne, IN 46852
Tel: 219-424-7241 ext. 2220
URL: http://www.fgs.org/~fgs/soc0087.htm

Jackson County Genealogical Society
415 Walnut Street
Seymour, IN 47274

Jay County Genealogical Society
P.O. Box 1086
Portland, IN 47371

Jennings County Genealogical Society
RR 1, Box 227
Scipion, IN 47273

LaPorte Genealogical Society
904 Indiana Avenue
LaPorte, IN 46350

Lawrence County Historical Genealogical Society
Courthouse
Bedford, IN 47421

Marion-Adams Historical and Genealogical Society
308 Main Street
Sheridan, IN 46069

Marshall County Genealogical Society
123 N. Michigan Street
Plymouth, IN 46563
URL: httP://www.fgs.org/~fgs/soc0120.htm

Martin County Genealogical Society
P.O. Box 45
Shoals, IN 47581

Miami County Genealogical Society
P.O. Box 542
Peru, IN 46970

Monroe County Genealogical Society
c/o Genealogy Library
202 East 6th Street
Bloomington, IN 47408
Tel: 812-332-2517
Email: julian@bluemarble.net
URL: http://www.bluemarble.net/~julian/monroe.html

Morgan County History and Genealogy Association, Inc.
P.O. Box 1012
Martinsville, IN 46151-1012
Tel: 317-349-1537
URL: http://www.scican.net/~scline/mchagai.html

Noble County Genealogical Society
109 N. York Street
Albion, IN 46701

North Central Indiana Genealogical Society
2300 Canterbury Drive
Kokomo, IN 46901

Northwest Indiana Genealogical Society
154 Granite Street
Valparaiso, IN 46383

Northwest Territory Genealogical Society
c/o Lewis Historical Library
Vincennes University LRC-22
Vincennes, IN 47591
URL: http://www.vinu.edu/lewis.edu

Orange County Genealogical Society
P.O. Box 344
Paoli, IN 47454
Tel: 812-723-3437
URL: http://copper.ucs.indiana.edu/~vheverly/gensoc.htm

Owen County Historical and Genealogical Society
110 East Market Street
Spencer, IN 47460
Tel: 812-829-3392
Email: peterson@ccrtc.com
URL: http://www.bluemarble.net/~julian/owen.html

Porter County Public Library Genealogical Group
103 Jefferson Street
Valparaiso, IN 46383

Pulaski County Genealogical Society
RR 4, Box 121
Winamac, IN 46996

Putnam County Genealogy Club
Rte. 1, Box 28
Bainbridge, IN 46105

Randolph County Genealogical Society
Route 3, Box 61
Winchester, IN 47394
Tel: 317-584-4323

Scott County Genealogical Society
RR 2, Box 169B
Lexington, IN 47138

Shelby County Genealogical Society
Grover Museum
52 West Broadway
Shelbyville, IN 46176

South Bend Area Genealogical Society
53119 Oakmont Park Drive, W
P.O. Box 1222
South Bend, IN 46624-1222

Southern Indiana Genealogical Society
P.O. Box 665
New Albany, IN 47151
URL: http://www.fgs.org/~fgs/soc0176.htm

Southern Indiana Genealogical Society
RR 1
Leavenworth, IN 47137

Starke County Genealogical Society
7720 E. Toto Road
Knox, IN 46534

Tippecanoe County Area Genealogical Society
909 South Street
Lafayette, IN 47901
http://www.fgs.org/~fgs/soc0189.htm

Tri-County Genealogy Society
23184 Pocket Road, W
P.O. Box 118
Batesville, IN 47006
URL: http://www.fgs.org/~fgs/soc0191.htm

Tri State Genealogical Society
c/o Willard Library
21 First Avenue
Evansville, IN 47710
Tel: 812-425-4309
Email: tsgs@evansville.net
URL: http://www.evansville.net/~tsgs/tsgs.html

Twin Oaks Genealogy
1371 East, 400 North
Bluffton, IN 46714
Wabash Valley Genealogical Society
P.O. Box 85
Terre Haute, IN 47808

Wayne County Genealogical Society
1150 North A Street
Richmond, IN 47374

White County Genealogy Society
609 South Maple Street, Box 884
Monticello, IN 47960

Whitley County, Genealogical Society of
P.O. Box 224
Columbia City, IN 46725-0224
URL: http://www.execpc.com/~drg/gswc.html

Historical Societies

Adams County Historical Society
420 W. Monroe Street
Decatur, IN 46733
Tel: 219-724-2341

African-American Historical & Genealogical Society (AAHGS)
502 Clover Terrace
Bloomington, IN 47404-1809

Alexandria-Monroe Township Historical Society
205 East Church Street
Alexandria, IN 46001
Tel: 317-724-2993

Allen County-Fort Wayne Historical Society/Museum & Archives
302 E. Berry Street
Fort Wayne, IN 46802
Tel: 219-426-2882
Fax: 219-424-4419
URL: http://www.ft-wayne.in.us/fort/FW_History/

Anson Wolcott Historical Society
Box 294
Wolcott, IN 47995

Bartholomew County Historical Society
524 Third Street
Columbus, IN 47201
Tel: 812-372-3541

Besancon Historical Society
15533 Lincoln Highway East
New Haven, IN 46774
Tel: 219-749-4525
URL: http://cvax.ipfw.indiana.edu/www/depts/history/historgs/besanco.html

Blackford County Historical Society/Museum
321 N. High Street
P.O. Box 264
Hartford City, IN 47348

Boone County Historical Society
P.O. Box 141
Lebanon, IN 46052

Brown County Historical Society
P.O. Box 668
Nashville, IN 47448

Carmel-Clay Historical Society
211 First SW
Carmel, IN 47201
Tel: 317-846-4564

Carroll County Historical Society/Museum
P.O. Box 277
Delphi, IN 46923
Tel: 317-564-3152

Cass County Historical Society
1004 E. Market Street
Logansport, IN 46947
Tel: 219-753-3866

Cedar Lake Historical Association
Lake of the Red Cedars Museum
P.O. Box 421
Cedar Lake, IN 46303
Tel: 219-374-6157

Clark County Historical Society
Howard Steamboat Museum, Inc.
1101 East Market Street
P.O. Box 606
Jeffersonville, IN 47130-0606
Tel: 812-283-3728

Clark's Grant Historical Society
P.O. Box 423
Charlestown, IN 47111

Clay County Historical Society
100 E. National Road
Brazil, IN 47834
Tel: 812-446-4036

Clinton County Historical Society/Museum
301 E. Clinton
Frankfort, IN 46041
Tel: 317-659-2030

Crawford County Historical & Genealogical Society
P.O. Box 133
Leavenworth, IN 47137
Tel: 812-739-2358

Daleville Historical Society
P.O. Box 586
Daleville, IN 47334

Daviess County Historical Society/Museum
Donaldson Road
Washington, IN 47501
Tel: 812-254-5122
URL: http://www.artcom.com/museums/nv/af/47501.htm

Dearborn County Historical Society
Courthouse
215 West High Street
Lawrenceburg, IN 47025
Tel: 812-537-4075

Decatur County Historical Society
P.O. Box 163
Greensburg, IN 47240

Decatur Township Historical Society
P.O. Box 42
West Newton, IN 46183
Tel: 317-856-6567

DeKalb County Historical Society
Box 686
Auburn, IN 46706

Delaware County Historical Alliance/Heritage Library
120 East Washington
P.O. Box 1266
Muncie, IN 47308
Tel: 317-282-1550
Email: dcha@iquest.net
URL: http://www.iquest.net/~dcha/

Dolan Historical Society
New Prospect Baptist Church
6055 North Old State Road 37
Dolan, IN 47401

Dubois County Historical Society
737 W. 8th Street
Jasper, IN 47546
Tel: 812-482-3074

Duneland Historical Society
P.O. Box 809
Chesterton, IN 46304

Dyer Historical Society
Dyer Town Hall
One Town Square
Dyer, IN 46311
Tel: 219-865-6108

East Chicago Historical Society
2401 East Columbus Drive
East Chicago, IN 46312
Tel: 219-397-2453

Elkhart County Historical Society/Museum
304 West Vistula Street
P.O. Box 434
Bristol, IN 46507
Tel: 219-848-4322

Ferdinand Historical Society
Box 194
Ferdinand, IN 47532

Floyd County Historical Society
P.O. Box 455
New Albany, IN 47151-0455

Fort Benjamin Harrison Historical Society
1028 N. Delaware Street
Indianapolis, IN 46202
Tel: 317-636-4646

Fort Wayne Railroad Historical Society, Inc.
P.O. Box 11017
Fort Wayne, IN 46855
Tel: 219-493-0765

Fountain County Historical Society
724 S. Layton
P.O. Box 148
Kingman, IN 47952

Franklin County Historical Society/Museum
P.O. Box 342
Brookville, IN 47012
Tel: 317-647-5413

Franklin Township Historical Society
P.O. Box 39015
Indianapolis, IN 46239

Fulton County Historical Society
37 East, 375 North
Rochester, IN 46975
Tel: 219-223-4436

Garrett Historical Society
210 East Quincy Street
P.O. Box 225
Garrett, IN 46738

Gary Historical & Cultural Society
2409 West Fifth Avenue
Gary, IN 46404
Tel: 219-882-3311

Gas City Historical Society
505 E. South F Street
P.O. Box 192
Gas City, IN 46933

Gibson County Historical Society
P.O. Box 516
Princeton, IN 47670

Goshen Historical Society
P.O. Box 701
Goshen, IN 46526

Grant County Historical Society
1713 North Quarry Road
P.O. Box 1951
Marion, IN 46952

Greene County Historical Society
P.O. Box 301
Bloomfield, IN 47424
Tel: 812-384-8441

Griffith Historical Society
P.O. Box 678
Griffith, In 46319
Tel: 219-924-7246

Guilford Township Historical Society
c/o Plainfield Public Library
1120 Stafford Road
Plainfield, IN 46168
Tel: 317-839-6602

Hamilton County Historical Society
Old Sheriff's Residence and Jail
P.O. Box 397
Noblesville, IN 46060
Tel: 317-770-0775
Email: historicalsociety@noblesville.com
URL: http://www.noblesville.com/history.htm

Hammond Historical Society
c/o Hammond Public Library
564 State Street
Hammond, IN 46320
Tel: 219-931-5100

Hancock County Historical Society
P.O. Box 375
Greenfield, IN 46140
Tel: 317-462-7780

Harrison County Historical Society
117 Beaver Street
Corydon, IN 47112

Hebron Historical Society, Inc.
P.O. Box 675
Hebron, IN 46341

Hendricks County Historical Society/Museum
170 South Washington
P.O. Box 128
Danville, IN 46122
Tel: 317-745-2992

Henry County Historical Society/Museum
606 South 14th Street
New Castle, IN 47362
Tel: 765-529-4028
Email: glennaw@nchcpl.lib.in.us
URL: http://www.nchcpl.lib.in.us/Museum/

Heritage Society of Northwest Indiana
P.O. Box 508
Chesterton, IN 46304-0508

Hessville Historical Society
7205 Kennedy Avenue
Hammond, IN 46323
Tel: 219-844-5666

Highland Historical Society
c/o Bank of Highland
2611 Highway Avenue
Highland, IN 46322

Historic Forks of the Wabash, Inc.
3010 West Park Drive
Huntington, IN 46750
Tel: 219-356-1903
Email: dericsson@huntcol.edu
URL: http://www.huntington.in.us/FORKS/forks.html

Hobart Historical Society
Mariam Library
706 East Fourth Street
P.O. Box 24
Hobart, IN 46342
Tel: 219-942-0970

Howard County Historical Society/Museum
1200 W. Sycamore Street
Kokomo, IN 46901
Tel: 317-452-4314

Huntington County Historical Society
1041 South Jefferson Street
P.O. Box 1012
Huntington, IN 46750

Indiana German Heritage Society
401 East Michigan Street
Indianapolis, IN 46204

Indiana Historical Bureau
140 North Senate Avenue, Room 408
Indianapolis, IN 46204
Tel: 317-232-2537
Fax: 317-232-3728
Email: ihb@statelib.lib.in.us
URL: http://www.statelib.lib.in.us/WWW/ihb/ihb.HTML

Indiana Historical Society/Library
315 W. Ohio Street, 3rd Floor
Indianapolis, IN 46202
(Moving Fall 1998 to Ohio and West Streets)
Tel: 317-232-1879
317-233-3109
URL: http://www.ihs1830.org/ihs.html

Indiana Jewish Historical Society
203 W. Wayne Street #312
Fort Wayne, IN 46802
Tel/Fax: 219-422-3862

Indiana Religious History Association
P.O. Box 88267
Indianapolis, IN 46208

Indians of Indiana
P.O. Box 9563
Fort Wayne, IN 46899-9563

Irvington Historical Society
Benton House
312 South Downey Avenue
Indianapolis, IN 46219
Tel: 317-357-0318

Jackson County Historical Society
115 N. Sugar Street
Brownstown, IN 47220

Jay County Historical Society
P.O. Box 1282
Portland, IN 47371
Tel: 219-726-2551

Jefferson County Historical Society
Madison Railroad Station
615 West First Street
Madison, IN 47250
Tel: 812-265-2335

Johnson County Historical Society
135 North Main Street
Franklin, IN 46131
Tel: 317-736-4655

Kennard Historical Society
Box 227
Kennard, IN 47351

Kosciusko County Historical Society/Library
Kosciusko County Jail Museum
P.O. Box 1071
Warsaw, IN 46580
Tel: 219-269-1078

LaGrange County Historical Society
RR 1
P.O. Box 134
LaGrange, IN 46761
Tel: 219-463-2632

Lake County Historical Society/Museum
5131 Canterbury Avenue
Portage, IN 46368
Tel: 219-662-3975

Lake Station Historical Society
P.O. Box 5253
Lake Station, IN 46405-2232
Tel: 219-962-2836

LaPorte Historical Society/Museum
LaPorte County Govt. Complex
1 Courthouse Square
LaPorte, IN 46350
Tel: 219-326-6808 x276
URL: http://www.adsnet.com/MichiganCity/Activities/HomePages/LPMuseum/LPMuseum.html

Lawrence County Historical Genealogical Society
12 Courthouse Museum
Bedford, IN 47421
Tel: 812-475-4141

Lexington Historical Society
P.O. Box 238
Lexington, IN 47138

Ligonier Historical Society
503 South Main Street
Ligonier, IN 46767
Tel: 219-894-4511

Linden-Madison Township Historical Society
P.O. Box 154
Linden, IN 47955
Tel: 317-339-7245

Madison County Historical Society
P.O. Box 523
Anderson, IN 46015
Tel: 317-641-2442

Marion-Adams Historical and Genealogical Society
308 Main Street
Sheridan, IN 46069

Marion County-Indianapolis Historical Society
P.O. Box 2223
Indianapolis, IN 46206
Tel: 317-274-2718
Email: reboomer@iquest.net
URL: http://www.iquest.net/~reboomer/mcihs.htm

Marshall County Historical Society, Inc.
123 N. Michigan Street
Plymouth, IN 46563
Tel: 219-936-2306

Martin County Historical Society
P.O. Box 564
Shoals, IN 47581

Merrillville-Ross Township Historical Society
6975 Broadway
Merrillville, IN 46410

Miami County Historical Society
Courthouse, Room 102
51 North Broadway
Peru, IN 46970
Tel: 317-473-9183

Michiana Jewish Historical Society
P.O. Box 11074
South Bend, IN 46634-0074
Tel: 219-233-9553

Michigan City Historical Society
P.O. Box 512
Michigan City, IN 46360
Tel: 219-872-6133

Middletown-Fall Creek Township Historical Society
707 West Mill Street
Middletown, IN 47356
Tel: 317-354-2791

Monon Historical Society
P.O. Box 193
Monon, IN 47959

Monroe County Genealogical/Historical Society
c/o Genealogy Library
202 East 6th Street
Bloomington, IN 47408
Tel: 812-332-2517
Email: julian@bluemarble.net
URL: http://www.bluemarble.net/~julian/monroe.html

Montgomery County Historical Society
212 Water Street
Crawfordsville, IN 47933
Tel: 317-362-3416

Montpelier Historical Society, Inc.
109 West Huntington Street
Montpelier, IN 47359
Tel: 317-728-8642

Morgan County Historic Preservation Society
P.O. Box 1377
Martinsville, IN 46151

Morgan County History and Genealogy Association, Inc.
P.O. Box 1012
Martinsville, IN 46151-1012
Tel: 317-349-1537
URL: http://www.scican.net/~scline/mchagai.html

Munster Historical Society
Townhall
1005 Ridge Road
Munster, In 46321
Tel: 219-836-8810

New Paris Historical Society
P.O. Box 101
New Paris, IN 46553

Noble County Historical Society
P.O. Box 152
Albion, IN 46701

North Manchester Historical Society
P.O. Box 131
North Manchester, IN 46962

Northern Indiana Historical Society
808 West Washington Blvd.
South Bend, IN 46601
Tel: 219-235-9664

Ohio County Historical Society
218 South Walnut Street
Rising Sun, IN 47040
Tel: 812-438-2056

Ogden Dunes, Historical Society of
101 Ogden Dunes
Portage, IN 46368-1268
Tel: 219-762-1268

Orange County Historical Society
Thomas Elwood Lindley House
P.O. Box 454
Paoli, IN 47454

Osceola Historical Society
P.O. Box 14
Osceola, IN 46561
Tel: 219-674-8956

Owen County Historical and Genealogical Society
110 East Market Street
Spencer, IN 47460
Tel: 812-829-3392
Email: peterson@ccrtc.com
URL: http://www.bluemarble.net/~julian/owen.html

Owen County Historical Society
P.O. Box 222
Spencer, IN 47460

Palmyra Historical Society
Palmyra Historical Museum
Palmyra Commercial Building
Palmyra, IN 47164

Park County Historical Society
503 E. Oak Drive
P.O. Box 332
Rockville, IN 47872
Tel: 317-569-2223

Perry County Historical Society
538 Eleventh Street
Tell City, IN 47586

Pike County Historical Society
c/o Pike County Public Library
1104 Main Street
Petersburg, IN 47567

Porter County, Historical Society of
Old Jail Museum
153 Franklin
Valparaiso, IN 46383
Tel: 219-465-3595

Portage Community Historical Society
2100 Willowcreek Road
Portage, IN 46368
Tel: 219-762-4218

Posey County Historical Society
P.O. Box 171
Mount Vernon, IN 47620

Pulaski County Historical Society
400 South Market Street
P.O. Box 135
Winamac, IN 46996
Tel: 219-946-3712

Putnam County Historical Society
c/o Roy O. West Library
Archives & Special Collections
DePauw University
Greencastle, IN 46135
Tel: 317-658-4406

Randolph County Historical Society/Museum
416 South Meridian
Winchester, IN 47394
Tel: 317-584-4323

Ripley County Historical Society
Local History & Genealogical Library
125 Washington Street
P.O. Box 525
Versailles, IN 47023
Tel: 812-689-3031
Email: rchslib@seidata.com
URL: http://www.seidata.com/~rchslib/

Rush County Historical Society
614 N. Jackson
P.O. Box 302
Rushville, IN 46173

St. John Historical Society
P.O. Box 134
St. John, IN 46373
Tel: 219-365-8550

Schererville Historical Society
P.O. Box 333
Schererville, IN 46375
Tel: 219-322-1699

Scotland Historical Society, Inc.
Box 173
Scotland, IN 47457

Scott County Historical Society
P.O. Box 245
Scottsburg, IN 47170

Shawnee Historical Association
5501 E. 200 N.
Lafayette, IN 47905
Tel: 317-589-8049

Shelby County Historical Society
52 West Broadway
P.O. Box 74
Shelbyville, IN 46176
Tel: 317-392-4634

Shirley Centennial Historical Society, Inc.
Historic Shirley Museum
P.O. Box 69
Shirley, IN 47384-0069
Tel: 317-737-6119

Society for Preservation of Indian Heritage
P.O. Box 23
Thorntown, IN 46071
Tel: 317-436-2202

Southwestern Indiana Historical Society
435 S. Spring Street
Evansville, IN 47714-1550

Spencer County Historical Society
c/o Rockport-Ohio Township Public Library
210 Walnut Street
Rockport, IN 47635

Starke County Historical Society/Museum
401 South Main Street
Knox, IN 46534
Tel: 219-772-5393

Stones Trace Historical Society
407 Johnson Street
Ligonier, IN 46767

Sullivan County Historical Society
P.O. Box 326
Sullivan, IN 47882
Tel: 812-268-6253

Swiss Heritage Society, Inc.
Swiss Heritage Village
Box 88
Berne, IN 46711
Tel: 219-589-8007

Switzerland County Historical Society
P.O. Box 201
Vevay, IN 47043
Tel: 812-427-3560

Tell City Historical Society
P.O. Box 728
Tell City, IN 47586
Tel: 812-547-2995

Three Creeks Historical Association
c/o Lowell Public Library
1505 Commercial Avenue
Lowell, IN 46356

Tippecanoe County Historical Association/Museum
909 South Street
Lafayette, IN 47901
Tel: 765-476-8411
Fax: 765-476-8414
Email: tcha@iquest.net
URL: http://www.iquest.net/tcha/

Topeka Area Historical Society
123 Indiana Street
P.O. Box 33
Topeka, IN 46571
Tel: 219-593-3613

United Methodist Historical Society
P.O. Box 331
Greencastle, IN 46135

Upland Area Historical Society
P.O. Box 577
Upland, IN 46989

Vanderburgh County Historical Society
P.O. Box 2626
Evansville, IN 47728-0626

Vermillion County Historical Society
220 E. Market Street
P.O. Box 273
Newport, IN 47966
Tel: 317-492-3570
URL: http://members.aol.com/KFether123/verhs.html

Vigo County Historical Society/Museum
1411 South Sixth Street
Terre Haute, IN 47807
Tel: 812-235-9717
Email: vchs@iquest.net
URL: http://web.indstate.edu/community/vchs/home.html

Wabash County Historical Society
Memorial Hall
89 West Hill Street
Wabash, IN 46992
Tel: 219-563-0661

Wakarusa Historical Society
Box 2
Wakarusa, IN 46573

Warren County Historical Society
P.O. Box 176
Williamsport, IN 47993

Washington County Historical Society
307 E. Market Street
Salem, IN 47167
Tel: 812-883-6495

Wayne County Historical Association
1150 North A Street
Richmond, IN 47374
Tel: 317-962-5756

Wayne Township Historical Society
1220 S. High School Road
Indianapolis, IN 46241

Wells County Historical Society/Museum
420 West Market Street
P.O. Box 143
Bluffton, IN 46714-0143
Tel: 219-824-9956
Email: pbender@parlorcity.com
URL: http://www.parlorcity.com/pbender/

West Baden Historical Society
P.O. Box 6
West Baden Springs, IN 47469
Tel: 812-936-9630

Whiting-Robertsdale Historical Society
1610 119th Street
Whiting, IN 46394
Tel: 219-659-1432

Whitley County Historical Society/Museum
108 West Jefferson Street
Columbia City, IN 46725
Tel: 219-244-6372
URL: http://www.execpc.com/~drg/gwsc.html#wchs

Winona Lake Historical Society
101 Fourth Street
Winona Lake, IN 46590

Zionsville Historical Society
714 Sugarbush Drive
Zionsville, IN 46077

LDS Family History Centers

Bloomington Family History Center
2411 East Second Street
Bloomington, IN 47401
Tel: 812-333-0050

Columbus Family History Center
3330 30th Street
Columbus, IN 47203
Tel: 812-376-7073

Evansville Family History Center
519 East Olmstead Avenue
Evansville, IN 47711
Tel: 812-423-9832

Fort Wayne Family History Center
5401 Saint Joe Road
Fort Wayne, IN 46835
Tel: 219-485-9581

Indianapolis Family History Center
900 East Stop 11 Road
Indianapolis, IN 46227
Tel: 317-888-6002

Muncie Family History Center
4800 Robinwood Drive
Muncie, IN 47304
Tel: 317-288-7278

New Albany Family History Center
1534 State Run Road
New Albany, IN 47150
Tel: 812-949-7532

Noblesville Family History Center
777 Sunblest Road
Noblesville, IN 46060
Tel: 317-857-8709

South Bend Family History Center
3050 Edison Road
South Bend, IN 46615
Tel: 219-233-6501

Terre Haute Family History Center
1845 North Center
Terre Haute, IN 47804
Tel: 812-234-0269

West Lafayette Family History Center
3224 Jasper Street
West Lafayette, IN 47906
Tel: 317-463-5079

Archives/Libraries/Museums

Akron Carnegie Public Library
204 E. Rochester Street
Akron, IN 46910

Alameda McCullough Library
Wetherill Historical Resource Center
1001 South Street
Lafayette, IN 47901
URL: http://www.iquest.net/tcha/library.html

Alexandria Public Library
117 E. Church Street
Alexandria, IN 46001

Alexandrian Public Library
115 W. Fifth Street
Mt. Vernon, IN 47620

Allen County Public Library
900 Webster Street
Fort Wayne, IN 46802
Tel: 219-424-7241
URL: http://www.acpl.lib.in.us/

Anderson Public Library
111 E. 12th Street
Anderson, IN 46016
Tel: 317-641-2456
Fax: 317-641-2468
URL: http://www.acsc.net/~apl/

Andrews/Dallas Township Public Library
P.O. Box 367
Andrews, IN 46702
Tel: 219-786-3574

Angola-Carnegie Public Library
322 S. Wayne Street
Angola, IN 46703
Tel: 219-665-3362

Atlanta/Jackson Township Public Library
100 S. Walnut St.
P.O. Box 68
Atlanta, IN 46031
Tel: 317-292-2521

Attica Public Library
305 S. Perry Street
Attica, IN 47918
Tel: 317-764-4194
URL: http://glenmar.com/~emoyhbo/atticalb.html

Aurora Public Library
414 Second Street
Aurora, IN 47001
Tel: 812-926-0646
URL: http://www.seidata.com/~aurplib/

Ball State University
Bracken Library
Muncie, IN 47306
Tel: 765-285-1101
765-285-5078 (Archives & Special Collections)
URL: http://www.library.bsu.edu/index.html

Bartholomew County Public Library
536 Fifth Street
Columbus, IN 47201
Tel: 812-379-1255

Batesville Memorial Public Library
131 N. Walnut Street
Batesville, IN 47006
Tel: 812-934-4706
Fax: 812-934-6288
Email: mkruse@ind.net
URL: http://batesville.venus.net/nonprofit/bmpl.html

Bedford Public Library
1323 K Street
Bedford, IN 47421
Tel: 812-275-4471

Beech Grove Public Library
1102 W. Main Street
Beech Grove, IN 46107
Tel: 317-788-4203

Beeson Library
314 N. High Street
Hartford City, IN 47348
Tel: 317-348-1720

Bell Memorial Public Library
306 N. Broadway
P.O. Box 368
Mentone, IN 46539
Tel: 219-353-7234

Benton County Public Library
102 N. Van Buren Avenue
Fowler, IN 47944
Tel: 317-884-1720

Berne Public Library
166 N. Sprunger
Berne, IN 46711
Tel: 219-589-2809

Bicknell/Vigo Township Public Library
201 W. Second Street
Bicknell, IN 47512
Tel: 812-735-2317

Blackford County Historical Society/Museum
321 N. High Street
P.O. Box 264
Hartford City, IN 47348

Bloomfield-Carnegie Public Library
125 South Franklin Street
Bloomfield, IN 47424
Tel: 812-384-4125
Fax: 812-384-0820

Bluffton/Wells County Public Library
200 West Washington
Bluffton, IN 46714
Tel: 219-824-1612

Boonville Public Library
611 W. Main Street
Boonville, IN 47601
Tel: 812-897-1500

Boswell-Grant Township Public Library
202 Main Street
Boswell, IN 47921
Tel: 317-869-5428

Bourbon Public Library
307 N. Main Street
Bourbon, IN 46504
Tel: 219-342-5655

Brazil Public Library
204 N. Walnut Street
Brazil, IN 47834
Tel: 812-448-1981

Bremen Public Library
304 N. Jackson St.
P.O. Box 130
Bremen, IN 46506
Tel: 219-546-2849

Bristol Public Library
505 N. Vistula Street
Bristol, IN 46507
Tel: 219-848-7458

Brook-Iroquois Township Public Library
100 West Main
P.O. Box 155
Brook, IN 47922
Tel: 219-275-2471

Brookston-Prairie Township Library
111 West Second Street
Brookston, IN 47923
Tel: 765-563-6511
Fax: 765-563-6833
Email: bptpl@dcwi.com
URL: http://dcwi.com/~bptpl/Welcome.html

Brookville Township Public Library
919 Main Street
Brookville, IN 47012
Tel: 317-647-4031

Brown County Public Library
246 E. Main Street
P.O. Box 8
Nashville, IN 47448
Tel: 812-988-2850

Brownsburg Public Library
450 S. Jefferson Street
Brownsburg, IN 47112-1310
Tel: 317-852-3167

Butler-Carnegie Library
201 E. Main Street
Butler, IN 46721
Tel: 219-868-2351

Cambridge City Public Library
33 W. Main Street
Cambridge, IN 47327

Camden-Jackson Township Public Library
258 Main Street
P.O. Box 24
Camden, IN 46917
Tel: 219-686-2120

Cannelton Public Library
West Sixth Street
P.O. Box 37
Cannelton, IN 47520
Tel: 812-547-6028

Carmel Public Library
515 East Main Street
Carmel, IN 46032
Tel: 317-844-3361
URL: http://www.carmel.lib.in.us/

Carthage Public Library
North Main
P.O. Box 35
Carthage, IN 46115
Tel: 317-565-6631

Cass County Public Library
616 E. Broadway
Logansport, IN 46947
Tel: 219-753-6383

Cedar Lake Historical Association
Lake of the Red Cedars Museum
P.O. Box 421
Cedar Lake, IN 46303
Tel: 219-374-6157

Centerville Township Public Library
115 West Main Street
Centerville, IN 47330
Tel: 317-855-5223

Charlestown/Clark County Public Library
51 Clark Road
Charlestown, IN 47111
Tel: 812-256-3337

Churubusco Public Library
116 N. Mulberry Street
Churubusco, IN 46723
Tel: 219-693-6466

Clay County Genealogical Society/Library
P.O. Box 56
Center Point, IN 47840-0056
Tel: 812-835-5005
Email: fred@indiana.net
URL: http://indiana.net/clay/ccgs.htm

Clayton/Liberty Township Public Library
124 Kentucky Street
P.O. Box E
Clayton, IN 46118
Tel: 317-539-2991

Clinton County Historical Society/Museum
301 E. Clinton
Frankfort, IN 46041
Tel: 317-659-2030

Clinton Public Library
313 S. 4th Street
Clinton, IN 47842
Tel: 765-832-8349
Fax: 765-832-3823
Email: clinpl@holli.com
URL: http://www.iquest.net/~clinpl/

Coatsville Public Library
North Milton Street
P.O. Box 147
Coatsville, IN 46121

Colfax Public Library
P.O. Box 308
Colfax, IN 46035
Tel: 317-324-2915

Corydon Public Library
117 W. Beaver Street
Corydon, IN 47112
Tel: 812-738-4110

Covington Public Library
622 5th Street
Covington, IN 47932
Tel: 317-793-2572
URL: http://glenmar.com/~emoyhbo/covlib.html

Crawford County Public Library
111 W. Fifth Street
P.O. Box 159
English, IN 47118
Tel: 812-338-2606

Crawfordsville Public Library
222 S. Washington Street
Crawfordsville, IN 47933
Tel: 317-362-2242
Fax: 317-362-7986

Crown Point Library
214 S. Court Street
Crown Point, IN 46307
Tel: 219-663-0270

Culver-Union Township Public Library
107 N. Main Street
Culver, IN 46511
Tel: 219-842-2941

Danville Township Public Library
101 S. Indiana Street
Danville, IN 46122
Tel: 317-745-2604

Darlington Public Library
203 W. Main Street
Darlington, IN 47940
Tel: 317-794-4813

Daviess County Historical Society/Museum
Donaldson Road
Washington, IN 47501
Tel: 812-254-5122
URL: http://www.artcom.com/museums/nv/af/47501.htm

Decatur Public Library
128 South 3rd Street
Decatur, IN 46733
Tel: 219-724-2605

Delphi Public Library
222 East Main Street
Delphi, IN 46923
Tel: 317-564-2929
Fax: 317-564-4746

DeMotte Public Library
901 Birch Street SW
DeMotte, IN 46310
Tel: 219-987-2221
Fax: 219-987-2220
Email: dplhist@netnitco.net
URL: http://birch.palni.edu/jcpl/

DePauw University
Roy O. West Library
Archives & Special Collections
Greencastle, IN 46135
Tel: 317-658-4406
URL: http://www.depauw.edu/lib/HomePg.htm

Dublin Public Library
P.O. Box 188
Dublin, IN 47335
Tel: 317-478-6206

Earl Park Public Library
400 East Fifth Street
P.O. Box 97
Earl Park, IN 47942
Tel: 219-474-6932

Earlham College
Earlham College Libraries
Arthur & Kathleen Postle Archives and Friends Collection
Richmond, IN 47374
URL: http://www.earlham.edu/www/library/files/tour/about.htm

East Chicago Public Library
2401 E. Columbus Drive
East Chicago, IN 46312
Tel: 219-397-2453

Eckhart Public Library
603 South Jackson Street
Auburn, IN 46706
URL: http://www.clearlake.com/epl/epl.htm

Edinburgh Public Library
119 West Main Cross Street
Edinburgh, IN 46124
Tel: 812-526-5487

Elkhart County Historical Society/Museum
304 West Vistula Street
P.O. Box 434
Bristol, IN 46507
Tel: 219-848-4322

Elkhart County Public Library
300 South Second Street
Elkhart, IN 46516
Tel: 219-522-2665

Elwood-North Madison County Public Library
124 North 16th Street
Elwood, IN 46036
Tel: 317-552-5001

Emline Fairbank Memorial Library
222 North 7th Street
Terre Haute, IN 47807
Tel: 812-232-1113

Evansville Public Library
22 SE Fifth Street
Evansville, IN 47708
Tel: 812-428-8200
Fax: 812-428-8215
URL: http://www.evcpl.lib.in.us/

Fairmount Public Library
205 South Main Street
P.O. Box 27
Fairmount, IN 46928
Tel: 317-948-3177

Farmland Public Library
106 S. Main Street
P.O. Box 188
Farmland, IN 47340
Tel: 317-468-7292

Fayette County Public Library
828 Grand Avenue
Connersville, IN 47331
Tel: 317-827-0883
URL: http://www.fcplibrary.com/

Flora-Monroe Public Library
109 North Center Street
Flora, IN 46929
Tel: 219-967-3912

Fort Branch Public Library
107 E. Locust Street
Fort Branch, IN 47648
Tel: 812-753-4212

Francesville-Salem Public Library
P.O. Box 577
Francesville, IN 47947
Tel: 219-567-9433

Frankfort Public Library
208 West Clinton Street
Frankfort, IN 46041
Tel: 765-654-8746
TDD: 765-659-3047
Fax: 765-654-8747

Fremont Public Library
Coffin Street
Fremont, IN 46975
Tel: 219-495-7157

Fulton County Public Library
320 West Seventh Street
Rochester, IN 46975
Tel: 219-223-2713
Fax: 219-223-5102
URL: http://www.townsquare.net/~jimkreft/resdir/aejt/aejt15b3.html

Garrett Public Library
107 West Houston Street
Garrett, IN 46738
Tel: 219-357-5485

Gary Public Library
220 West Fifth Avenue
Gary, IN 46402
Tel: 219-886-2484

Gas City/Mill Township Public Library
135 East Main Street
Gas City, IN 46933
Tel: 317-674-4718

Geneva Public Library
307 East Line Street
P.O. Box 187
Geneva, IN 46740
Tel: 219-368-7270

Goodland-Grant Township Public Library
P.O. Box 405
Goodland, IN 47948
Tel: 219-297-4431

Goshen Public Library
601 South Fifth Street
Goshen, IN 46526
Tel: 219-533-9531

Gosport History Museum
P.O. Box 56
Gosport, IN 47433

Greenfield Public Library
700 Broadway
Greenfield, IN 46140
Tel: 317-462-5141

Greentown Public Library
421 South Harrison Street
Greentown, IN 46936
Tel: 317-628-3534
Fax: 317-628-3759
URL: http://birch.palni.edu/~lhurst/gplhome/grentown.htm

Greenwood Public Library
310 South Meridian
Greenwood, IN 46143
Tel: 317-881-1953
Fax: 317-881-1963
Email: MHAMLTN@IQUEST.NET
URL: http://estel.uindy.edu/outReach/guestSchools/gpl/gpl.html

Hagerstown Public Library
10 West College
Hagerstown, IN 47346
Tel: 317-489-5632
Fax: 317-489-5808
Email: info@hagerstown.lib.in.us
URL: http://www.hagerstown.lib.in.us/

Hammond Public Library
564 State Street
Hammond, IN 46320
Tel: 219-931-5100
219-852-2230

Hartford City Public Library
314 N. High Street
Hartford City, IN 47348
Tel: 317-348-1720
URL: http://birch.palni.edu/~jkieffer/hcpl/libhome.htm

Hartman Museum
901 West Maumee Street
Angola, IN 46703

Hayden Historical Museum, Inc.
P.O. Box 58
Hayden, IN 47245
Tel: 812-346-8212

Hebron Public Library
201 E. Sigler Street
P.O. Box 97
Hebron, IN 46341
Tel: 219-996-3684

Hendricks County Historical Society/Museum
170 South Washington
P.O. Box 128
Danville, IN 46122
Tel: 317-745-2992

Henry County Historical Society/Museum
606 South 14th Street
New Castle, IN 47362
Tel: 765-529-4028
Email: glennaw@nchcpl.lib.in.us
URL: http://www.nchcpl.lib.in.us/Museum/

Howard County Historical Society/Museum
1200 W. Sycamore Street
Kokomo, IN 46901
Tel: 317-452-4314
URL: http://members.aol.com/kckokomo/hchs/

Howard Steamboat Museum, Inc.
Clark County Historical Society
1101 East Market Street
P.O. Box 606
Jeffersonville, IN 47130-0606
Tel: 812-283-3728

Huntingburg Public Library
419 Jackson Street
Huntingburg, IN 47542
Tel: 812-683-2052

Hussey Memorial Public Library
255 W. Hawthorne Street
P.O. Box 840
Zionsville, IN 46077
Tel: 317-873-3149

IUPUI University Library
Ruth Lilly Special Collections and Archives
755 West Michigan Street
Indianapolis, IN 46202-5195
Tel: 317-274-0464
Email: tdaniels@library.iupui.edu
URL: http://www-lib.iupui.edu/ecollects/archives.html

Indiana Historical Society/Library
315 W. Ohio Street, 3rd Floor
Indianapolis, IN 46202
(Moving Fall 1998 to Ohio and West Streets)
Tel: 317-232-1879
317-233-3109
800-IHS-1830
URL: http://www.ihs1830.org/ihs.html

Indiana State Library
140 N. Senate Avenue, Room 250 (Gen. Section)
Indianapolis, IN 46204
http://www.statelib.lib.in.us/

Indiana University - Bloomington
Main Library
1320 E. 10th Street
Bloomington, IN 47405-1801
Tel: 812-855-8028 (Reference)
812-855-8084 (Subject and Area Librarians)
812-855-3722 (Government Publications)
URL: http://www.indiana.edu/~librcsd/

Indiana State University
Cunningham Memorial Library
Terre Haute, IN 47802
Tel: 812-237-2610
Fax: 812-237-2567
Email: librbsc@cml.indstate.edu
URL: http://odin.indstate.edu/level1.dir/rare.dir/rare.htm

Indiana University - School of Medicine
Ruth Lilly Medical Library
975 W. Walnut Street

Indianapolis, IN 46202-5121
Tel: 317-274-2076
Fax: 317-278-2349
Email: Billings@indyvax.iupui.edu
URL: http://www.medlib.iupui.edu/hom/

Indianapolis-Marion County Public Library
40 East St. Clair Street
P.O. Box 211
Indianapolis, IN 46206
Tel: 317-269-1733
URL: http://www.imcpl.lib.in.us/

Jackson County Public Library
303 West 2nd Street
Seymour, IN 47274
Tel: 812-522-3412
Fax: 812-522-5456
Email: thill@japl.lib.in.us
URL: http://www.seymour.org/jcpl.htm

Jasper Public Library
116 Main Street
Jasper, IN 47546
Tel: 812-482-2712

Jay County Public Library
131 East Walnut Street
Portland, IN 47371
Tel: 219-726-7890
URL: http://birch.palni.edu/~jcpl/

Jefferson County Historical Society
Madison Railroad Station
615 West First Street
Madison, IN 47250
Tel: 812-265-2335

Jeffersonville Public Library
211 Court Avenue
P.O. Box 1548
Jeffersonville, IN 47131
Tel: 812-282-7765
812-285-5632

Jennings County Public Library
143 E. Walnut Street
North Vernon, IN 47265
Tel: 812-346-2091

Johnson County Public Library
401 South State Street
Franklin, IN 46131
Tel: 317-738-2833
Fax: 317-738-9635
URL: http://www.franklincoll.edu/comweb/libraries/jcpl/

Jonesboro Public Library
124 E. Fourth Street
Jonesboro, IN 46938
Tel: 317-674-8716
317-677-9080

Kendallville Public Library
126 West Rush Street
Kendallville, IN 46755
Tel: 219-347-2768

Kentland-Jefferson Township Library
201 East Graham Street
Kentland, IN 47951
Tel: 219-474-5044

Kewanna Public Library
P.O. Box 365
Kewanna, IN 46939
Tel: 219-653-2011

Kirklin Public Library
P.O. Box 8
Kirklin, IN 46050
Tel: 317-279-8258

Knox County Public Library
502 N. Seventh Street
Vincennes, In 47591
Tel: 812-886-4380

Knox County Records Library
819 Broadway
Vincennes, IN 47591

Kokomo-Howard County Public Library
Genealogy and Local History Dept.
220 North Union
Kokomo, IN 46901
Tel: 317-457-3242
Fax: 317-457-3683
Email: mmcnabb@kokomo.lib.in.us
URL: http://www.kokomo.lib.in.us/genealogy.html

Kosciusko County Historical Society/Library
Kosciusko County Jail Museum
Main & Indiana Streets
P.O. Box 1071
Warsaw, IN 46580
Tel: 219-269-1078

Ladoga Public Library
128 Main Street
Ladoga, IN 47954

Lake County Public Library
1919 West 81st Avenue
Merrillville, IN 46406
Tel: 219-769-3541

LaGrange Public Library
203 West Spring Street
LaGrange, IN 46761
Tel: 219-463-2841

LaPorte County Public Library
904 Indiana Avenue
LaPorte, IN 46350
Tel: 219-362-6156

LaPorte Historical Society/Museum
LaPorte County Govt. Complex
1 Courthouse Square
LaPorte, IN 46350
Tel: 219-326-6808 x276

Lawrence County Historical Genealogical Society
12 Courthouse Museum
Bedford, IN 47421
Tel: 812-475-4141

Lawrence County Railroad Historical Society
1420 I Street
Bedford, IN 47421

Lawrenceburg Public Library
123 West High Street
Lawrenceburg, IN 47025
Tel: 812-537-2857
URL: http://www.seidata.com/~lawplib/

Lebanon Public Library
104 East Washington
Lebanon, IN 46052
Tel: 317-482-3460

Ligonier Public Library
300 South Main Street
Ligonier, IN 46767
Tel: 219-894-4511

Linden-CarnegiePublic Library
102 South Main Street
P.O. Box 10
Linden, IN 47955
Tel: 317-339-4239

Logansport Public Library
616 East Broadway
Logansport, IN 46947
Tel: 219-753-6383

Loogootee Public Library
410 North Line Street
Loogootee, IN 47553
Tel: 812-295-3717

Madison-Jefferson County Public Library
420 West Main Street
Madison, IN 47250
Tel: 812-265-2744

Mariam Library
Hobart Historical Society
706 East Fourth Street, Box 24
Hobart, IN 46342

Marion Public Library
600 South Washington Street
Marion, IN 46953
Tel: 317-668-2900
Fax: 317-668-2911

Marshall County Historical Center
317 West Monroe Street
Plymouth, IN 46563

Melton Public Library
315 E. College Street
French Lick, IN 47432
Tel: 812-936-2177

Mennonite Historical Library
1700 S. Main
Goshen, IN 46526

Michigan City Public Library
100 E. Fourth Street
Michigan City, IN 46360
Tel: 219-879-3040

Milford Public Library
P.O. Box 247
Milford, IN 46542
Tel: 219-658-4312

Mishawaka Public Library
209 Lincoln Way E.
Mishawaka, IN 46544
Tel: 219-259-5277

Mitchell Public Library
804 W. Main Street
Mitchell, IN 47446
Tel: 812-849-2412

Monon Public Library
427 N. Market Street
P.O. Box 305
Monon, IN 47959
Tel: 219-253-6517

Monroe County Genealogical/Historical Society
c/o Genealogy Library
202 East 6th Street
Bloomington, IN 47408
Tel: 812-332-2517
Email: julian@bluemarble.net
URL: http://www.bluemarble.net/~julian/monroe.html

Monroe Public Library
Indiana Room

303 E. Kirkwood Avenue
Bloomington, IN 47408
Tel: 812-349-3080
812-349-3050
Email: ddevore@monroe.lib.in.us
URL: http://www.monroe.lib.in.us/indiana_room/indiana_room_home.html

Monterey-Tippecanoe Public Library
P.O. Box 38
Monterey, IN 46960
Tel: 219-542-2171

Montpelier Public Library
300 South Main Street
Montpelier, IN 47359
Tel: 317-728-5969

Mooresville Public Library
Indiana Library
220 West Harrison
Mooresville, IN 46158
Tel: 317-831-7323
URL: http://birch.palni.edu/~mvillepl

Morgan County Public Library
Genealogy Section
110 South Jefferson Street
Martinsville, IN 46151
Tel: 317-342-3451
Fax: 317-342-9992
Email: morglib@scican.net
URL: http://www.scican.net/~morglib/genasist/genasist.html

Morrison-Reeves Public Library
80 N. 6th Street
Richmond, IN 47374
Tel: 317-966-8291

Muncie Public Library
301 East Jackson St.
Muncie, IN 47305
Tel: 317-747-8200

Nappanee Public Library
157 N. Main Street
Nappanee, IN 46550
Tel: 219-773-7919

New Albany/Floyd County Public Library
180 W. Spring Street
New Albany, IN 47150
Tel: 812-949-3527

New Carlisle Public Library
124 E. Michigan Street
P.O. Box Q
New Carlisle, IN 46552
Tel: 219-654-3046

New Castle Public Library
376 South 15th Street
P.O. Box J
New Castle, IN 47362
Tel: 317-521-9354
317-529-0362

Noblesville Southeastern Public Library
One Library Plaza
Noblesville, IN 46060
Tel: 317-773-1384
URL: http://www.fgs.org/~fgs/soc0130.htm

North Judson Public Library
208 Keller Avenue
North Judson, IN 46366
Tel: 219-896-2841

North Manchester Public Library
204 West Main Street
North Manchester, IN 46962
Tel: 219-982-4773

Notre Dame Archives
607 Hesburgh Library
Notre Dame, IN 46556
Tel: 219-631-6448
Fax: 219-631-7980
Email: Archives.1@nd.edu
URL: archives1.archives.nd.edu/guidecom.htm

Oakland City Public Library
210 South Main Street
Oakland City, IN 47660
Tel: 812-749-3559

Odon Winkelpleck Memorial Library
202 West Main Street
Odon, IN 47562
Tel: 812-636-4805
812-636-4949

Ohio County Public Library
100 North High Street
Rising Sun, IN 47040
Tel: 812-438-2257

Ohio Township Public Library
23 West Jennings Street
Newburgh, In 47630
Tel: 812-853-5468

Orleans Public Library
174 N. Maple Street
Orleans, IN 47452
Tel: 812-865-3270

Osgood Public Library
136 West Ripley
Osgood, IN 47037
Tel: 812-689-4011

Otterbein Public Library
P.O. Box 550
Otterbein, IN 47970
Tel: 317-583-2107

Owen County Public Library
10 South Montgomery Street
Spencer, IN 47460
URL: http://www.countryconnect.com/ocpl/ocpl.htm

Owensville-Carnegie Public Library
110 Main Street
P.O. Box 219
Owensville, IN 47665
Tel: 812-724-3335

Oxford Public Library
200 East Smith Street
P.O. Box 6
Oxford, IN 47971
Tel: 317-385-2177

Paoli Public Library
NE Court Square
Paoli, IN 47454
Tel: 812-723-3841

Patrick Henry Sullivan Museum & Genealogy Library
225 W. Hawthorne Street
Zionsville, IN 46077
Tel: 317-873-4900
URL: http://www.artcom.com/museums/nv/mr/46077-16.htm

Peabody Library
203 Main Street
Columbia City, IN 46725
Tel: 219-244-5541

Pennville Public Library
195 N. Union
P.O. Box 206
Pennville, IN 47369
Tel: 219-731-3333

Peru Public Library
102 East Main Street
Peru, IN 46970
Tel: 317-473-3069

Pierceton Public Library
P.O. Box 328
Pierceton, IN 46562
Tel: 219-594-5474

Pike County Public Library
Barrett Memorial Library
1104 Main Street
Petersburg, IN 47567
Tel: 812-354-6257

Plainfield Public Library
1120 Stafford Road
Plainfield, IN 46168-2230
Tel: 317-839-6602
Fax: 317-839-4044
Email: plpl.plpl@incolsa.palni.edu
URL: http://www.plainfield.lib.in.us/

Plymouth Public Library
201 N. Center Street
Plymouth, IN 46563
Tel: 219-936-2324

Poseyville Public Library
P.O. Box 220
Poseyville, IN 47633
Tel: 812-874-3418

Princeton Public Library
124 South Hart
Princeton, IN 47670
Tel: 812-385-4464

Pulaski County Public Library
121 South Riverside Drive
Winamac, IN 46996
Tel: 219-946-3432

Putnam County Public Library
120 East Walnut Street
P.O. Box 116
Greencastle, IN 46135
Tel: 319-653-2755

Randolph County Historical Society/Museum
416 South Meridian
Winchester, IN 47394
Tel: 317-584-4323

Remington-Carpenter Township Library
Ohio Street
P.O. Box 65
Remington, IN 47977
Tel: 219-261-2543

Rensselaer Public Library
208 West Susan Street
Rensselaer, IN 47978
Tel: 219-866-5881
Fax: 219-866-7378
EMail: jcplref@netnitco.net
URL: http://birch.palni.edu/~jcpl/

Ridgeville Public Library
P.O. Box 63
Ridgeville, IN 47380
Tel: 317-857-2025

Ripley County Historical Society
Local History & Genealogical Library

125 Washington Street
P.O. Box 525
Versailles, IN 47023
Tel: 812-689-3031
Email: rchslib@seidata.com
URL: http://www.seidata.com/~rchslib/

Ripley County Historical Society Museum
Main and Water Streets
Versailles, IN 47023
Email: rchslib@seidata.com
URL: http://www.seidata.com/~rchslib/

Roachdale Public Library
P.O. Box 278
Roachdale, IN 46172

Roann-PawPaw Public Library
P.O. Box 248
Roann, IN 46974
Tel: 317-833-5231

Roanoke Public Library
126 N. Main Street
P.O. Box 249
Roanoke, IN 46783
Tel: 219-872-3306
219-872-8116

Rockport-Ohio Township Public Library
210 Walnut Street
Rockport, IN 47635
Tel: 812-649-4866

Rockville Public Library
106 N. Market Street
Rockville, IN 47872
Tel: 317-569-5544

Royal Center/Boone Township Public Library
P.O. Box 459
Royal Center, IN 46978
Tel: 219-643-3185

Rushville Public Library
130 West 3rd Street
Rushville, IN 46173
Tel: 317-932-3496
Fax: 317-932-4528

St. Joseph County Public Library
304 South Main Street
South Bend, IN
Tel: 219-282-4630
219-282-4621 (Local History & Genealogy)
Email: m.waterson@gomail.sjcpl.lib.in.us
URL: http://sjcpl.lib.in.us/homepage/LocalHist/Genealogy.html

Salem Public Library
212 N. Main Street
Salem, IN 47167
Tel: 812-883-5600

Scott County Public Library
108 S. Main Street
Scottsburg, IN 47170
Tel: 812-752-2751

Shelbyville Public Library
57 West Broadway
Shelbyville, IN 46176
Tel: 317-398-7121
Fax: 317-398-4430

Sheridan Public Library
214 S. Main Street
Sheridan, IN 46069
Tel: 317-758-5201

Shoals Public Library
Fourth and High Street
P.O. Box 188
Shoals, IN 47581
Tel: 812-247-3838

South Bend Public Library
122 West Wayne
South Bend, IN 46601

Speedway Public Library
5633 W. 25th Street
Speedway, IN 46224
Tel: 317-244-8959
Fax: 317-243-9373
Email: spdwylib@indy.net
URL: http://birch.palni.edu/~jriggle/spdwy3.htm

Spencer-Owen Public Library
110 E. Market Street
Spencer, IN 47460
Tel: 812-829-3392

Spiceland Public Library
106 Main Street
Spiceland, IN 47385
Tel: 317-987-7472

Sullivan County Public Library
100 S. Crowder Street
Sullivan, IN 47882
Tel: 812-268-4957

Swayzee Public Library
301 South Washington
P.O. Box 307
Swayzee, IN 46986
Tel: 317-922-7526

Switzerland County Public Library
210 Ferry Street
P.O. Box 133
Vevay, IN 47043
Tel: 812-427-3363
Fax: 812-427-3654

Syracuse Public Library
115 E. Main Street
Syracuse, IN 46567

Thorntown Public Library
124 N. Market Street
Thorntown, IN 46071
Tel: 317-436-7348
317-436-7518

Tippecanoe County Historical Association/Museum
909 South Street
Lafayette, IN 47901
Tel: 765-476-8411
Fax: 765-476-8414
Email: tcha@iquest.net
URL: http://www.iquest.net/tcha/

Tippecanoe County Public Library
627 South Street
Lafayette, IN 47901
Tel: 317-429-0100

Tipton County Public Library
127 E. Madison Street
Tipton, IN 46072
Tel: 317-675-8761

Union City Public Library
408 N. Columbia Street
Union City, IN 47390
Tel: 317-964-4748

Union County Public Library
2 East Seminary Street
Liberty, IN 47353
Tel: 317-458-5355

University of Southern Indiana
David L. Rice Library
Evansville, IN 47712
URL: http://www.usi.edu/library/library.htm

Valparaiso/Porter County Public Library
103 Jefferson Street
Valparaiso, IN 46383
Tel: 219-462-0524

Veedersburg Public Library
408 North Main Street
Veedersburg, IN 47987
Tel: 317-294-2808
URL: http://glenmar.com/~emoyhbo/vburglib.html

Vermillion County Public Library
P.O. Box 97
Newport, IN 47966
Tel: 765-492-3555
URL: http://members.aol.com/KFether123/verlib.html

Vigo County Historical Society/Museum
1411 South Sixth Street
Terre Haute, IN 47807
Tel: 812-235-9717
812-253-9717
Email: vchs@iquest.net
URL: http://web.indstate.edu/community/vchs/home.html

Vigo County Public Library
One Library Square
Terre Haute, IN 47807
Tel: 812-235-2121
Fax: 812-232-3208

Vincennes University
Lewis Historical Library
1002 N. 1st Street
Vincennes, IN 47591
Tel: 812-885-4330
Email: gstevens@wabash.vinu.edu
URL: http://www.vinu.edu/lewis.htm

Wabash County Historical Museum
89 West Hill Street
Wabash, IN 46992

Wabash-Carnegie Public Library
188 West Hill Street
Wabash, IN 46992
Tel: 219-563-2972

Wabash Valley Historical Museum
1411 South Sixth Street
Terre Haute, IN 47802
Tel: 812-235-9717

Wakarusa Public Library
124 N. Elkhart
P.O. Box 485
Wakarusa, IN 46573
Tel: 219-862-2465

Walkerton/Lincoln Township Public Library
607 Roosevelt Road
Walkerton, IN 46574-1296
Tel: 219-586-2933

Walton-Tipton Township Public Library
103 E. Bishop
P.O. Box 406
Walton, IN 46994
Tel: 219-626-2234

Wanatah Public Library
104 N. Main Street
P.O. Box 299
Wanatah, IN 46390
Tel: 219-733-9303

Warren Public Library
123 E. Third Street
P.O. Box 327
Warren, IN 46792
Tel: 219-375-3450

Warrick County Museum
611 W. Main
P.O. Box 581
Boonville, IN 47601-0581
Tel: 812-897-3100
812-897-1500

Warsaw Public Library
315 E. Center Street
Warsaw, IN 46580
Tel: 219-267-6011

Washington Township Public Library
498 N. State Road 267
Avon, IN 46168
Tel: 317-272-4818
URL: http://realty.mibor.net/sites/avon-library/

Washington-Carnegie Public Library
300 West Main Street
Washington, IN 47501
Tel: 812-254-4586

Waveland/Brown Township Public Library
P.O. Box 158
Waveland, IN 47989
Tel: 317-435-2700

West Lafayette Public Library
208 West Columbia Street
West Lafayette, IN 47906
Tel: 317-743-2261

Westchester Public Library
200 W. Indiana Avenue
Chesterton, IN 46304
Tel: 219-926-7696

Westfield Public Library
333 W. Hoover Road
Westfield, IN 46074
Tel: 317-896-9391

Westville-New Durham Public Library
P.O. Box 526
Westville, IN 46391
Tel: 219-785-2015

White County Historical Museum
101 S. Bluff
Monticello, IN 47960
Tel: 219-583-3998

Whiting Public Library
1735 Oliver Street
Whiting, IN 46394
Tel: 219-659-0269

Willard Library
21 North First Avenue
Evansville, IN 47710
Tel: 812-425-4309

Williamsport/Washington Township Public Library
9 Fall Street
Williamsport, IN 47993
Tel/Fax: 317-762-6555

Winchester Public Library
125 N. East Street
Winchester, IN 47394
Tel: 317-584-4824

Wolcott Public Library
101 E. North Street
P.O. Box 376
Wolcott, IN 47995
Tel: 219-279-2695

Worthington Public Library
26 N. Commercial Street
Worthington, IN 47471
Tel: 812-875-3815

York Township Public Library
8475 North, 885th West
Raub, IN 47976
Tel: 219-474-5689

Newspaper Repositories

Batesville Memorial Public Library
131 N. Walnut Street
Batesville, IN 47006
Tel: 812-934-4706
Fax: 812-934-6288
Email: mkruse@ind.net
URL: http://batesville.venus.net/nonprofit/bmpl.html

Indiana Historical Society/Library
315 W. Ohio Street, 3rd Floor
Indianapolis, IN 46202
(Moving Fall 1998 to Ohio and West Streets)
Tel: 317-232-1873
Email: rshoemaker@statelib.lib.in.us
URL: http://www.ihs1830.org/newsp.htm

Indiana State Library
Indiana Division
140 N. Senate Avenue
Indianapolis, IN 46204
http://www.statelib.lib.in.us/

Indiana University - Bloomington
Main Library, Serials Dept.
1320 E. 10th Street
Bloomington, IN 47405-1801
Tel: 812-855-5672
Email: shepher@indiana.edu
URL: http://www.indiana.edu/~librcsd/

St. Joseph County Public Library
304 South Main Street
South Bend, IN 46601
Tel: 219-282-4630
219-282-4621 (Local History & Genealogy)
Email: m.waterson@gomail.sjcpl.lib.in.us
URL: http://sjcpl.lib.in.us/homepage/LocalHist/Genealogy.html

Vital Records

Indiana State Department of Health
Vital Records Department
2 North Meridian Street
Indianapolis, IN 46204
Tel: 317-233-2700
317-233-1325 (Local Health Departments Assistance)
URL: http://www.state.in.us/doh/vital/vr1.html

Indiana on the Web

Allen County Public Library
http://www.acpl.lib.in.us/

Index of Indiana Marriages Through 1850
http://www.statelib.lib.in.us/www/indiana/genealogy/mirr.html

Indiana GenWeb Project
http://www.comsource.net/~kyseeker/indiana/

Indiana Historical Society/Library
http://www.ihs1830.org/ihs.html

Indiana History
http://cvax.ipfw.indiana.edu/www/depts/history//indihist.html

Indiana in the Civil War
http://www.thnet.com/~liggettkw/incw/cw.htm

Indiana State Archives
http://www.state.in.us/acin/icpr/index.html

Indiana State Library
http://www.statelib.lib.in.us/

Morgan County Public Library
http://www.scican.net/~morglib/genasist/genasist.html

Underground Railroad Operators Directory - Indiana
http://www.ugrr.org//names/map-in.htm

IOWA

ARCHIVES, STATE & NATIONAL

Iowa State Archives
State Historical Society of Iowa
Capitol Complex
State of Iowa Historical Building
600 East Locust
Des Moines, IA 50319
Tel: 515-281-3007

National Archives—Central Plains Region
2312 East Bannister Road
Kansas City, MO 64131
Tel: 816-926-6272
Fax: 816-926-6982
Email: archives@kansascity.nara.gov
URL: http://www.nara.gov/nara/regional/06nsgil.html

GENEALOGICAL SOCIETIES

Adams County Genealogical Society
P.O. Box 117
Prescott, IA 50859

Ankeny Genealogical Chapter
P.O. Box 136
Ankeny, IA 50021

Appanoose County Genealogy Society
1601 S. 16th Street
Centerville, IA 52544

Boone County Genealogical Society
P.O. Box 453
Boone, IA 50036

Botna Valley Genealogical Society of East Pottawattamie County
P.O. Box 633
Oakland, IA 51560

Bremer County Genealogical Society
Route 1, Box 132
Plainfield, IA 50666
URL: http://www.netins.net/showcase/celene/genweb/brmgnsoc.htm

Buchanan County Genealogical Society
103 4th Avenue, SE
P.O. Box 4
Independence, IA 50644

Buena Vista Genealogical Society/Library
609 Erie Street
Storm Lake, IA 50588
URL: http://www.digiserve.com/igs/bunavst.htm

Butler County Genealogy Society
c/o Clarksville Public Library
103 West Greene Street
Clarksville, IA 50619
URL: http://www.netins.net/showcase/winter/butler.htm

Carroll County Genealogical Society
P.O. Box 21
Carroll, IA 51401

Cass County Genealogical Society
706 Hazel Street
Atlantic, IA 50022

Central Iowa Genealogical Society
P.O. Box 945
Marshalltown, IA 50158

Chickasaw County Genealogical Society
P.O. Box 434
New Hampton, IA 50659

Clayton County Genealogical Society
P.O. Box 846
Elkader, IA 52043

Clarke County Genealogical Society
300 South Fillmore
Osceola, IA 50213

Crawford County Genealogical Society
P.O. Box 26
Vail, IA 51465

Dallas County Genealogical Society
P.O. Box 264
Dallas Center, IA 50063-0264

Decorah Genealogy Association
c/o Decorah Public Library
202 Winnebago Street
Decorah, IA 52101
Tel: 319-382-8559
URL: http://bl-12.rootsweb.com/~iawinnes/dga.htm

Des Moines County Genealogical Society
P.O. Box 493
Burlington, IA 52601
URL: http://www.fgs.org/~fgs/soc0041.htm

Dubuque County-Key County Genealogical Society
P.O. Box 13
Dubuque, IA 52004-0013
URL: http://www.fgs.org/~fgs/soc0043.htm

Fayette County Genealogical Society
100 North Walnut
West Union, IA 52175

Forest City Municipal Library
115 East L Street
Forest City, IA 50436
Tel: 515-582-4542

Franklin County Genealogical Society
c/o Hampton Public Library
4 Federal Street South
Hampton, IA 50441
Email: yankeez@willowtree.com
URL: http://www.willowtree.com/~yankeez/fcgs/page1.htm

Fremont County Genealogical Society
P.O. Box 671
Sidney, IA 51652

Gateway Genealogical Society
618 14th Avenue
Camanche, IA 52730

Greater Sioux County Genealogical Society
c/o Sioux Center Public Library
327 First Avenue, NE
Sioux Center, IA 51250

Greene County Genealogical Society
P.O. Box 133
Jefferson, IA 50129

Grundy County Genealogical Society
708 West Street
Reinbeck, IA 50669-1365

Guthrie County Genealogical Society
P.O. Box 96
Jamaica, IA 50128-0096

Hamilton Heritage Hunters Genealogical Society
P.O. Box 364
Webster City, IA 50595

Hancock County Genealogical Society
P.O. Box 81
Klemme, IA 50449
URL: http://www.netins.net/showcase/winter/hancock.htm

Hardin County Genealogical Society
P.O. Box 252
Eldora, IA 50627

Harrison County Genealogical Society
2810 190th Trail
Woodbine, IA 51579
Tel: 712-647-2593
Email: HCGS51579@aol.com
URL: http://www.rootsweb.com/~iaharris/hcgs.htm
Library at:
Merry Brook Museum
212 Lincoln Way
Woodbine, IA 51579

Henry County Genealogical Society
P.O. Box 81
Mt. Pleasant, IA 52641

Howard-Winneshieck Genealogy Society
P.O. Box 362
Cresco, IA 52136
URL: http://www.netins.net/showcase/winter/howwin.htm

Humboldt County Genealogical Society
c/o Humboldt Public Library
30 6th Street North
Humboldt, IA 50548
URL: http://www.netins.net/showcase/winter/humboldt.htm

Iowa City Genealogical Society
P.O. Box 822
Iowa City, IA 52244
URL: http://www.rootsweb.com/~iajohnso/icgensoc.htm

Iowa Genealogical Society/Library
6000 Douglas Avenue
Des Moines, IA 50322
Tel: 515-276-0287
Mail:
IGS-NET
P.O. Box 7735
Des Moines, IA 50322-7735
URL: http://www.digiserve.com/igs/igs.htm

Iowa Lakes Genealogy Society
600 West 11th Street
Spencer, IA 51301-3235
URL: http://www.pionet.net/~nwiowa/spencer/clubs/ilgs.htm

Jackson County Genealogical Chapter (IGS)
P.O. Box 1065
Maquoketa, IA 52060

Jasper County Genealogical Society
Jasper County Courthouse
P.O. Box 163
Newton, IA 50208
Tel: 515-792-1522
URL: http://www.rootsweb.com/~iajasper/jcgs.htm

Jefferson County Genealogical Society
Route 1
Fairfield, IA 52556

Jones County Genealogical Society
P.O. Box 174
Anomosa, IA 52205

Keomah Genealogical Society (Keokuk and Mahaska Counties)
P.O. Box 616
Oskaloosa, IA 52577-0616

Lee County Genealogical Society
P.O. Box 303
Keokuk, IA 52632

Lime Creek/Winnebago County Genealogical Society
115 East L Street
Forest City, IA 50436
URL: http://www.netins.net/showcase/winter/winnebgo.htm

Linn County Genealogical Society
101 8th Avenue, SE
Cedar Rapids, IA 52401
Tel: 319-369-0022

Louisa County Genealogical Society
607 Highway 61 North
Wapello, IA 52653
URL: http://bl-12.rootsweb.com/~ialouisa/lchspub.htm

Lucas County Genealogical Society
c/o Chariton Free Public Library
Family History Room
803 Braden Avenue
Chariton, IA 50049
Tel: 515-774-5514
Fax: 515-774-8695
Email: chariton@netins.net

Madison County Genealogy Society
P.O. Box 26
Winterset, IA 50273-0026

Marion County Genealogical Society
P.O. Box 385
Knoxville, IA 50138
Email: jean2gen@se-iowa.net
URL: http://www.rootsweb.com/~iamarion/resc.html#mcgs

Mid-American Genealogical Society
P.O. Box 316
Davenport, IA 52801

Mills County Genealogical Society
c/o Glenwood Public Library
109 North Vine Street
Glenwood, IA 51534

Monroe County Genealogical Society
c/o Albia Public Library
203 Benton Avenue, E
Albia, IA 52531

Montgomery County Genealogical Society
320A Coolbaugh
Red Oak, IA 51566

Nishnabotna Genealogical Society of Shelby County
847 Rd M56
Harlan, IA 51537
URL: http://www.rootsweb.com/~iashelby/scgs.htm

North Central Iowa Genealogical Society
P.O. Box 237
Mason City, IA 50402
URL: http://www.netins.net/showcase/winter/cerrogor.htm

Northeast Iowa Genealogical Society
c/o Grout Museum
503 South Street
Waterloo, IA 50701-1517
URL: http://iowa-counties.com/blackhawk/gene.html

Northwest Iowa Genealogical Society
c/o LeMars Public Library
46 First Street, SW
LeMars, IA 51031

Old Fort Genealogical Society
P.O. Box 1
Fort Madison, IA 52627

Page County Genealogical Society
RR 2, Box 236
Shenandoah, IA 51610

Palo Alto County Genealogical Society
207 North Wallace Street
Emmetsburg, IA 50536

Pioneer Sons & Daughters Genealogical Society
P.O. Box 2103
Des Moines, IA 50310

Pottawattamie County Genealogical Society
P.O. Box 394
Council Bluffs, IA 51502
Tel: 712-322-1171
Email: banders@nfinity.com
URL: http://www.rootsweb.com/~iapottaw/index.html#anchor1703570

Poweshiek County Historical and Genealogical Society
P.O. Box 280
Montezuma, IA 50171

Sac County Genealogical Society
P.O. Box 234
Lytton, IA 50561

Scott County Genealogical Society/Library
P.O. Box 3132
Davenport, IA 52808
Tel: 319-326-7902

Story County Chapter (IGS)
c/o Chamber of Commerce
205 Clark Avenue
Ames, IA 50010

Tama County Tracers Genealogical Society
200 North Broadway
Toledo, IA 52342

Taylor County Genealogical Society
RR 3
Bedford, IA 50833

Tree Stumpers
Route 1, Box 65
Meriden, IA 51037

Union County Genealogical Society
c/o Gibson Memorial Library
310 North Maple
Creston, IA 50801

Wapello County Genealogical Society/Library
Amtrack Depot
210 W. Main Street
P.O. Box 163
Ottumwa, IA 52501
Tel: 515-682-8676
URL: http://www.rootsweb.com/~iawapegs/

Warren County Genealogical Society
Route 2, 802 Kennedy Street
Indianola, IA 50125

Washington County Genealogical Society
P.O. Box 446
Washington, IA 52353
URL: http://www.rootsweb.com/~iawashin/wcgs.htm

Wayne County Genealogical Society
304 North Franklin
Corydon, IA 50060

Webster County Genealogical Society
P.O. Box 1584
Fort Dodge, IA 50501

Winneshieck County Genealogical Society
P.O. Box 344
Decorah, IA 52101

Woodbury County Genealogical Society
P.O. Box 624
Sioux City, IA 51102

Wright County Genealogical Searchers
P.O. Box 225
Clarion, IA 50525

Historical Societies

Benton County Historical Society
612 First Avenue
Vinton, IA 52349-1705

Boone County Historical Society
P.O. Box 1
Boone, IA 50036

Central Community Historical Society
RR 2, Box 98
DeWitt, IA 52742

Cherokee County Historical Society
P.O. Box 247
Cleghorn, IA 51014

Fayette County Helpers Club & Historical Society
100 North Walnut
West Union, IA 52175
Tel: 319-422-5797

Iowa, State Historical Society of
Library, Archives, & Museum
600 E. Locust
Des Moines, IA 50319-0290
Tel: 515-281-5111 (library/archives)
515-281-6412 (museum)
Library/Archives
402 Iowa Avenue
Iowa City, IA 52240-1806
Tel: 319-335-3916
URL: http://www.uiowa.edu/~shsi/index.htm

Johnson County Historical Society
P.O. Box 5081
Coralville, IA 52241

Kellogg Historical Society/Museum
218 High Street
P.O. Box 295
Kellogg, IA 50135-0295

Linn County Heritage Society
P.O. Box 175
Cedar Rapids, IA 52406

Linn County Historical Society/Museum
101 8th Avenue, SE
Cedar Rapids, IA 52401
Tel: 319-362-1501

Louisa County Historical Society
609 Highway 61 North
Wapello, IA 52653
URL: http://bl-12.rootsweb.com/~ialouisa/lchspub.htm

Pella Historical Society/Village
507 Franklin Street
Pella, IA 50219
Tel: 515-628-4311
Fax: 515-628-9192
Email: pellatt@kdsi.net
URL: http://www.kdsi.net/~pellatt/

Pottawattamie County, Historical Society of
Email: DENCATD@AOL.COM
or VERGAMI@CULAW.CREIGHTON.EDU
URL: http://www.geocities.com/Heartland/Plains/5660/

Poweshiek County Historical and Genealogical Society
P.O. Box 280
Montezuma, IA 50171

West Liberty Historical Society
600 E. Fourth Street
West Liberty, IA 52776

LDS Family History Centers

Ames Family History Center
2524 Hoover Avenue
Ames, IA 50010
Tel: 515-232-3634

Cedar Falls Family History Center
3006 Pleasant
Cedar Falls, IA 50613
Tel: 319-266-6374

Cedar Rapids Family History Center
4300 Trailridge Road, SE
Cedar Rapids, IA 52403
Tel: 319-363-7178

Davenport Family History Center
4929 Wisconsin Avenue
Davenport, IA 52806
Tel: 319-386-7547

Iowa City Family History Center
2730 Bradford Drive
Iowa City, IA 52240
Tel: 319-338-5306

Mason City Family History Center
1309 S. Kentucky Avenue
Mason City, IA 50401
Tel: 515-424-4211

Sioux City Family History Center
1201 West Clifton
Sioux City, IA 51104
Tel: 712-255-9686

West Des Moines Family History Center
3301 Ashworth Road
West Des Moines, IA 50265
Tel: 515-225-0416

Archives/Libraries/Museums

Ames Public Library
515 Douglas Avenue
Ames, IA 50010-6215
Tel: 515-239-5656
Fax: 515-232-4571
Email: lb.svd@isumvs.iastate.edu
URL: http://www.ames.lib.ia.us/

Buena Vista Genealogical Society/Library
609 Erie Street
Storm Lake, IA 50588
URL: http://www.digiserve.com/igs/bunavst.htm

Burlington Public Library
501 North Fourth Street
Burlington, IA 52601
Tel: 319-753-1647
URL: http://www.burlington.lib.ia.us

Carnegie-Eldon Public Library
608 W. Elm Street
Eldon, IA 52554-0430
Tel/Fax: 515-652-7517

Carnegie-Montezuma Public Library
200 S. 3rd
Montezuma, IA 50171
Tel: 515-623-3417
Fax: 515-623-3339
Email: zumapl@netins.net

Carnegie-Stout Public Library
360 W. 11th Street
Dubuque, IA 52001
Tel: 319-589-4225
Fax: 319-589-4217
URL: http://www.dubuque.lib.ia.us/

Carnegie-Vierson Public Library
823 Broadway
Pella, IA 50219
Tel: 515-628-4268
Fax: 515-628-1326
Email: cvpublib@central.edu

Carroll Public Library
118 E. 5th Street
Carroll, IA 51401
Tel: 712-792-3432
Fax: 712-792-0141

Cedar Falls Public Library
524 Main Street
Cedar Falls, IA 50613
Tel: 319-273-8643
Email: cfpljohn@iren.net
URL: http://www.iren.net/cfpl/

Cedar Rapids Historical Archives
1201 6th Street, SW
Cedar Rapids, IA 52404
Tel: 319-398-0419

Cedar Rapids Public Library
500 1st Street, SE
Cedar Rapids, IA 52401
Tel: 319-398-5123
Fax: 319-398-0476
URL: http://www.cedar-rapids.lib.ia.us/crpl/home.html

Chariton Free Public Library
803 Braden Avenue
Chariton, IA 50049
Tel: 515-774-5514
Fax: 515-774-8695
Email: chariton@netins.net

Clinton Public Library
306 8th Avenue, S
Clinton, IA 52732
Tel: 319-242-8441
Fax: 319-242-8162
Email: library@sanasys.com

Conrad Public Library
102 E. Grundy
Conrad, IA 50621
Tel: 515-366-2583
Fax: 515-366-3105
Email: conradlib@mtnia.com

Danish Immigrant Museum
2212 Washington Street
P.O. Box 178
Elk Horn, IA 51531
Tel: 800-759-9192

Davenport Public Library
321 N. Main Street
Davenport, IA 52801
Tel: 319-326-7832
Fax: 319-326-7809
URL: http://www.rbls.lib.il.us/lib/dpa.html

Decorah Public Library
202 Winnebago Street
Decorah, IA 52101
Tel: 319-382-8559
319-382-3717
Fax: 319-382-4524
Email: borowslo@martin.luther.edu

Des Moines Public Library
100 Locust
Des Moines, IA 50309
Tel: 515-283-4152
Email: dsmlib@netins.net
URL: http://www.netins.net/showcase/pldm/

Donnellson Public Library
Family History Department
500 Park
Donnellson, IA 52625
Email: donpulib@interl.net

Drake University
Cowles Library
28th and University
Des Moines, IA 50311
Tel: 515-271-3993
Fax: 515-271-3933
Email: RH7871r@acad.drake.edu
URL: http://www.drake.edu/lib.html

Eckels Memorial Library
207 S. Highway
P.O. Box 519
Oakland, IA 51560
Tel: 712-482-6668

Elgin Public Library
250 Center
Elgin, IA 52141
Tel/Fax: 319-426-5313

Elliott Public Library
401 Main Street
P.O. Box 306
Elliott, IA 51532
Tel: 712-767-2355

Emmetsburg Public Library
2018 East 10th Street
Emmetsburg, IA 50536
Tel/Fax: 712-852-4009
Email: emtsbgli@ncn.net

Ericson Public Library
702 Greene Street
Boone, IA 50036
Tel: 515-432-3727
Fax: 515-432-1103
Email: cwatson@netins.net

Fairfield Public Library
104 West Adams
Fairfield, IA 52556
Tel: 515-472-6551
Fax: 515-472-3249
Email: library@fairfield.com

Fort Dodge Public Library
605 1st Avenue, North
Fort Dodge, IA 50501-3899
Tel: 515-573-8167
Fax: 515-573-5422

Frontier Heritage Library
Broadway and Main Sts., 2nd Floor
Council Bluffs, IA 51501
Tel: 712-322-1171

Glenwood Public Library
109 N. Vine
Glenwood, IA 51534
Tel: 712-527-5252
Fax: 712-527-3619
Email: denise@netins.net

Greenfield Public Library
215 South 1st
P.O. Box 328
Greenfield, IA 50849
Tel: 515-743-6120

Grout Museum of History & Science
Hans J. Chryst Archival Library
503 South Street
Waterloo, IA 50701
Tel: 319-234-6357
Fax: 319-236-0500

Grundy Center Public Library
706 7th Street
Grundy Center, IA 50638
Tel: 319-824-3607
Fax: 319-824-5863

Guthrie Center Public Library
507 State
Guthrie Center, IA 50115
Tel/Fax: 515-747-8110

Hampton Public Library
4 Federal Street South
Hampton, IA 50441
Tel: 515-456-4451
Fax: 515-456-2377
Email: Hampublib@hampton-dumont.k12.ia.us

Harlan Community Library
718 Court
Harlan, IA 51537
Tel: 712-755-5934
Fax: 712-755-3952

Hawkins Memorial Library
308 Main
LaPorte, IA 50651
Tel: 319-342-3025
Fax: 319-342-3025
URL: http://www.cedarnet.org/library/laport.html

Independence Public Library
210 2nd Street, NE
Independence, IA 50644
Tel/Fax: 319-334-2470

Indianola Public Library
207 North B Street
Indianola, IA 50125
URL: http://www.indianola.ia.us/library/

Iowa City Public Library
123 S. Linn Street
Iowa City, IA 52240
Tel: 319-356-5200
Fax: 319-356-5494
Email: mclark@wade.iowa-city.lib.ia.us
URL: http://www.jeonet.com/city/library.htm

Iowa Genealogical Society/Library
6000 Douglas Avenue
Des Moines, IA 50322
Tel: 515-276-0287
Mail:
IGS-NET
P.O. Box 7735
Des Moines, IA 50322-7735
URL: http://www.digiserve.com/igs/igs.htm

Iowa Masonic Library
The Grand Lodge of Iowa, A.F. & A.M.
813 First Avenue, SE
Cedar Rapids, IA 52401-5001
Tel: 319-365-1438
Email: Grand_Lodge_IA@msn.com
URL: http://freemasonry.org/gl-ia/index.html

Iowa, State Historical Society of
Library, Archives, & Museum
600 E. Locust
Des Moines, IA 50319-0290
Tel: 515-281-5111 (library/archives)
515-281-6412 (museum)
Library/Archives
402 Iowa Avenue
Iowa City, IA 52240-1806
Tel: 319-335-3916
URL: http://www.uiowa.edu/~shsi/index.htm

Iowa, State Library of
1112 East Grand
Des Moines, IA 50319
Tel: 515-281-4105
Email: siloweb@www.silo.lib.ia.us
URL: http://www.silo.lib.ia.us

Iowa State University
Parks Library
Osborn and Morrill
Ames, IA 50011
Tel: 515-294-2345
Fax: 515-294-1885
URL: http://www.lib.iastate.edu/

Janesville Public Library
227 Main Street
P.O. Box 328
Janesville, IA 50647
Tel/Fax: 319-987-2925
URL: http://www.cedarnet.org/library/janesvil.htm

Kellogg Historical Society/Museum
218 High Street
P.O. Box 295
Kellogg, IA 50135-0295

Kendall Young Library
1201 Wilson Avenue
Webster City, IA 50595
Tel: 515-832-9100
Fax: 515-832-9102
Email: c.weiss@netins.net

Keokuk Public Library
210 N. 5th
Keokuk, IA 52632
Tel: 319-524-1483
Fax: 319-524-2320
Email: ddsystem@interl.net

Kinney Memorial Library
203 Main Street
Hanlontown, IA 50444
Tel/Fax: 515-896-2888

Knoxville Public Library
213 E. Montgomery
Knoxville, IA 50138
Tel/Fax: 515-828-0585
Email: Knoxlib@se-iowa.net

LeMars Public Library
46 First Street, SW
LeMars, IA 51031
Tel: 712-546-5004
Fax: 712-546-5797
Email: library@lemars.ia.frontiercomm.net

Linn County Historical Society/Museum
101 8th Avenue, SE
Cedar Rapids, IA 52401
Tel: 319-362-1501

Livermore Public Library
402 5th Street and 4th Avenue
Livermore, IA 50558
Tel: 515-379-2078
Fax: 515-379-1002
Email: libplib@trvnet.net
URL: http://www.trvnet.net/~livplib/

Living History Farms
2600 NW 111th Street
Urbandale, IA 50322
Tel: 515-278-5286
515-278-2400 (24-hour/event info)
Email: lhf@ioweb.com
URL: http://www.ioweb.com/lhf/

Loras College
Wahlert Memorial Library
1450 Alta Vista
Dubuque, IA 52001
Tel: 319-588-7009
Fax: 319-588-7292
Email: Klein@lcacl.loras.edu
URL: http://www.loras.edu/library/index.html

Lost Nation Public Library
301 Pleasant Street
Lost Nation, IA 52254-0397
Tel/Fax: 319-678-2114

Manchester Public Library
300 N. Franklin
Manchester, IA 52057
Tel: 319-927-3719
Fax: 319-927-3058
Email: mnchst00@iren.net

Marshalltown Public Library
36 N. Center Street
Marshalltown, IA 50158
Tel: 515-754-5738
Fax: 515-754-5708

Mason City Public Library
225 2nd Street, SE
Mason City, IA 50401
Tel: 515-421-3668
Fax: 515-423-2615
Email: mcpl@mach3ww.com

Matilda J. Gibson Memorial Library
124 North Maple
Creston, IA 50801
Tel: 515-782-2277
Fax: 515-782-4604
Email: cstanger@aea14.k12.ia.us

Merry Brook Museum
212 Lincoln Way
Woodbine, IA 51579
Tel: 712-647-2593

Montgomery Memorial Library
711 Main
P.O. Box 207
Jewell, IA 50130
Tel: 515-827-5112
Email: jewell_public.lib@s-hamilton.k12.ia.us

Musser Public Library
304 Iowa Avenue

Muscatine, IA 52761
Tel: 319-293-3068
Fax: 319-264-1033
Email: mtate@libby.rbls.lib.il.us
URL: http://www.rbls.lib.il.us/mus/index.html

Newberry Library
60 West Walton Street
Chicago, IL 60610-3305
Tel: 312-943-9090 (Main)
312-255-3506 (Reference)
312-255-3512 (Genealogy)
Email: furmans@newberry.org
URL: http://www.newberry.org/

Northwestern Community College
Ramaker Library
101 7th Street, SW
Orange City, IA 51041-1996
Tel: 712-737-7236
Fax: 712-737-7247
Email: richardr@nwc.iowa.edu

Oelwein Public Library
22 1st Avenue, NW
Oelwein, IA 50662
Tel/Fax: 319-283-1515
Email: olwein00@iren.net

Onawa Public Library
707 Iowa Avenue
Onawa, IA 51040
Tel: 712-423-1733
Fax: 712-423-3828
Email: onawa00@iren.net

Orange City Public Library
112 Albany Street, SE
Orange City, IA 51041
Tel: 712-737-4302
Fax: 712-737-4431
Email: orange00@iren.net

Osage Public Library
406 Main Street
Osage, IA 50461
Tel; 515-732-3323
Fax: 515-732-4419

Oskaloosa Public Library
301 South Market
Oskaloosa, IA 52577
Tel: 515-673-0441
Fax: 515-673-6237
Email: osklsapl@se-iowa.net

Ottumwa Public Library
129 North Court Street
Ottumwa, IA 52501
Tel: 515-682-7563

Pella Historical Society/Village
507 Franklin Street
Pella, IA 50219
Tel: 515-628-4311
Fax: 515-628-9192
Email: pellatt@kdsi.net
URL: http://www.kdsi.net/~pellatt/

Pioneer Heritage Public Library
204 N. Vine Street
P.O. Box 188
LeGrand, IA 50142
Tel/Fax: 515-479-2122
Email: pioner00@iren.net

Pocahontas Public Library
14 Second Avenue, NW
Pocahontas, IA 50574
Tel/Fax: 712-335-4471
Email: nokypl@ncn.net
URL: http://www.ncn.net/~pokypl/

Putnam Museum of History and Natural Science
Putnam Museum Library
1717 West 12th Street
Davenport, IA 52807
Tel: 319-324-1933
Fax: 319-324-6638

Red Oak Public Library
400 N. 2nd Street
Red Oak, IA 51566
Tel: 712-623-6516
Fax: 712-623-6518
Email: redoak00@iren.net

Richardson-Sloane Genealogical Library
1019 Mound Street, Suite 301
Davenport, IA 52803
Tel: 800-828-4363
Fax: 319-383-0008
URL: http://www.fgs.org/~fgs/soc0158.htm

Scott County Genealogical Society/Library
P.O. Box 3132
Davenport, IA 52808
Tel: 319-326-7902

Scott County Library System
215 N. 2nd Street
Eldridge, IA 52748
Tel: 319-285-4794
Fax: 319-285-4743

Shelby County Historical Museum
1805 Morse
Harlan, IA 51537
Tel: 712-755-2437

Sidney Public Library
604 Clay Street
P.O. Box 479
Sidney, IA 51652
Tel: 712-374-2223

Sioux Center Public Library
327 First Avenue, NE
Sioux Center, IA 51250

Sioux City Public Library
529 Pierce Street
Sioux City, IA 51101
Tel: 712-255-2933
Fax: 712-279-6432
Email: thompsb@scity.sc.lib.ia.us

Spencer Public Library
21 E. Third Street
Spencer, IA 51301
Tel: 712-264-7290
Email: spencerpl@ncn.net
URL: http://www.pionet.net/~nwiowa/spencer/library/hmpagfrt.htm

Storm Lake Public Library
609 Cayuga Street
Storm Lake, IA 50588
Tel: 712-732-8026
Fax: 712-732-7609
Email: slpl@ncn.net
URL: http://pionet.net/~nwiowa/stormlake/City/sl_lib.htm

Tama Public Library
901 McClellan
P.O. Box 308
Tama, IA 52339
Tel/Fax: 515-484-4484
Email: tamapl@mail.gte.net

University of Iowa
Main Library
Iowa City, IA 52242
TEL: 319-335-5299
URL: http://www.lib.uiowa.edu/main/index.html

University of Northern Iowa
Rod Library
Cedar Falls, IA 50613-3675
Tel: 319-273-2838
Fax: 319-273-2913
Email: lib-www@uni.edu
URL: http://www.uni.edu/library

Urbandale Public Library
7305 Aurora Avenue
Urbandale, IA 50322
Tel: 515-278-3945
Fax: 515-278-3918
Email: urgandal@netins.net

Vesterheim Norwegian American Museum/Library
502 West Water Street
Decorah, IA 52101
Tel: 319-382-9681
Fax: 319-382-8828

Waterloo Public Library
415 Commercial Street
Waterloo, IA 50701
Tel: 319-291-4521
319-291-4476 (information)
Fax: 319-291-6736
URL: http://www.wplwloo.org/index.html

Waukon Municipal Library
401 1st Avenue
Waukon, IA 52172
Tel/Fax: 319-568-4424
Email: robeylib@ptel.net

Webb Shadle Memorial Library
301 W. Dallas
Pleasantville, IA 50225
Tel: 515-848-5617

NEWSPAPERS REPOSITORIES

Iowa Genealogical Society/Library
6000 Douglas Avenue
Des Moines, IA 50322
Tel: 515-276-0287
Mail:
IGS-NET
P.O. Box 7735
Des Moines, IA 50322-7735
URL: http://www.digiserve.com/igs/igs.htm

Iowa, State Historical Society of
Library/Archives
402 Iowa Avenue
Iowa City, IA 52240-1806
Tel: 319-335-3916
Email: nekraft@blue.weeg.uiowa.edu
URL: http://www.uiowa.edu/~shsi/index.htm

VITAL RECORDS

Iowa Department of Health
Bureau of Vital Records
Lucas State Office Building, 1st Floor
Des Moines, IA 50319-0075
Tel: 515-281-4944
URL: http://idph.state.ia.us/pa/vr.htm

IOWA ON THE WEB

Iowa Genweb Project
http://www.rootsweb.com/~iagenweb/iowa.htm

Iowa Historical Information
http://www.iowa-counties.com/historical/index.shtml

Iowa Pioneers Project
http://www.digiserve.com/ladyhawk/IPL/ipl_main.htm

North Central Iowa Genealogy Connection
http://www.netins.net/showcase/pafways/

Underground Railroad Operators-Iowa
http://www.ugrr.org//names/map-ia.htm

KANSAS

ARCHIVES, STATE & NATIONAL

Kansas State Archives
Kansas State Historical Society/Library & Archives
The Kansas History Center
6425 SW Sixth Street
Topeka, KS 66615-1099
Tel: 913-272-8681
Email: webmaster@hspo.wpo.state.ks.us
URL: http://kuhttp.cc.ukans.edu/heritage/kshs/resource/archives.htm

National Archives—Central Plains Region
2312 East Bannister Road
Kansas City, MO 64131
Tel: 816-926-6272
Fax: 816-926-6982
Email: archives@kansascity.nara.gov
URL: http://www.nara.gov/nara/regional/06nsgil.html

GENEALOGICAL SOCIETIES

Atchison County Genealogical Society
c/o Atchison Library
401 Kansas
Atchison, KS 66002
Tel: 913-367-1902

Barton County Genealogical Society, Inc.
P.O. Box 425
Great Bend, KS 67530
Tel: 316-792-2409

Bluestem Genealogical Society
P.O. Box 582
Eureka, KS 67045

Branches and Twigs Genealogical Society
c/o Kingman Carnegie Library
445 North Main
Kingman, KS 67068
Tel: 316-532-3061

Bukovina Society of the Americas/Museum
722 Washington
P.O. Box 81
Ellis, KS 67637
Tel: 913-625-9492
913-726-4568
Email: owindholz@juno.com
URL: http://members.aol.com/LJensen/bukovina.html

Chanute Genealogical Society
1010 South Allen
Chanute, KS 66720
Tel: 316-431-1563

Cherokee County Kansas Genealogical/Historical Society
100 South Tennessee
P.O. Box 33
Columbus, KS 66725-0033
Tel: 316-429-2992
URL: http://history.cc.ukans.edu/~hersite/kcn-1/columbus/graphics/ckghs.html

Cloud County Genealogical Society
Route 3
P.O. Box 76
Concordia, KS 66901
Tel: 913-243-4676

Coffey County Genealogical Society
712 Sanders
Burlington, KS 66839
Tel: 316-364-8795

Cowley County Genealogical Society
P.O. Box 102
Arkansas City, KS 67005
Tel: 316-442-5635
316-442-6750

Crawford County Genealogical Society
c/o Pittsburg Public Library
211 West 4th
Pittsburg, KS 66762
Tel: 316-231-8110

Decatur County Genealogical Society
258 South Penn
Oberlin, KS 67749
Tel: 913-475-2712

Douglass County Genealogical Society, Inc.
P.O. Box 3664
Lawrence, KS 66046-0664

Family Researchers
c/o Geary County Historical Society
530 North Adams
P.O. Box 1161
Junction City, KS 66441
Tel: 913-238-1666

Finney County Genealogical Society
P.O. Box 592
Garden City, KS 67846
Tel: 316-272-3680

Flint Hills Genealogical Society
P.O. Box 555
Emporia, KS 66801
Tel: 316-343-2719

Fort Hays Genealogical Society
c/o Forsyth Library, Western Collection Room
Fort Hays State University
600 Park Street
Hays, KS 67601
Tel: 913-735-2230
Email: semk@fhsuvm.fhsu.edu

Four State Genealogy Society
922 Galena Avenue
Galena, KS 66739
Tel: 316-783-5132

Franklin County Genealogical Society
P.O. Box 145
Ottawa, KS 66067
Tel: 913-242-4097
URL: http://www.ukans.edu/~hisite/franklin/fcgs/

Genealogical Researchers
412 South Campbell
Abilene, KS 67410
Tel: 913-263-2681

Harper County Genealogical Society
c/o Harper Public Library
1002 Oak
Harper, KS 67058
Tel: 316-896-2959
URL: http://www.pe.net/~lucindaw/kansas/genealog/hgs.htm

Heritage Genealogical Society
c/o Rankin Memorial Library
502 Indiana
Neodesha, KS 66757
Tel: 316-325-3275

Hodgeman County Genealogical Society
P.O. Box 441
Jetmore, KS 67854
Tel: 316-357-6594

Jefferson County Genealogical Society
P.O. Box 174
Oskaloosa, KS 66066
Tel: 913-863-2070

Johnson County Genealogical Society/Library
8700 Shawnee Mission Parkway
P.O. Box 12666
Shawnee Mission, KS 66282
Tel: 913-780-4764
Email: kenl@sky.net
URL: http://history.cc.ukans.edu/heritage/society/jcgs/jcgs_main.html

Kansas Council of Genealogical Societies
P.O. Box 3858
Topeka, KS 66604
Email: mphil@parod.com
URL: http://ukanaix.cc.ukans.edu/kansas/seneca/kscoun/kscoun.html

Kansas Genealogical Society, Inc.
Village Square Mall, Lower Level
2601 Central Avenue
P.O. Box 103
Dodge City, KS 67801
Tel: 316-225-1951
URL: http://www.dodgecity.net/kgs/

Leavenworth County Genealogical Society
P.O. Box 362
Leavenworth, KS 66048-0362
Tel: 913-651-4835

Midwest Historical and Genealogical Society
1203 North Main
P.O. Box 1121
Wichita, KS 67201-1121
Tel: 316-264-3611

Montgomery County Genealogy Society
P.O. Box 444
Coffeyville, KS 67337
Tel: 316-251-0716

Morris County Genealogical Society
P.O. Box 114
White City, KS 66872

North Central Kansas Genealogical Society
P.O. Box 251
Cawker City, KS 67430
Tel: 913-781-4925
913-781-4343
URL: http://skyways.lib.ks.us/kansas/towns/Cawker/library.html#society

Northwest Kansas Genealogical and Historical Society
Oakley Library
700 West 3rd
Oakley, KS 67748
Tel: 913-672-4776

Norton County Genealogical Society
One Washington Square
Norton, KS 67654
Tel: 913-877-2481

Old Fort Genealogical Society of Southeastern Kansas, Inc.
502 South National
Fort Scott, KS 66701
Tel: 316-223-3300

Osborne County Genealogical and Historical Society, Inc.
213 North First Street
Osborne, KS 67473
Tel: 913-346-5486

Phillips County Genealogical Society
P.O. Box 114
Phillipsburg, KS 67661
Tel: 913-543-5325

Rawlins County Genealogical Society
P.O. Box 203
Atwood, KS 67730
Tel: 913-626-3805

Reno County Genealogical Society
P.O. Box 5
Hutchinson, KS 67504
Tel: 316-663-5441
URL: http://www.hplsck.org/gen.htm

Riley County Genealogical Society/Library
2005 Claflin Road
Manhattan, KS 66502
Tel: 913-537-2205

Santa Fe Trail Genealogical Society
P.O. Box 528
Syracuse, KS 67878
Tel: 316-384-7614

Smoky Valley Genealogical Society/Library
211 West Iron, Suite 205
Salina, KS 67401
Tel: 913-825-7573

Southeast Kansas Genealogy Society
P.O. Box 393
Iola, KS 66749

Stafford County Historical and Genealogical Society
100 South Main
P.O. Box 249
Stafford, KS 67578
Tel: 316-234-5664

Tonganoxie Genealogical Society
P.O. Box 354
Tonganoxie, KS 66086
Tel: 913-845-3281

Topeka Genealogical Society/Library
2717 SE Indiana Avenue
P.O. Box 4048
Topeka, KS 66604
Tel: 913-233-5762
URL: http://www.cjnetworks.com/~gaulding/tgs.htm

Washington County Historical and Genealogical Society
P.O. Box 31
Washington, KS 66968
Tel: 913-325-2198

Wichita Genealogical Society
P.O. Box 3705
Wichita, KS 67201
Tel: 316-262-0611
316-687-5925
Email: wardm@mail.dec.com
URL: http://kuhttp.cc.ukans.edu/kansas/wgs/wgs.html

Woodson County Genealogical Society
608 North Prairie
Yates Center, KS 66783
Tel: 316-625-2705

Historical Societies

Albany Historical Society, Inc.
415 Grant
Sabetha, KS 66534
Tel: 913-284-3446

Allen County Historical Society/Library
207 North Jefferson
Iola, KS 66749
Tel: 316-365-3051

Anderson County Historical Society/Library
6th and Maple
Garnett, KS 66032
Tel: 913-448-5962
913-448-5881

Argonia and Western Sumner County Historical Society
221 West Garfield
Argonia, KS 67004
Tel: 316-435-6990
316-435-6606

Arkansas City Historical Society
1400 North 3rd
Arkansas City, KS 67005
Tel: 316-442-0333

Atchison County Historical Society/Museum
200 South Main
P.O. Box 201
Atchison, KS 66002
Tel: 913-367-6238

Augusta Historical Society/Museum
303 State Street
P.O. Box 545
Augusta, KS 67010
Tel: 316-775-5655

Barton County Historical Society/Museum
85 South Highway 281
P.O. Box 1091
Great Bend, KS 67530
Tel: 316-793-5125
316-792-2204
Email: shorock@midusa.net
URL: http://homepage.midusa.net/~shorock/bchs.htm

Baxter Springs Historical Society/Museum
8th and East Avenue
P.O. Box 514
Baxter Springs, KS 66713
Tel: 316-856-2385

Black Historical Society
4230 East 25th North
Wichita, KS 67220
Tel: 316-683-1247

Black Jack Historical Society
163 East 2000 Road
Wellsville, KS 66092
Tel: 913-883-2584

Brown County Historical Society/Library
611 Utah
Hiawatha, KS 66434
Tel: 913-742-3330

Bunker Hill Historical Society
P.O. Box 112
Bunker Hill, KS 67626
Tel: 913-483-3637

Burns Community Historical Society
Main Street
Burns, KS 66840
Tel: 316-726-5528
316-732-5277

Butler County Historical Society/Museum
383 E. Central
P.O. Box 696
El Dorado, KS 67042
Tel: 316-321-9333

Butterfield Trail Association &
Historical Society of Logan County, Kansas, Inc.
Highway 25 and Museum Drive
P.O. Box 336
Russell Springs, KS 67755
Tel: 913-751-4242

Caney Valley Historical Society
4th & Wood
P.O. Box 354
Caney, KS 67333
Tel: 316-879-5198
316-879-2210

Chase County Historical Society/Library/Museum
301 Broadway
P.O. Box 375
Cottonwood Falls, KS 66845
Tel: 316-273-8500

Cherokee County Kansas Genealogical/Historical Society
100 South Tennessee
P.O. Box 33
Columbus, KS 66725-0033
Tel: 316-429-2992
URL: http://history.cc.ukans.edu/~hersite/kcn-1/columbus/graphics/ckghs.html

Cheyenne County Historical Society
West Highway 36
P.O. Box 611
St. Francis, KS 67756
Tel: 913-332-2504

Clark County Historical Society
Pioneer-Krier Museum
430 West 4th
P.O. Box 862
Ashland, KS 67831
Tel: 316-635-2227
316-635-2273

Clay County Historical Society
2121 7th
Clay Center, KS 67432
Tel: 913-632-3786

Clearwater Historical Society
149 North 4th
P.O. Box 453
Clearwater, KS 67026
Tel: 316-584-2444
316-584-2323

Clifton Historical Society
108 Clifton Street
Clifton, KS 66937
Tel: 913-455-3555

Clinton Lake Historical Society
261 North 851 Diag. Road
Overbrook, KS 66524
Tel: 913-748-9836
913-748-0800

Cloud County Historical Society
635 Broadway
Concordia, KS 66901
Tel: 913-243-2866

Comanche County Historical Society, Inc.
410 South Baltimore
P.O. Box 177
Coldwater, KS 67029
Tel: 316-582-2679

Cowley County Historical Society/Library
1011 Mansfield
Winfield, KS 67156
Tel: 316-221-4811
316-221-9353

Crawford County Historical Society/Museum
651 South Highway 69
Pittsburg, KS 66762
Tel: 316-231-1440

Dickinson County Historical Society
Heritage Center
412 South Campbell
Abilene, KS 67410
Tel: 913-263-2681
URL: http://history.cc.ukans.edu/heritage/abilene/herctr.html

Doniphan County Historical Society
c/o Library District #1
105 North Main
Troy, KS 66087
Tel: 913-985-2597

Douglas County Historical Society
Watkins Community Museum of History
1047 Massachusetts
Lawrence, KS 66044
Tel: 913-841-4109

Downs Carnegie Library, Historical Society of
504 South Morgan
Downs, KS 67437
Tel: 913-454-3958
913-454-3821

Edwards County Historical Society
Highway 56
Kinsley, KS 67547
Tel: 316-659-2420

Elk County Historical Society
Caney Valley Ranch
Route 1
Grenola, KS 67346
Tel: 316-358-2291

Ellinwood Community Historical Society
P.O. Box 111
Ellinwood, KS 67526

Ellis County Historical Society
100 West 7th
Hays, KS 67601
Tel: 913-628-2624

Ellsworth County Historical Society
104 West Main
Ellsworth, KS 67439
Tel: 913-472-3059

Eudora Area Historical Society
620 Elm
P.O. Box 370
Eudora, KS 66025
Tel: 913-542-2298
913-542-2210

Finney County Historical Society
Finnup Park
403 South 4th
P.O. Box 796
Garden City, KS 67846
Tel: 316-272-3664

First National Black Historical Society of Kansas
601 North Water
P.O. Box 2695
Wichita, KS 67201
Tel: 316-262-7651

Florence Historical Society
408 West 7th
Florence, KS 66851
Tel: 316-878-4474

Ford County Historical Society
P.O. Box 131
Dodge City, KS 67801
Tel: 316-227-3400
316-227-9791

Fort Larned Historical Society, Inc.
Santa Fe Trail Center
Route 3
Larned, KS 67550
Tel: 316-285-2054

Fort Leavenworth Historical Society
c/o Frontier Army Museum Gift Shop
Fort Leavenworth, KS 66027
Tel: 913-684-2262
913-651-7440

Franklin County Historical Society/Library
Franklin County Courthouse
P.O. Box 145
Ottawa, KS 66067
Tel: 913-242-1232
URL: http://www.ukans.edu/~hisite/franklin/fchs/

Frederic Remington Area Historical Society
P.O. Box 133
Whitewater, KS 67154
Tel: 316-799-2470

Geary County Historical Society
530 North Adams
P.O. Box 1161
Junction City, KS 66441
Tel: 913-238-1666

Graham County Historical Society
414 North West
Hill City, KS 67642
Tel: 913-674-5601

Grant County Museum and Historical Society
300 East Oklahoma Avenue
P.O. Box 906
Ulysses, KS 67880
Tel: 316-356-3009

Greeley County Historical Society/Library
P.O. Box 231
Tribune, KS 67879
Tel: 316-376-4996

Greenwood County Historical Society/Library/Museum
120 West 4th Street
Eureka, KS 67045-1445
Tel: 316-583-6682
Email: drwaff@mail.aros.net
URL: http://skyways.lib.ks.us/kansas/genweb/greenwoo/gchs.htm

Halstead Historical Society
P.O. Box 88
Halstead, KS 67056
Tel: 316-835-2360

Harper City Historical Society
c/o Harper Public Library
1002 Oak
Harper, KS 67058
Tel: 316-896-2959

Harvey County Historical Society/Library
206 N. Main
P.O. Box 4
Newton, KS 67114
Tel: 316-283-2221

Haskell County Historical Society
Fairgrounds
P.O. Box 101
Sublette, KS 67877
Tel: 316-675-8344

Heritage of the Plains Historical Society
Arnold, KS 67515
Tel: 913-731-2701
913-731-2280

High Plains Historical Association
Brewster Heritage Center
P.O. Box 284
Brewster, KS 67732
Tel: 913-694-2891

Hillsboro Historical Society
501 South Ash
Hillsboro, KS 67063
Tel: 316-947-3775

Historic Old Mission Enthusiasts
6029 Larsen Lane
Shawnee Mission, KS 66203
Tel: 913-631-8485

Historic Preservation Association of Bourbon County
117 South Main
Fort Scott, KS 66701
Tel: 316-223-5443

Hodgeman County Historical Society
Route 2
P.O. Box 114
Jetmore, KS 67854
Tel: 316-357-8794

Humboldt Historical Society
P.O. Box 63
Humboldt, KS 66748
Tel: 316-473-2886

Inman Heritage Association
P.O. Box 217
Inman, KS 67546
Tel: 316-585-6748

Iron Horse Historical Society
P.O. Box 8
Parsons, KS 67357
Tel: 316-421-1959

Jackson County Historical Society/Library
4th and New York
P.O. Box 104
Holton, KS 66436
Tel: 913-364-2087
913-364-4991

Jefferson County Historical Society
Old Jefferson Town
Highway 59
Mail:
P.O. Box 146
Oskaloosa, KS 66066
Tel: 913-863-2070

Jewell County Historical Society
201 North Commercial
Mankato, KS 66956
Tel: 913-378-3692

Kansas State Historical Society/Library & Archives
The Kansas History Center
6425 SW Sixth Street
Topeka, KS 66615-1099
Tel: 913-272-8681
Email: webmaster@hspo.wpo.state.ks.us
URL: http://kuhttp.cc.ukans.edu/heritage/kshs/kshs1.html

Kearny County Historical Society and Museum
111 South Buffalo Street
P.O. Box 329
Lakin, KS 67860
Tel: 316-355-7448

Kingman County Historical Society/Library/Museum
400 North Main
P.O. Box 281
Kingman, KS 67068
Tel: 913-532-2627

Lake Region Historical Society
121 East 2nd
Ottawa, KS 66067
Tel: 913-242-2073

Lane County Historical Society/Museum
333 North Main
P.O. Box 821
Dighton, KS 67839
Tel: 316-397-5652

Lansing Historical Society
115 East Kansas Avenue
P.O. Box 32
Lansing, KS 66043
Tel: 913-727-3731

Leavenworth County Historical Society/Museum
1128 5th Avenue
Leavenworth, KS 66048
Tel: 913-682-7759
Fax: 913-682-2089
URL: http://leavenworth-net.com/lchs/

Lecompton Historical Society
P.O. Box 372
Lecompton, KS 66050
Tel: 913-887-6285
913-887-6148

Lenexa Historical Society
14907 West 87th Street Pkwy.
Lenexa, KS 66215
Tel: 913-492-0038

Lincoln County Historical Society
214 West Lincoln Avenue
Lincoln, KS 67455
Tel: 913-524-4614

Linn County Historical Society
Dunlap Park
P.O. Box 137
Pleasanton, KS 66075
Tel: 913-352-8739

Luray Historical Society/Library
505 North Fairview Avenue
P.O. Box 216
Luray, KS 67649
Tel: 913-698-2371

Lyon County Historical Society/Museum
118 East 6th Avenue
Emporia, KS 66801
Tel: 316-342-0933
URL: http://www.emporia.edu/S/www/slim/resource/lchs/lyonco.htm

Marquette Historical Society, Inc.
202 North Washington
Marquette, KS 67464
Tel: 913-546-2252
913-546-2205

Marshall County Historical Society
1207 Broadway
Marysville, KS 66508
Tel: 913-562-5012

Medicine Lodge Historical Society
Highway 160
Medicine Lodge, KS 67104
Tel: 316-886-3417

Miami County Historical Society/Library
North Side of Square
P.O. Box 393
Paola, KS 66071

Midwest Historical and Genealogical Society
1203 North Main
P.O. Box 1121
Wichita, KS 67201-1121
Tel: 316-264-3611

Milan Historical Society
Park House Museum
Milan, KS 67105
Tel: 316-435-6632
316-435-6423

Mitchell County Historical Society/Museum
402 West 8th
Beloit, KS 67420
Tel: 913-738-5355
Fax: 913-738-9503

Montgomery County Historical Society
P.O. Box 100
Independence, KS 67301
Tel: 316-331-3770
316-331-1890

Morris County Historical Society
303 West Main
Council Grove, KS 66846
Tel: 316-767-5716

Morton County Historical Society
U.S. Highway 56
P.O. Box 1248
Elkhart, KS 67950
Tel: 316-345-8420

Moundridge Historical Association
P.O. Box 69
Moundridge, KS 67107
Tel: 316-345-8420

Mulvane Historical Society
300 West Main
P.O. Box 117
Mulvane, KS 67110
Tel: 316-777-0506

Nemaha County Historical Society/Library
6th and Nemaha
Seneca, KS 66538
Email: mphil@parod.com
URL: http://ukanaix.cc.ukans.edu/kansas/seneca/gensoc/gensoc.html

Ness County Historical Society
123 South Pennsylvania Avenue
Ness City, KS 67560
Tel: 913-798-3298

Nicodemus Historical Society
P.O. Box 131
Bogue, KS 67625
Tel: 913-674-3311

Northwest Kansas Genealogical and Historical Society
Oakley Library
700 West 3rd
Oakley, KS 67748
Tel: 913-672-4776

Norton County Historical Society
P.O. Box 303
Norton, KS 67654

Olathe Historical Society
12466 Twilight
Olathe, KS 66062
Tel: 913-782-5918

Old Fort Bissell/Phillips County Historical Society, Inc.
City Park
Route 2
P.O. Box 18A
Phillipsburg, KS 67661
Tel: 913-543-6212

Onaga Historical Society
310 East 2nd
Onaga, KS 66521
Tel: 913-889-4457

Osage County Historical Society
631 Topeka
P.O. Box 361
Lyndon, KS 66451
Tel: 913-828-3477

Osage Mission/Neosho County Historical Society
P.O. Box 113
St. Paul, KS 66771

Osborne County Genealogical and Historical Society, Inc.
213 North First Street
Osborne, KS 67473
Tel: 913-346-5486

Oswego Historical Society/Museum
410 Commercial
Oswego, KS 67356
Tel: 316-795-4500
316-795-4455

Parsons Historical Society
401 South Corning
Parsons, KS 67357
Tel: 3196-421-3382

Peabody Historical Society
East Division
Peabody, KS 66866
Tel: 316-983-2815
316-983-2174

Pratt County Historical Society/Library
208 South Ninnescah
Pratt, KS 67124
Tel: 316-672-7874

Rawlins County Historical Society/Museum
308 State
Atwood, KS 67730
Tel: 913-626-3885

Reno County Historical Society, Inc.
100 South Walnut
P.O. Box 664
Hutchinson, KS 67504-0664
Tel: 316-662-1184

Republic County Historical Society
West Highway 36
P.O. Box 218
Belleville, KS 66935
Tel: 913-527-5971

Rice County Historical Society
105 West Lyon
Lyons, KS 67554
Tel: 316-257-3941

Riley County Historical Society
2309 Claflin Road
Manhattan, KS 66502
Tel: 913-537-2210
913-565-6490

Rock Creek Valley Historical Society
P.O. Box 13
Westmoreland, KS 66549
Tel: 913-457-3624

Rooks County Historical Society
South Highway 183
Stockton, KS 67669
Tel: 913-425-7217
913-425-7396

Rush County Historical Society, Inc.
202 West First
P.O. Box 473
LaCrosse, KS 67548
Tel: 913-222-2719
913-222-2673

Russell County Historical Society/Library
331 Kansas
P.O. Box 245
Russell, KS 67665
Tel: 913-483-3637

St. Marys Historical Society/Library
106 East Mission
St. Marys, KS 66536
Tel: 913-437-6600

Saline County Historical Society/Library
216 West Bond
Salina, KS 67401
Tel: 913-825-7573

Santa Fe Trail Historical Society
1515 High Street
P.O. Box 443
Baldwin, KS 66006
Tel: 913-594-6595

Seward County Historical Society
567 East Cedar
Liberal, KS 67901
Tel: 316-624-7624

Shawnee County Historical Society
P.O. Box 2201
Topeka, KS 66601

Shawnee Historical Society
P.O. Box 3042
Shawnee, KS 67740
Tel: 913-675-3501

Sheridan County Historical Society
County Courthouse
817 Royal Avenue
P.O. Box 274
Hoxie, KS 67740
Tel: 913-675-3501

Sherman County Historical Society
P.O. Box 684
Goodland, KS 67735
Tel: 913-899-5461

Smith County Historical Society
P.O. Box 38
Kensington, KS 66951
Tel: 913-476-3214

Smoky Valley Historical Association
c/o Lindsborg Community Library
111 South Main
Lindsborg, KS 67456
Tel: 913-227-2710

Stafford County Historical and Genealogical Society
100 South Main
P.O. Box 249
Stafford, KS 67578
Tel: 316-234-5664

Stanton County Historical Society
104 East Highland
P.O. Box 806
Johnson, KS 67855
Tel: 316-492-1526

Sumner County Historical Society
P.O. Box 213
Mulvane, KS 67110
Tel: 316-777-1434

Swiss Mennonite Cultural and Historical Association
109 East Hirschler
Moundridge, KS 67107
Tel: 316-345-2844

Thomas County Historical Society
P.O. Box 465
Colby, KS 67701
Tel: 913-462-4590

Tonganoxie Community Historical Society
P.O. Box 325
Tonganoxie, KS 66086
Tel: 913-845-2102
913-845-2383

Trading Post Historical Society/Museum
Trading Post, KS (mile post 96)
Route 2
P.O. Box 145A
Pleasanton, KS 66075
Tel: 913-352-6441

Trego County Historical Society
Highway 283
P.O. Box 132
WaKeeney, KS 67672
Tel: 913-743-2964

Tri-County Historical Society/Archives/Museum
Railroad Baggage Car Annex
800 South Broadway
P.O. Box 9
Herington, KS 67449
Tel: 913-258-2842

Valley Center Historical and Cultural Society
112 North Meridian
P.O. Box 173
Valley Center, KS 67147
Tel: 316-755-7340

Valley Falls Historical Society
310 Broadway
Valley Falls, KS 66088
Tel: 913-945-6698

Wabaunsee County Historical Society
227 Missouri Street
P.O. Box 387
Alma, KS 66401
Tel: 913-765-2200

Wamego Historical Society
P.O. Box 84
Wamego, KS 66547
Tel: 913-456-2040

Washington County Historical and Genealogical Society
P.O. Box 31
Washington, KS 66968
Tel: 913-325-2198

Wichita County Historical Society, Inc.
Fourth and J
Leoti, KS 67861
Tel: 316-375-2316

Wilson County Historical Society/Library/Museum
420 North 7th
Fredonia, KS 66736
Tel: 316-378-3965

Woodson County Historical Society/Library
Route 1
P.O. Box 16
Yates Center, KS 66783
Tel: 316-625-2929

Wyandotte County Historical Society
Museum and Harry M. Trowbridge Research Library
631 North 126th
Bonner Springs, KS 66012
Tel: 913-721-1078
URL: http://history.cc.ukans.edu/kansas/wchs/mainpage.html

LDS Family History Centers

Dodge City Family History Center
2508 Sixth Avenue
Dodge City, KS 67801
Tel: 316-225-6540

Emporia Family History Center
2313 Graphic Arts Road
Emporia, KS 66801
Tel: 316-343-1304

Hutchinson Family History Center
18 17th Crestview
Hutchinson, KS 67502
Tel: 316-665-1187

Olathe Family History Center
15915 West 143rd Street
Olathe, KS 66062
Tel: 913-829-1775

Salina Family History Center
845 South Ohio Avenue
Salina, KS 67401
Tel: 913-827-2392

Topeka Family History Center
2401 SW Kingsrow Road
Topeka, KS 66614
Tel: 913-271-6818

Wichita Family History Center
7011 East 13th Street
Wichita, KS 67206
Tel: 316-683-2951

Archives/Libraries/Museums

Allen County Historical Society/Library
207 North Jefferson
Iola, KS 66749
Tel: 316-365-3051

Anderson County Historical Society/Library
6th and Maple
Garnett, KS 66032
Tel: 913-448-5962
913-448-5881

Anthony Public Library
104 N. Springfield
Anthony, KS 67003
Tel: 316-842-5344

Arkansas City Public Library
120 E. 5th Avenue
Arkansas City, KS 67005
Tel: 316-442-1280

Atchison County Historical Society/Museum
200 South Main
P.O. Box 201
Atchison, KS 66002
Tel: 913-367-6238

Atchison Public Library
401 Kansas Avenue
Atchison, KS 66002
Tel: 913-367-1902

Atwood Public Library
102 South 6th Street
Atwood, KS 67730
Tel: 913-626-3805

Augusta Historical Society/Museum
303 State Street
P.O. Box 545
Augusta, KS 67010
Tel: 316-775-5655

Baker University Archives
P.O. Box 65
Baldwin, KS 66006
Tel: 913-594-6451 ext. 380

Barton County Historical Society/Museum
85 South Highway 281
P.O. Box 1091
Great Bend, KS 67530
Tel: 316-793-5125
316-792-2204
Email: shorock@midusa.net
URL: http://homepage.midusa.net/~shorock/bchs.htm

Baxter Springs Historical Society/Museum
8th and East Avenue
P.O. Box 514
Baxter Springs, KS 66713
Tel: 316-856-2385

Boot Hill Museum and Front Street
Front Street
Dodge City, KS 67801

Brown County Historical Society/Library
611 Utah
Hiawatha, KS 66434
Tel: 913-742-3330

Bukovina Society of the Americas/Museum
722 Washington
P.O. Box 81
Ellis, KS 67637
Tel: 913-625-9492
913-726-4568
Email: owindholz@juno.com
URL: http://members.aol.com/LJensen/bukovina.html

Butler County Historical Society/Museum
383 E. Central
P.O. Box 696
El Dorado, KS 67042
Tel: 316-321-9333

Cassoday Historical Museum
Washington & Beaumont
Cassoday, KS 66842
Tel: 316-735-7286

Cawker City Public Library
802 Locust Street
Cawker City, KS 67430
Tel: 913-781-4925
URL: http://skyways.lib.ks.us/kansas/towns/Cawker/library.html

Chanute Genealogical Society
1010 South Allen
Chanute, KS 66720
Tel: 316-431-1563

Chase County Historical Society/Library/Museum
301 Broadway
P.O. Box 375
Cottonwood Falls, KS 66845
Tel: 316-273-8500

Cherokee County Kansas Genealogical/Historical Society
100 South Tennessee
P.O. Box 33
Columbus, KS 66725-0033
Tel: 316-429-2992
URL: http://history.cc.ukans.edu/~hersite/kcn-1/columbus/graphics/ckghs.html

Cherokee Strip Land Rush Museum
South Summit Street
P.O. Box 1002
Arkansas City, KS 67005
Tel: 316-442-6750

Chetopa Historical Museum
Route 1
P.O. Box 135
Chetopa, KS 67336
Tel: 316-236-7195

Chisholm Trail Museum
502 N. Washington Avenue
Wellington, KS 67152
Tel: 316-326-3820

Clay County Historical Society
2121 7th
Clay Center, KS 67432
Tel: 913-632-3786

Coffey County Historical Museum
1110 Neosho
Burlington, KS 66839
Tel: 316-364-2653

Coffeyville Historical Museum, Inc.
113 East Eighth
P.O. Box 843
Coffeyville, KS 67337
Tel: 316-251-1194

Columbus Public Library
205 N. Kansas
Columbus, KS 66725-1297
Tel: 316-429-2086

Combined Arms Research Library
Attn: Ed Burgess
U.S. Army Command & General Staff College
250 Gibbon Avenue
Fort Leavenworth, KS 66027
Tel: 913-758-3155
DSN 720-3155
URL: http://www-cgsc.army.mil/cgsc/CARL/archive.htm

Council Grove Library
303 W. Main Street
Council, KS 66846
Tel: 316-767-5716

Cowley County Historical Society/Library
1011 Mansfield
Winfield, KS 67156
Tel: 316-221-4811
316-221-9353

Crawford County Historical Society/Museum
651 South Highway 69
Pittsburg, KS 66762
Tel: 316-231-1440

Decatur County Museum
258 South Penn
Oberlin, KS 67749
Tel: 913-475-2712

Dickinson County Historical Society
Heritage Center
412 South Campbell
Abilene, KS 67410
Tel: 913-263-2681
URL: http://history.cc.ukans.edu/heritage/abilene/herctr.html

Dodge City Heritage Center
1000 Second Avenue
Dodge City, KS 67801

Dodge City Public Library
1001 Second Avenue
Dodge City, KS 67801

Douglass Historical Museum
314 S. Forest
Douglass, KS 67039
Tel: 316-747-2319

Downs Carnegie Library
504 South Morgan
Downs, KS 67437
Tel: 913-454-3958
913-454-3821

Emmett Kelly Historical Museum
202-204 East Main
Sedan, KS 67361
Tel: 316-725-3470

Emporia Public Library
110 E. 6th Avenue
Emporia, KS 66801
Tel: 316-342-6524

Fort Hays State University
Forsyth Library
600 Park Street
Hays, KS 67601
Tel: 913-628-4431

Fort Larned National Historic Site
Route 3
Larned, KS 67550
Tel: 316-285-6911
URL: http://www.cr.nps.gov/csd/collections/fols.html

Fort Wallace Memorial Association
Highway 40
Wallace, KS 67761
Tel: 913-891-3564

Franklin County Historical Society/Library
Franklin County Courthouse
P.O. Box 145
Ottawa, KS 66067
Tel: 913-242-1232
URL: http://www.ukans.edu/~hisite/franklin/fchs/

Friends University
Pioneer Historical Museum
Fellow-Reeve Museum of History and Science
2100 University
Wichita, KS 67213
Tel: 316-292-5594
URL: http://www.southwind.net/ict/wht/wht-09s.html

Frederic Remington Area Historical Society
P.O. Box 133
Whitewater, KS 67154
Tel: 316-799-2470

Frontier Army Museum
Department of the Army
Commander, HQ CAC LVN, ATTN ATZL GCT M
100 Reynolds Avenue
Fort Leavenworth, KS 66027-5072
Tel: 913-684-3191
913-684-3767
Fax: 913-684-3624
URL: http://leav-www.army.mil/museum/

Galena Public Library
City Municipal Building
315 W. 7th
Galena, KS 66739
Tel: 316-783-5132

Garden City Public Library
210 North 7th
Garden City, KS 67846

Geary County Historical Society
530 North Adams
P.O. Box 1161
Junction City, KS 66441
Tel: 913-238-1666

Grant County Museum and Historical Society
300 East Oklahoma Avenue
P.O. Box 906
Ulysses, KS 67880
Tel: 316-356-3009

Great Bend Public Library
1409 Williams Street
Great Bend, KS 67530
Tel: 316-792-2409

Greeley County Historical Society/Library
P.O. Box 231
Tribune, KS 67879
Tel: 316-376-4996

Greenwood County Historical Society/Library/Museum
120 West 4th Street
Eureka, KS 67045-1445
Tel: 316-583-6682
Email: drwaff@mail.aros.net
URL: http://skyways.lib.ks.us/kansas/genweb/greenwoo/gchs.htm

Hamilton County Library
P.O. Box 1307
Syracuse, KS 67878
Tel: 316-384-5622

Hamilton County Museum
108 E. Highway 50
P.O. Box 923
Syracuse, KS 67878
Tel: 316-384-7496

Harper Public Library
Harper City Building
1002 Oak
Harper, KS 67058
Tel: 316-896-2959

Harvey County Historical Society/Library
206 N. Main
P.O. Box 4
Newton, KS 67114
Tel: 316-283-2221

Hays Masonic Bodies (A.F. & A.M.)
107 W. 11th
Hays, KS 67601
Tel: 913-625-3127
URL: http://spidome.net/~masons/index.html

Hays Public Library
1205 Main Street
Hays, KS 67601-3693
Tel: 913-625-9014
Fax: 913-625-8683
Email: hayspublib@spidome.net
URL: http://spidome.net/~hayspublib

High Plains Museum
1717 Cherry
Goodland, KS 67735
Tel: 913-899-4595

Hutchinson Public Library
901 N. Main
Hutchinson, KS 67501
Tel: 316-663-5441
URL: http://www.hplsck.org/index.htm

Iola Public Library
218 E. Madison Avenue
Iola, KS 66749
Tel: 316-365-3262
Fax: 316-365-5137
Email: rogerc@midusa.net
URL: http://www.kumc.edu/kansas/sekls/iolapub/

Jackson County Historical Society/Library
4th and New York
P.O. Box 104
Holton, KS 66436
Tel: 913-364-2087
913-364-4991

Jefferson County Historical Society?library
Old Jefferson Town
Highway 59
Mail:
P.O. Box 146
Oskaloosa, KS 66066
Tel: 913-863-2070

Johnson County Genealogical Society/Library
8700 Shawnee Mission Parkway
P.O. Box 12666
Shawnee Mission, KS 66282
Tel: 913-780-4764
Email: kenl@sky.net
URL: http://history.cc.ukans.edu/heritage/society/jcgs/jcgs_main.html

Johnson County Library
9875 W. 87th Street
Overland, KS 66212
Tel: 913-495-2400
800-386-8501
TDD: 913-495-2433
Email: jcl@jcl.lib.ks.us
URL: http://www.jcl.lib.ks.us/Central.html

Johnson County Museum of History
6305 Lackman Road
Shawnee Mission, KS 66217
Tel: 913-631-6709

Johnston Public Library
210 W. 10th
Baxter Springs, KS 66713
Tel: 316-856-5591

Kansas Center for Historical Research
6425 SW 6th Avenue
Topeka, KS 66615
Tel: 913-272-8681 ext. 117
Fax: 913-272-8682

Kansas City Public Library
625 Minnesota Street
Kansas City, KS 66101
Tel: 913-551-3280
Fax: 913-551-3221
Email: jpack@kckpl.lib.ks.us
URL: http://www.grapevine.com/wcedc/kckpl/kckpl.htm

Kansas Genealogical Society, Inc.
Village Square Mall, Lower Level
2601 Central Avenue
P.O. Box 103
Dodge City, KS 67801
Tel: 316-225-1951
URL: http://www.dodgecity.net/kgs/

Kansas Heritage Center
1000 2nd Avenue
P.O. Box 1207

Dodge City, KS 67801-1207
Tel: 316-227-1616
Email: info@ksheritage.org
URL: http://ksheritage.org/

Kansas State Historical Society/Library & Archives
The Kansas History Center
6425 SW Sixth Street
Topeka, KS 66615-1099
Tel: 913-272-8681
Email: webmaster@hspo.wpo.state.ks.us
URL: http://kuhttp.cc.ukans.edu/heritage/kshs/kshs1.html

Kansas State Library
Statehouse, 3rd Floor
Topeka, KS 66612
Tel: 913-296-3296
800-432-3919 (in Kansas)
Fax: 913-296-6650
URL: http://skyways.lib.ks.us/kansas/KSL/ksl.html

Kansas State University
Seaton Memorial Library
323 Seaton Hall
Manhattan, KS 66506
Tel: 913-532-5968

Kearny County Historical Society and Museum
111 South Buffalo Street
P.O. Box 329
Lakin, KS 67860
Tel: 316-355-7448

Kingman Carnegie Library
445 North Main
Kingman, KS 67068
Tel: 316-532-3061

Kingman County Historical Society/Library/Museum
400 North Main
P.O. Box 281
Kingman, KS 67068
Tel: 913-532-262

Lane County Historical Society/Museum
333 North Main
P.O. Box 821
Dighton, KS 67839
Tel: 316-397-5652

Last Indian Raid Museum
258 South Penn Avenue
Oberlin, KS 67749

Lawrence Public Library
707 Vermont Street
Lawrence, KS 66044
Tel: 913-843-3833

Leavenworth County Historical Society/Museum
1128 5th Avenue
Leavenworth, KS 66048
Tel: 913-682-7759
Fax: 913-682-2089
URL: http://leavenworth-net.com/lchs/

Leavenworth Public Library
5th and Walnut Streets
Leavenworth, KS 66048
Tel: 913-682-5666

Liberal Memorial Library
519 N. Kansas Avenue
Liberal, KS 67901
Tel: 316-624-0148

Lindsborg Community Library
111 South Main
Lindsborg, KS 67456
Tel: 913-227-2710

Luray Historical Society/Library
505 North Fairview Avenue
P.O. Box 216
Luray, KS 67649
Tel: 913-698-2371

Lyndon Carnegie Library
127 E. 6th
P.O. Box 563
Lyndon, KS 66451
Tel: 913-828-4520

Lyon County Historical Society/Museum
118 East 6th Avenue
Emporia, KS 66801
Tel: 316-342-0933
URL: http://www.emporia.edu/S/www/slim/resource/lchs/lyonco.htm

Marion Historical Museum
625 East Main
Marion, KS 66861
Tel: 316-382-2287
316-382-3432

Marshall County Historical Society
1207 Broadway
Marysville, KS 66508
Tel: 913-562-5012

Mary Cotton Public Library
915 Virginia
P.O. Box 70
Sabetha, KS 66534
Tel: 913-284-3160

McPherson County Old Mill Museum and Park
120 Mill Street
P.O. Box 94
Lindsborg, KS 67456
Tel: 913-227-3595

Meade County Historical Museum
200 East Carthage
P.O. Box 893
Meade, KS 67864
Tel: 316-873-2359

Mennonite Library and Archives
Bethel College
300 East 27th
North Newton, KS 67117
Tel: 316-283-2500
Email: mla@bethelks.edu
URL: http://www.bethelks.edu/services/mla/

Miami County Historical Society/Library
North Side of Square
P.O. Box 393
Paola, KS 66071

Midwest Historical and Genealogical Society
1203 North Main
P.O. Box 1121
Wichita, KS 67201-1121
Tel: 316-264-3611

Mitchell County Historical Society/Museum
402 West 8th
Beloit, KS 67420
Tel: 913-738-5355
Fax: 913-738-9503

Morrill Public Library
431 Oregon
Hiawatha, KS 66434
Tel: 913-742-3831

Native American Heritage Museum at Highland Mission
Route 1
P.O. Box 152C
Highland, KS 66035
Tel: 913-442-3304
URL: http://kuhttp.cc.ukans.edu/heritage/kshs/places/highland.htm

Nemaha County Historical Society/Library
6th and Nemaha
Seneca, KS 66538
Email: mphil@parod.com
URL: http://ukanaix.cc.ukans.edu/kansas/seneca/gensoc/gensoc.html

North Central Kansas Genealogical Society
P.O. Box 251
Cawker City, KS 67430
Tel: 913-781-4925
913-781-4343
URL: http://skyways.lib.ks.us/kansas/towns/Cawker/library.html#society

Northwest Kansas Heritage Center
P.O. Box 284
Brewster, KS 67732
Tel: 913-694-2891
913-694-2401

Oakley Library
700 West 3rd
Oakley, KS 67748
Tel: 913-672-4776

Olathe Public Library
201 E. Park Street
Olathe, KS 66061-3456
Tel: 913-764-2259
913-829-1706

Osborne Public Library
325 W. Main Street
Osborne, KS 67473
Tel: 913-346-5486

Oswego Historical Society/Museum
410 Commercial
Oswego, KS 67356
Tel: 316-795-4500
316-795-4455

Ottawa County Historical Museum
110 S. Concord
Minneapolis, KS 67467
Tel: 913-392-3621

Ottawa Public Library
105 S. Hickory
Ottawa, KS 66067
Tel: 913-242-3080
URL: http://www.ott.net/~reedlr/library/

Pioneer-Krier Museum
430 West 4th
P.O. Box 862
Ashland, KS 67831
Tel: 316-635-2227
316-635-2273

Pittsburg Public Library
211 West 4th
Pittsburg, KS 66762
Tel: 316-231-8110

Pratt County Historical Society/Library
208 South Ninnescah
Pratt, KS 67124
Tel: 316-672-7874

Rawlins County Historical Society/Museum
308 State
Atwood, KS 67730
Tel: 913-626-3885

Riley County Genealogical Society/Library
2005 Claflin Road
Manhattan, KS 66502
Tel: 913-537-2205

Russell County Historical Society/Library
331 Kansas
P.O. Box 245
Russell, KS 67665
Tel: 913-483-3637

St. Mary College
DePaul Library
Leavenworth, KS 66048
Email: lonergan@hub.smcks.edu
URL: http://www.smcks.edu/lib/index.html

St. Marys Historical Society/Library
106 East Mission
St. Marys, KS 66536
Tel: 913-437-6600

Saline County Historical Society/Library
216 West Bond
Salina, KS 67401
Tel: 913-825-7573

Santa Fe Trail Center
Route 3
Larned, KS 67550
Tel: 316-285-2054
URL: http://www.amberwave.net/~chamber/tourism/sftc/sftc.htm

Scandia Museum
Main Street
Scandia, KS 66966
Tel: 913-335-2506
913-335-2271

Seneca Free Library
606 Main
Seneca, KS 66538
Tel: 913-336-2377

Smoky Valley Genealogical Society/Library
211 West Iron, Suite 205
Salina, KS 67401
Tel: 913-825-7573

Stafford County Historical and Genealogical Society
100 South Main
P.O. Box 249
Stafford, KS 67578
Tel: 316-234-5664

Topeka and Shawnee County Public Library
1515 SW 10th Avenue
Topeka, KS 66604
Tel: 913-233-2040
Fax: 913-233-2055
URL: http://www.tscpl.org/index.html

Topeka Genealogical Society/Library
2717 SE Indiana Avenue
P.O. Box 4048
Topeka, KS 66604
Tel: 913-233-5762
URL: http://www.cjnetworks.com/~gaulding/tgs.htm

Trading Post Historical Society/Museum
Trading Post, KS (mile post 96)
Route 2
P.O. Box 145A
Pleasanton, KS 66075
Tel: 913-352-6441

Tri-County Historical Society/Archives/Museum
Railroad Baggage Car Annex
800 South Broadway
P.O. Box 9
Herington, KS 67449
Tel: 913-258-2842

U.S. Cavalry Museum
Building 205
P.O. Box 2160
Fort Riley, KS 66442
Tel: 913-239-2737
913-239-2743

W.A. Rankin Memorial Library
Wilson County Kansas
502 Indiana
Neodosha, KS 66757
Tel: 316-325-3275
URL: http://www.telepath.com/sysjer/rankin.htm

Watkins Community Museum of History
1047 Massachusetts
Lawrence, KS 66044
Tel: 913-841-4109

Wichita City Library
223 South Main Street
Wichita, KS 67202
Tel: 316-262-0611
Email: webmaster@wichita.lib.ks.us
URL: http://www.wichita.lib.ks.us/

Wichita/Sedgwick County Historical Museum
204 South Main
Wichita, KS 67202
Tel: 316-265-9314

Wichita State University
Ablah Library/Special Collections
Wichita, KS 67260
URL: http://www.twsu.edu/library/specialcollections/sc.html

Wilson County Historical Society/Library/Museum
420 North 7th
Fredonia, KS 66736
Tel: 316-378-3965

Woodson County Historical Society/Library
Route 1
P.O. Box 16
Yates Center, KS 66783
Tel: 316-625-2929

Wyandotte County Historical Society
Museum and Harry M. Trowbridge Research Library
631 North 126th
Bonner Springs, KS 66012
Tel: 913-721-1078
URL: http://history.cc.ukans.edu/kansas/wchs/mainpage.html

Young Historical Library
2770 Avenue I
Little River, KS 67457
Tel: 316-897-6236
316-897-6757

Newspapers Repositories

Kansas State Historical Society/Library & Archives
The Kansas History Center
6425 SW Sixth Street
Topeka, KS 66615-1099
Tel: 913-272-8681 ext. 201
Email: dhaury@hspo.wpo.state.ks.us
URL: http://history.cc.ukans.edu/heritage/kshs/resource/lib.htm

Vital Records

Vital Statistics
Kansas Department of Health and the Environment
900 SW Jackson, Room 151
Topeka, KS 66612-2221
Tel: 913-296-1400
URL: http://www.ink.org/public/kdhe/ovs.html

Kansas on the Web

Dick Taylor's Ghostchaser
http://www.sky.net/~husker/kansas/chaser.htm

Kansas Collection
http://kuhttp.cc.ukans.edu/carrie/kancoll/index.html

Kansas GenWeb Project
http://skyways.lib.ks.us/kansas/genweb/index.html

Kansas Pioneers Project
http://history.cc.ukans.edu/heritage/pioneers/pion_main.html

Kansas State Historical Society
URL: http://kuhttp.cc.ukans.edu/heritage/kshs/kshs1.html

Orphan Trains of Kansas
http://kuhttp.cc.ukans.edu/carrie/kancoll/articles/orphan/index.html

Plains and Emigrant Tribes of Kansas
http://history.cc.ukans.edu/heritage/old_west/indian.html

Quantrill's Guerrillas in the Civil War
ftp://ftp.cac.psu.edu/pub/genealogy/roots-l/genealog/genealog.quantril

Underground Railroad Operators Directory—Kansas
http://www.ugrr.org//names/map-ks.htm

KENTUCKY

ARCHIVES, STATE & NATIONAL

Kentucky Department for Libraries and Archives
Public Records Division
Archives Research Room
300 Coffee Tree Road
P.O. Box 537
Frankfort, KY 40602-0537
Tel: 502-875-7000
URL: http://www.kdla.state.ky.us/arch/

National Archives—Southeast Region
1557 St. Joseph Avenue
East Point, GA 30344-2593
Tel: 404-763-7477
Fax: 404-763-7033
Email: archives@atlanta.nara.gov
URL: http://www.nara.gov/nara/regional/04nsgil.html

GENEALOGICAL SOCIETIES

Adair County Genealogical Society
P.O. Box 613
Columbia, KY 42728

Ballard-Carlisle Historical & Genealogical Society
P.O. Box 279
Wickliffe, KY 42087
Tel: 502-335-5059
Email: CCScotts@apex.net
URL: http://www.ballardconet.com/bchgs/

Boyle County Genealogical Association
321 Springhill Drive
Danville, KY 40422

Breathitt County Genealogical & Historical Society
c/o Nancy Herald
121 Turner Drive
Jackson, KY 41339

Bullitt County Genealogical Society
P.O. Box 960
Shepherdsville, KY 40165

Butler County Historical & Genealogical Society
P.O. Box 146
Morgantown, KY 42261

Campbell County Historical & Genealogical Society
Library
19 East Main Street
Alexandria, KY 41001
Tel: 606-635-6417

Carter County Historical & Genealogical Society
P.O. Box 1128
Grayson, KY 41143

Christian County Genealogical Society
1101 Bethel Street
Hopkinsville, KY 42240
URL: http://www.evansville.net/~mylines/ccgsbks.htm

Clay County Genealogical & Historical Society, Inc.
P.O. Box 394
Manchester, KY 40962

Crittenden County Genealogical Society
South Crittenden County Library
P.O. Box 61
Marion, KY 42064

Eastern Kentucky Genealogical Society
P.O. Box 1544
Ashland, KY 41105-1544
Email: ekygensoc@wwd.net
URL: http://www.wwd.net/user/sjackson/ekgs/ekgs.htm

Estill County Historical and Genealogical Society
P.O. Box 221
Ravenna, KY 40472

Fayette County Genealogical Society
P.O. Box 8113
Lexington, KY 40533

Floyd County Historical & Genealogical Society
P.O. Box 217
Auxier, KY 41602

Fulton County Genealogical Society
P.O. Box 1031
Fulton, KY 42041

Graves County Genealogical Society
c/o Beverly Gourley
Route 1, Box 171
Cunningham, KY 42035

Hancock County, Genealogical Society of
Old Courthouse
Hawesville, KY 42348

Harlan County Genealogical Society
P.O. Box 1498
Harlan, KY 40831

Harlan Heritage Seekers
P.O. Box 853
Harlan, KY 40831

Harrodsburg Historical Society
Genealogical Committee
220 Chiles Street
P.O. Box 316
Harrodsburg, KY 40330
Tel: 606-734-5985
URL: http://w3.one.net/~durp/hhs.htm

Henderson County Genealogical & Historical Society
P.O. Box 303
Henderson, KY 42420
Tel: 502-830-7514
Email: netta@hcc-uky.campus.mci.net
URL: http://www.comsource.net/~kyseeker/society.html

Hopkins County Genealogical Society
P.O. Box 51
Madisonville, KY 42431

Jewish Genealogical Society of Louisville
Israel T. Namani Library
3600 Dutchmans Lane
Louisville, KY 40205

Johnson County Historical & Genealogical Society
Johnson County Public Library
P.O. Box 788
Paintsville, KY 41240

Kentucky Genealogical Society
P.O. Box 153
Frankfort, KY 40602
URL: http://members.aol.com/bdharney2/bh3.htm

KYOWVA Genealogical Society
P.O. Box 1254
Huntington, WV 25715

Lee County Historical & Genealogical Society
P.O. Box V
Beattyville, KY 41311

Letcher County Historical & Genealogical Society
P.O. Box 312
Whitesburg, KY 41858

Louisville Genealogical Society
P.O. Box 5164
Louisville, KY 40255

Marshall County Historical & Genealogical Society
P.O. Box 373
Benton, KY 42025
Tel: 502-527-4749
Email: marcoky@vci.net

Mason County Genealogical Society
P.O. Box 266
Maysville, KY 41056

McCracken County Genealogical Society
4640 Buckner Lane
Paducah, KY 42001

Menifee County Roots
P.O. Box 114
Frenchburg, KY 40322

Muhlenberg County Genealogical Society
Harbin Memorial Library
117 S. Main Street
Greenville, KY 42345

Nelson County Genealogical Roundtable
P.O. Box 409
Bardstown, KY 40004

Pendleton County Historical & Genealogical Society
Route 5, Box 280
Falmouth, KY 41040

Perry County Genealogical & Historical Society
148 Chester Street
Haxard, KY 41701

Scott County Genealogical Society
c/o Scott County Public Library
East Main
Georgetown, KY 40324
Email: jogt@aol.com

South Central Kentucky Historical/Genealogical Society
P.O. Box 157
Glasgow, KY 42142-0157
Email: sgorin@scrtc.blue.net
URL: http://www.angelfire.com/pg1/Barren/
index.html#Society

Southern Kentucky Genealogical Society
P.O. Box 1782
Bowling Green, KY 42102
URL: http://members.aol.com/kygen/skgs/gen-1.htm

Tri-State Genealogical Society
c/o Willard Library
21 First Avenue
Evansville, KY 47710
Tel: 812-425-4309
URL: http://www.evansville.net/~tsgs/tsgs.html

Washington County Genealogical Society
210 E. Main Street
Springfield, KY 40069

Wayne County Historical & Genealogical Society
c/o Wayne County Public Library
159 S. Main Street
Mail:
P.O. Box 320
Monticello, KY 42633

Webster County Historical & Genealogical Society
P.O. Box 215
Dixon, KY 42409
URL: http://www.dsenter.com/~cpalmer/wch&gs.htm
West-Central Kentucky Family Research Association
P.O. Box 1932
Owensboro, KY 42302

HISTORICAL SOCIETIES

Ancestral Trails Historical Society
P.O. Box 573
Vine Grove, KY 40175
URL: http://kvnet.org/aths/home.htm

Ballard-Carlisle Historical & Genealogical Society
P.O. Box 279
Wickliffe, KY 42087
Tel: 502-335-5059
Email: CCScotts@apex.net
URL: http://www.ballardconet.com/bchgs/

Bell County Historical Society
P.O. Box 1344
Middlesboro, KY 40965

Bracken County Historical Society
Old Jail next to the Courthouse
P.O. Box 66
Brooksville, KY 41004

Breathitt County Genealogical & Historical Society
c/o Nancy Herald
121 Turner Drive
Jackson, KY 41339

Breckinridge County Historical Society
c/o Breckinridge County Clerk
Courthouse Square
P.O. Box 498
Hardinsburg, KY 40143-0538
Tel: 502-756-2246
Fax: 502-756-5444

Butler County Historical & Genealogical Society
P.O. Box 146
Morgantown, KY 42261

Caldwell County Historical Society
P.O. Box 1
Princeton, KY 42445

Campbell County Historical & Genealogical Society Library
19 East Main Street
Alexandria, KY 41001
Tel: 606-635-6417

Carter County Historical & Genealogical Society
P.O. Box 1128
Grayson, KY 41143

Clark County Historical Society
122 Belmont Avenue
Winchester, KY 40391

Clay County Genealogical & Historical Society, Inc.
P.O. Box 394
Manchester, KY 40962

Estill County Historical and Genealogical Society
P.O. Box 221
Ravenna, KY 40472

Filson Club Historical Society
1310 South Third Street
Louisville, KY 40208
Tel: 502-635-5083
Fax: 502-635-5086
URL: http://www.louisville.com/fchs.html

Floyd County Historical & Genealogical Society
P.O. Box 217
Auxier, KY 41653

Fulton County Historical Society
P.O. Box 1031
Fulton, KY 42041

Garrard County Historical Society
208 Danville Street
Lancaster, KY 40444

Grayson County Historical Society
Leitchfield, KY 42754
Tel: 502-259-9645

Green County Historical Society
P.O. Box 276
Greensburg, KY 42743

Harrodsburg Historical Society
Genealogical Committee
220 Chiles Street
P.O. Box 316
Harrodsburg, KY 40330
Tel: 606-734-5985
URL: http://w3.one.net/~durp/hhs.htm

Hart County Historical Society/Museum
Chapline Building
Main Street
P.O. Box 606
Munfordville, KY 42765
Tel: 502-524-0101
URL: http://www.ovnet.com/userpages/feenerty/history.html

Henry County Historical Society
P.O. Box 570
New Castle, KY 40050

Hickman County Historical Society
Route 3, Box 255
Clinton, KY 42031

Johnson County Historical & Genealogical Society
Johnson County Public Library
P.O. Box 788
Paintsville, KY 41240

Kentucky Historical Society/Library/Museum
Old Capitol Annex
Corner of Broadway and Lewis Streets
P.O. Box 1792
Frankfort, KY 40602-1792
Tel: 502-564-3016
Fax: 502-564-4701
URL: http://www.state.ky.us/agencies/khs/main_toc.htm

Knott County Historical Society
P.O. Box 1023
Hindman, KY 41822

Knox County Historical Society, Inc.
P.O. Box 528
Barbourville, KY 40906

Laurel County Historical Society/Library
Old City Hall
Broad Street & West 3rd Street
P.O. Box 816
London, KY 40741
Tel: 606-864-0607
Email: rmaggard@skn.net
URL: http://www.geocities.com/Heartland/2060/main.htm

Lee County Historical & Genealogical Society
P.O. Box V
Beattyville, KY 41311

Letcher County Historical & Genealogical Society
P.O. Box 312
Whitesburg, KY 41858

Lewis County Historical Society
P.O. Box 212
Vanceburg, KY 41179

Lyon County Historical Society
P.O. Box 894
Eddyville, KY 42038

Madison County Historical Society
P.O. Box 5066
Richmond, KY 40476
Tel: 606-622-2820
606-622-1792
URL: http://www.iclub.org/kentucky/madison/history/

Magoffin County Historical Society/Library
213 S. Church Street
P.O. Box 222
Salyersville, KY 41465
Tel: 606-349-1607
URL: http://www.geocities.com/Heartland/7612/index.html

Marshall County Historical & Genealogical Society
P.O. Box 373
Benton, KY 42025
Tel: 502-527-4749
Email: marcoky@vci.net

Metcalfe County Historical Society
c/o Kay Harbison
Route 1, Box 371
Summer Shade, KY 42166

Nelson County Historical Society
P.O. Box 311
Bardstown, KY 40004

Ohio County Historical Society
P.O. Box 44
Hartford, KY 42347

Pendleton County Historical & Genealogical Society
Route 5, Box 280
Falmouth, KY 41040

Perry County Genealogical & Historical Society
148 Chester Street
Haxard, KY 41701

Pulaski County Historical Society
Pulaski County Public Library Building
107 N. Main Street
P.O. Box 36
Somerset, KY 42502

Red River Historical Society
P.O. Box 195
Clay City, KY 40312

Rockcastle County Historical Society
P.O. Box 930
Mt. Vernon, KY 40456

Rowan County Historical Society
302 E. 2nd Street
Morehead, KY 40351

Simpson County Historical Society/Library and Archives
206 N. College Street
Franklin, KY 42134
Tel: 502-586-4228

South Central Kentucky Historical/Genealogical Society
P.O. Box 157
Glasgow, KY 42142-0157
Email: sgorin@scrtc.blue.net
URL: http://www.angelfire.com/pg1/Barren/index.html#Society

Taylor County Historical Society
P.O. Box 14
Campbellsville, KY 42719

Trimble County Historical Society
Route 1, Box 127A
Pendleton, KY 40055
URL: http://www.ole.net/~maggie/trimble/histsoc.htm

Union County Historical Society/Museum
221 W. McElroy
Morganfield, KY 42437
URL: http://www.comsource.net/~kyseeker/union/society.htm

Vanlear Historical Society
P.O. Box 12
Vanlear, KY 41265

Woodford County Historical Society
121 Rose Hill
Versailles, KY 40383
Tel: 606-873-6786

LDS Family History Centers

Corbin Family History Center
Highway 312
Corbin, KY 40701
Tel: 606-528-2898

Hopkinsville Family History Center
1118 Pin Oak Drive
Hopkinsville, KY 42240
Tel: 502-886-1616

Lexington Family History Center
1789 Tates Creek Pike
Lexington, KY 40502
Tel: 606-269-2722
URL: http://www.uky.edu/StudentOrgs/LDSSA/fhcpage.html

Louisville Family History Center
1000 Hurstborne Pl.
Louisville, KY 40222
Tel: 502-426-8174

Martin Family History Center
Highway 80
Martin, KY 41649
Tel: 606-285-3133

Morgantown Family History Center
108 Meadowlark Drive
Morgantown, KY 42261
Tel: 502-728-3491

Owingsville Family History Center
Highway 36 South
Owingsville, KY 40360
Tel: 606-674-6626

Paducah Family History Center
120 Augusta Street #3
Paducah, KY 42003
Tel: 502-554-7203

Archives/Libraries/Museums

Adair County Public Library
307 GReensburg Street
Columbia, KY 42728
Tel: 502-384-2472

Bath Memorial Library
P.O. Box 136
Owingsville, KY 40360
Tel: 606-674-2531

Boyd County Public Library
Eastern Kentucky Genealogy Room
1740 Central Avenue
Ashland, KY 41101
Tel: 606-329-0090

Breathitt County Public Library
1024 College Avenue
Jackson, KY 41339

Breckinridge County Public Library
Special Collections
Hardinsburg, KY 40143
Tel: 502-756-2323

Buffalo Trace/Fleming County Public Library
303 South Main Cross Street
Flemingsburg, KY 41041
Tel: 606-845-7851
606-845-9571

Bullitt County Public Library
127 North Walnut
P.O. Box 146
Shepherdsville, KY 40165
Tel: 502-543-7675
Fax: 502-543-5487

Campbell County Historical & Genealogical Society Library
19 East Main Street
Alexandria, KY 41001
Tel: 606-635-6417

Campbellsville University
American Civil War Institute
1 University Drive
Campbellsville, KY 42718

Clark County Public Library
109-111 South Main Street
Winchester, KY 40391
Tel: 606-744-5661

Cincinnati Public Library
800 Vine Street
Cincinnati, OH 45202-2071
Tel: 513-369-6900

Crittenden County Library
204 West Carlisle Street
Marion, KY 42064
Tel: 502-965-3354

Cynthiana-Harrison County Public Library
110 North Main Street
Cynthiana, KY 41031
Tel: 606-234-4881

Department of Military Affairs
Military Records & Research Branch
Pine Hill Plaza
1121 Louisville Road
Frankfort, KY 40601
Tel: 502-564-4873
URL: http://www.state.ky.us/agencies/military/mrrb.htm

Eastern Kentucky University
Crabbe Library, Room 126
Special Collections & Archives
Richmond, KY 40475-3121
Tel: 606-622-1792
Fax: 606-622-1174
URL: http://www.cob.eku.edu/library/sca/scahome.htm

Elizabethtown Community College
Media Center/Microfilm
600 College Street
Elizabethtown, KY 42701

Filson Club Historical Society
1310 South Third Street
Louisville, KY 40208
Tel: 502-635-5083
Fax: 502-635-5086
URL: http://www.louisville.com/fchs.html

Fulton County Public Library
312 Main Street
Fulton, KY 42041
Tel: 502-472-3439
Fax: 502-472-6241

Gallatin Free Public Library
209 W. Market Street
P.O. Box 258
Warsaw, KY 41095
Tel/Fax: 606-567-2786

Garrard County Public Library
101 Lexington Street
Lancaster, KY 40444
Tel/Fax: 606-792-3424

George Coon Public Library
114 South Harrison Street
P.O. Box 230
Princeton, KY 42445
Tel: 502-365-2884
502-365-6674

Graves County Public Library
601 North 17th Street
Mayfield, KY 42066
Tel: 502-247-2911
Fax: 502-247-2990

Green County Public Library
116 South Main Street
Greensburg, KY 42743
Tel: 502-932-7081

Greenup County Public Library
614 Main Street
Greenup, KY 41144
Tel: 606-473-6514

Harvey Helm Memorial Library
301 Third Street
Stanford, KY 40484
Tel/Fax: 606-365-7513

Henderson Public Library
101 South Main Street
Henderson, KY 42420
Tel: 502-826-3712

Henry M. Caudill Memorial Library
121 E. Main Street
Whitesburg, KY 41858
Tel: 606-633-7547

Hickman County Memorial Public Library
209 Mayfield Road
Clinton, KY 42031
Tel/Fax: 502-653-2225

Israel T. Namani Library
3600 Dutchmans Lane
Louisville, KY 40205

Jackson County Public Library
David Street
P.O. Box 160
McKee, KY 40447-0160
Tel: 606-287-8113
Fax: 606-287-7774

John Fox Memorial Library
D.A. Shrine
Duncan Tavern Street
Paris, KY 40361

Kenton County Public Library
5th & Scott
Covington, KY 41011

Kentucky Department for Libraries and Archives
Public Records Division
Archives Research Room
300 Coffee Tree Road
P.O. Box 537
Frankfort, KY 40602-0537
Tel: 502-875-7000
URL: http://www.kdla.state.ky.us/arch/

Kentucky Historical Society/Library/Museum
Old Capitol Annex
300 West Broadway
P.O. Box 1792
Frankfort, KY 40602-1792
Tel: 502-564-3016
Fax: 502-564-4701
URL: http://www.state.ky.us/agencies/khs/main_toc.htm

Laurel County Historical Society/Library
Old City Hall
Broad Street & West 3rd Street
P.O. Box 816
London, KY 40741
Tel: 606-864-0607
Email: rmaggard@skn.net
URL: http://www.geocities.com/Heartland/2060/main.htm

Laurel County Public Library
116 East 4th Street
London, KY 40741
Tel: 606-864-5759
Fax: 606-864-9061

Lee County Public Library
123 Center Street
P.O. Box V
Beattyville, KY 41311
Tel: 606-464-8014
Fax: 606-464-2052

Leslie County Public Library
P.O. Box 498
Hyden, KY 41749

Lexington Public Library
140 E. Main
Lexington, KY 40507
Tel: 606-231-5520
URL: http://www.lpl.lib.ky.us/reference/kyroom.html

Louisville Free Public Library
301 York Street
Louisville, KY 40203
Tel: 502-574-1600

Magoffin County Historical Society/Library
213 S. Church Street
P.O. Box 222
Salyersville, KY 41465
Tel: 606-349-1607
URL: http://www.geocities.com/Heartland/7612/index.html

Marion County Free Public Library
201 East Main
Lebanon, KY 40033
Tel: 502-692-4698

Martin County Public Library
Main Street
P.O. Box 1318
Inez, KY 41224
Tel: 606-298-7766

Mary Wood Weldon Memorial Library
107 W. College Street
Glasgow, KY 42141
Tel: 502-651-2824

Menifee County Library
P.O. Box 237
Frenchburg, KY 40322
Tel: 606-768-2212

Morehead State University
Camden-Carroll Library
Special Collections
Morehead, KY 40351
Tel: 603-783-5107
603-783-2829
URL: http://www.morehead-st.edu/units/library/special.html

Morganfield Public Library
126 S. Morgan Street
Morganfield, KY 42437
Tel: 502-389-1696
Fax: 502-389-3935

Mt. Sterling/Montgomery County Library
241 W. Locust Street
Mt. Sterling, KY 40353
Tel: 606-498-2404

Nelson County Government Library
90 Court Square
Bardstown, KY 40004
Tel: 502-348-3714

Nicholas County Library
223 N. Broadway Street
Carlisle, KY 40311
Tel: 606-289-5595

Ohio County Library
413 Main Street
Hartford, KY 42347
Tel: 502-298-3790

Owen County Public Library
104 N. Main Street
Owenton, KY 40359
Tel: 502-484-3450
Email: owencopl@mis.net
URL: http://members.aol.com/fgoerler/owen/lib.htm

Owensboro/Daviess County Public Library
Kentucky Room, Local History & Genealogy
450 Griffith Avenue
Owensboro, KY 42301
Tel: 502-684-0211

Owsley County Public Library
#2 Medical Plaza
P.O. Box 280
Booneville, KY 41314
Tel: 606-593-5700
Fax: 606-593-5708

Perry County Public Library
479 High Street
Hazard, KY 41701
Tel: 606-436-2475

Pikeville Public Library
210 Pike Street
Pikeville, KY 41501
Tel: 606-432-0789

Pulaski County Public Library
107 N. Main
Somerset, KY 42501
Tel: 606-679-8401
606-679-1779

Robertson County Public Library
P.O. Box 282
Mt. Olivet, KY 41064
Tel: 606-724-5746

Rockcastle County Public Library
60 Ford Drive
Mt. Vernon, KY 40456
Tel/Fax: 606-256-2388

Rowan County Public Library
129 Trumbo Road
Morehead, KY 40351
Tel: 606-784-7137

Rufus M. Reed Public Library
P.O. Box 359
Lovely, KY 41231
Tel/Fax: 606-395-5809

Scott County Public Library
East Main
Georgetown, KY 40324

Secretary of State Land Office
The Capitol
Frankfort, KY 40601
Tel: 502-564-3490

Simpson County Historical Society/Library and Archives
206 N. College Street
Franklin, KY 42134
Tel: 502-586-4228

Union County Historical Society/Museum
221 W. McElroy
Morganfield, KY 42437
URL: http://www.comsource.net/~kyseeker/union/society.htm

University of Kentucky
King Library, North
Special Collection and Archives
Lexington, KY 40506
Tel: 606-257-8611
URL: http://www.uky.edu/Libraries/Special/

Wayne County Public Library
159 S. Main Street
Monticello, KY 42633
Tel: 606-348-8565
Fax: 606-348-3829

Western Kentucky University
DLSC/Kentucky Library
Kentucky Building, Room 206
14th Street & Big Red Way
Bowling Green, KY 42101
Tel: 502-745-5083
Fax: 502-745-4878
URL: http://www2.wku.edu/www/library/dlsc/ky_lib.htm

NEWSPAPER REPOSITORIES

Filson Club Historical Society
1310 South Third Street
Louisville, KY 40208
Tel: 502-635-5083
Fax: 502-635-5086
URL: http://www.louisville.com/fchs.html

Kentucky Historical Society/Library/Museum
Old Capitol Annex
Corner of Broadway and Lewis Streets
P.O. Box 1792
Frankfort, KY 40602-1792
Tel: 502-564-3016
Fax: 502-564-4701
URL: http://www.state.ky.us/agencies/khs/main_toc.htm

Lexington Public Library
140 E. Main
Lexington, KY 40507
Tel: 606-231-5520
URL: http://www.lpl.lib.ky.us/reference/kyroom.html

Murray State University
Pogue Library
Special Collections
Murray, KY 42071
Tel: 502-762-6152
URL: http://www.mursuky.edu/msml/collect.htm#special

St. Joseph County Public Library
304 South Main Street
South Bend, IN 46601
Tel: 219-282-4630
219-282-4621 (Local History & Genealogy)
Email: m.waterson@gomail.sjcpl.lib.in.us
URL: http://sjcpl.lib.in.us/homepage/LocalHist/Genealogy.html

University of Kentucky
King Library, North
Special Collection and Archives
Lexington, KY 40506
Tel: 606-257-8393
EMail: bacrring@ukcc.uky.edu
URL: http://www.uky.edu/Libraries/pnm.html#news1

University of Louisville
Archives and Records Center
Ekstrom Library Building
Louisville, KY 40292
Tel: 502-852-6674
Fax: 502-852-6673
Email: archives@ulkyvm.louisville.edu
URL: http://www.louisville.edu/library/uarc/

VITAL RECORDS

Office of Vital Statistics
375 East Main Street
Frankfort, KY 40601
Tel: 502-564-4212
URL: http://www.kdla.state.ky.us/arch/vitastat.htm

KENTUCKY ON THE WEB

First Kentucky Brigade, CS, "The Orphan Brigade"
http://bl-12.rootsweb.com/~orphanhm/

Kentucky Biographies Project
http://www.starbase21.com/kybiog/

Kentucky Explorer (Magazine)
http://www.win.net/kyexmag/KEhome.html

Kentucky GenWeb Project
http://www.rootsweb.com/~kygenweb/

Kentucky in the Civil War
http://www.dsenter.com/~trice/ky/civilwar.html

Kentucky Vital Records Index
http://ukcc.uky.edu/~vitalrec/

Melungeon Ancestry Research and Information Page
http://www.bright.net/~kat/melung.htm

Ohio River Valley Families
http://www.trilithic.com/orvf/

Travellers Southern Families
http://genealogy.traveller.com/genealogy/

LOUISIANA

ARCHIVES, STATE & NATIONAL

Louisiana Secretary of State
Division of Archives
Records Management & History
3851 Essen Lane
P.O. Box 94125
Baton Rouge, LA 70809
Tel: 504-922-1200
504-922-1206 (Louisiana Room)
504-922-1184 (Genealogical/Vital Records)
504-922-1208 (Heritage Center)
URL: http://www.sec.state.la.us/arch-1.htm

National Archives—Southwest Region
501 West Felix Street
Building 1, Dock 1
P.O. Box 6216
Fort Worth, TX 76115-0216
Tel: 817-334-5525
Fax: 817-334-5621
Email: archives@ftworth.nara.gov
URL: http://www.nara.gov/nara/regional/07nsgil.html

GENEALOGICAL SOCIETIES

Allen Genealogical and Historical Society
P.O. Box 789
Kinder, LA 70648

Amite Genealogical Club
P.O. Box 578
Amite, LA 70422

Ark-La-Tex Genealogical Association
P.O. Box 4462
Shreveport, LA 71134
URL: http://www.softdisk.com/comp/aga

Baton Rouge Genealogical and Historical Society
SE Station
P.O. Box 80565
Baton Rouge, LA 70898
URL: http://www.fgs.org/~fgs/soc0011.htm

Cajun Clickers Computer Club
5700 Florida Blvd., Suite 1109
Baton Rouge, LA 70806
URL: http://www.intersurf.com/~cars/index999.html

Central Louisiana Genealogical Society
P.O. Box 12206
Alexandria, LA 71315-2006

East Ascension Genealogical and Historical Society
P.O. Box 1006
Gonzales, LA 70707-1006

Evangeline Genealogical and Historical Society
P.O. Box 664
Ville Platte, LA 70586

Florida Parishes Genealogical Society
P.O. Box 520
Livingston, LA 70754-0520

Friends of Genealogy
P.O. Box 17835
Shreveport, LA 71138

GENCOM PC User Group of Shreveport
9913 Dagger Point
Shreveport, LA 71115
Email: hr50@softdisk.com
URL: http://www.softdisk.com/comp/gencom/

Genealogy West, Inc.
West Bank of the Mississippi
5644 Abbey Drive
New Orleans, LA 70131-3808

German-Acadian Coast Historical and Genealogical Society
P.O. Box 517
Destrahan, LA 70047-0517

Imperial/St. Landry Genealogical and Historical Society
P.O. Box 108
Opelousas, LA 70571-0108
Tel: 318-942-3332

Jefferson Genealogical Society
P.O. Box 961
Metairie, LA 70004-0961
URL: http://www.fgs.org/~fgs/soc0093.htm

Jennings Genealogical Society
136 Greenwood Drive
Jennings, LA 70546

Jewish Genealogical Society of New Orleans
P.O. Box 7811
Metairie, LA 70010-7811

Lafayette Genealogical Society
105 Gill Drive
Lafayette, LA 70507

Le Comite des Archives de la Louisiane
Capitol Station
P.O. Box 44370
Baton Rouge, LA 70804-4370
Tel: 504-355-9906
504-387-4264

Louisiana Genealogical and Historical Society
P.O. Box 82060
Baton Rouge, LA 70884

Louisiana Roots
P.O. Box 383
Marksville, LA 71351
Tel: 318-253-5413
Fax: 318-253-7223

Natchitoches Genealogical and Historical Association
P.O. Box 1349
Natchitoches, LA 71458

New Orleans, Genealogical Research Society of
P.O. Box 51791
New Orleans, LA 70150

North Louisiana Genealogical Society
P.O. Box 324
Ruston, LA 71270

Plaquemines Deep Delta Genealogical Society
c/o Plaquemines Parish Library
203 Highway 11 South
Buras, LA 70041
Tel: 504-657-7121

Pointe de l'Eglise Genealogical and Historical Society
P.O. Box 160
Church Point, LA 70525
Email: ffwp26e@prodigy.com

St. Bernard Genealogical Society
P.O. Box 271
Chalmette, LA 70044-0271
URL: http://www.challenger.net/local/users/lindas/stbernard/stbgs.htm

St. Mary Genealogical and Historical Society
P.O. Box 662
Morgan City, LA 70381

St. Tammany Genealogical Society
310 W. 21st Street
Covington, LA 70434

Sons and Daughters of the Province and
Republic of West Florida 1763-1810
P.O. Box 82672
Baton Rouge, LA 70884-2672

Southwest Louisiana Genealogical Society
P.O. Box 5652
Lake Charles, LA 70606-5652
URL: http://cust2.iamerica.net/jcraven/swlgs.htm

Terrebonne Genealogical Society
Station 2, Box 295
Houma, LA 70360-0295
URL: http://www.rootsweb.com/~laterreb/tgs.htm

Vermilion Genealogical Society
307 N. Main Street
P.O. Box 117
Abbeville, LA 70511-0117

Vernon Genealogical and Historical Society
P.O. Box 159
Anacoco, LA 71403

Vicksburg Genealogical Society
P.O. Box 116
Vicksburg, MS 39181-1161

West Bank Genealogy Society
P.O. Box 872
Harvey, LA 70059-0872
URL: http://www.challenger.net/local/users/lindas/jefferson/wbgs.html

West Baton Rouge Genealogical Society
P.O. Box 1126
Port Allen, LA 70767

Winn Parish Genealogical and Historical Society
P.O. Box 652
Winnfield, LA 71483
Email: peggy@winnsurf.net

HISTORICAL SOCIETIES

Allen Genealogical and Historical Society
P.O. Box 789
Kinder, LA 70648

Action Cadienne (Cajun Action)
P.O. Box 30104
Lafayette, LA 70593
URL: http://www.rbmulti.nb.ca/cadienne/cadienne.htm

Baton Rouge Genealogical and Historical Society
SE Station
P.O. Box 80565
Baton Rouge, LA 70898
URL: http://www.fgs.org/~fgs/soc0011.htm

East Ascension Genealogical and Historical Society
P.O. Box 1006
Gonzales, LA 70707-1006

Edward Livingston Historical Association
P.O. Box 67
Livingston, LA 70754-0067

Evangeline Genealogical and Historical Society
P.O. Box 664
Ville Platte, LA 70586

Feliciana History Committee
P.O. Box 8341
Clinton, LA 70722

Feliciana Historical Society
P.O. Box 338
St. Francisville, LA 70775

German-Acadian Coast Historical and Genealogical Society
P.O. Box 517
Destrahan, LA 70047-0517

Imperial/St. Landry Genealogical and Historical Society
P.O. Box 108
Opelousas, LA 70571-0108
Tel: 318-942-3332

Lafourche Heritage Society
412 Menard Street
Thibodaux, LA 70301

Louisiana Genealogical and Historical Society
P.O. Box 82060
Baton Rouge, LA 70884

Natchitoches Genealogical and Historical Association
P.O. Box 1349
Natchitoches, LA 71458

North Caddo, Historical Society of
P.O. Box 500
Vivian, LA 71082

St. Augustine Historical Society
312 Pearl Street
Natchitoches, LA 71457
Email: colsonj@cp-tel.net
URL: http://www.cp-tel.net/creole/

St. Helena Historical Society
Route 1, Box 131
Amite, LA 70422-9415

St. Mary Genealogical and Historical Society
P.O. Box 662
Morgan City, LA 70381

St. Tammany Parish Historical Society
P.O. Box 1001
Mandeville, LA 70470

Southeast Louisiana Historical Society
P.O. Box 789
Hammond, LA 70401-0789

Tangipahoa Parish Historical Society
77139 N. River Road
Kentwood, LA 70444

Vermillion Historic Foundation
1600 Surrey Street
P.O. Box 2266
Lafayette, LA 70502-2266
Tel: 318-233-4077
800-99-BAYOU

Vernon Genealogical and Historical Society
P.O. Box 159
Anacoco, LA 71403

West Feliciana Historical Society/Museum
Ferdinand Street
P.O. Box 338
St. Francisville, LA 70775
Tel: 504-635-6330

Winn Parish Genealogical and Historical Society
P.O. Box 652
Winnfield, LA 71483
Email: peggy@winnsurf.net

LDS Family History Center

Alexandria Family History Center
611 Versailles Street
Alexandria, LA 71303
Tel: 318-448-1842

Baton Rouge Family History Center
10335 Highland Road
Baton Rouge, LA 70810
Tel: 504-769-8913

Denham Springs Family History Center
25367 Riverton Avenue
Denham Springs, LA 70726
Tel: 504-664-8979

Metairie Family History Center
5025 Cleveland Place
Metairie, LA 70003
Tel: 504-885-3936

Monroe Family History Center
909 North 33rd Street
Monroe, LA 71201
Tel: 318-322-7009

Shreveport Family History Center
200 Carroll Street
Shreveport, LA 71105
Tel: 318-868-5169

Slidell Family History Center
112 Rue Esplanade
Slidell, LA 70461
Tel: 501-641-3982

Archives/Libraries/Museums

Amistead Research Center
Tilton Hall
Tulane University
6823 St. Charles Avenue
New Orleans, LA 70118
Tel: 504-865-5535
Fax: 504-865-5580
URL: http://www.arc.tulane.edu/

Ascension Parish Library
708 S. Irma Avenue
Gonzales, LA 70707-1006
Tel: 504-647-3955

Assumption Parish Library
293 Napoleon Avenue
Napoleonville, LA 70390
Tel: 504-369-7070
Fax: 504-369-6019
Email: apl1@pelican.state.lib.la.us

Avoyelles Parish Library
101 North Washington Street
Marksville, LA 71351-2496
Tel: 318-253-7559
Fax: 318-253-6361
Email: xxx1137@ucs.usl.edu

Beauregard Parish Library
205 S. Washington Avenue
DeRidder, LA 70634
Tel: 318-463-6217
800-524-6239
URL: http://www.beau.lib.dtx.net/genie.htm

Bogalusa Branch/Washington Parish Library
304 Avenue F
Bogalusa, LA 70427
Tel: 504-735-1961

Centenary College of Louisiana
Magale Library
2911 Centenary Blvd.
P.O. Box 41188
Shreveport, LA 71134
Tel: 318-869-5170
Fax: 318-869-5094
URL: http://www.centenary.edu/centenar/campusrv/lib/library.html

East Baton Rouge Parish Library
Bluebonnet Regional Branch
9200 Bluebonnet Blvd.
Baton Rouge, LA 70810
Tel: 504-763-2283 (Genealogy Dept.)

Iberville Parish Library
24605 J. Gerald Berret Blvd.
Plaquemine, LA 70764-0736
Tel: 504-687-2520
Fax: 501-687-9719
Email: paibv1@Unix1.sncc.lsu.edu

Jackson Barracks Military Library
Office of the Adjutant General
Building 53, Jackson Barracks
New Orleans, LA 70146-0330
Tel: 504-278-8241
Fax: 504-278-6554

Jefferson Parish Library
3420 N. Causeway Blvd.
P.O. Box 7490
Metairie, LA 70010-7490
Tel: 504-838-1100
Fax: 504-838-1110

Lafayette Parish Public Library
301 West Congress Street
P.O. Box 3427
Lafayette, LA 70502-3427
Tel: 318-261-5775
Fax: 318-261-5782

Lafourche Parish Library
303 West 5th Street
Thibodaux, LA 70301
Tel: 504-446-1163
Fax: 504-446-3848
Email: lpl1@pelican.state.lib.la.us

Lincoln Parish Library
509 West Alabama
P.O. Box 637
Ruston, LA 71270
Tel: 318-255-1920

Louisiana State Library
Louisiana Section
760 North Third Street
P.O. Box 131
Baton Rouge, LA 70821-0131
Tel: 504-342-4914
URL: http://smt.state.lib.la.us/

Louisiana State Museum Historical Center
751 Chartres Street
P.O. Box 2448
New Orleans, LA 70116-2448
Tel: 504-568-6968
800-568-6968
Fax: 504-568-4995
Email: jrubin@crt.state.la.us
URL: http://www.crt.state.la.us/crt/museum/lsmnet3.htm

Louisiana State University
Hill Memorial Library
Special Collections Public Services
Baton Rouge, LA 70803-3300
Tel: 504-388-6568
504-388-6551 (Reading Room)
Email: lbyspc@lsuvm.sncc.lsu.edu
URL: http://www.lib.lsu.edu/special/hours.html

Louisiana State University/Shreveport
Noel Memorial Library
Shreveport, LA 71115
Tel: 318-797-5069
URL: http://www.lsus.edu/library/

Natchitoches Parish Library
431 Jefferson Street
Natchitoches, LA 71457
Tel: 318-357-3280
blackb@alpha.nsula.edu

New Orleans Public Library
219 Loyola Avenue
New Orleans, LA 70112-2044
Tel: 504-596-2610 (Louisiana Division)
URL: http://www.gnofn.org/~nopl/nutrias.htm

Ouachita Parish Public Library
Genealogy Room
1800 Stubbs Avenue
Monroe, LA 71201-5787
Tel: 318-327-1490
Fax: 318-327-1373
Email: ou_lib1@alpha.nlu.edu

Plaquemines Parish Library
203 Highway 11 South
Buras, LA 70041
Tel: 504-657-7121

Point Coupee Library
201 Clairborne Street
New Roads, LA 70760-3403
Tel: 504-638-7593
504-638-9841
Fax: 504-638-9847
Email: papcpl@Unix1.sncc.lsu.edu

Rapides Parish Library
Red Carpet Van Service
411 Washington Street
Alexandria, LA 71301-8338
Tel: 318-445-6436
Fax: 318-445-6478
318-445-6196

St. James Parish Library
1879 West Main Street
Lutcher, LA 70071-9704
Tel: 504-869-3618
Fax: 504-869-8435
Email: sjpl1@pelican.state.lib.la.us

St. John the Baptist Parish Library
1334 West Airline Highway
LaPlace, LA 70068-3797
Tel: 504-652-6857
Fax: 504-652-2144
Email: llbsj-ad@nich-nsunet.nich.edu

St. Martin Parish Library
201 Porter Street
P.O. Box 79
St. Martinsville, LA 70582-0079
Tel: 318-394-2207
Fax: 318-394-2248
Email: pastm1@Unix1.sncc.lsu.edu

Shreve Memorial Library
424 Texas Street
P.O. Box 21523
Shreveport, LA 71120
Tel: 318-226-5890 (Genealogy)
Email: jgahagan@smlnet.sml.lib.la.us
URL: http://www.prysm.net/~japrime/lagenweb/shreve.htm

Shreveport Exhibit Museum
3015 Greenwood Road
Shreveport, LA 71109
Tel: 318-632-2020
318-632-2019
URL: http://www.sec.state.la.us/shreve-1.htm

Southwest Louisiana Genealogical Library
411 Pujo Street
Lake Charles, LA 70601
Tel: 318-437-3490
Fax: 318-437-4198

Tangipahoa Parish Library
100 SE Central Avenue
P.O. Box 578
Amite, LA 70422
Tel: 504-748-7151

Terrebonne Parish Library
424 Roussell Street
Houma, LA 70360
Tel: 504-876-5861
Fax: 504-876-5864
Email: ter@pelican.state.lib.la.us

Tulane University
Howard/Tilton Memorial Library
Special Collections
New Orleans, LA 70118
Tel: 504-865-5643
Fax: 504-865-6773
Email: meneray@mailhost.tcs.tulane.edu
URL: http://www.tulane.edu/~lmiller/SpecCollHomePage.html

University of Southwest Louisiana
Edith Garland Dupre' Library
Jefferson Caffery Louisiana Room
302 E. St. Mary Street
Lafayette, LA 70504
Tel: 318-482-6031
URL: http://www.usl.edu/Departments/Library/index.html

Vernon Parish Library
1401 Nolan Trace
Leesville, LA 71446-4331
Tel: 318-239-2027
800-737-2231
Fax: 318-238-0666
Email: vernonpl@alpha.nsula.edu

Washington Parish Library
825 Free Street
Franklinton, LA 70438
Tel: 504-839-7806
Fax: 504-839-7808
Email: slou3012@selu.edu

West Baton Rouge Museum
845 N. Jefferson
Port Allen, LA 70767
Tel: 504-336-2422

West Baton Rouge Parish Library
830 N. Alexander
Port Allen, LA 70767-2327
Tel: 504-342-7920
Email: pawbr1@Unix1.sncc.lsu.edu

West Feliciana Historical Society/Museum
Ferdinand Street
P.O. Box 338
St. Francisville, LA 70775
Tel: 504-635-6330

West Feliciana Parish Library
Audubon Library
11757 Ferdinand Street
St. Francisville, LA 70775
Tel: 504-635-3364

Xavier University
Archives and Special Collections
7325 Palmetto Street
New Orleans, LA 70125
Tel: 504-483-7655
Fax: 504-486-2385
Email: lsullivan@mail.xula.edu

NEWSPAPER REPOSITORIES

Louisiana State University
Hill Memorial Library
Special Collections Public Services
Baton Rouge, LA 70803-3300
Tel: 504-388-6559
Email: notlbs@lsuvm.sncc.lsu.edu
URL: http://www.lib.lsu.edu/special/lnp.html

New Orleans Public Library
219 Loyola Avenue
New Orleans, LA 70112-2044
Tel: 504-596-2610 (Louisiana Division)
URL: http://www.gnofn.org/~nopl/nutrias.htm

VITAL RECORDS

Louisiana Department of Health
Vital Records Registry
Office of Public Health
325 Loyola Avenue
P.O. Box 60630
New Orleans, LA 70160
Tel: 504-568-5150

LOUISIANA ON THE WEB

Acadian Genealogy Homepage
http://www.freespace.net/~cajun/genealogy/

Cajun and Creole Pages
http://http.tamu.edu:8000/~skb8721/

Louisiana GenWeb Project
http://www.goldenbranches.com/la-state

Traveller Southern Families
http://genealogy.traveller.com/genealogy/

U.S. Civil War Center
http://www.cwc.lsu.edu/civlink.htm

MAINE

ARCHIVES, STATE & NATIONAL

Maine State Archives
LMA Building
State House Station 84
Augusta, ME 04333
Tel: 207-287-5795
URL: http://www.state.me.us/sos/arc/general/admin/mawww001.htm

National Archives—New England Region
380 Trapelo Road
Waltham, MA 02154-8104
Tel: 617-647-8100
Fax: 617-647-8460
Email: archives@waltham.nara.gov
URL: http://www.nara.gov/nara/regional/01nsbgil.html

GENEALOGICAL SOCIETIES

Lincoln County Genealogical Society
P.O. Box 61
Wiscasset, ME 04578

Maine Genealogical Society
P.O. Box 221
Farmington, ME 04938

New England Historical and Genealogical Society (NEHGS)
101 Newbury Street
Boston, MA 02116-3007
Tel: 617-836-5740
888-AT-NEHGS (Membership & Education)
888-BY-NEHGS (Sales)
888-90-NEHGS (Library Circulation)
Fax: 617-536-7307
Email: nehgs@nehgs.org
URL: http://www.nehgs.org/

HISTORICAL SOCIETIES

Acton/Shapleigh Historical Society
Rt. 109
Shapleigh, ME 04076
Tel: 207-636-2606

Alexander-Crawford Historical Society
Pokey Road
Alexander, ME 04694

Allagash Historical Society
Rte. 161
St. Francis, ME 04774
Tel: 207-398-3335
207-398-3159
207-398-3157

Alna Historical Society
Old Alna Meeting House
Route 218
Alna, ME 04535
Tel: 207-586-6928

Androscoggin Historical Society
2 Turner
Auburn, ME 04210
Tel: 207-784-0586

Bangor Historical Society/Museum
159 Union Street
Bangor, ME 04401
Tel: 207-942-5766

Bar Harbor Historical Society/Museum
34 Mt. Desert Street
Bar Harbor, ME 04609
Tel: 207-288-3807
207-288-4245

Bath Historical Society
c/o Patten Free Library
33 Summer Street
Bath, ME 04530-2687
Tel: 207-443-5141
Fax: 207-443-3514
URL: http://www.biddeford.com/~pfl/shgr.htm

Bethel Historical Society/Museum
14 Broad Street
P.O. Box 12
Bethel, ME 04217
Tel: 207-824-2908

Biddeford Historical Society
McArthur Library
270 Main Street
Biddeford, ME 04005
Tel: 207-283-4706

Blue Hill Historical Society
Holt House
Water Street
Blue Hill, ME 04614

Boothbay Region Historical Society
70 Oak Street
Boothbay, ME 04537
Tel: 207-633-3462

Border Historical Society
Washington Street
Eastport, ME 04631
Tel: 207-853-2328

Brewer Historical Society
Clewley Museum
199 Wilson Street
Brewer, ME 04412
Tel: 207-989-7468

Bridgton Historical Society/Museum
Gibbs Avenue
P.O. Box 44
Bridgton, ME 04009
Tel: 207-647-3699

Brooksville Historical Society/Museum
Route 176
Brooksville, ME 04617
Tel: 207-326-4900
207-326-4959
207-326-4167

Buckfield Historical Society
RR 1, Box 780
Buckfield, ME 04220

Camden Historical Society
80 Mechanic Street
Camden, ME 04843

Camden-Rockport Historical Society
Old Conway Complex & Museum
P.O. Box 747
Camden, ME 04843
Tel/Fax: 207-236-2257

Caribou Historical Society
Presque Isle Road, Route 1
Caribou, ME 04736
Tel: 207-498-2556

Chebeague Island Historical Society
Chebeague Island, ME 04017
Email: Etta137@aol.com

Cherryfield-Narraguagus Historical Society
Main Street
P.O. Box 96
Cherryfield, ME 04622
Tel: 207-546-7979

Cushing Historical Society/Museum
Hawthorne Point Road
Cushing, ME 04563
Tel: 207-354-8262
800-261-1369

Dead River Area Historical Society
172 Main Street
Stratton, ME 04982
Tel: 207-246-2271

Dexter Historical Society
Grist Mill Museum & Millers House
Main Street
Dexter, ME 04930
Tel: 207-924-5721

Dixfield Historical Society
63 Main Street
P.O. Box 182
Dixfield, ME 04224

Dresden Historical Society
Dresden Brick School House
Route 128
Dresden, ME 04342
Tel: 207-737-2839
207-737-8892

Durham Historical Society
15 Cyr Road
Durham, ME 04222

Easton Historical Society
Station Road
Easton, ME 04740
Tel: 207-488-6846
207-488-6652

Falmouth Historical Society
c/o Falmouth Memorial Library
5 Lunt Road
Falmouth, ME 04105
Tel: 207-781-2351
Fax: 207-781-4094
URL: http://www.falmouth.lib.me.us/hist_soc.html

Franklin Historical Society
Sullivan Road, Rt. 200
Tel: 207-565-3635
207-565-3323

Freeport Historical Society
Enoch Harrington House
45 Main Street
Freeport, ME 04032
Tel: 207-865-0477

Fryeburg Historical Society/Museum
96 Main Street
Fryeburg, ME 04037-1126
Tel: 207-935-4192

Gouldsboro Historical Society
Old Town House
Route 1
Gouldsboro, ME 04607
Tel: 207-963-5530

Guilford Historical Society
North Main Street
Guilford, ME 04443
Tel: 207-876-2787

Hampden Historical Society
Kinsley House Museum and Archives
83 Main Road
Hampden, ME 04444
Tel: 207-862-2027

Hancock Historical Society
Hancock Corner
Hancock, ME 04640
Tel: 207-422-3080

Harpswell Historical Society
Old Meeting House
Route 123
Harpswell, ME 04079
Tel: 207-721-8950

Harrison Historical Society
Haskell Hill Road
Harrison, ME 04040
Tel: 207-583-6225

Island Falls Historical Society
Burley Street
Island Falls, ME 04037
Tel: 207-463-2264

Islesboro Historical Society
Old Town Hall/School
Main Road
P.O. Box 301
Islesboro, ME 04848
Tel: 207-734-6733

Jay Historical Society
Holmes-Crafts Homestead
Rt. 4, Jay Hill
North Jay, ME 04262
Tel: 207-645-2732

Kennebec Historical Society
14 Smith Street
Augusta, ME 04330
Tel: 207-621-3486

Kennebunkport Historical Society
Town House School
135 North Street
P.O. Box 1173
Kennebunkport, ME 04046
Tel: 207-967-2751
URL: http://www.vrmedia.com/KHS/

Lee Historical Society/Museum
Main Street, Rt. 6
Lee, ME 04455
Tel: 207-738-3533
207-738-4022

Liberty Historical Society
Old Octagonal Post Office
Main Street, Route 173
Liberty, ME 04949
Tel: 207-589-4393

Lincoln County Historical Association
Federal Street
Wiscasset, ME 04578
Tel: 207-882-6817

Lincolnville Historical Society/Museum
Route 1
Lincolnville, ME 04849
Tel: 207-789-5445

Lisbon Historical Society
14 High Street
Lisbon, ME 04250

Lovell Historical Society
Lovell, ME 04051
Tel: 207-925-3234
207-925-3760

Machiasport Historical Society
Gates House
Route 92
P.O. Box 301
Machiasport, ME 04655
Tel: 207-255-8461
207-255-8557

Madawaska Historical Society
Library Building
Main Street
Madawaska, ME 04756
URL: http://www.freespace.net/~cajun/genealogy/mad-soc.html

Maine Historical Society
Center for Maine History
485 Congress Street
Portland, ME 04101
Tel: 207-774-1822
Fax: 207-775-4301

Maine Military Historical Society/Museum
Camp Keyes
Upper Winthrop Street
Augusta, ME 04330
Tel: 207-626-4338

Maine's Swedish Colony
P.O. Box 50
New Sweden, ME 04762
Tel: 207-896-3199
Fax: 207-896-3120
207-896-5624
URL: http://www.state.me.us/sos/arc/external/otherins.htm

Monmouth Historical Society
Monmouth Museum
751 Main Street
Monmouth, ME 04259
Tel: 207-933-2287
207-933-2752

Moosehead Historical Society
Pritham Avenue
Greenville, ME 04441-9727
Tel: 207-695-2909
207-695-3163
Email: eparker@agate.net

Mt. Desert Island (MDI) Historical Society/Museum
Main Street, Rt. 102
Mt. Desert, ME 04660
Tel: 207-244-9012

Naples Historical Society/Museum
Route 302, Village Green
Naples, ME 04055
Tel: 207-693-6790

New England Historical and Genealogical Society (NEHGS)
101 Newbury Street
Boston, MA 02116-3007
Tel: 617-836-5740
888-AT-NEHGS (Membership & Education)
888-BY-NEHGS (Sales)
888-90-NEHGS (Library Circulation)
Fax: 617-536-7307
Email: nehgs@nehgs.org
URL: http://www.nehgs.org/

Nobleboro Historical Society
198 Center Street, Old Rt. 1
Nobleboro, ME 04555
Tel: 207-563-5874

Norridgewock Historical Society
Mercer Road
Norridgewock, ME 04957
Tel: 207-634-4243

Norway Historical Society/Museum
232 Main Street
Norway, ME 04268
Tel: 207-743-7377

Old Berwick Historical Society
Counting House
Rt. 4
South Berwick, ME 03908
Tel: 207-384-8041

Old Orchard Beach Historical Society/Museum
Harmon Memorial
4 Portland Avenue
Old Orchard Beach, ME 04064
Tel: 207-934-4485

Old York Historical Society/Museum
140 Lindsay Road
P.O. Box 312
York, ME 03909
Tel: 207-363-4974
207-363-3872
207-351-1083
URL: http://www.nentug.org/museums/oldyork/

Orland Historical Society
Main Street, Rt. 175
Orland, ME 04472
Tel: 207-469-2476

Otisfield Historical Society
Otisfield Town Office Building
Route 121, Oxford Road
Otisfield, ME 04270
Tel: 207-539-2664
207-539-2521
Mail:
c/o Hankins
202 Scribner Hill Road
Otisfield, ME 04270
URL: http://www.geocities.com/Heartland/8853/otis.htm

Oxford Historical Society
683 Main Street
Oxford, ME 04270

Paris Cape Historical Society/Museum
19 Park Street
South Paris, ME 04281
Tel: 207-743-0604

Parsonfield/Porter Historical Society
Main Street
Porter, ME 04068
Tel: 207-625-4667

Pejepscot Historical Society/Museum
159 Park Row
Brunswick, ME 04011
Tel: 207-729-6606
Fax: 207-729-6012
Email: pejepscot@acornbbs.com
URL: http://www.curtislibrary.com/pejepscot.htm

Pemaquid Historical Society
23 Old Harrington Road
Pemaquid, ME 04558

Phillips Historical Society
Pleasant Street
Phillips, ME 04966
Tel: 207-639-3352
207-639-4001

Pittsfield Historical Society
Depot House Museum
Railroad Plaza
Pittsfield, ME 04967
Tel: 207-487-2254

Presque Isle Historical Society
16 3rd Street
Presque Isle, ME 04769
Tel: 207-762-1151

Rangeley Lakes Region Historical Society
Main and Richardson Streets
Rangeley, ME 04970
Tel: 207-864-3317

Raymond-Casco Historical Society
Main Street
Raymond, ME 04071
Tel: 207-627-4350

Readfield Historical Society
Union Meeting House
Church Road
Readfield, ME 04355
Tel: 207-685-3831

Richmond Historical Society
7 Gardiner Street
Richmond, ME 04357
Tel: 207-737-4166

Rumford Area Historical Society
Municipal Building
Rumford, ME 04276
Tel: 207-364-7528

St. Croix Historical Society
245 Maine Street
Calais, ME 04619

Ste. Agatha Historical Society
Rt. 162, Main Street
Ste. Agatha, ME 04772
Tel: 207-543-6364

Salmon Brook Historical Society of Washburn
Main Street
Washburn, ME 04786
Tel: 207-455-8110
207-455-8279

Scarborough Historical Society
649 U.S. Rt. 1
Scarborough, ME 04074
Tel: 207-883-3539

Searsport Historical Society
Main Street, Rt. 1
Searsport, ME 04974
Tel: 207-548-0245

Sedgwick/Brooklin Historical Society/Museum
Rt. 15, Caterpillar Hill
Sedgwick, ME 04676
Tel: 207-359-2251

Southern Maine Technical College
Spring Point Museum
2 Fort Road
South Portland, ME 04106
Tel: 207-799-6337

Standish Historical Society
Oak Hill Road
Standish, ME 04084
Tel: 207-642-4443
207-642-5170

Stockholm Historical Society
Main and Lake Street
P.O. Box 37
Stockholm, ME 04783
Tel: 207-896-5731

Strong Historical Society
Vance & Dorothy Hammond Museum
Main Street
Strong, ME 04983
Tel: 207-684-4137
207-684-3396

Sweden Historical Society
RR 1, Box 230
Bridgton, ME 04009
Tel: 207-647-8272
Email: sueblack@nbridgton.lib.me.us

Thomaston Historical Society
Knox
Thomaston, ME 04861
Tel: 207-354-2295

Vassalboro Historical Society/Museum
Rt. 32
Vassalboro, ME 04989
Tel: 207-923-3533

Vinalhaven Historical Society/Museum
High Street
P.O. Box 339
Vinalhaven, ME 04863
Tel: 207-863-4410
207-863-4318
Email: vhhissoc@midcoast.com

Waldoboro Historical Society/Museum
Rt. 220 South
Waldoboro, ME 04572

Waterford Historical Society/Museum
P.O. Box 201
Waterford, ME 04088

Waterville Historical Society
Redington Museum
64 Silver
Waterville, ME 04901
Tel: 207-872-9439

Weld Historical Society
Weld Village
Weld, ME 04285
Tel: 207-585-2586

Wells Historical Society
Meetinghouse Museum
Genealogical & Historical Research Library
Rt. 1, Post Road
Wells, ME 04090
Tel: 207-646-4775

Windham Historical Society
26 Dutton Hill Road
Gray, ME 04039
Tel: 207-892-9667

Winslow Historical Society
16 Benton Avenue
Winslow, ME 04901

Winterport Historical Association
760 N. Main Street
Winterport, ME 04496
Tel: 207-223-5556

Woodstock Historical Society/Museum
Route 26
Bryant Pond, ME 04219
Tel: 207-665-2450

Woolwich Historical Society
Route 1 and Nequasset Road
Woolwich, ME 04579
Tel: 207-443-4833
207-443-6571

Yarmouth Historical Society
Museum of Yarmouth History &
Merrill Memorial Library
Main Street
Yarmouth, ME 04096
Tel: 207-846-6259

LDS Family History Centers

Bangor Family History Center
639 Grandview Avenue
Bangor, ME 04401
Tel: 207-942-7310

Cape Elizabeth Family History Center
29 Ocean House Road
Cape Elizabeth, ME 04107
Tel: 207-767-5000

Caribou Family History Center
67 West Hardison Avenue
Caribou, ME 04736
Tel: 207-492-4381

Farmingdale Family History Center
4 Hasson Street
Farmingdale, ME 04344
Tel: 207-582-1827

Archives/Libraries/Museums

Acadia National Park
Mount Desert Island
P.O. Box 177
Bar Harbor, ME 04609
Tel: 207-288-5459
207-288-5507
URL: http://www.cr.nps.gov/csd/collections/acad.html

Acadian Village
Rt. 1
Van Buren, ME 04785
Tel: 207-868-5042

Aroostook County Historical & Art Museum
109 Main Street
Houlton, ME 04730
Tel: 207-532-4216

Auburn Public Library
Court & Spring Streets
Auburn, ME 04210

Bangor Public Library
145 Harlow Street
Bangor, ME 04401
Tel: 207-947-8336
URL: http://www.maineguide.com/bangor/library/bgrlibr.html

Bethel Historical Society/Museum
14 Broad Street
P.O. Box 12
Bethel, ME 04217
Tel: 207-824-2908

Bowdoin College
Hawthorne-Longfellow Library
Archives and Special Collections
3000 College Station
Brunswick, ME 04011-8421
Tel: 207-725-3288 (Special Collections)
207-725-3096 (Archives)
URL: http://www.bowdoin.edu/dept/library/arch/guide/genweb.htm

Brewer Historical Society
Clewley Museum
199 Wilson Street
Brewer, ME 04412
Tel: 207-989-7468

Bridgton Historical Society/Museum
Gibbs Avenue
P.O. Box 44
Bridgton, ME 04009
Tel: 207-647-3699

Brooksville Historical Society/Museum
Route 176
Brooksville, ME 04617
Tel: 207-326-4900
207-326-4959
207-326-4167

Camden-Rockport Historical Society
Old Conway Complex & Museum
P.O. Box 747
Camden, ME 04843
Tel/Fax: 207-236-2257

Cary Library
Genealogy Room
107 Main Street
Houlton, ME 04730
Tel: 207-532-1302
Email: bettyf@cary.lib.me.us
URL: http://ece.wpi.edu/~baud/carylib/index.html

Chebeague Island Library
511 South Road
Chebeague, ME 04017
Tel: 207-846-4351
URL: http://web.nlis.net/~bjohnson/library.html

Curtis Memorial Library
23 Pleasant Street
Brunswick, ME 04011
Tel: 207-725-5242
URL: http://www.curtislibrary.com/home.html

Cushing Historical Society/Museum
Hawthorne Point Road
Cushing, ME 04563
Tel: 207-354-8262
800-261-1369

Dexter Historical Society
Grist Mill Museum & Millers House
Main Street
Dexter, ME 04930
Tel: 207-924-5721

Ellsworth Public Library
46 State Street
Ellsworth, ME 04605
Tel: 207-667-6363
Fax: 207-667-4901
Email: pat@seth.ellsworth.lib.me.us
URL: http://downeast.net/users/ellslib/ellslib.html

Falmouth Memorial Library
5 Lunt Road
Falmouth, ME 04105
Tel: 207-781-2351
Fax: 207-781-4094
URL: http://www.falmouth.lib.me.us/index.html

Farmington Public Library
2 Academy Street
Farmington, ME 04938
Tel: 207-778-4312
Email: cutler@saturn.caps.maine.edu
URL: http://www.farmington.lib.me.us/

Fryeburg Historical Society/Museum
96 Main Street
Fryeburg, ME 04037-1126
Tel: 207-935-4192

Gardiner Public Library
Community Room
152 Water Street
Gardiner, ME 04345
Tel: 207-582-3312
Email: webmaster@gpl.lib.me.us
URL: http://www.gpl.lib.me.us/hist.htm

Hampden Historical Society
Kinsley House Museum and Archives
83 Main Road
Hampden, ME 04444
Tel: 207-862-2027

Islesford Historical Museum
Little Cranberry
Islesford, ME 04646
Tel: 207-288-3338

Kennebunk Free Library
112 Main Street
Kennebunk, ME 04043

Kittery Historical and Naval Museum
Rogers Road
P.O. Box 453
Kittery, ME 03904
Tel: 207-439-3080

Lawrence Public Library
Lawrence Avenue
Fairfield, ME 04937
Tel: 207-453-6867

Lee Historical Society/Museum
Main Street, Rt. 6
Lee, ME 04455
Tel: 207-738-3533
207-738-4022

Lewiston Public Library
200 Lisbon Street
Lewiston, ME 04240
Tel: 207-784-0135
Fax: 207-784-3011

Lincolnville Historical Society/Museum
Route 1
Lincolnville, ME 04849
Tel: 207-789-5445

Maine Historical Society
Center for Maine History
485 Congress Street
Portland, ME 04101
Tel: 207-774-1822
Fax: 207-775-4301

Maine Military Historical Society/Museum
Camp Keyes
Upper Winthrop Street
Augusta, ME 04330
Tel: 207-626-4338

Maine State Library
LMA Building
64 State House Station
Augusta, ME 04333-0064
Tel: 207-287-5600
URL: http://www.state.me.us/msl/mslhome.htm

Maine State Museum
LMA Building
83 State House Station
Augusta, ME 04333-0083
Tel: 207-287-2132
207-287-2301
Fax: 207-287-6633

McArthur Library
270 Main Street
Biddeford, ME 04005
Tel: 207-283-4706

Mt. Desert Island (MDI) Historical Society/Museum
Main Street, Rt. 102
Mt. Desert, ME 04660
Tel: 207-244-9012

Naples Historical Society/Museum
Route 302, Village Green
Naples, ME 04055
Tel: 207-693-6790

New England Historical and Genealogical Society (NEHGS)
101 Newbury Street
Boston, MA 02116-3007
Tel: 617-836-5740
888-AT-NEHGS (Membership & Education)
888-BY-NEHGS (Sales)
888-90-NEHGS (Library Circulation)
Fax: 617-536-7307
Email: nehgs@nehgs.org
URL: http://www.nehgs.org/

New Sweden Historical Museum
Capitol Hill Road
New Sweden, ME 04762
Tel: 207-896-3018

Norway Historical Society/Museum
232 Main Street
Norway, ME 04268
Tel: 207-743-7377

Nylander Museum
393 Main Street
P.O. Box 1062
Caribou, ME 04736
Tel: 207-493-4209
207-493-4474

Oakfield Historical Museum
Oakfield, ME 04763
Tel: 207-757-8575

Old Orchard Beach Historical Society/Museum
Harmon Memorial
4 Portland Avenue
Old Orchard Beach, ME 04064
Tel: 207-934-4485

Old Town Historical Museum
North Fourth Ext.
Old Town, ME 04468
Tel: 207-827-7256

Orono Public Library
Goodridge Drive
Orono, ME 04473
Email: molloy@saturn.caps.maine.edu
URL: http://www.caps.maine.edu/~molloy/

Otisfield Historical Society
Otisfield Town Office Building
Route 121, Oxford Road
Otisfield, ME 04270
Tel: 207-539-2664
207-539-2521
Mail:
c/o Hankins
202 Scribner Hill Road
Otisfield, ME 04270
URL: http://www.geocities.com/Heartland/8853/otis.htm

Paris Cape Historical Society/Museum
Route 26
South Paris, ME 04281
Tel: 207-743-0604

Patten Free Library
Sagadahoc History & Genealogy Room
33 Summer Street
Bath, ME 04530
Tel: 207-443-5141
Fax: 207-443-3514
URL: http://www.biddeford.com/~pfl/shgr.htm

Pejepscot Historical Society/Museum
159 Park Row
Brunswick, ME 04011
Tel: 207-729-6606
Fax: 207-729-6012
Email: pejepscot@acornbbs.com
URL: http://www.curtislibrary.com/pejepscot.htm

Penobscot Marine Museum
Stephen Phillips Memorial Library
Church Street at U.S. Route 1
P.O. Box 498
Searsport, ME 04974
Tel: 207-548-2529
Fax: 207-548-2520
URL: http://www.acadia.net/pmmuseum/

Penobscot Nation Museum
5 Center Street
Old Town, ME 04468
Tel: 207-827-4153

Portland Public Library
5 Monument Square
Portland, ME 04101
Tel: 207-871-1700
Fax: 207-871-1703
Email: skaye@www.portland.lib.me.us
URL: http://www.portlandlibrary.com/depts.html

Redington Museum
Waterville Historical Society
64 Silver
Waterville, ME 04901
Tel: 207-872-9439

Sedgwick/Brooklin Historical Society/Museum
Rt. 15, Caterpillar Hill
Sedgwick, ME 04676
Tel: 207-359-2251

University of Maine/Fort Kent
Acadian Archives
25 Pleasant Street
Fort Kent, ME 04743
Tel: 207-834-7535
Fax: 207-834-7518
Email: acadian@maine.maine.edu
URL: http://www.umfk.maine.edu/infoserv/archives/welcome.htm

University of Maine/Orono
Fogler Library
Special Collections
Orono, ME 04469
Tel: 207-581-1686
Fax: 207-581-1653
Email: muriels@ursus1.ursus.maine.edu
URL: http://libinfo.ume.maine.edu/Speccoll/speccol.htm

University of Maine/Orono
Maine Folklife Center
South Stevens 5773
Orono, ME 04469-5773
Tel: 207-581-1891
Email: Pauleena_MacDougall@voyager.umeres.maine.edu or Alaric_Faulkner@voyager.umeres.maine.edu
URL: http://www.ume.maine.edu/~folklife/

University of Maine/Presque Isle
Library/Special Collections
181 Main Street
Presque Isle, ME 04769
Tel: 207-768-9591
Email: young@polaris.umpi.maine.edu
URL: http://www.umpi.maine.edu/info/lib/specol.htm

Vassalboro Historical Society/Museum
Rt. 32
Vassalboro, ME 04989
Tel: 207-923-3533

Vinalhaven Historical Society/Museum
High Street
P.O. Box 339
Vinalhaven, ME 04863
Tel: 207-863-4410
Email: vhhissoc@midcoast.com

Waldoboro Historical Society/Museum
Rt. 220 South
Waldoboro, ME 04572

Walker Memorial Library
800 Main Street
Westbrook, ME 04092

Waponahki Resource Center & Sipayik Museum
Rt. 190
Perry, ME 04667
Tel: 207-853-4001

Waterford Historical Society/Museum
P.O. Box 201
Waterford, ME 04088

Wells Historical Society
Meetinghouse Museum
Genealogical & Historical Research Library
Rt. 1, Post Road
Wells, ME 04090
Tel: 207-646-4775

Wiscasset Public Library
P.O. Box 367
Wiscasset, ME 04578

Woodstock Historical Society/Museum
Route 26
Bryant Pond, ME 04219
Tel: 207-665-2450

Yarmouth Historical Society
Museum of Yarmouth History
Merrill Memorial Library
Yarmouth, ME 04096
Tel: 207-846-6259

Young Institute Museum/Dyer Library
371 Main Street
Saco, ME 04072
Tel: 207-282-3031
207-283-3861

NEWSPAPER REPOSITORIES

Maine Historical Society
Center for Maine History
485 Congress Street
Portland, ME 04101
Tel: 207-774-1822
Fax: 207-775-4301

Maine State Library
LMA Building
64 State House Station
Augusta, ME 04333-0064
Tel: 207-287-5791
Email: janet.roberts@state.me.us
URL: http://www.state.me.us/msl/mslhome.htm

University of Maine/Orono
Fogler Library
Special Collections
Orono, ME 04469
Tel: 207-581-1686
Fax: 207-581-1653
Email: muriels@ursus1.ursus.maine.edu
URL: http://libinfo.ume.maine.edu/Speccoll/speccol.htm

VITAL RECORDS

Maine Department of Human Services
Office of Vital Records
State House Station 11
Augusta, ME 04333-0011
Tel: 207-287-3181

MAINE ON THE WEB

Acadian Genealogy Homepage
http://www.freespace.net/~cajun/genealogy/

Colonial Massachusetts and Maine Genealogies
http://www.qni.com/~anderson/index.html

Index to Maine Marriages
http://www.state.me.us/sos/arc/archives/genealog/marriage.htm

Maine GenWeb Project
http://www.goldenbranches.com/me-state

Maine State Archives
URL: http://www.state.me.us/sos/arc/general/admin/mawww001.htm

Maine State Archives/Civil War Page
http://www.state.me.us/sos/arc/archives/military/civilwar/civilwar.htm

Visit Maine—Historical Sites and Museums
http://www.visitmaine.com/historic.html

MARYLAND

ARCHIVES, STATE & NATIONAL

Maryland State Archives
Hall of Records Building
350 Rowe Blvd.
Annapolis, MD 21401
Tel: 410-974-3914
800-235-4045
Fax: 410-974-2525
Email: archives@mdarchives.state.md.us
URL: http://www.mdarchives.state.md.us

National Archives—Mid Atlantic Region
Ninth and Market Streets
Philadelphia, PA 19107
Tel: 215-597-3000
Fax: 215-597-2303
Email: archives@philarch.nara.gov
URL: http://www.nara.gov/nara/regional/03nsgil.html

GENEALOGICAL SOCIETIES

Afro-American Historical & Genealogical Society/Baltimore (AAHGS)
P.O. Box 66265
Baltimore, MD 21218

Afro-American Historical & Genealogical Society/Central Maryland (AAHGS)
P.O. Box 2774
Columbia, MD 21045

Afro-American Historical & Genealogical Society
Prince George's County (AAHGS)
P.O. Box 44722
Fort Washington, MD 20744-9998

Allegany County Genealogical Society
P.O. Box 3103
LaVale, MD 21502

Allegheny Regional Family History Society (ARFHS)
P.O. Box 1804
Elkins, WV 26241
Tel: 304-636-1958
304-636-1959
URL: http://www.swcp.com/~dhickman/arfhs.html

Anne Arundel Genealogical Society
P.O. Box 221
Pasadena, MD 21123
URL: http://www.geocities.com/Yosemite/Trails/4256/gensoc.htm

Baltimore Genealogical Society
P.O. Box 10085
Towson, MD 21285-0085
URL: http://www.serve.com/bcgs/bcgs.html

Calvert County Genealogical Committee
Calvert County Historical Society
P.O. Box 358
Prince Frederick, MD 20678

Calvert County Genealogy Society
P.O. Box 9
Sunderland, MD 20689

Carroll County Genealogical Society
P.O. Box 1752
Westminster, MD 21158
Email: ccgs@ccpl.carr.lib.md.us
URL: http://www.carr.lib.md.us/ccgs/ccgs.html

Catonsville Historical & Genealogical Society
Townsend House
1824 Frederick Road
P.O. Box 9311
Catonsville, MD 21228

Cecil County Genealogical Society
P.O. Box 11
Charlestown, MD 21914

Frederick County Genealogical Society
P.O. Box 324
Monrovia, MD 21770

Genealogical Council of Maryland
12631 Prices Distillery Road
Damascus, MD 20872-1520

Harford County Genealogical Society
P.O. Box 15
Aberdeen, MD 21001
URL: http://www.rtis.com/reg/md/org/hcgs/default.htm

Howard County Genealogical Society
P.O. Box 274
Columbia, MD 21045
Email: castlewrks@aol.com
URL: http://members.aol.com/castlewrks/hcgs/index.html

Jewish Genealogy Society of Greater Washington, DC
P.O. Box 31122
Bethesda, MD 20824-1122
Tel: 301-530-3511
URL: http://www.jewishgen.org/jgsgw/

Lower DelMarVa Genealogical Society
P.O. Box 3602
Salisbury, MD 21802-3602
Tel: 410-742-3501
410-546-0314
URL: http://bay.intercom.net/ldgs/index.html

Lower Shore Genealogical Society
1133 Somerset Avenue
Princess Anne, MD 21853

Maryland Genealogical Society
201 West Monument Street
Baltimore, MD 21201-4674
Tel: 410-685-3750

Montgomery County Historical Society/Genealogy Club/Library
Beall Dawson House
103 West Montgomery Avenue
Rockville, MD 20850
Tel: 301-340-2974

Prince George's County Genealogical Society
P.O. Box 819
Bowie, MD 20718-0819

Saint Mary's County Genealogical Society
P.O. Box 1109
Leonardtown, MD 20650-1109
URL: http://www.pastracks.com/~ehayden/smcgs/welcome.html

Upper Shore Genealogical Society of Maryland
P.O. Box 275
Easton, MD 21601

HISTORICAL SOCIETIES

Accohannock Tribe
P.O. Box 404
Marion, MD 21838
Tel: 410-623-2660
Email: mapperti@shore.intercom.net
URL: http://skipjack.net/le_shore/heritage/nativam/

Afro-American Historical & Genealogical Society/Baltimore (AAHGS)
P.O. Box 66265
Baltimore, MD 21218

Afro-American Historical & Genealogical Society/Central Maryland (AAHGS)
P.O. Box 2774
Columbia, MD 21045

Afro-American Historical & Genealogical Society
Prince George's County (AAHGS)
P.O. Box 44722
Fort Washington, MD 20744-9998

Allegany County Historical Society
218 Washington Street
Cumberland, MD 21502

Anne Arundel Historical Society
P.O. Box 385
Linthicum, MD 21090

Baltimore County Historical Society
Agriculture Building
9811 Van Buren Lane
Cockeysville, MD 21030

Calvert County Historical Society
P.O. Box 358
Prince Frederick, MD 20678

Caroline County Historical Society
c/o Dora W. Mitchell
Preston, MD 21655

Carroll County Historical Society
210 East Main Street
Westminster, MD 21157
URL: http://www.carr.lib.md.us/carroll/history/histsoc.htm

Catonsville Historical & Genealogical Society
Townsend House
1824 Frederick Road
P.O. Box 9311
Catonsville, MD 21228

Cecil County Historical Society
135 East Main Street
Elkton, MD 21921
Tel: 410-398-1790
Email: info@cchistory.org
URL: http://cchistory.org/

Dorchester County Historical Society
Meredith House
904 LaGrange Street
Cambridge, MD 21613

Dundalk Patapsco Neck Historical Society
43 Shipping Place
P.O. Box 9235
Dundalk, MD 21222
Tel: 410-284-2331

Essex and Middle River, Heritage Society of
516 Eastern Blvd.
Essex, MD 21221-6701
Tel: 410-574-6934

Frederick County Historical Society
24 East Church Street
Frederick, MD 21701
Tel: 301-663-1188

Garrett County Historical Society
County Courthouse
Oakland, MD 21550

Harford County Historical Society
The Hayes House
324 Kenmore Avenue
Bel Air, MD 21014

Howard County Historical Society/Library
8324 Court Avenue
Ellicott City, MD 21043-4506
Tel: 410-461-1050
410-750-0370

Jewish Historical Society of Maryland
Jewish Heritage Center
15 Lloyd Street
Baltimore, MD 21202
Tel: 410-732-6400
Email: info@jhsm.org
URL: http://www.jhsm.org/

Kent County Historical Society
Church Alley
Chestertown, MD 21620

Maryland Historical Society
201 West Monument Street
Baltimore, MD 21201-4674
Tel: 410-685-3750

Middletown Valley Historical Society
305 W. Main Street
Middletown, MD 21769-8022
Tel: 301-371-7582

Montgomery County Historical Society/Genealogy Club/Library
Beall Dawson House
103 West Montgomery Avenue
Rockville, MD 20850
Tel: 301-340-2974

Prince George's County Historical Society
Montpelier Mansion
Laurel, MD 20810

Queen Anne's County Historical Society
Wright's Chance
Commerce Street
Centreville, MD 21617

Saint Mary's City Historical Society
11 Courthouse Drive
P.O. Box 212
Leonardtown, MD 20650

Sligo-Silver Springs Historical Society
Email: rjaeggi@pop.dn.net
URL: http://www.capaccess.org/com/silver_spring/ss_museu.html

Somerset County Historical Society
Treackle Mansion
Princess Anne, MD 21853

Talbot County Historical Society
25 Washington Street
P.O. Box 964
Easton, MD 21601
Tel: 410-822-0773
URL: http://www.covesoft.com/Eastern/Michaels/historic.html

Washington County Historical Society
The Miller House
135 West Washington Street
Hagerstown, MD 21740

Wicomico County Historical Society
Pemberton Historical Park
Pemberton Drive
Salisbury, MD 21801

Worcester County Historical Society
c/o Julia Robertson
3 E. 2nd Street
Pocomoke City, MD 21851

LDS Family History Centers

Annapolis Family History Center
1875 Ritchie Highway
Annapolis, MD 21401
Tel: 410-757-4173

Ellicott City Family History Center
4100 St. John's Lane
Ellicott City, MD 21042
Tel: 410-465-1642

Frederick Family History Center
199 North Place
Frederick, MD 21701
Tel: 301-698-0406

Germantown Family History Center
18900 Kingsview Road
Germantown, MD 20874
Tel: 301-972-5897

Kensington Family History Center
10000 Stoneybrook Drive
Kensington, MD 20895
Tel: 301-587-0042

Lutherville Family History Center
1400 Dulany Valley Road
Lutherville, MD 21093
Tel: 301-821-9880

Suitland Family History Center
5300 Auth Road
Suitland, MD 20746
Tel: 301-423-8294

ARCHIVES/LIBRARIES/MUSEUMS

Allegany Community College
Appalachian Collection
Willowbrook Road
Cumberland, MD 21502

Anne Arundel County Public Library
5 Harry S. Truman Pkwy.
Annapolis, MD 21401
Tel: 410-222-7371

Baltimore City Archives
211 E. Pleasant Street
Baltimore, MD 21202

Banneker-Douglass Museum
Mount Moriah A.M.E. Church
84 Franklin Street
Annapolis, MD 21401
Tel: 410-974-2893
URL: http://www2.ari.net/mdshpo/bdm.html

Bowie State University
Thurgood Marshall Library
Bowie, MD 20715-9465
Tel: 301-464-7228
Fax: 301-464-7843
URL: http://www.bsu.umd.edu/library/bsu-libr.html

C. Burr Artz/Frederick County Public Library
110 E. Patrick Street
Frederick, MD 21701
Tel: 301-694-1630
Fax: 301-695-2905
TDD: 301-663-6999

Caroline County Public Library
100 Market Street
Denton, MD 21629
Tel: 410-479-1343
Fax: 410-479-1443
TDD: 410-479-2468
URL: http://www.esrl.lib.md.us/counties/caroline/library/home.html

Catonsville Branch/Baltimore County Public Library
1100 Frederick Road
Catonsville, MD 21228-5092
Tel: 410-887-0951
Fax: 410-788-8166
Email: catonsvi@mail.bcpl.lib.md.us
URL: http://www.bcpl.lib.md.us/branchpgs/ca/cahome.html

Cecil County Public Library
301 Newark Avenue
Elkton, MD 21921-5441
Tel: 410-996-5600
Fax: 410-996-5604
TDD: 410-996-5609
URL: http://sailor.lib.md.us/mdlibs/ceci2.htm

Charles County Public Library
Charles & Garrett Streets
P.O. Box 490
LaPlata, MD 20646-0490
Tel: 301-870-3520
301-934-3082
Fax: 301-934-2297
TDD: 301-934-9090

Cheasapeake Bay Maritime Museum
Mill Street
P.O. Box 636
St. Michaels, MD 21663
Tel: 410-745-2916
URL: http://www.cbmm.org/

Dorchester County Public Library
303 Gay Street
Cambridge, MD 21613
Tel: 410-228-7331
Fax: 410-228-6313
TDD: 410-228-0454
Email: dorch@mail.esrl.lib.md.us
URL: http://www.esrl.lib.md.us/counties/dorchester/

Enoch Pratt Free Library
400 Cathedral Street
Baltimore, MD 21201
Tel: 410-396-5300
410-396-5468 (Maryland Room)
Fax: 410-396-9537
Email: mdx@epfl2.epflbalto.org
URL: http://www.pratt.lib.md.us/

Harford County Library
100 East Pennsylvania Avenue
Bel Air, MD 21014
Tel: 410-638-3151
Fax: 410-638-3155
TDD: 410-838-3371

Issac Franck Jewish Public Library
Board of Jewish Education
11710 Hunters Lane
Rockville, MD 20852-2363

John Hopkins University
George Peabody Library
1 East Mt. Vernon Pl.
Baltimore, MD 21202
Tel: 410-659-8257
Fax: 410-727-5101
Email: gstacy@peabody.jhu.edu

Kuethe Library
Historical & Genealogical Research Center
5 Crain Highway SE
Glen Burnie, MD 21061
Tel: 410-760-9679
URL: http://www.geocities.com/Yosemite/Trails/4256/gensoc.htm#kuethe

Maryland Historical Trust Library
100 Community Place
Crownsville, MD 21032
Tel: 410-514-7655
URL: http://www2.ari.net/mdshpo/

Maryland State Law Library
Court of Appeals Building
361 Rowe Boulevard
Annapolis, MD 21401
Tel: 410-974-3395

Montgomery County Historical Society/Genealogy Club/Library
Beall Dawson House
103 West Montgomery Avenue
Rockville, MD 20850
Tel: 301-340-2974

Queen Anne's County Free Library
121 S. Commerce Street
Centreville, MD 21617
Tel: 410-758-0980

Reistertown Branch/Baltimore County Public Library
History Room, 2nd floor
21 Cockeys Mill Road
Reistertown, MD 21136-1285
Tel: 410-887-1165
Fax: 410-833-8756
Email: reisters@mail.bcpl.lib.md.us
URL: http://www.bcpl.lib.md.us/branchpgs/re/rehome.html

Rockville Regional Library/Montgomery County Public Library
99 Maryland Avenue
Rockville, MD 20850
Tel: 301-217-3800
TTY: 301-217-3873
URL: http://www.mont.lib.md.us/ro.html

Ruth Enlow Branch/Garrett County Library
6 North 2nd Street
Oakland, MD 21550-1316
Tel: 301-334-3996

St. Mary's College
Library
St. Mary's City, MD 20686
Tel: 301-862-0264
URL: http://www.smcm.edu/library/

St. Mary's County Memorial Library
Route 1, Box 9E
Leonardtown, MD 20650-9601
Tel: 301-475-2846
301-475-4844 (Archives & Records Center)
Fax: 301-884-4415
TDD: 301-475-8003
Email: mwood@eagle.eagle1.com

Salisbury State University
Research Center for DelMarVa History & Culture
1101 Camden Avenue, PP 190
Salisbury, MD 21801
Tel: 410-543-6312
Fax: 410-548-3002
Email: rfmiller@ssu.edu
URL: http://www.ssu.edu/Schools/Fulton/DelmarvaCtr/DelmarvaCtr.html

Snow Hill Branch/Worcester County Public Library
Worcester Room
307 N. Washington Street
Snow Hill, MD 21863
Tel: 410-632-2600
Fax/TDD: 410-632-1159
URL: http://www.esrl.lib.md.us/counties/worcester/library/home.html

Talbot County Free Library
Maryland Room
100 W. Dover Street
Easton, MD 21601-2620
Tel: 410-822-1626
Fax: 410-820-8217
TDD: 410-822-8735
URL: http://www.esrl.lib.md.us/counties/talbot/library/home.html

Towson Branch/Baltimore County Public Library
320 York Road
Towson, MD 21204-5179
Tel: 410-887-6166
Fax: 410-887-3170
URL: http://www.bcpl.lib.md.us/

University of Baltimore
Langsdale Library
1420 Maryland Avenue
Baltimore, MD 21201
Tel: 410-837-4318
Fax: 410-837-4330
Email: swheeler@ubmail.ubalt.edu
URL: http://www.ubalt.edu/www/langlib/index.html

University of Maryland/Baltimore County
Albin O. Kuhn Library
5401 Wilkens Avenue
Catonsville, MD 21228
Tel: 301-455-2232
URL: http://umbc7.umbc.edu/~curnoles/aokweb.html

University of Maryland/College Park
McKeldin Library
The Maryland Collection
College Park, MD 20742
Tel: 301-405-9212
Email: marylandia@umail.umd.edu
URL: http://www.lib.umd.edu/UMCP/RARE/797hmpg.html

Washington County Free Library
100 S. Potomac Street
Hagerstown, MD 21740
Tel: 301-739-3250
TDD: 301-739-3253
URL: http://www.wash.lib.md.us/wcfl/

Westminster Branch/Carroll Public Library
50 E. Main
Westminster, MD 21157
Tel: 410-848-4250
410-876-6018
URL: http://www.carr.lib.md.us/carroll/library/wb.htm

Wicomico County Free Library
Maryland Room and Genealogical Collection
122-126 S. Division Street
Salisbury, MD 21801
Tel: 410-749-5435
410-749-5171
URL: http://www.co.wicomico.md.us/library.html

NEWSPAPER REPOSITORIES

Maryland State Archives
Hall of Records Building
350 Rowe Blvd.
Annapolis, MD 21401
Tel: 410-974-3914
Fax: 410-974-2525
Email: nancyb@mdarchives.state.md.us
URL: http://www.mdarchives.state.md.us/msa/speccol/html/0003.html

VITAL RECORDS

State of Maryland Department of Health & Mental Hygiene
Division of Vital Records
Metro Executive Building
4201 Patterson Avenue
P.O. Box 68760
Baltimore, MD 21215-0020
Tel: 410-225-5988
800-832-3277

MARYLAND ON THE WEB

Cindy's Genealogy on the Eastern Shore of MD, DE, & VA
http://www.shoreweb.com/cindy/index.html

Handley's Eastern Shore Genealogy Project
http://bay.intercom.net/handley/index.html

Maryland Catholics on the Frontier
http://www.pastracks.com/~ehayden/mcf/welcome.html

Maryland GenWeb Project
http://www.rootsweb.com/~mdgenweb/

Maryland Loyalists and the American Revolution
http://www.erols.com/candidus/index.htm

Searching for your African American Ancestors; Maryland GenWeb
http://www.rootsweb.com/~mdgenweb/mdafric.htm

U.S. Colored Troops Resident in Baltimore at the time of the 1890 Census
http://www.mdarchives.state.md.us/msa/speccol/3096/html/00010001.html

MASSACHUSETTS

ARCHIVES, STATE & NATIONAL

Massachusetts Archives
Reference Supervisor
220 Morrissey Blvd.
Boston, MA 02125
Tel: 617-727-2816
Fax: 617-288-4505
Email: archives@mecn.mass.edu
URL: http://www.magnet.state.ma.us/sec/arc/arcidx.htm

National Archives—New England Region
380 Trapelo Road
Waltham, MA 02154-8104
Tel: 617-647-8100
Fax: 617-647-8460
Email: archives@waltham.nara.gov
URL: http://www.nara.gov/nara/regional/01nsbgil.html

GENEALOGICAL SOCIETIES

Acadian Cultural Society
P.O. Box 2304
Fitchburg, MA 01460-8804
Email: r-m-s-frazier@worldnet.att.net
URL: http://www.angelfire.com/ma/1755/index.html

American Portugese Genealogical & Historical Society, Inc.
P.O. Box 644
Taunton, MA 02780-0644

Association for Gravestone Studies
278 Main Street
Greenfield, MA 01301
Tel: 413-772-0836
Email: ags@berkshire.net
URL: http://www.berkshire.net/ags/

Berkshire Family History Association
P.O. Box 1437
Pittsfield, MA 01201

Cape Cod Genealogical Society
P.O. Box 1394
East Harwich, MA 02645

Central Massachusetts Genealogical Society
P.O. Box 811
Westminster, MA 01473-0811
URL: http://www.fgs.org/~fgs/soc0023.htm

Colonial Society of Massachusetts
87 Vernon Street
Boston, MA 02108
Tel: 617-227-2782

Essex County Society of Genealogists
Lynn Public Library
18 Summer Street
P.O. Box 313
Lynnfield, MA 01940-0313

Falmouth Genealogical Society
P.O. Box 2107
Teaticket, MA 02536

Genealogical Round Table
P.O. Box 654
Concord, MA 01742-0654
URL: http://www.fgs.org/~fgs/soc0057.htm

General Society of Mayflower Descendants
Mayflower Society Museum
4 Winslow Street
P.O. Box 3297
Plymouth, MA 02361
Tel: 508-746-2590

Institute of Family History and Genealogy
99 Ash Street
New Bedford, MA 02740

Irish Ancestral Research Association (TIARA)
Dept. W
P.O. Box 619
Sudbury, MA 01776
URL: http://world.std.com/~ahern/TIARA.html

Jewish Genealogical Society of Greater Boston
P.O. Box 610366
Newton, MA 02161-0366
Tel: 617-283-8003
URL: http://www.jewishgen.org/boston/jgsgb.html

Massachusetts Genealogical Council
P.O. Box 5393
Cochituate, MA 01778

Massachusetts Society of Genealogists, Inc.
P.O. Box 215
Ashland, MA 01721

Massachusetts Society of Mayflower Descendants
376 Boylston Street, 2nd Floor
Boston, MA 02116
Tel: 617-266-1624
Email: msmd@tiac.net
URL: http://www.tiac.net/users/msmd/

New England Historical and Genealogical Society (NEHGS)
101 Newbury Street
Boston, MA 02116-3007
Tel: 617-836-5740
888-AT-NEHGS (Membership & Education)
888-BY-NEHGS (Sales)

888-90-NEHGS (Library Circulation)
Fax: 617-536-7307
Email: nehgs@nehgs.org
URL: http://www.nehgs.org/

Plymouth Colony Genealogists
60 Sheridan Street
Brockton, MA 02402-2852
URL: http://users.rootsweb.com/~maplymou/pcgsmain.htm

Polish Genealogical Society of Massachusetts
P.O. Box 381
Northampton, MA 01061
Tel: 413-584-3428 (A.M.)
413-586-1827 (P.M.)
URL: http://www.dcn.davis.ca.us/go/feefh/pol/frgpgsma.html

South Shore Genealogical Society
P.O. Box 396
Norwell, MA 02061-0396

Western Massachusetts Genealogical Society
Forest Park Station
P.O. Box 206
Springfield, MA 01108

Historical Societies

American Antiquarian Society/Library
185 Salisbury Street
Worcester, MA 01609
Tel: 508-755-5221
Fax: 508-753-3311
Email: jdc@mark.mwa.org
URL: gopher://mark.mwa.org/0briefaccount.text

American Jewish Historical Society
2 Thornton Road
Waltham, MA 02154

American Portugese Genealogical & Historical Society, Inc.
P.O. Box 644
Taunton, MA 02780-0644

Amherst Historical Society
Strong House Museum
67 Amity Street
Amherst, MA 01002
Tel: 413-256-0678

Andover Historical Society
97 Main Street
Andover, MA 01810
Tel: 508-475-2236

Arlington Historical Society
7 Jason Street
Arlington, MA 02174
Tel: 617-648-4300

Ashland Historical Society
2 Myrtle Street
Ashland, MA 01721
Tel: 508-881-8183

Association for Gravestone Studies
278 Main Street
Greenfield, MA 01301
Tel: 413-772-0836
Email: ags@berkshire.net
URL: http://www.berkshire.net/ags/

Barre Historical Society
18 Common Street
Barre, MA 01005
Tel: 508-355-2572

Bay State Historical League
The Vale Lyman Estate
185 Lyman Street
Waltham, MA 02254-9998
Tel: 617-899-3920
Fax: 617-893-7832

Berkley Historical Society
725 Berkley Street
Berkley, MA 02779
Tel: 617-824-5367

Berkshire County Historical Society
780 Holmes Road
Pittsfield, MA 01201
Tel: 413-442-1793
Fax: 413-443-1449

Berlin Art & Historical Society
Woodward Avenue
Berlin, MA 01503
Tel: 508-838-2502

Beverly Historical Society/Museum
117 Cabot Street
Beverly, MA 01915
Tel: 508-922-1186

Bolton Historical Society
Sawyer House
676 Main Street
Bolton, MA 01740
Tel: 508-779-6392

Bostonian Society
Museum:
206 Washington Street
Boston, MA 02109
Tel: 617-720-3290
Fax: 617-720-3289
Library:
15 State Street
Boston, MA 02109
Tel: 617-720-3285
URL: http://www.boston.com/arts/museums/musstate.htm

Bourne Historical Society
Aptucxet Trading Post
24 Aptucxet Road
Bourne, MA 02532
Tel: 508-759-9487

Braintree Historical Society
786 Washington Street
Braintree, MA 02184
Tel: 617-848-1640
URL: http://world.std.com/~ssn/Braintree/hist_soc.html

Brockton Historical Society/Museum
216 N. Pearl Street, Rte. 27
Brockton, MA 02401
Tel: 508-583-1039
Email: gerryb@brocktonma.com
URL: http://www.brocktonma.com/bhs/bhs_mus.html

Brookline Historical Society
347 Harvard Street
Brookline, MA 02146
Tel: 617-566-5747

Burlington Historical Commission/Museum
Corner of Bedford and Cambridge Streets
Burlington, MA 01803
Tel: 617-272-0606

Cambridge Historical Society
159 Brattle Street
Cambridge, MA 02138
Tel: 617-547-4252
Fax: 617-661-1623

Canton Historical Society
1400 Washington Street
Canton, MA 02021
Tel: 617-828-3747

Cape Ann Historical Association/Library
27 Pleasant Street
Gloucester, MA 01930
Tel: 617-283-0455

Centerville Historical Society
513 Main Street
Centerville, MA 02632
Tel: 508-775-0331

Charlestown Historical Society
Bunker Hill Museum
43 Monument Square
Charlestown, MA 02129

Chatham Historical Society
347 Stage Harbor Road
Chatham, MA 02633
Tel: 508-945-2493

Chelmsford Historical Society
40 Byam Road
Chelmsford, MA 01824
Tel: 508-256-2311

Chesterfield Historical Society
Edwards Memorial Museum
North Street
Chesterfield, MA 01012
Tel: 413-296-4759

Cohasset Historical Society
14 Summer Street
Cohasset, MA 02025
Tel: 617-383-6930

Congregational Christian Historical Society
14 Beacon Street
Boston, MA 02108

Danvers Historical Society
13 Page Street
P.O. Box 381
Danvers, MA 01923
Tel: 508-777-1666

Dedham Historical Society
612 High Street
P.O. Box 215
Dedham, MA 02027-0215
Tel: 617-326-1385
Email: dhs@dedham.com
URL: http://www.tiac.net/users/tangaroa/dedham.html

Dennis Historical Society
c/o Dennis Memorial Library Association
Old Bass River Road
Dennis, MA 02638
Tel: 508-385-2255

Dighton Historical Society
1217 Williams
Dighton, MA 02715
Tel: 617-669-5514

Dorchester Historical Society
195 Boston Street
Boston, MA 02125
Tel: 617-265-7802

Dukes County Historical Society
Vineyard Museum
Cooke and School Streets
Edgartown, MA 02539
Tel: 508-627-4441

Duxbury Rural & Historical Society, Inc.
685 Washington Street
Duxbury, MA 02331
Tel: 617-934-6106

Eastham Historical Society, Inc.
P.O. Box 8
Eastham, MA 02642

Essex Historical Society
Essex Shipbuilding Museum
28 Main Street
Essex, MA 01929
Tel: 508-768-7541

Fall River Historical Society
451 Rock Street
Fall River, MA 02720
Tel: 508-679-1071

Falmouth Historical Society
Palmer Avenue at Village Green
Falmouth, MA 02541
Tel: 508-548-4857

Fitchburg Historical Society
50 Grove Street
Fitchburg, MA 01420
Tel: 508-345-1157

Framingham Historical and Natural History Society
Old Academy Building
Vernon and Grove Streets
Framingham, MA 01701
Tel: 508-872-378

Freetown Historical Society/Museum
1 Slab Bridge Road
P.O. Box 253
Assonet, MA 02702
Tel: 508-644-5310

Greenfield, Historical Society of
43 Church Street
Greenfield, MA 01301
Tel: 413-772-0180

Groton Historical Society
172 Main Street
Groton, MA 01450
Tel: 508-448-2046

Hardwick Historical Society
Hardwick Common
Hardwick, MA 01037
Tel: 413-477-6635

Harvard Historical Society
Still River Road
Still River, MA 01467
Mail:
P.O. Box 542
Harvard, MA 01451
Tel: 508-456-8285

Harwich Historical Society
Brooks Academy Museum
80 Parallel Street
P.O. Box 17
Harwich, MA 02645
Tel: 508-432-8089

Haverhill Historical Society
Buttonwoods Museum
240 Water Street
Haverhill, MA 01830
Tel: 508-374-4626

Hingham Historical Society
Old Ordinary
21 Lincoln Street
Hingham, MA 02043
Tel: 617-749-0013

Ipswich Historical Society
Heard House Museum
54 South Main Street
Ipswich, MA 01938
Tel: 508-356-2641
URL: http://www.tiac.net/users/ncg/ihs.html

Jones River Village Historical Society
Major John Bradford House
Maple Street & Landing Road
Kingston, MA 02364
Tel: 617-585-6300

Lawrence and Its People, Historical Society of
Immigrant City Archives
6 Essex Street
Lawrence, MA 01840
Tel: 508-686-9230

Leverett Historical Society
North Leverett Road
Leverett, MA 01054
Tel: 413-367-2800

Lexington Historical Society
Munroe Tavern
1332 Massachusetts Avenue
P.O. Box 514
Lexington, MA 02173
Tel: 617-862-1703

Longmeadow Historical Society
697 Longmeadow Street
Longmeadow, MA 01106
Tel: 413-567-3600

Longyear Historical Society/Museum
120 Seaver Street
Brookline, MA 02146
Tel: 617-277-8943
URL: http://www.boston.com/arts/museums/muslong.htm

Lynn Historical Society/Library & Museum
125 Green Street
Lynn, MA 01902
Tel: 617-592-2465

Manchester Historical Society
10 Union Street
Manchester, MA 01944
Tel: 508-526-7230

Marblehead Historical Society
161 Washington Street
Marblehead, MA 01945
Tel: 617-631-1069

Marlborough Historical Society
377 Elm Street
Marlborough, MA 01752
Tel: 508-485-4763

Massachusetts Historical Commission
220 Morrissey Blvd.
Boston, MA 02125
Tel: 617-727-8470
Fax: 617-727-5128
TDD: 800-392-6090
URL: http://www.state.ma.us/sec/mhc/

Massachusetts Historical Society
1154 Boylston Street
Boston, MA 02215
Tel: 617-536-1608

Mattapoisett Historical Society
5 Church Street
Mattapoisett, MA 02739
Tel: 508-758-2844

Medford Historical Society
10 Governors Avenue
Medford, MA 02155

Middleborough Historical Association, Inc.
Jackson Street
P.O. Box 304
Middleborough, MA 02346
Tel: 508-947-1969
508-866-4414

Middleton Historical Society
Lura Watkins Museum
Pleasant Street
Middleton, MA 01949
Tel: 508-774-9301

Milton Historical Society
1370 Canton Avenue
Milton, MA 02186
Tel: 617-333-0644
URL: http://world.std.com/~ssn/Milton/mhs.html

Nantucket Historical Association
5 Washington Street
P.O. Box 1016
Nantucket, MA 02554
Tel: 508-228-1894
508-228-5618
URL: http://www.4cyte.com/NHA/

Narragansett Historical Society
The Common
Templeton, MA 01468
Tel: 508-939-8762

Natick Historical Society/Museum
Bacon Free Library Building, Lower Level
58 Eliot Street
South Natick, MA 01760
Tel: 508-647-4841
Email: eliot@ixl.net
URL: http://www.ixl.net/~natick/

Needham Historical Society
53 Glendoon Road
Needham, MA 02192
Tel: 617-444-5640

New England Historical and Genealogical Society (NEHGS)
101 Newbury Street
Boston, MA 02116-3007
Tel: 617-836-5740
888-AT-NEHGS (Membership & Education)
888-BY-NEHGS (Sales)
888-90-NEHGS (Library Circulation)
Fax: 617-536-7307
Email: nehgs@nehgs.org
URL: http://www.nehgs.org/

Newton Historical Society
Jackson Homestead
527 Washington Street
Newton, MA 02158
Tel: 617-552-7238
URL: http://www.boston.com/arts/museums/musjacksn.htm

North Andover Historical Society
153 Academy Road
North Andover, MA 01845
Tel: 508-686-4035

Northampton Historical Society
Historic Northampton
46 Bridge Street
Northampton, MA 01060
Tel: 413-584-6011

Northborough Historical Society, Inc.
50 Main Street
Northborough, MA 01532
Tel: 508-393-6389

Old Abington Historical Society
c/o Dyer Memorial Library
25 Centre Avenue (Route 123)
Abington, MA 02351
Tel: 617-878-8480

Old Bridgewater Historical Society
Memorial Building
162 Howard Street
West Bridgewater, MA 02379
Tel: 508-559-1510

Old Colony Historical Society
66 Church Green
Taunton, MA 02780
Tel: 508-822-1622

Old Dartmouth Historical Society
New Bedford Whaling Museum
18 Johnny Cake Hill
New Bedford, MA 02740
Tel: 508-997-0046

Old Newbury, Historical Society of
98 High Street
Newburyport, MA 01950
Tel: 617-462-2681

Old Yarmouth, Historical Society of
11 Strawberry Lane
Yarmouth Port, MA 02675
Tel: 508-362-3021

Osterville Historical Society, Inc.
155 Bay Road
Osterville, MA 02655
Tel: 508-428-5861
508-428-5658

Peabody Historical Society
35 Washington Street
Peabody, MA 01960

Pembroke Historical Society, Inc.
Center Street
Pembroke, MA 02359
Tel: 617-293-9083

Petersham Historical Society, Inc.
North Main Street
Petersham, MA 01366
Tel: 617-724-3380

Pilgrim Society
Pilgrim Hall Museum
75 Court Street
Plymouth, MA 02360
Tel: 508-746-1620

Plymouth Antuquarian Society
27 North Street
P.O. Box 1137
Plymouth, MA 02360
Tel: 508-746-0012

Quincy Historical Society
Adams Academy Building
8 Adams Street
Quincy, MA 02169
Tel: 617-773-1144

Ramapogue Historical Society
70 Park Street
West Springfield, MA 01089
Tel: 413-734-8322

Rowe Historical Society
Kemp-McCarthy Memorial Museum
Zoar Road
Rowe, MA 01966
Tel: 413-339-4238

Rowley Historical Society
233 Main Street
Rowley, MA 01969
Tel: 508-948-7483

Roxbury Historical Society
189 Roxbury Street, John Eliot Square
Roxbury, MA 02119
Tel: 617-445-3399

Rumford Historical Association
90 Elm Street
North Woburn, MA 01801
Tel: 617-933-0781

Sandwich Historical Society
Sandwich Glass Museum
Town Hall Square
129 Main Street
Sandwich, MA 02563
Tel: 508-888-0251

Sandy Bay Historical Society & Museums, Inc.
40 King Street
Rockport, MA 01966
Tel: 508-546-9533

Santuit and Cotuit, Historical Society of
1148 Main Street
Cotuit, MA 02635
Tel: 508-428-0461

Scituate Historical Society
Laidlaw Historical Center
43 Cudworth Road
Scituate, MA 02066
Tel: 617-545-1083
617-545-0474

Somerville Historical Society/Museum
1 Westwood Road
Somerville, MA 02143
Tel: 617-666-9810

Stoughton Historical Society
Lucius Clapp Memorial, Stoughton Center
6 Park Street
P.O. Box 542
Stoughton, MA 02072
Tel: 617-344-5456
Email: davidl@user1.channel1.com
URL: http://www.channel1.com/~com/~davidl/stough.htm

Swampscott Historical Society
99 Paradise Road
Swampscott, MA 01907
Tel: 617-598-4363

Topsfield Historical Society
One Howlett Street
Topsfield, MA 01983
Tel: 508-887-3998

Wakefield Historical Society
American Civic Center
467 Main Street
Wakefield, MA 01880
Tel: 617-245-0549

Waltham Historical Society
190 Moody Street
Waltham, MA 02154
Tel: 617-891-5815

Wayland Historical Society
12 Cochituate Road
Wayland, MA 01778
Tel: 508-358-7959

Wellesley Historical Society, Inc.
229 Washington Street
Wellesley Hills, MA 02181
Tel: 617-235-6690

Wellfleet Historical Society/Museum
Main Street
Wellfleet, MA 02667
Tel: 508-349-9157

Wenham Historical Association
132 Main Street, Route 1A
Wenham, MA 01984
Tel: 508-468-2377

Weston Historical Society
626 Boston Post Road
Weston, MA 02193
Tel: 617-891-3224

Williamstown House of Local History
Williamstown Public Library
762 Main Street, 2nd Floor
Williamstown, MA 01267
URL: http://bcn.net/~willieb/hlh.html

Winchendon Historical Society
50 Pleasant Street
Winchendon, MA 01475
Tel: 617-297-0300

Winchester Historical Society
1 Copley Street
Winchester, MA 01890

LDS Family History Centers

Foxboro Family History Center
76 N. Main Street
Foxboro, MA 02035
Tel: 508-543-0298

Hingham Family History Center
379 Gardiner Street
Hingham, MA 02043
Tel: 617-749-9835

Weston Family History Center-Boston Stake
150 Brown Street
Weston, MA 02193
Tel: 617-235-2164

Worcester Family History Center
67 Chester Street
Worcester, MA 01605
Tel: 508-852-7000

Archives/Libraries/Museums

Acton Public Library
486 Main Street
Acton, MA 01720
Tel: 508-264-9641
Fax: 508-635-0073

Afro American History, Museum of
Abiel Smith School
46 Joy Street
Boston, MA 02114
Tel: 617-742-1854
URL: http://www.boston.com/arts/museums/musafam.htm

Agawam Public Library
750 Cooper Street
Agawam, MA 01001
Tel: 413-789-1550
Fax: 413-789-1552

American Antiquarian Society/Library
185 Salisbury Street
Worcester, MA 01609
Tel: 508-755-5221
Fax: 508-753-3311
Email: jdc@mark.mwa.org
URL: gopher://mark.mwa.org/0briefaccount.text

Amesbury Public Library
149 Main Street
Amesbury, MA 01913
Tel: 508-388-8148
Email: todd@mvlc.lib.ma.us
URL: http://www.greennet.net/clients/ameslib/

Archdiocese of Boston Archives
2121 Commonwealth Avenue
Boston, MA 02135
Tel: 617-746-5797
Fax: 617-783-5642
Email: ROBERT_JOHNSON_LALLY@CHANCERY.RCAB.ORG

Armenian Library and Museum of America
65 Main Street
Watertown, MA 02172
Tel: 617-926-2562

Attleboro Public Library
74 North Main Street
Attleboro, MA 02703
Tel: 508-222-0157
Fax: 508-226-3326

Bacon Free Public Library
58 Eliot Street
Natick, MA 01760
Tel: 508-653-6730

Bedford Free Public Library
7 Mudge Way
Bedford, MA 01730
Tel: 617-275-9440
URL: http://www.tiac.net/users/spickett/library.html

Belmont Public Library
336 Concord Avenue
P.O. Box 125
Belmont, MA 02178
Tel: 617-489-2000
Fax: 617-489-5725
Email: belmails@mln.lib.ma.us

Berkshire Athenaeum
1 Wendell Avenue
Pittsfield, MA 01201
Tel: 413-499-9486
Fax: 413-499-9489

Beverly Historical Society/Museum
117 Cabot Street
Beverly, MA 01915
Tel: 508-922-1186

Boston Athenaeum
10 1/2 Beacon Street
Boston, MA 02108
Tel: 617-227-0270
Fax: 617-227-5266
Email: snonack@tiac.net

Boston Public Library
Copley Square
666 Boylston Street
Boston, MA 02117
Tel: 617-536-5400
URL: http://www.bpl.org/

Bostonian Society
Museum:
206 Washington Street
Boston, MA 02109
Tel: 617-720-3290
Fax: 617-720-3289
Library:
15 State Street
Boston, MA 02109
Tel: 617-720-3285
URL: http://www.boston.com/arts/museums/musstate.htm

Bourne Public Library
19 Sandwich Road
Bourne, MA 02532
Tel: 508-759-0644

Bridgewater Public Library
15 South Street
Bridgewater, MA 02324
Tel/TDD: 508-697-3331
Fax: 508-279-1467
Email: bwpl@ma.ultranet.com
URL: http://www.ultranet.com/~bwpl/index.shtml

Bridgewater State College
Clement C. Maxwell Library
Special Collections, 3rd Floor
Bridgewater, MA 02325
Tel: 508-697-1756
Email: smbates@bridgew.edu
URL: http://www.bridgew.edu/depts/maxwell/speccoll.htm

Brockton Historical Society/Museum
216 N. Pearl Street, Rte. 27
Brockton, MA 02401
Tel: 508-583-1039
Email: gerryb@brocktonma.com
URL: http://www.brocktonma.com/bhs/bhs_mus.html

Brockton Public Library
304 Main Street
Brockton, MA 02401
Tel: 508-580-7890
Fax: 508-580-7898
Email: brpublib@tiac.net

Brookline Public Library
361 Washington Street
Brookline, MA 02146
Tel: 617-730-2360
Fax: 617-232-7146

Brooks Academy Museum
80 Parallel Street
P.O. Box 17
Harwich, MA 02645
Tel: 508-432-8089

Burlington Historical Commission/Museum
Corner of Bedford and Cambridge Streets
Burlington, MA 01803
Tel: 617-272-0606

Buttonwoods Museum
240 Water Street
Haverhill, MA 01830
Tel: 508-374-4626

Caleb Lothrop House
14 Summer Street
Cohasset, MA 02025
Tel: 617-383-6930

Cambridge Public Library
449 Broadway
Cambridge, MA 02138
Tel: 617-349-4040
URL: http://www.ci.cambridge.ma.us/~CPL/

Cape Ann Historical Association/Library
27 Pleasant Street
Gloucester, MA 01930
Tel: 617-283-0455

Cary Memorial Library
1874 Massachusetts Avenue
Lexington, MA 02173
Tel: 617-862-6288
URL: http://link.ci.lexington.ma.us/WWW/Cary/Cary.html7

Chelmsford Public Library
25 Boston Road
Chelmsford, MA 01824
Tel: 508-256-5521
Fax: 508-256-4368
Email: mcd@mvlc.lib.ma.us

Concord Free Public Library
129 Main Street
Concord, MA 01742
Tel: 508-371-6240
Fax: 508-371-6244

Congregational Library and Archives
14 Beacon Street
Boston, MA 02108
Tel: 617-523-0470
Email: lplato@tiac.net
URL: http://www.tiac.net/users/lplato/mainmenu.htm

Connecticut Valley Historical Museum
194 State Street
Springfield, MA 01103
Tel: 413-732-3080
URL: http://www.spfldlibmus.org/home05.htm

Danvers Archival Center
Peabody Institute Library
15 Sylvan Street
Danvers, MA 01923
Tel: 508-774-0554

Dennis Memorial Library Association
Old Bass River Road
Dennis, MA 02638
Tel: 508-385-2255

Dyer Memorial Library
25 Centre Avenue (Route 123)
Abington, MA 02351
Tel: 617-878-8480

East Bridgewater Public Library
32 Union Street
East Bridgewater, MA 02333
Tel: 508-378-1616
Fax: 508-378-1617
Email: ebpl@tiac.net

Eastham Public Library
190 Samoset Road
RR 1, Box 338
Eastham, MA 02642
Tel: 508-255-3070

Edwards Memorial Museum
North Street
Chesterfield, MA 01012
Tel: 413-296-4759

Edwin Smith Historical Museum
6 Elm Street
Westfield, MA 01085
Tel: 413-568-7833

Eldredge Public Library
564 Main Street
Chatham, MA 02633
Tel: 508-945-0274

Essex Shipbuilding Museum
28 Main Street
Essex, MA 01929
Tel: 508-768-7541

Falmouth Public LIbrary
123 Katharine Lee Bates Road
Falmouth, MA
Tel: 508-457-2555
URL: http://www.capecod.net/fpl/welcome.html

Fitchburg Public Library
Willis Room
610 Main Street
Fitchburg, MA 01420
Tel: 508-345-9635
URL: http://www.net1plus.com/users/fpl

Fobes Memorial Library
Historical Room
Maple Street
Oakham, MA 01068
Tel: 508-882-3372
Email: dthistle@holycross.edu
URL: http://carver.holycross.edu/~dthistle/fobes/

Forbes Library
20 West Street
Northampton, MA 01060
Tel: 413-584-8399

Freetown Historical Society/Museum
1 Slab Bridge Road
P.O. Box 253
Assonet, MA 02702
Tel: 508-644-5310

Goodnow Public Library
21 Concord Road
Sudbury, MA 01776
Tel: 508-443-1035
Fax: 508-443-1036

Harvard University
Graduate School of Business Administration
Baker Library, Historical Collection Dept.
Soldiers Field
Boston, MA 02163
Tel: 617-495-6411
Fax: 617-495-5957
Email: histcollref@hbs.edu
URL: http://library.hbs.edu/collmu.htm#Historical Collections

Haverhill Public Library
99 Main Street
Haverhill, MA 01830
Tel: 508-373-1586

Heard House Museum
54 South Main Street
Ipswich, MA 01938
Tel: 508-356-2641
URL: http://www.tiac.net/users/ncg/ihs.html

Hingham Public Library
66 Leavitt Street
Hingham, MA 02043
Tel: 617-741-1406
Fax: 617-749-0956

Holyoke Public Library/Museum
335 Maple Street
Holyoke, MA 01040
Tel: 413-534-2211

Hyannis Public Library
401 Main Street
Hyannis, MA 02601-3903
Tel: 508-775-2280

J.V. Fletcher Library
50 Main Street
Westford, MA 01886
Tel: 508-692-5555
Fax: 508-692-0287
Email: mwf@mvlc.lib.ma.us

Jackson Homestead
527 Washington Street
Newton, MA 02158
Tel: 617-552-7238
URL: http://www.boston.com/arts/museums/musjacksn.htm

Jones Library, Inc.
Boltwood Local History & Genealogy Collection
43 Amity Street
Amherst, MA 01002
Tel: 413-256-4090
Fax: 413-256-4096
URL: http://k12.oit.umass.edu/masag/1440o.html

Joshua Hyde Public Library
Local History Room
306 Main Street
Sturbridge, MA 01566
Tel: 508-347-2512
Email: library@hey.net
URL: http://www.hey.net/Sturbridge/library/index.html

Kemp-McCarthy Memorial Museum
Zoar Road
Rowe, MA 01966
Tel: 413-339-4238

Kendall Whaling Museum
27 Everett Street
Sharon, MA 02067
Tel: 617-784-5642
URL: http://www.boston.com/arts/museums/muskwm.htm

Lawrence Free Public Library
51 Lawrence Street
Lawrence, MA 01841
Tel: 508-682-1727
Fax: 508-688-3142
URL: http://www.tiac.net/users/lfpl/

Longyear Historical Society/Museum
120 Seaver Street
Brookline, MA 02146
Tel: 617-277-8943
URL: http://www.boston.com/arts/museums/muslong.htm

Lucius Beebe Memorial Library
599 North Avenue, Door 9
Wakefield, MA 01880
Tel: 617-246-6334
Fax: 617-245-8748
Email: wakefieldlibrary@noblenet.org

Lynn Historical Society/Library & Museum
125 Green Street
Lynn, MA 01902
Tel: 617-592-2465

Lynn Public Library
5 North Common Street
Lynn, MA 01902
Tel: 617-595-0567
Email: lynlib@shore.net
URL: http://www1.shore.net/~lynnlib/

Lynnfield Public Library
18 Summer Street
Lynnfield, MA 01940
Tel: 617-334-5411
Fax: 617-334-2164
Email: lfd@noblenet.org

Malden Public Library
36 Salem Street
Malden, MA 02148
Tel: 617-324-0218
Fax: 617-324-4467
Email: maldensup@mbln.org.ma.us

Marlborough Public Library
35 West Main Street
Marlborough, MA 01752
Tel: 508-624-6900
Fax: 508-485-1494
URL: http://www.marlborough.com/mpl.html

Massachusetts Historical Society
1154 Boylston Street
Boston, MA 02215
Tel: 617-536-1608

Massachusetts Society of Mayflower Descendants
376 Boylston Street, 2nd Floor
Boston, MA 02116
Tel: 617-266-1624
Email: msmd@tiac.net
URL: http://www.tiac.net/users/msmd/

Massachusetts State Library
341 State House
Beacon Street
Boston, MA 02133
Tel: 617-727-2590

Mayflower Society Museum
4 Winslow Street
P.O. Box 3297
Plymouth, MA 02361
Tel: 508-746-2590

Melrose Public Library
69 West Emerson Street
Melrose, MA 02176-3173
Tel: 617-665-2313
Fax: 617-662-4229
Email: mel@noblenet.org

Memorial Hall Library
Andover Room
Elm Square
Andover, MA 01810
Tel: 508-623-8401
Email: webmaster@mhl.org
URL: http://www.mhl.org/

Milford Public Library
80 Spruce Street
Milford, MA 01757
Tel: 617-473-2145

Millicent Library
45 Center Street
Fairhaven, MA 02719
Tel: 508-992-5342
Fax: 508-993-7288
Email: millie@tiac.net
URL: http://www.tiac.net/users/millie/archives.htm

Milton Public Library
476 Canton Avenue
Milton, MA 02186
Tel: 617-698-5757
Email: miltonref@ocln.org
URL: http://www.tiac.net/users/mpl/

Morrill Memorial Library
Walpole Street
P.O. Box 220
Norwood, MA 02062
Tel: 617-769-0020
Fax: 617-769-6083

Morse Institute
14 E. Central Street
Natick, MA 01760
Tel: 508-651-7300

Museum of Our National Heritage
33 Marrett Road
Lexington, MA 02173
Tel: 617-861-6559
617-861-9638
Fax: 617-861-9846
URL: http://www.boston.com/arts/museums/musnaher.htm

Needham Free Public Library
1139 Highland Avenue
Needham, MA 02194
Tel: 617-455-7559
617-455-7562 (Reference)
Fax: 617-455-7591
URL: http://www.needhamonline.com/library/home.html

New Bedford Free Public Library
613 Pleasant Street
New Bedford, MA 02740
Tel: 617-991-6275
Fax: 508-979-5825

New England Historical and Genealogical Society (NEHGS)
101 Newbury Street
Boston, MA 02116-3007
Tel: 617-836-5740
888-AT-NEHGS (Membership & Education)
888-BY-NEHGS (Sales)
888-90-NEHGS (Library Circulation)
Fax: 617-536-7307
Email: nehgs@nehgs.org
URL: http://www.nehgs.org/

Newburyport Public Library
94 State Street
Newburyport, MA 01950
Tel: 508-465-4428
Fax: 508-463-0394
Email: mne@mvlc.lib.ma.usc

Newton Free Public Library
330 Homer Street
Newton, MA 02159
Tel: 617-552-7145
Fax: 617-964-9549
URL: http://www.ci.newton.ma.us/lib.html

North Adams State College
Freel Library, Special Collections
P.O. Box 9250
North Adams, MA 01247
Tel: 413-662-5321
Fax: 413-662-5286
Email: aterryberry@nasc.mass.edu
URL: http://www.nasc.mass.edu/nascinfo/library/index.html

Northborough Free Library
34 Main Street
Northborough, MA 01532
Tel: 508-393-5025
URL: http://www.pixielations.com/NborLibH.html

Norwell Public Library
64 South Street
Norwell, MA 02061
Tel: 617-659-2015
Fax: 617-659-6755

Peabody Essex Museum
Phillips Library
East Indian Square
Salem, MA 01970
Tel: 800-745-4054
800-745-1876 (library)
Fax: 508-744-0036
Email: pem@pem.org
URL: http://www.pem.org/

Pilgrim Hall Museum
75 Court Street
Plymouth, MA 02360
Tel: 508-746-1620
Fax: 508-747-4228
URL: http://media3.net/pilgrimhall/intro.htm

Plymouth Public Library
Plymouth Collection
132 South Street
Plymouth, MA 02360
Tel: 508-830-4250
Fax: 508-830-4258
Email: ppl@pcix.com

Pollard Memorial Library
401 Merrimack Street
Lowell, MA 01852
Tel: 508-970-4120
Fax: 508-970-4117
TDD: 508-970-4129
URL: http://www.uml.edu/Lowell/library.html

Randall Library
Common Road
Stow, MA 01775
Tel: 508-897-8572

Reading Public Library
64 Middlesex Avenue
Reading, MA 01867
Tel: 617-944-0840
Email: readingpl@noblenet.org
URL: http://www.netcasters.com/library/

Rockland Memorial Library
20 Belmont Street
Rockland, MA 02370
Tel: 617-878-1236
Fax: 617-878-4013
Email: roill@ocln.org

Salem Maritime National Historic Site
174 Derby Street
Salem, MA 01970
Tel: 508-744-4323

Salem Public Library
370 Essex Street
Salem, MA 01970
Tel: 508-744-0860
Fax: 508-745-8616
Email: sal@noblenet.org

Salem Witch Museum
19 1/2 Washington Square, North
Salem, MA 01970
Tel: 508-744-1692
Email: facts@salemwitchmuseum.com
URL: http://www.salemwitchmuseum.com/

Salisbury Public Library
17 Elm Street
Salisbury, MA 01952
Tel: 508-465-5071
Email: msa.@mvlc.lib.ma.us

Sandy Bay Historical Society & Museums, Inc.
40 King Street
Rockport, MA 01966
Tel: 508-546-9533

Scituate Town Library
85 Branch Street
Scituate, MA 02066
Tel: 617-545-8727
617-545-8728
Email: sclib@ocln.org

Sharon Public Library
11 North Main Street
Sharon, MA 02067-
Tel: 617-784-1578
Fax: 617-784-4728
Email: sharon@gateway.sharon.lib.ma

Shrewsbury Free Public Library
609 Main Street
Shrewsbury, MA 01545
Tel: 508-842-0081
Fax: 508-842-9140

Somerville Public Library
Local History Room
79 Highland Avenue
Somerville, MA 02143
Tel: 617-623-5000
TDD: 617-625-8808
Email: SOMHELP@MLN.LIB.MA.US
URL: http://www.ultranet.com/~somlib/

Springfield Libraries & Museums
Genealogy and Local History Library
220 State Street
Springfield, MA 01103
Tel: 413-263-6800 ext. 311
URL: http://ww.spfldlibmus.org/home05.htm

Strong House Museum
67 Amity Street
Amherst, MA 01002
Tel: 413-256-0678

Sturgis Library
3090 Main Street, Rte. 6A
P.O. Box 606
Barnstable, MA 02630
Tel: 508-362-6636

Swansea Free Public Library
69 Main Street
Swansea, MA 02777
Tel: 508-674-9609
Fax: 508-675-5444

Taft Public Library
Main Street
P.O. Box 35
Mendon, MA 01756
Tel: 508-473-3259
Fax: 508-473-7049

University of Massachusetts/Amherst
W.E.B. DuBois Library
Special Collections
Amherst, MA 01003
Tel: 413-545-0150
URL: http://www.library.umass.edu/index.html

Ventress Memorial Library
Library Plaza
Marshfield, MA 02050
Tel: 617-834-5535
Fax: 617-837-8362
Email: eriboldi@ocln.org
URL: http://www.ssih.com/Marshfield/library.html

Vineyard Haven Library
Main Street
Vineyard Haven, MA 02568
Tel: 508-696-4212
Fax: 508-696-7495
Email: vhpl@vineyard.net
URL: http://www.vineyard.net/org/vhpl/index.html

Vineyard Museum
Cooke and School Streets
Edgartown, MA 02539
Tel: 508-627-4441

Watertown Free Public Library
123 Main Street
Watertown, MA 02172
Tel: 617-972-6431
Fax: 617-924-5471
Email: watref@mln.lib.ma.us

Wayland Public Library
5 Concord Road
Wayland, MA 01778
Tel: 508-358-2311
URL: http://www.wayland.k12.ma.us/library/index.htm

Wenham Public Library
138 Main Street
Wenham, MA 01984
Tel: 508-468-5527
Fax: 508-468-5535
Email: mwn@mvlc.lib.ma.us

Westborough Public Library
55 West Main Street
Westborough, MA 01581
Tel: 508-366-3050
Fax: 508-366-3049

Weston Public Library
87 School Street
Weston, MA 02193
Tel: 617-893-3312
Fax: 617-893-9142
Email: weston@mln.lib.ma.us

Williamstown House of Local History
Williamstown Public Library
Elizabeth S. Botsford Memorial Building
762 Main Street, 2nd Floor
Williamstown, MA 01267
URL: http://bcn.net/~willieb/hlh.html

Winchester Public Library
80 Washington Street
Winchester, MA 01890
Tel: 617-721-7171
Fax: 617-721-7170
URL: http://www.tiac.net/users/mvz/winchest/library.html

Woburn Public Library
45 Pleasant Street
P.O. Box 298
Woburn, MA 01801
Tel: 617-933-0148
Fax: 617-938-7860
Email: woblib@ultranet.com
URL: http://www.ultranet.com/~woblib/

Worcester Public Library
Local History/Worcester Room
3 Salem Square
Worcester, MA 01608
Tel: 508-799-1655
URl: http://world.std.com/~sgreen/

Yarmouth Library
297 Main Street
Yarmouthport, MA 02675
Tel: 508-760-4822
Fax: 508-760-2699

Newspaper Repositories

Boston Public Library
Copley Square
666 Boylston Street
Boston, MA 02117
Tel: 617-536-5400 ext. 241
Email: mbdunhouse@bpl.org
URL: http://www.bpl.org/

Massachusetts State Library
341 State House
Beacon Hill
Boston, MA 02133
Tel: 617-727-2590

Vital Records

Massachusetts Department of Public Health
Registry of Vital Records & Statistics
470 Atlantic Avenue, 2nd Floor
Boston, MA 02210
Tel: 617-753-8600

Massachusetts on the Web

America's Homepage—Plymouth
http://media3.com/plymouth/

Ancestry's Library - Massachusetts Marriage Index
http://www.ancestry.com/

Colonial Massachusetts & Maine Genealogies
http://www.qni.com/~anderson/index.html

Historical Records of Tisbury, Massachusetts
http://www.vineyard.net/vineyard/history/index.html

Massachusetts GenWeb Project
http://www.rootsweb.com/~magenweb/

Mayflower Web Pages
http://members.aol.com/calebj/mayflower.html

MICHIGAN

ARCHIVES, STATE & NATIONAL

Michigan State Archives
Michigan Library and Historical Center
717 Allegan Street
Lansing, MI 48918
Tel: 517-373-1408
URL: http://www.sos.state.mi.us/history/archive/archive.html

National Archives—Great Lakes Region
7358 Pulaski Road
Chicago, IL 60629
Tel: 773-581-7816
Fax: 312-353-1294
Email: archives@chicago.nara.gov
URL: http://www.nara.gov/nara/regional/05nsgil.htm

GENEALOGICAL SOCIETIES

Bay County Genealogical Society
P.O. Box 27
Essexville, MI 48732

Bigelow Genealogical Society
P.O. Box 4115
Flint, MI 48504

Branch County Genealogical Society
P.O. Box 443
Coldwater, MI 49036
Email: woodwardcl@orion.branch-co.lib.mi.us
URL: http://www.geocities.com/TheTropics/1050/Gensociety.html

British Heritage Society
4177 Garrick Avenue
Warren, MI 48091
Tel: 810-757-4177
Email: Anton_The_Lord_Hartforth@msn.com

Calhoun County Genealogical Society
P.O. Box 777
Marshall, MI 49068
Email: THowell582@AOL.com

Charlevoix County Genealogical Society
c/o Boyne City Public Library
201 E. Main Street
Boyne City, MI 49712
Tel: 616-582-7861
Fax: 616-582-2998
URL: http://www.rootsweb.com/~micharle/cx-03.htm

Cheboygan County Genealogical Society
P.O. Box 51
Cheboygan, MI 49721

Dearborn Genealogical Society
P.O. Box 1112
Dearborn, MI 48121

Detroit Society for Genealogical Research
c/o Detroit Public Library
Burton Historical Collection
5201 Woodward Avenue
Detroit, MI 48202
Tel: 313-833-1480

Dickinson County Genealogical Society
401 Iron Mountain Street
Iron Mountain, MI 49801

Downriver Genealogical Society
1394 Cleophus
P.O. Box 476
Lincoln Park, MI 48146

Eaton County Genealogical Society
100 Lawrence Avenue
Charlotte, MI 48813

Farmington Genealogical Society
23500 Liberty
Farmington, MI 48024

Flemish Americans, Genealogical Society of
18740 Thirteen Mile Road
Roseville, MI 48066

Flint Genealogical Society
P.O. Box 1217
Flint, MI 48501
Email: ldnelson@tir.com

Ford Genealogy Club
Ford Motor Credit Company Building, Room 1491 (meetings only)
Dearborn, MI 48126
URL: http://www.wwnet.net/~krugman1/fgc/

Four Flags Area Genealogical Society
P.O. Box 414
Niles, MI 49120

French-Canadian Heritage Society of Michigan
Detroit Chapter
c/o Detroit Public Library
Burton Historical Collection
5201 Woodward Avenue
Detroit, MI 48202

French-Canadian Heritage Society of Michigan
Lansing Chapter
P.O. Box 10028
Lansing, MI 48901-0028

French-Canadian Heritage Society of Michigan
Traverse City Chapter
c/o Brenda Wolfgram Moore
430 S. Airport Road, East
Traverse City, MI 49686-4832

Gaylord Fact-Finders Genealogical Society
P.O. Box 1524
Gaylord, MI 49735

Grand Haven Genealogical Society
c/o Loutit Library
407 Columbus
Grand Haven, MI 49417

Grand Traverse Area Genealogical Society
P.O. Box 2015
Traverse City, MI 49685
URL: http://members.aol.com/VWilson577/gtags.html

Gratiot County Historical & Genealogical Society
P.O. Box 73
Ithaca, MI 48847
URL: http://www.rootsweb.com/~migratio/gchgs.html

Harrison Area Genealogical Society
P.O. Box 796
Harrison, MI 48625
URL: http://www.rootsweb.com/~miclare/harrison.htm

Holland Genealogical Society
c/o Herrick Pubic Library
300 River Avenue
Holland, MI 49423

Huron County Genealogical Society
c/o Ford & Marilyn Hebner
2843 Electric Avenue
Port Huron, MI 48060
Email: xvfp44b@prodigy.com

Huron Shores Genealogical Society
1909 Bobwhite
Oscoda, MI 48750
Huron Valley Genealogical Society
1100 Atlantic
Milford, MI 48042

Ionia County Genealogical Society
c/o Pam Swiler
13051 Ainsworth Road, Route 3
Lake Odessa, MI 48849
Tel: 616-374-3141
Email: pkswiler@juno.com
or bwills@ionia-mi.net
URL: http://bl-12.rootsweb.com/~miionia/icgs.htm

Jackson County Genealogical Society
c/o Jackson District Library
244 West Michigan Avenue
Jackson, MI 49201
URL: http://www.rootsweb.com/~mijackso/jcgs.htm

Jewish Genealogical Society of Michigan
P.O. Box 1361
Royal Oak, MI 48068

Jewish Historical Society of Michigan, Genealogical Branch
3345 Buckingham Trail
West Bloomfield, MI 48033

Kalamazoo Valley Genealogical Society
P.O. Box 405
Comstock, MI 49041
Email: 76635.231@compuserve.com
or tptm71a@prodigy.com
URL: http://www.rootsweb.com/~mikvgs/

Kalkaska Genealogical Society
P.O. Box 353
Kalkaska, MI 49646

Lapeer County Genealogical Society
c/o Lapeer County Library/Marguerite deAngeli Branch
921 Nepressing Street
Lapeer, MI 48446
URL: http://www.lapeer.lib.mi.us/Library/Genealogy/Index.html

Lenawee County Genealogical Society
P.O. Box 511
Adrain, MI 49221

Livingston County Genealogical Society
P.O. Box 1073
Howell, MI 48844-1073
URL: http://www.ismi.net/lcmigw/lcgslogo.htm

Luce-Mackinac Genealogical Society
P.O. Box 113
Engadine, MI 49827-0113
URL: http://www.rootsweb.com/~miluce/luce-mac.htm

Lyon Township Genealogical Society
c/o Lyon Township Public Library
27025 Milford Road
New Hudson, MI 48165

Macomb County Genealogy Group
c/o Mount Clemens Public Library
150 Cass Avenue
Mount Clemens, MI 48043
URL: http://www.macomb.lib.mi.us/mountclemens/genealog.htm

Marquette County Genealogical Society
c/o Peter White Public Library
217 North Front Street
Marquette, MI 49855
Email: MQTCGS@aol.com
URL: http://members.aol.com/MQTCGS/MCGS/mcgs.html

Mason County Genealogical Society
P.O. Box 352
Ludington, MI 49431

Michigan Genealogical Council
P.O. Box 80953
Lansing, MI 48908

Mid-Michigan Genealogical Society
P.O. Box 16033
Lansing, MI 48901

Midland Genealogical Society
c/o Grace A. Dow Library
1710 West St. Andrews Drive
Midland, MI 48640
URL: http://members.mdn.net/billword/mgs.htm

Monroe County, Genealogical Society of
P.O. Box 1428
Monroe, MI 48161
URL: http://www.tdi.net/havekost/gsmc.htm

Muskegon County Genealogical Society
c/o Hackley Library
316 W. Webster Avenue
Muskegon, MI 49440

National Society, Daughters of the Union 1861-1865, Inc.
11396 Grand Oak Drive
Grand Blanc, MI 48439

North Oakland Genealogical Society
c/o Orion Township Public Library
825 Joslyn Road
Lake Orion, MI 48362
Tel: 248-858-0159

Northeast Michigan Genealogical Society
c/o Jesse Besser Museum
491 Johnson Street
Alpena, MI 49707
URL: http://members.aol.com/alpenaco/migenweb/genealog.htm

Northville Genealogical Society
42164 Gladwin Drive
Northville, MI 48167

Oakland County Genealogical Society
P.O. Box 1094
Birmingham, MI 48012

Ogemaw Genealogical & Historical Society
c/o West Branch Public Library
West Branch, MI 48661

Palatines to America, Michigan Chapter
868 Beechwood Street, NE
Grand Rapids, MI 49505-3783

Polish Genealogical Society of Michigan
c/o Detroit Public Librar
Burton Historical Collection
5201 Woodward Avenue
Detroit, MI 48202

Pontiac Area Historical & Genealogical Society
P.O. Box 901
Pontiac, MI 48056

Presque Isle County Genealogical Society
c/o Onaway Library
P.O. Box 742
Onaway, MI 49765

Reed City Area Genealogical Society
c/o Reed City Public Library
410 West Upton Avenue
Reed City, MI 49677

Roseville Historical & Genealogical Society
c/o Roseville Public Library
29777 Gratiot Avenue
Roseville, MI 48066

Saint Clair County Family History Group
P.O. Box 611483
Port Huron, MI 48061-1483

Saginaw Genealogical Society
c/o Saginaw Public Library
505 Janes Avenue
Saginaw, MI 48507

Shiawassee County Genealogical Society
P.O. Box 841
Owosso, MI 48867

Southwest Michigan Genealogical Society
P.O. Box 573
St. Joseph, MI 49085

Southwestern Michigan, Genealogical Association of
P.O. Box 573
St. Joseph, MI 49085

Sterling Heights Genealogical & Historical Society
P.O. Box 1154
Sterling Heights, MI 48311-1154

Van Buren Regional Genealogical Society
P.O. Box 143
Decatur, MI 49045

Washtenaw County, Genealogical Society of
P.O. Box 7155
Ann Arbor, MI 48107

Western Michigan Genealogical Society
c/o Grand Rapids Public Library
60 Library Plaza, NE
Grand Rapids, MI 49503-3093
Email: wmgs@iserv.net
URL: http://www.iserv.net/~wmgs

Western Wayne County Genealogical Society
P.O. Box 530063
Livonia, MI 48153-0063

Historical Societies

Albion Historical Society
Gardner House Museum
509 South Superior Street
Albion, MI 49224

Ann Arbor Historical Foundation
312 South Division Street
Ann Arbor, MI 48104
Tel: 313-996-3008

Bellaire Area Historical Society
P.O. Box 646
Bellaire, MI 49615

Benzie Area Historical Society
6941 Traverse Avenue
P.O. Box 185
Benzonia, MI 49616

Berrien County Historical Association
North Cass
Berrien Springs, MI 49104
Tel: 616-471-1202

Branch County Historical Society
P.O. Box 107
Coldwater, MI 49036

Byron Center Historical Society
2506 Prescott
P.O. Box 20
Byron Center, MI 49315-0020

Chelsea Area Historical Society
125 Jackson Road
Chelsea, MI 48118
Tel: 313-475-9330
or 313-475-7047
URL: http://www.hvcn.org/info/libcahs.html

Elk Rapids Area Historical Society
401 River Street
P.O. Box 2
Elk Rapids, MI 49629
URL: http://www.ole.net/~maggie/antrim/elk.htm

Elsie Historical Society
c/o Elizabeth Hess
P.O. Box 125
Elsie, MI 48831

Flat River Historical Society
P.O. Box 188
Greenville, MI 48838

Flat Rock Historical Society
P.O. Box 386
Flat Rock, MI 48134

Fraser Historical Commission
16330 Fourteen Mile Road
Fraser, MI 48026
Tel: 810-293-4036

Grand Traverse Pioneer and Historical Society
232 Front Street
P.O. Box 1108
Traverse City, MI 49685

Grass Lake Area Historical Society
P.O. Box 53
Grass Lake, MI 49240

Gratiot County Historical & Genealogical Society
P.O. Box 73
Ithaca, MI 48847
URL: http://www.rootsweb.com/~migratio/gchgs.html

Grosse Ile Historical Society
P.O. Box 131
Grosse Ile, MI 48138

Huron County Historical Society
223 Third Street
Harbor Beach, MI 48441

Huron Valley RR Historical Society
3487 Broad Street
Dexter, MI 48130
Tel: 313-426-5100

Ionia County Historical Society
P.O. Box 1776
Ionia, MI 48846

Iosco Bay Historical Society
405 E. Bay Street
East Tawas, MI 48730

Jewish Historical Society of Michigan, Genealogical Branch
3345 Buckingham Trail
West Bloomfield, MI 48033

Keweenaw County Historical Society
HC-1, Box 265L
Eagle Harbor, MI 49950

Lake Odessa Historical Society
Page Building
839 4th Avenue
Lake Odessa, MI 48849

Lincoln Park Historical Society
P.O. Box 1776
Lincoln Park, MI 48146

Little Traverse Historical Society/Museum
100 Depot Court
Petoskey, MI 49770
Tel: 616-347-2620
URL: http://www.freeway.net/community/civic/historymuseum/

Livonia Historical Society
38125 Eight Mile Road
Livonia, MI 48152

Marine Historical Society of Detroit
Dept. W
606 Laurel Avenue
Port Clinton, OH 43452
URL: http://www.oakland.edu/~ncschult/mhsd/

Marquette County Historical Society
John M. Longyear Research Library
213 North Front Street
Marquette, MI 49855

Mason County Historical Society
Rose Hawley Museum
115 West Loomis Street
Ludington, MI 49431

Michigan Historical Commission
505 State Office Building
Lansing, MI 48913

Michigan, Historical Society of
2117 Washtenaw Avenue
Ann Arbor, MI 48104
Tel: 313-769-1828
Fax: 313-769-4267

Midland County Historical Society
c/o Midland Center for the Arts
1801 West Andrews Drive
Midland, MI 48640

Northville Historical Society
P.O. Box 71
Northville, MI 48167

Northwest Oakland County Historical Society
306 South Saginaw Street
Holly, MI 48442

Oakland County Pioneer & Historical Society/Archives
405 Oakland Avenue
Pontiac, MI 48342
Tel: 313-338-6732
URL: http://http2.sils.umich.edu/HCHS/REPOS-MICH/Oakland.html

Ogemaw Genealogical & Historical Society
c/o West Branch Public Library
West Branch, MI 48661

Plymouth Historical Society
155 South Main Street
Plymouth, MI 48170

Pontiac Area Historical & Genealogical Society
P.O. Box 901
Pontiac, MI 48056

Rockwood Area Historical Society
P.O. Box 68
Rockwood, MI 48173

Romulus Historical Society
c/o Romulus Public Library
11121 Wayne Road
Romulus, MI 48174

Rose City Area Historical Society, Inc.
c/o Ogemaw District Library
107 West Main
P.O. Box 427
Rose City, MI 48654

Roseville Historical & Genealogical Society
c/o Roseville Public Library
29777 Gratiot Avenue
Roseville, MI 48066

Saginaw River Marine Historical Society
Dept. W
P.O. Box 2051
Bay City, MI 48707
URL: http://www.concentric.net/~Djmaus/srmhs.htm

Sanilac County Historical Society
228 North Ridge Street
Port Sanilac, MI 48469
Tel: 810-622-9946

Washtenaw County Historical Society
500 North Main Street
Ann Arbor, MI 48104
Tel: 313-662-9092

Wayne Historical Society
1 Town Square
Wayne, MI 48184

Ypsilanti Historical Society/Museum/Archives
220 North Huron Street
Ypsilanti, MI 48197
Tel: 313-482-4990
Email: barr@hvcn.org
URL: http://www.hvcn.org/info/libyhma.html

Zeeland Historical Society
37 E. Main Street
Zeeland, MI 49464

LDS Family History Centers

Ann Arbor Family History Center
914 Hill Street
Ann Arbor, MI 48104
Tel: 313-995-0211

Bloomfield Hills Family History Center
425 North Woodward Avenue
Bloomfield Hills, MI 48304
Tel: 810-647-5671

East Lansing Family History Center
431 East Saginaw Street
East Lansing, MI 48823
Tel: 517-332-2932

Escanaba Family History Center
915 9th Avenue, South
Escanaba, MI 49829
Tel: 906-789-0370

Grand Blanc Family History Center
4285 McCandlish Road
Grand Blanc, MI 48439
Tel: 810-694-2964

Grand Rapids Family History Center
2780 Leonard, Northeast
Grand Rapids, MI 49505
Tel: 616-949-3343

Harvey Family History Center
350 Cherry Creek Road
Harvey, MI 49855
Tel: 906-249-1511

Hastings Family History Center
600 North Airport Road
Hastings, MI 49058
Tel: 616-948-2104

Howell Family History Center
1041 Grand River
Howell, MI
Mail:
Linda Philburn, Dir.
7445 Schrepfer Road
Howell, MI 48843
Tel: 517-546-2716
URL: http://www.ismi.net/lcmigw/howfhc.htm

Kalamazoo Family History Center
1112 North Drake Road
Kalamazoo, MI 49006
Tel: 616-342-1906

Ludington Family History Center
416 East Melendy Street
Ludington, MI 49431
Tel: 616-843-3358

Midland Family History Center
1700 West Sugnet Road
Midland, MI 48640
Tel: 517-631-1120

Muskegon Family History Center
1725 West Giles Road
Muskegon, MI 49445
Tel: 616-744-3283

Traverse City Family History Center
3746 Veterans Drive
Traverse City, MI 49684
Tel: 616-947-4646
URL: http://members.aol.com/VWilson577/fhc.html

Westland Family History Center
7575 North Hix Road
Westland, MI 48185
Tel: 313-459-4570

Archives/Libraries/Museums

Adrian Public Library
143 E. Maumee Street
Adrian, MI 49221
Tel: 517-265-2265

Albion Public Library
501 S. Superior Street
Albion, MI 49224
Tel: 517-629-3993
TDD: 517-629-3994
Email: albion@monroe.lib.mi.us
URL: http://monroe.lib.mi.us/~albion/library

Allen County Public Library
900 Webster Street
Fort Wayne, IN 46802
Tel: 219-424-7241
URL: http://www.acpl.lib.in.us/

Alpena County Library
11 North First Avenue
Alpena, MI 49707
Tel: 517-356-6188
Fax: 517-356-2765
Email: alpena1@northland.lib.mi.us
URL: http://members.aol.com/alpenaco/migenweb/library.htm

Ann Arbor Public Library
343 South 5th Avenue
Ann Arbor, MI 48104
Tel: 313-994-2333

Archdiocese of Detroit
Archives Department
1234 Washington Road
Detroit, MI 48226-1875
Tel: 313-237-5846
Fax: 313-237-4643

Bacon Memorial District Library
45 Vinewood,
Wyandotte, MI 48192

Bay County Library
708 Center Avenue
Bay City, MI 48708
Tel: 517-893-9566

Bay County Library/Sage Branch
100 East Midland Street
Bay City, MI 48706
Tel: 517-892-8555

Bay County Library-South Side Branch
311 Lafayette Avenue
Bay City, MI 48708
Tel: 517-893-1287

Birmingham Public Library
300 W. Merrill Street
Birmingham, MI 48009
Tel: 248-647-1700

Boyne City Public Library
201 E. Main Street
Boyne City, MI 49712
Tel: 616-582-7861
Fax: 616-582-2998
Email: boynecl@northland.lib.mi.us
URL: http://nlc.lib.mi.us/members/boyne_c.htm

Branch District Library
10 E. Chicago Street
Coldwater, MI 49036
Tel: 517-278-2341
Fax: 517-279-7134
Email: webmaster@orion.branch-co.lib.mi.us

Cadillac and Wexford County Public Library
411 South Lake Street
Cadillac, MI 49601
Tel: 616-775-6541

Central Michigan University
Clarke Historical Library
Mount Pleasant, MI 48859
Tel: 517-774-3352
517-774-3471 (Reference)
Fax: 517-774-4499
URL: http://www.lib.cmich.edu/clarke/clarke.htm

Cheboygan Area Public Library
107 S. Ball Street
Cheboygan, MI 49721
Tel/Fax: 616-627-2381
Email: cheboyl@northland.lib.mi.us
URL: http://nlc.lib.mi.us/members/cheboyga.htm

Comstock Township Library
6130 King Highway
Comstock, MI 49001
Tel: 616-345-0136

Detroit Public Library
Burton Historical Collection
5201 Woodward Avenue
Detroit, MI 48202
Tel: 313-833-1480
Fax: 313-832-0877
Email: nvangor@cms.cc.wayne.edu
URL: http://www.detroit.lib.mi.us/special_collections.htm

Dexter Area Museum
3433 Inverness
Dexter, MI 48130
Tel: 313-426-2519
Email: DexMuseum@aol.com
URL: http://www.hvcn.org/info/libdahs.html

Dickinson County Library
401 Iron Mountain Street
Iron Mountain, MI 49801
Tel: 906-774-1218

Ecorse Public Library
4184 Jefferson Avenue
Ecorse, MI 48229
Tel/TDD: 313-389-2030
Fax: 313-389-2032
URL: http://tln.lib.mi.us/~ecor/index.htm

Farmington Community Library
32737 West 12 Mile Road
Farmington Hills, MI 48334
Tel: 248-553-0300

Finnish-American Heritage Center
Suomi College
Hancock, MI 49930
Tel: 906-487-7367
Fax: 906-487-7383
URL: http://www.suomi.edu/lnk/FHC.html

Flint Public Library
1026 E. Kearsley Street
Flint, MI 48502
Tel: 810-232-7111
Fax: 810-232-8360
URL: http://www.flint.lib.mi.us/fpl/about/branches/main.html

Galesburg Memorial Library
188 E. Michigan
Galesburg, MI 49053
Tel: 616-665-7839

Grace A. Dow Library
1710 West St. Andrews Drive
Midland, MI 48640
Tel: 517-835-9599

Grand Rapids Public Library
60 Library Plaza, NE
Grand Rapids, MI 49503
Tel: 616-456-3640
URL: http://www.iserv.net/grpl/

Hackley Public Library
316 W. Webster Avenue
Muskegon, MI 49440
Tel: 616-722-7276
URL: http://www.remc4.k12.mi.us/muskegon/library/hackley.htm

Hall-Fowler Memorial Library
126 E. Main Street
Ionia, MI 48846
Tel: 616-527-3680
Fax: 616-527-6210

Harrison Community Library
102 N. Second Street
Harrison, MI 48625
Tel: 517-539-6711

Herrick Public Library
300 South River Avenue
Holland, MI 49423
Tel: 616-355-1400

Howell Carnegie District Library
314 W. Grand River
Howell, MI 48843
Tel: 517-546-0720

Iosco-Arenac District Library
951 Turtle Road
Tawas City, MI 48763
Tel: 517-362-2651

Jesse Besser Museum
491 Johnson Street
Alpena, MI 49707
Tel: 517-356-2202

Kalamazoo Public Library
315 South Rose Street (under construction until Dec. 1997)
121 West South (Temporary Address)
Kalamazoo, MI 49007
Tel: 616-342-9837
616-342-5745 (Local History Room)
Fax: 616-342-8342
URL: http://www.kpl.gov/home.htm

Lansing Public Library
401 South Capitol
Lansing, MI 48843
Tel: 517-325-6400
Fax: 517-325-6423
Email: morrowl@mlc.lib.mi.us
URL: http://www.mlc.lib.mi.us/~morrowl/

Lapeer County Library/Marguerite deAngeli Branch
921 West Nepressing
Lapeer, MI 48446
Tel: 810-664-6971
Fax: 810-664-5581
URL: http://www.lapeer.lib.mi.us/Library/Genealogy/Index.html

Mackinac Island Public Library
Box C
Mackinac Island, MI 49757
Tel: 906-847-3421
Email: MackPLIB@aol.com
URL: http://www.si.umich.edu/~twigs/Mackinac/library.html

Mackinaw Public Library
528 West Central Avenue
P.O. Box 67
Mackinaw City, MI 49701-0067
Tel: 616-436-5451
Fax: 616-436-7344
Email: mackinal@northland.lib.mi.us
URL: http://nlc.lib.mi.us/members/mackinaw.htm

Mancelona Public Library
202 East State Street
Mancelona, MI 49659
Tel: 616-587-9451

Manistee Public Library
95 Maple Street
Manistee, MI 49660
Tel: 616-723-2519

Marquette County Historical Society
John M. Longyear Research Library
213 North Front Street
Marquette, MI 49855

McKay Memorial Library
105 S. Webster
Augusta, MI 49012
Tel: 616-731-4000

Michigan Library & Historical Center
Library of Michigan
Genealogical & Local History Collection
717 Allegan Street
P.O. Box 30007
Lansing, MI 48909
Tel: 517-373-1580
URL: http://www.libofmich.lib.mi.us/citizens/collections/genealogy/genealogy.html

Michigan Technological University Archives and The Copper County Historical Collection
J. Robert Van Pelt Historical Collection
1400 Townsend Drive
Houghton, MI 49931-1295
Tel: 906-487-3209
Fax: 906-487-2357
Email: copper@mtu.edu
URL: http://www.lib.mtu.edu/jrvp/index.htm

Milan Public Library
151 Wabash Street
Milan, MI 48160
Tel: 313-439-1240
Fax: 313-439-5625
Email: milan@monroe.lib.mi.us/
URL: http://www.hvcn.org/info/milanlibrary/

Milford Township Library
1100 Atlantic Street
Milford, MI 48381
Tel: 248-684-0845
Email: milford@tln.lib.mi.us
URL: http://milf.tln.lib.mi.us

Mitchell Public Library
22 N. Manning Street
Hillsdale, MI 49242
Tel: 517-437-2581

Monroe County Library System
Ellis Reference and Information Center
3700 S. Custer Road
Monroe, MI 48161
Tel: 313-241-5277
Fax: 313-242-9037
URL: http://monroe.lib.mi.us:8000/

Mount Clemens Public Library
150 Cass Avenue
Mount Clemens, MI 48043
Tel: 810-469-6672

North Berrien Historical Museum
300 Coloma Avenue
Coloma, MI 49038-9724
Tel: 616-468-3330

Northville District Library
212 W. Cady Street
Northville, MI 48167
Tel: 248-349-3020
URL: http://tln.lib.mi.us/~nort/

Northwestern Michigan College
Helen and Mark Osterlin Library
1701 E. Front Street
Traverse City, MI 49686
Tel: 616-922-1060
Email: library@elmo.nmc.edu
URL: http://www.nmc.edu/~library/

Novi Public Library
45245 West Ten Mile Road
Novi, MI 48375
Tel: 248-349-0720
Fax/TDD: 248-349-6520
URL: http://tln.lib.mi.us/directory/members/novi

Ogemaw District Library
107 West Main
P.O. Box 427
Rose City, MI 48654

Onaway Library
P.O. Box 742
Onaway, MI 49765

Parchment Community Library
401 S. Riverview
Parchment, MI 49004
Tel: 616-343-7747

Peter White Public Library
217 North Front Street
Marquette, MI 49855
Tel: 906-228-9510

Petoskey Public Library
451 E. Mitchell Street
Petoskey, MI 49770
Tel: 616-347-4211
Fax: 616-347-3429
Email: petoskyl@northland.lib.mi.us
URL: http://nlc.lib.mi.us/members/Petoskey.htm

Portage Public Library
300 Library Lane
Portage, MI 49002
Tel: 616-329-4544

Reed City Public Library
410 West Upton Avenue
Reed City, MI 49677
Tel: 616-832-2131

Richland Community Library
330 N. Centre
Schoolcraft, MI 49087
Tel: 616-679-5959

Rochester Hills Public Library
Local History Room
500 Olde Towne Road
Rochester, MI 48307
Tel: 248-656-2900
URL: http://metronet.lib.mi.us/ROCH/rhpl.html

Romulus Public Library
1121 Wayne Road
Romulus, MI 48174

Tel/TDD: 313-942-7589
Fax: 313-941-3575
URL: http://tln.lib.mi.us/~rooms/index.htm

Roseville Public Library
29777 Civic Center Blvd.
Roseville, MI 48066
Tel: 810-445-5407

Royal Oak Public Library
222 E. Eleven Mile Road
Royal Oak, MI 48067
Tel: 248-541-1470
Fax: 248-545-6220
TDD: 248-546-6399

Saint Clair County Library
Michigan Room
210 McMorran Blvd.
Port Huron, MI 48060-4098
Tel: 313-987-READ

Saint Clair Shores Library
22500 East 11 Mile Road
St. Clair Shores, MI 48081
Tel: 810-771-9020

Saint Joseph Public Library
500 Market Street
St. Joseph, MI 49085
Tel: 616-983-7167

Saginaw Public Library
Hoyt Main Branch
505 Janes Avenue
Saginaw, MI 48607
Tel: 517-755-0904
Fax: 517-755-9828
Email: saginaw@saginaw.lib.mi.us
URL: http://www.saginaw.lib.mi.us/

Spies Public Library
940 First Street
Menominee, MI 49858
Tel: 906-863-3911

Sturgis Public Library
130 North Nottawa Street
Sturgis, MI 49091
Tel: 616-659-5911

Three Rivers Public Library
920 West Michigan Avenue
Three Rivers, MI 49093
Tel: 616-273-8666

Trenton Veterans Memorial Library
2790 Westfield
Trenton, MI 48183
Tel: 313-676-9777
Fax: 313-676-9895
TDD: 313-676-9773
URL: http://tln.lib.mi.us/~tren/index.htm

Troy Public Library
510 Big Beaver Road
Troy, MI 48084
Tel: 248-524-3538

University of Michigan/Ann Arbor
Bentley Historical Library
1150 Beall Avenue
Ann Arbor, MI 48109-2113
Tel: 313-764-3482
Fax: 313-936-1333
URL: http://www.umich.edu/~bhl/bhl/bhlmenu.htm

University of Michigan/Flint
Flint Library
Genesee History Collection Center
Flint, MI 48502
Tel: 313-762-3402

Van Buren District Library
200 North Phelps Street
Decatur, MI 49045
Tel: 616-423-4771

Vicksburg District Library
215 S. Michigan
Vicksburg, MI 49097
Tel: 616-649-1648

Wayne State University
Walter P. Reuther Library
5401 Cass Avenue
Detroit, MI 48202
Tel: 313-577-4024
Fax: 313-577-4300
URL: http://www.reuther.wayne.edu/collections.html

Western Michigan University
Archives and Regional History Collection
Room 111, East Hall
Kalamazoo, MI 49008-5081
Tel: 616-387-8490
Fax: 616-387-8484
Email: arch_collect@wmich.edu
URL: http://www.wmich.edu/library/archive/archives.html

Willard Library
7 W. Van Buren
Battle Creek, MI 49017
Tel: 616-968-8166
URL: http://www.willard.lib.mi.us/

Ypsilanti District Library/Peters Branch
1165 Ecorse Road
Ypsilanti, MI 48198
Tel: 313-482-5025
Fax: 313-482-0122
URL: http://tln.lib.mi.us/directory/members/petr/

Ypsilanti Historical Society/Museum/Archives
220 North Huron Street
Ypsilanti, MI 48197
Tel: 313-482-4990
Email: barr@hvcn.org
URL: http://www.hvcn.org/info/libyhma.html

Newspaper Repositories

Detroit Public Library
Burton Historical Collection
5201 Woodward Avenue
Detroit, MI 48202
Tel: 313-833-1480
Fax: 313-832-0877
Email: nvangor@cms.cc.wayne.edu
URL: http://www.detroit.lib.mi.us/special_collections.htm

Grand Rapids Public Library
60 Library Plaza, NE
Grand Rapids, MI 49503
Tel: 616-456-3640
URL: http://www.iserv.net/grpl/

Michigan Library & Historical Center
Library of Michigan
Genealogical & Local History Collection
717 Allegan Street
P.O. Box 30007
Lansing, MI 48909
Tel: 517-373-8927
Email: kamteaux@libofmich.lib.mi.us
URL: http://www.libofmich.lib.mi.us/libraries/services/usnewsproj.html

University of Michigan/Ann Arbor
Bentley Historical Library
1150 Beall Avenue
Ann Arbor, MI 48109-2113
Tel: 313-764-3482
Fax: 313-936-1333
URL: http://www.umich.edu/~bhl/bhl/bhlmenu.htm

Vital Records

Michigan Department of Public Health
Vital Records Section
3423 N. Logan Street
P.O. Box 30035
Lansing, MI 48914
Tel: 517-335-8656

Michigan on the Web

Farmington/Farmington Hills History and Genealogy
http://www.mich.com/~fafh/hag/hag.htm

Michigan County Clerks Genealogical Directory
http://www.sos.state.mi.us/history/archive/archgene.html

Michigan GenWeb Project
http://www.rootsweb.com/~migenweb

Michigan in the Civil War
http://users.aol.com/dlharvey/cwmireg.htm

Michigan Library & Historical Center
http://www.libofmich.lib.mi.us/citizens/collections/genealogy/genealogy.html

Native Genealogy
http://www.edwards1.com/rose/genealogy/native-gen/native-gen.htm

Sons of Union Veterans of the Civil War, Department of Michigan
http://www.centuryinter.net/suvcw.mi/index.html

MINNESOTA

ARCHIVES, STATE & NATIONAL

Minnesota State Archives
Minnesota Historical Society Research Center
345 Kellogg Boulevard
St. Paul, MN 55102
Tel: 612-296-0332
URL: http://www.mnhs.org/index.html

National Archives—Central Plains Region
2312 East Bannister Road
Kansas City, MO 64131
Tel: 816-926-6272
Fax: 816-926-6982
Email: archives@kansascity.nara.gov
URL: http://www.nara.gov/nara/regional/06nsgil.html

National Archives—Great Lakes Region
7358 Pulaski Road
Chicago, IL 60629
Tel: 773-581-7816
Fax: 312-353-1294
Email: archives@chicago.nara.gov
URL: http://www.nara.gov/nara/regional/05nsgil.htm

GENEALOGICAL SOCIETIES

Anoka County Genealogical Society
1900 3rd Avenue, S
Anoka, MN 55303
Tel: 612-421-0600

Association for Certification of Minnesota Genealogists, Inc.
c/o Applications Secretary
330 South Park
Mora, MN 55051

Carlton County, Genealogical Society of
P.O. Box 204
Cloquet, MN 55720

Chippewa County Genealogical Society
P.O. Box 303
Montevideo, MN 56265

Chisago County Genealogical Society
Chisago Historical Society
P.O. Box 360
Center City, MN 55012

Clarks Grove Area Heritage Society
P.O. Box 188
Clarks Grove, MN 56016

Crow River Genealogical Society
380 School Road, North
Hutchinson, MN 55350

Crow Wing County Genealogical Society
2103 Graydon Avenue
Brainerd, MN 56401

Czechoslovak Genealogical Society International
P.O. Box 16225
St. Paul, MN 55116-0225
Tel: 612-645-4585
URL: http://members.aol.com/CGSI/index.html

Dakota County Genealogical Society
P.O. Box 74
South St. Paul, MN 55075
Email: VAlbu@worldnet.att.net

Danish American Genealogical Group
c/o Minnesota Genealogical Society
P.O. Box 16069
St. Paul, MN 55116
URL: http://www.mtn.org/mgs/branches/danish.html

Dodge County Genealogical Society
P.O. Box 683
Dodge Center, MN 55927

Douglas County Genealogical Society
P.O. Box 505
Alexandria, MN 56308
URL: http://www.mtn.org/mgs/branches/douglas.html

English Genealogical Society
c/o Minnesota Genealogical Society
P.O. Box 16069
St. Paul, MN 55116
URL: http://www.mtn.org/mgs/branches/english.html

Freeborn County Genealogical Society
P.O. Box 403
Albert Lea, MN 56007
Tel: 507-373-9269
Email: rflisran@wolf.co.net
URL: http://fox.co.net/austin/arts/geneal.html

Fulda Heritage Society
P.O. Box 303
Fulda, MN 56131

German-Bohemian Heritage Society
P.O. Box 822
New Ulm, MN 56073
Email: lalgbhs.@newulmtel.net
URL: http://www.qrz.com/gene/reg/SUD/sudet_GBHS.html

Germanic Genealogical Society
c/o Minnesota Genealogical Society
P.O. Box 16069
St. Paul, MN 55116
URL: http://www.mtn.org/mgs/branches/german.html

Heart-O-Lakes Genealogical Society
1324 Jackson Avenue
Detroit Lakes, MN 56501
Tel: 218-847-6043
URL: http://perham.eot.com/~bolerud/heart.html

Irish Genealogical Society
P.O. Box 13585
St. Paul, MN 55116
URL: http://www.rootsweb.com/~irish/

Itasca County Genealogical Society
P.O. Box 261
Bovey, MN 55709

Jackson/Cottonwood Genealogical Group
343 Buckwheat Avenue
Windom, MN 56101
Mail:
P.O. Box 238
Lakefield, MN 56150
Tel: 507-662-5505

Kandiyohi County, Heritage Searchers of
P.O. Box 175
Willmar, MN 56201-0175

Martin County Genealogical Society
c/o Martin County Public Library
110 North Park Street
Fairmont, MN 56031

Meeker County Genealogical Society
308 Marshall Avenue, North
Litchfield, MN 55355

Minnesota Genealogical Society
1650 Carroll Avenue
P.O. Box 16069
St. Paul, MN 55116
Tel: 612-645-3671
URL: http://www.mtn.org/mgs/

Minnesota, Genealogical Society of
2642 University Avenue
St. Paul, MN 55114
Tel: 612-724-2101

Minnkota Genealogical Society
P.O. Box 126
East Grand Forks, MN 56721
URL: http://www.rootsweb.com/~minnkota/

Mower County Genealogical Society
P.O. Box 145
Austin, MN 55912
Tel: 507-437-6082

Nobles County Genealogical Society
407 12th Street, Suite 2
Worthington, MN 56187
URL: http://www.worthington.mn.frontiercomm.net/~demuth/page2.html

Norwegian American Bygdelagenes Fellesraad
c/o Marilyn Somdahl, Pres.
10129 Goodrich Circle
Bloomington, MN 55437
Tel: 612-831-4409
Email: rsylte@ix.netcom.com
URL: http://www.lexiaintl.org/sylte/bygdelag.html

Olmsted County Genealogical Society
P.O. Box 6411
Rochester, MN 55903
Tel: 507-282-9447
Email: sweetman@millcomm.com
URL: http://www.millcomm.com/~gzimmer/ochs.html

Otter Tail County Genealogical Society
1110 Lincoln Avenue, West
Fergus Falls, MN 56537
Tel: 218-736-6038

Pipestone County Genealogical Society
113 South Hiawatha
Pipestone, MN 56164

Polish Genealogical Society of Minnesota
c/o Minnesota Genealogical Society
P.O. Box 16069
St. Paul, MN 55116
URL: http://www.mtn.org/mgs/branches/polish.html

Prairieland Genealogical Society
Southwest Historical Center, Room 141
Southwest State University
Marshall, MN 56258
Tel: 507-537-7373

Rainy River Valley Genealogical Society
P.O. Box 1032
International Falls, MN 56649

Range Genealogical Society
P.O. Box 388
Chisholm, MN 55719

Red River Valley Genealogical Society
P.O. Box 9284
Fargo, ND 58106

Red River Valley Heritage Society
P.O. Box 733
Moorhead, MN 56560
Tel: 218-233-5604

Renville County Genealogical Society
211 North Main Street
P.O. Box 331
Renville, MN 56284

Rice County Genealogical Society
408 Division Street
Northfield, MN 55057

St. Cloud Area Genealogist, Inc.
P.O. Box 213
St. Cloud, MN 56302
Tel: 320-252-6673

Scandinavian American Genealogical Society
c/o Minnesota Genealogical Society
P.O. Box 16069
St. Paul, MN 55116
URL: http://www.mtn.org/mgs/branches/sags.html

South Central Minnesota Genealogical Society
110 North Park Street
Fairmont, MN 56031

Stevens County Genealogical Society
West 6th and Nevada
Morris, MN 56267

Swedish Genealogical Group of Minnesota
c/o Minnesota Genealogical Society
P.O. Box 16069
St. Paul, MN 55116
Email: pjsveria@mtn.org
URL: http://www.mtn.org/mgs/branches/swedish.html

Traverse des Sioux Genealogical Society/Mankato
815 Nicollet Avenue
North Mankato, MN 56001
Tel: 507-387-2290

Traverse des Sioux Genealogical Society/St. Peter
c/o Treaty Site History Center
1851 North Minnesota Avenue
St. Peter, MN 56082

Twin Ports Genealogical Society
P.O. Box 16895
Duluth, MN 55806

Waseca Area Genealogical Society
P.O. Box 264
Waseca, MN 56093
Tel: 507-835-7700

White Bear Lake Genealogical Society
P.O. Box 10555
White Bear Lake, MN 55110

Wilkin County Historical Society, Genealogy Committee
P.O. Box 330
Breckenridge, MN 56520
Tel: 218-643-3166

Winona County Genealogical Roundtable/Society
P.O. Box 363
Winona, MN 55987

Wright County Genealogical Society
911 2nd Avenue, South
Buffalo, MN 55313

Yankee Genealogical Society
c/o Minnesota Genealogical Society
P.O. Box 16069
St. Paul, MN 55116
URL: http://www.mtn.org/mgs/branches/yankee.html

Historical Societies

Afton Historical Society
P.O. Box 178
Afton, MN 55001
Tel: 612-436-3500

Aitkin County Historical Society
20 Pacific Street, SW
P.O. Box 215
Aitkin, MN 56431
Tel: 218-927-3348

Albany Historical Society
P.O. Box 25
Albany, MN 56307
Tel: 320-845-2982

Alden Community Historical Society
P.O. Box 323
Alden, MN 56009
Tel: 507-874-3462

American Historical Society of Germans from Russia (AHSGR)
North Star Chapter - Minnesota
175 Spring Valley Drive
Bloomington, MN 55420-5337
Email: SamFiske@aol.com
URL: http://www.teleport.com/nonprofit/ahsgr/mnnostar.html

Anishinabe Regional Historical Society
Bradley Building, Suite #320
10 East Superior Street
Duluth, MN 55802
Tel: 218-723-4659

Anoka County Historical Society
1900 3rd Avenue, S
Anoka, MN 55303
Tel: 612-421-0600

Atwater Area History Society
108 N. 3rd Street
Atwater, MN 56209
Tel: 320-974-8284

Barnesville Heritage Society
P.O. Box 126
Barnesville, MN 56514
Tel: 218-354-2364

Bay Area Historical Society
Outer Drive
P.O. Box 33
Silver Bay, MN 55614
Tel: 612-226-4870

Becker County Historical Society
c/o Becker County Museum
Summit & West Front St.
P.O. Box 622
Detroit Lakes, MN 56502
Tel: 218-847-2938
Fax: 218-847-5048
Email: bolerud@tekstar.com
URL: http://perham.eot.com/~bolerud/bchs.html

Belle Plaine Historical Society
South Cedar Avenue
P.O. Box 73
Belle Plaine, MN 56011
Tel: 612-873-6109

Beltrami County Historical Society
County Fairgrounds T.H. #71
P.O. Box 683
Bemidji, MN 56601
Tel: 218-751-7824

Benton County Historical Society
218 1st Street, North
P.O. Box 245
Sauk Rapids, MN 56379
Tel: 320-253-9614

Big Stone County Historical Society
RR 2, Box 31
Ortonville, MN 56278
Tel: 320-839-3359

Bloomington Historical Society
10200 Penn Avenue, South
Bloomington, MN 55431
Mail:
2525 W. Old Shakopee Road
Bloomington, MN 55431
Tel: 612-948-8881

Blue Earth County Historical Society/Museum
415 Cherry Street
Mankato, MN 56001
Tel: 507-345-5566
URL: http://www.ic.mankato.mn.us/reg9/bechs/bechs1.html

Brooklyn Center Historical Society
P.O. Box 29345
Brooklyn Center, MN 55429

Brown County Historical Society
2 North Broadway
P.O. Box 116
New Ulm, MN 56073
Tel: 507-354-2016

Browns Valley Historical Society
514 3rd Street, South
Browns Valley, MN 56219

Cannon Falls Area Historical Society
P.O. Box 111
Cannon Falls, MN 55009
Tel: 507-263-4080
507-263-4503

Canosia Historical Society
c/o Audrey Eaton, Dir.
5762 North Pike Lake
Duluth, MN 55811
Tel: 218-729-8963

Carlton County Historical Society
History & Heritage Center
406 Cloquet Avenue
Cloquet, MN 55720
Tel: 218-879-1938

Carver County Historical Society
119 Cherry Street
Waconia, MN 55387
Tel: 612-442-4234

Cass County Historical Society
P.O. Box 505
Walker, MN 56484
Tel: 218-547-3300 ext. 251

Center City Historical Society
P.O. Box 366
Center City, MN 55012
Tel: 612-257-9128

Chaska Historical Society
City Hall
Chaska, MN 55318
Tel: 612-448-4458

Chatfield Historical Society
RR 1
Chatfield, MN 55923

Chippewa County Historical Society
Junction 7 & 59
P.O. Box 303
Montevideo, MN 56265
Tel: 320-269-7636

Chisago County Historical Society
30495 Park Street
P.O. Box 146
Lindstrom, MN 55045-0146
Tel: 612-257-5310

Chisago County Historical Society, North Chapter
51245 Fairfield Avenue
Rush City, MN 55609
Tel: 612-674-4122

Christie Home Historical Society
110 2nd Avenue, North
Long Prairie, MN 56347

Clarks Grove Area Heritage Society
P.O. Box 188
Clarks Grove, MN 56016

Clay County Historical Society
Heritage Hjemkomst Interpretive Center
202 First Avenue, North
P.O. Box 501
Moorhead, MN 56560
Tel: 218-233-4604
Email: mpeihl@delphi.com
URL: http://www.gps.com/Pioneer_Spirit/THEN/authors.htm

Clearwater County Historical Society
112 2nd Avenue
P.O. Box 241
Bagley, MN 56621
Tel: 218-785-2000

Cokato-Finnish American Society
10783 County Road 3, SW
Cokato, MN 55321
Tel: 320-286-2833

Cokato Historical Society
Cokato Museum & Library Building
4th & Millard
P.O. Box 269
Cokato, MN 55321
Tel: 320-286-2427
Email: cokatomuseum@cmgate/com

Comfrey Area Historical Society
P.O. Box 218
Comfrey, MN 56019

Cook County Historical Society
Lightkeepers House
4 Broadway
P.O. Box 1293
Grand Marais, MN 55604
Tel: 218-387-2314

Coon Rapids Historical Society
1313 Coon Rapids Boulevard
Coon Rapids, MN 55433
Tel: 612-784-4920
612-755-2880

Cottonwood Area Historical Society
P.O. Box 106
Cottonwood, MN 56229

Cottonwood County Historical Society
Museum and Research Library
812 4th Avenue
Windom, MN 56101
Tel: 507-831-1134
URL: http://www.mtn.org/mgs/othersoc/cottonwd.html

Crosslake Area Historical Society
P.O. Box 369
Crosslake, MN 56442

Crow Wing Historical Society
320 Laurel Street
P.O. Box 722
Brainerd, MN 56401
Tel: 218-829-3268

Cuyuna Range Historical Society
101 1st Street, NE
P.O. Box 128
Crosby, MN 56441
Tel: 218-546-6178

Dakota County Historical Society
130 3rd Avenue, North
South St. Paul, MN 55075
Tel: 612-451-6260

Dodge County Historical Society
P.O. Box 433
Mantorville, MN 55955
Tel: 507-635-5508

Douglas County Historical Society
1219 South Nokomis
Alexandria, MN 56308
Tel: 320-762-0382

East Grand Forks, Heritage Foundation of
218 NW 4th Street
P.O. Box 295
East Grand Forks, MN 56721
Tel: 218-773-7481

East Otter Tail Historical Society
349 2nd Avenue, SE
Perham, MN 56573
Tel: 218-346-6262

Eden Prairie Historical Society
Eden Prairie City Hall
8950 Eden Prairie Road
Eden Prairie, MN 55344
Tel: 612-944-2486

Edina Historical Society
4711 West 70th St.
Edina, MN 55424
Tel: 612-920-8952

Ellendale Area Historical Society
P.O. Box 334
Ellendale, MN 56026

Ely-Winton Historical Society
1900 Camp Street
Ely, MN 55731

England Prairie Pioneer Club
P.O. Box 127
Verndale, MN 56481

Esko Historical Society
c/o Ray Mattinen
5 Elizabeth Avenue
Esko, MN 55733

Evansville Historical Foundation
P.O. Box 337
Evansville, MN 56326
Tel: 218-948-2010

Excelsior/Lake Minnetonka Historical Society
P.O. Box 305
Excelsior, MN 55331
Tel: 612-474-8956

Faribault County Historical Society
405 E. Sixth Street
Blue Earth, MN 56013
Tel: 507-526-5421

Fillmore County Historical Society
Route 1, Box 81-D
Fountain, MN 55935
Tel: 507-268-4449

Finland Historical Society
P.O. Box 583
Finland, MN 55603
Tel: 218-353-7393

Finnish-American Historical Society, Minnesota
P.O. Box 34
Wolf Lake, MN 56593

Freeborn County Historical Society
1031 Bridge Avenue
P.O. Box 105
Albert Lea, MN 56007
Tel: 507-373-8003
Email: rflisran@wolf.co.net

Fridley Historical Society
611 Mississippi Street, NE
Mail:
5273 NE Horizon Drive
Fridley, MN 55432
Tel: 612-571-5041

Golden Valley Historical Society
7800 Golden Valley Road
Golden Valley, MN 55427
Tel: 612-544-4547

Goodhue Area Historical Society
P.O. Box 3
Goodhue, MN 55027

Goodhue County Historical Society
1166 Oak Street
Red Wing, MN 55066
Tel: 612-388-6024

Goodridge Area Historical Society
Goodridge City Hall
P.O. Box 171
Goodridge, MN 56725

Grant County Historical Society
P.O. Box 1002
Elbow Lake, MN 56531

Hastings Historical Society
c/o Bertrand Goderstad
109 1/2 2nd Street, East
Hastings, MN 55033

Hennepin County Historical Society
Hennepin History Museum
2303 3rd Avenue, South
Minneapolis, MN 55404
Tel: 612-870-1329

Hesper/Mabel Area Historical Society
P.O. Box 56
Mable, MN 55954
Tel: 507-493-5018

Hibbing Historical Society
400 E. 23rd Street
Hibbing, MN 55746
Tel: 218-263-8522

Hill Farm Historical Society
28 Meadowlark Lane
North Oaks, MN 55127
Tel: 612-484-1434

Hollandale Area Historical Society
P.O. Box 184
Hollandale, MN 56045
Tel: 507-889-4491

Hopkins Historical Society
Hopkins Community Center
33 14th Street, North
Hopkins, MN 55343
Mail:
1010 1st Street, South
Hopkins, MN 55343
Tel: 612-938-8304

Houston County Historical Society
Museum on the fairgrounds
P.O. Box 173
Houston, MN 55943
Tel: 507-724-3884
507-896-2291

Hubbard County Historical Society
Old County Courthouse
P.O. Box 327
Park Rapids, MN 56470
Tel: 218-732-5237

Irish-American Cultural Institute
683 Osceola Avenue
St. Paul, MN 55105

Iron Range Historical Society
Gilbert City Hall, 2nd Floor
P.O. Box 786
Gilbert, MN 55741
Tel: 218-749-3150

Isanti County Historical Society
139 East 1st Avenue
P.O. Box 525
Cambridge, MN 55008
Tel: 612-689-4229

Itasca County Historical Society
10 5th Street, NW
P.O. Box 664
Grand Rapids, MN 55744
Tel: 218-326-6431

Jackson County Historical Society
307 North Highway 86
P.O. Box 238
Lakefield, MN 56150
Tel: 507-662-5505

Jasper Historical Society
217 2nd Street, SE
Jasper, MN 56144
Tel: 507-348-9841

Jewish Historical Society of the Upper Midwest
Hamline University
1536 Hewitt Avenue
St. Paul, MN 55104
Tel: 612-641-2407

Kanabec County Historical Society
P.O. Box 113
Mora, MN 55051

Kandiyohi County Historical Society
610 NE Highway 71
Willmar, MN 56201
Tel: 320-235-1881

Kenyon Area Historical Society
Gunderson House
Kenyon, MN 55946
Tel: 507-789-5365

Kittson County Historical Society
P.O. Box 100
Lake Bronson, MN 56734
Tel: 218-754-4100

Koochiching County Historical Society
Smoky Bear Park
214 6th Avenue.
P.O. Box 1147
International Falls, MN 56649
Tel: 218-283-4316

Lac Qui Parle County Historical Society
South T.H. #75
P.O. Box 124
Madison, MN 56256
Tel: 320-598-7678

La Societe Canadienne Française du Minnesota
4895 Bryant Avenue
Inver Grove Heights, MN 55075

Lake Benton Historical Society
115 1/2 South Center Street
P.O. Box 218
Lake Benton, MN 56149-0218
Tel: 507-368-4214

Lake City Historical Society
City Hall
Lake City, MN 55041

Lake County Historical Society
Railroad Depot Museum
P.O. Box 313
Two Harbors, MN 55616
Tel: 218-834-4898

Lake Crystal Historical Society
132 North Grove
Lake Crystal, MN 56055
Tel: 507-726-2687

Lake of the Woods County Historical Society
County Museum
119 8th Avenue, SE
Baudette, MN 56623
Mail:
c/o County Courthouse
Baudette, MN 56623
Tel: 218-634-1200
218-634-2075

Lake Park Area Historical Society
RR 1, Box 124A
Lake Park, MN 56544
Tel: 218-238-5896

Lakeville Area Historical Society
City Hall
20195 Holyoke Avenue
Lakeville, MN 55044

Lamberton Area Historical Society
Community Building
110 2nd Avenue, West
Lamberton, MN 56152
Tel: 507-752-7063

Lanesboro Historical Society
105 Parkway, South
P.O. Box 354
Lanesboro, MN 55949
Tel: 507-467-3439

Le Sueur County Historical Society
P.O. Box 240
Elysian, MN 56028
Tel: 507-627-4620

Le Sueur Historians
709 North 2nd Street
Le Sueur, MN 56058
Tel: 507-665-2050

Lincoln County Historical Society
610 West Elm
Hendricks, MN 56136
Mail:
406 Brooks Street
Hendricks, MN 56136
Tel: 507-275-3537

Lindstrom Historical Society
P.O. Box 12
Lindstrom, MN 55045
Tel: 612-257-2700

Little Canada Historical Society
515 East Little Canada Road
Little Canada, MN 55117
Tel: 612-484-4783

Lyon County Historical Society
114 North Third Street
Marshall, MN 56258
Tel: 507-537-6580

Madison Lake Area Historical Society
525 Main Street
Madison Lake, MN 56063

Mahnomen County Historical Society
P.O. Box 123
Mahnomen, MN 56557
Tel: 218-935-5490

Marine Historical Society
Stone House Museum
5th & Oak Streets
Marine on St. Croix, MN 55047

Marshall County Historical Society
Historical Visitor Center
P.O. Box 103
Warren, MN 56762
Tel: 218-745-4803

Martin County Historical Society
304 East Blue Earth Avenue
Fairmont, MN 56031
Tel: 507-235-5178

Masonic Historical Society and Museum, Minnesota
200 E. Plato Blvd.
St. Paul, MN 55107
Tel: 612-222-6051
Fax: 612-222-6144

McLeod County Historical Society
380 North School Road
Hutchinson, MN 55350
Tel: 320-587-2109

Meeker County Historical Society
308 Marshall Avenue, North
Litchfield, MN 55355
Tel: 320-693-8911

Menahga Area Historical Society
P.O. Box 299
Menahga, MN 56464

Mendota/West St. Paul Historical Society
1160 Dodd Road
Mendota Heights, MN 55118

Military Historical Society of Minnesota
c/o Minnesota Military Museum
Box 150, Camp Riley
Little Falls, MN 56345
Tel: 320-632-7374

Mille Lacs County Historical Society
Depot Museum
104 10th Avenue
P.O. Box 42
Princeton, MN 55371
Tel: 612-389-1296

Minnesota Historical Society
345 Kellogg Boulevard
St. Paul, MN 55102
Tel: 612-296-0332
URL: http://www.mnhs.org/index.html

Minnesota Lake Area Historical Society
Kremer House
P.O. Box 225
Minnesota Lake, MN 56068
Tel: 507-462-3420

Minnetonka Historical Society
Burwell House
13209 McGinty Road, East
Minnetonka, MN 55343
Tel: 612-933-1611
612-476-4042

Missabe Railroad Historical Society
719 Northland Avenue
Stillwater, MN 55082
URL: http://www1.minn.net/~mspanton/mrhs.html

Moose Lake Historical Society
Village Hall Museum
205 Elm
Moose Lake, MN 55767
Tel: 218-485-4680

Morrison County Historical Society
Charles A. Weyerhaeuser Memorial Museum
1600 Lindbergh Drive, South
P.O. Box 239
Little Falls, MN 56345
Tel: 320-632-4007
URL: http://www.upstel.net/~johns/History/MorrisonCo.html

Morristown Historical Society
P.O. Box 113
Morristown, MN 55052

Mower County Historical Society
12th Street & 6th Street SW
P.O. Box 804
Austin, MN 55912
Tel: 507-437-6082
URL: http://fox.co.net/austin/arts/geneal.html

Murray County Historical Society
2980 Broadway
Slayton, MN 56172
Tel: 507-836-6533

New Brighton Area Historical Society
850 Emerald Court
New Brighton, MN 55112

New York Mills/Finnish American Society
P.O. Box 316
New York Mills, MN 56567
Tel: 218-385-2075
218-385-2085

Nicollet County Historical Society
Treaty Site History Center
1851 North Minnesota Avenue
St. Peter, MN 56082
Tel: 507-931-2160
Fax: 507-931-0172
Email: nicolletco@aol.com
URL: http://tourism.st-peter.mn.us/nicollet.html

Nobles County Historical Society
407 12th Street, Suite 2
Worthington, MN 56187
Tel: 507-376-4432
507-376-3125
Email: demuth@worthington.mn.frontiercomm.net
URL: http://www.worthington.mn.frontiercomm.net/~demuth/page13.html

Norman County Historical Society
409 East 1st Avenue
Ada, MN 56510
Tel: 218-784-4989

North St. Paul Historical Society
2666 E. 7th Avenue
North St. Paul, MN 55109
Tel: 612-779-6402

Northfield Historical Society
408 Division Street
Northfield, MN 55057
Tel: 507-645-9268

Norwegian-American Historical Association (NAHA)
1510 St. Olaf Avenue
Northfield, MN 55057
Fax: 507-646-3734
Email: naha@stolaf.edu
URL: http://www.stolaf.edu/stolaf/other/naha/naha.html

Olmsted County Historical Society
1195 County Road 22, SW
Rochester, MN 55902
Tel: 507-282-9447
Email: sweetman@millcomm.com
URL: http://www.millcomm.com/~gzimmer/ochs.html

Otter Tail County Historical Society
1110 West Lincoln
Fergus Falls, MN 56537
Tel: 218-736-6038

Paul Bunyan Historical Society
Route 2, Box 131
Akeley, MN 56433

Paynesville Historical Society
570 River Street
Paynesville, MN 56362

Pennington County Historical Society
Peder Engelstad Pioneer Village
Oakland Park Road
P.O. Box 127
Thief River Falls, MN 56701
Tel: 218-681-5767

Pine County Historical Society
305 Governors Way
Sandstone, MN 55704
Tel: 320-245-2574

Pipestone County Historical Society
113 South Hiawatha
Pipestone, MN 56164
Tel: 507-825-2563
Email: pipctymu@rconnect.com
URL: http://www.pipestone.mn.us/Museum/Homepa~1.HTM

Plymouth Historical Society
3605 Fernbrook Lane
Plymouth, MN 55447
Mail:
3400 Plymouth Blvd.
Plymouth, MN 55447
Tel: 612-559-9201

Polk County Historical Society
US Hwy. 2
P.O. Box 214
Crookston, MN 56716
Tel: 218-281-1038

Pope County Historical Society
809 S. Lakeshore Drive
Glenwood, MN 56334
Tel: 320-634-3293

Preston Historical Society
c/o Richard Nelson
Houston & Preston Streets
Preston, MN 55965
Tel: 507-765-4555

Ramsey County Historical Society
75 West 5th Street, Room 323
St. Paul, MN 55102
Tel: 612-222-0701

Red Lake County Historical Society
Lake Pleasant School House
Route 1, Box 298
Red Lake Falls, MN 56750
Tel: 218-253-2833

Red River Valley Heritage Society
P.O. Box 733
Moorhead, MN 56560
Tel: 218-233-5604

Redwood County Historical Society
507 Morten Drive
Redwood Falls, MN 56283
Mail:
RR 2, Box 12
Redwood Falls, MN 56283
Tel: 507-637-3329

Renville County Historical Society
441 North Park Drive
P.O. Box 266
Morton, MN 56270
Tel: 507-697-6147

Rice County Historical Society
Museum and Genealogical Research Center
1814 NW 2nd Avenue
Faribault, MN 55021
Tel: 507-332-2121

Richfield Historical Society
6900 Lyndale Avenue, South
P.O. Box 23304
Richfield, MN 55423
Tel: 612-869-2049
612-869-4761

Rock County Historical Society
Hinkly House
P.O. Box 741
Luverne, MN 56156
Tel: 507-283-4810

Rockford Area Historical Society
Ames-Florida-Stork House
P.O. Box 186
Rockford, MN 55373
Tel: 612-477-5383

Roseau County Historical Society
Roseau County Museum and Center
505 2nd Avenue, NE
Roseau, MN 56751
Tel: 218-463-1918

Rosemount Area Historical Society
3130 145th Street, West
Rosemount, MN 55068

Roseville Historical Society
2107 North Hamline Avenue
Roseville, MN 55113

Royalton Historical Society
P.O. Box 196
Royalton, MN 56373
Tel: 320-584-5641

Rushford Area Historical Organization
c/o Alton Morken, Pres.
403 East North Street
Rushford, MN 55971
Tel: 507-864-7223

Sacred Heart Area Historical Society
Rural Route 2
Sacred Heart, MN 56285
Tel: 320-765-2274

St. Francis Historical Society
c/o Dennis Bentilla
22731 Rum River Blvd., NW
St. Francis, MN 55070
Tel: 612-753-1224

St. Louis County Historical Society
506 West Michigan Street
Duluth, MN 55802
Tel/Fax: 218-727-8025
Email: CVB@Visit.Duluth.MN.US
URL: http://www.visit.duluth.com/Depot/historic.html

St. Louis Park Historical Society
Jovig Park
6210 West 37th Street
St. Louis Park, MN 55426
Tel: 612-929-9486

Sauk Centre Area Historical Society
1725 Sinclair Lewis Avenue
Sauk Centre, MN 56378

Schroeder Area Historical Society
9248 W. Highway 61
Schroeder, MN 55613
Tel: 218-663-7589

Scott County Historical Society
Stans Historical Center
235 South Fuller
Shakopee, MN 55379
Tel: 612-445-0378

Sherburne County Historical Society
13122 First Street
Becker, MN 55308
Tel: 612-261-4433

Sibley County Historical Society
700 Main Street
P.O. Box 407
Henderson, MN 56044
Tel: 612-248-3350

Sleepy Eye Historical Society
316 Walnut, SE
Sleepy Eye, MN 56085

South St. Paul Historical Society
345 7th Avenue, South
South St. Paul, MN 55075

Spencer Brook Historical Society
RR 3
Princeton, MN 55371

Spring Valley Community Historical Society, Inc.
112 South Washington Avenue
Spring Valley, MN 55975
Mail:
909 South Broadway
Spring Valley, MN 55975
Tel: 507-346-2763

Stearns County Historical Society
Stearns County Heritage Center
235 33rd Avenue, South
P.O. Box 702
St. Cloud, MN 56302
Tel: 320-253-8424

Steele County Historical Society
Steele County Fairgrounds
P.O. Box 204
Owatonna, MN 55060
Tel: 507-451-1420

Stevens County Historical Society
West 6th & Nevada
Morris, MN 56267
Tel: 320-589-1719
Email: history@infolink.morris.mn.us

Swift County Historical Society
Route 2, Box 4D1
Benson, MN 56215
Tel: 320-843-4467

Taylors Falls Historical Society
505 Folsom Street
Taylors Falls, MN 55084
Tel: 612-465-3125

Territorial Pioneers
1395 McKinley
St. Paul, MN 55108

Todd County Historical Society
215 1st Avenue, North
Long Prairie, MN 56347

Tofte Historical Society
P.O. Box 2312
Tofte, MN 55615-2312

Tower Soudan Historical Society
Train Coach
P.O. Box 413
Tower, MN 55790
Tel: 218-753-3039

Traverse County Historical Society
507 12th Street, North
Wheaton, MN 56396
Mail:
RR 1, Box 42
Wheaton, MN 56396

Upsala Area Historical Society
Borgstrom House
Highway 238
P.O. Box 35
Upsala, MN 56384
Tel: 320-573-4208
URL: http://www.upstel.net/~johns/History/History.html

Verndale Historical Society
North 3rd Street & Main Street
Verndale, MN 56481

Virginia Area Historical Society
P.O. Box 736
Virginia, MN 55792
Tel: 218-744-1136

Wabasha County Historical Society
503 West Center Street
Lake City, MN 55041

Wabasso County Historical Society
564 South Street
Wabasso, MN 56293

Wadena County Historical Society
603 North Jefferson
Wadena, MN 56482

Warroad Historical Society
Warroad Heritage Center
202 Main Avenue, NE
P.O. Box 688
Warroad, MN 56763
Tel: 218-386-1283

Waseca County Historical Society
315 2nd Avenue, NE
P.O. Box 314
Waseca, MN 56093
Tel: 507-835-7700

Washington County Historical Society
602 North Main Street
P.O. Box 167
Stillwater, MN 55082
Tel: 612-439-5956

Watonwan County Historical Society
423 Dill Avenue, SW
P.O. Box 126
Madelia, MN 56062
Tel: 507-642-3247

Wawina Area Historical Society
P.O. Box 102
Wawina, MN 55794
Tel: 218-488-6588

Wayzata Historical Society
At the Depot
402 East Lake Street
Wayzata, MN 55391

Welcome Historical Society
109 Hulseman
Welcome, MN 56181
Tel: 507-728-8806

West Concord Historical Society
P.O. Box 346
West Concord, MN 55985
Tel: 507-527-2177

West Side Historical Society
c/o Joe Hoover, Pres.
615 Stryker Avenue
St. Paul, MN 55107

Western Hennepin County Pioneers Association
1953 West Wayzata Blvd.
P.O. Box 332
Long Lake, MN 55356
Tel: 612-473-6557

Westonka Historical Society
3740 Enchanted Lane
Mound, MN 55364

Wilkin County Historical Society
704 Nebraska Avenue
P.O. Box 212
Breckenridge, MN 56520
Tel: 218-643-1303

Winnebago Historical Society/Museum
18 1st Street, NE
P.O. Box 218
Winnebago, MN 56098
Tel: 507-893-4660

Winona County Historical Society
160 Johnson Street
Winona, MN 55987
Tel: 507-454-2723
Fax: 507-454-0006

Winona Heritage Association
369 W. Broadway
Winona, MN 55987

Wright County Historical Society
2001 Highway 25, North
Buffalo, Mn 55313
Tel: 612-339-6881 ext. 7323
612-682-7323

Yellow Medicine County Historical Society
Junction T.H. 67 & 23
P.O. Box 145
Granite Falls, MN 56241
Tel: 612-564-4479
612-564-3574

LDS Family History Centers

Bemidji Family History Center
3033 Birchmont Drive
Bemidji, MN 56601
Tel: 218-751-9129

Brooklyn Park Family History Center
4700 Edinbrook Terrace
Minneapolis, MN 55443
Tel: 612-425-1865

Duluth Family History Center
521 Upham Road
Duluth, MN 55811
Tel: 218-726-1361

Minneapolis Family History Center
2801 North Douglas Drive
Minneapolis, MN 55422
Tel: 612-544-2479

Rochester Family History Center
2300 Viola Heights Drive, NE
Rochester, MN 55906
Tel: 507-281-6641

St. Paul Family History Center
2200 North Hadley
St. Paul, MN 55128
Tel: 612-770-3213

Archives/Libraries/Museums

Amador Heritage Center
Route 2, Box 191
North Branch, MN 55056
Tel: 612-583-2883

American Swedish Institute
2600 Park Avenue
Minneapolis, MN 55407
Tel: 612-871-4907

Anoka County/Northtown Central Library
707 Highway 10, NE
Blaine, MN 55434
Tel: 612-784-1100
Fax: 612-784-3233
TDD: 612-784-7013
URL: http://anoka.lib.mn.us/

Archdiocese of St. Paul & Minneapolis
226 Summit Avenue
St. Paul, MN 55102
Tel: 612-291-4429

Austin-Mower County Public Library
201 Second Avenue, NW
Austin, MN 55912
Tel: 507-433-2391
Fax: 507-433-8787

Bemidji State University
A.C. Clark Library
1500 Birchmont Drive, NE
Bemidji, MN 56601
Tel: 218-755-3342
Fax: 21/-755-2051
Email: library@beaver.bemidji.msus.edu
URL: http://bsuweb.bemidji.msus.edu/~library/

Bethel Theological Seminary Library/Archives
3949 Bethel Drive
St. Paul, MN 55112
Tel: 612-638-6282

Blue Earth County Historical Society/Museum
415 Cherry Street
Mankato, MN 56001
Tel: 507-345-5566
URL: http://www.ic.mankato.mn.us/reg9/bechs/
bechs1.html

Carleton College
Lawrence McKinley Gould Memorial Library
Northfield, MN 55057
Tel: 507-663-4266
Fax: 507-663-4204
URL: http://www.library.carleton.edu/

Cleveland Historical Center
303 Broadway
Cleveland, MN 56017
Tel: 507-931-2054
507-931-1510

Concordia College
Carl B. Ylvisaker Library
Moorhead, MN 56560
Tel: 218-299-4239
Email: library@cord.edu
URL: http://home.cord.edu/dept/library/

Dakota County Library
1340 Wescott Road
Eagan, MN 55123
Tel: 612-688-1500
Fax: 612-688-1515
URL: http://knidos.cc.metu.edu.tr:8002/us4/us478

Duluth Public Library
520 West Superior Street
Duluth, MN 55802
Tel: 218-723-3802
218-723-3821
Fax: 218-723-3815

Ethnic Cultural Center of Minnesota
400 Third Avenue, South
South St. Paul, MN 55075
Tel: 612-455-4449

Gustavus Adolphus College
Folke Bernadotte Memorial Library
St. Peter, MN 56082
Tel: 507-933-7572
507-933-7569
Fax: 507-933-6292
Email: folke@gac.edu
URL: http://www.gac.edu/Academics/Resources/Library

Hamline University
School of Law Library
1536 Hewitt Avenue
St. Paul, MN 55104
Tel: 612-641-2308
Fax: 612-641-2435

Henderson Public Library
110 South 6th Street
Henderson, MN 56044
Tel: 507-248-3880

Hennepin County Historical Society
Hennepin History Museum
2303 3rd Avenue, South
Minneapolis, MN 55404
Tel: 612-870-1329

Hennepin County Public Library/Southdale
7001 York Avenue
Edina, MN 55435
Tel: 612-830-4900
612-830-4933
Fax: 612-830-4976
URL: http://www.hennepin.lib.mn.us/

Heritage/Hjemkomst Interpretive Center
202 1st Avenue, North
Moorhead, MN 56560
Tel: 218-233-5604

Immigration History Research Center
University of Minnesota
826 Berry Street
St. Paul, MN 55114
Tel: 612-627-4208
Fax: 612-627-4190
Email: ihrc@gold.tc.umn.edu
URL: http://www.umn.edu/ihrc/

Iron Range Research Center
Ironworld Complex
Highway 169 West
P.O. Box 392
Chisholm, MN 55719
Tel: 218-254-3321
URL: http://www.mtn.org/mgs/othersoc.html

Kanabec History Center
West Forest Avenue
P.O. Box 113
Mora, MN 55051
Tel: 320-679-1665

Luther Seminary
Gullixson Hall
Region 3 Archives, 3rd floor
2481 Como Avenue
St. Paul, MN 55108
Tel: 612-641-3205

Mankato State University
Memorial Library
Southern Minnesota Historical Center
Maywood and Ellis
MSU #19, P.O. Box 8419
Mankato, MN 56002
Tel: 507-389-5952
507-389-5953
Fax: 507-389-5155
Email: libweb@mankato.msus.edu
URL: http://www.lib.mankato.msus.edu/

Masonic Historical Society and Museum, Minnesota
200 E. Plato Blvd.
St. Paul, MN 55107
Tel: 612-222-6051
Fax: 612-222-6144

Mayo Foundation Archives & Historical Area
200 1st Street, SW
Rochester, MN 55901
Tel: 507-282-2511 ext. 2585

Minneapolis Public Library
Minneapolis Collection
300 Nicollet Mall
Minneapolis, MN 55401
Tel: 612-372-6500 (Information)
612-372-6648 (Special Collections)
Fax: 612-372-6623
TTY: 612-372-6533
URL: http://www.mpls.lib.mn.us/

Minneapolis Regional Native American Center
1530 East Franklin Avenue
Minneapolis, MN 55404
Tel: 612-348-5600

Minnesota Alliance of Local Historical Museums
c/o Stearns County Historical Society
P.O. Box 702
St. Cloud, MN 56302

Minnesota Genealogical Society
1650 Carroll Avenue
P.O. Box 16069
St. Paul, MN 55116
Tel: 612-645-3671
URL: http://www.mtn.org/mgs/

Minnesota Historical Society
345 Kellogg Boulevard
St. Paul, MN 55102
Tel: 612-296-0332
URL: http://www.mnhs.org/index.html

Minnesota Military Museum
Box 150, Camp Riley
Little Falls, MN 56345

Minnesota State Law Library
Minnesota Judicial Center
25 Constitution Avenue
St. Paul, MN 55155-6122
Tel: 612-297-7661
612-296-2775
Fax: 612-296-6740
TDD: 612-282-5352
URL: http://www.courts.state.mn.us/library/index.html

Monastic Heritage Museum
Sisters of the Order of St. Benedict
104 Chapel Lane
St. Joseph, MN 56374
Tel: 612-363-7100

Moorhead State University
Livingston Lord Library
Northwest Minnesota Historical Center
1104 7th Avenue, South
Moorhead, MN 56563
Tel: 218-236-2346
Email: shoptaug@mhdli.moor
URL: http://www.moorhead.msus.edu/~library/index.htm

Nicollet County Historical Society
Treaty Site History Center
1851 North Minnesota Avenue
St. Peter, MN 56082
Tel: 507-931-2160
Fax: 507-931-0172
Email: nicolletco@aol.com
URL: http://tourism.st-peter.mn.us/nicollet.html

Nobles County Library & Information Center
407 12th Street
Worthington, MN 56187

Old Home Town Museum
608 5th Street
P.O. Box 593
Stephen, MN 56757
Tel: 218-478-3092

Olmsted County Historical Society
1195 County Road 22, SW
Rochester, MN 55902
Tel: 507-282-9447
Email: sweetman@millcomm.com
URL: http://www.millcomm.com/~gzimmer/ochs.html

Osakis Heritage Center
Todd County Highway 46E
P.O. Box 327
Osakis, MN 56360
Tel: 320-859-3777

Otter Tail County Genealogical Society
1110 Lincoln Avenue, West
Fergus Falls, MN 56537
Tel: 218-736-6038

Owatonna Public Library
105 N. Elm
Owatonna, MN 55060
Tel/TDD: 507-451-4660
Fax: 507-451-3909
Email: info@owatonna.lib.mn.us
URL: http://www.ic.owatonna.mn.us/lib

Polish American Cultural Institute of Minnesota
4935 Abbott Avenue, North
Minneapolis, MN 55429

Ramsey County/Roseville Public Library
2180 N. Hamline Avenue
Roseville, MN 55113
Tel: 612-631-0494
Fax: 612-631-0615
URL: http://library.usask.ca/hytelnet/us4/us479.html

Renville County Genealogical Society
211 North Main Street
P.O. Box 331
Renville, MN 56284

Rice County Historical Society
Museum and Genealogical Research Center
1814 NW 2nd Avenue
Faribault, MN 55021
Tel: 507-332-2121

Rochester Public Library
101 2nd Street, SE
Rochester, MN 55904
Tel: 507-285-8000
Email: judith@selco.lib.mn.us
URL: http://www2.isl.net/city/publi.html

St. Cloud State University
Learning Resources Services
Central Minnesota Historical Center
720 Fourth Avenue, South
St. Cloud, MN 56301
Tel: 612-255-2086
Fax: 612-255-4778
URL: http://lrs.stcloud.msus.edu/

St. John's University
Alcuin Library
Collegeville, MN 56321
Tel: 612-363-2122
Fax: 612-363-2126
URL: http://www.csbsju.edu/library/index.html

St. Olaf College
Rolvaag Memorial Library
Northfield, MN 55057
Tel: 507-646-3452 (Reference)
507-646-3229 (Archives)
URL: http://www.stolaf.edu/library/

St. Paul Public Library
90 West 4th Street
St. Paul, MN 55102
Tel: 612-292-6311
Fax: 612-292-6141
URL: http://www.stpaul.lib.mn.us/

Sandstone History and Art Center
4th and Main
P.O. Box 398
Sandstone, MN 55072
Tel: 320-245-2271

South St. Paul Public Library
106 3rd Avenue, North
South St. Paul, MN 55075
Tel: 612-451-1093
Fax: 612-451-9136

Southwest State University
Southwest Minnesota Historical Center
Marshall, MN 56258
Tel: 507-537-6176
Fax: 507-537-6200
URL: http://www.southwest.msus.edu/AcadSuppServ/hist_center

Stillwater Library
St. Croix Valley Room
216 North 4th Street
Stillwater, MN 55082

Todd County Historical Museum
333 Central Avenue
Long Prairie, MN 56347
Tel: 320-732-4426

United Methodist Church
Commission on Archives and History
122 West Franklin Avenue
Minneapolis, MN 55404
Tel: 612-339-7716

University of Minnesota/Duluth
Northeast Minnesota Historical Center
Library 375
10 University Drive
Duluth, MN 55812-2495
Tel: 218-726-8526
218-726-8100
Fax: 218-726-6205
Email: pmaus@d.umn.edu
URL: http://www.d.umn.edu/lib/collections/nemn.html

University of Minnesota/Minneapolis
Government Publications Library
409 Wilson Library
309 19th Avenue, South
Minneapolis, MN 55455
Tel: 612-624-5073
Fax: 612-626-9353
URL: http://www.lib.umn.edu/gov/

University of Minnesota/Minneapolis
Law Library
229 19th Avenue, South
Minneapolis, MN 55455
Tel: 612-625-4309
Fax: 612-625-3478
URL: http://www.umn.edu/law/library/welcome.htm

University of Minnesota/Morris
Rodney A. Briggs Library
West Central Minnesota Historical Center
600 E. 4th Street
Morris, MN 56267
Tel: 612-589-6176
Fax: 612-589-6168
URL: http://www.mrs.umn.edu/library/

University of Minnesota/St. Paul
St. Paul Campus Central Library
1984 Buford Avenue
St. Paul, MN 55108
Tel: 612-624-1212 (Reference)
Fax: 612-624-3793
URL: http://www-stplib.umn.edu/stp/

Waseca-LeSueur Regional Library
408 North State
Waseca, MN 56093
Tel/Fax: 507-835-3700

William Mitchell College of Law
Warren E. Burger Law Library
871 Summit Avenue
St. Paul, MN 55105

Tel: 612-290-6424
Fax: 612-290-6318
URL: http://www.wmitchell.edu/library/index.html

Winona State University
Maxwell Library
Sanborn and Johnson Sts.
Winona, MN 55987
Tel: 507-457-5144
Fax: 507-457-5586
Email: Refdesk@vax2.winona.msus.edu
URL: http://www.winona.msus.edu/is-f/library-f/libhome.htm

NEWSPAPER REPOSITORIES

Mankato State University
Memorial Library
Southern Minnesota Historical Center
Maywood and Ellis
MSU #19, P.O. Box 8419
Mankato, MN 56002
Tel: 507-389-5952
507-389-5953
Fax: 507-389-5155
Email: libweb@mankato.msus.edu
URL: http://www.lib.mankato.msus.edu/

Minnesota Historical Society
345 Kellogg Boulevard
St. Paul, MN 55102
Tel: 612-297-4367
Email: toni.anderson@mnhs.org
URL: http://www.mnhs.org/research/dl.htm

Moorhead State University
Livingston Lord Library
Northwest Minnesota Historical Center
1104 7th Avenue, South
Moorhead, MN 56563
Tel: 218-236-2346
Email: shoptaug@mhdli.moor
URL: http://www.moorhead.msus.edu/~library/index.htm

St. Cloud State University
Learning Resources Services
Central Minnesota Historical Center
720 Fourth Avenue, South
St. Cloud, MN 56301
Tel: 612-255-2086
Fax: 612-255-4778
URL: http://lrs.stcloud.msus.edu/

Southwest State University
Southwest Minnesota Historical Center
Marshall, MN 56258
Tel: 507-537-6176
Fax: 507-537-6200
URL: http://www.southwest.msus.edu/AcadSuppServ/hist_center

University of Minnesota/Duluth
Northeast Minnesota Historical Center
Library 375
10 University Drive
Duluth, MN 55812-2495
Tel: 218-726-8526
218-726-8100
Fax: 218-726-6205
Email: pmaus@d.umn.edu
URL: http://www.d.umn.edu/lib/collections/nemn.html

University of Minnesota/Morris
Rodney A. Briggs Library
West Central Minnesota Historical Center
600 E. 4th Street
Morris, MN 56267
Tel: 612-589-6176
Fax: 612-589-6168
URL: http://www.mrs.umn.edu/library/

Vital Records
Minnesota Department of Health
Section of Vital Statistics Registration
717 Delaware Street, SE
P.O. Box 9441
Minneapolis, MN 55440
Tel: 612-623-5121

MINNESOTA ON THE WEB

Minnesota GenWeb Project
http://www.rootsweb.com/~mngenweb/

Minnesota Historical Society
http://www.mnhs.org/index.html

Pig's Eye's Notepad—Historical Encyclopedia of St. Paul, MN 1830-1850
http://wavefront.wavefront.com/~pjlareau/pep1.html

MISSISSIPPI

ARCHIVES, STATE & NATIONAL

Mississippi Department of Archives and History
War Memorial Building
120 North State Street
P.O. Box 571
Jackson, MS 39205-0571
Tel: 601-359-6850
URL: http://www.mdah.state.ms.us/

National Archives—Southeast Region
1557 St. Joseph Avenue
East Point, GA 30344-2593
Tel: 404-763-7477
Fax: 404-763-7033
Email: archives@atlanta.nara.gov
URL: http://www.nara.gov/nara/regional/04nsgil.html

GENEALOGICAL SOCIETIES

Aberdeen Genealogical Society
c/o General Delivery
Aberdeen, MS 39730

Adams County, Genealogical Society of
P.O. Box 187
Washington, MS 39190

Alcorn County Genealogical Society
P.O. Box 1808
Corinth, MS 38835
Email: gjudkins@avsia.com

Calhoun County Historical and Genealogical Society
P.O. Box 114
Pittsboro, MS 38951
Email: thallum@teclink.htm
URL: http://home.teclink.net/~michaelc/cchgs.html

Central Mississippi, Family Research Association of
P.O. Box 13334
Jackson, MS 39236

Chickasaw County Historical & Genealogical Society
P.O. Box 42
Houston, MS 38851

Claiborne/Jefferson County Genealogical Society
P.O. Box 1017
Port Gibson, MS 39150

Columbus-Lowndes Genealogical Society
314 Seventh Street, North
Columbus, MS 39701

Dancing Rabbit Genealogical Society
c/o Carthage Leake Library
114 East Franklin Street
Carthage, MS 39051
Fax: 601-267-7874
Email: payne4@ali.intop.net
URL: http://www.rootsweb.com/~drcgs/index.html

DeSoto County, Genealogical Society of
DeSoto County Courthouse
P.O. Box 303
Hernando, MS 38632

Jackson County Genealogical Society
P.O. Box 984
Pascagoula, MS 39567
Tel: 601-841-9013

Jones County Genealogical Organization
321 Ira Odom Road
Ellisville, MS 39437

Lowndes County Genealogical Society
c/o Lowndes County Library System
314 7th Street, North
Columbus, MS 39701
Tel: 601-329-5300

Mississippi, Family Research Association
P.O. Box 13334
Jackson, MS 39236

Mississippi Coast Genealogical and Historical Society
P.O. Box 513
Biloxi, MS 39530

Mississippi Genealogical Society
P.O. Box 5301
Jackson, MS 39216-5301

Mississippi, Historical and Genealogical Association of
618 Avalon Road
Jackson, MS 39206
Tel: 601-362-3079

Northeast Mississippi Historical and Genealogical Society
P.O. Box 434
Tupelo, MS 38802-0434
Tel: 601-841-9013

Ocean Springs Genealogical Society
P.O. Box 1055
Ocean Springs, MS 39564-1055
Tel: 601-388-3071

Panola County, Historical and Genealogical Society of (Pan Gens)
c/o Betty Jo Randolph
7020 Highway 35 South

Batesville, MS 38606
URL: http://www.iocc.com/~swright/pansoc.html#PHGS

Pontotoc County Pioneers
207 North Main Street
Pontotoc, MS 38863

Skipwith Historical and Genealogical Society, Inc.
P.O. Box 1382
Oxford, MS 38655
Tel: 601-234-1074
URL: http://www.rootsweb.com/~mslafaye/books.htm

South Mississippi Genealogical Society
Southern Station
P.O. Box 15271
Hattiesburg, MS 39404
Email: CLARISE@prodigy.net
URL: http://oscar.teclink.net/~bfhenny/forrest/smgs.html

Tate County Genealogical and Historical Society
102B Robinson Street
P.O. Box 974
Senatobia, MS 38668
Tel: 601-562-0390

Tippah County Historical and Genealogical Society
308 North Commerce Street
Ripley, MS 38663
Tel: 601-837-7773

Vicksburg Genealogical Society, Inc.
P.O. Box 1161
Vicksburg, MS 39181-1161

Wayne County Genealogy Organization
c/o Patsy Brewer
712 Wayne Street
Waynesboro, MS 39367

West Chickasaw County Genealogy and Historical Society
P.O. Box 42
Houston, MS 38851

Winston County Genealogical and Historical Society
P.O. Box 428
Louisville, MS 39339

Historical Societies

Bolivar County Historical Society
1615 Terrace Road
Cleveland, MS 38732
Tel: 601-843-8204

Calhoun County Historical and Genealogical Society
P.O. Box 114
Pittsboro, MS 38951
Email: thallum@felix.teclink.htm

Hancock County Historical Society
108 Cue Street
Bay St. Louis, MS 39520
Tel: 601-467-4090
URL: http://www.gulfcoastplus.com/hancock/hancock1.htm

Itawamba County Historical Society
P.O. Box 7
Mantachie, MS 38855
Tel: 601-282-7664
Email: robfra@network-one.com
URL: http://www.network-one.com/~ithissoc/

Marshall County Historical Society
P.O. Box 806
Holly Springs, MS 38635

Mississippi Baptist Historical Society
Mississippi College Library
P.O. Box 51
Clinton, MS 39056

Mississippi Coast Genealogical and Historical Society
P.O. Box 513
Biloxi, MS 39530

Mississippi, Historical and Genealogical Association of
618 Avalon Road
Jackson, MS 39206
Tel: 601-362-3079

Mississippi Historical Society
100 South State Street
Jackson, MS 39205

Northeast Mississippi Historical and Genealogical Society
P.O. Box 434
Tupelo, MS 38801-0434
Tel: 601-841-9013

Noxubee County Historical Society
P.O. Box 392
Macon, MS 39341
URL: http://www2.netdoor.com/~rtaylor/society.htm

Panola County, Historical and Genealogical Society of (Pan Gens)
c/o Betty Jo Randolph
7020 Highway 35 South
Batesville, MS 38606
URL: http://www.iocc.com/~swright/pansoc.html#PHGS

Pearl River Historical Group
c/o Books & Things
120 Tate Street
Picayune, MS 39466
Tel: 601-795-6773
URL: http://www.gulfcoastplus.com/histsoc/pearlriv.htm

Pontotoc County Pioneers
207 North Main Street
Pontotoc, MS 38863

Rankin County Historical Society
P.O. Box 841
Brandon, MS 39042

Skipwith Historical and Genealogical Society, Inc.
P.O. Box 1382
Oxford, MS 38655
Tel: 601-234-1074
URL: http://www.rootsweb.com/~mslafaye/books.htm

Sunflower County Historical Society, Inc.
201 Cypress Drive
Indianola, MS 38751

Tate County Genealogical and Historical Society
P.O. Box 974
Senatobia, MS 38668
Tel: 601-562-0390

Tippah County Historical and Genealogical Society
308 North Commerce Street
Ripley, MS 38663
Tel: 601-837-7773

Tishomingo County Historical and Genealogical Society
P.O. Box 437
Iuka, MS 38852

Vicksburg and Warren County Historical Society
c/o Old Court House Museum
1008 Cherry Street
Vicksburg, MS 39180
Tel: 601-636-0741

Webster County Historical Society
Route 3, Box 14
Elepora, MS 39744
Tel: 601-258-6898

West Chickasaw County Genealogy and Historical Society
P.O. Box 42
Houston, MS 38851

Wilkinson County Historical Society
c/o Wilkinson County Museum
P.O. Box 1055
Woodville, MS 39669
Email: Wilkmuseum@aol.com

Winston County Genealogical and Historical Society
P.O. Box 428
Louisville, MS 39339

Woodville Civic Club
Friends of the Museum
P.O. Box 814
Woodville, MS 39669

Yalobusha County Historical Society
P.O. Box 258
Coffeeville, MS 38922

Yazoo Historical Society
332 North Main Street
P.O. Box 575
Yazoo City, MS 39194
Tel: 601-746-2273

LDS Family History Centers

Booneville Family History Center
204 George Allen Drive
Booneville, MS 38829
Tel: 601-728-9011

Clinton Family History Center
1301 Pinehaven Road
Clinton, MS 39056
Tel: 601-924-2686

Columbus Family History Center
708 Airline Road
Columbus, MS 39702
Tel: 601-328-2788

Gulfport Family History Center
11148 Klein Road
Gulfport, MS 39503
Tel: 601-832-0195

Hattiesburg Family History Center
2215 Highway 11, South
Hattiesburg, MS 39401
Tel: 601-268-3733

Archives/Libraries/Museums

Attala County Library
201 South Huntington Street
Kosciusko, MS 39090
Tel: 601-289-5141

Batesville Public Library
106 College Street
Batesville, MS 38606
Tel: 601-563-6644

Biloxi Public Library
139 Lameuse Street
P.O. Box 467
Biloxi, MS 39533
Tel: 601-374-0330

Bolivar/Robinson-Carpenter Memorial Library
401 S. Court Street
Cleveland, MS 38732
Tel: 601-843-2774

Carnegie Public Library
114 Delta Avenue
Clarksdale, MS 38614
Tel: 601-624-4461

Carthage Leake Library
114 East Franklin Street
Carthage, MS 39051
Tel: 601-267-7821

Center for the Study of Southern Culture
University of Mississippi
University, MS 38677
Tel: 601-232-5993
Fax: 601-232-5814
URL: http://imp.cssc.olemiss.edu/

Columbus Public Library
314 North 7th Street
Columbus, MS 39701
Tel: 601-329-5300

Corinth/Northeast Regional Library
1023 N. Fillmore Street
Corinth, MS 38834
Tel: 601-287-2441

DeKalb Library
P.O. Box 710
DeKalb, MS 39328
URL: http://www.rootsweb.com/~mskemper/library.html

Evans Memorial Library
105 N. Long Street
Aberdeen, MS 39730
Tel: 601-369-4601

Forrest Library
723 N. Main Street
Hattiesburg, MS 39401
Tel: 601-582-4461

Greenville/Percy Memorial Library
341 Main Street
Greenville, MS 38701
Tel: 601-335-2331

Greenwood/Leflore Public Library
405 W. Washington Street
Greenwood, MS 38930
Tel: 601-453-3634

Gulfport Public Library
130 21st Avenue
P.O. Box 4018
Gulfport, MS 39501
Tel: 601-863-6411

Harriet Person Memorial Library
1005 College Street
P.O. Box 1017
Port Gibson, MS 39150
Tel: 601-437-5202

Historical Trails Library
Route 1, Box 373
Philadelphia, MS 39350
Tel: 601-656-3506

Iuka Library
204 North Main Street
Iuka, MS 38852
Tel: 601-423-6300

Jefferson County Public Library
428 North Main
Fayette, MS 39069
Tel: 601-786-3982

Jennie Stephens Smith Library
Court Avenue & Main Street
P.O. Box 846
New Albany, MS 38652

Judge George W. Armstrong Library
220 Commerce Street
Natchez, MS 39120
Tel: 601-445-8862

Lauderdale County, Dept. of Archives and History
Courthouse Annex
P.O. Box 5511
Meridian, MS 39302

Laurel/Jones County Library
503 Commerce Street
Laurel, MS 39440
Tel: 601-428-4313

Lauren Rogers Memorial Library/Museum
5th and 7th Streets
P.O. Box 1108
Laurel, MS 39440

Lee County Library
219 North Madison
Tupelo, MS 38801
Tel: 601-841-9029

Lincoln Public Library
100 S. Jackson Street
Brookhaven, MS 39601
Tel: 601-833-3369

Lowndes County Library System
314 7th Street, North
Columbus, MS 39701
Tel: 601-329-5300

Marks/Quitman County Library
315 East Main
Marks, MS 38646
Tel: 601-326-7141

McComb Public Library
114 State Street
McComb, MS 39648
Tel: 601-684-2661

Meridian Public Library
2517 7th Street
Meridian, MS 39301
Tel: 601-693-6771

Mississippi State University
Mitchell Memorial Library/Special Collections
Starkville, MS 39759
Tel: 601-325-7679
Email: lmueller@library.MsState.edu
or blove@library.MsState.edu
URL: http://www.msstate.edu/Library/spcoll.html

Noxubee County Library
103 King Street
Macon, MS 39341

Oxford/Lafayette County Public Library
401 Bramlett Boulevard
Oxford, MS 38655
Tel: 601-234-5751

Pascagoula Public Library
3214 Pascagoula Street
Pascagoula, MS 39567
Tel: 601-769-3000

Philadelphia/Neshoba County Library
230 Beacon Street
Philadelphia, MS 39350
Tel: 601-656-4911

Ripley Public Library
308 North Commerce
Ripley, MS 38663
Tel: 601-837-7773

Starkville/Oktibbeha County Public Library
326 University Drive
P.O. Box 1406
Starkville, MS 39759
Tel: 601-323-2766
Fax: 601-323-9140
Email: starkvillelib@hotmail.com
URL: http://www.chamber.starkville.ms.us/library/index.html

Sunflower County Library
201 Cypress Drive
Indianola, MS 38751
Tel: 601-887-2298
Fax: 601-887-2153

Union County Library
219 King Street
P.O. Box 846
New Albany, MS 38652
Tel: 601-534-1991

Union Public Library
101 Peachtree
Union, MS 39365
Tel: 601-774-8597

University of Mississippi
John Davis Williams Library
Department of Archives and Special Collections
University, MS 38677
Tel: 601-234-6091
Fax: 601-234-6381
Email: libweb@www.olemiss.edu
URL: http://sunset.backbone.olemiss.edu/depts/general_library/files/archhome.htm

University of Southern Mississippi
McCain Library
Southern Station, Box 5148
Hattiesburg, MS 39406
Tel: 601-266-4347
601-266-4345
URL: http://www.lib.usm.edu/mccain.html

Vicksburg/Warren Public Library
700 Veto Street
P.O. Box 511
Vicksburg, MS 39181-0511
Tel: 601-636-6411

William Carey College
L.W. Anderson Genealogical Library
P.O. Box 1647
Gulfport, MS 39502
Tel: 601-865-1554

Newspaper Repositories

Mississippi Department of Archives and History
War Memorial Building
120 North State Street
P.O. Box 571
Jackson, MS 39205-0571
Tel: 601-359-6850
Email: hth@mdah.state.ms.us

Vital Records

State Department of Health
Vital Records
2423 North State Street
Jackson, MS 39216
Tel: 601-960-7981

Mississippi on the Web

Christine's Genealogy Website
http://www.concentric.net/~ccharity/

Dayna's Southern Genealogy Page
http://home.texoma.net/~mmcmullen/welcome.html

Mississippi Civil War History Sources
http://home.teclink.net/~moorerga/cw/list-hx.html

Mississippi GenWeb Project
http://www.insolwwb.net/~rholler/ms/

Southern Roots
http://www.gower.net/bclayton/index.html

Traveller Southern Families
http://genealogy.traveller.com/genealogy/

Missouri

Archives, State & National

Missouri State Archives
600 West Main Street
P.O. Box 778
Jefferson City, MO 65102
Tel: 314-751-3280
Email: archref@mail.sos.state.mo.us
URL: http://mosl.sos.state.mo.us/arch.html

National Archives—Central Plains Region
2312 East Bannister Road
Kansas City, MO 64131
Tel: 816-926-6272
Fax: 816-926-6982
Email: archives@kansascity.nara.gov
URL: http://www.nara.gov/nara/regional/06nsgil.html

Genealogical Societies

Afro-American Historical and Genealogical Society (AAHGS)
Landon Creek
P.O. Box 23804
St. Louis, MO 63121-0804

Afro-American Historical and Genealogical Society (AAHGS)
Magic
3700 Blue Parkway
Kansas City, MO 64130

American Family Records Association
P.O. Box 15505
Kansas City, MO 64106
URL: http://www.fgs.org/~fgs/soc0008.htm

Audrain County Area Genealogical Society
c/o Mexico/Audrain County Public Library
305 West Jackson Street
Mexico, MO 65265

Barry County Genealogical Society
P.O. Box 291
Cassville, MO 65625
URL: http://www.rootsweb.com/~mobarry/society.html

Butler County, Genealogical Society of
P.O. Box 426
Poplar Bluff, MO 63901

Campbell Area Genealogical and Historical Society
P.O. Box 401
Campbell, MO 63933-0401

Cape Girardeau County Genealogical Society
c/o Riverside Regional Library
204 South Union Avenue
P.O. Box 389
Jackson, MO 63755
Email: GTPD45B@prodigy.com
URL: http://www.rosecity.net/genealog.html

Carthage Genealogical Society
Southwest Missouri Genealogical Library
Route 3, Box 117
Carthage, MO 64836
Tel: 417-358-6494

Central Missouri, Genealogical Society of
3801 Ponderosa Drive
P.O. Box 26
Columbia, MO 65205
Tel: 573-443-8936
Email: KTEH59A@prodigy.com
URL: http://www.coin.missouri.edu/community/genealogy/cent-mo/

Dade County Genealogical Society
P.O. Box 155
Greenfield, MO 65661

Daughters of Old Westport
8124 Pennsylvania Lane
Kansas City, MO 64114

Douglas County Historical and Genealogical Society
P.O. Box 986
Ava, MO 65608

Dunklin County Genealogical Society
c/o Dunklin County Library
226 N. Main
Kennett, MO 63857

Excelsior Springs Genealogical Society
1000 Magnolia West
Excelsior, MO 64024

Family Tree Climbers
P.O. Box 422
Lawson, MO 64062

Genealogy Friends of the Library
507 W. Hickory
P.O. Box 314
Neosho, MO 64850

Gentry County Genealogical Society
802 E. Canady
Albany, MO 64402

Grundy County Genealogical Society
P.O. Box 223
Trenton, MO 64683

Harrison County Genealogical Society
2243 Central Street
P.O. Box 65
Bethany, MO 64424

Heart of America Genealogical Society
c/o Kansas City Public Library, Valley Room
311 East 12th Street
Kansas City, MO 64106

Howard County Genealogical Society
206 North Linn Avenue, Rte. 1
Fayette, MO 65248
Tel: 816-248-3247

Jackson County Genealogical Society
P.O. Box 2145
Independence, MO 64055

Jefferson County Genealogical Society
c/o Jefferson County Library
3033 High Ridge Blvd.
High Ridge, MO 63049
Tel: 314-677-8186
Email: wyz004@mail.connect.more.net
or cosmergen@ninenet.com
URL: http://www.rootsweb.com/~mojcgs/jcgsinde.htm

Jewish Genealogical Society of St. Louis (JGSSTL)
c/o United Hebrew Congregation
One Gudder Campus
13788 Conway Road
Creve Coeur, MO 63141
Email: letvak@aol.com
URL: http://www.stlcyberjew.com/jgs-stl/

Joplin Genealogical Society
P.O. Box 152
Joplin, MO 64802
Tel: 417-623-7953

Laclede County Genealogical Society
P.O. Box 350
Lebanon, MO 65536

Lincoln County Genealogical Society
P.O. Box 192
Hawk Point, MO 63349
Tel: 573-338-4639

Linn County Genealogy Researchers
771 Tomahawk
Brookfield, MO 64628

Livingston County Genealogical Society
409 Clay Street
Chillicothe, MO 64601

Mid-Missouri Genealogical Society
P.O. Box 715
Jefferson, MO 65102

Mississippi County Genealogical Society
P.O. Box 5
Charleston, MO 63834

Missouri State Genealogical Association
P.O. Box 833
Columbia, MO 65205-0833
URL: http://www.umr.edu/~mstauter/mosga/

Native Sons of Kansas City
P.O. Box 10046
Kansas City, MO 64113

Newton County Historical Society/Genealogy Study Group
P.O. Box 675
Neosho, MO 64850

Nodaway County Genealogical Society
P.O. Box 214
Maryville, MO 64468

Northeast Missouri Genealogical Society
c/o Jean Purvines
614 Clark Street
Canton, MO 63435

Northwest Missouri Genealogical Society
Buchanan County Research Center
412 Felix Street
P.O. Box 382
St. Joseph, MO 64502
Tel: 816-233-0524
URL: http://www.smartnet.net/~stjoed/nwmgs.html

Oregon County Genealogical Society
Courthouse
Alton, MO 65606

Ozarks Genealogical Society/Library
534 West Catalpa
P.O. Box 3945 G.S.
Springfield, MO 65808
Tel: 417-831-2773
URL: http://www.orion.org/community/history/ogs/libogs.htm

Phelps County Genealogical Society
P.O. Box 571
Rolla, MO 65402
Tel: 573-364-5977
URL: http://www.umr.edu/~whmcinfo/pcgs/

Pike County Genealogical Society
P.O. Box 364
Bowling Green, MO 63334

Platte County Genealogical Society
P.O. Box 103
Platte City, MO 64079

Pulaski County, Genealogy Society of
P.O. Box 226
Crocker, MO 65452

Ray County Genealogical Association
901 W. Royle Street
Richmond, MO 64085

Reynolds County Genealogy and Historical Society
P.O. Box 281
Ellington, MO 63638

Ripley County Historical and Genealogical Society
101 Washington Street
Doniphan, MO 63935

St. Charles County Genealogical Society
Historic Courthouse
Third and Jefferson, Room 106
P.O. Box 715
St. Charles, MO 63302-0715
Tel: 314-947-1762

St. Louis Genealogical Society
9011 Manchester Road, Ste. 3
St. Louis, MO 63144
URL: http://library.wustl.edu/~spec/archives/aslaaa/genealogical.html

Santa Fe Trail Researchers Genealogical Society
c/o Karen Boggs
Route 1, Box 84
Franklin, MO 65250
Tel: 816-848-2962

Seeking 'n Searching Ancestors
c/o Peggy Smith Hake
Route 1, Box 52
St. Elizabeth, MO 65075

South-Central Missouri Genealogical Society
939 Nichols Drive
West Plains, MO 65775

South Vernon Genealogical Society
c/o Wilma Lathrop
Route 2, Box 280
Sheldon, MO 64784

Southwest Missouri Genealogical Society
c/o Carthage Public Library
Seventh and Garrison Streets
Carthage, MO 64836

Texas County Genealogical and Historical Society
P.O. Box 12
Houston, MO 65483
Tel: 417-967-2946

Thrailkill Genealogical Society
2018 Gentry Street
North Kansas City, MO 64116

Vernon County Genealogical Society
c/o Nevada Public Library
225 West Austin
Nevada, MO 64772

Warren County Genealogical Society
c/o Dorris Keeven
401 Oak Drive
Warrenton, MO 63383

Webb City Area Genealogical Society
101 South Liberty Street
Webb City, MO 64870

West Central Missouri Genealogical Society/Library
705 Broad
Warrensburg, MO 64093

Wright County Historical and Genealogical Society
P.O. Box 66
Hartville, MO 65667
Tel: 417-741-6265

HISTORICAL SOCIETIES

Adair County Historical Society/Library
308 South Franklin Street
Kirksville, MO 63501

African Historical Society
P.O. Box 4964
St. Louis, MO 63106

Afro-American Historical and Genealogical Society (AAHGS)
Landon Creek
P.O. Box 23804
St. Louis, MO 63121-0804

Afro-American Historical and Genealogical Society (AAHGS)
Magic
3700 Blue Parkway
Kansas City, MO 64130

Andrew County Historical Society
P.O. Box 12
Savannah, MO 64485

Ash Grove Historical Society
606 West Boone
Ash Grove, MO 65604
Tel: 417-672-2025

Audrain County Historical Society
P.O. Box 3
Mexico, MO 65265

Augusta Historical Society
498 Schell Road
Augusta, MO 63332
Tel: 314-228-4821

Boone County Historical Society/Museum
Wilson-Huff History and Genealogical Library
3801 Ponderosa Drive (Nifong Park)
Columbia, MO 65201
Tel: 573-443-8936
URL: http://www.coin.missouri.edu/community/genealogy/cent-mo/boco-mus.html
or http://www.synapse.com/bocomogenweb/GSCMLIB.HTM

Boone-Duden Historical Society
3565 Mill Street
P.O. Box 82
New Melle, MO 63365
Tel: 314-828-5887
Email: 314-828-5887
URL: http://norn.org/pub/other_orgs/bdhissoc/

Boonslick Historical Society of Cooper and Howard Counties
811 7th Street Terrace
P.O. Box 324
Booneville, MO 65233
Tel: 816-882-6370

Campbell Area Genealogical and Historical Society
P.O. Box 401
Campbell, MO 63933-0401

Cass County Historical Society
400 East Mechanic
P.O. Box 406
Harrisonville, MO 64701

Centralia Historical Society, Inc.
319 East Sneed
Centralia, MO 65240
Tel: 573-682-5711

Chariton County Historical Society
402 E. 6th
Salisbury, MO 65281

Clay County Historical Society/Museum
14 North Main Street
Liberty, MO 64068
Tel: 816-792-1849

Cole County Historical Society/Museum
109 Madison Street
Jefferson City, MO 65101
Tel: 573-635-1850

Cooper County Historical Society
5236 Highway A
Bunceton, MO 65237
Email: cchs@solar.sky.net

Dallas County Historical Society
P.O. Box 594
Buffalo, MO 65622
URL: http://www.smsu.edu/contrib/bms/county/dallas.htm#SOCIETY

DeKalb County Historical Society
P.O. Box 477
Maysville, MO 64469

Douglas County Historical and Genealogical Society
P.O. Box 986
Ava, MO 65608

Florissant Valley Historical Society
Taille de Noyer
P.O. Box 298
Florissant, MO 63032
Tel: 314-524-1100

Foristell Area Historical Society
626 Ball Street
Wentzville, MO 63385
Tel: 314-327-8234

Franklin County Historical Society
P.O. Box 352
Washington, MO 63090
Tel: 573-239-5426

Friends of Florida
Route 1
Stoutsville, MO 65283
Tel: 573-672-3330

Friends of Historic Boonville
614 E. Morgan
P.O. Box 1776
Boonville, MO 65233
Tel: 816-882-7977

Friends of Keytesville, Inc.
408 Bridge Street
Keytesville, MO 65261

Friends of the Neosho Library, Genealogy
P.O. Box 314
Neosho, MO 64850

Friends of Rocheport
P.O. Box 122
Rocheport, MO 65279
Tel: 573-698-2129

Glascow Area Historical and Preservation Society
100 Market
Glascow, MO 65254
Tel: 816-338-2377

Graham Historical Society
417 South Walnut
Marysville, MO 64468

Green County Missouri Historical Society
P.O. Box 3466 G.S.
Springfield, MO 65808
Tel: 417-881-6147
Email: gsociety@mail.orion.org
URL: http://www.rootsweb.com/~gcmohs/

Henry County Historical Society/Genealogy Library
203 West Franklin Street
P.O. Box 65
Clinton, MO 64735
Tel: 816-885-8414

Heritage League of Greater Kansas City
Newcomb Hall
5100 Rockhill Road
Kansas City, MO 64110

Higbee Area Historical Society
P.O. Box 38
Higbee, MO 65257

Huntsville Historical Society
107 North Main
Huntsville, MO 65259

Iron County Historical Society
123 West Wayne
Irontown, MO 63650

Johnson County Historical Society
Heritage Library
300 North Main
Warrensburg, MO 64093
Tel: 816-747-6480

Kimmswick Historical Society
P.O. Box 41
Kimmswick, MO 63053

Kingdon of Callaway Historical Society
331 West 7th Street
P.O. Box 6073
Fulton, MO 65251

Lawrence County Historical Society
P.O. Box 406
Mt. Vernon, MO 65712

Lewis County Historical Society, Inc.
614 Clark Street
Canton, MO 63435

Lincoln County Historical Society
Court and Collier Streets
P.O. Box 29
Troy, MO 63370

Macon County Historical Society
120 Bennett Avenue
Macon, MO 63552
Tel: 816-385-2826

Madison County Historic Society
HCR 78, Box 427
Fredericktown, MO 63645

Maries County, Historical Society of
P.O. Box 289
Vienna, MO 65582

Missouri Historical Society
Jefferson Memorial Building
225 S. Skinker
P.O. Box 11940
St. Louis, MO 63112
Tel: 313-746-4510
URL: http://library.wustl.edu/~spec/archives/aslaa/mo-hist-archives.html

Missouri Methodist Historical Society
c/o C.W. Orvall
10516 E. 35th Terrace
Independence, MO 64052
URL: http://cmc2.cmc.edu/soc.html

Missouri Pacific Historical Society
Museum of Transportation
3015 Barrett Station
St. Louis, MO 63122
Tel: 314-937-7941
314-234-8622
URL: http://library.wustl.edu/~spec/archives/aslaa/mopac-historical.html

Missouri State Historical Society
Ellis Library Building
1020 Lowry Street
Columbia, MO 65201
Tel: 573-882-7083
Fax: 573-882-4950
Email: shsofmo@ext.missouri.edu
URL: http://www.system.missouri.edu/shs/

Missouri Territorial Pioneers
3929 Milton Drive
Independence, MO 64055

Moniteau County Historical Society
P.O. Box 263
California, MO 65018

Montgomery County Historical Society/Museum
112 West Second Street
Montgomery City, MO 63361

Morgan County Historical Society
P.O. Box 177
Versailles, MO 65084

Newton County Historical Society
P.O. Box 675
Neosho, MO 64850

Northern Cherokee Nation
P.O. Box 1121
Independence, MO 64051

O'Fallon Historical Society
Civic Park Drive
O'Fallon, MO 63366

Old Mines Area Historical Society
Route 1, Box 300Z
Cadet, MO 63630

Osage County Historical Society
402 East Main Street
P.O. Box 402
Linn, MO 65051
Tel: 573-897-2932

Perry County Historical Society
P.O. Box 97
Perryville, MO 63775

Phelps County Historical Society
Dillon Log Cabin/Phelps County Museum
302 Third Street
P.O. Box 1535
Rolla, MO 65402
Tel: 573-364-5977
URL: http://www.umr.edu/~whmcinfo/pchs/

Randolph County Historical Society
P.O. Box 116
Moberly, MO 65270

Ray County Historical Society
P.O. Box 2
Richmond, MO 64085

Reynolds County Genealogy and Historical Society
P.O. Box 281
Ellington, MO 63638

Ripley County Historical and Genealogical Society/Library
Current River Heritage Museum
101 Washington Street
Doniphan, MO 63935

St. Charles Historical Society/Archives
101 South Main St.
St. Charles, MO 63301
Tel: 314-946-9828
URL: http://library.wustl.edu/~spec/archives/aslaa/stcharles-historical.html

Saline County Historical Society
P.O. Box 4028
Marshall, MO 65340
Tel: 816-886-8013

Scotland County Historical Society
P.O. Box 263
Memphis, MO 63555

South Howard County Historical Society
P.O. Box 13
New Franklin, MO 65274

Stone County Historical Society
P.O. Box 63
Galena, MO 65656

Texas County Genealogical and Historical Society
P.O. Box 12
Houston, MO 65483

Union Cemetery Historical Society
2727 Main Street, Suite 120
Kansas City, MO 64108

Vernon County Historical Society
231 North Main Street
Nevada, MO 64772

Warren County Historical Society/Museum and History Library
Walton and Market St.
P.O. Box 12
Warrenton, MO 63383
Tel: 573-456-3820

Washington Historical Society
314 West Main Street
P.O. Box 146
Washington, MO 63090
Tel: 573-239-0280

Wentzville Community Historical Society/Archives
506 South Lynn Avenue
P.O. Box 122
Wentzville, MO 63385

White River Valley Historical Society
P.O. Box 565
Point Lookout, MO 65726

Wright County Historical and Genealogical Society
P.O. Box 66
Hartville, MO 65667
Tel: 417-741-6265

LDS Family History Centers

Cape Girardeau Family History Center
1048 West Cape Rock Drive
Cape Girardeau, MO 63701
Tel: 314-334-9298

Columbia Stake Family History Center
904 Old Highway 63
Columbia, MO 65203
Tel: 573-443-2048
URL: http://www.synapse.com/bocomgenweb/LDSFHC.HTM

Farmington Family History Center
709 South Henry Street
Farmington, MO 63640
Tel: 314-756-6521

Frontenac Family History Center
10445 Clayton Road
St. Louis, MO 63131
Tel: 314-993-2328

Hazelwood Family History Center
6386 Howdershell Road
Hazelwood, MO 63042
Tel: 314-731-5373

Independence Family History Center
705 West Walnut
Independence, MO 64050
Tel: 816-461-0245

Joplin Family History Center
22nd and Indiana
Joplin, MO 64801
Tel: 417-623-6506

Kansas City Family History Center
13025 Wornall Road
Kansas City, MO 64145
Tel: 816-941-7389

Liberty Family History Center
1130 Clayview Drive
Liberty, MO 64068
Tel: 816-781-8295

Monett Family History Center
South Highway 37
Monett, MO 65708
Tel: 417-235-5147

Nevada Family History Center
1101 North Olive
Nevada, MO 64772
Tel: 417-667-2781

Springfield Family History Center
1357 South Ingram Mill Road
Springfield, MO 65804
Tel: 417-887-8229

St. Joseph Family History Center
#7 North Carriage Drive
St. Joseph, MO 64506
Tel: 816-232-2428

ARCHIVES/LIBRARIES/MUSEUMS

Adair County Historical Society/Library
308 South Franklin Street
Kirksville, MO 63501

Adair County Public Library
One Library Lane
Kirksville, MO 63501
Tel: 816-665-6038
Fax: 816-627-0028
URL: http://www.nemostate.edu/kirksville/library.html

Barry County/Cassville Branch Library
1007 Main Street
Cassville, MO 65625
Tel: 417-847-2121

Boone County Historical Society/Museum
Wilson-Huff History and Genealogical Library
3801 Ponderosa Drive
Columbia, MO 65201
URL: http://www.coin.missouri.edu/community/genealogy/cent-mo/boco-mus.html

Boonslick Regional Library
219 West 3rd Street
Sedalia, MO 65301
Tel: 816-827-7111
816-827-6195

Callaway County Public Library
712 Court Street
Fulton, MO 65251-1992
Tel: 573-642-7261
TDD: 573-642-0662
URL: http://gopher.coin.missouri.edu/library/dbrl/ccpl.htm

Central Missouri, Genealogical Society of
3801 Ponderosa Drive
P.O. Box 26
Columbia, MO 65205
Tel: 573-443-8936
Email: KTEH59A@prodigy.com
or rtaylor@mail.coin.missouri.edu
URL: http://www.coin.missouri.edu/community/genealogy/cent-mo/

Clay County Archives and Historical Library
210 East Franklin Street
P.O. Box 99
Liberty, MO 64068
Tel: 816-781-3611

Clay County Museum/Library
14 North Main Street
Liberty, MO 64068
Tel: 816-781-8062

Cole County Historical Society/Museum
109 Madison Street
Jefferson City, MO 65101
Tel: 573-635-1850

Concordia Historical Institute
301 DeMun Avenue
St. Louis, MO 63105

Dallas County Library
219 W. Main
Buffalo, MO 65622
Tel: 417-345-2667

Daniel Boone Regional Library
100 W. Broadway
Columbia, MO 65201
Tel: 573-443-3161

Doniphan/Ripley County Public Library
207 Locust Street
Doniphan, MO 63935
Tel: 573-996-2616

Dunklin County Library
226 N. Main
Kennett, MO 63857
Tel: 573-888-3561
Fax: 573-888-6393
URL: http://dunklin-co.lib.mo.us/index.html

Frenchtown Museum
1400 North Second Street
St. Charles, MO 63301
Tel: 314-946-2865
URL: http://home.stlnet.com/~tgodwin/vinson.html

Garst Memorial Library
219 West Jackson Street
Marshfield, MO 65706
Tel: 417-468-3335

Henry County Historical Society/Genealogy Library
203 West Franklin Street
P.O. Box 65
Clinton, MO 64735
Tel: 816-885-8414

Heritage Library
300 North Main
Warrensburg, MO 64093
Tel: 816-747-6480

Jefferson County Library
3033 High Ridge Blvd.
High Ridge, MO 63049

Johnson County Historical Society
Heritage Library
300 North Main
Warrensburg, MO 64093
Tel: 816-747-6480

Joplin Public Library
300 S. Main Street
Joplin, MO 64801
Tel: 417-624-5465
417-623-7953
Fax: 417-624-5217

Kansas City Public Library
Local History Research/Special Collections
311 East 12th Street
Kansas City, MO 64106
Tel: 816-221-2698
URL: http://www.kcpl.lib.mo.us/sc/default.htm

Keytesville Library
406 W. Bridge Street
Keytesville, MO 65261
Tel: 816-288-3204

Livingston County Library
450 Locust
Chillicothe, MO 64601
Tel: 816-646-0547
Fax: 816-646-5504
Email: ugy001@mail.connect.more.net
URL: http://vax2.rain.gen.mo.us/~lclibrary/index.html

Maryville Public Library
Genealogy Division
509 N. Main
Maryville, MO 64468
Tel: 816-582-5281

Mercer County Library
601 Grant
Princeton, MO 64673
Tel: 816-748-3725

Mexico/Audrain County Public Library
Audrain County Area Genealogical Society Section
305 West Jackson Street
Mexico, MO 65265
Tel: 573-581-4939
Fax: 573-581-7510
URL: http://www.llion.org/maain/library.html

Mid-Continent Public Library
Genealogy and Local History Department
317 West 24 Highway
Independence, MO 64050
Tel: 816-252-0950
Email: ge@mcpl.lib.mo.us
URL: http://www.mcpl.lib.mo.us/gen.htm

Missouri State Library
600 West Main Street
Jefferson City, MO 65101
Tel: 573-751-3615
URL: http://mosl.sos.state.mo.us/libserv.html

Montgomery County Historical Society/Museum
112 West Second Street
Montgomery City, MO 63361

Neosho City/County Library
403 South Jefferson
Neosho, MO 64850
Tel: 417-451-4231

Newton County Museum/Library
121 N. Washington
P.O. Box 675
Neosho, MO 64850
Tel: 417-451-4940

Northwest Missouri Genealogical Society
Buchanan County Research Center
412 Felix Street
P.O. Box 382
St. Joseph, MO 64502
Tel: 816-233-0524
URL: http://www.smartnet.net/~stjoed/nwmgs.html

Ozarks Genealogical Society/Library
634 West Catalpa
P.O. Box 3945 G.S.
Springfield, MO 65808
URL: http://www.orion.org/community/history/ogs/libogs.htm

Phelps County Archives
Phelps County Courthouse, Room 315
200 North Main
Rolla, MO 65401
Tel: 573-364-1891

Phelps County Historical Society
Dillon Log Cabin/Phelps County Museum
302 Third Street
P.O. Box 1535
Rolla, MO 65402
Tel: 573-364-5977
URL: http://www.umr.edu/~whmcinfo/pchs/

Putnam County Library
115 South 16th Street
P.O. Box 305
Unionville, MO 63565
Tel: 816-947-3192

Richland Library
P.O. Box 340
Richland, MO 65556
Tel: 573-765-3642

Ripley County Historical and Genealogical Society/Library
Current River Heritage Museum
101 Washington Street
Doniphan, MO 63935

Riverside Regional Library
204 South Union Avenue
P.O. Box 389
Jackson, MO 63755
Tel: 573-243-8141
URL: http://www.showme.net/rrl/home2.html

St. Charles County Genealogical Society
Historic Courthouse
Third and Jefferson, Room 106
P.O. Box 715
St. Charles, MO 63302-0715
Tel: 314-947-1762

St. Charles Historical Society/Archives
101 South Main St.
St. Charles, MO 63301
Tel: 314-946-9828
URL: http://library.wustl.edu/~spec/archives/aslaa/stcharles-historical.html

St. Charles Library/Kathryn Linneman Branch
2323 Elm Street
St. Charles, MO 63301
Tel: 314-723-0232
314-946-6294
Email: aking01@mail.win.org
URL: http://www.win.org/library/services/lhgen/cinmenu.htm

St. Joseph Museum/Library
1100 Charles Street
St. Joseph, MO 64501
Tel: 816-232-8471
Fax: 816-232-8482

St. Louis Public Library
1301 Olive Street
St. Louis, MO 63103
Tel: 314-241-2288
Fax: 314-539-0393
TDD: 314-539-0364
Email: webmaster@slpl.lib.mo.us
URL: http://www.slpl.lib.mo.us/

Scenic Regional Library/New Haven Branch
901 Maupin
New Haven, MO 63068
Tel: 573-237-2189

Shelbina/Carnegie Public Library
102 North Center Street
P.O. Box 247
Shelbina, MO 63468
Tel: 573-588-2271

Southeast Missouri State College
Kent Library
1 University Plaza
Cape Girardeau, MO 63701
Tel: 573-651-2235
Fax: 573-651-5103

Southwest Missouri Genealogical Library
Route 3, Box 117
Carthage, MO 64836
Tel: 417-358-6494

Southwest Missouri State University
Meyer Library/Lena Wills Collection
901 S. National
Springfield, MO 65804
Tel: 417-836-4535 (Reference/Information)
417-836-4532 (Govt. Documents)
Fax: 417-836-6799
TDD: 417-836-6794
URL: http://www.smsu.edu/contrib/library/library.html

Springfield Public Library
Shepard Room
397 East Central Street
Springfield, MO 65802
Tel: 417-837-5000
417-869-0320
URL: http://www.orion.org/library/sgcl/

Stephens Museum
Central Methodist College
Fayette, MO 65248
Tel: 816-248-3391

Summers Memorial Library
Missouri Room
135 Harwood
Lebanon, MO 65536
Tel: 417-532-2148

Fax: 417-532-7424
Email: mkinion@mail.llion.org
URL: http://www.llion.org/library/gen.html

University City Library
6701 Delmar Blvd.
University City, MO 63130
Tel: 314-968-2763

University of Missouri/Columbia
Western Historical Manuscript Collection
23 Ellis Library
Columbia, MO 65201
Tel: 573-882-6028
Fax: 573-884-4950
Email: whmc@ext.missouri.edu
URL: http://www.system.missouri.edu/whmc/

University of Missouri/Kansas City
Western Historical Manuscript Collection
302 Newcomb Hall
5100 Rockhill Road
Kansas City, MO 64110
Tel: 816-235-1543
Email: WHMCKC@smtpgate.umkc.edu
URL: http://cctr.umkc.edu/www/w3/dept/whmckc/homepage.html

University of Missouri/Rolla
Western Historical Manuscript Collection
Curtis Laws Wilson Library
1870 Miner Circle
Rolla, MO 65409-0060
Tel: 573-341-4874
Email: whmcinfo@umr.edu
URL: http://www.umr.edu/whmcinfo/

University of Missouri/St. Louis
Western Historical Manuscript Collection
Thomas Jefferson Library, Room 221
8001 Natural Bridge Road
St. Louis, MO 63121
Tel: 314-516-6034 (Information)
314-516-5060 (Reference)
Fax: 314-516-5853
TDD: 314-516-5212
Email: silvest@umslvma.umsl.edu
URL: http://www.umsl.edu/~whmc/

Warren County Historical Society/Museum and History Library
Walton and Market St.
P.O. Box 12
Warrenton, MO 63383
Tel: 573-456-3820

Waynesville Library
306 Route 66
Waynesville, MO 65583
Tel: 573-774-2965
Fax: 573-774-2965

Westminster College
Winston Churchill Memorial Library
501 Westminster
Fulton, MO 65251
Tel: 573-642-3361
573-642-6648

Wright County Library
Courthouse
Main Street
P.O. Box 70
Hartville, MO 65667
Tel: 417-741-7595

Newspaper Repositories

State Historical Society of Missouri
1020 Lowry Street
Columbia, MO 65201
Tel: 573-882-7083
Fax: 573-882-4950
Email: shsofmo@ext.missouri.edu
URL: http://www.system.missouri.edu/shs/

Vital Records

Missouri Department of Health
Bureau of Vital Records
930 Wildwood
P.O. Box 570
Jefferson, MO 65102
Tel: 573-751-6400
URL: http://www.health.state.mo.us/cgi-bin/uncgi/BirthAndDeathRecords

University of Missouri/Kansas City
5100 Rockhill Road
Kansas City, MO 64110
Tel: 816-235-1531
Email: sheldont@smtpgate.umkc.edu
URL: http://www.umkc.edu/lib/collec.html#other

Missouri on the Web

Anne Hood's Missouri Page
http://home.sprynet.com/sprynet/Hood/missouri.htm

COIN Genealogy Center
http://www.coin.missouri.edu/community/genealogy/

Directory of Archives and Manuscript Repositories in the St. Louis Area
http://library.wustl.edu/~spec/archives/aslaa/intro.html

Missouri GenWeb Project
http://www.rootsweb.com/~mogenweb/mo.htm

Missouri Maps and Vital Records Requisition Forms (zip files)
http://www.cchat.com/cupido/records.htm

Missouri Pioneers
http://www.rootsweb.com/~mopionee/

Osage County Missouri Genealogy Resources
http://www.mindspring.com/~mgentges/

MONTANA

ARCHIVES, STATE & NATIONAL

Montana State Archives
Montana Historical Society
Memorial Building
225 Roberts Street
P.O. Box 201201
Helena, MT 59601
Tel: 800-243-9900
406-444-4774/5
Fax: 406-444-2696
URL: http://www.his.mt.gov/

National Archives—Rocky Mountain Region
Denver Federal Center, Building 48
P.O. Box 25307
Denver, CO 80225
Tel: 303-236-0817
Fax: 303-236-9354
Email: archives@denver.nara.gov
URL: http://www.nara.gov/nara/regional/08nsgil.html

GENEALOGICAL SOCIETIES

Beaver-Head-Hunters Genealogical Society
c/o Beaverhead County Museum
15-25 South Montana
P.O. Box 830
Dillon, MT 59725

Big Horn County Genealogical Society
P.O. Box 51
Hardin, MT 59034

Bitterroot Genealogical Society
P.O. Box 350022
Grantsdale, MT 59835-0022

Broken Mountains Genealogical Society
P.O. Box 261
Chester, MT 59522

Fort Assiniboine Genealogical Society
P.O. Box 321
Havre, MT 59501

Gallatin Genealogy Society
P.O. Box 1783
Bozeman, MT 59715

Great Falls Genealogy Society
c/o Cascade County Historical Museum
1400 First Avenue
Great Falls, MT 59401
Tel/Fax: 406-452-3462

Lewis and Clark County Genealogical Society
P.O. Box 5313
Helena, MT 59604
Tel: 406-447-1690 ext. 28
Email: TATWOOD@mt.gov
URL: http://www.mth.mtlib.org/LCLHomepage/HoursServices/Services/Genealogical_Soc.html

Lewistown Genealogy Society
701 West Main
Lewitton, MT 59457

Miles City Genealogical Society
c/o Miles City Public Library
1 South 10th Street
P.O. Box 711
Miles City, MT 59301

Montana State Genealogical Society
P.O. Box 555
Chester, MT 59522

Park County Genealogy Society
c/o Park County Public Library
228 West Callender Street
Livingston, MT 59047

Powder River Genealogical Society
P.O. Box 614
Broadus, MT 59317
Email: emmov@mcn.net

Powell County Genealogical Society
912 Missouri Avenue
Deer Lodge, MT 59722

Root Diggers Genealogical Society
P.O. Box 249
Glasgow, MT 59230

Western Montana Genealogical Society
P.O. Box 2714
Missoula, MT 59806

Yellowstone Genealogy Forum
c/o Parmly Billings Library
510 North Broadway
Billings, MT 59101
Tel: 406-657-8259
URL: http://www.fgs.org/~fgs/soc0204.htm

Historical Societies

Anaconda Deer Lodge County Historical Society
401 E. Commercial Street
Anaconda, MT 59711-2327
Tel: 406-563-2220

Carbon County Historical Society
P.O. Box 476
Red Lodge, MT 59068

Cascade County Historical Society/Museum
1400 First Avenue, North
Great Falls, MT 59401
Tel/Fax: 406-452-3462

Gallatin County Historical Society/Pioneer Museum
Old County Jail
317 W. Main Street
Bozeman, MT 59715-4576
Tel: 406-582-3195

Montana Historical Society
225 North Roberts Street
P.O. Box 201201
Helena, MT 59601
Tel: 800-243-9900
406-444-4774/5
Fax: 406-444-2696
URL: http://www.his.mt.gov/

Phillips County Historical Society/Museum
133 S. 1st West
Malta, MT 59538
Tel: 406-654-1037
URL: http://icstech.com/~mteast/museum.html

Stumptown Historical Society
Central Avenue, Rm 301
Whitefish, MT 59937
Tel: 406-862-0067

Upper Blackfoot Valley Historical Society
P.O. Box 922
Lincoln, MT 59639
Tel: 406-362-4099

Upper Musselshell Historical Society/Museum
11 S. Central Avenue
Harlowton, MT 59036
Tel: 406-632-5519

LDS Family History Centers

Billings Family History Center
1000 Wicks Lane
Billings, MT 59105
Tel: 406-259-3348

Billings Family History Center
2929 Belvedere Drive
Billings, MT 59102
Tel: 406-656-5559

Bozeman Family History Center
2915 Colter Drive
Bozeman, MT 59715
Tel: 406-586-3880 ext. 15

Butte Family History Center
3400 East Four Mile Vue Road
Butte, MT 59701
Tel: 406-494-9909

Glasgow Family History Center
800 Fourth Avenue, North
Glasgow, MT 59230
Tel: 406-228-2382

Glendive Family History Center
1900 North Anderson Avenue
Glendive, MT 59330
Tel: 406-365-4609

Great Falls Family History Center
1015 15th Avenue, South
Great Falls, MT 59404
Tel: 406-454-1611

Great Falls Family History Center
1401 Ninth Street, NW
Great Falls, MT 59404
Tel: 406-453-1625

Havre Family History Center
1315 Washington Avenue
Havre, MT 59501
Tel: 406-265-7982

Helena Family History Center
1610 East 6th Avenue
Helena, MT 59601
Tel: 406-443-0713

Kalispell Family History Center
61 Bountiful Drive
Kalispell, MT 59901
Tel: 406-752-5446

Lewistown Family History Center
900 Casino Creek Drive
Lewistown, MT 59457
Tel: 406-538-9058

Missoula Family History Center
3201 Bancroft Street
Missoula, MT 59801
Tel: 406-543-6148

Stevensville Family History Center
Eastside Highway and Middle Burnt Fork Road
Stevensville, MT 59870
Tel: 406-777-2489

ARCHIVES/LIBRARIES/MUSEUMS

Beaverhead County Museum
15-25 South Montana
P.O. Box 830
Dillon, MT 59725
Tel: 406-683-5027

Big Horn County Historical Museum
P.O. Box 1206A
Hardin, MT 59034
Tel: 406-665-1671

Blackfoot Cultural Program
P.O. Box 850
Browning, MT 59417
Tel: 406-338-7406

Bureau of Land Management
Granite Tower
222 North 32nd Street
P.O. Box 36800
Billings, MT 59107
Tel: 406-255-2939

Butte/Silver Bow County Archives
17 West Quartz Street
P.O. Box 81
Butte, MT 59703
Tel: 406-723-8262
URL: http://www.mtech.edu/silvrbow/ARCHIVES.HTM

Butte/Silver Bow County Public Library
106 West Broadway Street
Butte, MT 59701
Tel: 406-723-8262
Fax: 406-782-6637

Carter County Library
Ekalaka, MT 59324
Tel: 406-775-6336

Cascade County Historical Museum
Paris Gibson Square
1400 First Avenue, North
Great Falls, MT 59401
Tel/Fax: 406-452-3462

Crow Tribal Council
P.O. Box 159
Crow Agency, MT 59022
Tel: 406-638-2601

Daniels County Museum
7 Country Road
Scobey, MT 59263
Tel: 406-487-5965

Diocese of Great Falls
121 23rd Street, South
P.O. Box 1399
Great Falls, MT 59403

Diocese of Helena
515 North Ewing
P.O. Box 1729
Helena, MT 59624

Fallon County Library
10 West Fallon Avenue
P.O. Box 1037
Baker, MT 59313
Tel: 406-778-2883

Flathead Cultural Committee
P.O. Box 418
St. Ignatius, MT 59865
Tel: 406-745-4572

Fort Missoula Historical Museum
Fort Missoula Building 322
Missoula, MT 59804
Tel: 406-728-3476
Fax: 406-728-5063

Gallatin County Historical Society/Pioneer Museum
Old County Jail
317 W. Main Street
Bozeman, MT 59715-4576
Tel: 406-582-3195

Glasgow Library
408 Third Avenue, South
Glasgow, MT 59230
Tel: 406-228-2731
URL: http://www.mtgl.mtlib.org/

Great Falls Public Library
301 2nd Avenue, North
Great Falls, MT 59401
Tel: 406-453-0349
URL: http://orion.mtgr.mtlib.org/www/library/index.html

Hardin Historical Museum
East of Hardin
Hardin, MT 59034
Tel: 406-665-1671

Havre/Hill County Library
402 3rd Street
P.O. Box 1151
Havre, MT 59501
Tel: 406-265-2123

Kootenai Cultural Center
P.O. Box 1452
Elmo, MT 59917
Tel: 406-849-5541

Lewis & Clark Library
120 Last Chance Gulch
Helena, MT 59601
Tel: 406-447-1690
Fax: 406-447-1687
Email: pdunham@mtlib.org
URL: http://www.mth.mtlib.org/homepage.html

Libby Heritage Museum
1367 U.S. Highway 2, South
Libby, MT 59923-9011
Tel: 406-293-7521

Lincoln County Library/Eureka Branch
318 Dewey Avenue
Eureka, MT 59917
Tel: 406-296-2613
URL: http://www.libby.org/Library/libhome.html

Miles City Public Library
1 South 10th Street
P.O. Box 711
Miles City, MT 59301
Email: UWPA28B@prodigy.com
URL: http://pages.prodigy.com/mc_library/library.htm

Mineral County Historical Society
P.O. Box 301
Superior, MT 59872
Tel: 406-822-4626

Missoula Public Library
301 East Main
Missoula, MT 59802
Tel: 406-721-2665
Fax: 406-728-5900
Email: mslaplib@ism.net
URL: http://www.ism.net/~mslaplib/

Mon Dak Heritage Center
120 3rd Avenue, SE
Sidney, MT 59270-4324
Tel: 406-482-3500

Montana Historical Society
225 North Roberts Street
P.O. Box 201201
Helena, MT 59601
Tel: 800-243-9900
406-444-4774/5
Fax: 406-444-2696
URL: http://www.his.mt.gov/

Montana State Library
1515 East Sixth Avenue
P.O. Box 201800
Helena, MT 59620-1800
Tel: 406-444-3004
Fax: 406-444-5612
URL: http://msl.mt.gov/

Montana State University/Billings
Library
1500 North 30th Street
Billings, MT 59101
Tel: 406-657-2262
URL: http://www.msubillings.edu/technology/lib/lib.html

Montana State University/Bozeman Library
Merrill C. Burlingame Special Collections
P.O. Box 173320
Bozeman, MT 59717-3320
Tel: 406-994-3119
Fax: 406-994-2851
URL: http://www.lib.montana.edu/SPCOLL/index.html

Montana State University/Northern
Vande Bogard Library
P.O. Box 7751
Havre, MT 59501

Montana College of Mineral Science and Technology
Library/Govt. Documents
1300 West Park Street
Butte, MT 59701
Tel: 406-496-4284
URL: http://www.mtech.edu/library/menu1.htm

Northern Cheyenne Cultural Center
Dull Knife Community College
P.O. Box 98
Lame Deer, MT 59043
Tel: 406-477-6215

O'Fallon Historical Museum
723 S. Main
Baker, MT 59313
Tel: 406-778-3265

Old Trail Museum
823 North Main Street
Choteau, MT 59422
Tel: 406-466-5332

Park County Public Library
228 West Callender Street
Livingston, MT 59047

Parmly Billings Library
510 North Broadway
Billings, MT 59101
Tel: 406-657-8259

Phillips County Historical Society/Museum
133 S. 1st West
Malta, MT 59538
Tel: 406-654-1037
URL: http://icstech.com/~mteast/museum.html

Powder River Historical Museum
Broadus, MT 59317
Tel: 406-436-2977

Powell County Museum
1119 Main Street
Deer Lodge, MT 5972

Rocky Mountain College
Paul M. Adams Memorial Library
1511 Poly Drive
Billings, MT 59102
Tel: 406-657-1087
Fax: 406-657-1085

Sheridan County Library
100 West Laurel Avenue
Plentywood, MT 59254
Tel: 406-765-2317

University of Montana/Missoula
Mansfield Library
Missoula, MT 59812
Tel: 406-243-6800
Email: mullin@selway.umt.edu
URL: http://www.lib.umt.edu/

Upper Musselshell Historical Society/Museum
11 S. Central Avenue
Harlowton, MT 59036
Tel: 406-632-5519

Valley County Pioneer Museum
816 U.S. Highway 2, West
Glasgow, MT 59230
Tel: 406-228-8697

Victor Heritage Museum
Blake and Main
Victor, MT 59875
Tel: 406-642-3997

Western Heritage Center
2822 Montana Avenue
Billings, MT 59101
Tel: 406-256-6809
Fax: 406-256-6850

NEWSPAPER REPOSITORIES

Montana College of Mineral Science and Technology
Library/Govt. Documents
1300 West Park Street
Butte, MT 59701
Tel: 406-496-4284
URL: http://www.mtech.edu/library/menu1.htm

Montana Historical Society
225 North Roberts Street
P.O. Box 201201
Helena, MT 59620
Tel: 406-444-4787
Fax: 406-444-2696
URL: http://www.his.mt.gov/

Vital Records

Department of Public Health and Human Services (DPHHS)
111 North Sanders
P.O. Box 4210
Helena, MT 59604-4210

Montana on the Web

Montana Genealogy Information
http://www.digisys.net/users/scarlett/

Montana GenWeb
http://www.imt.net/~corkykn/montana.html

Native American Research in Montana
http://www.imt.net/~corkykn/native.html

Nebraska

Archives, State & National

Nebraska State Historical Society/State Archives Division
1500 R Street
P.O. Box 82554
Lincoln, NE 68501
Tel: 402-471-3270
402-471-4771 (library)
Fax: 402-471-3100
URL: http://www.dsenter.com/nebraska/societies/stsoclib.html#nesthst

National Archives—Central Plains Region
2312 East Bannister Road
Kansas City, MO 64131
Tel: 816-926-6272
Fax: 816-926-6982
Email: archives@kansascity.nara.gov
URL: http://www.nara.gov/nara/regional/06nsgil.html

Genealogical Societies

Adams County Genealogical Society
1330 N. Burlington
P.O. Box 424
Hastings, NE 68902
Tel: 402-463-5838
Email: acgs@tcgcs.com
URL: http://www.cnweb.com/hastings/commnet/community/acgs/

Arnold Kinseekers
P.O. Box 135
Arnold, NE 69120

Boone-Nance County Genealogical Society
P.O. Box 231
Belgrade, NE 68623

Cairo Roots
c/o Mrs. Delmar Perkins
Route 1, Box 42
Cairo, NE 68824

Chase County Genealogical Society
P.O. Box 303
Imperial, NE 69033

Cherry County Genealogical Society
P.O. Box 380
Valentine, NE 69201

Cheyenne County Genealogical Society
P.O. Box 802
Sidney, NE 69162

Cozad Genealogy Club
c/o Cozad Public Library
910 Meridian Avenue
P.O. Drawer C
Cozad, NE 69130

Dakota County Genealogical Society
P.O. Box 18
Dakota City, NE 68850

Dawson Genealogical Society
c/o Mrs. Gus Anderson
514 E. 8th Street
Cozad, NE 69130

Eastern Nebraska Genealogical Society
P.O. Box 541
Fremont, NE 68025

Fillmore Heritage Genealogical Society
c/o Mrs. Merlin Hulse
Route 2, Box 28
Exeter, NE 68351

Flatwater Genealogical Society
P.O. Box 324
Gibbon, NE 68840

Fort Kearney Genealogical Society
P.O. Box 22
Kearney, NE 68847

Frontier County Genealogical Society
P.O. Box 507
Curtis, NE 69025

Furnas County Genealogical Society
P.O. Box 166
Beaver City, NE 68926

Genealogical Seekers
871 West 6th
Wahoo, NE 68066

Greater Omaha Genealogical Society
P.O. Box 4011
Omaha, NE 68104
Email: dclear@ix.netcom.com

Greater York Area Genealogical Society
c/o Kilgore Memorial Library
6th and Nebraska
York, NE 68467

Holdrege Area Genealogical Club
Phelps County Museum/Library
P.O. Box 164
Holdrege, NE 68949
Email: rs55453@navix.net
URL: http://www.4w.com/pages/psimpson/phelpsgen.html

Holt County Genealogical Society
P.O. Box 376
O'Neill, NE 68763

Hooker County Genealogical Society
P.O. Box 280
Mullen, NE 69152

Howard County Kinquesters
c/o Emma Osterman
317 7th Street
St. Paul, NE 68873

Jefferson County Genealogical Society
P.O. Box 163
Fairbury, NE 68352-0163
Email: eb72539@navix.net
URL: http://www.dsenter.com/ne/jefferson/jcgs1.html

Lexington Genealogy Society
P.O. Box 778
Lexington, NE 68850

Lincoln/Lancaster County Genealogy Society
P.O. Box 30055
Lincoln, NE 68503-0055

Madison County Genealogical society
P.O. Box 347
Norfolk, NE 68701

Nebraska D.A.R./Library
202 West 4th Street
Alliance, NE 69301

Nebraska S.A.R.
6731 Summer Street
Lincoln, NE 68506

Nebraska State Genealogical Society
P.O. Box 5608
Lincoln, NE 68505
Tel: 402-266-8881

Nemaha Valley Genealogy Society
Nemaha Valley Museum
P.O. Box 25
Auburn, NE 68305

Northern Central Nebraska Genealogical Society
P.O. Box 362
O'Neill, NE 68763

North Platte Genealogical Society
P.O. Box 1452
North Platte, NE 69101

Northeastern Nebraska Genealogical Society (NENGS)
P.O. Box 169
Lyons, NE 68038

Northern Antelope County Genealogical Society
P.O. Box 267
Orchard, NE 68764

Northwest Genealogical Society
P.O. Box 6
Alliance, NE 64337

Nuckolls County Genealogical Society
P.O. Box 441
Superior, NE 68978-0441

Pawnee Genealogy Scouters
P.O. Box 112
Albion, NE 68620

Perkins County Genealogical Society
P.O. Box 418
Grant, NE 69140

Plains Genealogical Society
c/o Kimball Public Library
208 South Walnut Street
Kimball, NE 69145

Platte Valley Kinseekers
P.O. Box 153
Columbus, NE 68601

Prairie Pioneer Genealogical Society
P.O. Box 1122
Grand Island, NE 68802

Ravenna Genealogical Society
c/o Mrs. Robert Johnson
105 Alba Street
Ravenna, NE 68869

Rebecca Winters Genealogical Society
1121 Avenue L
P.O. Box 323
Scottsbluff, NE 69361

Saline County Genealogical Society
P.O. Box 24
Crete, NE 68333

Sarpy County Genealogical Society
2402 Sac Place
Bellevue, NE 68005

Saunders County Genealogy Seekers
c/o G. Cajka
462 E. 13th
Wahoo, NE 68066

Seward County Genealogical Society
P.O. Box 72
Seward, NE 68434

South Central Genealogical Society
c/o Mrs. Haldine Johnson
Route 2, Box 57
Minden, NE 68959

Southeast Nebraska Genealogical Society
P.O. Box 562
Beatrice, NE 68310-0562
URL: http://www.dsenter.com/ne/gage/sengs.html

Southwest Nebraska Genealogical Society
P.O. Box 156
McCook, NE 69001

Thayer County Genealogical Society
P.O. Box 388
Belvidere, NE 68315

Thomas County Genealogical Society
P.O. Box 136
Thedford, NE 69166

Tri-State Corners Genealogical Society
c/o Lydia Brun Woods Memorial Library
120 E. 18th Street
Falls City, NE 68355

Valley County Genealogical Society
619 South 10th
Ord, NE 68862

Wahoo Genealogical Seekers
871 West 6th
Wahoo, NE 68066

Washington County Genealogical Society
c/o Blair Public Library
Blair, NE 68008

Historical Societies

Adams County Historical Society/Archives
1330 N. Burlington
P.O. Box 102
Hastings, NE 68902
Tel: 402-463-5838
URL: http://www.cnweb.com/hastings/commnet/community/achs/

American Historical Society of Germans from Russia (AHSGR)
Lincoln Chapter
631 D Street
Lincoln, NE 68502
Tel: 402-474-3363
URL: http://www.teleport.com/nonprofit/ahsgr/nelincol.html

American Historical Society of Germans from Russia (AHSGR)
Northeast Nebraska Chapter
c/o Ruthie Galitz
314 S. 13th Place
Norfolk, NE 68701-4809
URL: http://www.teleport.com/nonprofit/ahsgr/nenorthe.html

Brownville Historical Society
Brownville, NE 68321
Tel: 402-825-6001

Butler County Historical Society
c/o Don Ditzler
1125 3rd Street
David City, NE 68632
Tel: 402-367-3500

Cheyenne County Historical Association
6th and Jackson
Sidney, NE 69162
Tel: 308-254-2150

Custer County Historical Society, Inc./Museum & Archives
445 South 9th Avenue
P.O. Box 334
Broken Bow, NE 68822
Tel: 308-872-2203
URL: http://www.rootsweb.com/~necuster/

Dakota County Historical Society
RR 1
Chadron, NE 68731-9801
Tel: 402-698-2288

Dawson County Historical Society
P.O. Box 369
Lexington, NE 68850

Dodge County Historical Society
1643 N. Nye
P.O. Box 766
Fremont, NE 68026-0766

Douglas County Historical Society
Fort Omaha
P.O. Box 11398
Omaha, NE 68111-0398
Tel: 402-455-9990

Gage County Historical Society
2nd and Court Streets
P.O. Box 793
Beatrice, NE 68310
Tel: 402-228-1679
URL: http://www4.infoanalytic.com/gage/

High Plains Historical Society/Museum
413 Norris Avenue
McCook, NE 69001-2003
Tel: 308-345-3661

Holt County Historical Society
P.O. Box 231
O'Neill, NE 68763

Naponee Historical Society
Naponee, NE 68960
URL: http://www.4w.com/pages/psimpson/naponeehist.html

Nebraska State Historical Society
1500 R Street
P.O. Box 82554
Lincoln, NE 68501
Tel: 402-471-3270
402-471-4771 (library)
Fax: 402-471-3100
URL: http://www.dsenter.com/nebraska/societies/stsoclib.html#nesthst

Phelps County Historical Society
North Burlington
Holdrege, NE 68949
Tel: 308-995-5015

Platte County Historical Society/Museum
2916 16th Street
Columbus, NE 68601
Tel: 402-564-1856

Railroad Station Historical Society
430 Ivy Avenue
Crete, NE 68333
Tel: 402-826-3356

Saunders County Historical Society
240 N. Walnut Street
Wahoo, NE 68066
Tel: 402-443-3090
URL: http://wahoo.esu2.k12.ne.us/hist/history.html

Thurston County Historical Society
General Delivery
Pender, NE 68047

Washington County Historical Association
Highway 75 & Monroe St.
P.O. Box 25
Fort Calhoun, NE 68023
Tel: 402-468-5740

LDS Family History Centers

Gordon Family History Center
800 North Ash
Gordon, NE 69343
Tel: 308-282-9969

Grand Island Family History Center
212 West 22nd Avenue
Grand Island, NE 68801
Tel: 308-382-9418

Lincoln Family History Center
3100 Old Cheney Road
Lincoln, NE 68516
Tel: 402-423-4561

North Platte Family History Center
4100 West A and Lakeview Blvd.
North Platte, NE 69101
Tel: 308-532-0940

Omaha Family History Center
11027 Martha Street
Omaha, NE 68144
Tel: 402-393-7641

Papillion Family History Center
12009 South 84th Street
Papillion, NE 68046
Tel: 402-339-0461

Archives/Libraries/Museums

Adams County Historical Society/Archives
1330 N. Burlington
P.O. Box 102
Hastings, NE 68902
Tel: 402-463-5838
URL: http://www.cnweb.com/hastings/commnet/community/achs/

Alice M. Farr Library
1603 L Street
Aurora, NE 68818
Tel: 402-694-2200
URL: http://www.hamilton.net/aurora/city/library5.htm

Alliance Public Library
520 Box Butte Avenue
Alliance, NE 69301
Tel: 308-762-1387

Antelope County Historical Museum
509 L Street
Neligh, NE 68756
Tel: 402-887-4275

Bayard Public Library
509 Avenue A
P.O. Box B
Bayard, NE 69334
Tel: 308-586-1141

Beatrice Public Library
100 N. 16th Street
Beatrice, NE 68310
Tel: 402-223-3584

Bennett Martin Public Library
136 South 14th Street
Lincoln, NE 68508
Tel: 402-441-8500
Fax: 402-441-8586
Email: library@ci.lincoln.ne.us
URL: http://interlinc.ci.lincoln.ne.us/InterLinc/city/library/index.htm

Big Springs Public Library
P.O. Box 192
Big Springs, NE 69122
Tel: 308-889-3482

Black Americana Historical Museum
1240 S. 13th Street
Omaha, NE 68108
Tel: 402-341-6908

Blair Public Library
210 S. 17th Street
Blair, NE 68008
Tel: 402-426-3617

Bridgeport Public Library
722 Main
P.O. Box 940
Bridgeport, NE 69336
Tel: 308-262-0326

Broadwater Public Library
Broadwater, NE 69125
Tel: 308-262-0326

Cass County Historical Museum
646 Main Street
Plattsmouth, NE 68048
Tel: 402-296-4770

Catholic Chancery Office
Diocese of Lincoln
3400 Sheridan Blvd.
Lincoln, NE 68506
Tel: 402-488-0921

Chadron Public Library
507 Bordeaux Street
Chadron, NE 69337
Tel: 308-432-0531

Chadron State College
Mari Sandoz Heritage High Plains Center
Chadron, NE 69337
URL: http://www.csc.edu/library/resources/SANDOZ/SANDOZ2.HTML

Chadron State College
Chadron State Library
Nebraska State Historical Society Room
Chadron, NE 69337

Chappell Public Library
P.O. Box 248
Chappell, NE 69129
Tel: 308-874-2626

Columbus Public Library
2504 14th Street
Columbus, NE 68601
Tel: 402-564-7116
URL: http://www.megavision.com/~cisweb/columbus/cpl.htm

Cozad Public Library
910 Meridian Avenue
Cozad, NE 69130
Tel: 308-784-2019

Crawford Public Library
601 2nd Street
Crawford, NE 69339
Tel: 308-665-1780

Creighton University
Reinert/Alumni Library
2500 California Plaza
Omaha, NE 68178
Tel: 402-280-2927
402-280-2746 (Archives)
Fax: 402-280-2435
URL: http://reinert.creighton.edu/archives.htm

Crete Public Library
305 E. 13th Street
P.O. Box 156
Crete, NE 68333-0156
Tel: 402-826-3809

Dalton Public Library
Dalton, NE 69131
Tel: 308-376-2413

Dana College
Dana Immigrant Archives
C.A. Dana/LIFE Library
Blair, NE 68008
Tel: 402-426-7300
Fax: 402-426-7332
URL: http://www.eskimo.com/~fwg/nnon/dana.html

Dawes County Historical Museum
RR 1
Chadron, NE 69337
Tel: 308-432-4999

Douglas County Historical Society
Fort Omaha
P.O. Box 11398
Omaha, NE 68111-0398
Tel: 402-455-9990

Garfield County Historical Museum
P.O. Box 66
Burwell, NE 68823
Tel: 308-346-4521

Geneva Public Library
1043 G Street
Geneva, NE 68361
Tel: 402-759-3416
URL: http://www.ci.geneva.ne.us/General.htm#library

Gering Public Library
1055 P Street
Gering, NE 69341
Tel: 308-436-7443
URL: http://www.prairieweb.com/gering/g_librar.htm

Gordon Public Library
101 W. 5th Street
Gordon, NE 69343
Tel: 308-282-1198

Gothenburg Public Library
1104 Lake Avenue
Gothenburg, NE 69138
Tel: 308-537-2591

Grand Island/Edith Abbott Memorial Library
211 South Washington
Grand Island, NE 68801
Tel: 308-385-5333
URL: http://www.gi.lib.ne.us/

Hay Springs/Cravath Memorial Library
243 North Main Street
P.O. Box 309
Hay Springs, NE 69347
Tel: 308-638-4541
308-638-4421

Hemingford Public Library
P.O. Box 6
Hemingford, NE 69348
Tel: 308-487-3454

High Plains Historical Society/Museum
413 Norris Avenue
McCook, NE 69001-2003
Tel: 308-345-3661

Holdrege Area Genealogical Club
Phelps County Museum/Library
P.O. Box 164
Holdrege, NE 68949
Email: rs55453@navix.net
URL: http://www.4w.com/pages/psimpson/phelpsgen.html

Kearney Public Library
2020 1st Avenue
Kearney, NE 68847
Tel: 308-233-3282
Fax: 308-233-3291
URL: http://rip.physics.unk.edu/library/

Keene Memorial Library
1030 North Broad Street
Fremont, NE 68025
Tel: 402-727-2694
Fax: 402-727-2826
Email: kemeli01@nol.nol.org

Kilgore Memorial Library
520 Nebraska Avenue
York, NE 68467
Tel: 402-363-2620
URL: http://www.ci.york.ne.us/communit.htm#kilgore

Kimball Public Library
208 South Walnut Street
Kimball, NE 69145
Tel: 308-235-4523
URL: http://www.ci.kimball.ne.us/library.htm

Lewellen Public Library
P.O. Box 58
Lewellen, NE 69147
Tel: 308-778-5421

Lexington Public Library
103 E. Tenth Street
P.O. Box 778
Lexington, NE 68850
Tel: 308-324-2151
308-324-2140
Email: lp85039@navix.net

Lincoln County Historical Museum
2403 N. Buffalo
North Platte, NE 69101
Tel: 308-534-5640

Lincoln Public Library
136 South 14th Street
Lincoln, NE 68508

Lisco Library
P.O. Box 137
Lisco, NE 69148
Tel: 308-772-3345

Lydia Brun Woods Memorial Library
120 E. 18th Street
Falls City, NE 68355
Tel: 402-245-2913

Lyman Public Library
313 Jeffers Avenue
P.O. Box 384
Lyman, NE 69352
Tel: 308-787-1366

Minatare Public Library
405 Main
P.O. Box 483
Minatare, NE 69356
Tel: 308-783-2514
308-783-1414

Morrill Public Library
119 E. Webster
P.O. Box 402
Morrill, NE 69358
Tel: 308-247-2611

Nancy Fawcett Memorial Library
P.O. Box 318
Lodgepole, NE 69149
Tel: 308-483-5714

Nebraska D.A.R./Library
202 West 4th Street
Alliance, NE 69301

Nebraska Library Commission
The Atrium
1200 N. Street, Suite 120
Lincoln, NE 68508-2023
Tel: 402-471-2045
800-307-2665 (in Nebraska only)
Fax: 402-471-2086
URL: http://www.nlc.state.ne.us/

Nebraska State Law Library
Statehouse, 3rd Floor South
P.O. Box 94926
Lincoln, NE 68502
Tel: 402-471-3189

Nebraska United Methodist Archives & History Center
5000 St. Paul Avenue
Lincoln, NE 68504
Tel: 402-465-2175

Nebraska Veterans Administration Office
5631 S. 48th Street
Lincoln, NE 68516
Tel: 800-827-1000

Nemaha Valley Museum
P.O. Box 25
Auburn, NE 68305

Norfolk Public Library
308 Prospect Avenue
Norfolk, NE 68701
Tel: 402-644-8711
Fax: 402-370-3260
URL: http://www.norfolk.ne.us/norpub.htm

Omaha Public Library
215 South 15th Street
Omaha, NE 68102
Tel: 402-444-4800
402-444-4826 (Genealogy Dept.)
URL: http://www.omaha.lib.ne.us/

Oshkosh Public Library
355 West 1st
P.O. Box 140
Oshkosh, NE 69154
Tel: 308-772-4554

Platte County Historical Society/Museum
2916 16th Street
Columbus, NE 68601
Tel: 402-564-1856

Potter Public Library
333 Chestnut
P.O. Box 317
Potter, NE 69156
Tel: 308-879-4345

Quivey Memorial Library
1447 Center Avenue
Mitchell, NE 69357
Tel: 308-623-2222

Ralston Archives/Museum
8311 Park Drive
Ralston, NE 68127
Tel: 402-331-3366

Rushville Public Library
207 Sprague Street
P.O. Box 473
Rushville, NE 69360
Tel: 308-327-2740

Scottsbluff Public Library
1809 3rd Avenue
Scottsbluff, NE 69361
Tel: 308-632-0050
URL: http://www.ci.scottsbluff.ne.us/community/htm#library

Stuhr Museum of the Prairie Pioneer
3133 W. U.S. Highway 34
Grand Island, NE 68801-7280
Tel: 308-385-5316
URL: http://www.gionline.net/arts/stuhr/

Thurston County Historical Museum
500 Ivan Street
Pender, NE 68047
Tel: 402-385-3210

Union College Library
3800 South 48th Street
Lincoln, NE 68506
Tel: 402-486-2514

University of Nebraska/Kearney
Calvin T. Ryan Library
905 W. 25th Street
Kearney, NE 68849
Tel: 308-865-8535
308-865-8544 (Archives/Special Collections)
Fax: 308-865-8722
Email: lillis@platte.unk.edu
URL: http://www.unk.edu/buildings/library/

University of Nebraska/Lincoln
Love Library, City Campus 0410
14th and R Streets
Lincoln, NE 68588
Tel: 402-472-2848 (Reference)
402-472-2531 (Special Collections)
Email: infomail@unllib.unl.edu
URL: http://www.unl.edu/lovers/libs.html

University of Nebraska/Omaha
University Library
Omaha, NE 68182-0237
Tel: 402-554-2661 (Information)
402-554-3202 (Government Documents)
402-554-2884 (Special Collections)
URL: http://revelation.unomaha.edu/

Washington County Historical Museum
102 North 14th
Fort Calhoun, NE 68023
Tel: 402-468-5740

Wayne Public Library
410 Main Street
Wayne, NE 68787
Tel: 402-375-3135

Webster County Historical Museum
721 W. 4th Avenue
Red Cloud, NE 68970-2221
Tel: 402-746-2444

Western Heritage Museum
801 South 10th Street
Omaha, NE 68108
Tel: 402-444-5071

Newspaper Repositories

Lincoln/Lancaster County Genealogy Society
P.O. Box 30055
Lincoln, NE 68503-0055

Nebraska State Genealogical Society
P.O. Box 5608
Lincoln, NE 68505
Tel: 402-266-8881

Nebraska State Historical Society
1500 R Street
P.O. Box 82554
Lincoln, NE 68501
Tel: 402-471-3270
402-471-4771 (library)
Fax: 402-471-3100
URL: http://www.dsenter.com/nebraska/societies/stsoclib.html#nesthst

University of Nebraska/Lincoln
Love Library, City Campus 0410
14th and R Streets
Lincoln, NE 68588
Tel: 402-472-3939
Email: kayw@unllib.unl.edu
URL: http://www.unl.edu/nebnews/nnphome.html

Vital Records

Nebraska Department of Health & Human Services/Vital Records
P.O. Box 95065
Lincoln, NE 68509-5065
Tel: 402-471-2871
URL: http://www.nol.org/home/Health/services.htm

Nebraska on the Web

Andreas' History of the State of Nebraska (publ. 1885)
http://www.ukans.edu/carrie/kancoll/andreas_ne/

Heritage Village
http://www.sky.net/~husker/nebraska/

Nebraska GenWeb Project
http://www.dsenter.com/nebraska/

Nebraska GenWeb Project
http://www.dsenter.com/nebraska/

Nebraska State Government Publications Online
(Guide to Genealogical Research & Historical Society Reference Information Guide)
http://www.nlc.state.ne.us/docs/pilot/pilot.html

Nevada

Archives, State & National

National Archives—Pacific Southwest Region
24000 Avila Road, First Floor-East Entrance
Laguna Niguel, CA 92607-6719
Tel: 714-360-2641
Fax: 714-360-2644
Email: archives@laguna.nara.gov
URL: http://www.nara.gov/nara/regional/09nslgil.html
(Serves Clark County)

National Archives—Pacific Sierra Region
1000 Commodore Drive
San Bruno, CA 94066
Tel: 415-876-9009
Fax: 415-876-9233
Email: archives@sanbruno.nara.gov
URL: http://www.nara.gov/nara/regional/09nssgil.html
(Serves Nevada, except for Clark County)

Nevada State Library and Archives
100 N. Stewart Street
Carson City, NV 89710
Tel: 702-687-5160 (Library)
702-687-5210 (Archives)
URL: http://www.clan.lib.nv.us/docs/NSLA/nsla.htm

Genealogical Societies

Churchill County Historical & Genealogical Society
c/o Churchill County Museum & Archives
1050 South Main Street
Fallon, NV 89406
Tel: 702-423-3677

Clark County Genealogical Society
P.O. Box 1929
Las Vegas, NV 89125-1929

Humboldt County Genealogical Society
c/o Humboldt County Library
85 East 5th Street
Winnemucca, NV 89445

Jewish Genealogical Society of Las Vegas, Nevada
P.O. Box 29342
Las Vegas, NV 89126

Jewish Genealogical Society of Southern Nevada
c/o Rhoda Liss
2653 Topaz Square
Las Vegas, NV 89121

Nevada State Genealogical Society
P.O. Box 20666
Reno, NV 89515

Northeastern Nevada Genealogical Society
1515 Idaho Street
Elko, NV 89801

Round Mountain Genealogical Group
P.O. Box 330
Round Mountain, NV 89045

HISTORICAL SOCIETIES

Carson Valley Historical Society
P.O. Box 957
Minden, NV 89423
Tel: 702-782-2738

Central Nevada Historical Society
P.O. Box 326
Tonopah, NV 89049
Tel: 702-482-3454

Churchill County Historical & Genealogical Society
c/o Churchill County Museum & Archives
1050 South Maine Street
Fallon, NV 89406
Tel: 702-423-3677

Eureka County Historical Society
Eureka Sentinel Museum
P.O. Box 178
Eureka, NV 89316

Goldfield Historical Society
P.O. Box 225
Goldfield, NV 89013

Inter-Tribal Council History Project
806 Holman Way
Sparks, NV 89502
Tel: 702-355-0600

Lake Tahoe Historical Society
P.O. Box 404
South Lake Tahoe, NV 95705

Nevada Historical Society/Library
1650 North Virginia Street
Reno, NV 89503
Tel: 702-688-1190

Nevada State Museum and Historical Society
State Mall Complex
700 Twin Lakes Drive
Las Vegas, NV 89158
Tel: 702-486-5205
Fax: 702-486-5172
URL: http://www.clan.lib.nv.us/docs/MUSEUMS/LV/mus-lv.htm

North Central Nevada Historical Society
c/o Humboldt County Museum
P.O. Box 819
Winnemucca, NV 89445
Tel: 702-623-2912

North Lake Tahoe Historical Society
P.O. Box 6141
Tahoe City, NV 95730

Southern Nevada Historical Society
P.O. Box 1358
Las Vegas, NV 89101

Story County Historical Society
P.O. Box 846
Virginia City, NV 89440

White Pine Historical Society
McGill Highway
Ely, NV 89310

LDS FAMILY HISTORY CENTERS

Carson City Family History Center
411 N. Saliman Road
Carson City, NV 89701
Tel: 702-884-2064

Elko Family History Center
3001 North 5th Street
Elko, NV 89801
Tel: 702-738-4565

Ely Family History Center
900 Avenue East
Ely, NV 89301
Tel: 702-289-2287

Fallon Family History Center
450 North Taylor
Fallon, NV 89406
Tel: 702-423-8888

Henderson Family History Center
19 East Ocean Avenue
Henderson, NV 89015
Tel: 702-566-8190

Las Vegas Family History Center
509 South 9th Street
P.O. Box 1360
Las Vegas, NV 89125
Tel: 702-382-9695

Logandale Family History Center
2555 North St. Joseph
Logandale, NV 89021
Tel: 702-398-3266

Mesquite Family History Center
100 North Arrowhead
Mesquite, NV 89024
Tel: 702-346-2342

Reno Family History Center
4751 Neil Road
Reno, NV 89502
Tel: 702-826-1130

Tonapah Family History Center
Smokey Valley Road
Tonapah, NV 89049
Tel: 702-482-5492

Winnemucca Family History Center
111 West McArthur Avenue
Winnemucca, NV 89445
Tel: 702-623-4448

ARCHIVES/LIBRARIES/MUSEUMS

African American Museum and Research Center
The Walker Foundation
705 W. Van Buren Avenue
Las Vegas, NV 89106
Tel: 702-647-2242

Boulder City Historical Association/Museum
444 Hotel Plaza
P.O. Box 60516
Boulder City, NV 89006
Tel: 702-294-1988
URL: http://www.accessnv.com/bcmha/index.htm

Boulder City Library
813 Arizona Street
Boulder City, NV 89005
Tel: 702-293-1281
Email: duncan@accessnv.com
URL: http://www.accessnv.com/bclibrary/

Churchill County Museum & Archives
1050 South Main Street
Fallon, NV 89406
Tel: 702-423-3677

Douglas County Library
1625 Library Lane
P.O. Box 337
Minden, NV 89423
Tel: 702-782-9841
Email: ldeacy@douglas.lib.nv.us
URL: http://douglas.lib.nv.us/

East Ely Railroad Depot Museum
1100 Avenue
P.O. Box 151100
Ely, NV 89301
Tel: 702-289-1663
Fax: 702-289-1664
URL: http://www.clan.lib.nv.us/docs/MUSEUMS/ELY/mus-ely.htm

Eureka Sentinel Museum
P.O. Box 178
Eureka, NV 89316

Humboldt County Library
85 East 5th Street
Winnemucca, NV 89445

Humboldt County Museum
P.O. Box 819
Winnemucca, NV 89445
Tel: 702-623-2912

Las Vegas Public Library
833 Las Vegas Blvd., North
Las Vegas, NV 89101
Tel: 702-382-3493
URL: http://post-office.lvccld.lib.nv.us/index.htm

Lincoln County Museum
Pioche, NV 89043
Tel: 702-962-5207

Lost City Museum
721 S. Moapa Valley Blvd.
P.O. Box 807
Overton, NV 89040
Tel: 702-397-2193
Fax: 702-397-8987
URL: http://www.clan.lib.nv.us/docs/MUSEUMS/LOST/mus-lost.htm

Lyon County Museum
215 South Main
Yerington, NV 89447
Tel: 702-463-3842

Mineral County Museum
P.O. Box 1584
Hawthorne, NV 89415
Tel: 702-945-2395

Nevada Historical Society/Library
1650 North Virginia Street
Reno, NV 89503
Tel: 702-688-1190
Fax: 702-688-2917
URL: http://www.clan.lib.nv.us/docs/MUSEUMS/HIST/his-soc.htm

Nevada State Museum
600 North Carson
Carson City, NV 89710
Tel: 702-687-4810

Nevada State Museum and Historical Society
State Mall Complex
700 Twin Lakes Drive
Las Vegas, NV 89158
Tel: 702-486-5205
Fax: 702-486-5172
URL: http://www.clan.lib.nv.us/docs/MUSEUMS/LV/mus-lv.htm

Northeastern Nevada Museum
P.O. Box 503
Elko, NV 89801
Tel: 702-738-3418

Portola Railroad Museum
P.O. Box 608
Crystal Bay, NV 89402
Tel: 702-832-4131

Southern Nevada Museum
1830 S. Boulder Hwy.
Henderson, NV 89015

Sparks Heritage Foundation/Museum
820 Victorian Avenue
Sparks, NV 89431
Tel: 702-355-1144

University of Nevada/Las Vegas (UNLV)
James R. Dickinson Library
4505 Maryland Parkway
Las Vegas, NV 89154
Tel: 702-895-3285
URL: http://www.nscee.edu/unlv/Libraries/services/speccoll/sc.html

University of Nevada/Reno
Getchell Library
Special Collections Dept. 322
Reno, NV 89557
Tel: 702-784-6500
702-784-6538
Email: specarch@unr.edu
URL: http://gordo.library.unr.edu/~speccoll/index.html

Washoe Archive and Cultural Resource Center
861 Crescent Drive
Carson City, NV 89701
Tel: 702-888-0936

Washoe County Library
301 South Center Street
P.O. Box 2151
Reno, NV 89501
Tel: 702-785-4190
Fax: 702-785-4692
TDD: 702-785-4083
Email: jkup@washoe.lib.nv.us
URL: http://www.washoe.lib.nv.us/

Western Railroaders Hall of Fame & Museum
2533 N. Carson Street
Carson City, NV 89706
Tel: 702-883-5926

White Pine Public Museum
2000 Aultman Street
Ely, NV 89301
Tel: 702-289-4710

NEWSPAPER REPOSITORIES

Nevada Historical Society/Library
1650 North Virginia Street
Reno, NV 89503
Tel: 702-688-1190
Fax: 702-688-2917
URL: http://www.clan.lib.nv.us/docs/MUSEUMS/HIST/his-soc.htm

Nevada State Library and Archives
100 N. Stewart Street
Carson City, NV 89710
Tel: 702-687-5160 (Library)
702-687-5210 (Archives)
URL: http://www.clan.lib.nv.us/docs/NSLA/nsla.htm

University of Nevada/Las Vegas (UNLV)
James R. Dickinson Library
4505 Maryland Parkway
Las Vegas, NV 89154
Tel: 702-895-3285
URL: http://www.nscee.edu/unlv/Libraries/services/speccoll/sc.html

University of Nevada/Reno
Getchell Library
Special Collections Dept. 322
Reno, NV 89557
Tel: 702-784-6500 ext. 317
Email: blesse@admin.unr.edu
URL: http://www.library.unr.edu/~speccoll/index.html

VITAL RECORDS

State Office of Vital Records
Capitol Complex
505 E. King Street, Room 102
Carson City, NV 89710
Tel: 702-687-4480

NEVADA ON THE WEB

Nevada GenWeb Project
http://www.rootsweb.com/~nvgenweb/

Pony Express Home Page
http://users.ccnet.com/~xptom/

NEW HAMPSHIRE

ARCHIVES, STATE & NATIONAL

National Archives—New England Region
380 Trapelo Road
Waltham, MA 02154-8104
Tel: 617-647-8100
Fax: 617-647-8460
Email: archives@waltham.nara.gov
URL: http://www.nara.gov/nara/regional/01nsbgil.html

New Hampshire Division of Records Management and Archives
71 South Fruit Street
Concord, NH 03301
Tel: 603-271-2236
Fax: 603-271-2272
Email: FMEVERS@lilac.nhsl.lib.nh.us
or BBURFORD@lilac.nhsl.lib.nh.us
URL: http://www.state.nh.us/state/archives.htm

GENEALOGICAL SOCIETIES

American Canadian Genealogical Society/Library
378 Notre Dame Avenue
P.O. Box 668
Manchester, NH 03105

American-Canadian Genealogical Society (ACGS)
4 Elm Street
P.O. Box 6478
Manchester, NH 03108
Email: 102475.2260@compuserve.com
URL: http://ourworld.compuserve.com/homepages/ACGS/homepage.htm

Grafton County Historic & Genealogy Society
P.O. Box 1163
Ashland, NH 03217
Email: rbhicks@cyberportal.net

New England Historical and Genealogical Society (NEHGS)
101 Newbury Street
Boston, MA 02116-3007
Tel: 617-836-5740
888-AT-NEHGS (Membership & Education)
888-BY-NEHGS (Sales)
888-90-NEHGS (Library Circulation)
Fax: 617-536-7307
Email: nehgs@nehgs.org
URL: http://www.nehgs.org/

New Hampshire Society of Genealogists
P.O. Box 2316
Concord, NH 03302-2316
Tel: 603-225-3381
Email: milliken@tiac.net
URL: http://www.tiac.net/users/nhsog/

Piscataqua Pioneers
University of New Hampshire
Dimond Library/Piscataqua Pioneers Genealogical Collection
Durham, NH 03824
Tel: 603-862-2714 (Special Collections)
603-862-0277 (Archives)
Email: wer@christa.unh.edu
URL: http://wwwsc.library.unh.edu/specoll/

Rockingham Society of Genealogists
P.O. Box 81
Exeter, NH 03833-0081

HISTORICAL SOCIETIES

Acworth Historical Society
c/o Acworth Silsby Library
Acworth, NH 03601

Alton Historical Society
P.O. Box 536
Alton, NH 03809

Amherst, Historical Society of
P.O. Box 717
Amherst, NH 03031

Andover Historical Society
P.O. Box 167
Andover, NH 03216

Ashland Historical Society
P.O. Box 175
Ashland, NH 03217

Association of Historical Societies of New Hampshire
11 Ironwood Lane
Atkinson, NH 03811

Atkinson Historical Society
Academy Avenue
Atkinson, NH 03811

Bedford Historical Society
24 N. Amherst Road
Bedford, NH 03110

Bennington Historical Society
P.O. Box 50
Bennington, NH 03442

Boscawen Historical Society
P.O. Box 3067
Boscawen, NH 03303

Brentwood Historical Society
1 Dalton Road
Brentwood, NH 03833

Bridgewater Historical Society
RFD 2, Box 390
Plymouth, NH 03264

Canaan Historical Society/Museum
P.O. Box 38
Canaan, NH 03741

Candia Historical Society
P.O. Box 300
Candia, NH 03034

Canterbury Historical Society
P.O. Box 206
Canterbury, NH 03224

Center Harbor Historical Society
P.O. Box 98
Center Harbor, NH 03226

Charlestown Historical Society
P.O. Box 253
Charlestown, NH 03603

Cheshire County, Historical Society & Archives
246 Main Street
P.O. Box 803
Keene, NH 03431
Tel: 603-352-1895

Chester Historical Society
P.O. Box 34
Chester, NH 03036

Chesterfield Historical Society
P.O. Box 204
Chesterfield, NH 03443

Chichester Historical Society
c/o Chichester Library
Main Street
Chichester, NH 03263

Claremont Historical Society
26 Mulberry Street
Claremont, NH 03743

Colebrook Area Historical Society
P.O. Box 32
Colebrook, NH 03576

Conway Historical Society
100 Main Street
P.O. Box 1949
Conway, NH 03818
Tel: 603-447-5551

Cornish Historical Society
RR 2, Box 416
Cornish, NH 03745

Deerfield Heritage Commission
60 South Road
Deerfield, NH 03037
Tel/Fax: 603-463-7151

Deering Historical Society
RR 1, Box 69
Deering, NH 03244

Derry Historical Society/Museum
65 Birch Street
Derry, NH 03038

Durham Historic Association
P.O. Box 305
Durham, NH 03824

Effingham Historical Society
P.O. Box 33
South Effingham, NH 03882

Epping Historical Society
P.O. Box 348
Epping, NH 03042

Exeter Historical Society
47 Front Street
P.O. Box 924
Exeter, NH 03833
Tel: 603-778-2335

Franklin Historical Society
P.O. Box 43
Franklin, NH 03235

Gilmanton Historical Society
P.O. Box 236
Gilmanton, NH 03237

Gilsum Historical Society
P.O. Box 205
Gilsum, NH 03448

Goffstown Historical Society
P.O. Box 284
Goffstown, NH 03045

Grafton County Historic & Genealogy Society
P.O. Box 1163
Ashland, NH 03217
Email: rbhicks@cyberportal.net

Greenland Historical Society
459 Portsmouth Avenue
Greenland, NH 03840

Hampton Historians, Inc.
3 Thomsen Road
Hampton, NH 03842

Hancock Historical Society
P.O. Box 138
Hancock, NH 03049

Hanover Historical Society
P.O. Box 142
Hanover, NH 03755

Harold Gilman Historical Museum
P.O. Box 428
Alton, NH 03809

Hawke Historical Society of Danville
P.O. Box 402
Danville, NH 03819

Henniker Historical Society
P.O. Box 674
Henniker, NH 03242

Hill Historical Society
P.O. Box 193
Hill, NH 03243

Hillsborough Historical Society
P.O. Box 896
Hillsboro, NH 03244

Hinsdale Historical Society
RR 2, River Street, Box 9
Hinsdale, NH 03451

Holderness Historical Society
P.O. Box 319
Holderness, NH 03245

Hollis Historical Society
P.O. Box 754
Hollis, NH 03049

Jackson Historical Society
P.O. Box 8
Jackson, NH 03846

Jaffrey Historical Society
123 Main Street
Jaffrey, NH 03452

Kensington Historical Society
c/o Kensington Public Library
126 Amesbury Road
Kensington, NH 03833

Laconia Historical Society
P.O. Box 1126
Laconia, NH 03247

Lancaster Historical Society
226 Main Street
P.O. Box 473
Lancaster, NH 03584
Tel: 603-788-3004

Lee Historical Society
Lee Town Hall
7 Mast Road
Lee, NH 03824

Littleton Area Historical Society
2 Cottage Street
Littleton, NH 03561

Londonderry Historical Society
P.O. Box 136
Londonderry, NH 03053

Madbury Historical Society
13 Town Hall Road
Madbury, NH 03820

Madison Historical Society
P.O. Box 335
Madison, NH 03849

Manchester Historic Association
129 Amherst Street
Manchester, NH 03101
Tel: 603-622-7531

Marlborough Historical Society, Inc.
P.O. Box 202
Marlborough, NH 03455

Meredith Historical Society
P.O. Box 920
Meredith, NH 03253

Merrimack Historical Society
P.O. Box 1525
Merrimack, NH 03054

Milford Historical Society
P.O. Box 609
Milford, NH 03055

Milton Township Historical Society
P.O. Box 621
Milton, NH 03851

Moultonborough Historical Society
P.O. Box 6549
Moultonborough, NH 03254

Nashua Historical Society
5 Abbott Street
Nashua, NH 03060

New England Historical and Genealogical Society (NEHGS)
101 Newbury Street
Boston, MA 02116-3007
Tel: 617-836-5740
888-AT-NEHGS (Membership & Education)
888-BY-NEHGS (Sales)
888-90-NEHGS (Library Circulation)
Fax: 617-536-7307
Email: nehgs@nehgs.org
URL: http://www.nehgs.org/

New Hampshire Antiquarian Society
300 Main Street
Hopkinton, NH 03229
Tel: 603-746-3825

New Hampshire Historical Society/Library
30 Park Street
Concord, NH 03301-6384
Tel: 603-225-3381
Fax: 603-224-0463
Email: swilding@aol.com
URL: http://newww.com/org/nhhs/

New Hampton Historical Society
P.O. Box 422
New Hampton, NH 03256

New London Historical Society
P.O. Box 965
New London, NH 03257

Newmarket Historical Society
Granite Street
Newmarket, NH 03857

Newbury Historical Society
P.O. Box 176
Newbury, NH 03255

Newfields Historical Society
P.O. Box 126
Newfields, NH 03856

Northwood Historical Society
P.O. Box 114
Northwood, NH 03261

Nottingham Historical Society
P.O. Box 241
Nottingham, NH 03290

Ossipee Historical Society
P.O. Box 245
Ossipee, NH 03864

Pelham Historical Society
8 Nashua Road
Pelham, NH 03076

Peterborough Historical Society
Grove Street
P.O. Box 58
Peterborough, NH 03458
Tel: 603-924-3235

Piermont Historical Society
P.O. Box 273
Piermont, NH 03779

Pittsburg Historical Society
P.O. Box 128
Pittsburg, NH 03592

Plainfield Historical Society
P.O. Box 125
Plainfield, NH 03781

Plaistow Historical Society
P.O. Box 434
Plaistow, NH 03865

Raymond Historical Society
P.O. Box 94
Raymond, NH 03077

Rindge Historical Society
South Main Street
Rindge, NH 03461

Rochester Historical Society
P.O. Box 65
Rochester, NH 03867

Rye Historical Society
P.O. Box 583
Rye, NH 03870

Salem Historical Society
79 Brady Avenue
Salem, NH 03079

Sanbornton Historical Society
P.O. Box 2
Sanbornton, NH 03269

Sandown Historical Society/Museum
P.O. Box 300
Sandown, NH 03873

Sandwich Historical Society/Museum
Maple Street
P.O. Box 106
Center Sandwich, NH 03227
Tel: 603-284-6269

Seabrook, Historical Society of
P.O. Box 500
Seabrook, NH 03874

Stoddard Historical Society
HCR 32, Box 551
Stoddard, NH 03464

Strafford Historical Society
P.O. Box 33
Center Strafford, NH 03815

Stratham Historical Society
P.O. Box 39
Stratham, NH 03885

Somersworth Historical Society
6 Drew Road
Somersworth, NH 03878

Sutton Historical Society
P.O. Box 503
South Sutton, NH 03273

Tamworth Historical Society
P.O. Box 13
Tamworth, NH 03886

Temple Historical Society
P.O. Box 114
Temple, NH 03084

Thompson/Ames Historical Society
P.O. Box 252
Laconia, NH 03247

Tilton Historical Society
P.O. Box 351
Tilton, NH 03276

Tuftonboro Historical Society
P.O. Box 372
Melvin Village, NH 03850

Wakefield/Brookfield Historical Society
P.O. Box 795
Brookfield, NH 03872

Walpole Historical Society
P.O. Box 292
Walpole, NH 03608

Warner Historical Society
P.O. Box 189
Warner, NH 03278

Warren Historical Society
P.O. Box 114
Warren, NH 03279

Washington Historical Society
P.O. Box 90
Washington, NH 03280

Weare Historical Society
P.O. Box 33
Weare, NH 03281

Wilmot Historical Society
Town Office Building
Wilmot Flat, NH 03287

Windham Historical Society
P.O. Box 441
Windham, NH 03087

Wolfeboro Historical Society
Pleasant Valley Schoolhouse
P.O. Box 1066
Wolfeboro, NH 03894
URL: http://www.wolfeboro.com/histsoc.htm

LDS Family History Centers

Concord Family History Center
90 Clinton Street
Concord, NH 03301
Tel: 603-225-2848

Nashua Family History Center
110 Concord Street
Nashua, NH 03060
Tel: 508-649-9233

Portsmouth Family History Center
Andres Jarvis Drive
Portsmouth, NH 03801
Tel: 603-433-4428

Archives/Libraries/Museums

Acworth Silsby Library
P.O. Box 179
Acworth, NH 03601
Tel: 603-835-2150
Email: acworthlibrary@top.monad.net
URL: http://top.monad.net/~acworthlibrary/

American Canadian Genealogical Society/Library
378 Notre Dame Avenue
P.O. Box 668
Manchester, NH 03105

American Independence Museum
One Governers Lane
Exeter, NH 03833-2420
Tel: 603-772-2622
Fax: 603-772-0861
Email: aim@nh.ultranet.com
URL: http://www.nh.ultranet.com/~aim/

Cheshire County, Historical Society & Archives
246 Main Street
P.O. Box 803
Keene, NH 03431
Tel: 603-352-1895

Chichester Library
Main Street
P.O. Box 582
Chichester, NH 03234
Tel: 603-798-5613

Conant Public Library/Historical Museum
Main Street
P.O. Box 6
Winchester, NH 03470
Tel: 603-239-4331
Email: conantpl@top.monad.net/~conantpl/home.htm

Dartmouth College Archives
Baker Library
Hanover, NH 03755
Tel: 603-646-2037
URL: http://www.dartmouth.edu/~library/Special_Collections/BG_revised.html

Dover Public Library
73 Locust Street
Dover, NH 03820
Tel: 603-742-5313

Exeter Public Library
Founders Park
Exeter, NH 03833
Tel: 603-772-3101

Fiske Free Library
108 Broad Street
Claremont, NH 03743
Tel: 603-542-7017
603-542-4393
Fax: 603-542-7029
URL: http://www.claremontnh.com/library_index.html

Gilsum Public Library
Main Street
P.O. Box 57
Gilsum, NH 03448
Tel: 603-357-0320
URL: http://www.keenesentinel.com/communit/libraries/gilsum.shtml

Keene Public Library
Wright Room
60 Winter Street
Keene, NH 03431
Tel: 603-352-0157
Fax: 603-352-1101
URL: http://www.ci.keene.nh.us/library/

Kensington Social and Public Library
126 Amesbury Road
Exeter, NH 03833
Tel: 603-772-5022

Lane Memorial Library
2 Academy Avenue
Hampton, NH 03842
Tel: 603-926-3368
Fax: 603-926-1348
Email: bteschek@hampton.lib.nh.us (Local History & Genealogy)
URL: http://www.hampton.lib.nh.us/

Manchester Library
Carpenter Memorial Building
405 Pine Street
Manchester, NH 03104
Tel: 603-624-6550

New England Historical and Genealogical Society (NEHGS)
101 Newbury Street
Boston, MA 02116-3007
Tel: 617-836-5740
888-AT-NEHGS (Membership & Education)
888-BY-NEHGS (Sales)
888-90-NEHGS (Library Circulation)
Fax: 617-536-7307
Email: nehgs@nehgs.org
URL: http://www.nehgs.org/

New Hampshire Historical Society/Library
30 Park Street
Concord, NH 03301-6384
Tel: 603-225-3381
Email: swilding@aol.com
URL: http://newww.com/org/nhhs/

New Hampshire Museum of History
6 Eagle Square
Concord, NH 03301
Tel: 603-226-3189
URL: http://newww.com/org/nhhs/

New Hampshire State Library
20 Park Street
Concord, NH 03301
Tel: 603-271-2144
603-271-2239
Fax: 603-271-2205
Email: tepare@lilac.nhsl.lib.nh.us
URL: http://www.state.nh.us/nhsl/

Pelham Public Library
5 Main Street
Pelham, NH 03076
Tel/Fax: 603-635-7581
Email: library@pelham-nh.com
URL: http://www.pelham-nh.com/library/

Pillsbury Free Library
18 East Main Street
Warner, NH 03278
Tel: 603-456-2289
Email: pillsburylib@conknet.com
URL: http://www.conknet.com/~pillsburylib/pflhome.htm

Plymouth Historical Museum
Court Street
Plymouth, NH 03264
Tel: 603-536-2337

Portsmouth Athenaeum
9 Market Square
Portsmouth, NH 03801
Tel: 603-431-2538

Sandown Historical Society/Museum
P.O. Box 300
Sandown, NH 03873

Sandwich Historical Society/Museum
Maple Street
P.O. Box 106
Center Sandwich, NH 03227
Tel: 603-284-6369

Silsby Free Public Library
Main Street
P.O. Box 307
Charlestown, NH 03603
Tel: 603-826-7793
URL: http://www.keenesentinel.com/communit/libraries/chastown.shtml

Strawbery Banke Museum
Thayer Cumings Library and Archives
454 Court Street
P.O. Box 300
Portsmouth, NH 03802-0300
Tel: 603-433-1101
URL: http://wwwsc.library.unh.edu/specoll/Sbanke/library.htm

Sugar Hill Historical Museum
Village Green
Sugar Hill, NH 03585

University of New Hampshire
Dimond Library/Piscataqua Pioneers Genealogical Collection
Durham, NH 03824
Tel: 603-862-2714 (Special Collections)
603-862-0277 (Archives)
Email: wer@christa.unh.edu
URL: http://wwwsc.library.unh.edu/specoll/

Westmoreland Public Library
New England Collection
South Village Road
Westmoreland, NH 03467
Tel: 603-399-7750
URL: http://www.keenesentinel.com/communit/libraries/westmlnd.shtml

Wolfeboro Historical Society
Pleasant Valley Schoolhouse
P.O. Box 1066
Wolfeboro, NH 03894
URL: http://www.wolfeboro.com/histsoc.htm

Wolfeboro Public Library
South Main STreet
P.O. Box 710
Wolfeboro, NH 03894
Tel: 603-569-2428
URL: http://wolfeboro.com/library.htm

Newspaper Repositories

Dartmouth College Archives
Baker Library
Hanover, NH 03755
Tel: 603-646-3187
Email: john.g.crane@dartmouth.edu
URL: http://www.dartmouth.edu/~library/thelibs/baker.html

New Hampshire Historical Society/Library
30 Park Street
Concord, NH 03301-6384
Tel: 603-225-3381
Email: swilding@aol.com
URL: http://newww.com/org/nhhs/

New Hampshire State Library
20 Park Street
Concord, NH 03301
Tel: 603-271-2144
603-271-2239
Fax: 603-271-2205
Email: tepare@lilac.nhsl.lib.nh.us
URL: http://www.state.nh.us/nhsl/

Vital Records

Bureau of Vital Records
6 Hazen Drive
Concord, NH 03301
Tel: 603-271-4651

New Hampshire on the Web

Irish in 19th-Century Portsmouth, New Hampshire
http://www.geocities.com/CollegePark/9887/pintro.html

New Hampshire GenWeb Project
http://www.geocities.com/Heartland/5275/nh.htm

New Hampshire Historical Society Searchable Collection
http://newww.com/org/nhhs/databases/index.html

New Jersey

Archives, State & National

National Archives—Northeast Region
201 Varick Street
New York, NY 10014
Tel: 212-337-1300
Fax: 212-337-1306
Email: archives@newyork.nara.gov
URL: http://www.nara.gov/nara/regional/02nsgil.html

New Jersey State Archives
State Library Building
185 West State Street, Level 2
CN 307
Trenton, NJ 08625-0307
Tel: 609-292-6260
Fax: 609-396-2454
URL: http://www.state.nj.us/state/darm/archives.html

Genealogical Societies

Afro-American Historical & Genealogical Society
c/o AAHS Museum, 2nd Floor
1841 Kennedy Blvd.
Jersey City, NJ 07305
Tel: 201-547-5262

Bergen County Genealogy Society
P.O. Box 432
Midland Park, NJ 07432
http://maple.nis.net/~wardell/BCAssoc.htm

Burlington County Genealogy Club
Woodlane Road
P.O. Box 2449, RD 2
Mount Holly, NJ 08060
Tel: 609-267-0881

Cape May Historical & Genealogical Society/Library
Route 9
Cape May Courthouse, NJ 08210-3070
Tel: 609-465-3535
URL: http://www.cyberenet.net/~gsteiner/njgenweb/cmhgs.html

Central Jersey Genealogy Club
P.O. Box 9903
Hamilton, NJ 08650
http://members.aol.com/DSSaari.cjgc.htm

Genealogical Society of New Jersey
141 Linden Avenue
Westfield, NJ 07090

Jewish Genealogical Society of North Jersey
c/o Evan Stolbach
1 Bedford Road
Pompton Lakes, NJ 07442
Tel: 201-839-4045

Mayflower Descendants in New Jersey
P.O. Box 172
Chatham, NJ 07928

Metuchen/Edison Genealogy Club
c/o Vivian Hight
48 Elliot Place
Edison, NJ 08817
Tel: 908-985-3914

Monmouth County Genealogical Club
c/o Monmouth County Historical Association
70 Court Street
Freehold, NJ 07728
Tel: 908-462-1466
Fax: 908-462-8346
URL: http://nj5.injersey.com/~kjshelly/mcgc.html

Morris Area Genealogy Society
P.O. Box 105
Convent Station, NJ 07961

New Jersey Genealogical Society
P.O. Box 1291
New Brunswick, NJ 08903

New Jersey Historical Society/Library
Genealogy Club
230 Broadway
Newark, NJ 07104
Tel: 201-483-3939
Fax: 201-483-1988

Ocean County Genealogical Society
c/o Tom Jackson
135 Nautilus Drive
Manahawkin, NJ 08050

Passaic County Genealogy Club
430 Mt. Pleasant Avenue
West Paterson, NJ 07424

Salem County, Genealogical Society of
P.O. Box 231
Woodstown, NJ 08098
URL: http://www.cyberenet.net/~gsteiner/njgenweb/gsscnj.html

Warren County Historical & Genealogical Society/Museum & Library
313 Mansfield Street
P.O. Box 313
Belvidere, NJ 07823
Tel: 908-475-4246

West Fields, Genealogical Society of the
c/o Westfield Memorial Library
550 East Broad Street
Westfield, NJ 07090
Tel: 908-789-4090
Email: gswf@westfieldnj.com
URL: http://www.westfieldnj.com/gswf/index.htm

Historical Societies

Absecon Historical Society
618 Franklin Blvd.
Absecon, NJ 08201

Afro-American Historical & Genealogical Society
1841 Kennedy Blvd.
Jersey City, NJ 07305
Tel: 201-547-5262

Alexandria Township Historical Society
174 Warsaw Road
Frenchtown, NJ 08825

Allendale Historical Society
P.O. Box 294
Allendale, NJ 07401

Allentown/Upper Freehold Historical Society
76 North Main Street
P.O. Box 328
Allentown, NJ 08501
Tel: 609-259-3171

Alpine Historical Society
P.O. Box 59
Alpine, NJ 07620
Tel: 201-768-1360

American-Italian Historical Association
Historic Dorothea's House
120 John Street
Princeton, NJ 08540

Andover Boro, Historical Society of
189 Main Street
Andover, NJ 07821
Tel: 201-786-6829

Association of New Jersey County Cultural & Heritage Agencies
c/o Camden County Cultural & Heritage Commission (headquarters)
Hopkins House
250 S. Park Drive
Haddon Township, NJ 08108
Tel: 609-858-0040

Atlantic County Cultural & Heritage Commission
40 Farragut Avenue
Mays Landing, NJ 08330
Tel: 609-625-2776

Atlantic County Historical Society/Library & Museum
907 Shore Road
P.O. Box 301
Somers Point, NJ 08244
Tel: 609-927-5218

Atlantic Highlands Historical Society
27 Prospect Avenue
P.O. Box 108
Atlantic Highlands, NJ 07716
Tel: 908-291-1861

Audubon Historical Society
238 Washington Terrace
Audubon, NJ 08106

Barnegat Light Historical Society
West 5th & Central Avenue
P.O. Box 386
Barnegat Light, NJ 08006
Tel: 609-494-8578

Battleground Historical Society
P.O. Box 61
Tennent, NJ 07763
Tel: 908-446-9760

Bay Head Historical Society
P.O. Box 127
Bay Head, NJ 08742

Bayonne Historical Society
P.O. Box 3034
Bayonne, NJ 07002
Tel: 201-823-4840

Belleville Historical Society
c/o Belleville Public Library
221 Washington Avenue
Belleville, NJ 07109

Bergen County Division of Cultural & Historic Affairs
Administration Building
Court Plaza South
21 Main Street
Hackensack, NJ 08601-7000
Tel: 201-646-2786

Bergen County Historical Society
120 Main Street
P.O. Box 55
River Edge, NJ 07661
Tel: 201-487-1739
201-343-9492
URL: http://maple.nis.net/~wardell/BCAssoc.htm

Berkeley Heights, Historical Society of
P.O. Box 237
Berkeley Heights, NJ 07922

Berkeley Township Historical Society
759 U.S. Highway 9
Bayville, NJ 08721
Tel: 908-269-9527

Bethlehem Township Historical Society
P.O. Box 56
Asbury, NJ 08802

Bloomfield, Historical Society of
47 Clark Avenue
Bloomfield, NJ 07003
Tel: 201-429-8387

Blue Hills Historical Society
311 West End Avenue
North Plainfield, NJ 07060

Boonton Historic Society
619 Main Street
Boonton, NJ 07005
Tel: 201-627-6205

Boonton Township, Historical Society of
RD 2, Box 152
Boonton, NJ 07005

Bordentown Historical Society
Old City Hall
211 Crosswicks Road
P.O. Box 182
Bordentown, NJ 08505
Tel: 609-298-1740
URL: http://bc.emanon.net/bhs/

Bradley Beach Historical Society
Bradley Beach Library
511 4th Avenue
Bradley Beach, NJ 07720
Tel: 908-775-2175

Brick Township Historical Society
P.O. Box 160
Brick, NJ 08723
Tel: 908-477-4513

Brigantine Historical Society
470 West Shore Drive
Brigantine, NJ 08203

Burlington City Historical Society
Dr. Nicholas P. Kamaras
City Hall
Burlington City, NJ 08016
Tel: 609-386-3993
URL: http://bc.emanon.net/cgi-bin/burl/city_historical_society

Burlington County Cultural & Heritage Department
49 Rancocas Road
Mount Holly, NJ 08060
Tel: 609-265-5068

Burlington County Historical Society
457 High Street
Burlington, NJ 08016
Tel: 609-386-4773
Fax: 609-386-4828
URL: http://bc.emanon.net/cgi-bin/burl/county_historical_society

Byram Township Historical Society
3 Ghost Pony Road
Andover, NJ 07821
Tel: 201-347-4585

Califon Historical Society
25 Academy Street
P.O. Box 424
Califon, NJ 07830
Tel: 908-832-0878

Camden County Cultural & Heritage Commission
Hopkins House
250 South Park Drive
Haddon Township, NJ 08108
Tel: 609-858-0400

Camden County Historical Society/Library
Park Blvd. & Euclid Avenue
Camden, NJ 08103-3697
Tel: 609-964-3333
URL: http://www.cyberenet.net/~gsteiner/cchs/
or http://www.fieldtrip.com/nj/99643333.htm

Cape May County, Department of Culture & Heritage
Crest Haven Complex
4 Moore Road
Cape May Courthouse, NJ 08210
Tel: 609-465-1005

Cape May Historical & Genealogical Society/Library
John Holmes House
504 Route 9
Cape May Courthouse, NJ 08210-3070
Tel: 609-465-3535
URL: http://www.cyberenet.net/~gsteiner/njgenweb/cmhgs.html
or http://www.fieldtrip.com/nj/94653535.htm

Cedar Grove Historical Society
P.O. Box 461
Cedar Grove, NJ 07009
Tel: 201-239-5414

Chatham Historical Society
P.O. Box 682
Chatham, NJ 07928

Chester Historical Society
245 W. Main Street
P.O. Box 376
Chester, NJ 07930
Tel: 908-879-2761

Chesterfield Township Historical Society
P.O. Box 86
Crosswicks, NJ 08515

Clark Historical Society
Municipal Building, Room 18
430 Westfield Avenue
Clark, NJ 07066
Tel: 908-381-3600 ext. 3025

Colts Neck Historical Society
15 Enclosure
Colts Neck, NJ 07722
Tel: 908-946-4921

Cranbury History & Preservation Society
4 Park Place, E
Cranbury, NJ 08512
Tel: 609-655-2611

Cranford Historical Society
124 N. Union Avenue
Cranford, NJ 07016
Tel: 908-276-0082
Email: bdevlin@bobdevlin.com
URL: http://www.bobdevlin.com/crhissoc.html

Cumberland County Cultural & Heritage Commission
422 Rhonda Drive
Millville, NJ 08332
Tel: 609-825-9662

Cumberland County Historical Society
Gibbon House
P.O. Box 16
Greenwich, NJ 08323
Tel: 609-455-4055
URL: http://www.cyberenet.com/~gsteiner/njgenweb/cumbernj.html

Dennis Township Historical Society
P.O. Box 109
South Dennis, NJ 08245
Tel: 609-861-2925

Denville Historical Society
Diamond Spring Road
P.O. Box 466
Denville, NJ 07834
Tel: 201-625-1165

Dover Area Historical Society
P.O. Box 609
Dover, NJ 07801

Dunellen Historical Society
322 Whittier Avenue
Dunellen, NJ 08812

East Brunswick Historical Association
43 Sullivan Way
East Brunswick, NJ 08816
Tel: 908-249-3522

East Hanover Historical Society
181 Mount Pleasant Avenue
East Hanover, NJ 07936
Tel: 201-884-0038

Eatontown Historical Committee/Museum
75 Broad Street
Eatontown, NJ 07724
Tel: 908-542-4026

Edison Township Historical Society
328 Plainfield
Edison, NJ 08817

Egg Harbor City Historical Society
533 London Avenue
Egg Harbor City, NJ 08215
Tel: 609-965-9073

Elizabethtown Historical Foundation
P.O. Box 1
Elizabeth, NJ 07207

Elmwood Park Historical Society
210 Lee Street
Elmwood Park, NJ 07407
Tel: 201-797-2109

Englewood Historical Society
500 Liberty Street
Englewood, NJ 07631
Tel: 201-568-0678

English Neighborhood Historical Society
656 Elm Street
Maywood, NJ 07607

Essex County, Department of Parks, Recreation, Cultural & Historic Affairs
160 Fairview Avenue
Cedar Grove, NJ 07009
Tel: 201-484-6733

Essex Fells Historical Society
96 Forest Way
Essex Fells, NJ 07021

Evesham Historical Society
10 Madison Court
Marlton, NJ 08053
Tel: 609-988-0995

Ewing Township Historical Preservation Society/Library
27 Federal City Road
Ewing, NJ 08638
Tel: 609-530-1220

Fair Haven Historical Society
P.O. Box 72
Fair Haven, NJ 07704
Tel: 908-842-4453

Fairfield Historical Society
221 Hollywood Avenue
Fairfield, NJ 07006

Farmingdale Historical Society
2 Goodenough Road
Farmingdale, NJ 07727
Tel: 908-938-2008

Florham Park, Historical Society of
P.O. Box 193
Florham, NJ 07932
Tel: 201-377-6291

Fort Lee Historical Society
Borough Hall
309 Main Street
Fort Lee, NJ 07024
Tel: 201-592-3580

Fortescue Historical Society
Pier #1, Bayside
Fortescue, NJ 08321

Frenchtown Historical Association
Borough Hall
2nd Street
Frenchtown, NJ 08825

Garfield Historical Society
201 Outwater Lane
Garfield, NJ 07026
Tel: 201-478-9022

Glen Ridge Historical Society
P.O. Box 164
Glen Ridge, NJ 07028
Tel: 201-748-1784

Glen Rock Historical & Preservation Society
Municipal Building, Borough Hall
Glen Rock, NJ 07452
Tel: 201-447-2414

Gloucester County Cultural & Heritage Commission
406 Swedesboro Road
Gibbstown, NJ 08027
Tel: 609-423-0916

Gloucester County Historical Society/Library
17 Hunter Street
Woodbury, NJ 08096
Tel: 609-845-4771
URL: http://www.rootsweb.com/~njglouce/gchs/

Great Egg Harbor Township Historical Society
Township Hall
RD 1, Box 262
Linwood, NJ 08221

Greater Cape May Historical Society
Colonial House
653 1/2 Washington Street
P.O. Box 495
Cape May, NJ 08204
Tel: 609-889-0587
609-884-8344

Green Township Historical Society
P.O. Box 203
Tranquility, NJ 07879
Tel: 201-383-5829

Griggstown Historical Society
RD 1, Canal Road
Princeton, NJ 08554

Hackettstown Historical Society
106 Church Street
Hackettstown, NJ 07840
Tel: 908-852-8797
908-850-0568

Haddon Heights Historical Society
c/o Haddon Heights Library
Station Avenue
Haddon Heights, NJ 08035

Haddon Township Historical Society
109 Emerald Avenue
Westmont, NJ 08108

Haddonfield Historical Society
Greenfield Hall
343 Kingshighway East
Haddonfield, NJ 08033
Tel: 609-429-7375
URL: http://www.haddonfield.com/org/

Hamilton Township Historical Society
2200 Kuser Road
Trenton, NJ 08650
Tel: 609-585-1686

Hammonton Historical Society
767 Central Avenue
Hammonton, NJ 08037
Tel: 609-561-2830

Harding Township Historical Society
Village & Millbrook Roads
P.O. Box 1776
New Vernon, NJ 07976
Tel: 201-292-0161

Hardwick Township Historical Society
P.O. Box 722
Blairstown, NJ 07925

Hardyston Heritage Society
North Woods Trail
P.O. Box 434
Stockholm, NJ 07460
Tel: 201-697-8733

Harrington Park Historical Society
10 Herring Street
Harrington Park, NJ 07640

Harrison Township Historical Society
Main Street
P.O. Box 4
Mullica Hill, NJ 08062
Tel: 609-478-4949

Hazlet Township Historical Society
Municipal Offices
319 Middle Road
Hazlet, NJ 07730

Helmetta Historical Society
60 Main Street
Helmetta, NJ 08828
Tel: 908-521-2402

Highland Park Historical Commission
P.O. Box 1330
Highland Park, NJ 08904
Tel: 908-572-3400

Highlands, Historical Society of
P.O. Box 13
Highlands, NJ 07732

Hightstown/East Windsor Historical Society
164 North Main Street
Hightstown, NJ 08520
Tel: 609-371-9580

Hillsborough Historical Society
P.O. Box 720
Neshanic, NJ 08853

Hillside Historical Society
111 Conant Avenue
Hillside, NJ 07205
Tel: 908-353-8828

Holland Township Historical Society
P.O. Box 434
Milford, NJ 08848
Tel: 908-995-9197

Holmdel Historical Society
P.O. Box 282
Holmdel, NJ 07733

Hope Historical Society
High Street
P.O. Box 52
Hope, NJ 07844

Hopewell Valley Historical Society
State Highway 579 & 601
P.O. Box 371
Pennington, NJ 08534
Tel: 609-737-7751

Howell Historical Society
427 Lakewood Farmingdale Road
Howell, NJ 07731
Tel: 908-938-2212
908-938-5868

Hudson County Division of Cultural & Heritage Affairs
Murdoch Hall
114 Clifton Place
Jersey City, NJ 07304
Tel: 201-915-1212

Hunterdon County Cultural & Heritage Commission
Administration Building
Flemington, NJ 08822
Tel: 908-788-1256

Hunterdon County Historical Society
Hiram E. Deats Memorial Library
114 Main Street
Flemington, NJ 08822
Tel: 908-782-1091

Indian Mills Historical Society
Atsion Road
RD 5, Box 252
Vincentown, NJ 08088

Irvington Historical Society
34 Clinton Terrace
Irvington, NJ 07111
Tel: 201-374-7500

Island Heights Cultural & Heritage Association
P.O. Box 670
Island Heights, NJ 08732

Jamesburg Historical Association
203 Buckelew Avenue
Jamesburg, NJ 08831
Tel: 908-521-2040

Jefferson Township Historical Society
Dover Milton Road
P.O. Box 1776
Oak Ridge, NJ 07438
Tel: 201-697-0258
201-697-8675

Jewish Historical Society of Central Jersey
c/o Robert S. Kramer
228 Livingston Avenue
New Brunswick, NJ 08901
Tel: 908-249-4894
URL: http://www.jewishgen.org/jhscj/genealogyinfo.html

Jewish Historical Society of MetroWest
901 Route 10 East
Whippany, NJ 07981
Tel: 201-884-4800 ext 565
Fax: 201-428-4720
Email: jfien@aol.com
URL: http://www.fiengroup.com/jhs/jhs.htm

Jewish Historical Society of Northern New Jersey
P.O. Box 708
West Paterson, NJ 07424

Jewish Historical Society of Trenton
865 Lower Ferry Road
Trenton, NJ 08628
Tel: 609-883-2228

Kearny Cottage Historical Association
63 Catalpa Avenue
Perth Amboy, NJ 08861
Tel: 908-826-1826

Keyport Historical Society
2 Broad Street
P.O. Box 312
Keyport, NJ 07735
Tel: 908-739-6390

Kingwood Township Historical Society
Kingwood Township Municipal Building
P.O. Box 199
Baptistown, NJ 08803

Kinnelon Historical Commission
25 Kiel Avenue
Kinnelon, NJ 07405
Tel: 201-838-0185

Lacey Historical Society
P.O. Box 412
Forked River, NJ 08731

Lake Hopatcong Historical Society
P.O. Box 119
Lake Hopatcong, NJ 07849
Tel: 201-663-2460

Lakehurst Historical Society
505 Oak Street
Lakehurst, NJ 08733
Tel: 908-657-7209
URL: http://www.fieldtrip.com/nj/86577209.htm

Lambertville Historical Society
62 Bridge Street
P.O. Box 2
Lambertville, NJ 08530
Tel: 609-397-0770

Lawnside Historical Society
P.O. Box 608
Lawnside, NJ 08045-0608
Tel: 609-547-8489

Lawrence Historical Society
P.O. Box 6025
Lawrenceville, NJ 08648
Tel: 609-987-8196

League of Historical Societies of New Jersey
P.O. Box 909
Madison, NJ 07940
Tel: 908-463-8363
URL: http://scils.rutgers.edu/~macan/leaguelist.html

Leonia Historical Society
199 Christie Street
Leonia, NJ 07605
Tel: 201-947-5647

Linwood Historical Society
16 Poplar Avenue
Linwood, NJ 08221
Tel: 609-927-8293

Little Falls Township Historical Society
8 Douglas Drive
Little Falls, NJ 07424

Little Silver Historical Society
Borough Hall
480 Prospect Avenue
Little Silver, NJ 07739
Tel: 908-842-2400

Livingston Historical Society
P.O. Box 220
Livingston, NJ 07039

Long-a-Coming Historical Society
59 S. White Horse Pike
Berlin, NJ 08009
Tel: 609-767-6221

Long Beach Island Historical Association
Engelside & Beach Avenue
P.O. Box 1222
Beach Haven, NJ 08008
Tel: 609-492-0700

Long Branch Historical Museum
1260 Ocean Avenue
Long Branch, NJ 07740
Tel: 908-222-9879

Long Hill Township Historical Society
1336 Valley Road
Stirling, NJ 07087
Tel: 908-647-5762

Longport Historical Society
Borough Hall
2305 Atlantic Avenue
Longport, NJ 08403
Tel: 609-823-1115

Lumberton Historical Society
P.O. Box 22
Lumberton, NJ 08048

Lyndhurst Historical Society
P.O. Box 135
Lyndhurst, NJ 07071
Tel: 201-804-2513

Madison Township Historical Society
Box 150 Morristown Road
Matawan, NJ 07747

Mahwah Historical Society
310 Forest Road
Mahwah, NJ 07430
Tel: 201-891-9049

Manchester Historical Society
18 Bowie Drive
Whiting, NJ 08759

Mansfield Township Historical Society
3121 Route 206
Columbus, NJ 08022-9530
Tel: 609-298-4174

Maple Shade Historical Society
P.O. Box 368
Maple Shade, NJ 08052

Matawan Historical Society
94 Main Street
P.O. Box 41
Matawan, NJ 07747
Tel: 908-566-5605

Mauricetown Historical Society
Front Street
Mauricetown, NJ 08329
Tel: 609-785-0457

Medford Historical Society
Church Road
Medford, NJ 08055
Tel: 609-654-7767

Mercer County Cultural & Heritage Commission
640 S. Broad Street
Trenton, NJ 08650
Tel: 609-989-6899

Merchantville Historical Society
West Maple Avenue
Merchantville, NJ 08109
Tel: 609-665-1819

Metuchen/Edison Regional Historical Society
Genealogy Club
P.O. Box 61
Metuchen, NJ 08840
Tel: 908-906-0529

Middlesex County Cultural & Heritage Commission
841 Georges Road
North Brunswick, NJ 08902
Tel: 908-745-4489

Middletown Township Historical Society
Leonardville Road
Leonardo, NJ 07737
Mail:
P.O. Box 434
Middletown, NJ 07748
Tel: 908-291-8739

Midland Park Historical Society
212 Park Avenue
Midland Park, NJ 07432

Millburn/Short Hills Historical Society
4 Fox Hill Lane
P.O. Box 243
Short Hills, NJ 07078
Tel: 201-376-7048

Milltown Historical Society
P.O. Box 96
Milltown, NJ 08850

Millville Historical Society
2nd and Main Street
Millville, NJ 08332
Tel: 609-327-4944
609-825-0789

Monmouth County Historical Association
70 Court Street
Freehold, NJ 07728
Tel: 908-462-1466
Fax: 908-462-8346
Email: mchalib@aol.com
URL: http://www.monmouth.com/~mcha/

Monmouth County Historical Commission
27 E. Main Street
Freehold, NJ 07728
Tel: 908-431-7413

Monroe Township Historical Society
Hall Street
P.O. Box 474
Williamstown, NJ 08094
Tel: 609-728-0458

Montclair Historical Society
Terhune Library
110 Orange Road
Montclair, NJ 07043
Tel: 201-744-1796
URL: http://interactive.net/~upper/crane.html

Montville Historical Society
415 Boyd Street
P.O. Box 497
Boonton, NJ 07005

Moorestown, Historical Society of
Smith-Cadbury Mansion
12 High Street
P.O. Box 477
Moorestown, NJ 08057
Tel: 609-235-0353
URL: http://www.moorestown.com/community/history/

Morris County Heritage Commission
County Court House
Morristown, NJ 07960
Tel: 201-829-8117

Morris County Historical Society/Research Library
Acorn Hall
68 Morris Avenue
P.O. Box 170M
Morristown, NJ 07960
Tel: 201-267-3465

Mount Holly Historical Society
307 High Street
P.O. Box 4081
Mount Holly, NJ 08060
Tel: 609-267-8844

Neptune Township Historical Society/Museum
25 Neptune Blvd.
P.O. Box 1125
Neptune, NJ 07753
Tel: 908-775-8241
908-922-3154

New Egypt Historical Society
P.O. Box 295
New Egypt, NJ 08533

New Jersey Graveyard Preservation Society
P.O. Box 5
East Brunswick, NJ 08816

New Jersey Historical Society/Library
230 Broadway
Newark, NJ 07104
Tel: 201-483-3939
Fax: 201-483-1988

New Providence Historical Society
1350 Springfield Avenue
Mail:
360 Elkwood Avenue
New Providence, NJ 07974
Tel: 908-464-0163

Newfield Historical Society
Newfield Borough Hall
107 N.E. Blvd.
Newfield, NJ 08344
Tel: 609-697-1100
609-697-3811

North Arlington Historical Society
89 Canterbury Avenue
North Arlington, NJ 07032
Tel: 201-998-6290

North Brunswick Historical Society
690 Cranbury Crossroad
North Brunswick, NJ 08902

North Jersey Highlands Historical Society
P.O. Box 248
Ringwood, NJ 07456

Nutley Historical Society
65 Church Street
Nutley, NJ 07110
Tel: 201-667-1528

Oakland Historical Society
Van Allen House
P.O. Box 296
Oakland, NJ 07436
Tel: 201-825-9049

Ocean City Historical Society/Museum
1735 Simpson Avenue
Ocean City, NJ 08226
Tel: 609-399-1801

Ocean County Cultural & Heritage Commission
101 Hooper Avenue, Room 225
CN 2191
Toms River, NJ 08754-2191
Tel: 908-929-4779

Ocean County Historical Society
Strickler Research Library
26 Hadley Avenue
P.O. Box 2191
Toms River, NJ 08754
Tel: 908-341-1880
URL: http://www.fieldtrip.com/nj/83411880.htm

Ocean Gate Historical Society/Museum
Cape May and Asbury Avenues
P.O. Box 895
Ocean Gate, NJ 08740
Tel: 908-269-3468
URL: http://www.fieldtrip.com/nj/82693468.htm

Ocean Grove, Historical Society of
53 Central Avenue
P.O. Box 446
Ocean Grove, NJ 07756
Tel: 908-774-1869

Ogdensburg Historical Society
15 Richards Street
Ogdensburg, NJ 07439

Old Randolph Historical Society
P.O. Box 1776
Ironia, NJ 07845
Tel: 201-989-7095

Old Schralenburgh Historical Society
43 Overlook Road
Dumont, NJ 07628

Old Wall Historical Society
1701 New Bedford Road
P.O. Box 1203
Wall, NJ 07719
Tel: 908-974-1430

Oldman Township Historical Society
Railroad Avenue
P.O. Box 158208
Pedricktown, NJ 08067
Tel: 609-299-1743

Oliver Cromwell Black History Society
c/o Afri-Mail Institute
348 High Street
Burlington, NJ 08016
Tel: 609-387-8133
609-877-1449
Fax: 609-387-8144
URL: http://bc.emanon.net/cgi-bin/burl/oliver_cromwell_society

Oxford Historical Society
P.O. Box 277
Oxford, NJ 07863
Tel: 908-453-2204

Paramus Historical and Preservation Society
650 E. Glen Avenue
Ridgewood, NJ 07450
Tel: 201-447-3242
201-652-4584
URL: http://maple.nis.net/~wardell/BCAssoc.htm

Parsippany Historical Society
93 Intervale Road
Boonton, NJ 07005
Tel: 201-334-2116

Pascack Historical Society
19 Ridge Avenue
P.O. Box 285
Park Ridge, NJ 07656
Tel: 201-573-0307
201-664-4934
URL: http://maple.nis.net/~wardell/BCAssoc.htm

Passaic County Cultural & Heritage Council
Passaic County College
College Blvd.
Paterson, NJ 07509
Tel: 201-684-6555

Passaic County Historical Society/Library
Lambert Castle
Valley Road
Paterson, NJ 07503
Tel: 201-881-2761

Pennsauken Historical Society
9201 Burrough Dover Lane
P.O. Box 56
Pennsauken, NJ 08110
Tel: 609-662-3002

Pennsville Township Historical Society
86 Church Landing Road
Pennsville, NJ 08070
Tel: 609-678-4453

Perth Amboy Historical Society
1 Lewis Street
Perth Amboy, NJ 08861

Phillipsburg Area Historical Society
Municipal Building
Corliss Avenue
Phillipsburg, NJ 08865
Tel: 908-454-5500
908-454-3478

Piscataway Historical & Heritage Society
1001 Maple Avenue
Piscataway, NJ 08854
Tel: 908-752-5252

Plainfield, Historical Society of
602 West Front Street
Plainfield, NJ 07060-1004
Tel; 908-755-5831

Plainsboro Historical Society
641 Plainsboro Road
P.O. Box 278
Plainsboro, NJ 08536
Tel: 609-799-0909

Pohatcong Historical Society
Rte. 1, Box 251
Phillipsburg, NJ 08865
Tel: 908-995-7107

Point Pleasant Historical Society
P.O. Box 1273
Point Pleasant Beach, NJ 08742

Port Republic Historical Society
P.O. Box 215
Port Republic, NJ 08241
Tel: 609-652-1352

Princeton Historical Society/Library
158 Nassau Street
Princeton, NJ 08542
Tel: 609-921-6748
Email: PHS@injersey.com
URL: http://princetonol.com/groups/histsoc/

Rahway Historical Society
1632 Saint Georges Avenue
P.O. Box 1842
Rahway, NJ 07065
Tel: 908-381-0441
908-388-0053

Ramsey Historical Association
538 Island Road
P.O. Box 76
Ramsey, NJ 07446
Tel: 201-825-1126
201-825-8226
URL: http://maple.nis.net/~wardell/BCAssoc.htm

Red Bank Historical Society
P.O. Box 712
Red Bank, NJ 07701
Riverfront Historical Society
P.O. Box 175
Beverly, NJ 08010

Riverside Township Historical Society
220 Heulings Avenue
Riverside, NJ 08075

Riverton, Historical Society of
405 Midway
Riverton, NJ 08077
Tel: 609-829-6315

Rockaways, Historical Society of
Faesch House
Mount Hope Road
Rockaway, NJ 07866
Mail:
P.O. Box 100
Hibernia, NJ 07842
Tel: 201-366-6730
URL: http://www.gti.net/rocktwp/commdir.html#historical

Roebling Historical Society
140 Third Avenue
Roebling, NJ 08554
Tel: 609-499-2415

Roseland Historical Society
126 Eagle Rock Avenue
P.O. Box 152
Roseland, NJ 07068
Tel: 201-228-1812

Roselle Historical Society
116 E. 4th
Roselle, NJ 07203
Tel: 908-245-9010

Roselle Park Historical Society/Museum
9 West Grant Avenue
P.O. Box 135
Roselle Park, NJ 07204
Tel: 908-245-5422
908-245-9260
URL: http://www.acgnj.org/ourtown/rosellpk/upclose/history.html

Roxbury Township Historical Society
P.O. Box 18
Succasunna, NJ 07876

Rumson Historical Society
Wilson Circle
Rumson, NJ 07760
Tel: 908-842-0338

Salem County Cultural & Heritage Commission
Salem Court House
92 Market Street
Salem, NJ 08079
Tel: 609-935-7510 ext. 292

Salem County Historical Society/ Museum & Research Library
79-83 Market Street
Salem, NJ 08079
Tel: 609-935-5004
URL: http://www.cyberenet.net/~gsteiner/njgenweb/salemnj.html

Sayreville Historical Society
425 Main Street
P.O. Box 18
Sayreville, NJ 08872
Tel: 908-257-0893

Scotch Plains & Fanwood, Historical Society of
P.O. Box 261
Scotch Plains, NJ 07076

Sewaren Historical Club
434 Cliff Street
Sewaren, NJ 07077

Shrewsbury Historical Society
419 Sycamore Avenue
P.O. Box 333
Shrewsbury, NJ 07702
Tel: 908-530-7974

Somers Point Historical Society
P.O. Box 517
Somers Point, NJ 08244

Somerset County Cultural & Heritage Commission
Historic Court House
P.O. Box 3000
Somerville, NJ 08876
Tel: 908-231-7110

Somerset County Historical Society
Van Veghten Drive
Bridgewater, NJ 08807
Tel: 908-218-1281

Somerset Hills, Historical Society of
15 W. Oak Street
P.O. Box 136
Basking Ridge, NJ 07920
Tel: 908-221-1770

Somerville Historical Society
16 E. Summit Street
Somerville, NJ 08876

South Orange Historical & Preservation Society
P.O. Box 213
South Orange, NJ 07079
Tel: 201-761-0038

South Plainfield Historical Society
P.O. Box 11
South Plainfield, NJ 07080

South River Historical Society
129 Main Street
South River, NJ 08882
Tel: 908-257-2200

Southampton Historical Society
17 Mill
Vincentown, NJ 08088
Tel: 609-859-9237

Spring Lake Historical Society
Municipal Building
5th & Warren Avenue
P.O. Box 703
Spring Lake, NJ 07762
Tel: 908-449-0772

Springfield Historical Society
126 Morris Avenue
Springfield, NJ 07081
Tel: 201-912-4464

Squan Village Historical Society
Main Street
P.O. Box 262
Manasquan, NJ 08736
Tel: 908-223-6770

Stillwater Township Historical Society
P.O. Box 23
Stillwater, NJ 07855
Tel: 201-383-4822

Summit Historical Society
90 Butler Parkway
P.O. Box 464
Summit, NJ 07901
Tel: 908-277-1747

Sussex County Arts & Heritage Council, Inc.
P.O. Box 275
Lafayette, NJ 07848
Tel: 201-383-0027

Sussex County Historical Society
82 Main Street
P.O. Box 913
Newton, NJ 07860
Tel: 201-383-6010

Tabernacle Historical Society
162 Carranza Road
Tabernacle, NJ 08088

Tewsksberry Historical Society
P.O. Box 457
Oldwick, NJ 08858-0457
Tel: 908-832-2562

Toms River Seaport Society
78 Water Street
Toms River, NJ 08753
Tel: 908-349-9209

Trenton Historical Society
P.O. Box 1112
Trenton, NJ 08606-1112
Tel: 609-989-3111

Tuckerton Historical Society
P.O. Box 43
Tuckerton, NJ 08087

Union County Historical Society
P.O. Box 3562, Chestnut St. Branch
Union, NJ 07083

Union County Office of Cultural & Heritage Affairs
24-52 Rahway Avenue, 4th Floor
Elizabeth, NJ 07202

Union Landing Historical Society
P.O. Box 473
Brielle, NJ 08730

Union Township Historical Society
Caldwell Parsonage Museum
909 Caldwell Avenue
Union, NJ 07083

United Association of Railroad Veterans
187 Illinois Street
Paterson, NJ 07503

United Railroad Historical Society
W-11 Avon Drive
East Windsor, NJ 08520

Upper Saddle River Historical Society
245 Lake Street
Upper Saddle River, NJ 07458
Tel: 201-327-2236
URL: http://maple.nis.net/~wardell/BCAssoc.htm

Van Harlingen Historical Society
Ludlow Avenue
Belle Mead, NJ 08502
Tel: 908-359-2415

Vernon Township Historical Society
P.O. Box 803
Vernon, NJ 07462
Tel: 201-764-4055 ext. 258

Verona Historical Society
21 Grove Avenue
Verona, NJ 07044
Tel: 201-239-5600

Vineland Historical and Antiquarian Society/Library
108 S. 7th Street
P.O. Box 35
Vineland, NJ 08360
Tel: 609-691-1111

Voorhees Township Historical Society
820 Berlin Road
Voorhees, NJ 08043

Waldwick Historical Society
P.O. Box 273
Waldwick, NJ 07463

Wallpack Historical Society
Wallpack Center
P.O. Box 3
Branchville, NJ 07890
Tel: 201-948-6671

Warren County Cultural & Heritage Commission
Shippen Manor
8 Belvidere Avenue
Oxford, NJ 07863
Tel: 908-453-4381
Fax: 908-453-4981
Email: wcchc@nac.net
URL: http://www.wcchc.org/

Warren County Historical & Genealogical Society/Museum & Library
313 Mansfield Street
P.O. Box 313
Belvidere, NJ 07823
Tel: 908-475-4246

Washington Township Historical Society
6 Fairview Avenue
P.O. Box 189
Long Valley, NJ 07853
Tel: 908-876-9696

Watchung Historical Society
105 Turtle Road
Watchung, NJ 07060

West Caldwell, Historical Society of
278 Westville Avenue
West Caldwell, NJ 07006

West Long Branch Historical Society
P.O. Box 151
West Long Branch, NJ 07764

West Paterson Historical Society
Municipal Building
5 Brophy Land
West Paterson, NJ 07424

West Portal Historical Society
P.O. Box 134
Asbury, NJ 08802

West Windsor, Historical Society of
P.O. Box 38
Princeton Junction, NJ 08550
Tel: 609-452-8598

Westfield Historical Society/Library & Archives
Town Hall, 2nd Floor
425 E. Broad Street
P.O. Box 613
Westfield, NJ 07091
Tel: 908-789-4047
Email: history@westfieldnj.com
URL: http://www.westfieldnj.com/history/index.htm

Wharton Historical Society
10 North Main Street
P.O. Box 424
Wharton, NJ 07885

White Township Historical Society/Museum
RD 3
Belvidere, NJ 07823
Tel: 908-689-7677
908-453-2704

Wildwood Crest Historical Society
Crest Borough Hall
6101 Pacific Avenue
West Cape May, NJ 08210

Wildwood Historical Society
c/o George F. Boyer Historical Museum
Holly Beach Mall
3907 Pacific Avenue
Wildwood, NJ 08260
Tel: 609-523-0277
URL: http://www.beachcomber.com/Ocean/Chamber/ocmuse.html

Willingboro Historical Society
Municipal Complex
Willingboro, NJ 08046

Wyckoff Historical Society
P.O. Box 73
Wyckoff, NJ 07481

LDS Family History Centers

Cherry Hill Family History Center
252 Evesham Avenue
Cherry Hill, NJ 08003
Tel: 609-795-8841

East Brunswick Family History Center
303 Dunham's Corner Road
East Brunswick, NJ 08816
Tel: 908-254-1480

Morristown Family History Center
283 James Street
Morristown, NJ 07960
Tel: 908-539-5362

North Caldwell Family History Center
209 Mountain Avenue
North Caldwell, NJ 07006
Tel: 906-226-8975

Princeton Family History Center
Alexander Road & U.S. Highway 1
Princeton, NJ 08540
Tel: 609-452-0802

Short Hills Family History Center
140 White Oak Ridge Road
Short Hill, NJ 07078
Tel: 201-379-7315

Vineland Family History Center
110 Highland Avenue
Vineland, NJ 08360
Tel: 609-696-5002

ARCHIVES/LIBRARIES/MUSEUMS

Asbury Park Public Library
500 First Avenue
Asbury Park, NJ 07712
Tel: 908-774-4221
Fax: 908-988-6101

Atlantic City Free Public Library
1 North Tennessee Avenue
Atlantic City, NJ 08401
Tel: 609-345-2269
Email: brynk@library.atlantic.city.lib.nj.us
URL: http://library.atlantic.city.lib.nj.us/

Atlantic County Historical Society/Library & Museum
907 Shore Road
P.O. Box 301
Somers Point, NJ 08244
Tel: 609-927-5218

Atlantic County Library/Mays Landing Branch
Reference Center/New Jersey Collection
40 South Farragut Avenue
Mays Landing, NJ 08330
Tel: 609-646-8699
609-625-2776
Fax: 609-625-8143
URL: http://commlink.atlantic.county.lib.nj.us/aclsref.htm

Barnegat Bay Decoy & Bayman's Museum
137 W. Main Street
P.O. Box 52
Tuckerton, NJ 08087
Tel: 609-296-8868
URL: http://www.oceancountygov.com/decoy/default.htm

Belleville Public Library & Information Center
221 Washington Avenue
Belleville, NJ 07109
Tel: 201-450-3434
Fax: 201-450-9518
URL: http://www.intac.com/~bpllibn/hpfront.htm

Bloomfield Public Library
90 Broad Street
Bloomfield, NJ 07003
Tel: 201-429-9292

Boonton/Holmes Public Library
621 Main Street
Boonton, NJ 07005
Tel: 201-334-2980
Fax: 201-334-3272
URL: http://www.boonton.org/library/index.htm

Bridgeton Free Public Library
150 Commerce Street, E
Bridgeton, NJ 08302
Tel: 609-451-2620

Brookdale Community College
Learning Resource Center
765 Newman Springs Road
Lincroft, NJ 07738
Tel: 908-224-2706

Burlington County Library
Special Collections
5 Pioneer Blvd.
Westampton, NJ 08060
Tel: 609-267-9660
609-298-0063
609-235-6552
URL: http://www.burlco.lib.nj.us/

Camden County Historical Society/Library
Park Blvd. & Euclid Avenue
Camden, NJ 08103-3697
Tel: 609-964-3333
URL: http://www.cyberenet.net/~gsteiner/cchs/

Camden County Library
203 Laurel Road
Voorhees, NJ 08043
Tel: 609-772-1636
Email: pagemaster@camden.lib.nj.us
URL: http://www.camden.lib.nj.us/

Cape May County Library
30 West Mechanic Street
Cape May Courthouse, NJ 08210
Tel: 609-465-1040
URL: http://yyy.algorithms.com/cmclib/

Cape May Historical & Genealogical Society/Library
John Holmes House
504 Route 9
Cape May Courthouse, NJ 08210-3070
Tel: 609-465-3535
URL: http://www.cyberenet.net/~gsteiner/njgenweb/cmhgs.html
or http://www.fieldtrip.com/nj/94653535.htm

Centenary College
Taylor Memorial Museum
400 Jefferson Street
Hackettstown, NJ 07840-2100
Tel: 908-852-1400
URL: http://www.centenarycollege.edu/ce07000.html

Chathams, Library of the
214 Main Street
Chatham, NJ 07928
Tel: 201-635-0603
Email: obrien@main.morris.org
URL: http://www.csnet.net/chatlib/library.html

Clark Public Library
303 Westfield Avenue
Clark, NJ 07066
Tel: 908-388-5999
Fax: 908-388-7866
Email: clark@castle.net
URL: http://www.castle.net/~clark/

Clinton Historical Museum
56 Main Street
Clinton, NJ 08809
Tel: 908-735-4101

Drew University
United Methodist Archives
Madison, NJ 07940
Tel: 201-408-3590
Email: drewlib@drew.edu
URL: http://www.drew.edu/infosys/library/uma.html

East Orange Public Library
21 South Arlington Avenue
East Orange, NJ 07018
Tel: 201-266-5612

Easton Area Public Library
Marx History Room
6th & Church Street
Easton, PA 18042
Tel: 610-258-2917

Eatontown Historical Committee/Museum
75 Broad Street
Eatontown, NJ 07724
Tel: 908-542-4026

Edison Public Library
340 Plainfield Avenue
Edison, NJ 08817
Tel: 908-287-2298
Fax: 908-819-9134

Ewing Township Historical Preservation Society/Library
27 Federal City Road
Ewing, NJ 08638
Tel: 609-530-1220

Fairleigh Dickinson University
Messler Library
207 Montross Avenue
Rutherford, NJ 07070
Tel: 201-460-5067
Fax: 201-460-1187

Glassboro State College
Savitz Library, Stewart Room
Glassboro, NJ 08028
Tel: 609-863-6101
Fax: 609-863-6313

Gloucester County Historical Society/Library
17 Hunter Street
Woodbury, NJ 08096
Tel: 609-845-4771
URL: http://www.rootsweb.com/~njglouce/gchs/

Hackettstown Public Library
110 Church Street
Hackettstown, NJ 07840
Tel: 908-852-4936
Fax: 908-852-7850

Haddonfield Public Library
60 Haddon Avenue
Haddonfield, NJ 08033
Tel: 609-429-1304
Fax: 609-429-3760
URL: http://arginine.umdnj.edu/~swartz/hadlib.html

Hamilton Township Public Library
1 Municipal Drive
Trenton, NJ 08619
Tel: 609-581-4060
Fax: 609-581-4067

Hopewell Museum
28 E. Broad Street
Hopewell, NJ 08525
Tel: 609-466-0103
URL: http://www.fieldtrip.com/nj/94660103.htm

Hunterdon County Historical Society
Hiram E. Deats Memorial Library
114 Main Street
Flemington, NJ 08822
Tel: 908-782-1091

Hunterdon County Library
RR 12
Flemington, NJ 08822
Tel: 908-788-1444

Indian Heritage Museum
P.O. Box 225
Rancocas, NJ 08073
Tel: 609-261-4747

Irvington Public Library
346 16th Avenue
Irvington, NJ 07111
Tel: 201-372-6403

Jersey City Public Library
New Jersey Room
472 Jersey Avenue
Jersey City, NJ 07303
Tel: 201-547-4500

Kinnelon Public Library
132 Kinnelon Road
Kinnelon, NJ 07405
Tel: 201-838-1321

Livingston/Ruth L. Rockwood Memorial Library
Livingston Memorial Park
10 Robert Harp Drive
Livingston, NJ 07039
Tel: 201-992-4600
Fax: 201-994-2346
URL: http://www.new-jersey.com/livingston/govern/govern1a.htm#library

Long Branch Historical Museum
1260 Ocean Avenue
Long Branch, NJ 07740
Tel: 908-222-9879

Long Branch Public Library
328 Broadway
Long Branch, NJ 07740
Tel: 908-222-3900
Email: nsmith@hawkmail.monmouth.edu
URL: http://www.monmouth.edu/irs/library/melon/lbpub/library.htm

Madison Public Library
39 Keep Street
Madison, NJ 07940
Tel: 201-377-0722

Maplewood Memorial Library
51 Baker Street
Maplewood, NJ 07040
Tel: 201-762-1622
Fax: 201-762-4573
URL: http://berniann.com/maplewood/library.htm

Meadowlands Museum
91 Crane Avenue
P.O. Box 3
Rutherford, NJ 07070
Tel: 201-935-1175
URL: http://www.fieldtrip.com/nj/19351175.htm

Mercer County Public Library
2751 Brunswick Pike
Lawrenceville, NJ 08648
Tel: 609-989-6918
Fax: 609-538-1208

Metuchen Public Library
480 Middlesex Avenue
Metuchen, NJ 08840
Tel: 201-632-8526
URL: http://www.metuchen.com/library.html

Middletown Public Library
55 New Monmouth Road
Middletown, NJ 07748
Tel: 908-671-3700
Fax: 908-671-5839
URL: http://www.monmouth.edu/irs/library/melon/middletown/welcome.html

Monmouth County Archives
125 Symmes Drive
Manalapan, NJ 07726
Tel: 908-308-3772
Fax: 908-409-4888

Monmouth University
Guggenheim Library/Special Collections
Cedar Avenue
West Long Branch, NJ 07764
Tel: 908-571-3450
Fax: 908-571-3636
URL: http://www.monmouth.edu/irs/library/special.html

Montclair Historical Society
Terhune Library
110 Orange Road
Montclair, NJ 07043
Tel: 201-744-1796
URL: http://interactive.net/~upper/crane.html

Morris County Historical Society/Research Library
Acorn Hall
68 Morris Avenue
P.O. Box 170M
Morristown, NJ 07960
Tel: 201-267-3465

Morris County Library
New Jersey Collection
30 East Hanover Avenue
Whippany, NJ 07981
Tel: 201-285-6974
Email: heagney@main.morris.org
URL: http://www.gti.net/mocolib1/MCL.html

Morris Genealogical Library
228 Elberon Avenue
Allenhurst, NJ 07711

Morristown & Morris Township, Joint Free Public Library of
1 Miller Road
Morristown, NJ 07960
Tel: 201-537-6161
201-537-3473 (Local History & Genealogy)
Email: douthwaite@main.morris.org
URL: http://makcom.com/jfpl/gene.htm

Neptune Public Library/Historical Society Museum
25 Neptune Blvd.
P.O. Box 1125
Neptune, NJ 07753
Tel: 908-775-8241 (ext. 302—Front Desk, ext. 306—Museum)
Fax: 908-774-1132
URL: http://www.monmouth.edu/irs/library/melon/neptune/library.htm

New Jersey Catholic Historical Records Commission
238 E. Blancke Street
P.O. Box 1246
Linden, NJ 07036
Tel: 908-486-1022

New Jersey Catholic Historical Records Commission
@ Seton Hall University
Walsh Library/Special Collections
South Orange, NJ 07079-2696
Tel: 201-761-9476
Email: somersma@lanmail.shu.edu
URL: http://www.shu.edu/library/catholicrec/index.html

New Jersey Historical Commission
20 West State Street
CN 305
Trenton, NJ 08625-0305
Tel: 609-292-6062
Fax: 609-633-8168
URL: http://www.state.nj.us/state/history/hisidx.html

New Jersey Historical Society/Library
230 Broadway
Newark, NJ 07104
Tel: 201-483-3939
Fax: 201-483-1988

New Jersey State Library
State Library Building
Level 4 (Genealogy & Local History Office)
185 West State Street
CN 520
Trenton, NJ 08625-0520
Tel: 609-292-6220 (General Information)
609-292-6274 (Genealogy & Local History)
Fax: 609-984-7901
URL: http://www.state.nj.us/statelibrary/njlib.htm

New Jersey State Museum
205 West State Street
CN 530
Trenton, NJ 08625
Tel: 609-292-6464 (24 hour information)
609-292-6308 (Mon-Fri, 8-4)
Fax: 609-599-4098
URL: http://www.state.nj.us/state/museum/musidx.html

New Jersey State Police Museum
River Road
P.O. Box 7068
West Trenton, NJ 08628
Tel: 609-882-2000 ext. 6400

New Sweden Farmstead
50 E. Broad Street
Bridgeton, NJ 08302
Tel: 609-451-4802
URL: http://www.fieldtrip.com/nj/94514802.htm

Newark Public Library
New Jersey Department
5 Washington Street
P.O. Box 630
Newark, NJ 07101-0630
Tel: 201-733-7784
201-733-7776

Nutley Free Public Library
93 Booth Drive
Nutley, NJ 07110
Tel: 201-667-0405
Email: tropiano@bccls.org
URL: http://www.bccls.org/www/images/nutl.html

Ocean City Historical Museum
1735 Simpson Avenue
Ocean City, NJ 08226
Tel: 609-399-1801

Ocean County Historical Society
Strickler Research Library
26 Hadley Avenue
Toms River, NJ 08753
Tel: 908-341-1880

Ocean County Library
Bishop Building
101 Washington Street
Toms River, NJ 08753
Tel: 908-349-6200
URL: http://netra.oceancounty.lib.nj.us/bish.htm

Ocean Gate Historical Society/Museum
Cape May and Asbury Avenues
P.O. Box 895
Ocean Gate, NJ 08740
Tel: 908-269-3468
URL: http://www.fieldtrip.com/nj/82693468.htm

Ocean Township Historical Museum
163 Monmouth Road
Oakhurst, NJ 07755
Tel: 908-531-2136

Paramus Public Library
116 E. Century Road
Paramus, NJ 07652
Tel: 201-599-1302
Fax: 201-599-0059
Email: abrams@bccls.org
URL: http://www.bccls.org/www/images/para.html

Passaic County Historical Society/Library
Lambert Castle
Valley Road
Paterson, NJ 07503
Tel: 201-881-2761

Phillipsburg Free Public Library
200 Frost Avenue
Phillipsburg, NJ 08865
Tel: 908-454-3712

Princeton Historical Society/Library
158 Nassau Street
Princeton, NJ 08542
Tel: 609-921-6748
Email: PHS@injersey.com
URL: http://princetonol.com/groups/histsoc/

Princeton Public Library
65 Witherspoon Street
Princeton, NJ 08540
Tel: 609-924-9529
Fax: 609-924-7937
Email: pplwebmaster@princeton.lib.nj.us
URL: http://www.princeton.lib.nj.us/info.html

Princeton University
Firestone Library
One Washington Road
Princeton, NJ 08544
Tel: 609-258-3180
URL: http://infoshare1.princeton.edu:2003/

Ramsey Free Public Library
30 Wyckoff Avenue
Ramsey, NJ 07446
Tel: 201-327-1445
Email: rfpl@nic.com
URL: http://www.nic.com/~rfpl/

Red Bank Public Library
84 West Front Street
Red Bank, NJ 07701
Tel: 908-842-0690

Richard Stockton College Library
Jim Leeds Road
Pomona, NJ 08240
Tel: 609-652-4343
URL: http://loki.stockton.edu/~millerr/libhome.htm

Roselle Park Historical Society/Museum
9 West Grant Avenue
P.O. Box 135
Roselle Park, NJ 07204
Tel: 908-245-5422
908-245-9260
URL: http://www.acgnj.org/ourtown/rosellpk/upclose/history.html

Roxbury Public Library
103 Main Street
Succasunna, NJ 07876
Tel: 201-584-2400
TDD: 800-852-7899
URL: http://www.roxbury.org/library.htm

Rutgers University
Archibald Stevens Alexander Library
Special Collections & Archives
169 College Avenue
New Brunswick, NJ 08903
Tel: 908-932-7510
Fax: 908-932-7012
URL: http://www.libraries.rutgers.edu/rulib/spcol/spcol.htm

Salem County Historical Society/Museum & Research Library
79-83 Market Street
Salem, NJ 08079
Tel: 609-935-5004
URL: http://www.cyberenet.net/~gsteiner/njgenweb/salemnj.html

Sea Isle City Historical Museum
4416 Landis Avenue
Sea Isle City, NJ 08243
Tel: 609-263-2992

Seton Hall University
Walsh Library/Special Collections
South Orange, NJ 07079-2696
Tel: 201-761-9476
Email: somersma@lanmail.shu.edu
URL: http://www.shu.edu/library/speccoll.html

Sparta Public Library
22 Woodport Road
Sparta, NJ 07871
Tel: 201-729-3101
URL: http://home.ptd.net/~spartapl/

Sussex County Library
RD #3, Box 170
Newton, NJ 07860
Tel: 201-948-3660

Teaneck Public Library
840 Teaneck Road
Teaneck, NJ 07666
Tel: 201-837-4171
URL: http://soho.ios.com/~teaneck/

Tenafly Public Library
401 Tenafly Road
Tenafly, NJ 07670
Tel: 201-568-8680
Email: tenpubli@intac.com
URL: http://www.borough.tenafly.nj.us/lib.htm

Trenton Public Library/Main Branch
Trentoniana Dept.
120 Academy Street
Trenton, NJ 08608
Tel: 609-392-7188
Fax: 609-392-7655
Email: tplnj@pluto.njcc.com
URL: http://www.prodworks.com/library/

Vineland Historical and Antiquarian Society/Library
108 S. 7th Street
P.O. Box 35
Vineland, NJ 08360
Tel: 609-691-1111

Warren County Historical & Genealogical Society/Museum & Library
313 Mansfield Street
P.O. Box 313
Belvidere, NJ 07823
Tel: 908-475-4246

Warren County Free Public Library/Main Branch
Court House Annex
199 Hardwick Street
Belvidere, NJ 07823
Tel: 908-475-5361
908-475-6322

Washington Public Library
20 Carlton Avenue
Washington, NJ 07882
Tel: 908-689-0201

Wayne Public Library
The Lockett Room
12 Nellis Drive
Wayne, NJ 07470
Tel: 201-694-4272
Email: library@waynetownship.com
URL: http://www.waynetownship.com/library/

Westfield Memorial Library
550 East Broad Street
Westfield, NJ 07090
Tel: 908-789-4090

White Township Historical Society/Museum
RD 3
Belvidere, NJ 07823
Tel: 908-689-7677
908-453-2704

Wildwood Historical Society
c/o George F. Boyer Historical Museum
Holly Beach Mall
3907 Pacific Avenue
Wildwood, NJ 08260
Tel: 609-523-0277
URL: http://www.beachcomber.com/Ocean/Chamber/ocmuse.html

Willingboro Township Library
1 Salem Road
Willingboro, NJ 08046
Tel: 609-877-6668

Woodbridge Free Public Library
George Frederick Plaza
Woodbridge, NJ 07095
Tel: 908-634-4450

Yesteryear Museum
Regina Place & Harriet Drive
Whippany, NJ 07981
Tel: 201-386-1920

NEWSPAPER REPOSITORIES

New Jersey State Archives
State Library Building
185 West State Street, Level 2
CN 307
Trenton, NJ 08625-0307
Tel: 609-530-3200
Fax: 609-396-2454
Email: djones@archive.sos.state.nj.us
URL: http://www.state.nj.us/state/darm/darmidx.html

Rutgers University
Archibald Stevens Alexander Library
Special Collections & Archives
169 College Avenue
New Brunswick, NJ 08903
Tel: 908-932-7510
Fax: 908-932-7012
URL: http://www.libraries.rutgers.edu/rulib/spcol/spcol.htm

VITAL RECORDS

New Jersey State Dept. of Health
Health/Agriculture Building, Room 504
Front & Market Streets
Trenton, NJ
Mail:
New Jersey State Department of Health
Vital Statistics Registration
CN 370
Trenton, NJ 08625-0370
Tel: 609-292-4087
609-633-2860 (Vital Chek Operator)
Fax: 609-292-4292
URL: http://www.state.nj.us/health/vital/vs11/htm

NEW JERSEY ON THE WEB

Descendants of Edward Ball of New Jersey
Gedcom Repository Site
http://www.altlaw.com/edball/biged1.htm

Horseneck Founders of New Jersey
http://www.rootsweb.com/~genepool/nj.htm

New Jersey GenWeb Project
http://www.cyberenet.net/~gsteiner/njgenweb/

New Jersey History
http://scils.rutgers.edu/~macan/nj.history.html

NEW MEXICO

ARCHIVES, STATE & NATIONAL

National Archives—Rocky Mountain Region
Denver Federal Center, Building 48
P.O. Box 25307
Denver, CO 80225-0307
Tel: 303-236-0817
Fax: 303-236-9354
Email: archives@denver.nara.gov
URL: http://www.nara.gov/nara/regional/08nsgil.html

New Mexico State Records Center & Archives
404 Montezuma
Santa Fe, NM 87503
Tel: 505-827-7332
Fax: 505-827-7331
URL: http://www.nmculture.org/HTML/oca.htm

GENEALOGICAL SOCIETIES

Alamogordo Genealogy Society (AGeS)
1417 1/2 Porto Rico
Alamogordo, NM 88310
Tel: 505-437-6602

Albuquerque, Genealogy Club of
c/o Albuquerque Public Library
423 Central Avenue, NE
Albuquerque, NM 87102

Artesia Historical & Genealogical Society
P.O. Box 803
Artesia, NM 88211

Chavez County Genealogical Society
2201 W. Country Club
Roswell, NM 88201
Tel: 505-622-8306

Curry County Genealogy Society
c/o Clovis-Carver Public Library
701 Main Street
Clovis, NM 88101
Tel: 505-762-5408

Eddy County Genealogical Society
P.O. Box 461
Carlsbad, NM 88220
Tel: 505-887-7167

Grand Lodge of New Mexico
Ancient Free and Accepted Masons
P.O. Box 25004
Albuquerque, NM 87125-0004
URL: http://204.134.124.1/leon/gmm.htm

Grant County Genealogical Society
Tel: 505-538-2329

Hispanic Genealogical Research Center—New Mexico
1331 Juan Tabo, NE
Suite P, No. 18
Albuquerque, NM 87112
Tel: 505-836-5438
Email: HGRC@HGRC-NM.ORG
URL: http://www.hgrc-nm.org/

Las Vegas Genealogical Society
c/o Las Vegas/Carnegie Public Library
500 National Avenue
Las Vegas, NM 87701

Lea County Genealogical Society
P.O. Box 1044
Lovington, NM 88260
Tel: 505-396-2608

Los Alamos Family History Society
P.O. Box 900
Las Alamos, NM 87544
Tel: 505-672-9584

New Mexico Genealogical Society
P.O. Box 8283
Albuquerque, NM 87198-8283

New Mexico Jewish Historical Society
Genealogy & Family History Committee
P.O. Box 155989, Cielo Court Station
Santa Fe, NM 87506
Tel: 505-438-0738
URL: http://www.nmculture.org/HTML/northc.htm

Roosevelt County Searchers
Tel: 505-359-0772

Roswell Genealogical Society
c/o Roswell Adult Center
807 N. Missouri
Mail:
P.O. Box 994
Roswell, NM 88201
Tel: 505-622-6725

Sierra County Genealogical Society
c/o Truth or Consequences Public Library
325 Library Lane
Mail:
P.O. Box 311
Truth or Consequences, NM 87901
Tel: 505-894-3027

Southeastern New Mexico Genealogical Society/Library
P.O. Box 5725
Hobbs, NM 88240
Tel: 505-393-3658

Southern New Mexico Genealogical Society
P.O. Box 2563
Las Cruces, NM 88004-2563
Email: wheelerwc@zianet.com
URL: http://www.zianet.com/wheelerwc/GenSSNM/

Totah Tracers Genealogical Society
c/o Salmon Ruins
Bloomfield Highway
P.O. Box 125
Bloomfield, NM 87413
Tel: 505-632-3668

Historical Societies

Artesia Historical & Genealogical Society
P.O. Box 803
Artesia, NM 88211

Cimarron Historical Society
c/o Old Mill Museum
NM 21
P.O. Box 58
Cimarron, NM 87714
Tel: 505-376-2913
URL: http://www.nmculture.org/HTML/northe.htm

Columbus Historical Society/Museum
Highway 9 & 11
P.O. Box 562
Columbus, NM 88029
Tel: 505-531-2620
URL: http://www.nmculture.org/HTML/southw.htm

Historical Society for Southeast New Mexico/Museum & Archives
200 North Lea Avenue
Roswell, NM 88201
Tel: 505-622-8333
URL: http://www.nmculture.org/HTML/southe.htm

Los Alamos Historical Society/Museum & Archives
1921 Juniper Street
P.O. Box 43 VLA
Los Alamos, NM 87544
Tel: 505-662-6272 (Office & Archives)
505-662-4493 (Museum & Shop)
URL: http://www.vla.com/lahistory/

Moriarty Historical Society/Museum
777 Old U.S. Route 66, SW
P.O. Box 1366
Moriarty, NM 87035
Tel: 505-832-4764
URL: http://www.nmculture.org/HTML/central.htm

New Mexico Jewish Historical Society
P.O. Box 155989, Cielo Court Station
Santa Fe, NM 87506
Tel: 505-438-0738
URL: http://www.nmculture.org/HTML/northc.htm

Sacramento Mountains Historical Society/Museum
U.S. 82
P.O. Box 435
Cloudcroft, NM 88317
Tel: 505-682-2932
URL: http://www.nmculture.org/HTML/southe.htm

Santa Fe Trail Association
Santa Fe Trail Center
RR 3
Larned, KS 67550
Email: olsen_m@venus.nmhu.edu
URL: http://www.nmhu.edu/research/sftrail/sfta.htm

Socorro Historical Society/Hammel Museum
P.O. Box 923
Socorro, NM 87801
URL: http://www.nmt.edu/~nmtlib/LOCAL/hammel.html

Tularosa Basin Historical Society/Museum
1501 White Sands Blvd.
P.O. Box 518
Alamogordo, NM 88310
Tel: 505-437-6120
URL: http://www.nmculture.org/HTML/southe.htm

Union County Historical Society/Museum
23 S. 2nd
Clayton, NM 88415
Tel: 505-374-2977

Valencia County Historical Society
Harvey House Museum
104 N. 1st Street
Belen, NM 87002
Tel: 505-861-0581
URL: http://www.nmculture.org/HTML/central.htm

LDS Family History Centers

Alamogordo Family History Center
1800 23rd Street
Alamogordo, NM 88310
Tel: 505-437-8772

Albuquerque Family History Center
1100 Montano Road, NW
Albuquerque, NM 87107
Tel: 505-343-0456

Albuquerque Family History Center
4109 Eubank Blvd., NE
Albuquerque, NM 87111
Tel: 505-293-5610

Albuquerque Family History Center
5709 Haines Avenue, NE
Albuquerque, NM 87110
Tel: 505-266-4867

Carlsbad Family History Center
1211 West Church & Oak Street
Carlsbad, NM 88220
Tel: 505-885-1368

Clovis Family History Center
Manana at Lore
Clovis, NM 88101
Tel: 505-762-2021

Farmington Family History Center
400 West Apache
Farmington, NM 87401
Tel: 505-325-5813

Gallup Family History Center
601 Susan Avenue
Gallup, NM 87301

Grants Family History Center
1010 Bondad
Grants, NM 87020
Tel: 505-287-2305

Las Cruces Family History Center
3210 Venus Street
Las Cruces, NM 88012
Tel: 505-382-0618

Los Alamos Family History Center
18th Street
Los Alamos, NM 87544
Tel: 505-662-3186

Roswell Family History Center
2201 W. Country Club Road
Roswell, NM 87505
Tel: 505-623-4492

Santa Fe Family History Center
410 Rodeo Road
Santa Fe, NM 87505
Tel: 505-986-8254

Silver City Family History Center
3755 North Swan Street
Silver City, NM 88061
Tel: 505-388-5033

Archives/Libraries/Museums

Acoma Pueblo Museum
NM 23
P.O. Box 309
Acoma Pueblo, NM 87034
Tel: 505-252-1139
URL: http://www.nmculture.org/HTML/northw.htm

Alamogordo Public Library
920 Oregon Avenue
Alamogordo, NM 88310
Tel: 505-439-4140
Fax: 505-439-4108
TTY: 505-439-4149
Email: alamopl@wazoo.com
URL: http://www.alamogordo.com/library/index.html

Albuquerque Public Library/Rio Grande Valley Library System
Special Collections Branch
423 Central Avenue, NE
Albuquerque, NM 87102
Tel: 505-848-1376
URL: http://www.cabq.gov/rgvls/specol.html

Archdiocese of Santa Fe Museum
223 Cathedral Place
Santa Fe, NM 87501-2028
Tel: 505-983-3811

Artesia Historical Museum & Arts Center
505 W. Richardson Avenue
Artesia, NM 88210
Tel: 505-748-2390
Fax: 505-746-3886 (Attn: Museum)
URL: http://www.vpa.org/museumsnm.html

Artesia Public Library
306 W. Richardson
Artesia, NM 88210
Tel: 505-746-4252
Email: apublib@artesia.net
URL: http://www.artesia.net/~apublib/

Aztec Museum/Archives & Pioneer Village
125 North Main Avenue
Aztec, NM 87410
Tel: 505-334-9829
URL: http://www.nmculture.org/HTML/northw.htm

Cimarron Historical Society
c/o Old Mill Museum
NM 21
P.O. Box 58
Cimarron, NM 87714
Tel: 505-376-2913
URL: http://www.nmculture.org/HTML/northe.htm

Clovis-Carver Public Library
701 N. Main Street
Clovis, NM 88101
Tel: 505-769-7840
Fax: 505-769-7842
URL: http://www.andinfo.com/clovis/library/

College of Santa Fe
Fogelson Library
1600 St. Michaels Drive
Santa Fe, NM 87505-7615
Tel: 505-473-6577
Fax: 505-473-6593

Columbus Historical Society/Museum
Highway 9 & 11
P.O. Box 562
Columbus, NM 88029
Tel: 505-531-2620
URL: http://www.nmculture.org/HTML/southw.htm

Deming Luna Mimbres Museum
301 S. Silver
Deming, NM 88030
Tel: 505-546-2382
505-546-2677 (Archives)
URL: http://www.nmculture.org/HTML/southw.htm

Deming/Marshall Memorial Library
301 S. Tin
Deming, NM 88030
Tel: 505-546-9202
Fax: 505-546-9649
Email: demingpl@nm-us.campus.mci.net
URL: http://www.zianet.com/demingpl/

Eastern New Mexico University
Golden Library
Station 32
Portales, NM 88130
Tel: 505-562-2624
Fax: 505-562-2647
Email: dowline@golden.enmu.edu
URL: http://www.enmu.edu/golden.html

Farmington Museum
302 N. Orchard
Farmington, NM 87401-6227
Tel: 505-599-1174
Fax: 505-599-1185
URL: http://www.nmculture.org/HTML/northw.htm

General Douglas L. McBride Military Museum
New Mexico Military Institute
101 W. College Blvd.
P.O. Box J
Roswell, NM 88201
Tel: 505-624-8220/2
Fax: 505-624-8107
URL: http://www.nmmi.cc.nm.us/home/campustour.html

Hispanic Genealogical Research Center-New Mexico
1331 Juan Tabo, NE
Suite P, No. 18
Albuquerque, NM 87112
Tel: 505-836-5438
Email: HGRC@HGRC-NM.ORG
URL: http://www.hgrc-nm.org/

Historical Society for Southeast New Mexico/Museum & Archives
200 North Lea Avenue
Roswell, NM 88201
Tel: 505-622-8333
URL: http://roswell-usa.com/historic/index.html

Kit Carson Home & Museums
Kit Carson Road
P.O. Drawer CCC
Taos, NM 87571
Tel: 505-758-0505
URL: http://taoswebb.com/nmusa/TAOS/MAT/kit.html

Las Vegas/Carnegie Public Library
500 National Avenue
Las Vegas, NM 87701
Tel: 505-454-1403

Las Vegas City Museum & Rough Rider Memorial
729 Grand Avenue
Las Vegas, NM 87701
Tel: 505-425-8726
URL: http://www.nmculture.org/HTML/northe.htm

Los Alamos Historical Society/Museum & Archives
1921 Juniper Street
P.O. Box 43 VLA
Los Alamos, NM 87544
Tel: 505-662-6272 (Office & Archives)
505-662-4493 (Museum & Shop)
URL: http://www.vla.com/lahistory/

Lovington Public Library
115 S. Main
Lovington, NM 88260
Tel: 505-396-3144

Mescalero Apache Cultural Center
P.O. Box 176
Mescalero, NM 88340
Tel: 505-671-4494

Million Dollar Museum
White's City, NM 88268
URL: http://www.caverns.com/~chamber/rec.htm

Moriarty Historical Society/Museum
777 Old U.S. Route 66, SW
P.O. Box 1366
Moriarty, NM 87035
Tel: 505-832-4764
URL: http://www.nmculture.org/HTML/central.htm

New Mexico Highlands University (NMHU)
Donnelly Library
Las Vegas, NM 87701
Tel: 505-425-7511 (University)
URL: http://www.nmhu.edu/camplife/resources/library.htm

New Mexico State Library
325 Don Gaspar
Santa Fe, NM 87501-2777
Tel: 505-827-3800
505-827-3805 (Southwest Room)
Fax: 505-827-3888
URL: http://www.stlib.state.nm.us/

New Mexico State University/Las Cruces
Branson Library
Box 30006, Dept. 3475
Las Cruces, NM 88003-8006
Tel: 505-646-6928
505-646-3737 (Govt. Documents)
Fax: 505-646-1287 (Govt. Documents)
Email: library@lib.nmsu.edu
or govdocs@lib.nmsu.edu
URL: http://lib.nmsu.edu/

Palace of the Governors
Museum of New Mexico-History Library
105 W. Palace Avenue
P.O. Box 2087
Santa Fe, NM 87504-2087
Tel: 505-827-6483
Fax: 505-827-6521
URL: http://www.nmculture.org/HTML/oca.htm

Portales Public Library
218 South Avenue B
Portales, NM 88130
Tel: 505-356-3940

Pueblo Cultural Center
2401 12th Street, NW
Albuquerque, NM 87192
Tel: 505-843-7270
800-766-4406
Fax: 505-842-6959
URL: http://hanksville.phast.umass.edu/defs/independent/PCC/PCC.html

Raton Museum
216 S. First Street
Raton, NM 87740
Tel: 505-445-8979
URL: http://www.nmculture.org/HTML/northe.htm

Roosevelt County Historical Museum
Eastern New Mexico University (ENMU)
Station No. 30
Portales, NM 88130
Tel: 505-562-2592
Fax: 505-562-2578
URL: http://www.nmculture.org/HTML/southe.htm

Roswell Public Library
301 North Pennsylvania Avenue
Roswell, NM 88201-4695
Tel: 505-622-7101
URL: http://roswell-usa.com/library/

Sacramento Mountains Historical Society/Museum
U.S. 82
P.O. Box 435
Cloudcroft, NM 88317
Tel: 505-682-2932
URL: http://www.nmculture.org/HTML/southe.htm

Santa Fe History Library
110 Washington Avenue
Santa Fe, NM 87501
Tel: 505-827-6470

Santa Fe Public Library
1730 Llano Street
Santa Fe, NM 87505
Tel: 505-473-7262
Fax: 505-473-7261
Email: lafargepl@nm-us.campus.mci.net

Santa Fe Trail Historical Society/Museum
614 Maxwell Avenue
P.O. Box 323
Springer, NM 87747
Tel: 505-483-2682
URL: http://www.nmculture.org/HTML/northc.htm

Silver City Museum/Local History Research Library
312 W. Broadway
Silver City, NM 88061
Tel: 505-538-5921
Fax: 505-388-1096
Email: SCMuseum@zianet.com
URL: http://www.zianet.com/silverweb/museum/index.html

Silver City Public Library
515 W. College Avenue
Silver City, NM 88061
Tel: 505-538-3672
Fax: 505-388-3757
Email: silvercitypl@nm-us.campus.mci.net
URL: http://www.nmculture.org/HTML/southw.htm

Socorro Historical Society/Hammel Museum
P.O. Box 923
Socorro, NM 87801
URL: http://www.nmt.edu/~nmtlib/LOCAL/hammel.html

Socorro Public Library
401 Park Street
Socorro, NM 87801
Tel: 505-835-1114
Email: library@sdc.org
URL: http://www.sdc.org/~library/

Southeastern New Mexico Genealogical Society/Library
P.O. Box 5725
Hobbs, NM 88240
Tel: 505-393-3658

Thomas Branigan Memorial Library
200 E. Picacho Avenue
Las Cruces, NM 88001
Tel: 505-526-1045

Truth or Consequences Public Library
325 Library Lane
Truth or Consequences, NM 87901-2375
Tel: 505-894-3027
Fax: 505-894-2068
Email: torcpl@nm-us.campus.mci.net
URL: http://village.globaldrum.com/rvnewmexico/library.htm

Tularosa Basin Historical Society/Museum
1501 White Sands Blvd.
P.O. Box 518
Alamogordo, NM 88310
Tel: 505-437-6120
URL: http://www.nmculture.org/HTML/southe.htm

Union County Historical Society/Museum
23 S. 2nd
Clayton, NM 88415
Tel: 505-374-2977

University of New Mexico
Center for Southwestern Research/Museum of New Mexico
General Library
Albuquerque, NM 87131
Tel: 505-277-6451
Fax: 505-277-6019
Email: cswrref@unm.edu
URL: http://www.umn.edu/~cswrref/

Valencia County Historical Society
Harvey House Museum
104 N. 1st Street
Belen, NM 87002
Tel: 505-861-0581
URL: http://www.nmculture.org/HTML/central.htm

Western New Mexico University Museum
1000 W. College Avenue
P.O. Box 680
Silver City, NM 88061
Tel: 505-538-6386
Fax: 505-538-6178
URL: http://www.nmculture.org/HTML/wnmu.htm

NEWSPAPER REPOSITORIES

Santa Fe History Library
110 Washington Avenue
Santa Fe, NM 87501
Tel: 505-827-6470

University of New Mexico
General Library
Albuquerque, NM 87131
Tel: 505-277-7212
Fax: 505-277-6019
Email: mfletch@unm.edu
URL: http://www.umn.edu/~cswrref/

Vital Records

New Mexico Department of Health
Bureau of Vital Records & Health Statistics
1190 St. Francis Drive
P.O. Box 26110
Santa Fe, NM 87504-6110
Tel: 505-827-2321
505-827-2338 (Recorded Message)

New Mexico on the Web

La Herencia Del Norte—Hispanic Heritage Magazine
http://www.herencia.com/

New Mexico Cultural Treasures
http://www.nmculture.org/

New Mexico GenWeb Project
http://www.abq.com/nmgenweb/index.htm

New York

Archives, State & National

National Archives—Northeast Region
201 Varick Street
New York, NY 10014
Tel: 212-337-1300
Fax: 212-337-1306
Email: archives@newyork.nara.gov
URL: http://www.nara.gov/nara/regional/02nsgil.html

New York State Archives
Cultural Education Center, Room 11D40
Albany, NY 12230
Tel: 518-474-8955
Email: refserv@unix6.nysed.gov
URL: http://www.sara.nysed.gov/
or http://unix6.nysed.gov/holding/fact/genea-fa.htm

Genealogical Societies

Adirondack Genealogical-Historical Society
Saranac Lake Free Library
100 Main Street
Saranac Lake, NY 12983
Tel: 518-891-4190

Afro-American Historical & Genealogical Society (AAHGS)
Jean Sampson Scott Chapter-Greater New York
P.O. Box 022340
Brooklyn, NY 11202

Amherst Museum Genealogy Society
c/o Amherst Museum Colony Park
3755 Tonawanda Creek Road
Amherst, NY 14228

Ballston Spa Genealogy Club
c/o Ballston Spa Library
Ballston, NY 12020

Brooklyn Historical Society, Genealogy Workshop
128 Pierrepont Street
Brooklyn, NY 11201
(Closed for remodeling until 1998)

Buffalo & Western New York Italian Genealogy Society
171 Fowler Avenue
Kenmore, NY 14217-1503
Tel: 716-877-8124
URL: http://freenet.buffalo.edu/~roots/italian.htm

Capital District Genealogical Society
P.O. Box 2175, Empire State Plaza Station
Albany, NY 12220
URL: http://www.vivanet.com/~halsey/NY/capital.htm

Central New York Genealogical Society
P.O. Box 104, Colvin Station
Syracuse, NY 13205

Chautauqua County Genealogical Society
P.O. Box 404
Fredonia, NY 14063
URL: http://www.rootsweb.com/~nychauta/CCGS.HTM

Computer Genealogy Society of Long Island
c/o LDS Family History Center
160 Washington Avenue
Plainview, NY 11803
URL: http://www.maconnect.com/~vitev/genesocli/next.html

Creole-American Genealogical Society, Inc.
P.O. Box 2666, Church Street Station
New York, NY 10008

Dutch Settlers Society of Albany
23 Dresden Court
Albany, NY 12203
Tel: 518-456-7202

Dutchess County Genealogical Society
P.O. Box 708
Poughkeepsie, NY 12602

Finger Lakes Genealogical Society
P.O. Box 47
Seneca Falls, NY 13148

German Genealogy Group of Long Island
c/o LDS Family History Center
160 Washington Avenue
Plainview, NY 11803
Email: germ-genealogy@geocities.com
URL: http://www.geocities.com/Athens/Forum/2833/index.html

Heritage Hunters
P.O. Box 1389
Saratoga Springs, NY 12866

Huntington Historical Society, Genealogy Workshop
209 Main Street
Huntington, NY 11743
Tel: 516-427-7045

Irish Family History Forum, Inc.
P.O. Box 351
Rockville Center, NY 11571-0351
URL: http://www.fgs.org/~fgs/soc0090.htm

Italian Genealogical Group, Inc.
7 Grayon Drive
Dix Hills, NY 11746
Fax: 516-499-5524
Email: jdelalio@aol.com
URL: http://www.fgs.org/~fgs/soc0091.htm

Jefferson County New York Genealogical Society
P.O. Box 6453
Watertown, NY 13601
Email: jcnygs@imcnet.net
URL: http://www.rootsweb.com/~nyjeffer/jeffsoc.htm
or http://www.flash.net/~robinl/jcnygs.htm

Jewish Genealogical Society, Inc.
P.O. Box 6398
New York, NY 10128
Tel: 212-330-8257
URL: http://www.fgs.org/~fgs/soc0096.htm

Jewish Genealogical Society of Albany
P.O. Box 3850
Albany, NY 12208

Jewish Genealogical Society of Capital District
55 Sycamore Street
Albany, NY 12208

Jewish Genealogical Society of Greater Buffalo
174 Peppertree Drive #7
Amherst, NY 14228

Jewish Genealogical Society of Long Island
37 West Cliff Drive
Dix Hills, NY 11746

Jewish Genealogical Society of Rochester
c/o Dr. Bruce Kahn
265 Viennawood Drive
Rochester, NY 14618
URL: http://www.memo.com/jcc/jgsr/
or http://JGSR.HQ.net/

Kodak Genealogical Society
c/o Eastman Kodak Company
Kodak Recreation Building 28
Rochester, NY 14652-3404
URL: http://www.fgs.org/~fgs/soc0106.htm

Livingston-Steuben County Genealogical Society
9297 Shaw Road
Nunda, NY 14517

National Society-Daughters of the American Revolution
New York State Chapter
URL: http://www.borg.com/~emilies/nydar/nys.html

New York Genealogical & Biographical Society
122 East 58th Street
New York, NY 10022-1939
Tel: 212-755-8532
URL: http://www.tnp.com/nycgenweb/NYG&BS.htm

New York State Council of Genealogical Organizations
P.O. Box 2593
Syracuse, NY 13220-2593

Niagara County Genealogical Society
2650 Hess Road
Appleton, NY 14008

Niagara County Genealogical Society/Library
215 Niagara Street
Lockport, NY 14094
Tel: 716-433-1033

Northeastern New York Genealogical Society
c/o Joan Aldous, Treas.
80 Sunnyside North
Queensbury, NY 12804
URL: http://freenet.buffalo.edu/~ae487/nnygs.html

Northern New York American-Canadian Genealogical Society
P.O. Box 1256
Plattsburgh, NY 12901

Nyando Roots Genealogical Society
P.O. Box 175
Massena, NY 13662

Oneida County Genealogical Club
c/o Oneida County Historical Society
318 Genesee Street
Utica, NY 13502

Ontario County Genealogical Society
55 North Main Street
Canandaigua, NY 14424
Tel: 716-394-4975

Orange County Genealogical Society/Research Room
Historic Courthouse
101 Main Street
Goshen, NY 10924

Penfield Foundation, Inc.
Ironville Road
P.O. Box 126
Crown Point, NY 12928
Tel: 518-597-3804

Polish Genealogical Society of Western New York State (PGSWNY)
299 Barnard Street
Buffalo, NY 14206-3212
URL: http://feefhs.org/pol/frgpgswn.html

Puerto Rican/Hispanic Genealogical Society
25 Ralph Avenue
Brentwood, NY 11717-2421
Tel: 516-834-2511
Email: prgen@aol.com
URL: http://www.linkdirect.com/hispsoc/

Queens Genealogy Workshop
1820 Flushing Avenue
Ridgewood, NY 11385
Tel: 718-456-1776

Rochester Genealogical Society
P.O. Box 10501
Rochester, NY 14610-0501
Email: halsey@vivanet.com
URL: http://home.eznet.net/~halsey/rgs.html

Rockland County, Genealogical Society of
c/o Historical Society of Rockland County
20 Zukor Road
New City, NY 10956
Tel: 914-634-9629
URL: http://www.vivanet.com/~halsey/NY/rockland.htm

St. Lawrence Valley Genealogical Society
P.O. Box 341
Colton, NY 13625-0341
Email: eickhoff@aldus.northnet.org

Southern Tier Genealogy Club
Location:
Vestal Public Library
320 Vestal Parkway East
Vestal, NY 13850
Mail:
P.O. Box 680
Vestal, NY 13851-0680
Email: ann@spectra.net
URL: http://www.spectra.net/~ann/stgs.htm

Twin Tiers Genealogical Society
P.O. Box 763
Elmira, NY 14902
URL: http://www.rootsweb.com/~nychemun/tths.htm

Ulster County Genealogical Society
P.O. Box 536
Hurley, NY 12443

Westchester County Genealogical Society
P.O. Box 518
White Plains, NY 10603-0518
URL: http://pages.prodigy.com/HFBK19A/wcgs.htm

Western New York Genealogical Society/Library & Museum
5859 South Park Avenue, Route 62
P.O. Box 338
Hamburg, NY 14075
URL: http://www.localnet.com/andrle/erie/erwnygs.htm

Yates County Genealogical & Historical Society
200 Main Street
Penn Yan, NY 14527

Historical Societies

Adirondack Genealogical-Historical Society
100 Main Street
Saranac Lake, NY 12983

Afro-American Historical & Genealogical Society (AAHGS)
P.O. Box 022340
Brooklyn, NY 11202

Alabama Historical Society
c/o Alabama Town Historian
Jean Richardson
7079 Maple Street
Basom, NY 14013
Tel: 716-948-9886

Albany County Historical Association
Ten Broeck Mansion
9 Ten Broeck Place
Albany, NY 12210
Tel: 518-436-9826

Albany South End Historical Society
20 Second Avenue
Albany, NY 12202
Tel: 518-463-0249

Amagansett Historical Society
P.O. Box 7077
Amagansett, NY 11930
Tel: 516-267-3020

Amenia Historical Society
P.O. Box 22
Amenia, NY 12501

American Baptist Historical Society
Samuel Colgate Historical Library
1106 South Goodman Street
Rochester, NY 14620-2532
Tel: 716-473-1740

Amityville Historical Society/Library
Lauder Museum
170 Broadway
P.O. Box 764
Amityville, NY 11701
Tel: 516-598-1486

Anderson Falls Heritage Society
P.O. Box 1825
Keeseville, NY 12944
Tel: 518-384-2839

Ardsley Historical Society
9 American Legion Drive
Ardsley, NY 10502
Tel: 914-693-6027

Attica Historical Society
130 Main Street
P.O. Box 24
Attica, NY 14011
Tel: 716-591-2161

Babylon Village Historical and Preservation Society
117 West Main Street
Babylon, NY 11702
Tel: 516-669-7086

Baldwin Historical Society/Museum
1980 Grand Avenue
Baldwin, NY 11510
Tel: 516-223-6900

Beacon Historical Society
P.O. Box 89
Beacon, NY 12508

Bedford Historical Society
38 Village Green
Bedford, NY 10506
Tel: 914-234-9751
914-234-9328

Beekman Historical Society
P.O. Box 165
Poughquag, NY 12570

Bellport-Brookhaven Historical Society/Museum
31 Bellport Lane
Bellport, NY 11713
Tel: 516-286-0888
516-286-8773

Berne Historical Society
Berne Town Hall
P.O. Box 34
Berne, NY 12023
Tel: 518-768-2445

Bethlehem Historical Association
Old Cedar Hill Schoolhouse
Route 144 at Clapper Road
Selkirk, NY 12158
Tel: 518-767-9432

Bohemia Historical Society
P.O. Box 67
Bohemia, NY 11716
Tel: 516-244-2707

Bowdoin Park Historical & Archaeological Association
85 Sheafe Road
Wappingers Falls, NY 12590

Briarcliff Manor/Scarborough Historical Society
P.O. Box 11
Briarcliff Manor, NY 10510

Bridge Line Historical Society
Historical Society for the Delaware & Hudson Railroad
P.O. Box 7242, Capitol Station
Albany, NY 12224
URL: http://www.fileshop.com/personal/jashaw/rhs/blhs.html

Bridgehampton Historical Society/Museum
Montauk Highway
Bridgehampton, NY 11932
Tel: 516-537-1088

Brooklyn Historical Society
128 Pierrepont Street
Brooklyn, NY 11201
Tel: 718-624-0890
Fax: 718-875-3869
URL: http://www.brooklynhistory.org/index.htm
(Closed for remodeling until 1998)

Broome County Historical Society
30 Front Street
Binghamton, NY 13905
Tel: 607-772-0660

Bronx County Historical Society
3309 Bainbridge Avenue
Bronx, NY 10467
Tel: 718-881-8900

Brunswick Historical Society
P.O. Box 1776
Cropseyville, NY 12052

Buffalo and Erie County Historical Society/Library
25 Nottingham Court
Buffalo, NY 14216
Tel: 716-873-9612
Fax: 716-873-8754
URL: http://freenet.buffalo.edu/~library/local/histsoc.html

Castile Historical Society
17 Park Road
Castile, NY 14427
Tel: 716-493-5370

Cayuga-Owasco Lakes Historical Society
Luther Research Center and Archives
14 West Cayuga Street
P.O. Box 247
Moravia, NY 13118
Tel: 315-497-3206
URL: http://www.rootsweb.com/~nycayuga/colhs.htm

Charleston Historical Society
Baptist Church
Polin Point (off Route 30A)
Esperance, NY 12066
Tel: 518-875-6533

Charlotte-Genesee Lighthouse Historical Society
70 Lighthouse Street
Rochester, NY 14612
Tel: 716-621-6179

Chautauqua County Historical Society
P.O. Box 7
Westfield, NY 14787
Tel: 716-326-2977

Chautauqua Township Historical Society
Route 394
Mayville, NY 14757
Tel: 716-753-7535
URL: http://c1web.com/local_info/artsed/chs.html

Chemung County Historical Society
415 East Water Street
Elmira, NY 14901
Tel: 607-734-4167
URL: http://www.rootsweb.com/~nychemun/cchsres.htm

Chenango County Historical Society/Museum
45 Rexford Street
Norwich, NY 13815
Tel: 607-334-9227

Clinton County Historical Association
48 Court Street
Plattsburgh, NY 12901
Tel: 518-561-0340

Colonie, Historical Society of the Town of
Memorial Town Hall
207 Old Niskayuna Road, Box 212
Newtonville, NY 12128
Tel: 518-782-2593
518-783-1435

Colton Historical Society
Main Street
P.O. Box 223
Colton, NY 13625
Tel: 315-262-2524

Columbia County Historical Society/Museum & Research Library
5 Albany Avenue
P.O. Box 311
Kinderhook, NY 12106
Tel: 518-758-9265

Conesus Historical Society
Town Hall
Conesus, NY 14435
Tel: 716-346-2201

Constable Hall Association, Inc.
Constable Hall
P.O. Box 36
Constableville, NY 13325

Cortland County Historical Society
Sugget House Museum
25 Homer Avenue
Cortland, NY 13045
Tel: 607-756-6071

Cow Neck Peninsula Historical Society
Sands Williet House
336 Port Washington Blvd.
Port Washington, NY 11050
Tel: 516-365-9074

Cutchogue/New Suffolk Historical Council
Route 25
P.O. Box 575
Cutchogue, NY 11935
Tel: 516-734-7122

Dayton (Town of) Historical Society
P.O. Box 15
Dayton, NY 14041

Delaware County Historical Association/Library & Archives
RD 2, Box 201C
Delhi, NY 13753
Tel: 607-746-3849
Fax: 607-746-7326
Email: eckstrom@norwich.net
URL: http://www.rootsweb.com/~nydelaha/

DeWitt Historical Society of
Tompkins County Museum
401 East State Street
Ithaca, NY 14850
Tel: 607-273-8284

Dobbs Ferry Historical Society
12 Elm
Dobbs Ferry, NY 10522
Tel: 914-674-1007

Dr. Asa Fitch Historical Society
Email: jchilds1@aol.com
or jchilds1@juno.com
URL: http://www.sover.net/~salemny/histhl3.html

Dutchess County Historical Society
Clinton House
549 Main Street
P.O. Box 88
Poughkeepsie, NY 12602
Tel: 914-471-1630

East Bloomfield, Historical Society of Bloomfield Academy Museum
8 South Avenue
East Bloomfield, NY 14443
Tel: 716-657-7244
URL: http://www.rootsweb.com/~nyontari/ebhist.htm

East Hampton Historical Society
101 Main Street
East Hampton, NY 11937
Tel: 516-324-6850

Eastchester Historical Society
Town Hall
40 Mill Road, Box 37
Eastchester, NY 10709

Egbert Benson Historical Society of Red Hook
P.O. Box 1813
Red Hook, NY 12571-0397

Esquatak Historical Society
P.O. Box 151
Castleton, NY 12033

Essex Community Heritage Organization, Inc.
P.O. Box 260
Essex, NY 12936
Tel: 518-963-7088

Essex County Historical Society
Adirondack Center Museum
Court Street
Elizabethtown, NY 12932
Tel: 518-873-6466

Fenton Historical Society
67 Washington Street
Jamestown, NY 14701
Tel: 716-664-6256
Fax: 716-483-7524

Fishkill Historical Society
Van Wyck Homestead Museum
Route 9 and I-84
P.O. Box 133
Fishkill, NY 12524
Tel: 914-896-9560

Franklin County Historical Society/Museum
51 Milwaukee Street
Malone, NY 12953
Tel: 518-483-2750

Freeport Historical Society/Museum
350 S. Main Street
Freeport, NY 11520
Tel: 516-623-9632

Frontenac Historical Society/Museum
State Route 90
Union Springs, NY 13160
Tel: 315-889-5836

Fulton, Historical Society of
177 South First Street
P.O. Box 157
Fulton, NY 13069
Tel: 315-598-4616

Geneva Historical Society
Prouty Chew House
543 S. Main Street
Geneva, NY 14456-3194
Tel: 315-789-5151
Fax: 315-789-0314
URL: http://www.rootsweb.com/~nyontari/genhist.htm

Genoa Historical Society
Rural Life Museum
Route 34B
Genoa, NY 13071
Tel: 315-364-7550

Goshen Historical Society
Goshen Public Library
203 Main Street
Goshen, NY 10924
Tel: 914-294-6606

Gouverneur Historical Association
30 Church Street
Gouverneur, NY 13642
Tel: 315-287-0570

Greater Ridgewood Historical Society/Library
Onderdonk House
1820 Flushing Avenue
Ridgewood, NY 11385

Greece, Historical Society of
Greece Historical Center and Museum
595 Long Pond Road
Rochester, NY 14612
Tel: 716-225-7221

Greenbush Historical Society
P.O. Box 66
East Greenbush, NY 12061

Greenlawn/Centerport Historical Association
Harborfields Public Library Building
31 Broadway
P.O. Box 354
Greenlawn, NY 11740
Tel: 516-754-1180

Guilderland Historical Society
162 Main Street
P.O. Box 76
Guilderland Center, NY 12085
Tel: 518-861-8071

Hannibal Historical Society
P.O. Box 150
Hannibal, NY 13074
Tel: 315-564-5471

Harmony Historical Society
Open Meadows Road (Off Route 474)
Blockville, NY 14710
Tel: 716-782-3598
716-763-2381
URL: http://c1web.com/local_info/artsed/

Harrisville/Bonaparte History Association
c/o Gladys Van Wyck, Town Historian
High Street
P.O. Box 321
Harrisville, NY 13648
Tel: 315-543-2987

Hastings Heritage & History Club
Irene Meyers, Town & Village Historian
RR #3, County Rt. 33
Central Square, NY 13036
Tel: 315-668-2178

Hastings-on-Hudson Historical Society
41 Washington Avenue
Hastings-on-Hudson, NY 10706
Tel: 914-478-2249

Henderson Historical Society
P.O. Box 322
Henderson, NY 13650
Tel: 315-938-7169

Heritage Foundation of Oswego
156 West 2nd Street
Oswego, NY 13126
Tel: 315-342-3354

Herkimer County Historical Society
400 North Main Street
Herkimer, NY 13350

Historic Cherry Hill
523 1/2 South Pearl Street
Albany, NY 12202
Tel: 518-434-4791

Holland Society of New York
122 E. 58th Street
New York, NY 10022
Tel: 212-758-1875

Hoosick Township Historical Society
166 Main Street
Hoosick Falls, NY 12090

Hopkinton Historical Group
Hopkinton, NY 12965
Tel: 315-328-4684

Hudson Valley Railroad Society
Hyde Park Railroad Station
River Road
P.O. Box 135
Hyde Park, NY 12538
Tel: 914-331-9233

Huguenot Historical Society
P.O. Box 339
New Paltz, NY 12561
Tel: 914-255-1660
Email: Huguenothistoricalsociety@worldnet.att.net
URL: http://home.earthlink.net/~rctwig/hhs1.htm

Huntington Historical Society/Resource Center & Archives
209 Main Street
Huntington, NY 11743
Tel: 516-427-7045
Fax: 516-427-7056
Email: hunthistory@juno.com
URL: http://www.huntingtonli.org/hunthistorical/

Hyde Park Historical Society
Vanderbilt Mansion
Route 9
P.O. Box 182
Hyde Park, NY 12538
Tel: 914-229-8438

Interlaken Historical Society/Museum & Genealogical Res. Library
Main Street (Route 96)
Interlaken, NY 14847
Tel: 607-532-4341
607-532-4430

Irvington Historical Society
P.O. Box 23
Irvington, NY 10533

Italian Historical Society of America
111 Columbia Hts
Brooklyn, NY 11201
Tel: 718-852-2929

Jefferson County Historical Society
228 Washington Street
Watertown, NY 13601
Tel: 315-782-3491

Klyne-Esopus Historical Society/Museum
Route 9W
Ulster Park, NY 12487
Tel: 914-338-8109
Email: karlwick@mhv.net
URL: http://www1.mhv.net/~kehsm/

Knickerbocker Historical Society
P.O. Box 29
Schaghticoke, NY 12154

Knox Historical Society
P.O. Box 11
Knox, NY 12107
Tel: 518-872-2137
518-872-2551

LaGrange Historical Society
P.O. Box 412
LaGrange, NY 12540

Lake Placid/North Elba Historical Society
P.O. Box 189
Lake Placid, NY 12946
Tel: 518-523-1608

Lake Ronkonkoma Historical Society/Museum
328 Hawkins Avenue
P.O. Box 716
Lake Ronkonkoma, NY 11779
Tel: 516-467-3152

Lansing Historical Association
P.O. Box 100
Lansing, NY 14882
URL: http://www.lightlink.com/dagra/lanhist/join.htm
Outhouse Project
URL: http://www.lightlink.com/dagra/lanhist/outhouse.sht

Lansingburgh Historical Society
P.O. Box 219
Lansingburgh, NY 12182

Larchmont Historical Society
740 West Boston Post Road
Mamaroneck, NY 10543
Tel: 914-381-2239

Lewis County Historical Society
High Street
P.O. Box 277
Lyons Falls, NY 13368
Tel: 315-348-8089

Lindenhurst Historical Society
Old Village Hall Museum
215 S. Wellwood Avenue
P.O. Box 296
Lindenhurst, NY 11757
Tel: 516-957-4385

Little Nine Partners Historical Society
P.O. Box 243
Pine Plains, NY 12567

Little Red Schoolhouse Historical Society
P.O. Box 25
Coeymans Hollow, NY 12046
Tel: 518-756-2562
518-756-8166

Livingston County Historical Society
30 Center Street
Geneseo, NY 14454

Lloyd Harbor Historical Society
Lloyd Harbor Road
Lloyd Harbor, NY 11743
Tel: 516-424-6110

Lodi Historical Society
Main Street (Route 414)
Lodi, NY 14860
Tel: 607-582-6006

Madison County Historical Society/Library
Cottage Lawn House
435 Main Street
P.O. Box 415
Oneida, NY 13421
Tel: 315-363-4136

Mamaroneck Historical Society
P.O. Box 776
Mamaroneck, NY 10543

Manlius Historical Society
109 Pleasant Street
Manlius, NY 13104
Tel: 315-682-6660

Mannsville/Ellisburg, Historical Society of
110 Lilac Park Drive
Mannsville, NY 13661
Tel: 315-465-4049

Massapequas, Historical Society of the
106 Toronto Avenue
Massapequa, NY 11758
Tel: 516-799-4676

Massena Historical Association/Town Museum
200 East Orvis Street
Massena, NY 13669
Tel: 315-769-8571

Mattituck Historical Society
Main Road, Rte. 25
P.O. Box 766
Mattituck, NY 11952
Tel: 516-298-5248

Maybrook Railroad Historical Society
Route 208E
Maybrook, NY 12543
Tel: 914-427-2845

Merricks, Historical Society of the
2279 South Merrick Avenue
Merrick, NY 11566
Tel: 516-379-3476

Mexico Historical Society
South Jefferson Street
P.O. Box 331
Mexico, NY 13114
Tel: 315-963-8542

Middlebury Historical Society
c/o Middlebury Academy Museum
Academy Street
Wyoming, NY 14591
Tel: 716-495-6692
716-495-6582

Middletown & Walkill Precinct, Historical Society of
25 East Avenue
Middletown, NY 10940

Miller Place/Mount Sinai Historical Society
William Miller House
North Country Road & Honey Lane
P.O. Box 651
Miller Place, NY 11764
Tel: 516-473-3449

Minisink Valley Historical Society
127 West Main Street
Port Jervis, NY 12771
Tel: 914-856-2375

Montauk Historical Society
Montauk Highway
RFD 2, Box 112
Montauk, NY 11954
Tel: 516-668-5340

Moriches Bay Historical Society
Haven's House Museum
Montauk Highway and Chet Sweezy Road
P.O. Box 31
Center Moriches, NY 11934
Tel: 516-878-1776

Mount Pleasant Historical Society
1 Town Hall Plaza
Valhalla, NY 10595

National Maritime Historical Society
5 John Walsh Blvd.
Peekskill, NY 10566
Tel: 914-737-7878
Email: nmhs@marineart.com
URL: http://www.marineart.com/nmhs/

National Railway Historical Society
Mohawk/Hudson Chapter
74 Brookline Avenue
Albany, NY 12203
Tel: 518-489-2829

New Scotland (Town of) Historical Association
Old New Scotland Road
P.O. Box 511
Slingerlands, NY 12159
Tel: 518-765-2071

New York Historical Society
170 Central Park West
New York, NY 10024
Tel: 212-873-3400
Fax: 212-875-1591

New York State Historical Association
Fenimore House
Lake Road
P.O. Box 800
Cooperstown, NY 13326
Tel: 607-547-1400
607-547-1500 (Recorded Message)
Fax: 607-547-1404
Email: nyshal@aol.com
URL: http://www.cooperstown.net/nysha/

Newfane (Town of) Historical Society
Van Horn Mansion
2165 Lockport Olcott Road
Burt, NY 14028
Email: zeus@localnet.com
URL: http://www.localnet.com/~zeus/

North Castle Historical Society
312 King Street
Chappaqua, NY 10514
Tel: 914-238-4666
URL: http://nyslgti.gen.ny.us/newcastle/nchs.html

Northern New York Agricultural Historical Society
P.O. Box 108
LaFargeville, NY 13656
Tel: 315-658-2353
315-788-2882

Northport Historical Society
215 Main Street
Northport, NY 11768
Tel: 516-757-9859

Norwood Historical Association/Museum
P.O. Box 163
Norwood, NY 13668
Tel: 315-353-2167

Old Brutus Historical Society
8943 N. Seneca Street
Weedsport, NY 13166
Tel: 315-834-9342

Onondaga County Historical Association/Research Center
311 Montgomery Street
Syracuse, NY 13202
Tel: 315-428-1862
URL: http://www.syracusecvb.org/Visitor/Fun/Museums/onandaga.html
or http://maple.lemoyne.edu/~CERIOJL/oha.html

Ontario & Western Railway Historical Society, Inc.
P.O. Box 713
Middletown, NY 10940

Ontario County Historical Society
55 North Main Street
Canandaigua, NY 14424
Tel: 716-394-4975
URL: http://www.rootsweb.com/~nyontari/onthist.htm

Ossining Historical Society
196 Croton Avenue
Ossining, NY 10562
Tel: 914-941-0001

Oswego County Historical Society
135 East 3rd Street
Oswego, NY 13126
Tel: 315-343-1342

Otego Historical Society
c/o Harris Memorial Library
69 Main STreet
Otego, NY 13825
Tel: 607-988-6661 (Library)
607-988-2225 (Historical Society)
URL: http://lib.4cty.org/dialups/OTEGO.HTML

Oyster Bay Historical Society/Library & Museum
Earle-Wightman House
20 Summit Street
P.O. Box 297
Oyster Bay, NY 11771-0297
Tel: 516-922-5032
Fax: 516-922-6892
Email: OBHistory@aol.com
URL: http://members.aol.com/OBHistory/index.html

Oysterponds Historical Society
Village Lane
Orient, NY 11957
Tel: 516-323-2480

Palatine Settlement Society
Nellis Tavern
Route 5
St. Johnsville, NY 13452
Tel: 518-568-2952

Parishville Historical Association
P.O. Box 534
Parishville, NY 13672
Tel: 315-265-7619

Phelps Community Historical Society
c/o Ted Mullin, Pres.
29 Banta Street
Phelps, NY 14532
Tel: 315-548-3522 (John M. Parmelee, Town Historian)

Piseco Lake Historical Society
P.O. Box 607
Lake Pleasant, NY 12108
Tel: 518-548-8739

Plattekill Historical Society
P.O. Box 357
Clintondale, NY 12515

Pleasant Valley Historical Society
P.O. Box 309
Pleasant Valley, NY 12569

Poestenkill Historical Society
P.O. Box 140
Poestenkill, NY 12140-0140

Port Jefferson Historical Society
Mather House Museum
115 Prospect Street
P.O. Box 586
Port Jefferson, NY 11777
Tel: 516-473-2665

Pulaski Historical Society
3428 Maple Avenue
Pulaski, NY 13142
Tel: 315-298-4650

Pultneyville Historical Society
P.O. Box 92
Pultneyville, NY 14538
Tel: 315-589-9962 (Paula Carey, Archivist)

Putnam County Historical Society
Foundry Museum/Reference Library
63 Chestnut Street
Cold Spring, NY 10516
Tel: 914-265-4010
Email: PCHS@highlands.com

Quaker Hill and Pawling, Historical Society
P.O. Box 99
Pawling, NY 12564
Tel: 914-855-9316
914-855-5891

Regional Council of Historical Agencies
P.O. Box 28
Cooperstown, NY 13326
Tel: 800-895-1648

Rensselaer (City of) Historical Society
Agents House
15 Forbes Avenue
Rensselaer, NY 12144

Rensselaer County Historical Society/Genealogy Library
Hart-Cluett Mansion
59 Second Street
Troy, NY 12180
Tel: 518-272-7232
Fax: 518-273-1264
URL: http://crisny.org/not-for-profit/rchs/

Rensselaerville Historical Society
P.O. Box 8
Rensselaerville, NY 12147
Tel: 518-797-5154

Rhinebeck Historical Society
P.O. Box 291
Rhinebeck, NY 12572

Richville Historical Association
RD #1, Box 171
Hermon, NY 13652
Tel: 315-347-3221
315-287-0375

Rochester Historical Society
485 East Avenue
Rochester, NY 14607
Tel: 716-271-2705

Rockland County Historical Society/History Center
20 Zukor Road
New City, NY 10956
Tel: 914-634-9629

Rocky Point Historical Society
P.O. Box 1720
Rocky Point, NY 11778

Roe-Jan Historical Society/Museum
Route 344
Copake Falls, NY 12517
Tel: 518-329-2376

Rome Historical Society/Museum & Archives
200 Church Street
Rome, NY 13440
Tel: 315-336-5870
URL: http://www.rny.com/town/points/29romehistoricalsociety.html

Sag Harbor Historical Society
P.O. Box 1709
Sag Harbor, NY 11963
Tel: 516-725-5092

St. Lawrence County Historical Association
3 East Main Street
P.O. Box 8
Canton, NY 13617
Tel: 315-386-8133

Sand Lake Historical Society
P.O. Box 492
West Sand Lake, NY 12196

Sayville Historical Society
Edwards Homestead
39 Edwards Street
P.O. Box 41
Sayville, NY 11782
Tel: 516-563-0186

Schenectady County Historical Society
32 Washington Avenue
Schenectady, NY 12305
Tel: 518-374-0263
URL: http://www.scpl.org/schs.html

Schroon-North Hudson Historical Society, Inc.
Main Street
Schroon Lake, NY 12870
Tel: 518-532-7854

Schuyler County Historical Society/Library
108 North Catherine Street, Rte. 14
P.O. Box 651
Montour Falls, NY 14865

Scriba Town Historical Association
Scriba Municipal Building
RD #8
Oswego, NY 13126
Tel: 315-342-6420

Seaford Historical Society
2234 Jackson Avenue
Seaford, NY 11783
Tel: 516-826-1150

Shaker Heritage Society
Shaker Meeting House
Shaker Road
Albany, NY 12211
Tel: 518-456-7890

Shelter Island Historical Society
Old Havens House
16 S. Ferry Road
P.O. Box 847-24
Shelter Island, NY 11964
Tel: 516-749-1116
516-749-0025

Skaneateles Historical Society/Archives
The Creamery
28 Hannum Street
Skaneateles, NY 13152
URL: http://www.skaneateles.com/genealogy.html

Smithtown Historical Society/Library
Caleb Smith II House
North Country Road (Rte. 25A)
Smithtown, NY 11787
Tel: 516-265-6768

South Jefferson, Historical Association of
9 East Church Street
Adams, NY 13605
Tel: 315-232-2616
URL: http://www.rootsweb.com/~nyjeffer/sjef.htm

Southampton Historical Society
17 Meeting House Lane
Southampton, NY 11968
Tel: 516-283-2494

Southold Historical Society
Main Road & Maple Lane
P.O. Box 1
Southold, NY 11971
Tel: 516-765-5500

Southport Historical Society
P.O. Box 146
Pine City, NY 14871

Spencer Historical Society/Museum
Center Street
Spencer, NY 14883
Tel: 607-589-6906

Staten Island Historical Society
441 Clarke Avenue
Staten Island, NY 10306-1198
Tel: 718-351-1617
Fax: 718-351-6057

Steamship Historical Society of America
Hudson Valley Chapter
55 Indian Ledge Road
Voorheesville, NY 12186
Tel: 518-765-4446

Steamship Historical Society of America
Long Island Chapter
30 Shenandoah Blvd.
Nesconset, NY 11767

Stephentown Historical Society
P.O. Box 11
Stephentown, NY 12168

Sterling Historical Society
Main Street
P.O. Box 590
Greenport, NY 11944
Tel: 516-477-0099

Steuben County Historical Society
P.O. Box 349
Bath, NY 14810

Stony Brook Historical Society
P.O. Box 802
Stony Brook, NY 11790

Suffolk County Historical Society/Library
300 West Main Street
Riverhead, NY 11901
Tel: 516-727-2881
URL: http://www.lieast.com/museum.html

Sullivan County Historical Society
265 Main Street
Hurleyville, NY 12747
Tel: 914-434-8044

Taconic Valley Historical Society
Hilltop Road
P.O. Box 400
Berlin, NY 12022-0400

Tarrytowns, Historical Society of the
1 Grove Street
Tarrytown, NY 10591
Tel: 914-631-8374

Three Village Historical Society
P.O. Box 76
East Setauket, NY 11733
Tel: 516-331-1849
URL: http://members.aol.com/TVHS1/index.html

Ticonderoga Historical Association
Hancock House
1 Moses Circle
Ticonderoga, NY 12883
Tel: 518-585-7868

Tioga County Historical Society/Museum
110-112 Front Street
Owego, NY 13827
Tel: 607-687-2460

Tonawanda-Kenmore Historical Society
St. Peter's Church
Knoche Road near Elmwood Avenue
Tonawanda, NY 14150
Tel: 716-873-5774
URL: http://freenet.buffalo.edu/~tot/htm/o_hsoc.htm

Ulster & Delaware Railroad Historical Society, Inc.
P.O. Box 404
Margaretville, NY 12455-0404

Ulster County Historical Society/Museum
Route 209
Marbletown, NY 12401
Tel: 914-338-5614

Ulysses Historical Society
61 East Main Street
Trumansburg, NY 14886
Tel: 607-387-5659

Union Vale Historical Society
P.O. Box 100
Verbank, NY 12585

Wading River Historical Society
North Country Road
Wading River, NY 11792
Tel: 516-929-4082

Walworth Historical Society/Museum
2257 Academy Street
P.O. Box 142
Walworth, NY 14568
Tel: 315-524-9528

Wappinger Historical Society
P.O. Box 974
Wappingers Falls, NY 12590

Warwick (Town of), Historical Society of
P.O. Box 353
Warwick, NY 10990
Tel: 914-986-4833

Waterloo Library & Historical Society
Terwilliger Museum
31 East Williams Street
Waterloo, NY 13165
Tel: 315-539-0533

Watervliet Historical Society
P.O. Box 123
Watervliet, NY 12189
Tel: 518-235-6699

Wayne County Historical Society
21 Butternut Street
Lyons, NY 14489
Tel: 315-946-4943

Westchester County Historical Society
c/o Westchester County Archives
2199 Saw Mill River Road
Elmsford, NY 10523
Tel: 914-592-4323

Western New York Association of Historical Agencies
131 West Main Street
Batavia, NY 14020
Tel: 716-345-0023

Wheatland Historical Association
Sage-Marlowe House
69 Main Street
Scottsville, NY 14546
Tel: 716-889-4574

Woodbury Historical Society/Cemetery of the Highlands
Main Street
Woodbury, NY 11797
Tel: 914-928-6770

Woodstock, Historical Society of
Comeau Drive
81 Tinker Street
Woodstock, NY 12498
Tel: 914-679-6744

Wyoming Historical Pioneer Association
18 East Main Street
Arcade, NY 14009

Yaphank Historical Society
Hawkins-Jacobson House
Yaphank Road
Yaphank, NY 11980
Tel: 516-924-3879

Yates County Genealogical & Historical Society
Oliver House Museum & Research Room
200 Main Street
Penn Yan, NY 14527
Tel: 315-536-7318

Municipal and County Historians/Archives

Albany (City of) Historian
Town Hall
Albany, NY 12207
Tel: 518-434-5100

Albany County Hall of Records
250 South Pearl Street
Albany, NY 12202
Tel: 518-447-4500
Email: achor@nyslgti.gen.ny.us
URL: http://nyslgti.gen.ny.us/ACHOR/

Albany County Historian
Mr. John Travis
112 State Street, Room 820
Albany, NY 12207
Tel: 518-447-7057

Allegany County Historian
Allegany County Museum
Court House
11 Wells Lane
Belmont, NY 14813
Tel: 716-268-9293
Fax: 716-268-9446

Brooklyn Historian
(See Kings County)

Broome County Historian
Gerald Smith
Broome County Public Library
78 Exchange Street
Binghamton, NY 13901
Tel: 607-778-2076
URL: http://www.wskg.com/Ancestors_Resources.htm
#Broome Cty Historian

Bronx County Historian
Rev. William A. Tieck, Ph.D., Litt. D.
3930 Bailey Avenue
Bronx, NY 10463

Cattaraugus County Historian
Historical Museum
Court Street
Little Valley, NY 14755
Tel: 716-938-9111
URL: http://www.rootsweb.com/~nycattar/society.htm

Cayuga County Historian
Historic Old Post Office Building, Main Floor
157 Genesee Street
Auburn, NY 13021
Tel: 315-253-1300
URL: http://www.rootsweb.com/~nycayuga/cayhsltr.htm

Chautauqua County Historian
Elizabeth Crocker
131 Center Street
Fredonia, NY 14063
Tel: 716-672-6306

Chemung County Historian
Mr. Thomas E. Bryne
1448 W. Water Street
Elmira, NY 14901

Chenango County Historian
Chenango County Historical Society/Museum
45 Rexford Street
Norwich, NY 13815
Tel: 607-334-9227

Clinton County Historian/County Clerk
Clinton County Government Center
137 Margaret Street
Plattsburgh, NY 12901
Tel: 518-565-4749
518-565-4700 (County Clerk)

Columbia County Historian
122 Main Street, Box 00
Philmont, NY 12565
Tel: 518-672-7032

Cortland County Historian
Cortland County Courthouse
P.O. Box 5590
Cortland, NY 13045-5590
Tel: 607-753-5360

Delaware County Historian
Mrs. Clara Stewart
195 Main Street
Delhi, NY 13753

Dutchess County Historian
Joyce Ghee
22 Market Street
Poughkeepsie, NY 12601

Erie County Historian
c/o Buffalo & Erie County Historical Society
25 Nottingham Court
Buffalo, NY 14216
Tel: 716-873-9644
716-873-9612
Fax: 716-873-8754
URL: http://freenet.buffalo.edu/~library/local/histsoc.html

Essex County Historian
Adirondack Center Museum
Elizabethtown, NY 12932

Franklin County Historian
c/o Franklin County Historical Society
51 Milwaukee Street
Malone, NY 12953
Tel: 518-483-2750

Fulton County Historian
Lewis G. Decker
187 Bleeker Street
Gloversville, NY 12078
Tel: 518-725-0473

Genesee County History Department
Susan L. Conklin, Historian & Records Management Officer
131 W. Main Street
Batavia, NY 14020
Tel: 716-343-1164
Fax: 716-344-2442
Email: conklins@nyslgti.gen.ny.us

Greene County Historian
288-292 Main Street
Catskill, NY 12414

Hamilton County Historian
Frederick C. Aber
P.O. Box 3
Indian Lake, NY 12842

Herkimer County Historian
c/o Herkimer County Historical Society
400 North Main Street
Herkimer, NY 13350

Jefferson County Historian
Charles Dunham
P.O. Box 367
Chaumont, NY 13622

Kings County Historian (Brooklyn)
John Manbeck, Brooklyn Borough Historian
16 Court Street
Brooklyn, NY 11241
URL: http://webhost.brooklyn.lib.ny.us/world/manbeck.htm

Lewis County Historian
P.O. Box 277
Lyons Falls, NY 13368
Tel: 315-348-8089

Livingston County Historian
30 Center Street
Geneseo, NY 14454
Tel: 716-243-2311
716-243-9147

Madison County Historian
Isabel Bracy
616 McDonald Street
Chittenango, NY 13037

Monroe County Historian
Rochester Regional Library Council
Rundel Memorial Library, Room 230
115 South Avenue
Rochester, NY 14604
Tel: 716-428-7375
Fax: 716-428-7313
URL: http://www.rrlc.org/guide/arc25.shtml

Montgomery County, Department of History & Archives
Old Court House
9 Park Street
P.O. Box 1500
Fonda, NY 12068-1500
Tel: 518-853-8187
URL: http://www.superior.net/~emogen34/history.htm

Nassau County Historian
c/o Nassau County Museum
1864 Muttontown Road
Syosset, NY 11791

New York City Municipal Archives
31 Chambers Street, Room 103
New York, NY 10007
Tel: 212-788-8580
Fax: 212-385-0984
URL: http://www.ci.nyc.ny.us/html/doris/html/archives.html
or http://www.tnp.com/nycgenweb/municipal.htm

New York County Historian (Manhattan)
Paul O'Dwyer, Borough Historian
99 Wall Street, 17th Floor
New York, NY 10005

Niagara County Historian
Civil Defense Building
Niagara & Hawley Streets
Lockport, NY 14094
Tel: 716-439-7324

Ontario County Historian
3871 County Road #46
Canandiagua, NY 14424
Tel: 716-396-4034

Ontario County Records & Archives Center
3869 County Road #46
Canandiagua, NY 14424
Tel: 716-396-4376
Fax: 716-396-4390
Email: http://nyslgti.gen.ny.us/nylocal/Ontario/hist_records.html

Orange County Historian
101 Main Street
Goshen, NY 10924
Tel: 914-294-6644

Orleans County Historian
C.W. Lattin
34 East Park Street
Albion, NY 14411
Tel: 716-589-4174

Oswego County Clerk/Historian
46 E. Bridge Street
Oswego, NY 13126
Tel: 315-349-8385

Otsego County Historian
Nancy Milavec
RD #2, Box 297
Worcester, NY 12197

Putnam County Historian
Records Center
121 Main Street
Brewster, NY 10509
Tel: 914-278-7209
Fax: 914-278-1435

Queens County Historian
c/o Queens Borough Hall
120-55 Queens Blvd.
Kew Gardens, NY 11424

Rensselaer County Historian
c/o Rensselaer County Historical Society
Hart-Cluett Mansion
59 Second Street
Troy, NY 12180
Tel: 518-272-7232
Fax: 518-273-1264
URL: http://crisny.org/not-for-profit/rchs/

Richmond County Historian (Staten Island)
Loring McMillen, P.E.
3531 Richmond Road
Staten Island, NY 10306

Rochester (City of) Archives & Records Center
414 Andrews Street
Rochester, NY 14604
Tel: 716-428-7331
Fax: 716-428-6092
URL: http://www.rochester.lib.ny.us/cityhall/about_r/records/records.htm

Rochester City Historian
Ruth Rosenberg-Naparsteck
Rochester Public Library
115 South Avenue, 2nd Floor
Rochester, NY 14604-1896
Tel: 716-428-7340
Fax: 716-428-6383
Email: rrosenbe@mcls.rochester.lib.ny.us
URL: http://www.rochester.lib.ny.us/cityhall/about_r/history/history.htm

Rockland County Historian
Thomas F.X. Casey
12 Ashwood Lane
Garnerville, NY 10923

Saratoga County Historical Office
Municipal Center
McMaster Street
Ballston Spa, NY 12020
Tel: 518-885-5381

Schenectady City History Center Library
City Hall
Schenectady, NY 12305
Tel: 518-377-7061

Schenectady (City and County) Historian
Larry Hart
c/o Daily Gazette
2345 Maxon Road
Schenectady, NY 12308
Tel: 518-399-3466

Schoharie County Historian
Mildred L. Bailey
RD #1, Box 300
Stamford, NY 12167

Schuyler County Historian
Barbara Bell
RD #1, Box 192
Watkins Glen, NY 14891

Seneca County Historian
1 DiPronia Drive
Waterloo, NY 13165

Staten Island Historian
(See Richmond County)

Steuben County Historian
Steuben County Office Building
3 E. Pulteney Square
Bath, NY 14810
Tel: 607-776-9631 ext. 3411
URL: http://nyslgti.gen.ny.us/Steuben/hstorian.html

Suffolk County Historian
Division of Cultural & Historical Services
Montauk Highway
P.O. Box 144
West Sayville, NY 11796

Sullivan County Historian
c/o Sullivan County Museum
Hurleyville, NY 12747

Tioga County Historian
Tioga County Office Building
56 Main Street
Owego, NY 13827

Tompkins County Historian
c/o DeWitt Historical Society of
401 East State Street
Ithaca, NY 14850
Tel: 607-273-8284

Ulster County Historian
401 Route 208
New Paltz, NY 12561

Warren County Historian
Warren County Municipal Center
Lake George, NY 12845
Tel: 518-761-6544

Washington County Historian/Archives
383 Broadway
Fort Edward, NY 12828
Tel: 518-746-2178 (Historian)
518-746-2136 (Archivist)

Wayne County Historian
Pearl Street
Lyons, NY 14489
Tel: 315-946-5470

Westchester County Archives
2199 Saw Mill River Road
Elmsford, NY 10523
Tel: 914-592-5614
Fax: 914-592-5160
URL: http://nyslgti.gen.ny.us/Westchester/arcintro.html

Westchester County Historian
Michaelian Building, Room 618
White Plains, NY 10601

Wyoming County Historian
26 Linwood Avenue
Warsaw, NY 14569
Tel: 716-786-8818

Yates County Historian
Yates County Building
110 Court Street
Penn Yan, NY 14527

LDS Family History Centers

Albany Family History Center
411 Loudon Road
Loudonville, NY 12211
Tel: 518-463-4581

Binghampton Family History Center
305 Murray Hill Road
Vestal, NY 13805
Tel: 607-797-3900

Brighton Family History Center
1400 Westfall Road
Brighton, NY 14618
Tel: 716-271-9454

Brockport Family History Center
4088 Lake Road
Brockport, NY 14420
Tel: 716-637-2030

Brooklyn Family History Center
1212 Glenwood Road
Brooklyn, NY 11230
Tel: 718-434-8245

Buffalo Family History Center
305 Murray Hill Road
Williamsville, NY 14221
Tel: 716-688-6438

Elmhurst Family History Center (Spanish Speaking)
Rego Park
86-16 60th Road
Elmhurst, NY 11373
Tel: 718-478-5337

Ithaca Family History Center
114 Burleigh Drive
Ithaca, NY 14850
Tel: 607-257-1334

Jamestown Family History Center
851 Forest Avenue
Jamestown, NY 14701
Tel: 716-487-0830

Lake Placid Family History Center
Old Military & John Brown Road
Lake Placid, NY 12946
Tel: 518-523-2889

New York Family History Center
125 Columbus Avenue at Lincoln Square
New York, NY 10023
Tel: 212-873-1690

Orchard Park Family History Center
S-4003 Baker Road
Orchard Park, NY 14127
Tel: 716-662-3117
URL: http://www.localnet.com/~andrle/erie/orchard_park/opfhc.htm

Owego Family History Center
Montrose Turnpike
Owego, NY 13827
Tel: 607-687-3822
607-687-5137

Pittsford Family History Center
460 Kreag Road
Pittsford, NY 14534
Tel: 716-248-9930
716-637-2030

Plainview Family History Center
160 Washington Avenue
Plainview, NY 13137
Tel: 516-433-0122
URL: http://www.maconnect.com/~vitev/genesocli/fhc.html

Rochester Family History Center
1400 Westfall Road
Rochester, NY 14618
Tel: 716-271-9454

Scarsdale Family History Center
60 Wayside Lane
Scarsdale, NY 10583
Tel: 914-723-4022

Syracuse Family History Center
4889 Bear Road
Liverpool, NY 13088
Tel: 315-457-5172

Yorktown Family History Center
Route 134
Yorktown, NY 10598
Tel: 914-941-9754

ARCHIVES/LIBRARIES/MUSEUMS

Adriance Memorial Library/Poughkeepsie Library District
93 Market Street
Poughkeepsie, NY 12601
Tel: 914-485-3445
800-804-0092
Fax: 914-485-3789
Email: adriance@ulysses.sebridge.org
URL: http://midhudson.org/member/adriance.html

Ainsworth Memorial Library
6064 South Main Street
P.O. Box 69
Sandy Creek, NY 13145
Tel: 315-387-3732
URL: http://www.tce.vcomm.net/library/

Akwesasne Library
RR #1, Box 14C
Hogansburg, NY 13655
Tel: 518-358-2240

Albany Institute of History & Art/Museum & Library
125 Washington Avenue
Albany, NY 12210
Tel: 518-463-4478

Albany Public Library
161 Washington Avenue
Albany, NY 12210
Tel: 518-449-3380

Albany South End Historical Society
20 Second Avenue
Albany, NY 12202
Tel: 518-463-0249

Alfred University
Herrick Memorial Library
Special Collections
Saxon Drive
Alfred, NY 14802
Tel: 607-871-2184
607-871-2385
Fax: 607-871-2992
URL: http://www.herr.alfred.edu/speccoll.htm

Allegany County Museum
Court House
11 Wells Lane
Belmont, NY 14813
Tel: 716-268-9293
Fax: 716-268-9446

Altamount Archives/Museum
Village Hall
115 Main Street
Altamount, NY 12009
Tel: 518-861-8554

American Baptist Historical Society
Samuel Colgate Historical Library
1106 South Goodman Street
Rochester, NY 14620-2532
Tel: 716-473-1740

American Merchant Marine Museum
U.S.M.M.A.
Kings Point, NY 11024
Tel: 516-773-5515

American Veterans Historical Museum
P.O. Box 115
Pleasantville, NY 10570
Tel: 914-769-5297

Amherst Museum Colony Park
Nederlander Research Library/Archives
3755 Tonawanda Creek Road
Amherst, NY 14228
Tel: 716-689-1440
Fax: 716-689-1409
URL: http://www.localnet.com/~andrle/erie/eramcp.htm

Amityville Historical Society/Library
Lauder Museum
170 Broadway
P.O. Box 764
Amityville, NY 11701
Tel: 516-598-1486

Ancient Order of Hibernians
1021 Ninth Avenue
Watervliet, NY 12189
Tel: 518-274-2871

Ardsley Public Library
9 American Legion Drive
Ardsley, NY 10502
Tel: 914-693-6636

Babylon Public Library
24 S. Carll Avenue
Babylon, NY 11702-3403
Tel: 516-669-1624

Baldwin Historical Society/Museum
1980 Grand Avenue
Baldwin, NY 11510
Tel: 516-223-6900

Baldwinsville Public Library
Local History Room
33 East Genesee Street
Baldwinsville, NY 13027
Tel: 315-635-5631
Fax: 315-635-6760
Email: info@bville.lib.ny.us
URL: http://www.bville.lib.ny.us/

Bayville Free Library
34 School Street
Bayville, NY 11709
Tel: 516-628-2765
Fax: 516-628-2738
URL: http://www.516web.com/library/bayville/menu.htm

Bellport-Brookhaven Historical Society/Museum
31 Bellport Lane
Bellport, NY 11713
Tel: 516-286-0888
516-286-8773

Bethlehem Public Library
451 Delaware Avenue
Delmar, NY 12054
Tel: 518-439-9314

Binghamton University
Glenn G. Bartle Library
Vestal Parkway East
Vestal, NY 13850
Tel: 607-777-2800
URL: http://library.lib.binghamton.edu/

Blauvelt Free Library
86 South Western Highway
Blauvelt, NY 10913

Bodman Memorial Library/Museum
8 Aldrich Street
Philadelphia, NY 13673
Tel: 315-642-3323

Brentwood Public Library
2nd Avenue & 4th Street
Brentwood, NY 11717
Tel: 516-273-7883
URL: http://www.suffolk.lib.ny.us/libraries/bren/

Bridgehampton Historical Society/Museum
Montauk Highway
Bridgehampton, NY 11932
Tel: 516-537-1088

Brighton Memorial Library
2300 Elmwood Avenue
Rochester, NY 14618
Tel: 716-473-5420
TDD: 716-442-5619
Email: kbolan@mcls.rochester.lib.ny.us
URL: http://www.rochester.lib.ny.us/brighton/

Bronx County Historical Society
3309 Bainbridge Avenue
Bronx, NY 10467
Tel: 718-881-8900

Bronx Public Library
Reference Center
2555 Marion Avenue
Bronx, NY 10458

Brooklyn College/City University of New York (CUNY)
Harry D. Gideonse Library
Brooklyn, NY 11210
Tel: 718-951-5336
URL: http://www.brooklyn.cuny.edu/bc/fac/bclib.html

Brooklyn Museum/Wilbour Library & Archives
200 Eastern Parkway
Brooklyn, NY 11238-6052
Tel: 716-638-5000
Fax: 716-638-3731

Brooklyn Public Library/Central Library
Grand Army Plaza
Brooklyn, NY 11238
Tel: 718-780-7700
Email: bplweb@bway.net
URL: http://www.brooklyn.lib.ny.us/

Broome County Historical Society
30 Front Street
Binghamton, NY 13905
Tel: 607-772-0660

Broome County Public Library
78 Exchange Street
Binghampton, NY 13901
Tel: 607-778-6451
URL: http://www.tier.net/bcpl/

Bryant Library
Local History Collection
2 Paper Mill Road
Roslyn, NY 11576
Tel: 516-621-2240

Buffalo and Erie County Historical Society/Library
25 Nottingham Court
Buffalo, NY 14216
Tel: 716-873-9612
Fax: 716-873-8754
URL: http://freenet.buffalo.edu/~library/local/histsoc.html

Buffalo and Erie County Public Library
Lafayette Square
Buffalo, NY 14203
Tel: 716-858-7113
Fax: 716-858-6211
URL: http://freenet.buffalo.edu/~library/local/becpl.html

Canajoharie Library & Art Gallery
2 Erie Blvd.
Canajoharie, NY 13317
Tel: 518-673-2314

Canisius College
Andrew Bouwhuis Library
Archives Department
Buffalo, NY 14208
Tel: 716-888-2530
URL: http://www.canisius.edu/canhp/canlib/archives.html

Cape Vincent Historical Museum
James Street
P.O. Box 302
Cape Vincent, NY 13618
Tel: 315-654-4400
315-654-3640

Carthage Free Library
Heritage Room
412 Budd Street
Carthage, NY 13619
Tel: 315-493-2620

Cattaraugus County Memorial Historical Museum
Court Street
Little Valley, NY 14755
Tel: 716-938-9111

Cayuga Community College
Norman F. Bourke Memorial Library
Special Collections
Auburn, NY 13021
Tel: 315-255-1743 ext. 290
Email: brownk@caylib.cayuga-cc.edu
URL: http://www.cayuga-cc.edu/library/library/special.htm

Cayuga Museum of History & Art
203 Genesee Street
Auburn, NY 13021
Tel: 315-253-8051
URL: http://170.158.2.6/other/museums.html

Cayuga-Owasco Lakes Historical Society
Luther Research Center and Archives
14 West Cayuga Street
P.O. Box 247
Moravia, NY 13118
Tel: 315-497-3206
URL: http://www.rootsweb.com/~nycayuga/colhs.htm

Central Islip Public Library
33 Hawthorne Avenue
Central Islip, NY 11722
Tel: 516-234-9333
URL: http://www.suffolk.lib.ny.us/libraries/cisp/

Central Square Library
637 S. Main
P.O. Box 368
Central Square, NY 13036
Tel: 315-668-6104

Charles Dawson History Center
P.O. Box 1696
Harrison, NY 10528
Tel: 914-948-2550

Chautauqua Institution
Smith Memorial Library/Archives
21 Miller Avenue
P.O. Box 1093
Chautauqua, NY 14722
Tel: 716-357-6332
716-357-6306
Fax: 716-357-9014
URL: http://www.chautauqua-inst.org/

Clinton House State Historic Site
Dutchess County Historical Society
549 Main Street
Poughkeepsie, NY 12602
Tel: 914-471-1630

Coburn Free Library
275 Main Street
Owego, NY 13827
Tel: 607-687-3520

Columbia University
Journalism Library
New York, NY 10027
Tel: 212-854-4854
URL: http://www.columbia.edu/acis/documentation/journ/journnew.html

Cornell University
Croch Library
Ithaca, NY 14853-5302
Tel: 607-255-3530

Cornell University
John Henrik Clarke Africana Library
310 Triphammer Road
Ithaca, NY 14850
Tel: 607-255-3822
607-255-5229
Fax: 607-255-0784
Email: afrlib-mail@cornell.edu
URL: http://www.library.cornell.edu/africana/

Cornell University
John M. Olin Library
Ithaca, NY 14853
Tel: 607-255-5258
607-255-9567 (Newspapers Dept.)

Cortland County Historical Society
25 Homer Avenue
Cortland, NY 13045
Tel: 607-756-6071

Crandall Library
Holden Room
251 Glen Street
Glen Falls, NY 12801
Tel: 518-792-6508

Croghan Free Library
Main Street
P.O. Box 8
Croghan, NY 13327
Tel: 315-346-6521

Crown Point State Historic Site
RD #1, Box 219, Bridge Road
Crown Point, NY 12928
Tel: 518-597-3666

Dansville Public Library
200 Main Street
Dansville, NY 14437
Tel: 716-335-6720
Fax: 716-335-6133
Email: dpl@servtech.com

Darwin R. Barker Library/Museum
7 Day Street
Fredonia, NY 14063
Tel: 716-672-8051
716-672-2114

Daughters of the American Revolution
Irondequoit Chapter, DAR
11 Livingston Park
Rochester, NY 14608
Tel: 716-232-4509

Daughters of Charity Archives
DePaul Provincial House
96 Menands Road
Albany, NY 12204
Tel: 518-462-5593

Dexter Free Library
East Kirby Street
P.O. Box 544
Dexter, NY 13634
Tel: 315-639-6785

Dodge Memorial Library
144 Lake Street
Rouses Point, NY 12979
Tel: 518-297-6242

Dunkirk Historical Museum
513 Washington Avenue
Dunkirk, NY 14048
Tel: 716-366-3797
URL: http://c1web.com/local_info/artsed/dhm.html

Durham Center Museum/Research
Route 145
East Durham, NY 12433
Tel: 518-239-8461
518-239-4313

East Bloomfield, Historical Society of
Bloomfield Academy Museum
8 South Avenue
East Bloomfield, NY 14443
Tel: 716-657-7244
URL: http://www.rootsweb.com/~nyontari/ebhist.htm

East Hampton Free Library
Long Island Collection
159 Main Street
East Hampton, NY 11937
Tel: 516-324-0222
Fax: 516-324-5947
Email: ehamlib@suffolk.lib.ny.us
URL: http://www.peconic.net/easthampton/library/

Edmeston Free Library/Museum
6 West Street
P.O. Box 167
Edmeston, NY 13335-0167
Tel: 607-965-8208 (Library)
607-965-8902 (Museum)
URL: http://lib.4cty.org/dialups/edmeston.html

Ellenville Public Library/Museum
40 Center Street
Ellenville, NY 12428
Tel: 914-647-5530

Ellis Island Immigration Museum
American Family Immigration History Center
Liberty Island
New York, NY 10004
Tel: 212-363-3200
212-269-5755 (Circle Line Ferry for schedules/rates)
URL: http://www.ellisisland.org/

Elting Memorial Library
Haviland-Heidgerd Historical Collection
93 Main Street
New Paltz, NY 12561
Tel: 914-255-5030
Fax: 914-255-5818
Email: elting@sebridge.org
URL: http://midhudson.org/member/newpaltz.html

Emma Clark Library
120 Main Street
Setauket, NY 11733
Tel: 516-941-4080
Email: emsclib@suffolk.lib.ny.us
URL: http://emma.suffolk.lib.ny.us/

Episcopal Church Home Archives
505 Mount Hope Avenue
Rochester, NY 14620
Tel: 716-546-8400
Fax: 716-325-6553

Episcopal Diocese of Rochester Archives
935 East Avenue
Rochester, NY 14607
Tel: 716-473-2977
Fax: 716-473-3195

Essex County Historical Society
Adirondack Center Museum
Court Street
Elizabethtown, NY 12932
Tel: 518-873-6466

Fenton Historical Center
67 Washington Street
Jamestown, NY 14701
Tel: 716-664-6256
URL: http://c1web.com/local_info/artsed/fhc.html

Field Library
Peekskill Archives Collection
4 Nelson Avenue
Peekskill, NY 10566
Tel: 914-737-1212
Fax: 914-737-0714
URL: http://www.wls.lib.ny.us/libs/peekskill/pks.html

First Unitarian Universalist Society of Albany
405 Washington Avenue
Albany, NY 12206
Tel: 518-463-7135

Floral Park Public Library
Tulip Avenue & Caroline Place
Floral Park, NY 11001
Tel: 516-326-6330
516-437-6959

Flower Memorial Library
Genealogical Committee
229 Washington Street
Watertown, NY 13601
Tel: 315-788-2352

Frank J. Basloe Library
245 Main Street
Herkimer, NY 13350-1918
Tel: 315-866-1733

Franklin County Historical Society/Museum
51 Milwaukee Street
Malone, NY 12953
Tel: 518-483-2750

Freeport Historical Society/Museum
350 S. Main Street
Freeport, NY 11520
Tel: 516-623-9632

Fryer Memorial Museum
West Peterboro Street
Munnsville, NY 13409
Tel: 315-495-5395

Fulton Public Library
160 South First Street
Fulton, NY 13069
Tel: 315-592-5159

Garden City Public Library
60 7th Street
Garden City, NY 11530-2800
Tel: 516-742-8405

Gates Public Library
1605 Buffalo Road
Rochester, NY 14624
Tel: 716-247-6446
Fax: 716-426-5766
Email: sswanton@mcls.rochester.lib.ny.us
URL: http://mcls.rochester.lib.ny.us/gates/gatesinfo.html
or http://www.ggw.org/freenet/g/GatesPublicLibrary/

Genesee County Library
Department of History
131 West Main Street
Batavia, NY 14020

Genesis HealthCare Library
218 Stone Street
Watertown, NY 13601
Tel: 315-782-7400 ext. 2152

Geneva Free Library
244 Main Street
Geneva, NY 14456
Tel: 315-789-5303
Fax: 315-789-9835

Gilbertsville Library
Local History Department
Commercial Street
P.O. Box 332
Gilbertsville, NY 13776
Tel: 607-783-2832
Email: glibrary@tri-town.net
URL: http://lib.4cty.org/dialups/GI.HTML

Glen Cove Public Library
Glen Cove Avenue
Glen Cove, NY 11542-2885
Tel: 516-676-2130
Fax: 516-676-2788

Goff Nelson Memorial Library
41 Lake Street
Tupper Lake, NY 12986
Tel: 518-359-9421

Goshen Public Library
203 Main Street
Goshen, NY 10924
Tel: 914-294-6606

Great Neck Library
Bayview Avenue at Gristmill
Great Neck, NY 11024
Tel: 516-466-8055

Greater Ridgewood Historical Society/Library
Onderdonk House
1820 Flushing Avenue
Ridgewood, NY 11385

Guernsey Memorial Library
Otis A. Thompson Local History Room
3 Court Street
Norwich, NY 13815
Tel: 607-334-4034
URL: http://lib.4cty.org/otis.html

Hamilton Public Library
13 Broad Street
Hamilton, NY 13346
Tel: 315-824-3060

Harris Memorial Library
Otego Historical Society
69 Main STreet
Otego, NY 13825
Tel: 607-988-6661 (Library)
607-988-2225 (Historical Society)
URL: http://lib.4cty.org/dialups/OTEGO.HTML

Haviland Records Room (Quaker)
c/o New York Yearly Meeting
15 Rutherford Place
New York, NY 10016

Hawn Memorial Library
220 John Street
Clayton, NY 13624
Tel: 315-686-3762

Hempstead Public Library
115 Nichols Court
Hempstead, NY 11550
Tel/Fax: 516-481-6719

Email: hemplib@li.net
URL: http://www.516w.com/library/hempstead/

Henderson Free Library
Route 178
P.O. Box 302
Henderson, NY 13650
Tel: 315-938-5032

Henrietta Public Library
455 Calkins Road
Rochester, NY 14623
Tel: 716-359-7092

Hepburn Library
P.O. Box 86
Lisbon, NY 13658
Tel: 315-393-0111

Hofstra University
Long Island Studies Institute
Axinn Library, 9th Floor
Hempstead Turnpike
Hempstead, NY 11550
Tel: 516-560-5097
516-560-5846

Holland Land Office Museum
131 W. Main Street
Batavia, NY 14020
Tel: 716-343-4727

Holland Library
Market Street
Alexandria Bay, NY 13607
Tel: 315-482-2241

Holocaust Library & Research Center
557 Bedford Avenue
Brooklyn, NY 11211
Tel: 718-599-5833

Huntington Historical Society/Resource Center & Archives
209 Main Street
Huntington, NY 11743
Tel: 516-427-7045
Fax: 516-427-7056
Email: hunthistory@juno.com
URL: http://www.huntingtonli.org/hunthistorical/

Huntington Memorial Library
New York State History Room
62 Chestnut Street
Oneonta, NY 13820
Tel: 607-432-1980
URL: http://lib.4cty.org/oneonta/onnysr.html

Huntington Public Library
338 Main Street
Huntington, NY 11743-6956
Tel: 516-427-5165

Ilion Free Public Library
Municipal Building
78 West Street
Ilion, NY 13357-1725
Tel: 315-894-5028
Fax: 315-894-9980

Institute for Jewish Research
1048 Fifth Avenue
New York, NY 10028

Interlaken Historical Society/Museum & Genealogical Res. Library
Main Street (Route 96)
Interlaken, NY 14847
Tel: 607-532-4341
607-532-4430

Irish American Heritage Museum
19 Clinton Avenue
Albany, NY 12207
Tel: 518-432-6598

Irondequoit Public Library
Helen McGraw Branch
2180 E. Ridge Road
Rochester, NY 14622
Tel: 716-336-6060

Jefferson Community College
Melvil Dewey Library
Outer Coffeen Street
Watertown, NY 13601
Tel: 315-786-2224
315-786-2225

Jericho Public Library
1 Merry Lane
Jericho, NY 11753-1792
Tel: 516-935-6790

Jervis Library
613 N. Washington Street
Rome, NY 13440-4203
Tel: 315-336-4570

Johnstown Public Library
38 South Market Street
Johnstown, NY 12095

Keene Public Library
HCR #1, Box 63A
Keene, NY 12942
Tel: 518-576-2200

Keene Valley Library Archives
Main Street
Keene Valley, NY 12943
Tel: 518-576-4335

Klyne-Esopus Historical Society/Museum
Route 9W
Ulster Park, NY 12487
Tel: 914-338-8109
Email: karlwick@mhv.net
URL: http://www1.mhv.net/~kehsm/

Lake Placid Public Library
67 Main Street
Lake Placid, NY 12946
Tel: 518-523-3200

Lake Ronkonkoma Historical Society/Museum
328 Hawkins Avenue
P.O. Box 716
Lake Ronkonkoma, NY 11779
Tel: 516-467-3152

Lehman College Library/City University of New York
Special Collections
250 Bedford Park Blvd., West
Bronx, NY 10468
Tel: 718-960-8603
URL: http://www.lehman.cuny.edu/library/library2.htm

Leo Baeck Institute
German-Jewish Families
129 East 73rd Street
New York, NY 10021
Tel: 212-744-6400

Little Red Schoolhouse
Panama Rocks Road
Clymer Center, NY 14724
Tel: 716-355-6391
URL: http://c1web.com/local_info/artsed/lrs.html

Lockport Public Library
23 East Avenue
Lockport, NY 14094
Tel: 716-433-5935

Locust Valley Library
170 Buckram Road
Locust Valley, NY 11560
Tel: 516-671-1837
Fax: 516-676-8164

Lorenzo-New York State Historic Site
RD #2
Cazenovia, NY 13035
Tel: 315-655-3200
URL: http://cazenovia.com/lorenzo/index.html

Louise Adelia Read Memorial Library/Museum
12 Read Street
Hancock, NY 13783
Tel: 607-637-2519
URL: http://lib.4cty.org/dialups/HANCOCK.HTML A

Lower East Side Tenement Museum
90 Orchard Street (at Broome Street)
Mail:
66 Allen Street
New York, NY 10002
Tel: 212-431-0233
Fax: 212-431-0402
URL: http://www.wnet.org/tenement/
or http://www.high5tix.com/events/organizations/tenement.html

Lyme Heritage Center
12165 Main Street
Chaumont, NY 13622
Tel: 315-649-5452

Madison County Historical Society/Library
Cottage Lawn House
435 Main Street
P.O. Box 415
Oneida, NY 13421
Tel: 315-363-4136

Mamaroneck Public Library
136 Prospect Avenue
Mamaroneck, NY 10543
Tel: 914-698-1250

Margaret Reaney Memorial Library/Museum
19 Kingsburg Avenue
St. Johnsville, NY 13452
Tel: 518-568-7822

Military Heritage Museum
195 Washington Avenue
Albany, NY 12205
Tel: 518-436-0103

Montgomery Academy
Village Hall
133 Clinton Street
Maybrook, NY 12543
Tel: 914-457-5135

Montour Falls Memorial Library
406 W. Main Street
Montour Falls, NY 14865
Tel: 607-535-7489

Moore Memorial Library
59 Genesee Street
Green, NY 13778
Tel: 607-656-9349
URL: http://lib.4cty.org/gr/GREENE.HTML

Mount Vernon Public Library
Local History Room
28 S. First Avenue
Mount Vernon, NY 10550
Tel: 914-668-1840 ext. 32
Fax: 914-668-1018
URL: http://www.wls.lib.ny.us/libs/mount_vernon/mtv.html

Nassau County Museum
1864 Muttontown Road
Syosset, NY 11791

Nazarene College of Rochester
Lorette Wilmot Library
4245 East Avenue
Rochester, NY 14610
Tel: 716-586-2525 ext. 450
Fax: 716-248-8766
URL: http://www.naz.edu/dept/library/index.html

New City Library
Rockland Room
220 North Main Street
New City, NY 10956
Tel: 914-634-4997
914-634-4963
Fax: 914-634-0173
URL: http://www.naz.edu/dept/library/index.html

New Netherland Project
New York State Library
Cultural Education Center, 8th Floor
Empire State Plaza
Albany, NY 12230
Tel: 518-474-6067
518-486-4815 (Friends of the New Netherland Project)
Fax: 518-474-5786
Email: cgehring@unix2.nysed.gov
URL: http://nnp.nysed.gov/

New York Division of Military & Naval Affairs
330 Old Niskayuna Road
Latham, NY 12110

New York Genealogical & Biographical Society
122 East 58th Street
New York, NY 10022-1939
Tel: 212-755-8532
URL: http://www.tnp.com/nycgenweb/NYG&BS.htm

New York Historical Society
170 Central Park West
New York, NY 10024
Tel: 212-873-3400
Fax: 212-875-1591

New York Public Library
U.S. History, Local History, and Genealogy Resources
5th Avenue and 42nd Street, Room 315S
New York, NY 10016
Tel: 212-340-0849
URL: http://www.nypl.org/research/chss/lhg/genea.html

New York State Association of Museums
189 Second Street
Troy, NY 12181
Tel: 518-273-3416

New York State Bureau of Historic Sites
Office of Parks, Recreation, & Historic Preservation
Peebles Island
P.O. Box 219
Waterford, NY 12188
Tel: 518-237-8643 ext. 200

New York State Division of Military & Naval Affairs
330 Old Niskayuna Road
Latham, NY 12110
Tel: 518-436-0218

New York State Library
Cultural Education Center
Empire State Plaza
Albany, NY 12230
Tel: 518-474-5355 (Information/Reference)
518-474-6282 (Special Collections)
Email: nyslweb@unix2.nysed.gov
URL: http://unix2.nysed.gov/gengen.htm
or http://www.nysl.nysed.gov/gengen.htm

New York/Ulster County Library
(See Elting Memorial Library)

Newburgh Free Library
124 Grand Street
Newburgh, NY 12550
Tel: 914-561-1985
Fax: 914-561-2401

Niagara County Community College
Library Learning Center, Special Collections
3111 Saunders Settlement Road
Sanborn, NY 14132
Tel: 716-731-3271 ext. 401
Fax: 716-731-7118
URL: http://www.sunyniagara.cc.ny.us/library/special.html

Niagara County Genealogical Society/Library
215 Niagara Street
Lockport, NY 14094

Niagara Falls Public Library
1425 Main Street
Niagara Falls, NY 14305
Tel: 716-286-4899
Fax: 716-286-4885
URL: http://freenet.buffalo.edu/~library/local/nfpl.html

Norfolk Town Historical Museum
105 River Road
Norfolk, NY 13667
Tel: 315-384-3136
315-384-4575

North Merrick Public Library
1691 Meadowbrook Road
North Merrick, NY 11566
Tel: 516-378-7474
URL: http://www.516web.com/library/nomerrick/menu.htm

North Rockland History Museum
20 Oak Street
Garnerville, NY 10923

North Tonawanda Public Library
505 Meadow Drive
North Tonawanda, NY 14120
Tel: 716-693-4132
Fax: 716-693-0719

Ogdensburg Dioceses Archives
622 Washington Street
P.O. Box 369
Ogdensburg, NY 13669
Tel: 315-393-2920

Ogdensburg Public Library
312 Washington Street
Ogdensburg, NY 13669
Tel: 315-393-4325
Fax: 315-393-4344
URL: http://www.northnet.org/ogbpublib/

Oneida Library
220 Broad Street
Oneida, NY 13421
Tel: 315-363-3050

Onondaga County Historical Association/Research Center
311 Montgomery Street
Syracuse, NY 13202
Tel: 315-428-1862
URL: http://www.syracusecvb.org/Visitor/Fun/Museums/onandaga.html
or http://maple.lemoyne.edu/~CERIOJL/oha.html

Onondaga County Public Library
Local History/Special Collections
447 South Salina Street
Syracuse, NY 13202-2494
Tel: 315-435-1900
Email: anagle@mailbox.syr.edu
URL: http://www.cny.com/OCPL/

Ontario County Historical Society
55 North Main Street
Canandaigua, NY 14424
Tel: 716-394-4975

Orange County Genealogical Society/Research Room
Historic Courthouse
101 Main Street
Goshen, NY 10924

Oswego City Library
120 East 2nd Street
Oswego, NY 13126
Tel: 315-341-5867

Otis A. Thompsom Local History Room
3 Court Street
Norwich, NY 13815

Paine Memorial Free Library
1 School Street
Willsboro, NY 12996
Tel: 518-963-4478

Patchogue Medford Library
Local History Room
54-60 E. Main Street
Patchogue, NY 11722
Tel: 516-654-4700
Fax: 516-289-3999
URL: http://pml.suffolk.lib.ny.us/refhome.htm

Patterson Library
40 South Portage Street
Westfield, NY 14787
Tel: 716-326-2154
Fax: 716-326-2554
Email: wlibrary@epix.net
URL: http://www.cecomm.com/wlibrary/libhome.htm

Penfield Public Library
1985 Baird Road
Penfield, NY 14526
Tel: 716-383-0500
716-383-0800 (Hours & Programs)
TDD: 716-383-8712
Email: infodesk@mcls.rochester.lib.ny.us
URL: http://www.rochester.lib.ny.us/penfield/

Peru Free Library
N. Main St.
Peru, NY 12972
Tel: 518-643-8618

Pickering-Beach Museum
West Main Street
P.O. Box 204
Sackets Harbor, NY 13685
Tel: 315-646-2052

Plattsburgh Public Library/Local History Room
19 Oak Street
Plattsburgh, NY 12901
Tel: 518-563-0921

Polish American Museum
16 Bellview Avenue
Port Washington, NY 11050
Tel: 516-883-6542
URL: http://www.liglobal.com/t_i/attractions/museums/polish/

Port Chester Public Library
1 Haseco Avenue
Port Chester, NY 10573

Port Jervis Free Library
138 Pike Street
Port Jervis, NY 12771
Tel: 914-856-7313
Fax: 914-858-8710

Port Leyden Museum
Lincoln & Main Street
P.O. Box 252
Port Leyden, NY 13433
Tel: 315-348-6190

Port Washington Library
One Library Drive
Port Washington, NY 11050
Tel: 516-883-4400
Fax: 516-883-7927
TDD: 516-767-7235
Email: pwpl@lilrc.org
URL: http://www.516web.com/library/pw/menu.htm

Potsdam Public Museum
Civic Center
Potsdam, NY 13676
Tel: 315-265-6910

Pulaski Public Library
Snow Memorial Building
Jefferson Street
Pulaski, NY 13142
Tel: 315-298-2717

Purchase Free Library
Purchase Street
Purchase, NY 10577
Tel: 914-948-0550
URL: http://www.wls.lib.ny.us/libs/purchase/pur.html

Queens Borough Public Library
89-11 Merrick Blvd.
Jamaica, NY 11432
Tel: 718-990-0770

Queens County Land Records
88-11 Sutphin Blvd.
Jamaica, NY 11435

Queens Genealogy Workshop
1820 Flushing Avenue
Ridgewood, NY 11385
Tel: 718-456-1776

Rensselaer County Historical Society/Genealogy Library
Hart-Cluett Mansion
59 Second Street
Troy, NY 12180
Tel: 518-272-7232
Fax: 518-273-1264
URL: http://crisny.org/not-for-profit/rchs/

Richmond Memorial Library
19 Ross Street
Batavia, NY 14020
Tel: 716-343-9550
URL: http://www2.www.batavia.ny.us/batavia/bat5.html

Roberts Wesleyan College
Kenneth B. Keating Library
Archives and Chesbrough-Roberts Historical Center
2301 Westside Drive
Rochester, NY 14624
Tel: 716-594-6016

Rochester Public Library
Local History Division
115 South Avenue
Rochester, NY 14604
Tel: 716-428-7300
716-428-7338 (Local History/Genealogy Dept.)
Email: cdoyle@mcls.rochester.lib.ny.us
URL: http://www.rochester.lib.ny.us/central/

Rochester Regional Research Library Council
Documentary Heritage Program
390 Packett's Landing
P.O. Box 66160
Fairport, NY 14450
Tel: 716-223-7570
Fax: 716-223-7712
Email: swalker@rrlc.rochester.lib.ny.us

Rogers Memorial Library
9 Jobs Lane
Southampton, NY 11968
Tel: 516-283-0774
URL: http::www.thehamptons.com/showhouse/library.html

Roman Catholic Diocese of Albany
40 North Main Avenue
Albany, NY 12203
Tel: 518-453-6633

Roman Catholic Diocese of Rochester
1150 Buffalo Road
Rochester, NY 14624
Tel: 716-328-3210

Rome Historical Society/Museum & Archives
200 Church Street
Rome, NY 13440
Tel: 315-336-5870
URL: http://www.rny.com/town/points/29romehistorical-society.html

Roxbury Library Association
Main Street
P.O. Box 186
Roxbury, NY 12474
Tel: 607-326-7901
URL: http://lib.4cty.org/dialups/ROXBURY.HTML

St. Lawrence County Historical Association
3 East Main Street
P.O. Box 8
Canton, NY 13617
Tel: 315-386-8133

St. Lawrence University
Owen D. Young Library
Special Collections
Canton, NY 13617
Tel: 315-379-5476
Email: lekf@music.stlawu.edu
URL: http://www.stlawu.edu/library:http/hompage.html

Saint Mary's Hospital Library
89 Genesee Street
Rochester, NY 14611-3201

St. Peter's Armenian Church
110 Troy-Schenectady Road
Watervliet, NY 12189
Tel: 518-274-3673

Saranac Lake Free Library
Adirondack Collection
100 Main Street
Saranac Lake, NY 12983
Tel: 518-891-4190

Saratoga Springs Public Library
Putnam Street
Saratoga Springs, NY 12866
Tel: 518-584-7860

Scarsdale Public Library
Post and Olmsted Roads
Scarsdale, NY 10583
Tel: 914-722-1300
URL: http://www.wls.lib.ny.us/libs/scarsdale/welcome.html

Schenectady County Historical Society
32 Washington Avenue
Schenectady, NY 12305
Tel: 518-374-0263
URL: http://www.scpl.org/schs.html

Schenectady County Public Library
99 Clinton Street
Schenectady, NY 12305-2083
Tel: 518-388-4500
Email: scpl@scpl.org
URL: http://www.scpl.org/index.html

Schenectady Museum & Planetarium
Nott Terr Heights
Schenectady, NY 12308
Tel: 518-382-7891
Fax: 518-382-7898

Schomburg Center for Research/Branch New York Public Library
515 Malcolm X Blvd.
New York, NY 10037-1801
Tel: 212-491-2200
URL: http://www.nypl.org/research/sc/sc.html

Scottsville Free Library
Cox Room
28 Main Street
Scottsville, NY 14546
Tel: 716-889-2023
Email: jdinolfo@mcls.rochester.lib.ny.us
URL: http://www.rochester.lib.ny.us/scottsville/

Sea Cliff Village Museum
95 Tenth Street
Sea Cliff, NY 11579
Tel: 516-671-0090

Seymour Library
Local History Room
178 Genesee Street
Auburn, NY 13021
Tel: 315-252-2571
Fax: 315-252-7985
Email: seymourlib@ns1.relex.com
URL: http://www.flls.org/auburn.html

Shandaken Historical Center
Academy Street
Pine Hill, NY 12465
Tel: 914-254-4460

Sherman Free Library
4 Church Street
Port Henry, NY 12974
Tel: 518-546-7461

Smithtown Historical Society/Library
Caleb Smith II House
North Country Road
Smithtown, NY 11787
Tel: 516-265-6768
Email: smithlib@suffolk.lib.ny.us
URL: http://www.suffolk.lib.ny.us/libraries/smth/smith2.html

Smithtown Library
Long Island History Room
1 North Country Road
Smithtown, NY 11787
Tel: 516-265-2072

South Central Research Library Council
Documentary Heritage Program
215 North Cayuga Street
Ithaca, NY 14850
Tel: 607-273-9106
Fax: 607-272-0740
Email: jbeechen@stny.lrun.com

Southeastern New York Library Resources Council
Route 299
P.O. Box 879
Highland, NY 12528
Tel: 914-691-1258

Southold Free Library
Whitaker Historical Collection
Main Road
Southold, NY 11971
Tel: 516-765-2077

Spencer Historical Society/Museum
Center Street
Spencer, NY 14883
Tel: 607-589-6906

Stamford Village Library
117 Main Street
Stamford, NY 12167
Tel: 607-652-5001
URL: http://lib.4cty.org/dialups/STAMFORD.HTML

State University of New York/Albany (SUNY)
University Library B-3
Special Collections & Archives
1400 Washington Avenue
Albany, NY 12222
Tel: 518-442-3544
URL: http://www.albany.edu/library/oldlib/services/specoll.html

State University of New York/Brockport (SUNY)
Drake Memorial Library
College Archives, Special Collections
Brockport, NY 14420
Tel: 716-395-5667
Fax: 716-395-5651
Email: ccowling@acspr1.acs.brockport.edu
URL: http://cc.brockport.edu/~library1/archives.htm

State University of New York/Fredonia (SUNY)
Daniel E. Reed Library
Fredonia, NY 14063
Tel: 716-673-3183
Fax: 716-673-3185
URL: http://freenet.buffalo.edu/~library/local/fredonia.html

State University of New York/Oswego (SUNY)
Penfield Library
Special Collections
Oswego, NY 13126
Tel: 315-341-3567
Fax: 315-341-3194
Email: osborne@oswego.oswego.edu
URL: http://www.oswego.edu/library/speccoll.html

Steele Memorial Library
One Library Plaza
Elmira, NY 14901
Tel: 607-733-9173
Fax: 607-733-9176
Email: staff@steele.org

Strong Museum Library and Archives
One Manhattan Square
Rochester, NY 14607
Tel: 716-263-2700
Fax: 716-263-2493
URL: http://www.strongmuseum.org/

Suffern Village Museum
61 Washington Avenue
Suffern, NY 10901
Tel: 914-357-2600

Suffolk County Historical Society/Library
300 West Main Street
Riverhead, NY 11901
Tel: 516-727-2881
URL: http://www.lieast.com/museum.html

Susan B. Anthony House National Historic Landmark
17 Madison Street
Rochester, NY 14608
Tel: 716-235-6124
URL: http://www.frontier.net/~lhurst/sbahouse/sbahome.htm

Syosset Public Library
225 S. Oyster Bay Road
Syosset, NY 11791-5897
Tel: 516-921-7161
URL: http://lilrc1.lilrc.org/~syossorg/

Tarrytowns, Historical Society of the
1 Grove Street
Tarrytown, NY 10591
Tel: 914-631-8374

Theresa Free Library
301 Main Street
Theresa, NY 13691
Tel: 315-628-5972

Tioga County Historical Society/Museum
110-112 Front Street
Owego, NY 13827
Tel: 607-687-2460

Tompkins County Museum
401 East State Street
Ithaca, NY 14850
Tel: 607-273-8284

Troy Public Library
Troy Room Collection
100 Second Street
Troy, NY 12180
Tel: 518-274-7071

Union College
Schaffer Library
807 Union St.
Schenectady, NY 12308
Tel: 518-370-6620

University of Rochester
Department of History
364 Rush Rhees Library
Rochester, NY 14627
Tel: 716-275-2052
Fax: 716-442-2749
Email: rahz@dbv.cc.rochester.edu
URL: http://www.history.rochester.edu/rochhist/

University of Rochester
Rare Books & Special Collections-Local History & Archives Room
Rush Rhees Library
Rochester, NY 14627
Tel: 716-275-4477
Fax: 716-273-1032
URL: http://rodent.lib.rochester.edu/rbk/about.htm

Utica Public Library
303 Genesee Street
Utica, NY 13501
Tel: 315-733-6316
315-735-2279

Valley Historical Society
Main Street
Sinclairville, NY 14782
Tel: 716-962-2635
URL: http://c1web.com/local_info/artsed/vhs.html

Vestal Public Library
320 Vestal Parkway East
Vestal, NY 13850
Tel: 607-754-4244
Fax: 607-754-7936
URL: http://lib.4cty.org/vestal/vestal_r.html

Voorheesvillle School District Public Library
51 School Road
Voorheesville, NY 12186
Tel: 518-765-2791

Waterloo Library & Historical Society
Terwilliger Museum
31 East Williams Street
Waterloo, NY 13165
Tel: 315-539-0533

Waterloo Memorial Day Museum
35 East Main Street
Waterloo, NY 13165
Tel: 315-539-5033

Wead Library
64 Elm Street
Malone, NY 12953
Tel: 518-483-5251

Wenrich Memorial Library
133 South Fitzhugh Street
Rochester, NY 14608
Tel: 716-546-7029
Fax: 716-546-4788

West Islip Public Library
3 Higbie Lane
West Islip, NY 11795
Tel: 516-661-7080
Fax: 516-661-7137
Email: wislip@suffolk.lib.ny.us
URL: http://lilrc1.lilrc.org/~wispagen

Western New York Genealogical Society/Library & Museum
5859 South Park Avenue, Route 62
P.O. Box 338
Hamburg, NY 14075
URL: http://www.localnet.com/andrle/erie/erwnygs.htm

Western New York Heritage Institute
Resource Center
Briarwood Square
5450 Southwestern Blvd.
Hamburg, NY 14075
Mail:
P.O. Box 192
Buffalo, NY 14205-0192
Tel: 716-649-2300
Fax: 716-649-2329
Email: athcah@buffnet.net
URL: http://intotem.buffnet.net/bhw/wnyhi/wnyhi.htm

Western New York Library Resources Council
Calspan Building, 2nd Floor
4455 Genesee Street
P.O. Box 400
Buffalo, NY 14225-0400
Tel: 716-633-0705
716-633-1736
Email: hbamford@wnylrc.org (Heidi Bamford-Regional Archivist)
URL: http://ww.wnylrc.org/

Westport Library Association
Waddington Street
Westport, NY 12993
Tel: 518-962-8964

William H. Bush Memorial Library
P.O. Box 141
Martinsburg, NY 13404
Tel: 315-376-7490

William K. Sanford Town Library
629 Albany-Shaker Road
Loudonville, NY 12211
Tel: 518-458-9274
URL: http://www.crisny.org/libraries/capreg/colonie/index.html

Wyckoff House Association
Clarendon & Ralph Avenue
P.O. Box 100376
Brooklyn, NY 11210
Tel/Fax: 718-629-5400

Yivo Institute for Jewish Research
555 West 57th Street (Temporary Location)
New York, NY 10019
or
15 West 16th Street (Sometime in 1997)
New York, NY 10011
URL: http://spanky.osc.cuny.edu/~rich/yivo/

Newspaper Repositories

New York State Library
Cultural Education Center
Empire State Plaza
Albany, NY 12230
Tel: 518-474-5355 (Information/Reference)
518-474-6282 (Special Collections)
Email: nyslweb@unix2.nysed.gov
URL: http://unix2.nysed.gov/gengen.htm
or http://www.nysl.nysed.gov/gengen.htm

New York State Newspaper Project
New York State Library
Cultural Education Center, 6th Floor
Empire State Plaza
Albany, NY 12220
Tel: 518-474-7491
Fax: 518-474-5786
Email: wvann@unix2.nysed.gov
URL: http://www.nysl.nysed.gov/nysnp/

State University of New York/Albany (SUNY)
University Library B-3
Special Collections & Archives
1400 Washington Avenue
Albany, NY 12222
Tel: 518-442-3544
URL: http://www.albany.edu/library/oldlib/services/specoll.html

State University of New York/Oswego (SUNY)
Penfield Library
Special Collections
Oswego, NY 13126
Tel: 315-341-3567
Fax: 315-341-3194
Email: osborne@oswego.oswego.edu
URL: http://www.oswego.edu/library/speccoll.html

Vital Records

New York City Department of Health
Division of Vital Records
125 Worth Street
P.O. Box 3776, Church Street Station
New York, NY 10007
URL: http://www.tnp.com/nycgenweb/vital.htm

New York City Municipal Archives
31 Chambers Street, Room 103
New York, NY 10007
Tel: 212-788-8580
URL: http://www.tnp.com/nycgenweb/municipal.htm

New York State Department of Health
Vital Records Section
Corning Tower Building, Empire State Plaza
Albany, NY 12237-0023
Tel: 518-474-3077
518-486-1863
Email: nyhealth@health.state.ny.us
URL: http://www.health.state.ny.us/nysdoh/consumer/vr/geninst.htm

New York on the Web

Chris Andrle's New York State Genealogical Resources
http://www.localnet.com/~andrle/nyres.htm

Eagle Byte Historical Research
http://home.eznet.net/~dminor/

Ed Nugent's Links to Links
http://www.geocities.com/Heartland/Plains/8622/gen_idx.html

History of Rochester
http://www.history.rochester.edu/rochhist/

Hudson Valley Network
http://www.hvnet.com/

Jeffco/Upstate New York Resources by Robin L. Holden, Sr.
http://www.flash.net/~robinl/j

Index of Marriages and Deaths in the New York Weekly Museum
1788-1817
http://www.itsnet.com/~pauld/newyork/

New York Addresses for Genealogy
http://www.geocities.com/~agiroux/

New York GenWeb Project
http://www.rootsweb.com/~nygenweb/

New York History Net
http://www.nyhistory.com/

New York State Archives
http://unix6.nysed.gov/holding/fact/genea-fa.htm

New York State Library
http://unix2.nysed.gov/gengen.htm
or
http://www.nysl.nysed.gov/gengen.htm

New York State Newspaper Project
http://www.nysl.nysed.gov/nysnp/

Rochester Regional Library Council (RRLC)
http://www.rrlc.org/index.html

NORTH CAROLINA

ARCHIVES, STATE & NATIONAL

National Archives—Southeast Region
1557 St. Joseph Avenue
East Point, GA 30344-2593
Tel: 404-763-7477
Fax: 404-763-7033
Email: archives@atlanta.nara.gov
URL: http://www.nara.gov/nara/regional/04nsgil.html

North Carolina State Archives
Archives and History/State Library Building
109 East Jones Street
Raleigh, NC 27601-2807
Tel: 919-733-3952
Fax: 919-733-1354
Email: archives@ncsl.dcr.state.nc.us
URL: http://www.ah.dcr.state.nc.us/archives/arch/archhp.htm

GENEALOGICAL SOCIETIES

Alamance County Genealogical Society
P.O. Box 3052
Burlington, NC 27215-3052

Albemarle Genealogical Society
Route 1, Box 15
Coinjock, NC 27923

Alexander County Ancesstry Association, Inc.
P.O. Box 241
Hiddenite, NC 28636

Alexander County Genealogical Society, Inc.
Route 2, Box 87A
Hiddenite, NC 28636

Alleghany Historical & Genealogical Society
P.O. Box 817
Sparta, NC 28675

Anson County, Genealogical Society of
108 Sunset Drive
Wadesboro, NC 28170

Beaufort County Genealogical Society
P.O. Box 1089
Washington, NC 27889-1089

Broad River Genealogical Society
P.O. Box 2261
Shelby, NC 28151-2261
URL: http://www.rootsweb.com/~ncclevel/brgs.htm

Burke County Genealogical Society
P.O. Box 661
Morganton, NC 28680

Cabarrus Genealogical Society
P.O. Box 2981
Concord, NC 28025-2981

Caldwell County Genealogical Society
P.O. Box 2476
Lenoir, NC 28645-2476

Carolinas Genealogical Society
P.O. Box 397
Monroe, NC 28111
Tel: 704-289-6737

Catawba County Genealogical Society
P.O. Box 2406
Hickory, NC 28603-2406
URL: http://www.co.catawba.nc.us/otheragency/ccgs/ccgsmain.htm

Coastal Genealogical Society
P.O. Box 1421
Swansboro, NC 28584

Craven County Kinfolk Trackers
Route 65, Box 8A
Arapahoe, NC 28510

Cumberland County Genealogical Society
P.O. Box 53299
Fayetteville, NC 28305

Davidson County, Genealogical Society of
P.O. Box 1665
Lexington, NC 27293-1665

Davie County Historical & Genealogical Society
371 N. Main Street
Mocksville, NC 27028

Durham-Orange County Genealogical Society
P.O. Box 4703
Chapel Hill, NC 27515-4703
Email: dogs@rtpnet.org
URL: http://rtpnet.org/~dogs/index.html

Eastern North Carolina Genealogical Society
P.O. Box 395
New Bern, NC 28563

Forsyth County Genealogical Society
P.O. Box 5715
Winston-Salem, NC 27113-5715
Email: ccasey@mail.netunlimited.net
URL: http://www.erols.com/fmoran/gensoc/gensoc.html

Gaston-Lincoln Genealogical Society
P.O. Box 584
Mount Holly, NC 28120

Granville County Genealogical Society, Inc.
P.O. Box 1746
Oxford, NC 27565

Guilford County Genealogical Society
P.O. Box 9693
Greensboro, NC 27429

Halifax County Genealogical Society
P.O. Box 447
Halifax, NC 27839

Hampstead Historical & Genealogical Society
P.O. Box 8
Hampstead, NC 28443

Harnett County Genealogical Society
P.O. Box 219
Buies Creek, NC 27506-0219

Haywood County Genealogical Society, Inc.
P.O. Box 1331
Waynesville, NC 28786

Henderson County Genealogical & Historical Society, Inc.
P.O. Box 2616
Hendersonville, NC 28793-2616

Hyde County Historical & Genealogical Society
Route 1, Box 74
Fairfield, NC 27826

Iredell County, Genealogical Society of
P.O. Box 946
Statesville, NC 28687

Jackson County Genealogical Society
P.O. Box 2108
Cullowhee, NC 28723

Johnston County Genealogical Society
305 Market Street
Smithfield, NC 27577

Lee County Genealogical & Historical Society, Inc.
P.O. Box 3216
Sanford, NC 27331-3216

Loyalist Descendants, Society of
P.O. Box 848, Desk 120
Rockingham, NC 28379

Martin County Genealogical Society
P.O. Box 468
Williamston, NC 27892-0121

Moore County Genealogical Society
P.O. Box 1183
Pinehurst, NC 28374-1183

North Carolina Genealogical Society
Dept. E
P.O. Box 1492
Raleigh, NC 27602
Email: ncgs.info@moobasi.com
URL: http://www.moobasi.com/genealogy/ncgs/

Northeastern North Carolina, Family Research Society of
Route 1, Box 159
Belvidere, NC 27919

Old Buncombe County Genealogical Society
Innsbruck Mall, Suite 22
85 Tunnel Road
P.O. Box 2122
Asheville, NC 28802
Tel: 704-253-1894
URL: http://main.nc.us/OBCGS/obcgs.htm

Old Dobbs County Genealogical Society
P.O. Box 617
Goldsboro, NC 27533

Old New Hanover Genealogical Society
P.O. Box 2536
Wilmington, NC 28402-2536
URL: http://www.co.new-hanover.nc.us/lib/oldnew.htm

Old Tryon County, Genealogical Society of
P.O. Box 938
Forest City, NC 28043

Olde Mecklenburg Genealogical Society
P.O. Box 32453
Charlotte, NC 28232
Email: omgs002@ibm.net

Onslow County Genealogical Association
P.O. Box 1739
Jacksonville, NC 28541-1739

Pasquotank Historical & Genealogical Society
P.O. Box 523
Elizabeth City, NC 27907

Personal Computer Club of Charlotte
Genealogy Special Interest Group
P.O. Box 114
Paw Creek, NC 28130-0114
URL: http://www.chem.uncc.edu/pccc/gensig/

Pitt County Family Researchers
P.O. Box 20339
Greenville, NC 27858-0339
URL: http://www.geocities.com/Heartland/7591/

Randolph County Genealogical Society
P.O. Box 4394
Asheboro, NC 27203

Richmond County Descendants, Society of
P.O. Box 848, Desk 120
Rockingham, NC 28379

Rockingham-Stokes Counties, Genealogical Society of
P.O. Box 152
Mayodan, NC 27027-0152
URL: http://ns.netmcr.com/~lonabec/gsrsinfo.html

Rowan County, Genealogical Society of
P.O. Box 4305
Salisbury, NC 28145-4305
URL: http://www.lib.co.rowan.nc.us/hr/ges.htm

Scotland County Genealogical Society
P.O. Box 496
Laurel Hill, NC 28351

Southeastern North Carolina Genealogical Society
Route 2, Box 291E
Whiteville, NC 28472

Southwestern North Carolina Genealogical Society
101 Blumenthal
Murphy, NC 28906

Stanly County Genealogical Society
P.O. Box 31
Albemarle, NC 28002-0031

Surry County Genealogical Association
P.O. Box 997
Dobson, NC 27017

Swain County Genealogical & Historical Society
P.O. Box 267
Bryson City, NC 28713

Tar River Connections Genealogical Society
c/o Billie Jo Matthews
101 Wildwood Avenue
Rocky Mount, NC 27803

Toe Valley Genealogical Society
491 Beaver Creek Road
Spruce Pine, NC 28777

Tyrell County Genealogical & Historical Society
P.O. Box 686
Columbia, NC 27825

VA-NC Piedmont Genealogical Society
P.O. Box 2272
Danville, VA 24541

Wake County Genealogical Society
P.O. Box 17713
Raleigh, NC 27619

Washington County Genealogical Society
P.O. Box 567
Plymouth, NC 27962

Watauga County, Genealogical Society of
P.O. Box 126 (DTS)
Boone, NC 28607

Wilkes Genealogical Society, Inc.
P.O. Box 1629
North Wilkesboro, NC 28659

Wilson County Genealogical Society, Inc.
P.O. Box 802
Wilson, NC 27894-0802

Yadkin County Historical & Genealogical Society, Inc.
P.O. Box 1250
Yadkinville, NC 27055

HISTORICAL SOCIETIES

Alleghany Historical-Genealogical Society
P.O. Box 817
Sparta, NC 28675

Anson County Historical Society, Inc.
206 East Wade Street
Wadesboro, NC 28170
Tel: 704-694-6694
URL: http://www.ghgcorp.com/sellers/html/socnews.htm

Apex Historical Society
P.O. Box 502
Apex, NC 27502

Ashe County Historical Society
Route 1, 148 Library Drive
West Jefferson, NC 28694

Avery County Historical Society
P.O. Box 266
Newland, NC 28657

Beaufort Historical Association
P.O. Box 1709
Beaufort, NC 28516-1709

Black Creek Historical Society
P.O. Box 204
Black Creek, NC 27813

Bladen County Historical Society
P.O. Box 848
Elizabethtown, NC 28337

Brunswick County Historical Society
P.O. Box 874
Shallotte, NC 28459

Burke County Historical Society
P.O. Box 151
Morganton, NC 28655

Cabarrus, Historic
P.O. Box 966
Concord, NC 28025

Carteret County Historical Society, Inc.
P.O. Box 481
Morehead City, NC 28557

Cary Historical Society
P.O. Box 134
Cary, NC 27511

Caswell County Historical Association, Inc.
P.O. Box 278
Yanceyville, NC 27379

Catawba County Historical Association
P.O. Box 73
Newton, NC 28658

Chapel Hill Historical Society, Inc.
P.O. Box 503
Chapel Hill, NC 27514-0503

Chatham County Historical Association, Inc.
P.O. Box 913
Pittsboro, NC 27312

Cherokee Historical Association
P.O. Box 398
Cherokee, NC 28719

China Grove, Historical Society of
113 N. Main Street
China Grove, NC 28023
Tel: 704-857-1176

Cleveland County Historical Association
P.O. Box 1335
Shelby, NC 28150

Columbus County Historical Society
P.O. Box 339
Whiteville, NC 28472

Cooleemee Historical Association
131 Church Street
P.O. Box 667
Cooleemee, NC 27014
Tel: 704-284-6040

Davie County Historical & Genealogical Society
371 N. Main Street
Mocksville, NC 27028

Duplin County Historical Society
P.O. Box 130
Rose Hill, NC 28458-0130

Edenton Historical Commission
P.O. Box 474
Edenton, NC 27932

Fair Bluff Historical Society
339 Railroad Street
P.O. Box 285
Fair Bluff, NC 28439
Tel: 910-649-7707

Federation of North Carolina Historical Societies
109 East Jones Street, Room 305
Raleigh, NC 27601
Tel: 919-733-7305

Gaston County Historical Society
P.O. Box 429
Dallas, NC 28034

Gates County Historical Society
P.O. Box 98
Gates, NC 27937

Halifax County Historical Association
P.O. Box 12
Halifax, NC 27839

Hampstead Historical & Genealogical Society
P.O. Box 8
Hampstead, NC 28443

Henderson County Genealogical & Historical Society, Inc.
P.O. Box 2616
Hendersonville, NC 28793-2616

Hillsborough Historical Society
P.O. Box 871
Hillsborough, NC 27278

Hyde County Historical & Genealogical Society
RR 1, Box 74
Fairfield, NC 27826
Tel: 919-926-2506

Jackson County Historical Association
P.O. Box 173
Sylva, NC 28779

Lee County Genealogical & Historical Society, Inc.
P.O. Box 3216
Sanford, NC 27331-3216

Lower Cape Fear Historical Society
126 S. 3rd Street
P.O. Box 813
Wilmington, NC 28402
Tel: 910-762-0492

Macon County Historical Society
P.O. Box 822
Franklin, NC 28734

Malcolm Blue Historical Society
P.O. Box 603
Aberdeen, NC 28315

Martin County Historical Society, Inc.
P.O. Box 468
Williamston, NC 27892

Mitchell County Historical Society
P.O. Box 651
Bakersville, NC 28705

Montgomery County Historical Society
P.O. Box 664
Troy, NC 27306

Murfreesboro Historical Association
P.O. Box 3
Murfreesboro, NC 27855

Nash County Historical Association
100 Salem Court
Rocky Mt., NC 27804

New Bern Historical Society Foundation, Inc.
P.O. Box 119
New Bern, NC 28536

North Carolina Afro-American Heritage Society
P.O. Box 26334
Raleigh, NC 27611

North Carolina Society of Historians
P.O. Box 848
Rockingham, NC 28379

Onslow County Historical Society
P.O. Box 5203
Jacksonville, NC 28540

Pasquotank Historical & Genealogical Society
P.O. Box 523
Elizabeth City, NC 27907

Pender County Historical Society
P.O. Box 1380
Burgaw, NC 28425

Person County Historical Society
P.O. Box 887
Roxboro, NC 27573

Pitt County Historical Society
P.O. Box 1554
Greenville, NC 17835-1554

Randolph County Historical Society
P.O. Box 4394
Asheboro, NC 27204

Richmond County Historical Society
P.O. Box 1041
Rockingham, NC 28379

Roanoke Island Historical Association
P.O. Box 40
Manteo, NC 27954

Robeson, Historic
P.O. Box 159
Lumberton, NC 28359

Rockingham County Historical Society
P.O. Box 84
Wentworth, NC 27375

Rockingham Society for Research and Preservation
P.O. Box 848
Rockingham, NC 28380-0848
Tel: 919-997-6641

Rutherford County Historical Society
P.O. Box 1044
Rutherfordton, NC 28139

Sampson County Historical Society
P.O. Box 1084
Clinton, NC 28328

Southport Historical Society
501 North Atlantic Avenue
Southport, NC 28461

Stokes County Historical Society
P.O. Box 250
Germantown, NC 27019

Surry County Historical Society
P.O. Box 70
Siloam, NC 27047

Swain County Genealogical & Historical Society
P.O. Box 267
Bryson City, NC 28713

Tyrell County Genealogical & Historical Society
P.O. Box 686
Columbia, NC 27825

Union County Historical Society
P.O. Box 222
Monroe, NC 28110

Vance County Historical Society
P.O. Box 2284
Henderson, NC 27536

Wake County Historical Society
P.O. Box 2
Raleigh, NC 27602

Warren County Historical Association
210 Plummer Street
Warrenton, NC 27589

Washington County Historical Society
P.O. Box 296
Plymouth, NC 27962

Watauga County Historical Society
P.O. Box 1306
Boone, NC 28607

Wayne County Historical Association, Inc.
P.O. Box 665
Goldsboro, NC 27533

Yancey History Association
108 Town Square
Burnsville, NC 28714

LDS Family History Centers

Chapel Hill Family History Center
1050 Airport Road
Chapel Hill, NC 27514
Tel: 919-967-0988

Charlotte Family History Center
3020 Hilliard Drive
Charlotte, NC 28205
Tel: 704-535-0238

Charlotte Family History Center
5815 Carmel Road
Charlotte, NC 28226
Tel: 704-541-1451

Fayetteville Family History Center
6720 Morganton Road
Fayetteville, NC 28314
Tel: 910-860-1350

Goldsboro Family History Center
1000 Eleventh Street
Goldsboro, NC 27534
Tel: 919-731-2130

Greensboro Family History Center
3719 Pinetop Road
Greensboro, NC 27410
Tel: 910-288-6539

Hickory Family History Center
Highway 127 North
Hickory, NC 28602
Tel: 704-324-2823

Kinston Family History Center
3006 Carey Road
Kinston, NC 28504
Tel: 919-522-4671

Raleigh Family History Center
5060 Six Forks Road
Raleigh, NC 27609
Tel: 919-783-7752

Skyland Family History Center
3401 Sweeten Creek Road
Skyland, NC 28776
Tel: 704-687-8339

Wilmington Family History Center
514 South College Road
Wilmington, NC 28403
Tel: 910-395-4456

Winston Salem Family History Center
4780 Westchester Dr.
Winston Salem, NC 27103
Tel: 910-768-8878

ARCHIVES/LIBRARIES/MUSEUMS

Alamance County Historical Museum
4777 South NC Highway 62
Burlington, NC 27215
Tel: 910-226-8254

Appalachian State University
Carol Grotnes Belk Library, 2nd Floor
W.L. Eury Appalachian Collection
Boone, NC 28608
Tel: 704-262-4041
Fax: 704-262-2553
Email: hayfj@appstate.edu
URL: http://www1.appstate.edu/dept/library/appcoll/history.html

Bladen County Public Library
Cypress Street
Elizabethtown, NC 28337
Tel: 910-862-6990

Blount-Bridgers House
Archives Room
130 Bridgers Street
Tarboro, NC 27886
Tel: 919-823-4159

Burke County Public Library
204 South King Street
Morganton, NC 28655
Tel: 704-437-5638

Caldwell County Public Library/Lenoir Headquarters
Local History Collection
120 Hospital Avenue
Lenoir, NC 28645
Tel: 704-757-1270
Fax: 704-757-1413
URL: http://ils.unc.edu/nclibs/caldwell/home.htm

Catawba County Main Library
Rhodes Room
115 West C Street
Newton, NC 28658
Tel/TDD: 704-464-2421
Fax: 704-465-8293
Email: lreed@ncsl.dcr.state.nc.us
URL: http://www.co.catawba.nc.us/depts/library/library.htm

Charles A. Cannon Memorial Library
27 Union Street, N
Concord, NC 28025-4726
Tel: 704-788-3167

Charlotte-Mecklenburg County Public Library
Robinson-Spangler Carolina Room
310 N. Tryon Street
Charlotte, NC 28202
Tel: 704-336-4140
704-336-2980 (Carolina Room)
Email: ncr@plcmc.lib.nc.us
URL: http://www.plcmc.lib.nc.us/branch/main/default.htm

Cherokee County Historical Museum
205 Peachtree Street
Murphy, NC 28906
Tel: 704-837-6792

Cleveland County Memorial Library
104 Howie Drive
P.O. Box 1120
Shelby, NC 28151-1120
Tel: 704-487-9069
704-481-1234

Cumberland County Library
Local & State History Room
300 Maiden Lane
Fayetteville, NC 28301-5000
Tel: 910-483-3745 (Local & State History Room)
TDD: 910-483-7878
URL: http://www.cumberland.lib.nc.us/hisroom.htm

Currituck County Public Library
Joseph Palmer Knapp Section
Star Route, Box 826
Barco, NC 27917
Tel: 919-453-8345
Fax: 919-453-8717
URL: http://ils.unc.edu/nclibs/currituck/c_home.htm

Davidson County Public Library
602 South Main Street
Lexington, NC 27292
Tel: 910-242-2040
Fax: 910-248-2141
Email: ncs0271@interpath.com
URL: http://ils.unc.edu/nclibs/davidson/third.htm

Duke University
William R. Perkins Library
Special Collections
Durham, NC 27708
Tel: 919-660-5800
919-660-5820 (Special Collections)
919-660-5840 (Newspapers & Microforms)
Fax: 919-684-2855
URL: http://www.lib.duke.edu/

Durham County Public Library
North Carolina Collection
300 North Roxboro Street
P.O. Box 3809
Durham, NC 27702
Tel: 919-560-0100
919-560-0171 (North Carolina)
TTY: 919-560-0299
URL: http://ils.unc.home/nclibs/durham/dclhome.htm

East Carolina University
Joyner Library
North Carolina Collection
Greenville, NC 27858
Tel: 919-328-6671
Fax: 919-328-0268
URL: http://fringe.lib.ecu.edu/JoynerLib/LibraryDepts/SpclColl/NCColl.html

Eden Public Library
North Carolina Collection
598 S. Pierce Street
Eden, NC 27288
Tel: 910-623-3168
Fax: 910-623-1171
URL: http://www.rcpl.org/lib2.html

Edgecombe Community College
Learning Resource Center
North Carolina and Local History Collection
2009 W. Wilson Street
Tarboro, NC 27886
Email: keenj@sco.ncdcc.cc.nc.us
URL: http://www.edgecombe.cc.nc.us/LRC/LRCWEB.HTM

Edgecombe County Memorial Library
Allsbrook Room
909 North Main Street
Tarboro, NC 27886-3800
Tel: 919-823-1141
Fax: 919-641-7004

Elbert Ivey Memorial Library
420 Third Avenue, NW
Hickory, NC 28601
Tel: 704-322-2905
Fax: 704-322-3479
Email: jdeal@ncsl.dcr.state.nc.us (Genealogy Asst.)

Forsyth County Library
North Carolina Room
660 West 5th Street
Winston Salem, NC 27101
Tel: 910-727-8100
910-727-2152 (North Carolina Room)
URL: http://www.erols.com/fmoran/gensoc/library.html

Gaston County Public Library
North Carolina Collection
1555 E. Garrison Blvd.
Gastonia, NC 28054
Tel: 704-868-2168
URL: http://www.gaston.net/glrl/glrlncc.htm

Greensboro Historical Museum
130 Summit Avenue
Greensboro, NC 27401-3004
Tel: 910-373-2043
Fax: 910-373-2204

Greensboro Public Library
201 N. Greene Street
Greensboro, NC 27401
Future Location:
NW Corner of Church Street & YMCA Place (Fall, 1998)
Tel: 910-373-2471
910-373-2159
URL: http://www.greensboro.com/library/central.htm

High Point Public Library
411 S. Main Street
P.O. Box 2530
High Point, NC 27261-2530
Tel: 910-887-3631
910-887-3006

Iredell County Public Library
James Iredell History & Genealogy Room
135 E. Water Street
Statesville, NC 28677
Tel: 704-878-3093
URL: http://www.charweb.org/education/iredell/jir.html

Lawrence Memorial Public Library
204 Dundee Street
Windsor, NC 27983-1210
Tel: 919-794-2244

Lincoln County Public Library
North Carolina Collection
306 West Main Street
Lincolnton, NC 28092-2616
Tel: 704-735-8044
URL: http://www.gaston.net/glrl/glrlncc.htm

Macon County Public Library
45 Wayah Street
Franklin, NC 28734-3329
Tel: 704-524-3600

Madison Public Library
Genealogy Room
140 E. Murphy Street
Madison, NC 27025
Tel: 910-548-6553
Fax: 910-548-2010
URL: http://www.rcpl.org/lib3.html

May Memorial Library
342 South Spring Street
Burlington, NC 27215
Tel: 910-229-3588
URL: http://ils.unc.edu/nclibs/centralnc/may.htm

Murphy Public Library
101 Blumenthal Street
Murphy, NC 28906
Tel: 704-837-2417
Fax: 704-837-6416
Email: bstiles@grove.net
URL: http://www.grove.net/~nrl/mpl.htm

New Bern-Craven County Public Library
400 Johnson Street
New Bern, NC 28560
Tel: 919-638-7800

New Hanover County Public Library
State & Local History Department
North Carolina Collection
201 Chestnut Street
Wilmington, NC 28401
Tel: 910-341-4394
URL: http://www.co.new-hanover.nc.us/lib/localhis.htm

North Carolina State Land Records Management Division
512 North Salisbury Street, Room 725
Raleigh, NC 27604
Tel: 919-733-7006
URL: http://www.secstate.state.nc.us/secstate/land.htm

North Carolina, State Library of
Archives and History/State Library Building
109 East Jones Street
Raleigh, NC 27601-2807
Tel: 919-733-3270 (Reference)
919-733-7222 (Gen. Services)
Fax: 919-33-5679
URL: http://hal.dcr.state.nc.us/nclhome.htm
http://hal.dcr.state.nc.us/iss/gr/genealog.htm

Olivia Raney Local History Library
4016 Carya Drive
Raleigh, NC 27610
Tel: 919-250-1196
Email: szolkowski@co.wake.nc.us
URL: http://www.state.nc.us/Wake/depts/CommServ/Library/
branches/orl/orl.htm

Onslow County Public Library
58 Doris Avenue, E
Jacksonville, NC 28540
Tel: 910-455-7350
Fax: 910-455-1661
Email: frosenth@ncsl.dcr.state.nc.us
URL: http://www.onslow.com/library/

Pack Public Library
67 Haywood Street
Asheville, NC 28801
Tel: 704-255-5203
Fax: 704-255-5213
URL: http://ils.unc.edu/nclibs/asheville/pack.htm
or http://ils.unc.edu/nclibs/asheville/genealog.htm

Person County Public Library
319 S. Main Street
Roxboro, NC 27573
Tel: 910-597-7881

Reidsville Library
North Carolina Collection
204 W. Morehead Street
Reidsville, NC 27320
Tel: 910-349-8476
Fax: 910-342-4824
URL: http://www.rcpl.org/lib5.html

Richard H. Thornton Memorial Library
210 Main Street
P.O. Box 339
Oxford, NC 27565
Tel: 919-693-1121

Robersonville Public Library
North Main Street
Robersonville, NC 27871
Tel: 919-795-3591

Robeson County Public Library
101 North Chestnut Street
P.O. Box 988
Lumberton, NC 28359-0988
Tel: 910-738-4859

Rowan Public Library
Edith M. Clark History Room
201 West Fisher Street
P.O. Box 4039
Salisbury, NC 28145-4039
Tel: 704-638-3021
Fax: 704-638-3013
URL: http://www.lib.co.rowan.nc.us/hr/home.htm

Sandhill Regional Library
412 E. Franklin Street
Rockingham, NC 28379
Tel: 910-997-3388

Scotland County Memorial Library
312 W. Church Street
Laurinburg, NC 28352-3720
Tel: 910-276-0563
Email: rbusko@ncsl.dcr.state.nc.us
URL: http://soca.sapc.edu/~scotland/library.htm

Scottish Tartans Museum/Heritage Center
33 E. Main Street
Franklin, NC 28734-3025
Tel: 704-524-7472

Stanly County Public Library/Main Branch
133 E. Main Street
Albemarle, NC 28001-4939
Tel: 704-983-6118

Thomas Hackney Braswell Memorial Library
344 Falls Road
Rocky Mount, NC 27801
Tel: 919-442-1951

Union County Public Library
316 East Windsor
Monroe, NC 28112-4842
Tel: 704-283-8184

University of North Carolina/Asheville
D. Hiden Ramsey Library
Special Collections/Southern Highlands Research Center
One University Heights
Asheville, NC 28804
Tel: 704-251-6336
Email: hwykle@unca.edu
URL: http://www.unca.edu/library/find.html

University of North Carolina/Chapel Hill
Louis Round Wilson Library
North Carolina Collection/Southern History Collection/Manuscripts
CB# 3914
Chapel Hill, NC 27514
Tel: 919-962-1301
919-933-1172 (North Carolina Coll.)
919-962-1345 (Manuscripts Dept.)
Fax: 919-962-4452
Email: MSS@email.unc.edu
URL: http://ils.unc.edu/nccoll/ncc.html
or http://www.unc.edu/lib/mssinv/index.html
or http://www.unc.edu/lib/mssinv/shc.html

University of North Carolina/Charlotte
J. Murrey Atkins Library, 10th Floor
Special Collections
Charlotte, NC 28223
Tel: 704-547-2449
Email: speccoll@email.uncc.edu
URL: http://www.uncc.edu/lis/library/collections/special/family.htm0

Wayne Count Public Library
1001 E. Ashe Street
Goldsboro, NC 27530
Tel: 919-735-1824

Wilkes Public Library
Genealogy Research Room
913 C Street
North Wilkesboro, NC 28659
Tel: 910-838-2818

Wilson County Public Library
249 W. Nash Street
P.O. Box 400
Wilson, NC 27894-0400
Tel: 919-237-5355

Newspaper Repositories

North Carolina Newspaper Project
North Carolina Department of Cultural Resources
109 E. Jones Street
Raleigh, NC 27601-2807
Tel/Fax: 919-733-2570
Email: jwelch@hal.dcr.state.nc.us
URL: http://hal.dcr.state.nc.us/tss/newspape.htm

Vital Records

North Carolina Vital Records
P.O. Box 29537
Raleigh, NC 27626-0537
Tel: 919-733-3000

North Carolina on the Web

Charlotte's Web
http://www.charweb.org/gen/

North Carolina Genealogical Societies/Resources
by Avery J. Parker
http://www.arrowweb.com/ajparker/ncgensr.htm

North Carolina GenWeb Project
http://www.goldenbranches.com/nc-state/

North Carolina State Archives—Genealogy Page
http://www.ah.dcr.state.nc.us/archives/arch/gen-res.htm

North Carolina, State Library of
http://hal.dcr.state.nc.us/iss/gr/genealog.htm

Traveller Southern Families
http://genealogy.traveller.com/genealogy/

North Dakota

Archives, State & National

National Archives—Central Plains Region
2312 East Bannister Road
Kansas City, MO 64131
Tel: 816-926-6272
Fax: 816-926-6982
Email: archives@kansascity.nara.gov
URL: http://www.nara.gov/nara/regional/06nsgil.html

National Archives—Rocky Mountain Region
Denver Federal Center, Building 48
P.O. Box 25307
Denver, CO 80225-0307
Tel: 303-236-0817
Fax: 303-236-9354
Email: archives@denver.nara.gov
URL: http://www.nara.gov/nara/regional/08nsgil.html

State Archives and Historical Research Library
State Historical Society of North Dakota
North Dakota Heritage Center
612 East Boulevard Avenue
Bismarck, ND 58505-0830
Tel: 701-328-2091
Email: ccmail.histsoc@ranch.state.nd.us
URL: http://www.state.nd.us/hist/sal.htm

Genealogical Societies

Bismarck-Mandan Historical & Genealogical Society
P.O. Box 485
Bismarck, ND 58502-0485
Email: DEarlSmith@prodigy.net
URL: http://soli.inav.net/~dsenne/bmhgs_html/bmhgs.html

Bowman County Genealogical Society
206 9th Avenue, NW
Bowman, ND 58623

Bottineau Genealogical Society
614 West Pine Circle
Bottineau, ND 58318

Germans From Russia Heritage Society
1008 East Central Avenue
Bismarck, ND 58501
Tel: 701-223-6167
Email: grhs@btigate.com
URL: http://www.teleport.com/nonprofit/grhs/

Griggs County Genealogical Society
Griggs County Court House
P.O. Box 237
Cooperstown, ND 58425

James River Genealogical Society
651 4th Street, N.
Carrington, ND 58421

McLean County Genealogical Society
P.O. Box 84
Garrison, ND 58540

Minnkota Genealogical Society
P.O. Box 126
Grand Forks, ND 56721
URL: http://www.rootsweb.com/~minnkota/

Mouse River Loop Genealogical Society
P.O. Box 1391
Minot, ND 58702-1391
Email: marockem@donnybrook.ndak.net
URL: http://www.geocities.com/Athens/Forum/2079/mrlgs.html

Red River Valley Genealogical Society/Library
Manchester Building, Suite L-116
112 N. University Drive
P.O. Box 9284
Fargo, ND 58106
Tel: 701-239-4129
URL: http://www.atpfargo.com/hjem/rrvgs/index.html

Richland County, ND and Wilkin County, MN Genealogy Guild
c/o Leach Public Library
417 2nd Avenue N.
Wahpeton, ND 58075

South Western North Dakota Genealogical Society
HCR 01, Box 321
Regent, ND 58650

Williams County Genealogical Society
703 West 7th Street
Williston, ND 58801-4908

Historical Societies

Barnes County Historical Society, Inc.
2030 W. Main Street
Valley City, ND 58072-4404
Tel: 701-845-0966

Bismarck-Mandan Historical & Genealogical Society
P.O. Box 485
Bismarck, ND 58502-0485
Email: DEarlSmith@prodigy.net
URL: http://soli.inav.net/~dsenne/bmhgs_html/bmhgs.html

Cass County Historical Society
Bonanzaville, USA
1351 West Main Avenue (Interstate 94, Exit 85)
West Fargo, ND 58078
Tel: 701-282-2822

Crosby Historical Society and Pioneer Village
West of City
Crosby, ND 58730
Tel: 701-965-6705

Dunn County Historical Society
HC 1, Box 42
Dunn Center, ND 58626
Tel: 701-548-8111

Grand Forks Country Historical Society
2405 Belmont Road
Grand Forks, ND 58201-7505
Tel: 701-775-2216

North Dakota, State Historical Society of
North Dakota Heritage Center
612 East Boulevard Avenue
Bismarck, ND 58505-0830
Tel: 701-328-2666
Fax: 701-328-3710
Email: ccmail.histsoc@ranch.state.nd.us
URL: http://www.state.nd.us/hist/

Richland County Historical Society
11 7th Avenue, N.
Wahpeton, ND 58075-3931
Tel: 701-642-3075

Steele County Historical Society
Steele Avenue
P.O. Box 144
Hope, ND 58046
Tel: 701-945-2394

Turtle Mountain Indian Historical Society
Chippewa Heritage Center
Belcourt, ND 58316
Tel: 701-477-6140

LDS Family History Centers

Bismarck Family History Center
1500 Country West Road
Bismarck, ND 58501
Tel: 701-222-2794

Fargo Family History Center
2502 17th Avenue, S.
Fargo, ND 58103
Mail:
c/o Dorothy Hanks
1518 13 1/2 Street, S.
Fargo, ND 58103
Tel: 701-232-4003
URL: http://www.atpfargo.com/hjem/lds/index.html

Grand Forks Family History Center
2814 Cherry Street
Grand Forks, ND 58201
Tel: 218-746-6126

Minot Family History Center
2025 Ninth Street, NW
Minot, ND 58703
Tel: 701-838-4486

ARCHIVES/LIBRARIES/MUSEUMS

Bureau of Land Management
P.O. Box 36800
Billings, MT 59107

Cape Hancock State Historic Site
101 West Main
Bismarck, ND 58501

Carnegie Regional Library
49 West 7th Street
Grafton, ND 58237-1409
Tel: 701-352-2754

Divide County Library
204 1st Street, NE
Crosby, ND 58730
Tel: 701-965-6305

Fargo Public Library
102 North 3rd Street
Fargo, ND 58102
Tel: 701-241-1491/2
TDD: 701-241-8809
URL: http://www.atpfargo.com/hjem/fpl/index.html

Fort Totten State Historic Site
Pioneer Daughters Museum
P.O. Box 224
Fort Totten, ND 58335
Tel: 701-766-4441
800-233-8048 (Devils Lake Convention and Visitors Bureau)
Email: rgreene@ranch.state.nd.us

Grand Forks Public Library
2110 Library Circle
Grand Forks, ND 58201-6324
Tel: 701-772-8116

Leach Public Library
417 2nd Avenue, N
Wahpeton, ND 58075-4488
Tel: 701-642-5732
701-642-1428
Email: maciver@senditt.nodak.edu

Minot Public Library
516 Second Avenue, SW
Minot, ND 58701
Tel: 701-852-1045

North Dakota, State Historical Society of
North Dakota Heritage Center
612 East Boulevard Avenue
Bismarck, ND 58505-0830
Tel: 701-328-2666
Fax: 701-328-3710
Email: ccmail.histsoc@ranch.state.nd.us
URL: http://www.state.nd.us/hist/

North Dakota State Library
State Capitol Grounds
604 E. Boulevard
Bismarck, ND 58505-0800
Tel: 800-472-2104
701-328-4622
Fax: 701-328-2040
Email: msmail,statelib@ranch.state.nd.us
URL: http://www.sendit.nodak.edu/ndsl/index.html

North Dakota State University
Germans from Russia Heritage Society Collection
NDSU Library
Corner of 12th Avenue and Albrecht Blvd.
P.O. Box 5599
Fargo, ND 58105-5599
Tel: 701-231-8416
Fax: 701-231-7138
Email: mmmiller@badlands.nodak.edu
URL: http://www.lib.ndsu.nodak.edu/gerrus/index.html

North Dakota State University
Institute for Regional Studies
NDSU Library, Lower Level, Room 6
Corner of 12th Avenue and Albrecht Blvd.
P.O. Box 5599
Fargo, ND 58105-5599
Tel: 701-231-8914
Fax: 701-231-7138
Email: nulibarc@plains.nodak.edu

Red River Valley Genealogical Society/Library
Manchester Building, Suite L-116
112 N. University Drive
P.O. Box 9284
Fargo, ND 58106
Tel: 701-239-4129
URL: http://www.atpfargo.com/hjem/rrvgs/index.html

University of North Dakota
Chester Fritz Library
Elwyn B. Robinson Department of Special Collections
North Dakota Room and Family History/Genealogy Room
P.O. Box 9000
Grand Forks, ND 58202-9000
Tel: 701-777-4625
Fax: 701-777-3319
URL: http://www.und.nodak.edu/dept/library/Collections/spk.html

Newspaper Repositories

North Dakota, State Historical Society of
North Dakota Heritage Center
612 East Boulevard Avenue
Bismarck, ND 58505-0830
Tel: 701-328-2668
Fax: 701-328-3710
Email: ccmail.histsoc@ranch.state.nd.us
URL: http://www.state.nd.us/hist/infnews.htm

Vital Records

Division of Vital Records, Dept. of Health
600 East Boulevard Avenue
Bismarck, ND 58505
Tel: 701-328-2360
URL: http://www.state.nd.us/hist/infvit.htm

North Dakota on the Web

Dakota Territory during the Civil War
Roster of the 1st Dakota Cavalry
http://www.rootsweb.com/~usgenweb/sd/military/cw.htm

North Dakota GenWeb Project
http://www.rootsweb.com/~ndgenweb/

Red River Valley Heritage Resource Center
http://www.atpfargo.com/hjem/

State Historical Society of North Dakota,
Materials Available for Genealogical Research
http://www.state.nd.us/hist/infgen.htm

Ohio

Archives, State & National

National Archives—Great Lakes Region
7358 South Pulaski Road
Chicago, IL 60629-5898
Tel: 773-581-7816
Fax: 312-353-1294
Email: archives@chicago.nara.gov
URL: http://www.nara.gov/nara/regional/05nsgil.html

Ohio State Archives
Ohio State Historical Society
1982 Velma Avenue
Columbus, OH 43211-2497
Tel: 614-297-2510
Fax: 614-297-2411
Email: ohswww@winslo.ohio.gov
URL: http://winslo.ohio.gov/ohswww/ohshome.html

Genealogical Societies

Adams County Genealogical Society
P.O. Box 231
West Union, OH 45693

African-American Historical & Genealogical Society/Cleveland (AAHGS)
P.O. Box 200382
Cleveland, OH 44120

Allen County Genealogical Society (OGS)
620 Market Street
Lima, OH 45801-4665

Alliance Genealogical Society (OGS)
P.O. Box 3630
Alliance, OH 44601-7630

Arizona Chapter (OGS)
P.O. Box 677
Gilbert, AZ 85234-0677

Ashland County Genealogical Society (OGS)
P.O. Box 681
Ashland, OH 44805-0681

Ashtabula County Genealogical Society (OGS Chapter #83)
c/o Geneva Public Library
861 Sherman Street
Geneva, OH 44041
Email: acgs@interlaced.net
URL: http://www.interlaced.net/~tom/acgs/

Athens County Genealogical Society (OGS)
65 North Court Street
Athens, OH 45701-2506
Tel: 614-592-2280
Email: gwright@eurekanet.com
URL: http://www.seorf.ohiou.edu/~xx024/

Auglaize County Genealogical Society (OGS)
P.O. Box 2021
Wapakoneta, OH 45895-0521

Belmont County Genealogical Society (OGS)
P.O. Box 285
Barnesville, OH 43713-0285

Brown County Genealogical Society (OGS)
P.O. Box 83
Georgetown, OH 45121-0083

Butler County Genealogical Society (OGS)
P.O. Box 2011
Middletown, OH 45044-2011

Carroll County Genealogical Society (OGS)
59 3rd Street, NE
Carrollton, OH 44615-1205

Champaign County Genealogical Society (OGS)
P.O. Box 680
Urbana, OH 43078-0680

Clark County Genealogical Society (OGS)
102 E. Main Street, Suite 204
Springfield, OH 45501-1412

Clermont County Genealogical Society (OGS)
P.O. Box 394
Batavia, OH 45103-0394

Clinton County Genealogical Society (OGS)
149 E. Locust Street
P.O. Box 529
Wilmington, OH 45177-0529
Tel: 937-382-4684
URL: http://www.postcom.com/ccgshs/

Colorado Chapter (OGS)
P.O. Box 1106
Longmont, CO 80502-1106

Columbiana County Genealogical Society (OGS)
P.O. Box 861, Dept. I
Salem, OH 44460-0861
Email: clark13@ibm.net
or frantta@valunet.com
URL: http://www.rootsweb.com/~ohcccogs/

Coshocton County Genealogical Society (OGS)
P.O. Box 128
Coshocton, OH 43812-0128
Email: C05H0CT0N@aol.com
URL: http://www.pe.net/~sharyn/ccogs.html

Crawford County Genealogical Society (OGS)
P.O. Box 92
Galion, OH 44833-0092

Cuyahoga Valley Genealogical Society (OGS)
P.O. Box 41414
Brecksville, OH 44141-0414

Cuyahoga West Genealogical Society (OGS)
P.O. Box 26196
Fairview Park, OH 44126-0196

Darke County Genealogical Society (OGS)
P.O. Box 908
Greenville, OH 45331-0908
http://www.calweb.com/~wally/darke/society.htm

Daughters of the American Revolution, Ohio Society
Email: osdar@aol.com
URL: http://members.aol.com/osdar/index.html

Defiance County Genealogical Society (OGS)
P.O. Box 7006
Defiance, OH 43512-7006

Delaware County Genealogical Society (OGS)/Library
157 E. William Street
P.O. Box 1126
Delaware, OH 43015-8126
Tel: 614-369-3831
Email: dchsdcgs@midohio.net
URL: http://www.midohio.net/dchsdcgs/

East Cuyahoga Genealogical Society (OGS)
P.O. Box 24182
Lyndhurst, OH 44124-0182

Erie County Genealogical Society (OGS)
P.O. Box 1301
Sandusky, OH 44871-1301

Fairfield County Genealogical Society (OGS)
P.O. Box 1470
Lancaster, OH 43130-0570
Email: grwheel@juno.com
URL: http://www.greenapple.com/~ksmith/

Fayette County Genealogical Society (OGS)
P.O. Box 342
Washington Court House, OH 43160-0342

Florida Chapter (OGS)
c/o W. Friis
1679 Holiday Drive
Casselberry, FL 32707

Franklin County Genealogical Society (OGS)
570 West Broad Street
P.O. Box 2503
Columbus, OH 43216-2406

Fulton County Genealogical Society (OGS)
P.O. Box 337
Swanton, OH 43558-0337

Gallia County Genealogical Society (OGS)
P.O. Box 295
Gallipolis, OH 45631-0295

Geauga County Genealogical Society (OGS)
110 E. Park Street
Chardon, OH 44024-1213

Greater Cleveland Genealogical Society (OGS)
P.O. Box 40254
Cleveland, OH 44140-0254

Greene County Genealogical Society (OGS)
P.O. Box 706
Xenia, OH 45385-0706
Email: Blin4012@aol.com
URL: http://www.dsenter.com/ohio/greene/chapter.htm

Guernsey County Genealogical Society (OGS)
8583 Georgetown Road
P.O. Box 661
Cambridge, OH 43725-0661

Hamilton County Genealogical Society (OGS)
P.O. Box 15851
Cincinnati, OH 45215-0851
Tel: 513-956-7078
Email: egan@fuse.net
URL: http://members.aol.com/ogshc/index.htm

Hancock County Genealogical Society (OGS)
P.O. Box 672
Findlay, OH 45839-0672
URL: http://www.bright.net/~hanogs/

Hardin County Genealogical Society (OGS)
P.O. Box 520
Kenton, OH 43326-0520

Harrison County Genealogical Society (OGS)/Library
45507 Unionvale Road
Cadiz, OH 43907-9723

Henry County Genealogical Society (OGS)
P.O. Box 231
Deshler, OH 43516

Hocking County Genealogical Society (OGS)
P.O. Box 115
Rockbridge, OH 43149-0115

Holmes County Genealogical Society (OGS)
P.O. Box 136
Millersburg, OH 44654-0136

Hudson Chapter (OGS)
Hudson Library & Historical Society
22 Aurora Street, #G
Hudson, OH 44236

Huron County Genealogical Society (OGS)
P.O. Box 923
Norwalk, OH 44857-0923
URL: http://www.accnorwalk.com/~jkelble/

International Society for British Genealogy & Family History
P.O. Box 20425
Cleveland, OH 44120

Jackson County Genealogical Society (OGS)
P.O. Box 807
Jackson, OH 45640-0807

Jefferson County Genealogical Society (OGS)
P.O. Box 4712
Steubenville, OH 43952-8712

Johnstown Genealogy Society
P.O. Box 345
Johnstown, OH 43031

Knox County Genealogical Society (OGS)
P.O. Box 1098
Mount Vernon, OH 43050-1098

KYOWVA Genealogical Society
P.O. Box 1254
Huntington, WV 25715

Lake County Genealogical Society (OGS)
Morley Library
184 Phelps
Painesville, OH 44077-3927

Lawrence County Genealogical Society (OGS)
P.O. Box 945
Ironton, OH 45638-0955

Licking County Genealogical Society (OGS)
P.O. Box 4037
Newark, OH 43058-4037

Logan County Genealogical Society (OGS)
P.O. Box 36
Bellefontaine, OH 43311

Lorain County Genealogical Society (OGS)
P.O. Box 865
Elyria, OH 44036-0865

Lucas County Genealogical Society (OGS)
325 N. Michigan Street
Toledo, OH 43624-1614

Madison County Genealogical Society (OGS)
P.O. Box 102
London, OH 43140-0102

Mahoning County Genealogical Society (OGS)
P.O. Box 9333
Boardman, OH 44513

Marion Area Genealogical Society (OGS)
Heritage Hall
169 E. Church Street
P.O. Box 844
Marion, OH 43301-0844
URL: http://www.genealogy.org/~smoore/marion.html
or http://emcee.com/~smoore/marion.html

Medina County Genealogical Society (OGS)
P.O. Box 804
Medina, OH 44258-0804

Meigs County Genealogical Society (OGS)
P.O. Box 346
Pomeroy, OH 45769-0346

Mercer County Genealogical Society (OGS)
P.O. Box 437
Celina, OH 45822-0437

Miami County Historical and Genealogical Society (OGS)
P.O. Box 305
Troy, OH 45373-0305

Miami Valley Genealogical Society (OGS)
P.O. Box 1364
Dayton, OH 45401-1364

Monroe County Genealogical Society (OGS)
P.O. Box 641
Woodsfield, OH 43793-0641

Montgomery County Genealogical Society (OGS)
P.O. Box 1584
Dayton, OH 45401-1584

Morgan County Genealogical Society (OGS)
P.O. Box 418
McConnelsville, OH 43756-0418

Morrow County Genealogical Society (OGS)
P.O. Box 401
Mount Gilead, OH 43338-0401
Email: b.j.gameier@juno.com
URL: http://www.rootsweb.com/~ohmorrow/

Muskingum County Genealogical Society (OGS)
P.O. Box 3066
Zanesville, OH 43702-3066

National Capital Buckeye Chapter (OGS)
P.O. Box 105
Bladensburg, MD 20710

Noble County Genealogical Society (OGS)
P.O. Box 174
Caldwell, OH 43724-0174

Northwestern Ohio Genealogical Society
P.O. Box 17066
Toledo, OH 43615

Ohio Genealogical Society (OGS)
713 South Main Street
P.O. Box 2625
Mansfield, OH 44906-0625
Tel: 419-522-9077
Email: ogs@freenet.richland.oh.us
URL: http://www.ogs.org/public/default.htm

Ottawa County Genealogical Society (OGS)
P.O. Box 193
Port Clinton, OH 43452-0193

Parma/Cuyahoga Genealogical Society (OGS)
6428 Nelwood Road
Parma Heights, OH 44130-3211

Paulding County Genealogical Society (OGS)
205 E. Main Street
Paulding, OH 45879-1492

Perry County Genealogical Society (OGS)
P.O. Box 275
Junction City, OH 43748-0275

Pickaway County Chapter (OGS)/Library
Pickaway County Historical Society
P.O. Box 85
Circleville, OH 43113

Pike County Genealogical Society (OGS)
P.O. Box 224
Waverly, OH 45690-0224

Polish Genealogical Society of Greater Cleveland
906 College Avenue
Cleveland, OH 44113

Portage County Genealogical Society (OGS)
P.O. Box 821
Ravenna, OH 44266
URL: http://www2.clearlight.com/~pchs/pccogs.htm

Preble County Genealogical Society (OGS)
Preble County District Library
450 S. Barron Street
Eaton, OH 45320-1705
Email: pcroom@infinet.com
URL: http://www.pcdl.lib.oh.us/pcgs.htm

Putnam County Genealogical Society (OGS)
P.O. Box 403
Ottawa, OH 45875-0403

Richland County Genealogical Society (OGS)
P.O. Box 3823
Mansfield, OH 44907-0823
URL: http://www.rootsweb.com/~ohrichgs/

Richland County/Shelby Genealogical Society (OGS)
P.O. Box 766
Shelby, OH 44875-0766

Ross County Genealogical Society (OGS)
270 S. Paint Street
P.O. Box 6352
Chillicothe, OH 45601-6352

Sandusky County Kin Hunters (OGS)
1337 Hayes Avenue
Fremont, OH 43420

Scioto County Genealogical Society (OGS)
P.O. Box 812
Portsmouth, OH 45662-0812

Seneca County Genealogical Society (OGS)
P.O. Box 157
Tiffin, OH 44883-0157

South Cuyahoga Genealogical Society (OGS)
13305 Pearl Road
Strongsville, OH 44136

Southern California Chapter (OGS)
P.O. Box 5057
Los Alamitos, CA 90721-5057

Southern Ohio Genealogical Society (OGS)
229 Crestview Drive
P.O. Box 414
Hillsboro, OH 45133

Southwest Butler County Genealogical Society
c/o Soldiers, Sailors, & Pioneers Monument
South Monument Avenue
Hamilton, OH 45011

Stark County Genealogical Society (OGS)
7300 Woodcrest, NE
North Canton, OH 44721-1949
Email: dms@netcom.com
http://www.webcom.com/schori/starkogs.html

Summit County Genealogical Society (OGS)
P.O. Box 2232
Akron, OH 44309-2232

Trumbull County Genealogical Society (OGS)
P.O. Box 309
Warren, OH 44482-0309

Tuscarawas County Genealogical Society (OGS)
P.O. Box 141
New Philadelphia, OH 44663-0141

Union County Genealogical Society (OGS)
P.O. Box 438
Marysville, OH 43040-0438

Van Wert County Genealogical Society (OGS)
P.O. Box 485
Van Wert, OH 45891-0485

Vinton County Genealogical Society (OGS)
P.O. Box 306
Hamden, OH 45634-0306

Warren County Genealogical Society (OGS)/Research Center
300 E. Silver Street
Lebanon, OH 45036-1800
Tel: 513-933-1144

Washington County Genealogical Society (OGS)
P.O. Box 2174
Marietta, OH 45750-2174

Wayne County Genealogical Society (OGS)
P.O. Box 856
Wooster, OH 44691

Wellington Genealogical Workshop
P.O. Box 224
Wellington, OH 44090

West Augusta Historical & Genealogical Society
1510 Prairie Drive
Belpre. OH 45714

Williams County Genealogical Society (OGS)
P.O. Box 293
Bryan, OH 43506-0293

Wood County Genealogical Society (OGS)
P.O. Box 722
Bowling Green, OH 43402-0722

Wyandot County Genealogical Society (OGS)
P.O. Box 414
Upper Sandusky, OH 43351-0414

HISTORICAL SOCIETIES

Adjutant General's Department Library
2825 W. Dublin Granville Road
Columbus, OH 43235-2712
Tel: 614-889-7038

Allen County Historical Society
Allen County Museum &
Elizabeth M. MacDonell Memorial Library
620 West Market Street
Lima, OH 45801
Tel: 419-222-9426
Email: acmuseum@nala.worcnet.gen.oh.us
URL: http://www.worcnet.gen.oh.us/~acmuseum/

American West Research Center and Historical Society, Inc.
10605 Chester Avenue
Cleveland, OH 44106-2240
Tel: 216-721-9594

Amherst Historical Society
Quigley Museum
710 Milan Avenue
Amherst, OH 44001-1311
Tel: 216-988-7255

Athens County Historical Society
65 N. Court Street
Athens, OH 45701-2506
Tel: 614-592-2280
URL: http://www.seorf.ohiou.edu/~xx023/

Auglaize County Historical Society
223 S. Main Street
Saint Marys, OH 45885-2208
Tel: 419-394-70696

Bedford Historical Society
30 South Park Avenue
Bedford, OH 44146
Tel: 216-323-0796

Berea Historical Society
Mahler Museum & History Center
118 E. Bridge Street
P.O. Box 173
Berea, OH 44017
Tel: 216-243-2541
URL: http://members.aol.com/bereahist/index.html

Black River Historical Society
309 W. 5th Street
Lorain, OH 44052
Tel: 216-245-2563

Botkins Historical Society
P.O. Box 256
Botkins, OH 45306
Email: BotkinsHS@aol.com
URL: http://members.aol.com/BotkinsHS/history/bhshome.html

Brecksville Historical Association
History Center & Archives
Blossom Hill Complex
Brecksville, OH 44141
Tel: 216-526-7165

Brooklyn Historical Society
4442 Ridge Road
Cleveland, OH 44144-3353
Tel: 216-749-2804

Brookville Historical Society/Library
P.O. Box 82
Brookville, OH 45309

Centerville Historical Society
89 W. Franklin Street
Dayton, OH 45459-4735
Tel: 937-433-0123

Chagrin Falls Historical Society
21 Walnut Street
Chagrin Falls, OH 44022-3125
Tel: 216-247-4695

Champaign County Historical Society
809 East Lawn Avenue
Urbana, OH 43078

Chesterland Historical Foundation
P.O. Box 513
Chesterland, OH 44026-0513
Tel: 216-729-1830

Cincinnati Historical Society/Library & Collections
Cincinnati Museum Center at Union Terminal
1301 Western Avenue
Cincinnati, OH 45203
Tel: 513-287-7041
URL: http://www.cincymuseum.org/chscoll.htm

Cleveland Police Historical Society/Museum
Ontario Street
Cleveland, OH 44113
Tel: 216-623-5055

Clinton County Historical Society
149 E. Locust Street
P.O. Box 529
Wilmington, OH 45177-0529
Tel: 937-382-4684
URL: http://www.postcom.com/ccgshs/

Conneaut Historical Railroad Society
363 Depot Street
Conneaut, OH 44030-2468
Tel: 216-599-7878

Delaware County Historical Society/Library
157 E. William Street
P.O. Box 317
Delaware, OH 43015
Tel: 614-369-3831
Email: dchsdcgs@midohio.net
URL: http://www.midohio.net/dchsdcgs/

Dover Historical Society
325 E. Iron Avenue
Dover, OH 44622-2105
Tel: 330-343-7040

East Liverpool Historical Society
305 Walnut Street
East Liverpool, OH 43920-3427
Tel: 330-385-2550

East Palestine Area Historical Society
555 Bacon Avenue
East Palestine, OH 44413-1530

Enon Community Historical Society
P.O. Box 442
Enon, OH 45323
Tel: 513-864-7080

Fayette County Historical Society/Museum
517 Columbus Avenue
Washington Court House, OH 43160-1427
Tel: 614-335-2953
URL: http://www.washingtonch.com/faytrav/museum.htm

Firelands Historical Society
4 Case Avenue
P.O. Box 572
Norwalk, OH 44857-0572
Tel: 419-668-6038

Franklin Area Historical Society
302 Park Avenue
Franklin, OH 45005

Gahanna Historical Society
101 S. High Street
Columbus, OH 43215-3408
Tel: 614-475-3342

Gallia County Historical Society
P.O. Box 295
Gallipolis, OH 45631

Gates Mills Historical Society/Museum
7580 Old Mill Road
Gates Mills, OH 44040-0249
URL: http://clio1.cuyahoga.lib.oh.us/home/locations/GAT.html

Geauga County Historical Society
14653 E. Park Street
Burton, OH 44021
Tel: 216-834-1492

Germantown, Historical Society of
47 W. Center Street
Germantown, OH 45327-1341
Tel: 937-855-7951

Granger Historical Society/Library
1261 Granger Road
Medina, OH 44256-7337
Tel: 330-239-1523

Highland County Historical Society
151 East Main Street
Hillsboro, OH 45133

Indian Hill Historical Society
8100 Given Road
Cincinnati, OH 45243-1520
Tel: 513-891-1873

Jefferson County Historical Association/Library
426 Franklin Avenue
P.O. Box 4268
Steubenville, OH 43952
Tel: 614-283-1133

Knox County Historical Society
997 Harcourt Road
Mount Vernon, OH 43050-4434
Tel: 614-393-5247

Lake County Historical Society
8610 King Memorial Road
Mentor, OH 44060-7959
Tel: 216-255-8979

Lake Erie Islands Historical Society
Put-in-Bay, OH 43456
Tel: 419-285-2804
Email: history@leihs.org
URL: http://www.leihs.org/

Lakewood Historical Society
14710 Lake Avenue
Lakewood, OH 44107
Tel: 216-221-7343
URL: http://www.lkwdpl.org/histsoc/

Licking County Historical Society/Museum
6 N. 6th Street
Newark, OH 43055-4902
Tel: 614-345-4898

Logan County Historical Society
521 E. Columbus Avenue
Bellefontaine, OH 43311-2401
Tel: 937-593-7557

Loghurst Western Reserve Historical Society
3967 Boardman Canfield Road
Canfield, OH 44406-9030
Tel: 330-533-4330

Lorain County Historical Society
509 Washington Avenue
Elyria, OH 44035
Tel: 216-322-3341

Loveland Historical Society
201 E. Kemper Road
Loveland, OH 45140
Tel: 513-683-5692

Marion County Historical Society
Heritage Hall
169 E. Church Street
P.O. Box 844
Marion, OH 43301-0844
Tel: 614-387-4255
URL: http://www.genealogy.org/~smoore/marion.html
or http://emcee.com/~smoore/marion.html

Mayfield Township Historical Society
606 Som Center Road
Cleveland, OH 44143-2311
Tel: 216-461-0055

Miami County Historical and Genealogical Society (OGS)
P.O. Box 305
Troy, OH 45373-0305

Middlefield Historical Society
14979 S. State Street
Middlefield, OH 44062
Tel: 216-632-0400

Middletown African-American Historical Society
4521 Poppy Drive
Middletown, OH 45044-5228
Tel: 513-424-1791

Middletown Historical Society/Canal Museum
1605 N. Verity Parkway
Middletown, OH 45042
Tel: 513-422-7161

Milford Area Historical Society
906 Main Street
Milford, OH 45150-1767
Tel: 513-248-0324

Mohican Historical Society/Museum
203 E. Main Street
Loudonville, OH 44842-1214
Tel: 419-994-4050

Montgomery County Historical Society
7 N. Main Street
Dayton, OH 45402-1903
Tel: 937-228-6271

Niles Historical Society
503 Brown Street
Niles, OH 44446
Tel: 330-544-2143

North Canton Heritage Society, Inc.
400 S. Main Street
Canton, OH 44720
Tel: 330-494-4791

Oakwood Historical Society
1947 Far Hills Avenue
Dayton, OH 45419-2536
Tel: 937-299-3793

Ohio Division of Veterans' Affairs
30 E. Broad Street, Room 1825
Columbus, OH 43266-0422
Tel: 614-466-5453

Ohio Historical Society
1982 Velma Avenue
Columbus, OH 43211-2497
Tel: 614-297-2300
614-297-2510 (Archives/Library)
Fax: 614-297-2411
Email: ohswww@winslo.ohio.gov
` ohsref@winslo.ohio.gov (Reference Requests)
URL: http://winslo.ohio.gov/ohswww/ohshome.html

Perry County Historical Society
105 S. Columbus Street
P.O. Box 746
Somerset, OH 43783-0746
Tel: 614-743-2591
Email: pchs@netpluscom.com
URL: http://www.netpluscom.com/~pchs/

Pickaway County Historical Society
P.O. Box 85
Circleville, OH 43113

Muskingum County, Pioneer and Historical Society of
304 Woodlawn Avenue
Zanesville, OH 43701-4940
Tel: 614-454-9500

Plymouth Area Historical Society
7 E. Main Street
Plymouth, OH 44865-1201
Tel: 419-687-5411

Portage County Historical Society
6549 N. Chestnut Street
Ravenna, OH 44266
Tel: 330-296-3523
Email: pchs@bardo.clearlight.com
URL: http://www2.clearlight.com/~pchs/

Reynoldsburg Truro Historical Society
1399 1/2 Lancaster Avenue
Columbus, OH 43207
Tel: 614-863-6969

Salem Historical Society/Museum
208 S. Broadway
Salem, OH 44460
Tel: 216-337-8514

Sandusky County Historical Society
1337 Hayes Avenue
Fremont, OH 43420

Shelby County Historical Society
P.O. Box 376
Sidney, OH 45365
Email: lodges@bright.net
URL: http://www.bright.net/~richnsus/index.html

Stark County Historical Society
749 Hazlett Avenue, NW
Canton, OH 44708

Summit County Historical Society
550 Copley Road
Akron, OH 44320
Tel: 330-535-1120
Email: invision@interramp.com
URL: http://www.neo.lrun.com/l
Summit_County_Historical_Society/

Twinsburg Historical Society
P.O. Box 7
Twinsburg, OH 44087

Warren County Historical Society/Library & Museum
105 S. Broadway
P.O. Box 223
Lebanon, OH 45036-0223
Tel: 513-932-1817
URL: http://www2.eos.net/edsale/cities/lebanon/
warrencomuseum.html

Wayne County Historical Society
546 East Bowman Street
Wooster, OH 44691

**Union Township Historical Museum/
Quaker Heritage Center**
47 N. Miami Street
West Milton, OH 45383-1831
Tel: 937-698-3820

Wayne County Historical Society
546 E. Bowman Street
Wooster, OH 44691
Tel: 330-264-8856

Wellsville Historical Society
1003 Riverside Avenue
Wellsville, OH 43968
Tel: 330-532-1018

West Carrollton Historical Society
323 East Central Avenue
Dayton, OH 45449
Tel: 937-859-5912

Western Lake Erie Historical Society
2319 Torrey Hill Drive
Toledo, OH 43606-4351
Tel: 419-473-9534

Western Reserve Historical Society/Library
10825 East Boulevard
Cleveland, OH 44106
Tel: 216-721-5722

Wood County Historical Society
13660 County Home Road
Bowling Green, OH 43402
Tel: 419-352-0967
URL: http://www-wbgu.bgsu.edu/nwoetf/ode/
historical_society.html

Worthington Historical Society
50 W. New England Avenue
Columbus, OH 43085-3536
Tel: 614-885-1247

Wyandot County Historical Society
130 S. 7th Street
Upper Sandusky, OH 43351
Tel: 419-294-3857

LDS Family History Centers

Cincinnati Family History Center
5505 Bosworth Place
Cincinnati, OH 45212
Tel: 513-531-5624

Cincinnati Family History Center
Cornell and Snider Road
Cincinnati, OH 45247
Tel: 513-489-3036

Dayton Family History Center
1500 Shiloh Springs Road
Dayton, OH 45426
Tel: 513-854-4566

Dublin Family History Center
7135 Coffman Road
Dublin, OH 43017
Tel: 614-761-1898

Grove City Family History Center
2400 Red Rock Blvd.
Grove City, OH 43123

Kirtland Family History Center
8751 Kirtland Road
Kirtland, OH 44094
Tel: 216-256-8808

Middletown Family History Center
4930 Central Avenue
Middletown, OH 45044
Tel: 513-423-9642

Perrysburg Family History Center
11050 Avenue Road
Perrysburg, OH 43551
Tel: 419-872-9491

Reynoldsburg Family History Center
2135 Baldwin Road
Reynoldsburg, OH 43068
Tel: 614-866-7686

Tallmadge Family History Center
106 E. Howe Road
Tallmadge, OH 44278
Tel: 330-630-3365

Westerville Family History Center
307 Huber Village Blvd.
Westerville, OH 43081

Westlake Family History Center
25000 Westwood Road
Westlake, OH 44145
Tel: 216-777-1518

Wilmington Family History Center
State Route 73
Wilmington, OH 45177
Tel: 513-382-1510

Wintersville Family History Center
Powells Lane
Wintersville, OH 43952
Tel: 614-266-6334

ARCHIVES/LIBRARIES/MUSEUMS

Akron/Summit County Public Library
55 South Main Street
Akron, OH 44326-0001
Tel: 330-643-9000
Fax: 330-643-9033
URL: http://www.neo.lrun.com/Akron_Summit_County_Public_Library/

American Jewish Archives
Hebrew Union College/Jewish Institute of Religion
3101 Clifton Avenue
Cincinnati, OH 45220-2488
Tel: 513-221-7444 ext. 403
Fax: 513-221-7812
Email: AJA@fuse.net
URL: http://home.fuse.net/aja/

American West Research Center and Historical Society, Inc.
10605 Chester Avenue
Cleveland, OH 44106-2240
Tel: 216-721-9594

Amos Memorial Public Library
230 East North Street
Sidney, OH 45365-2733
Tel: 937-492-8354
Fax: 937-492-9229

Arms Family Museum of Local History
648 Wick Avenue
Youngstown, OH 44502-1215
Tel: 330-743-2589

Bellevue Public Library
224 E. Main Street
Bellevue, OH 44811
Tel: 419-483-4769
URL: http://www.bellevue.lib.oh.us/

Bluffton/Richland Public Library
145 S. Main Street
Bluffton, OH 45817
Tel: 419-358-5016
Fax: 419-358-9653
Email: schirmsh@oplin.lib.oh.us
URL: http://library.norweld.lib.oh.us/Bluffton/

Bowling Green State University
Jerome Library
Center for Archival Collections
Bowling Green, OH 43403-0175
Tel: 419-372-2411
URL: http://www.bgsu.edu/colleges/library/cac/cac.html

Brookville Historical Society/Library
P.O. Box 82
Brookville, OH 45309

Camp Dennison Civil War Museum (Scheduled to open Spring, 1998)
SR 126
Camp Dennison, OH 45111
For more information:
Mrs. Charles R. Wright
Museum Chairwoman, DAR
1779 Cottontail Drive
Milford, OH 45150
Tel: 513-575-9284
http://www.intcom.net/~tomt/dennison/dennison.html

Carnegie Public Library
127 South North Street
Washington Court House, OH 43160-2283
Tel: 614-335-2540
Fax: 614-335-8409

Chagrin Falls Branch/Cuyahoga County Public Library
100 E. Orange Street
Chagrin Falls, OH 44022-2799
Tel: 216-247-3556
Fax: 216-247-0179
URL: http://clio1.cuyahoga.lib.oh.us/home/locations/CHF.html

Champaign County Library
160 West Market Street
Urbana, OH 43078
Tel: 937-653-3811
Fax: 937-653-5679

Chillicothe/Ross County Public Library
140-146 South Paint Street
Chillicothe, OH 45601-3214
Tel: 614-702-4145
Fax: 614-702-4156
Email: chl0lib@winslo.ohio.gov

Cincinnati/Hamilton County, Public Library of
Library Square
800 Vine Street
Cincinnati, OH 45202-2071
Tel: 513-369-6900
513-369-6905 (History and Genealogy)
Fax: 513-369-6067
Email: comments@plch.lib.oh.us
URL: http://plch.lib.oh.us/

Cincinnati Historical Society/Library & Collections
Cincinnati Museum Center at Union Terminal
1301 Western Avenue
Cincinnati, OH 45203
Tel: 513-287-7041
URL: http://www.cincymuseum.org/chscoll.htm

Clark County Public Library
201 South Fountain Avenue
P.O. Box 1080
Springfield, OH 45501-1080
Tel: 937-328-6901
Fax: 934-328-6908
Email: clark@ohionet.org
URL: http://www.ccpl.lib.oh.us/

Cleveland Police Historical Society/Museum
Ontario Street
Cleveland, OH 44113
Tel: 216-623-5055

Cleveland Public Library
325 Superior Avenue
Cleveland, OH 44114-1271
Tel: 216-623-2800
Fax: 216-623-7015
Email: info@library.cpl.org
URL: http://www.cpl.org/

Columbus/Franklin County, Public Library of
96 South Grant Avenue
Columbus, OH 43215
Tel: 614-645-2610
Fax: 614-645-2051

Croatian Heritage Museum & Library
34900 Lake Shore Blvd.
Willoughby, OH 44095-2043
Tel: 216-946-2044

Dayton/Montgomery County Public Library
215 E. Third Street
Dayton, OH 45402-2103
Tel: 513-227-9531
513-227-9500
Fax: 513-227-9539
URL: http://www.dayton.lib.oh.us/

Delaware County Genealogical Society (OGS)/Library
157 E. William Street
P.O. Box 1126
Delaware, OH 43015-8126
Tel: 614-369-3831
Email: dchsdcgs@midohio.net
URL: http://www.midohio.net/dchsdcgs/

Fairfield County District Library
219 N. Broad Street
Lancaster, OH 43130
Tel: 614-653-2745

Fairview Park Regional Library/Cuyahoga County Public Library
4449 W. 213th Street
Fairfield Park, OH 44126-2189
Tel: 216-333-4700
Fax: 216-333-4887
TDD: 216-333-4898
URL: http://clio1.cuyahoga.lib.oh.us/home/locations/FPR.html

Fayette County Historical Society/Museum
517 Columbus Avenue
Washington Court House, OH 43160-1427
Tel: 614-335-2953
URL: http://www.washingtonch.com/faytrav/museum.htm

Firelands Historical Society Library
Laning-Young Research Center
9 Case Avenue
P.O. Box 572
Norwalk, OH 44857-0572
Tel: 419-663-0392
URL: http://www.accnorwalk.com/credits/norwalk/firelands/index.html

Garst Museum
205 N. Broadway
Greenville, OH 45331
Tel: 937-548-5250

Gates Mills Branch/Cuyahoga County Public Library and Gates Mills Historical Society/Museum
7580 Old Mill Road
P.O. Box 249
Gates Mills, OH 44040-0249
Tel: 216-423-4808
Fax: 216-423-1363
URL: http://clio1.cuyahoga.lib.oh.us/home/locations/GAT.html

Geauga West Library
13455 Chillicothe Road
Chesterland, OH 44026
Tel: 216-729-4250
Fax: 216-729-7517

Geneva Public Library
861 Sherman Street
Geneva, OH 44041

Grand Rapids Branch/Weston Public Library
17620 Bridge Street
P.O. Box 245
Grand Rapids, OH 43522
Tel: 419-832-5231
Fax: 419-832-8104
Email: dfroman@wcnet.org
URL: http://library.norweld.lib.oh.us/weston/br.htm

Granville Public Library
217 E. Broadway
Granville, OH 43023-1398
Tel: 614-587-0196

Greenville Public Library
Genealogy Department
520 Sycamore Street
Greenville, OH 45331-1438
Tel: 937-548-3915
Fax: 937-548-3837
Email: gplibrary@wesnet.com

Guernsey County District Public Library
800 Steubenville Avenue
Cambridge, OH 43725-2354
Tel: 614-432-5946
Fax: 614-432-7142

Harrison County Genealogical Society (OGS)/Library
45507 Unionvale Road
Cadiz, OH 43907-9723

Henderson Memorial Library Association
54 East Jefferson Street
Jefferson, OH 44047
Tel: 216-576-3761
Fax: 216-576-8402
Email: jfr0por@winslo.ohio.gov

Hudson Library and Historical Society
22 Aurora Street
Hudson, OH 44236
Tel: 216-653-6658

Huron County Historical Library
Administration Building (Basement)
180 Milan Avenue
Norwalk, OH 44857
Tel: 419-668-4383
URL: http://www.accnorwalk.com/~jkelble/resources/library/hist.html

Huron Historical & Cultural Center
401 Williams Street
Huron, OH 44839-1642
Tel: 419-433-4660

Jefferson County Historical Association/Library
426 Franklin Avenue
P.O. Box 4268
Steubenville, OH 43952
Tel: 614-283-1133

Kaubisch Library
205 Perry Street
Fostoria, OH 44830
Tel: 419-435-2813
Fax: 419-435-5350
Email: kmpl@ohionet.org
URL: http://library.norweld.lib.oh.us/Kaubisch/

Lakewood Public Library
15425 Detroit Avenue
Lakewood, OH 44107-3890
Tel: 216-226-8275
Fax: 216-521-4327
Email: lpl@lkwdpl.org
URL: http://www.lkwdpl.org/

Lorain Public Library
351 6th Street
Lorain, OH 44052-1770
Tel: 216-244-1192
Fax: 216-244-1733
Email: loradm@library.cpl.org

Mansfield/Richland County Public Library
John Sherman Room
43 West Third Street
Mansfield, OH 44902-1295
Tel: 419-521-3100
Fax: 419-525-4750
URL: http://www.mrcpl.lib.oh.us/shermrm/

McComb Public Library
Local History and Genealogy Dept.
113 S. Todd Street
P.O. Box 637
McComb, OH 45858
Tel: 419-293-2425
Email: grosede@oplin.lib.oh.us
URL: http://library.norweld.lib.oh.us/McComb/

McKinley Museum/Ramsayer Research Library
800 McKinley Monument Drive, NW
Canton, OH 44708-4832
Tel: 330-455-7043
URL: http://www.neo.lrun.com/McKinley_Museum/index.html

Medina Branch/Medina County District Library
Franklin Sylvester Genealogy Room
210 S. Broadway
Medina, OH 44256
Tel: 330-725-0588
Fax: 330-725-2053
URL: http://www.medina.lib.oh.us/

Middletown Public Library
125 S. Broad Street
Middletown, OH 45042
Tel: 513-424-1251
Fax: 513-424-6585

Milan/Berlin Township Public Library
East Church Street
P.O. Box 1550
Milan, OH 44846
Tel: 419-499-4117
Fax: 419-499-4697

Minerva Public Library
677 Lynnwood Drive
Minerva, OH 44657-1200
Tel: 330-868-4101
Fax: 330-868-4267
URL: http://www.minervaohio.com/library.htm

Monroeville Public Library
34 Monroe Street
Monroeville, OH 44847-9722
Tel: 419-465-2035
URL: http://www.accnorwalk.com/~jkelble/resources/library/monpub.html

Morley Library
184 Phelps Street
Painesville, OH 44077
Tel: 216-352-3383
Fax: 216-352-1069

Mount Gilead Public Library
Genealogy Dept.
35 E. High Street
Mount Gilead, OH 43338-1429
Tel: 419-947-5866
Fax: 419-947-9252

New London Public Library
67 S. Main Street
New London, OH 44851
Tel: 419-929-3981
Fax: 419-929-0007
URL: http://www.accnorwalk.com/~jkelble/resources/library/monpub.html

Norwalk Public Library
46 W. Main Street
Norwalk, OH 44857
Tel: 419-668-6063
Fax: 419-663-2190
Email: norwalk@oplin.blib.oh.us
URL: http://www.accnorwalk.com/~jkelble/resources/library/norpub.html

Ohio Genealogical Society (OGS)
713 South Main Street
P.O. Box 2625
Mansfield, OH 44906-0625
Tel: 419-522-9077
Email: ogs@freenet.richland.oh.us
URL: http://www.ogs.org/public/default.htm

Ohio Historical Society
1982 Velma Avenue
Columbus, OH 43211-2497
Tel: 614-297-2300
614-297-2510 (Archives/Library)
Fax: 614-297-2411
Email: ohswww@winslo.ohio.gov
` ohsref@winslo.ohio.gov (Reference Requests)
URL: http://winslo.ohio.gov/ohswww/ohshome.html

Ohio Society of Military History Museum
316 Lincoln Way, E.
Massillon, OH 44646
Tel: 330-832-5553

Ohio State Land Office, Auditor
88 East Broad Street
Columbus, OH 43266-0040

Ohio State Library
65 South Front Street
Columbus, OH 43215-4163
Tel: 614-644-7061
800-686-1531 (Ohio only)
Fax: 614-466-3584
URL: http://winslo.ohio.gov/

Ohio University
Vernon R. Alden Library
Park Place
Athens, OH 45701-2978
Tel: 614-593-2710
Fax: 614-593-0138
URL: http://www.library.ohiou.edu/libinfo/depts/microforms/geneal.htm

Paulding County Carnegie Library
Genealogy Department
205 South Main Street
Paulding, OH 45879
Tel: 419-399-2032
Fax: 419-399-2114
URL: http://library.norweld.lib.oh.us/Paulding/

Pemberville Public Library
375 East Front Street
Pemberville, OH 43450
Tel: 419-287-4012
Fax: 419-287-4620
Email: pemlib@wcnet.org
URL: http://library.norweld.lib.oh.us/Pemberville/

Pike Heritage Museum
110 S. Market Street
Waverly, OH 45690-1317
Tel: 614-947-5281

Portsmouth Public Library
Local History Department
1220 Gallia Street
Portsmouth, OH 45662
Tel: 614-354-5304
Fax: 614-353-1249
URL: http://ppl.library.net/

Preble County District Library
Preble County Room
450 S. Barron Street
Eaton, OH 45320-1705
Tel: 937-456-4250
Fax: 937-456-6092
Email: pcroom@infinet.com
URL: http://www.pcdl.lib.oh.us/

Reed Memorial Library
167 E. Main Street
Ravenna, OH 44266-3197
Tel: 330-296-2827
Fax: 330-296-3780
Email: reedmem@ohionet.org

Rodman Public Library
Alliance Room
215 E. Broadway
Alliance, OH 44601
Tel: 330-821-2665
Fax: 330-821-5053
URL: http://www.rodman.lib.oh.us/rpl/home.htm

Rutherford B. Hayes Presidential Center
Library and Archives
Spiegel Grove
Fremont, OH 43420
Tel: 419-332-2081
Fax: 419-332-4952
Email: hayeslib@nwohio.com
URL: http://www.rbhayes.org/rbhlibry.htm

Saint Paris Library
127 East Main Street
St. Paris, OH 43072
Tel: 513-663-4349
Fax: 513-663-0297

Salem Public Library
821 E. State Street
Salem, OH 44460-2298
Tel: 330-332-0042
Fax: 330-332-4488
Email: library@salemohio.com
URL: http://www.salemohio.com/library/

Schiappa Branch Library
4141 Mall Drive
Steubenville, OH 43952
Tel: 614-264-6166
Fax: 614-264-7397

Stark County District Library
715 Market Avenue, North
Canton, OH 44702-1080
Tel: 216-452-0665
Fax: 216-452-0403
Email: scdl@cannet.com
URL: http://www.molo.lib.oh.us/home/stark/gene.html

Toledo/Lucas County Public Library
Local History & Genealogy Department
325 Michigan Street
Toledo, OH 43624-1628
Tel: 419-259-5207
Fax: 419-255-1334
TTY: 419-259-5252
URL: http://www.library.toledo.oh.us/history/index.html

Ukrainian Museum/Archives
1202 Kenilworth Avenue
Cleveland, OH 44113-4417
Tel: 216-781-4329

University of Akron Libraries
Polsky Building
Archival Services

225 S. Main, Room LL10
Akron, OH 44325-1702
Tel: 330-972-7670
Fax: 330-972-6170
Email: jvmiller@uakron.edu
URL: http://www.uakron.edu/archival/home.htm

University of Cincinnati
808 Belgen Library
Archives and Rare Books Department
ML 0113
Cincinnati, OH 45221-0113
Tel: 513-556-1959
Fax: 513-556-2113
URL: http://www.libraries.uc.edu/libinfo/arb.html

Warren County Genealogical Society (OGS)/Research Center
300 E. Silver Street
Lebanon, OH 45036-1800
Tel: 513-933-1144

Warren/Trumbull County Public Library
444 Mahoning Avenue
Warren, OH 44483
Tel: 330-399-8807 ext. 120
Fax: 330-395-3988
TDD: 330-393-0784
URL: http://www.wtcpl.lib.oh.us/lh&g.htm

Washington County Public Library
615 Fifth Street
Marietta, OH 45750-1973
Tel: 614-373-1057
Fax: 614-373-2860
Email: joeller@state.lib.oh.us

Way Public Library
Local History Room
101 E. Indiana Avenue
Perrysburg, OH 43551
Tel/TDD: 419-874-3135
Fax: 419-874-6129
Email: kelleyna@oplin.lib.oh.us
URL: http://www.wcnet.org/~waylib/

Wayne County Public Library
304 North Market Street
Wooster, OH 44691
Tel: 330-262-0916
Fax: 330-262-7313

Wayne Public Library
Local History Room
137 E. Main Street
Wayne, OH 43466
Tel: 419-288-2708
Fax: 419-288-3766
Email: waynelib@wcnet.org
URL: http://library.norweld.lib.oh.us/Wayne/

Western Reserve Historical Society
Case Western Reserve University
History Library
10825 East Boulevard
Cleveland, OH 44106
Tel: 216-721-5722
URL: http://www.cwru.edu/CWRU/buildings/cultural/historical_society_annex.html

Westerville Public Library
Ohio Room
126 S. State Street
Westerville, OH 43081-2095
Tel: 614-882-7277
URL: http://www.wpl.lib.oh.us/library/index.html

Wood County District Public Library
Local History Department
251 N. Main Street
Bowling Green, OH 43402
Tel: 419-352-5102
Fax: 419-354-0405
Email: WCDPL@wcnet.org
URL: http://www.wcnet.org/WCDPL/

Wright State University
Paul Laurence Dunbar Library, 4th Floor
Archives and Special Collections
Dayton, OH 45435-0001
Tel: 937-775-2092
Email: archive@library.wright.edu
URL: http://www.libraries.wright.edu/staff/dunbar/arch/schome.htm

Xenia Community Library
Greene County Room, 2nd Floor
76 East Market Street
Xenia, OH 45385
Tel: 937-376-2996 ext. 221
Email: gcr@gcpl.lib.oh.us
URL: http://www.gcpl.lib.oh.us/services/genealogy/genealogy.htm

Youngstown Historical Center of Industry and Labor
Archives and Library
151 W. Wood Street
P.O. Box 533
Youngstown, OH 44501-0533
Tel: 330-743-5934
Email: yhcillibrary@cisnet.com
URL: http://winslo.ohio.gov/ohswww/youngst/arch_lib.html

Youngstown/Mahoning County, Public Library of
305 Wick Street
Youngstown, OH 44503-1003
Tel: 330-744-8636
Fax: 330-744-3355
Email: ygs0lib@winslo.ohio.gov

Newspaper Repositories

Bowling Green State University
Jerome Library
Center for Archival Collections
Bowling Green, OH 43403-0175
Tel: 419-372-2411
URL: http://www.bgsu.edu/colleges/library/cac/cac.html

Ohio Historical Society
1982 Velma Avenue
Columbus, OH 43211-2497
Tel: 614-297-2510 (Archives/Library)
Fax: 614-297-2411
Email: gparkins@winslo.ohio.gov
URL: http://winslo.ohio.gov/ohswww/newspape.html

Ohio University
Vernon R. Alden Library
Park Place
Athens, OH 45701-2978
Tel: 614-593-2710
Fax: 614-593-0138
URL: http://www.library.ohiou.edu/libinfo/depts/microforms/geneal.htm

Vital Records

Ohio Department of Health
Division of Vital Statistics
P.O. Box 15098
Columbus, OH 43215-0098
Tel: 614-466-2531
URL: http://www.state.oh.us/doh/heovri.html

Ohio Historical Society
1982 Velma Avenue
Columbus, OH 43211-2497
Tel: 614-297-2300
614-297-2510 (Archives/Library)
Fax: 614-297-2411
Email: ohswww@winslo.ohio.gov
ohsref@winslo.ohio.gov (Reference Requests)
URL: http://winslo.ohio.gov/ohswww/brthdth1.html

Ohio on the Web

African Americans in Southeastern Ohio (AFROAMSEO)
http://www.seorf.ohiou.edu/~xx057

Camp Dennison Civil War Museum
http://www.intcom.net/~tomt/dennison/dennison.html

Darke County Ohio Genealogical Researchers
http://php.ucs.indiana.edu/~jetorres/dco.html

Miami Valley Genealogical Index
http://www.pcdl.lib.oh.us/miami/miami.htm

Ohio GenWeb Project
http://www.netwalk.com/~coliver/ohio/

Ohio Historical Society—Home Page
URL: http://winslo.ohio.gov/ohswww/ohshome.html

Ohio Historical Society
Ohio Online Death Certificate Index 1913-1917
http://www.on-library.com/cgi-onlib/ohiohist/dindex.pl

Ohio in the Civil War
http://www.infinet.com/~lstevens/a/civil.html

Ohio River Valley Families
http://www.tbox.com/orvf/

OKLAHOMA

ARCHIVES, STATE & NATIONAL

National Archives—Southwest Region
501 West Felix Street, Building 1
P.O. Box 6216
Fort Worth, TX 76115-0216
Tel: 817-334-5525
Fax: 817-334-5621
Email: archives@ftworth.nara.gov
URL: http://www.nara.gov/nara/regional/07nsgil.html

Oklahoma State Archives
Office of Archives and Records
Oklahoma Department of Libraries
200 NE 18th Street
Oklahoma City, OK 73105-3298
Tel: 405-521-2502
Fax: 405-525-7804
Email: tkremm@oltn.odl.state.ok.us
URL: http://www.state.ok.us/~odl/oar/archives.htm

GENEALOGICAL SOCIETIES

Atoka County Genealogical Society
P.O. Box 83
Atoka, OK 74525

Bartlesville Genealogical Society
c/o Bartlesville Public Library
600 S. Johnstone
Bartlesville, OK 74003
Tel: 918-337-5333

Beaver River Genealogical & Historical Society
Route 1, Box 79
Hooker, OK 73945

Broken Arrow Genealogical Society
P.O. Box 1244
Broken Arrow, OK 74013

Caddo County Genealogical Society
c/o Janet Langley
Route 1, Box 400
Fort Cobb, OK 73038
Tel: 405-643-5100

Canadian County Genealogical Society
P.O. Box 866
El Reno, OK 73036
Tel: 405-262-2409
Email: elreno@oltn.state.ok.us
(Attn: CCGS)
URL: http://www.rootsweb.com/~okccgs/

Choctaw County Genealogical Society
P.O. Box 1056
Hugo, OK 74743-1056
Tel: 405-326-7568
Fax: 405-326-7569
URL: http://www2.1starnet.com/goodland/history/hsge_01.html

Cleveland County Genealogical Society
1005 N. Flood, Suite 136
P.O. Box 6176
Norman, OK 73070
Tel: 405-329-9180
405-329-4481 (Library)
Email: rdwilsoni@aol.com
URL: http://www.geocities.com/Heartland/Plains/4006/

Coal County Historical & Genealogical Society
111 West Ohio
Coalgate, OK 74538

Craig County Genealogical Society
P.O. Box 484
Uinita, OK 74301

Cushing Genealogical Society
c/o Cushing County Library
P.O. Box 551
Cushing, OK 74023

Delaware County Genealogical Society
c/o Grove Public Library
206 South Elk
Grove, OK 74344
Tel: 918-786-2945
URL: http://www.rootsweb.com/~okdelawa/dcgs.htm

Federation of Oklahoma Genealogical Societies
P.O. Box 26151
Oklahoma City, OK 73126-0151

First Families of the Twin Territories
c/o Oklahoma Genealogical Society
P.O. Box 12986
Oklahoma City, OK 73157
URL: http://www.rootsweb.com/~okgenweb/fftt.htm

Fort Gibson Genealogical & Historical Society
P.O. Box 416
Fort Gibson, OK 74434

Garfield County Genealogists, Inc.
P.O. Box 1106
Enid, OK 73702-1106
URL: http://www.harvestcomm.net/org/garfield_genealogy/

Grady County Genealogical Society
P.O. Box 792
Chickasha, OK 73023

Greer County Genealogical & Historical Society
240 W. Lincoln
Mangum, OK 73554
Tel: 405-782-3185
405-782-2477

Haskell County Genealogy Society
P.O. Box 481
Stigler, OK 74462
Tel: 918-967-8681
URL: http://www.rootsweb.com/~okhaskel/hasksoc.htm

Kiowa County Genealogical Society
P.O. Box 191
Hobart, OK 73651-0191

Latimer County Genealogical & Historical Society
c/o Hoyt Duncan
101 W. Durant
Wilburton, OK 74578
Email: hoyt@juno.com

Logan County Genealogical Society
P.O. Box 1419
Guthrie, OK 73044

Major County Genealogical Society
c/o Fairview City Library
P.O. Box 419
Fairview, OK 73737

Mayes County Genealogical Society
P.O. Box 924
Chouteau, OK 74337

McClain County Historical & Genealogical Society/Museum
203 W. Washington Street
Purcell, OK 73080-4227
Tel: 405-527-5894

McCurtain County Genealogy Society
P.O. Box 1832
Idabel, OK 74745

Muldrow Genealogical Society
P.O. Box 1253
Muldrow, OK 74948

Muskogee County Genealogical Society
c/o Muskogee Public Library
801 West Okmulgee
Muskogee, OK 74401
Tel: 918-682-6657

Noble County Genealogy Society
P.O. Box 785
Perry, OK 73077

North Caddo Genealogical Society
P.O. Box 309
Hinton, OK 73047

Northwest Oklahoma Genealogical Society
P.O. Box 834
Woodward, OK 73801

Oklahoma Genealogical Society
P.O. Box 12986
Oklahoma City, OK 73157-2986
URL: http://www.rootsweb.com/~okgs/

Okmulgee County Genealogical Society
P.O. Box 805
Okmulgee, OK 74447

Ottawa County Genealogical Society
P.O. Box 1383
Miami, OK 74355-1383

Pawhuska Genealogical Society
P.O. Box 807
Pawhuska, OK 74056

Payne County Genealogical Society
c/o Stillwater Public Library
206 W. 6th
Stillwater, OK 74074

Pioneer Genealogical Society
P.O. Box 1965
Ponca City, OK 74602
Email: famfox@pcok.com
URL: http://www.brigadoon.com/~nipperb/pgs/piogenhp.htm

Pittsburg County Genealogical & Historical Society
113 East Carl Albert Pkwy.
McAlester, OK 74501

Pontotoc County Historical & Genealogical Society
221 West 16th Street
Ada, OK 74820

Poteau Valley Genealogical Society
P.O. Box 1031
Poteau, OK 74953
Email: dbrown@clnk.com
URL: http://www.rootsweb.com/~okleflor/pvgs.htm

Rogers County Genealogical Society
P.O. Box 2493
Claremore, OK 74018

Sequoyah Genealogical Society
P.O. Box 1112
Sallisaw, OK 74955

Sons & Daughters of the Cherokee Strip Pioneers
P.O. Box 465
Enid, OK 73702

Southwest Oklahoma Genealogical Society
P.O. Box 148
Lawton, OK 73502-0148
Email: lgarris@sirinet.net
URL: http://www.sirinet.net/~lgarris/swogs/

Stephens County Genealogical Society/Library
301 North 8th Street
Duncan, OK 73534

Texas-Oklahoma Panhandle Genealogical Society
c/o Perry Memorial Library
22 SE 5th Street
Perryton, OK 79070
Tel: 806-435-5801

Three Forks Genealogical Society
102 South State Street
Wagoner, OK 74467

Tulsa Genealogical Society
P.O. Box 585
Tulsa, OK 74101-0585
URL: http://ourworld.compuserve.com/homepages/bsr/tgspage.htm

Western Plains Weatherford Genealogical Society
P.O.Box 1672
Weatherford, OK 73096

Western Trails Genealogical Society
P.O. Box 70
Altus, OK 73522
URL: http://www.rootsweb.com/~okjackso/wtgs.htm

Woods County Genealogists
P.O. Box 234
Alva, OK 73717

HISTORICAL SOCIETIES

1889er Society/Museum
Harn Homestead
313 NE 16th Street
Oklahoma City, OK 73104
Tel: 405-235-4058

American Historical Society of Germans from Russia
Central Oklahoma Chapter
Membership:
Delbert Amen
2400 Ashley Drive
Oklahoma City, OK 73120
Email: beideckpaf@aol.com
URL: http://www.teleport.com/nonprofit/ahsgr/okcentra.html

Arbuckle Historical Society
113 W. Muskogee Street
Sulphur, OK 73086
Tel: 405-622-2824

Atoka County Historical Society/Museum
Highway 69 North
P.O. Box 245
Atoka, OK 74525
Tel: 405-889-7192

Beaver River Genealogical & Historical Society
Route 1, Box 79
Hooker, OK 73945
Tel: 405-652-2716

Broken Arrow Historical Society
1800 S. Main Street
Broken Arrow, OK 74012-6503
Tel: 918-258-2616

Bryan County Heritage Society
P.O. Box 153
Calera, OK 74730

Canadian County Historical Society
600 W. Wade
El Reno, OK 73036
Tel: 405-262-5121

Cherokee Dixieland Historical Society/Museum
Downtown
Webbers Falls, OK 74470
Tel: 918-464-2728

Cherokee National Historical Society/Museum
Cherokee Heritage Center
P.O. Box 515
Tahlequah, OK 74465
Tel: 918-456-6007
918-456-6165
URL: http://www.powersource.com/powersource/heritage/

Cheyenne Arapaho Cultural Preservation Committee
212 S. Rock Island Avenue
El Reno, OK 73036
Tel: 405-422-4813

Chickasaw Council
House Museum
Court House Square
P.O. Box 717
Tishomingo, OK 73460
Tel: 405-371-3351

Cleveland County Historical Society
508 N. Peters
P.O. Box 260
Norman, OK 73069
Tel: 405-321-0156

Coal County Historical & Genealogical Society
111 West Ohio
Coalgate, OK 74538

Delaware County Historical Society
Jay, OK 74346
Tel: 918-253-4345

Drumright Community Historical Society
Broadway & Harley Streets
Mail:
118 S. Creek
Drumright, OK 74030
Tel: 918-352-2898

Eastern Oklahoma Historical Society
Kerr Museum
P.O. Box 111
Poteau, OK 74953
Tel: 918-647-8221

Edmond Historical Society/Museum
431 S. Boulevard
Edmond, OK 73034
Tel: 405-340-0078
Fax: 405-340-2771

Fort Gibson Genealogical & Historical Society
P.O. Box 416
Fort Gibson, OK 74434

Grady County Historical Society
P.O. Box 495
Chickasha, OK 73018

Grant County Historical Society/Museum
RR3, Box 301
Medford, OK 73759
Tel: 405-395-2822
405-395-2888
Fax: 405-395-2343

Greer County Genealogical & Historical Society
240 W. Lincoln
Mangum, OK 73554
Tel: 405-782-3185
405-782-2477

Haskell County Historical Society
204 E. Main Street
Stigler, OK 74462
URL: http://www.rootsweb.com/~okhaskel/hasksoc.htm

Hughes County Historical Society
114 N. Creek Street
Holdenville, OK 74848
Tel: 405-379-6723

Lincoln County Historical Society
Museum of Pioneer History
717 Manvel Avenue
Chandler, OK 74834-2842
Tel: 405-258-2425

Logan County Historical Society
223 S. 1st Street
Guthrie, OK 73044-4707
Tel: 405-282-4446

Love County Historical Society
Pioneer Museum
101 SW Front Street
P.O. Box 134
Marietta, OK 73448
Tel: 405-276-5888

Major County Historical Society
Fairview, OK 73737
Tel: 405-227-2265

Mayes County Historical Society
Coo-Y-Yah Country Museum
Old Depot
Pryor, OK 74361
Tel: 918-476-5493
URL: http://www.pryorwebdesign.com/pryor/pryor.html

McClain County Historical & Genealogical Society/Museum
203 W. Washington Street
Purcell, OK 73080-4227
Tel: 405-527-5894

Newkirk Community Historical Society
101 S. Maple Street
Newkirk, OK 73647
Tel: 405-362-3330

No Man's Land Historical Society/Museum
207 W. Sewell Street
Goodwell, OK 73939
Tel: 405-349-2670

North Central Oklahoma Historical Association
417 E. Grand Avenue
P.O. Box 2811 Dept. DP
Ponca City, OK 74602
Tel: 405-765-4600
405-765-7169
Email: nipperb@brigadoon.com
URL: http://www.brigadoon.com/~famfox/ncohafrt.htm

Nowata County Historical Society
121 S. Pine Street
Nowata, OK 74048-3413
Tel: 918-273-1191

Okfuskee County Historical Society
407 W. Broadway Street
Okemah, OK 74859-2401
Tel: 918-623-2027

Oklahoma Baptist Historical Society
1141 N. Robinson
Oklahoma City, OK 73103
Tel: 405-236-4341

Oklahoma Heritage Association
Oklahoma Heritage Center
201 NW 14th Street
Oklahoma City, OK 73103
Mail:
1500 N. Robinson
Oklahoma City, OK 73103
Tel: 405-235-4458
888-501-2059
Fax: 405-235-2714
Email: oha@telepath.com
URL: http://www.telepath.com/oha/

Oklahoma Historical Society/Library and Archives
2100 N. Lincoln Blvd.
Oklahoma City, OK 73105-4997
Archives & Manuscripts Division:
Tel: 405-522-5209
Fax: 405-521-2492
Library Resources Division:
Tel: 405-522-5225
Fax: 405-521-2492
URL: http://www.rootsweb.com/~okgenweb/ohsrlib.htm

Osage County Historical Society
700 N. Lnn Avenue
P.O. Box 267
Pawhuska, OK 74056
Tel: 918-287-9924

Piedmont Historical Society
Old Bank Building
Piedmont, OK 73078

Pittsburg County Genealogical & Historical Society
113 East Carl Albert Pkwy.
McAlester, OK 74501

Pontotoc County Historical & Genealogical Society
221 West 16th Street
Ada, OK 74820

Pottawatomie County, Historical Society of
1301 East Farrall
Shawnee, OK 74801
Tel: 405-273-5062

Pushmataha County Historical Society
125 W. Main
P.O. Box 285
Antlers, OK 74523

Red River Valley Historical Association
Southeastern Oklahoma State University
P.O. Box 4014
Durant, OK 74701
Tel: 405-924-0121 ext. 203

Sacred Heart (Konawa) Historical Society
c/o Kennedy Library of Konawa
Konawa High School
Route 1, Box 3
Konawa, OK 74849
Tel: 405-925-3662
URL: http://www.konawa.k12.ok.us/sacredheart.html

Sapulpa Historical Society
100 E. Lee
P.O. Box 278
Sapulpa, OK 74067
Tel: 918-224-4871

Sayre Historical Society
106 E. Poplar Avenue
Sayre, OK 73662
Tel: 405-928-5757

Seminole Historical Society
1717 Highway 9, West
Seminole, OK 74868-2041
Tel: 405-382-1500

Seminole Nation Historical Society/Museum
524 S. Wewoka Avenue
Wewoka, OK 74884-3239
Tel: 405-257-5580

Shortgrass Country Historical Society/Museum
106 E. Poplar Avenue
Sayre, OK 73662-2933
Tel: 405-928-5757

Sod House Museum & Historical Society
RR 1
Aline, OK 73716
Tel: 405-463-2441
405-463-2241

Southwestern Oklahoma Historical Society
P.O. Box 3693
Lawton, OK 73502

Sunbelt Railroad Historical Society
110 West A Street
Jenks, OK 74037
Tel: 918-298-7246

Tillman County Historical Society/Museum
201 N. 9th Street
Frederick, OK 73542
Tel: 405-335-7541
405-335-2989
405-335-2805
Email: brad_l_benson@compuserve.com
URL: http://www.mindspring.com/~sl-sf/msw/mswtil

Tonkawa Historical Society
P.O. Box 336
Tonkawa, OK 74653
Tel: 405-628-2702

Top of Oklahoma Historical Society/Museum
303 S. Main Street
Blackwell, OK 74631-3347
Tel: 405-363-0209

Tulsa County Historical Society
2501 W. Newton Street
Tulsa, OK 74127-5161
Tel: 918-585-9263
918-585-5520

Turley Historical Society
6540 N. Peoria Avenue
Tulsa, OK 74126
Tel: 918-425-8429

Washington County Historical Society
P.O. Box 255
Bartlesville, OK 74003
Tel: 918-333-0073

Washita County Historical Society
105 East First
P.O. Box 440
Cordell, OK 73632
Tel: 405-343-2554

Waynoka Historical Society
103 Missouri
Waynoka, OK 73860
Tel: 405-824-1886

Webbers Falls Historical Society/Museum
Commercial & Main Streets
Webbers Falls, OK 74470
Tel: 918-464-2728

Yukon Historical Society
Farm Museum
Third Street and Cedar
Yukon, OK 73099

LDS Family History Centers

Ardmore Family History Center
Prairie Valley Road
Ardmore, OK 73401
Tel: 405-226-2134

Bartlesville Family History Center
1501 Swan Drive
Bartlesville, OK 74006
Tel: 918-333-3135

Claremore Family History Center
1701 North Chambers Terrace
Claremore, OK 74017
Tel: 918-342-0101

Enid Family History Center
419 N. Eisenhower Street
Enid, OK 73503
Tel: 405-234-1518

Lawton Family History Center
7002 SW Drakestone
Lawton, OK 73505
Tel: 405-536-1303

Muskogee Family History Center
3008 East Hancock
Muskogee, OK 74403
Tel: 918-687-8861

Norman Family History Center
Imhoff Road & Highway 9
Norman, OK 73071
Tel: 405-364-8337

Oklahoma City Family History Center
12915 South Santa Fe
Oklahoma City, OK 73170
Tel: 405-794-3800

Oklahoma City Family History Center
5020 Northwest 63rd
Oklahoma City, OK 73132
Tel: 405-721-8455

Owasso Family History Center
9300 North 129th East Avenue
Owasso, OK 74055
Tel: 918-272-2048

Sapulpa Family History Center
920 Pioneer Road
Sapulpa, OK 74066
Tel: 918-224-7585

Seminole Family History Center
2500 John Street
Seminole, OK 74868
Tel: 405-382-5111

Shawnee Family History Center
1501 East Independence
Shawnee, OK 74801
Tel: 405-273-7943

Stillwater Family History Center
1720 East Virginia
Stillwater, OK 74075
Tel: 405-377-4122

Tulsa East Stake Family History Center
12110 East Seventh Street
Tulsa, OK 74128
Tel: 918-437-5690

Tulsa Stake Family History Center
3640 South New Haven
Tulsa, OK 74135
Tel: 918-747-3966

Woodward Family History Center
2023 Main Street
Woodward, OK 73801
Tel: 405-256-5113

ARCHIVES/LIBRARIES/MUSEUMS

Altus Library/Southern Prairie Library System
421 N. Hudson Street
Altus, OK 73521
Tel: 405-477-2890

Alva Public Library
504 Seventh Street
Alva, OK 73717
Tel: 405-327-1833

American Heritage Library
P.O. Box 176
Davis, OK 73030

Atoka County Library
205 East 1st
Atoka, OK 74525
Tel: 405-889-3555

Bartlesville Public Library/History Museum
600 S. Johnstone
Bartlesville, OK 74003
Tel: 918-337-5333 (Local and Family History Room)
918-337-5336 (History Museum)
Fax: 918-337-5338
TDD: 918-337-5359
Email: webmaster@bartlesville.lib.ok.us
URL: http://netra.bartlesville.lib.ok.us:8080/

Cherokee City/County Public Library
602 South Grand Avenue
Cherokee, OK 73728
Tel: 405-596-2366

Cherokee National Historical Society/Museum
Cherokee Heritage Center
Tsa-La-Gi
Tahlequah, OK 74464
Tel: 918-456-6007
918-456-6195
URL: http://www.powersource.com/powersource/heritage/museum.html

Cherokee Strip Museum Association
901 14th Street
Alva, OK 73717
Tel: 405-327-2030

Cherokee Strip, Museum of
507 S. 4th Street
Enid, OK 73701
Tel: 405-237-1907

Chickasha Public Library
527 W. Iowa Avenue
Chickasha, OK 73018
Tel: 405-222-6075

Chisholm Trail Historical Museum
Highways 70 & 81
Waurika, OK 73573
Tel: 405-228-2166

Choctaw County Library
208 E. Jefferson
Hugo, OK 74743
Tel: 405-326-5591
Email: hugolib@1starnet.com
URL: http://www2.1starnet.com/hugolib/

Cushing County Library
215 North Steele
P.O. Box 551
Cushing, OK 74023
Tel: 918-225-4188

El Reno Carnegie Library
Archives Room
215 E. Wade
El Reno, OK 73036
Tel: 405-262-2409

Enid Public Library
Great Plains Room
120 W. Maine Avenue
P.O. Box 8002
Enid, OK 73701
Tel: 405-234-6313
Fax: 405-233-2948

Fairview City Library
115 S. 6th Street
P.O. Box 419
Fairview, OK 73737
Tel: 405-227-2190

Five Civilized Tribes Museum
Agency Hill & Honor Heights Drive
Muskogee, OK 74401
Tel: 918-683-1701

Gilcrease Museum
1400 N. Gilcrease Museum Road
Tulsa, OK 74127
Tel: 918-596-2700

Grove Public Library
206 South Elk
Grove, OK 74344
Tel: 918-786-2945

Idabel Public Library
2 SE Avenue D
P.O. Box 778
Idabel, OK 74745
Tel: 405-286-6406

John F. Henderson Memorial Library
P.O. Box 580
Westville, OK 74965
Tel: 918-723-5002

Lawton Public Library
Family History Room
110 SW Fourth Street
Lawton, OK 73501
Tel: 405-581-3450

Layland Museum
201 N. Caddo
Cleburne, TX 76031
Tel: 817-641-3321

Martin East Regional Library
2601 S. Garnett Road
Tulsa, OK 74129
Tel: 918-669-6340

Metropolitan Library System/Downtown Library
Charles E. France Room, Oklahoma Collection
131 Dean McGee Avenue
Oklahoma City, OK 73102
Tel: 405-231-8650
URL: http://www.mls.lib.ok.us/dn.htm

Muldrow Public Library
City Hall Building
100 S. Main Street
P.O. Box 449
Muldrow, OK 74948
Tel: 918-427-6703

Museum of the Western Prairie
1100 N. Hightower
Altus, OK 73521
Tel: 405-482-1044

Muskogee Public Library
801 West Okmulgee
Muskogee, OK 74401
Tel: 918-682-6657

Norman Public Library
225 N. Webster
Norman, OK 73069
Tel: 405-321-1481
Fax: 405-360-7007

Northeastern State University
John Vaughan Library
Special Collections, Room 221
or
Ballenger Reading Room, Room 126
Tahlequah, OK 74464
Tel: 918-456-5511 ext. 3252 (Special Collections)
918-456-5511 ext. 3220 (University Archives)
Email: library@cherokee.nsuok.edu
URL: http://www.nsuok.edu/jvl/jvlspc.html

Oklahoma Department of Libraries
200 NE 18th Street
Oklahoma City, OK 73105-3298
Tel: 405-521-2502
Fax: 405-525-7804
URL: http://www.state.ok.us/~odl/

Oklahoma Heritage Association
Oklahoma Heritage Center
201 NW 14th Street
Oklahoma City, OK 73103
Mail:
1500 N. Robinson
Oklahoma City, OK 73103
Tel: 405-235-4458
888-501-2059
Fax: 405-235-2714
Email: oha@telepath.com
URL: http://www.telepath.com/oha/

Oklahoma Historical Society/Library and Archives
2100 N. Lincoln Blvd.
Oklahoma City, OK 73105-4997
Archives & Manuscripts Division:
Tel: 405-522-5209
Fax: 405-521-2492
Library Resources Division:
Tel: 405-522-5225
Fax: 405-521-2492
URL: http://www.rootsweb.com/~okgenweb/ohsrlib.htm

Oklahoma State University
204 Edmon Low Library
Stillwater, OK 74078
Tel: 405-744-6311
URL: http://www.library.okstate.edu/dept/scua/scuahp.htm

Oklahoma Territorial Museum
406 E. Oklahoma Avenue
Guthrie, OK 73044-3317
Tel: 405-282-1889

Old Greer County Museum & Hall of Fame
222 W. Jefferson Street
Mangum, OK 73554-4022
Tel: 405-782-2851

Pawnee Historical & Cultural Museum
657 Harrison Street
Pawnee, OK 74058-2520
Tel: 918-762-3706

Pioneer Museum & Art Center
2009 Williams Avenue
Woodward, OK 73801-5717
Tel: 405-256-6136

Pioneer Woman State Museum
701 Monument Road
Ponca City, OK 74604-3910
Tel: 405-765-6108

Ponca City Cultural Center & Museum Library
1000 E. Grand Avenue
Ponca City, OK 74601
Tel: 405-767-0427

Ponca City Library
515 East Grand Avenue
Ponca City, OK 74601-5499
Tel: 405-767-0345

Potawatomi Tribal Museum
1901 S. Gordon Cooper Drive
Shawnee, OK 74801-8604
Tel: 405-275-3119

Prague Historical Museum
1008 N. Broadway
Prague, OK 74864
Tel: 405-567-4750

Ralph Ellison Library
2000 North East 23rd
Oklahoma City, OK 73111
Tel: 405-424-1437
URL: http://www.mls.lib.ok.us/re.htm

Rudisill North Regional Library
1520 N. Hartford
Tulsa, OK 74106
Tel: 918-596-7280

Sapulpa Public Library
27 West Dewey Avenue
Sapulpa, OK 74066-3909
Tel: 918-224-5624

Stanley Tubbs Memorial Library
101 East Cherokee Street
Sallisaw, OK 74955-4621
Tel/Fax: 918-775-4481

Stephens County Historical Museum
Highway 81 & Beech
Duncan, OK 73533
Tel: 405-252-0717

Talbot Library & Museum
406 S. Colcord Avenue
P.O. Box 349
Colcord, OK 74338
Tel: 918-326-4532

Tillman County Historical Society/Museum
201 N. 9th Street
Frederick, OK 73542
Tel: 405-335-7541
405-335-2989
405-335-2805
Email: brad_l_benson@compuserve.com
URL: http://www.mindspring.com/~sl-sf/msw/mswtil

University of Oklahoma Library
Western History Collection
Monnet Hall, Room 452
630 Parrington Oval
Norman, OK 73069
Tel: 405-325-3641
Fax: 405-325-6069
URL: http://www-lib.uoknor.edu/depts/west/index.htm

University of Tulsa
McFarlin Library
2933 E. 6th Street
Tulsa, OK 74104
Tel: 918-631-2352
Fax: 918-631-3791
URL: http://www.lib.utulsa.edu/general/speccoll.htm

Vinita Public Library
Maurice Haynes Memorial Bldg.
215 West Illinois Avenue
Vinita, OK 74301
Tel: 918-256-2115
Fax: 918-256-2309

Watonga Public Library
301 N. Prouty Avenue
Watonga, OK 73772
Tel: 405-623-7748
Email: bookwoman@pldi.net
URL: http://www.watonga.com/library/

Weatherford Public Library
219 East Franklin Avenue
Weatherford, OK 73096
Tel: 405-772-3591

Newspaper Repositories

Muskogee Public Library
801 West Okmulgee
Muskogee, OK 74401
Tel: 918-682-6657

Oklahoma Department of Libraries
200 NE 18th Street
Oklahoma City, OK 73105-3298
Tel: 405-521-2502
Fax: 405-525-7804
URL: http://www.state.ok.us/~odl/

Oklahoma Historical Society/Library and Archives
2100 N. Lincoln Blvd.
Oklahoma City, OK 73105-4997
Tel: 405-522-5206
Fax: 405-521-2492
URL: http://www.keytech.com:80/~Frizzell/

Vital Records

Oklahoma Department of Health
Division of Vital Records
1000 Northeast 10th Street, Room 117
P.O. Box 53551
Oklahoma City, OK 73152-3551
Tel: 405-271-4040

Oklahoma on the Web

Application for Search & Certified Copy of Birth Certificate
http://home.earthlink.net/~scburn1/certificates.htm

Application for Search & Certified Copy of Death Certificate
http://home.earthlink.net/~scburn1/birth.htm

BJ's Place—Genealogy Home Page
http://www.harvestcomm.net/personal/bjsbytes/index.html

Cheyenne Genealogy Research
http://www.mcn.net/~hmscook/roots/cheyenne.html

Electric Cemetery Home Page—Civil War Site
http://www.ionet.net/~cousin/index.html

Federal Tract Books of Oklahoma Territory (SWOGS)
http://www.sirinet.net/~lgarris/swogs/tract.html

History of the Cherokee—Genealogy
http://www.phoenix.net/~martikw/geneal.html

Native American Resources
http://www.cowboy.net/native/indian.links.html

Oklahoma Department of Libraries/Archives—Genealogical Materials
http://www.state.ok.us/~odl/oar/arcgene.htm

Oklahoma GenWeb Project
http://www.rootsweb.com/~okgenweb/okindex.htm

Oklahoma Tribes and Officials
http://www.cowboy.net/native/tribes.html
or
http://www.codetalk.fed.us/tribes.html

OREGON

ARCHIVES, STATE & NATIONAL

National Archives—Pacific Northwest Region
6125 Sand Point Way, NE
Seattle, WA 98115
Tel: 206-526-6507
Fax: 206-526-4344
Email: archives@seattle.nara.gov
URL: http://www.nara.gov/nara/regional/10nsgil.html

Oregon State Archives
800 Summer Street, NE
Salem, OR 97310
Tel: 503-373-0701
Fax: 503-373-0953
Email: reference.archives@state.or.us
(Reference requests welcome)
URL: http://arcweb.sos.state.or.us/

GENEALOGICAL SOCIETIES

ALSI Historical & Genealogical Society
P.O. Box 822
Waldport, OR 97394

Baker County Genealogy Club
c/o Baker County Public Library
2400 Resort Street
Baker City, OR 97814

Belgian Researchers, Inc.
62073 Fruitdale Lane
LaGrande, OR 97850
Fax: 541-962-7604
Email: linghels@eosc.osshe.edu

Bend Genealogical Society
P.O. Box 8254
Bend, OR 97708

Blue Mountain Genealogical Society
P.O. Box 1801
Pendleton, OR 97801
Tel: 541-276-6000

Clackamas County Family History Society/Library
211 Tumwater Drive
P.O. Box 995
Oregon City, OR 97045-2900
Tel: 503-655-5574
URL: http://www.rootsweb.com/~genepool/ccfhs.htm

Clatsop County Genealogical Society
c/o Astoria Public Library
450 10th Street
Astoria, OR 97103

Columbia Gorge Genealogical Society
c/o The Dalles/Wasco County Public Library
722 Court Street
The Dalles, OR 97058
Tel: 541-296-2815
Fax: 541-296-4179

Coos Bay Genealogical Forum/Library
P.O. Box 1067
North Bend, OR 97459

Cottage Grove Genealogical Society/Library
Cottage Grove Community Building
207 H Street
P.O. Box 388
Cottage Grove, OR 97424
Tel: 541-942-4088
541-942-2936

Crook County Genealogical Society
c/o A.R. Bowman Memorial Museum
246 North Main Street
Prineville, OR 97754-1852
Tel: 541-447-3715 (Museum)

Daughters of the American Revolution
Oregon State Society
URL: http://www.teleport.com/~dareth/DAR/

Deschutes County Historical & Genealogical Society
P.O. Box 5252
Bend, OR 97708

Douglas County, Genealogical Society of
P.O. Box 579
Roseburg, OR 97470

Genealogical Council of Oregon
P.O. Box 15169
Portland, OR 97215

Genealogical Forum of Oregon/Library
2130 SW Fifth Avenue, Suite 220
Portland, OR 97201-4934
Tel: 503-227-2398
URL: http://www.rootsweb.com/~genepool/forum.htm

Genealogical Heritage Council of Oregon
P.O. Box 628
Ashland, OR 97520-0021

Grant County Genealogical Society
c/o Grant County Museum
101 South Canyon Boulevard
Canyon City, OR 97820
Tel: 541-575-0362 (Museum)

Grants Pass Genealogical Society
P.O. Box 1834
Grants Pass, OR 97526

Juniper Branch of the Family Finders
P.O. Box 652
Madras, OR 97741

Klamath Basin Genealogical Society
c/o Klamath Falls Public Library
126 S. 3rd Street
Klamath Falls, OR 97601
Tel: 541-882-8894 (library)

LaPine Genealogy Society
P.O. Box 1081
LaPine, OR 97739

Lebanon Genealogical Society
c/o Lebanon Public Library
626 2nd Street
Lebanon, OR 97355
Tel: 541-451-7461 (Library)

Linn Genealogical Society
P.O. Box 1222
Albany, OR 97321

Mid-Valley Genealogical Society
P.O. Box 1511
Corvallis, OR 97339

Milton-Freewater Genealogucal Club
c/o Carmen Buff
127 SE 6th Street
Milton-Freewater, OR 97862

Mount Hood Genealogical Forum
950 South End Road
P.O. Box 744
Oregon City, OR 97045

Oregon Genealogical Society
Oregon Research Room
223 N. A Street, Suite F
Springfield, OR
Mail:
P.O. Box 10306
Eugene, OR 97440-2306
Tel: 541-746-7924
URL: http://www.rootsweb.com/~genepool/ogs.htm

Polk County Genealogical Society
Katherine Johnson
535 SE Ash Street
Dallas, OR 97338

Rogue Valley Genealogical Society/Library
133 South Central Avenue
Medford, OR 97501-7221
Tel: 541-770-5848
URL: http://www.grrtech.com/rvgs/

Scandinavian Genealogical Society of Oregon
1123 7th Street, NW
Salem, OR 97304

Siuslaw Genealogical Society
P.O. Box 1540
Florence, OR 97439

Sons and Daughters of Oregon Pioneers
P.O. Box 6685
Portland, OR 97228

Sweet Home Genealogical Society
c/o Sweet Home Library
13th & Kalmia Streets
Sweet Home, OR 97386
Tel: 503-367-5007

Tillamook County Historical Society/Genealogy Study Group
P.O. Box 123
Tillamook, OR 97141

Willamette Valley Genealogical Society
P.O. Box 2083
Salem, OR 97308
URL: http://webfoot.osl.state.or.us/oslhome/wvgs.html

Yamhill County Genealogical Society
P.O. Box 568
McMinnville, OR 97128

Yaquina Genealogical Society
c/o Toledo Public Library
173 NW Seventh Street
Toledo, OR 97391

HISTORICAL SOCIETIES

Aurora Colony Historical Society
Old Aurora Colony Museum
P.O. Box 202
Aurora, OR 97002
Tel: 503-678-5754

Bandon Historical Society/Museum
West First Street
P.O. Box 737
Bandon, OR 97411
Tel: 514-347-2164

Benton County Historical Society/Museum & Library
1101 Main Street
P.O. Box 35
Philomath, OR 97370
Tel: 541-929-6230
Email: bchm@peak.org
URL: http://www.peak.org/~lewisb/Museum.html

Boston Mill Society
222 First Avenue, W.
Albany, OR 97321
Tel: 541-928-5008
URL: http://www.rootsweb.com/~genepool/boston.htm

Clatsop County Historical Society
Clatsop County Heritage Museum
1618 Exchange Street
Astoria, OR 97103-3615
Tel: 503-325-2203

Big Butte Historical Society
432 Pine Street
Butte Falls, OR 97522
Tel: 541-865-3332

Brooks Historical Society
3995 Brooklake Road, NE
Salem, OR 97303-9728
Tel: 503-390-0690

Cannon Beach Historical Society
1387 S. Spruce
Cannon Beach, OR 97110
Tel: 503-436-9301

Chetco Valley Historical Society/Museum
15461 Museum Road
Brookings, OR 97415-9519
Tel: 541-469-6651

Clatsop County Historical Society
Clatsop County Heritage Museum
1618 Exchange Street
Astoria, OR 97103-3615
Tel: 503-325-2203

Coos County Historical Society/Museum
1220 Sherman Avenue
North Bend, OR 97459-3666
Tel: 541-756-6320

Crook County Historical Society
A.R. Bowman Memorial Museum
246 North Main Street
Prineville, OR 97754
Tel: 541-447-3715

Curry County Historical Society/Museum
920 S. Ellensburg Avenue
Gold Beach, OR 97444-9705
Tel: 541-247-6113

Deschutes County Historical & Genealogical Society
129 NW Idaho Avenue
P.O. Box 5252
Bend, OR 97708
Tel: 541-389-1813

Gilliam County Historical Society
Highway 19 at Burns Park
Condon, OR 97823
Tel: 541-384-4233

Gold Hill Historical Society
504 1st Street
Gold Hill, OR 97525-9609
Tel: 541-855-1182

Gresham Historical Society
P.O. Box 65
Gresham, OR 97030
Tel: 503-661-0347

Harney County Historical Society/Museum
18 West D Street
P.O. Box 388
Burns, OR 97720-1226
Tel: 541-573-5618
541-573-2636

Josephine County Historical Society
508 SW 5th Street
Grants Pass, OR 97526
Tel: 541-479-7827

Junction City Historical Society
Lee House
655 Holly Street
Junction City, OR 97448
Tel: 541-998-3657

Lake County Historical Society
35 South G Street
Lakeview, OR 97630

Lincoln County Historical Society/Library
545 SW 9th Street
Newport, OR 97365-4726
Tel: 541-265-7509
URL: http://www.newportnet.com/newport/library/LCHS.htm

Manon County Historical Society
260 12th Street, SE
Salem, OR 97301
Tel: 503-364-2128

Marion County Historical Society/Museum
260 12th Street, SE
Salem, OR 97301-4101
Tel: 503-364-2128

North Santiam Historical Society
143 Wall, NE
Mill City, OR 97360
Tel: 503-897-4088

Oregon-California Trails Association
P.O. Box 1019
Independence, MO 64051-0519
Tel: 816-252-2276
Fax: 816-836-0919
Email: jansen@plains.uwyo.edu
URL: http://bobcat.etsu.edu/octa/octahome.htm

Oregon Electric Railway Historical Society
P.O. Box 702
Forest Grove, OR 97116
Email: reyn@reed.edu
URL: http://www.reed.edu/~reyn/oerhs.html

Oregon Historic Cemeteries Association
P.O Box 802
Boring, OR 97009
Tel: 503-658-4522

Oregon Historical Society
1200 SW Park Avenue
Portland, OR 97205-2483
Tel: 503-222-1741
503-306-5280 (Education & Outreach)
Fax: 503-221-2035
Email: orhist@ohs.org
URL: http://www.ohs.org/

Polk County Historical Society
Brunk House
751 SE Miller
Dallas, OR 97338
Tel: 503-623-2669
503-371-3831

Santiam Historical Society
260 N. 2nd Avenue
Stayton, OR 97383-1710
Tel: 503-769-1406

Seaside Museum & Historical Society
570 Necanicum Drive
P.O. Box 1024
Seaside, OR 97138-6040
Tel: 503-738-7065

Sherman County Historical Society/Museum
P.O. Box 173
Moro, OR 97039
Tel: 541-565-3232

South Umpqua Historical Society/Museum
421 W. Fifth
Canyonville, OR 97417
Tel: 541-839-4845

Southern Oregon Historical Society/Library
106 N. Central Avenue
Medford, OR 97501
Tel: 541-773-6536 ext. 238

Umatilla County Historical Society
108 SW Frazer
P.O. Box 253
Pendleton, OR 97801
Tel: 541-276-0012
URL: http://www.tricity.wsu.edu/~pkeller/tc/museums/Umatilla.html

Wasco County Historical Society
300 West 13th Street
The Dalles, OR 97058-2010
Tel: 541-296-1867

Washington County Historical Society/Museum
PCC, Rock Creek Campus
17677 NW Springville Road
Portland, OR 97229-1743
Tel: 503-645-5353

LDS Family History Centers

Astoria Family History Center
Third and Niagara
Astoria, OR 97103
Tel: 503-325-3929

Baker City Family History Center
2625 Hughes Lane
Baker City, OR 97814
Tel: 503-523-4901

Beaverton Family History Center
4195 SW 99th Street
Beaverton, OR 97005
Tel: 503-644-7782

Bend Family History Center
1260 NE Thompson Drive
Bend, OR 97701
Tel: 503-382-9947

Brookings Family History Center
770 Elk Drive
Brookings, OR 97415
Tel: 503-469-4079

Central Point Family History Center
2305 Taylor Road
Central Point, OR 97502
Tel: 503-664-5356

Corvallis Family History Center
4141 NW Harrison
Corvallis, OR 97330
Tel: 503-758-1156

Eugene Family History Center
3550 West 11th Avenue
Eugene, OR 97402
Tel: 503-343-3741

Grants Pass Family History Center
1969 Williams Highway
Grants Pass, OR 97527
Tel: 541-476-1926

Gresham Family History Center
3600 SE 182nd Avenue
Gresham, OR 97030
Tel: 503-665-1524

Hermiston Family History Center
850 SW Eleventh
Hermiston, OR 97838
Tel: 541-567-3445

Hillsboro Family History Center
2200 NE Jackson School Road
Hillsboro, OR 97124
Tel: 503-640-6458

John Day Family History Center
East Highway
John Day, OR 97845
Tel: 503-575-1817

Klamath Falls Family History Center
6630 Alva Avenue
Klamath Falls, OR 97603
Tel: 541-884-7998

La Grande Family History Center
2504 North Fir
La Grande, OR 97850
Tel: 503-963-5003

Lake Oswego Family History Center
1271 Overlook Drive
Lake Oswego, OR 97034
Tel: 503-638-1410

Lebanon Family History Center
1955 5th Street
Lebanon, OR 97355
Tel: 503-451-3992

McMinnville Family History Center
1645 NW Baker Creek Road
McMinnville, OR 97128
Tel: 503-434-5681

Medford Family History Center
2900 Juanipero Way
Medford, OR 97504
Tel: 503-773-3363

Milwaukie Family History Center
7880 SE Milwaukie Avenue
Portland, OR 97202
Tel: 503-238-1671

Newport Family History Center
2229 NE Crestview Drive
Newport, OR 97365
Tel: 541-265-7333
URL: http://www.newportnet.com/newport/library/FamHist.htm

North Bend Family History Center
3355 Virginia Avenue
North Bend, OR 97459
Tel: 503-756-3575

Nyssa Family History Center
1309 Park Avenue
Nyssa, OR 97913
Tel: 503-372-5255

Ontario Family History Center
1705 NW 4th Avenue
Ontario, OR 97914
Tel: 503-889-7835

Oregon City Family History Center
14340 South Donovan Road
Oregon City, OR 97045
Tel: 503-655-9908 ext. 5

Portland Family History Center
1975 SE 30th Avenue
Portland, OR 97214
Tel: 503-235-9090

Portland Family History Center
2215 NE 106th Street
Portland, OR 97220
Tel: 503-252-1081

Prineville Family History Center
333 South Idlewood Street
Prineville, OR 97754
Tel: 503-447-1488

Rainier Family History Center
Parkdale Road
Rainier, OR 97048
Tel: 503-556-9694

Roseburg Family History Center
1864 NW Calkins Road
Roseburg, OR 97470
Tel: 541-672-1237

Salem Family History Center
4550 Lone Oak, SE
Salem, OR 97302
Tel: 503-363-0374

Salem Family History Center
862 45th, NE
Salem, OR 97301
Tel: 503-371-0453

Salem Family History Center
1375 Lockhaven Drive, NE
Salem, OR 97303
Tel: 503-390-2095

Sandy Family History Center
16317 SE Bluff Road
Sandy, OR 97055
Tel: 503-668-4811 ext. 17

Scio Family History Center
1955 Fifth Street
Scio, OR 97374
Tel: 503-451-3992

Seaside Family History Center
1403 Wahanna Road
Seaside, OR 97138
Tel: 503-738-7543

St. Helens Family History Center
2735 Sykes Road
St. Helens, OR 97051
Tel: 503-397-1300

The Dalles Family History Center
1815 East 15th Street
The Dalles, OR 97058
Tel: 503-298-5815

Tualatin Family History Center
22284 SW Grahams Ferry Road
Tualatin, OR 97062
Tel: 503-692-0481

ARCHIVES/LIBRARIES/MUSEUMS

Albany Public Library/Main Branch
1390 Waverly Drive, SE
Albany, OR 97321
Tel: 541-967-4307
Fax: 541-967-4345

Astoria Public Library
450 10th Street
Astoria, OR 97103
Tel: 503-325-READ
Fax: 503-325-2017

Baker County Public Library
2400 Resort Street
Baker City, OR 97814
Tel: 541-523-6419
Fax: 541-523-9088

Benton County Historical Society/Museum & Library
1101 Main
P.O. Box 35
Philomath, OR 97370
Tel: 541-929-6230
Email: bchm@peak.org
URL: http://www.peak.org/~lewisb/Museum.html

Benton County History Center
110 NW 3rd Street
Corvallis, OR 97330-4701
Email: bchm@peak.org
URL: http://www.peak.org/lewisb/histcent.htm

Clackamas County Family History Society/Library
211 Tumwater Drive
P.O. Box 995
Oregon City, OR 97045-2900
Tel: 503-655-5574
URL: http://www.rootsweb.com/~genepool/ccfhs.htm

Clatsop County Historical Society
Clatsop County Heritage Museum
1618 Exchange Street
Astoria, OR 97103-3615
Tel: 503-325-2203

Columbia River Maritime Museum Library
1792 Marine Drive
Astoria, OR 97103-3525
Tel: 503-325-2323

Coos Bay Genealogical Forum/Library
P.O. Box 1067
North Bend, OR 97459

Coos Bay Public Library
Oregon Archives
525 W. Anderson
Coos Bay, OR 97420
Tel: 541-269-1101
Email: cblib@mail.coos.or.us
URL: http://mail.coos.or.us/~cblib/

Crook County Historical Society
A.R. Bowman Memorial Museum
246 North Main Street
Prineville, OR 97754
Tel: 541-447-3715

Dallas Public Library
Oregon Collection
950 Main Street
Dallas, OR 97338
Tel: 503-623-2633
URL: http://www.ccrls.org/dallas/

Douglas County Library System
County Courthouse
Roseburg, OR 97470
Tel: 541-440-4308
Fax: 541-440-4315

Douglas County Museum of History and Natural History
123 Museum Drive
P.O. Box 1550
Roseburg, OR 97470

Tel: 541-957-7007
541-440-4507
Fax: 541-440-6023
Email: museum@rosenet.net

Eastern Oregon Museum
P.O. Box 6
Haines, OR 97833
Tel: 541-856-3568

Eastern Oregon State University
Walter M. Pierce Library
1410 L Avenue
La Grande, OR 97850
Tel: 541-962-3579
541-962-3605 (Reference)
Fax: 541-962-3335
URL: http://lib.www.eosc.osshe.edu/

Elgin Public Library
P.O. Box 67
Elgin, OR 97827
Tel: 541-437-5931

Grant County Museum
101 South Canyon Boulevard
Canyon City, OR 97820
Tel: 541-575-0362

Hermiston Public Library/Archives
235 E. Gladys Avenue
Hermiston, OR 97838
Tel: 541-567-2882
541-567-3551

Hillsboro Public Library
775 SE 10th Avenue
Hillsboro, OR 97123
Tel: 503-681-6115
Fax: 503-681-6112

Hudson's Bay Company Archives
Provincial Archives of Manitoba
200 Vaughan Street
Winnipeg, Manitoba R3C 1T5
Tel: 204-945-4949
Fax: 204-948-3236
Email: hbca@chc.gov.mb.ca
URL: http://www.gov.mb.ca/chc/archives/hbca/index.html

Hutson Museum
4967 Baseline Drive
Mount Hood Parkdale, OR 97041-9727
Tel: 541-352-6808

Independence Public Library
Local History
311 S. Monmouth Street
Independence, OR 97351
Tel: 503-838-1811
Fax: 503-838-4486
URL: http://www.ccrls.org/independence/

Jackson County Public Library/Main Branch
413 W. Main Street
Medford, OR 97501
Tel: 541-746-7287
TTY: 541-776-7281

Josephine County Library System/Main Branch
200 NW C STreet
Grants Pass, OR 97526
Tel: 541-474-5482

Klamath Falls Public Library
126 S. 3rd Street
Klamath Falls, OR 97601
Tel: 541-882-8894

Lake Oswego Public Library
706 4th Street
Lake Oswego, OR 97034
Tel: 503-636-7628
URL: http://www.ci.oswego.or.us/library/library.htm

Lebanon Public Library
626 2nd Street
Lebanon, OR 97355
Tel: 541-451-7461

Lewis & Clark College
Aubrey R. Watzek Library
615 SW Palatine Hill Road
Portland, OR 97219
Tel: 503-768-7270
Email: refdesk@lclark.edu
URL: http://www.lclark.edu/~refdesk/

Lincoln County Historical Society/Library
545 SW 9th Street
Newport, OR 97365-4726
Tel: 541-265-7509
URL: http://www.newportnet.com/newport/library/
LCHS.htm

McMinnville Public Library
225 N. Adams
McMinnville, OR 97128
Tel: 503-434-7308

Monmouth Public Library
238 E. Jackson Street
Monmouth, OR 97361
Tel: 503-838-1932

Morrow County Museum
Genealogical Research Center
444 N. Main
Heppner, OR 97836
Tel: 541-676-5524
URL: http://ourworld.compuserve.com/homepages/
MCMuseum/genealog.htm

Multnomah County Library/Central Branch
John Wilson Room
801 SW 10th
Portland, OR 97205
Tel: 503-248-5123
URL: http://www.multnomah.lib.or.us/lib/

North Bend Public Library
1800 Sherman Avenue
North Bend, OR 97459
Tel: 541-756-0400
Fax: 541-756-1073

Oregon City Public Library
606 John Adams Street
Oregon City, OR 97045
Tel: 503-657-8269

Oregon Genealogical Society/Library
Oregon Research Room
223 N. A Street, Suite F
Springfield, OR
Mail:
P.O. Box 10306
Eugene, OR 97440-2306
Tel: 541-746-7924
URL: http://www.rootsweb.com/~genepool/ogs.htm

Oregon Historical Society
1200 SW Park Avenue
Portland, OR 97205-2483
Tel: 503-222-1741
503-306-5280 (Education & Outreach)
Fax: 503-221-2035
Email: orhist@ohs.org
URL: http://www.ohs.org/

Oregon State Library
State Library Building
250 Winter Street, NE
Salem, OR 97310-0641
Tel: 503-378-4243
Fax: 503-588-7119
TTY/TDD: 503-378-4276
Email: websters@sparkie.osl.state.or.us
URL: http://webfoot.osl.state.or.us/oslhome.html
http://webfoot.osl.state.or.us/oslhome/gen.html
(Genealogy)

Oregon State University
Valley Library
Corvallis, OR 97331-4501
Tel: 541-737-2971 (Map Room)
541-737-2075 (Special Collections)
URL: http://www.orst.edu/dept/library/

Polk County Museum
187 SW Court Street
Dallas, OR 97338-3112
Tel: 503-623-6251
503-623-2287

Rogue Valley Genealogical Society/Library
133 South Central Avenue
Medford, OR 97501-7221
Tel: 541-770-5848
URL: http://www.grrtech.com/rvgs/

Schmidt House Museum
508 SW 5th Street
Grants Pass, OR 97526-2804
Tel: 541-479-7827

Schminck Memorial Memorial
128 S. East Street
Lakeview, OR 97630-1721
Tel: 541-947-3134

Sherman County Historical Society/Museum
P.O. Box 173
Moro, OR 97039
Tel: 541-565-3232

Silverton Public Library
410 South Water Street
Silverton, OR 97381
Tel: 503-873-5770
Fax: 503-873-7452

Southern Oregon Historical Society/Library
106 N. Central Avenue
Medford, OR 97501
Tel: 541-773-6536 ext. 238
Fax: 541-776-7994

Southern Oregon State College Library
1250 Siskiyou Blvd.
Ashland, OR 97520-5076
Tel: 541-552-6839
Fax: 541-552-6429

The Dalles/Wasco County Library
City Hall
313 Court Street
The Dalles, OR 97058
Tel: 541-296-2815
Fax: 541-296-4179

Tigard Public Library
13125 SW Hall Blvd.
Tigard, OR 97223
Tel: 503-684-6537
Fax: 503-598-7515
Email: lauterva@tpl.wccls.lib.or.us
URL: http://www.ci.tigard.or.us/tplmain.htm

Tillamook County Library
210 Ivy Street
Tillamook, OR 97141
Tel: 503-842-4792
Fax: 503-842-1120

University of Oregon
Knight Library
Eugene, OR 97403-1299
Tel: 503-346-1818 (Reference)
503-346-3465 (Maps)
503-346-3054 (Hours)
Email: libref@oregon.uoregon.edu
URL: http://libweb.uoregon.edu/

Washington County Historical Society
Washington County Museum
17677 NW Springville Road
Portland, OR 97229
Tel: 503-645-5353

Western Oregon State College Library
345 N. Monmouth Avenue
Monmouth, OR 97361
Tel: 503-838-8890
Fax: 503-838-8474

Newspaper Repositories

Oregon Historical Society
1200 SW Park Avenue
Portland, OR 97205-2483
Tel: 503-222-1741
503-306-5280 (Education & Outreach)
Fax: 503-221-2035
Email: orhist@ohs.org
URL: http://www.ohs.org/

University of Oregon
Knight Library
Eugene, OR 97403-1299
Tel: 503-346-1896
Email: mrwatson@oregon.uoregon.edu
URL: http://libweb.uoregon.edu/preservn/usnp/usnp.html

Vital Records

Oregon State Archives
800 Summer Street, NE
Salem, OR 97310
Tel: 503-373-0701
Fax: 503-373-0953
Email: reference.archives@state.or.us
(Reference requests welcome)
URL: http://arcweb.sos.state.or.us/

Oregon State Registrar
Oregon Center for Health Statistics, Suite 205
State Office Building
800 NE Oregon Street
Portland, OR 97232
Tel: 503-731-4108

Oregon on the Web

Census of Overland Emigrant Documents (COED)
http://bobcat.etsu.edu/octa/coed.htm

Gene Pool, by Joanne Todd Rabun
http://www.rootsweb.com/~genepool/

Oregon GenWeb Project
http://www.rootsweb.com/~orgenweb/

Oregon Pioneers, by Mike Ransom
http://www.peak.org/~mransom/pioneers.html

Oregon State Archives—Genealogical Name Database Search
http://arcweb.sos.state.or.us/databases/searchgeneal.html

Oregon Trail
http://www.isu.edu/~trinmich/Oregontrail.html

Records of Interest to Genealogists at the Oregon State Archives
http://arcweb.sos.state.or.us/geneal.html

PENNSYLVANIA

ARCHIVES, STATE & NATIONAL

National Archives—Mid Atlantic Region
Ninth and Market Streets
Philadelphia, PA 19107-4292
Tel: 215-597-3000
Fax: 215-597-2303
Email: archives@philarch.nara.gov
URL: http://www.nara.gov/nara/regional/03nsgil.html

Pennsylvania State Archives
Third and Forster Streets
P.O. Box 1026
Harrisburg, PA 17108-1026
Tel: 717-783-3821
URL: http://www.state.pa.us/PA-Exec/Historical_Museum/DAM/genie1.htm

GENEALOGICAL SOCIETIES

African-American Genealogy Group (AAGG)
P.O. Box 1798
Philadelphia, PA 19105-1798
Tel: 215-572-6063
Fax: 215-885-7244
URL: http://www.libertynet.org/~gencap/aagg.html

Allegheny Regional Family History Society (ARFHS)
P.O. Box 1804
Elkins, WV 26241
Tel: 304-636-1958
304-636-1959
URL: http://www.swcp.com/~dhickman/arfhs.html

Armstrong County Historical Museum & Genealogical Society
300 North McKean Street
Kittanning, PA 16201-1345
Tel: 412-548-5707

Beaver County Genealogical Society
c/o Carnegie Free Library
Beaver County Research Center
1301 Seventh Avenue
Beaver Falls, PA 15010
Tel: 412-846-4340
Fax: 412-846-0370

Berks County Genealogical Society
15197 Kutztown Road
P.O. Box 305
Kutztown, PA 19530-0305
Tel: 610-683-9420
Email: berksgensoc@geocities.com (General inquiries)
bcgs@juno.com (Library)
URL: http://www.geocities.com/Heartland/Hills/7727/

Blair County Genealogical Society
P.O. Box 855
Altoona, PA 16603
Tel: 814-942-3681

Bradford County Genealogical Society
21 Main Street
Towanda, PA 18848

Bucks County Genealogical Society
P.O. Box 1092
Doylestown, PA 18901
Tel: 215-230-9410 ext. 41
URL: http://libertynet.org/~gencap/bcgs.html

Cameron County Genealogical Society
102 West 4th Street
Emporium, PA 15834
Tel: 814-486-2162

Capital Area Genealogical Society
P.O. Box 4502
Harrisburg, PA 17111-4502
Tel: 717-543-2622

Carpatho/Rusyn Society
125 Westland Drive
Pittsburgh, PA 15217
Email: ggressa@carpatho-rusyn.org
URL: http://www.carpatho-rusyn.org/

Central Pennsylvania Genealogical Pioneers
Priestly-Forsythe Library
100 King Street
Northumberland, PA 17857

Central Susquehanna Valley Genealogical Society
c/o Columbia County Historical Society
P.O. Box 197
Orangeville, PA 17859

Centre County Genealogical Society
P.O. Box 1135
State College, PA 16804-1135

Cornerstone Genealogical Society
519 4th Anenue
P.O. Box 547
Waynesburg, PA 15370
Tel: 412-627-5653
412-627-5896
URL: http://www.vicoa.com/cornerstone/

Crawford County Genealogical Society
848 North Main Street
Meadville, PA 16335
Tel: 814-724-6080

Descendants of the Signers of the Constitution, Society of
325 Chestnut Street
Philadelphia, PA 19106

Elk County Genealogical Society
P.O. Box 142
Johnsonburg, PA 15845

Erie Society for Genealogical Research
P.O. Box 1403
Erie, PA 16512-1403
Tel: 814-454-1813

Fayette County Genealogical Society
24 Jefferson Street
Uniontown, PA 15401-3699

Genealogical Computing Association of Pennsylvania (GENCAP)
c/o M.A. Miller, Treas.
51 Hillcrest Road
Barto, PA 19504
BBS: 215-438-2858
Email: gencap@libertynet.org
URL: http://libertynet.org/~gencap/index.html

Indiana County, Historical & Genealogical Society of
200 South 6th Street
Indiana, PA 15701
Tel: 412-463-9600

Jefferson County Historical & Genealogical Society
232 Jefferson Street
P.O. Box 51
Brookville, PA 15825
Tel: 814-849-0077
814-849-7833

Jewish Genealogical Society of Philadelphia
c/o Leonard Markowitz
1279 June Road
Huntingdon Valley, PA 19006-8405
Email: priluki@voicenet.com
URL: http://www.jewishgen.org/jgsp/

Jewish Genealogical Society of Pittsburgh
c/o Julian Falk
2131 Fifth Avenue
Pittsburgh, PA 15219
Tel: 412-471-0772

Lycoming County Genealogical Society
P.O. Box 3625
Williamsport, PA 17701-3625
Tel: 717-326-3326
Email: LCGSgen@aol.com
URL: http://members.aol.com/LCGSgen/lcgs.htm

McKean County Genealogical Society
P.O. Box 207A
Derrick City, PA 16727

Mercer County Genealogical Society
P.O. Box 812
Sharon, PA 16146-0812
Tel: 412-346-5117

Montgomery Area Genealogical Society
c/o Montgomery Public Library
1 South Main Street
Montgomery, PA 17751
Tel: 717-547-6212

Montgomery County, Historical Society of
Library and Genealogy Study Group
1654 DeKalb Street
Norristown, PA 19401
Tel: 610-272-0297
URL: http://libertynet.org/~gencap/montcopa.html

North Hills Genealogists
c/o Northland Public Library
300 Cumberland Road
Pittsburgh, PA 15237-5410
Tel: 412-366-8100
412-931-5406

Northampton County Historical & Genealogical Society
101 South 4th Street
Easton, PA 18042
Tel: 610-253-1222

Northeast Pennsylvania Genealogical Society
P.O. Box 1776
Shavertown, PA 18708-0776
URL: http://home.ptd.net/~tamlamb/gene.htm

Northeastern Pennsylvania, Genealogical Research Society of
P.O. Box 1
Olyphant, PA 18447-0001
Tel: 717-383-7661
Fax: 717-383-7466
Email: genealogy@usnetway.com (General Information)
searcher@microserve.net (Research Requests)
URL: http://www.clark.net/pub/mjloyd/grsnp/grsnp.html

Old York Road Genealogical Society
1030 Old York Road
Abington, PA 19001
Tel: 215-887-7683

Palatines to America/Pennsylvania Chapter
P.O. Box 280
Strasburg, PA 17579
URL: http://genealogy.org/~palam/

Pennsylvania, Genealogical Society of
1305 Locust Street
Philadelphia, PA 19107
Tel: 215-545-0391
URL: http://libertynet.org/~gencap/gsp.html

Pennsylvania Society of Mayflower Descendants
1201 Knox Road
Wynnewood, PA 19096

Perry Historians/Genealogical Society
P.O. Box 73
Newport, PA 17074
Tel: 717-566-0990

Punxsutawney Area Historical & Genealogical Society
Bennis House Museum
401 West Mahoning Street
P.O. Box 286
Punxsutawney, PA 15767
Tel: 814-938-2555
814-938-7221
Email: mweimer@penn.com
URL: http://users.penn.com/~mweimer/historcl.html

Slovenian Genealogy Society
c/o Al Peterlin, Pres.
52 Old Farm Road
Harrisburg, PA 17011-2604
Tel: 717-731-8804
URL: http://feefhs.org/slovenia/frg-sgsi.html

Somerset County, Historical & Genealogical Society of
RD 2, Box 238
Somerset, PA 15501-9802
Tel: 814-445-6077

South Central Pennsylvania Genealogical Society
P.O. Box 1824
York, PA 17405
Tel: 717-843-6169

Southwestern Pennsylvania, Genealogical Society of
P.O. Box 894
Washington, PA 153010

Swedish Colonial Society
c/o Wallace Richter, Registrar
336 South Devon Avenue
Wayne, PA 19087
Tel: 610-688-1766
URL: http://libertynet.org/~gencap/scs.html

Tarentum Genealogical Society
c/o Community Library of Allegheny Valley
315 East 6th Avenue
Tarentum, PA 15084
Tel: 412-226-0770

Troy Genealogical Associates
10 Cherry Street
Brookville, PA 15825

Venango County Genealogical Club
P.O. Box 811
Oil City, PA 16301-0811
Tel: 814-678-3077

Warren County Genealogical Society
c/o Virginia Roberts
50 2nd Street
Youngsville, PA 16371
Tel: 814-563-9696

Welcome Society of Pennsylvania
316 S. Juniper Street
Philadelphia, PA 19107

Western Pennsylvania Genealogical Society
4400 Forbes Avenue
Pittsburgh, PA 15213-4080
Tel: 412-622-3114
URL: http://www.clpgh.org/CLP/Pennsylvania/oak_pennag.html

Windber-Johnstown Area Genealogical Society
1401 Graham Avenue
Windber, PA 15963
Tel: 814-467-4950

HISTORICAL SOCIETIES

Adams County Historical Society
111 N. West Confederate Avenue
P.O. Box 4325
Gettysburg, PA 17325
Tel: 717-334-4723

Afro American Historical & Cultural Museum
7th and Arch Streets
Philadelphia, PA 19106
Tel: 215-574-0380
URL: http://www.fieldtrip.com/pa/55740380.htm

Allegheny Foothills Historical Society
675 Old Frankstown Road
Export, PA 15632
Tel: 412-325-4933

Allegheny-Kiski Historical Society
224 E. 7th Avenue
Tarentum, PA 15084-1513
Tel: 412-224-7666

Apollo Area Historical Society
219 North Penn
Apollo, PA 15613
Tel: 412-478-4214

Armstrong County Historical Museum & Genealogical Society
300 North McKean Street
Kittanning, PA 16201-1345
Tel: 412-548-5707

Beaver County Historical Research & Landmarks Foundation
1216 L. Fourth Street
Beaver, PA 15009

Beaver Falls Historical Society/Museum
c/o Carnegie Public Library
Beaver County Research Center
1301 7th Avenue
Beaver Falls, PA 15010
Tel: 412-843-4340
Fax: 412-846-0370

Bedford County Historical Commission
231 S. Juliana Street
Bedford, PA 15522

Bedford County Pioneers Historical Society/Library
242 E. John Street
Bedford, PA 15522-1750
URL: http://www.rootsweb.com/~pabedfor/plibrary.html

Bell Township Historical Preservation Society
RR 2
Saltsburg, PA 15681-9802
Tel: 412-697-4092

Bellefonte Historical Railroad Society
Train Station
Bellefonte, PA 16823
Tel: 814-355-0311

Berks County, Historical Society of
Library and Museum
940 Centre Avenue
Reading, PA 19601
Tel: 610-375-4375
URL: http://www.berksweb.com/histsoc.html

Berlin Historical Society
400 Vine Street
Berlin, PA 15530-0011
Tel: 814-267-5987

Berwick Historical Society
5th & Market Streets
Berwick, PA 18603

Blair County Historical Society
Baker Mansion Museum
3500 Baker Blvd.
P.O. Box 1083
Altoona, PA 16602-1828
Tel: 814-942-3916

Blairsville Area, Historical Society of the
116 E. Campbell Street
Blairsville, PA 15717
Tel: 412-459-0580

Bloomingrove Historical Society
Dunkard Church Road
Cogan Station, PA 17728
Tel: 717-435-2997

Boyertown Area Historical Society
43 S. Chestnut Street
Boyertown, PA 19512-1508
Tel: 610-367-5255

Braddock Field Historical Society
419 Library Street
Pittsburgh, PA 15234
Tel: 412-351-5356

Bradford County Historical Society/Museum
21 Main Street
Towanda, PA 18848-1803
Tel: 717-265-2240
URL: http://www.rootsweb.com/~sgrp/bchsmain.htm

Bristol Cultural & Historical Foundation
321 Cedar Street
Bristol, PA 19007-5001
Tel: 215-781-9895

Broad Top Area Coal Miners Historical Society
Reality Theatre
Robertsdale, PA 16674
Tel: 814-635-3807

Brownsville Historical Society
P.O. Box 24
Brownsville, PA 15417

Bucks County Historical Society
Spruance Library/Mercer Museum
84 S. Pine Street
Doylestown, PA 18901-4999
Tel: 215-345-0210
Fax: 215-230-0823
Email: bchs@philadelphia.libertynet.org
URL: http://www.libertynet.org/~bchs/index.html

Butler County Historical Society
Butler County Heritage Center
119 W. New Castle Street
P.O. Box 414
Butler, PA 16003-0414
Tel: 412-283-8116
Fax: 412-283-2505
URL: http://www.butlercounty.com/local/historical/

California Area Historical Society
429 Wood Street
California, PA 15419-1139
Tel: 412-938-3250

Cambria County Historical Society
615 N. Center Street
Ebensburg, PA 15931
Tel: 814-472-6674

Cameron County Historical Society
139 E. Fourth Street
Emporium, PA 15834

Carbondale Historical Society
1 North Main Street, 3rd Floor
P.O. Box 151
Carbondale, PA 18407-2356
Tel: 717-282-0385
Email: silasrobert@juno.cm

Carnegie, Historical Society of
140 E. Main Street
Carnegie, PA 15106
Tel: 412-276-7447

Centre County Historical Society
1001 East College Avenue
State College, PA 16801
Tel: 814-234-4779

Chadds Ford Historical Society
Route 100
Chadds Ford, PA 19317
Tel: 610-388-7376
Email: gwf1@psu.edu
URL: http://www.de.psu.edu/cfhs/

Chester County Historical Society
225 North High Street
West Chester, PA 19380
Tel: 610-692-4800
Email: cchs@chesco.com
URL: http://www.chesco.com/~cchs/

Clarion County Historical Society
18 Grant Street
Clarion, PA 16214-1015
Tel: 814-226-4450

Clearfield County Historical Society
104 East Pine Street
Clearfield, PA 16830-2517
Tel: 814-765-6125

Clinton County Historical Society
362 East Water Street
Lock Haven, PA 17745
Tel: 717-748-7254

Cocalico Valley, Historical Society of
249 West Main Street
Ephrata, PA 17522
Tel: 717-733-1616

Cochranton Heritage Society
P.O. Box 598
Cochranton, PA 16314

Columbia County Historical Society
410 Main Street
P.O. Box 197
Orangeville, PA 17859
Tel: 717-683-6011

Conemaugh Township Historical Society
100 South Main Street
Davidsville, PA 15928
URL: http://www.ctcnet.net/ConemaughTwp/history.htm

Conneaut Valley Area Historical Sociey (CVAHS)
P.O. Box 266
Conneautville, PA 16406
Email: bkovac@toolcity.net
URL: http://www.granniesworld.com/cvahs/

Connellsville Area Historical Society
410 East Cedar Avenue
Connellsville, PA 15425
Tel: 412-628-5640

Corry Area Historical Society
945 Mead Avenue
Corry, PA 16407
Tel: 814-664-4749

Crawford County Historical Society
848 North Main Street
Meadville, PA 16335-2673
Tel: 814-724-6080

Croatian Fraternal Union of America
100 Delaney Street
Pittsburgh, PA 15235
Tel: 412-351-3909

Cumberland County Historical Society
Hamilton Library
21 North Pitt Street
Carlisle, PA 17013
Tel: 717-249-7610
URL: http://www1.trib.com/CUMBERLINK/cumb/hist.groups.html

Dauphin County, Historical Society of
219 South Front Street
Harrisburg, PA 17104
Tel: 717-233-3462

Delaware County Historical Society
Delaware County Community College (Temporary Hdqtrs.)
Malin Road Center, Room 208
85 North Malin Road
Broomall, PA 19008-1928
Tel: 610-359-1148
URL: http://libertynet.org/~gencap/delcopa.html

Derry Area Historical Society
P.O. Box 176
Loyalhanna, PA 15661
Tel: 412-694-8243
412-537-2165
Email: cheetles@westol.com
pjsbears@westol.com
URL: http://www.westol.com/~cheetles/The_Derry_Area_Historical_SocietyThe-Derry-Area-Historical-Society.html

Derry Township Historical Society
East Granada Avenue
Hershey, PA 17033
Tel: 717-520-0748

DuBois Area Historical Society
30 West Long Avenue
P.O. Box 401
DuBois, PA 15801-0401
Tel: 814-371-9006

Elizabeth Township Historical Society
5811 Smithfield Street
Boston, PA 15135-1136
Tel: 412-754-2030

Elk County Historical Society
109 Center Street
Ridgway, PA 15853
Tel: 814-776-1032

Erie County Historical Society
419 State Street
Erie, PA 16501-1106
Tel: 814-454-1813

Evangelical & Reformed Church, Historical Society of Archives
West James Street and College Avenue
Lancaster, PA 17604
Tel: 717-393-0654

Evans City Historical Society
220 Wahl Avenue
Evans City, PA 16033
Tel: 412-538-3629

Fairview Area Historical Society
4302 Garwood Street
Fairview, PA 16415
Tel: 814-474-5855

Fayette County Historical Society
Route 40W
Uniontown, PA 15401
Tel: 412-439-4422

Forest County Historical Society
Court House
Tionesta, PA 16353

Fort Loudon Historical Society
1720 Brooklyn Road
Fort Loudon, PA 17224
Tel: 717-369-3473

Fort Manson Historical Society
548 N. Main Street
Masontown, PA 15461
Tel: 412-583-9944

Fort Washintton, Historical Society of
473 Bethlehem Pike
Fort Washington, PA 19034
Tel: 215-646-6065

Frankford, Historical Society of
1507 Orthodox Street
Philadelphia, PA 19124
Tel: 215-743-6030
URL: http://libertynet.org/~gencap/frankford.html

Fulton County Historical Society
P.O. Box 115
McConnellsburg, PA 17233

German Society of Pennsylvania
611 Spring Garden Street
Philadelphia, PA 19123
Tel: 215-627-2332
215-627-4365 (Library)
Fax: 215-627-5297
URL: http://libertynet.org/~gencap/germanpa.html

Germantown Historical Society
5501 Germantown Avenue (Market Square)
Philadelphia, PA 19144-2291
Tel: 215-844-0514 (Museum)
215-844-8428 (Library/Archives)
URL: http://libertynet.org/~gencap/germantown.html

Goschenhoppen Historians
Redmen's Hall
Route 29
Green Lane, PA 18054
Tel: 215-234-8953

Governor Wolf Historical Society
6600 Jacksonville Road
Bath, PA 18014
Tel: 610-837-9015

Green Tree, Historical Society of
10 West Manilla Avenue
Pittsburgh, PA 15220
Tel: 412-921-9292

Greene County Historical Society/Library & Museum
RR 2
P.O. Box 127
Waynesburg, PA 15370
Tel: 412-627-3204
URL: http://www.greenepa.net/~museum/

Greenville Historical Society
94 College Avenue
Greenville, PA 16125
Tel: 412-588-7150

Hanover Area Historical Society
113 W. Chestnut Street
Hanover, PA 17331
Tel: 717-632-3207
Fax: 717-632-5199

Hazleton Historical Society
55 N. Wyoming Street
Hazleton, PA 18201
Tel: 717-455-8576

Hellertown Historical Society
150 W. Walnut Street
Hellertown, PA 18055
Tel: 610-838-1770

Heritage Society of Pennsylvania
P.O. Box 146
Laughlintown, PA 15655

Highlands Historical Society
7001 Sheaff Lane
Fort Washington, PA 19034
Tel: 215-641-2687

Historic Catasauqua Preservation Association
P.O. Box 186
Catasauqua, PA 18032
Tel: 610-266-2948
URL: http://www.ncpa.org/

Historic Schaefferstown
P.O. Box 1776
Schaefferstown, PA 17088
Tel: 717-949-2244

Homestead Historical Society
1110 Silvan Avenue
Homestead, PA 15120

Huguenot Society of Pennsylvania
1313 Spruce Street
Philadelphia, PA 19107

Hummelstown Area Historical Society
P.O. Box 252
Hummelstown, PA 17036
Tel: 717-566-6314

Huntingdon County Historical Society
100 4th Street
Hundingdon, PA 16652
Tel: 814-643-5449

Indiana County, Historical & Genealogical Society of
200 South 6th Street
Indiana, PA 15701
Tel: 412-463-9600

Jacobsburg Historical Society
402 Henry Road
Nazareth, PA 18064
Tel: 610-759-9029

Jamestown Area Historical Society
405 Summit Street
Jamestown, PA 16134
Tel: 412-932-5997

Jefferson County Historical & Genealogical Society
232 Jefferson Street
P.O. Box 51
Brookville, PA 15825
Tel: 814-849-0077

Juniata County Historical Society
498 Jefferson Street
Mifflintown, PA 17059
Tel: 717-436-5152

Kittochtinny Historical Society
175 East Kint Street
Chambersburg, PA 17201
Tel: 717-264-1667

Kutztown Area Historical Society
Normal & White Avenue
Kutztown, PA 19530
Tel: 610-683-7697

Lackawanna Historical Society
232 Monroe Avenue
Scranton, PA 18510
Tel: 717-344-3841

Lancaster County Historical Society/Library and Museum
230 North President Avenue
Lancaster, PA 17603
Tel: 717-392-4633
Fax: 717-293-2739
Email: lchs@ptd.net (Research requests)
lchs@juno.com (Information)
URL: http://lanclio.org/

Lancaster Mennonite Historical Society
2215 Millstream Road
Lancaster, PA 17602
Tel: 717-393-9745
URL: http://lanclio.org/lmhs.htm

Lansdale Historical Society
137 Jenkins Avenue
Lansdale, PA 19446
Tel: 215-855-1872

Latrobe Historical Society
1501 Ligonier Street
Latrobe, PA 15650
Tel: 412-539-8889

Lawrence County Historical Society
408 N. Jefferson Street
New Castle, PA 16101
Tel: 412-658-4022

Lebanon County Historical Society
924 Cumberland Street
Lebanon, PA 17042
Tel: 717-272-1473

Lehigh County Historical Society
501 Hamilton Street
Allentown, PA 18102
Tel: 610-435-4664

Lenni Lenape Historical Society of Pennsylvania
2825 Fish Hatchery Road
Allentown, PA 18102
Tel: 610-797-2121

Levittown Historical Society
7200 New Falls Road
P.O. Box 1641
Levittown, PA 19058

Ligonier Valley Historical Society
Star Route East
Ligonier, PA 15655
Tel: 412-238-6818

Limerick Township Historical Society
545 West Ridge Pike
Limerick, PA 19468
Tel: 610-495-5229

Lititz Historical Foundation
145 E. Main
Lititz, PA 17543
Tel: 717-627-4636

Lower Macungie Township Historical Society
P.O. Box 3722
Wescosville, PA 18106
URL: http://www.geocities.com/Heartland/3955/LMTHS.htm

Lycoming County Historical Society
858 West 4th Street
Williamsport, PA 17701
Tel: 717-326-3326

Manheim Historical Society
210 S. Charlotte Street
Manheim, PA 17545
Tel: 717-664-3486

Masontown Historical Society
P.O. Box 769
Masontown, PA 15461

Mauch Chunk Historical Society
14 W. Broadway
Jim Thorpe, PA 18229
Tel: 717-325-4439

McKean County Historical Society
Courthouse
Smethport, PA 16749
Tel: 814-887-5142

Mennonite Historians of Eastern Pennsylvania
Mennonite Heritage Center
565 Yoder Road
P.O. Box 82
Harleysville, PA 19438
Tel: 215-256-3020
Fax: 215-256-3023
Email: mennhist@pond.com
URL: http://www.pond.com/~mennhist/

Mercer County Historical Society
119 South Pitt Street
Mercer, PA 16137
Tel: 412-662-3490

Mifflin County Historical Society
1 West Market Street, #1
Lewiston, PA 17044
Tel: 717-242-1022

Military Order of the Loyal Legion of the United States
1805 Pine Street
Philadelphia, PA 19103
Tel: 215-546-2425
Email: YJNW42A@prodigy.com
URL: http://suvcw.org/mollus.htm

Millersburg & Upper Paxton Township, Historical Society of
Center Street
Millersburg, PA 17061
Tel: 717-692-4084

Milton Historical Society
River Road
Milton, PA 17847
Tel: 717-742-7057

Monroe County Historical Association
900 Main Street
Stroudsburg, PA 18360
Tel: 717-421-7703

Monroeville Historical Society
2700 Monroeville Boulevard
Monroeville, PA 15146
Tel: 412-372-9133

Montgomery County, Historical Society of
Library and Genealogy Study Group
1654 DeKalb Street
Norristown, PA 19401
Tel: 610-272-0297
URL: http://libertynet.org/~gencap/montcopa.html

Montour County Historical Society
1 Bloom Street
Danville, PA 17821

Moravian Historical Society
214 E. Center Street
Nazareth, PA 18064
Tel: 610-759-5070

Muncy Historical Society & Museum of History
131 S. Main Street
Muncy, PA 17756
URL: http://members.aol.com/LCGSgen/muncy.htm

National Historical Society
6405 Flank Drive
Harrisburg, PA 17112
Tel: 717-657-9555

National Railway Historical Society
100 N. 17th Street
Philadelphia, PA 19102
Tel: 215-557-6606

New Hope Historical Society
South Main
New Hope, PA 18938
Tel: 215-862-5652

Newtown Historic Association
Centre Avenue and Court Street
P.O. Box 303
Newtown, PA 18940
Tel: 215-968-4004

Newville Historical Society
Dougherty-Welch House
69 S. High Street
Newville, PA 17241
Tel: 717-776-6210
URL: http://www1.trib.com/CUMBERLINK/cumb/hist.groups.html

Northampton County Historical & Genealogical Society
101 South 4th Street
Easton, PA 18042
Tel: 610-253-1222

Northumberland County Historical Society
1150 North Front Street
Sunbury, PA 17801
Tel: 717-286-4083

Oil City Heritage Society
P.O. Box 862, Oil Creek Station
Oil City, PA 16301

Old York Road Historical Society
York and Vista Roads
Jenkintown, PA 19046
Tel: 215-884-0593

Pennsylvania German Society
P.O. Box 397
Birdsboro, PA 19508
Tel: 610-582-1441

Pennsylvania, Historical Society of
Library & Museum (Closed 11/27/97 - 4/13/98)
1300 Locust Street
Philadelphia, PA 19107
Tel: 215-732-6201
Fax: 215-732-2680
Email: hsppr@aol.com
URL: http://www.libertynet.org/~pahist/

Perry County Historical Society
129 North Second Street
Newport, PA 17074

Phoenixville Area, Historical Society of
Main and Church
Phoenixville, PA 19453
Tel: 610-935-7646

Pike County Historical Society
608 Broad Street
Milford, PA 18337
Tel: 717-296-8126

Pioneer Historical Society of Bedford County/Library
242 E. John Street
Bedford, PA 15522
Tel: 814-623-2011

Pittsburgh History & Landmarks Foundation
Old Post Office
One Landmarks Square
Pittsburgh, PA 15212

Plymouth Historical Society
115 Gaylord Avenue
Plymouth, PA 18651
Tel: 717-779-5840

Plymouth Meetint Historical Society
2130 Sierra Road
Plymouth Meeting, PA 19462
Tel: 610-828-8111

Potter County Historical Society
308 North Main Street
Coudersport, PA 16915

Presbyterian Historical Society
425 Lombard Street
Philadelphia, PA 19147
Tel: 215-627-1852
URL: http://libertynet.org/~gencap/presbyhs.html

Punxsutawney Area Historical & Genealogical Society
Bennis House Museum
401 West Mahoning Street
P.O. Box 286
Punxsutawney, PA 15767
Tel: 814-938-2555
814-938-7221
Email: mweimer@penn.com
URL: http://users.penn.com/~mweimer/historcl.html

Quakertown Historical Society
26 N. Main Street
Quakertown, PA 18951-1114
Tel: 215-536-3298

Radnor Historical Society
113 W. Beechtree Lane
Wayne, PA 19087-3212
Tel: 610-688-2668

Reading Company Technical & Historical Society
P.O. Box 15143
Reading, PA 19612
Tel: 610-372-5513
610-434-1289 (Sales)
Email: reading@vicon.net
URL: http://www.vicon.net/~reading/

Red Lion Area Historical Society
10 E. Broadway
Red Lion, PA 17356
Tel: 717-244-1912

St. Marys/Benzinger Township, Historical Society of
319 Erie Avenue
St. Marys, PA 15857
Tel: 814-834-6525

Schuylkill County, Historical Society of
14 N. Third Street
Pottsville, PA 17901-2905
Tel: 717-622-7540

Scotch-Irish Society of the U.S.A.
3 Parkway, 20th Floor
Philadelphia, PA 19102

Scottish Historic & Research Society of the Delaware Valley
102 St. Paul's Road
Ardmore, PA 19003
Tel: 610-649-4144

Sewickley Valley Historical Society
200 Broad Street
Sewickley, PA 15143
Tel: 412-741-5315

Shippensburg Historical Society/Library
52 W. King Street
Shippensburg, PA 17257
Tel: 717-532-6727

Snyder County Historical Society
30 East Market Street
P.O. Box 276
Middleburg, PA 17842
Tel: 717-837-6191

Somerset County, Historical & Genealogical Society of
RD 2, Box 238
Somerset, PA 15501-9802
Tel: 814-445-6077

South Bethlehem Historical Society
479 Brighton Street
Bethlehem, PA 18015
Tel: 610-758-8790

Springford Area Historical Society
1 Reading Railroad Plaza
Royersford, PA 19468
Tel: 610-948-7127

Stoneboro Community & Historical Society
Lake Street
Stoneboro, PA 16153

Sullivan County Historical Society
Court House Square
LaPorte, PA 18626

Susquehanna County Historical Society
c/o Susquehanna County Free Library
2 Monument Square, 2nd Floor
Montrose, PA 18801
Tel: 717-278-1881
Email: suspulib@epix.net
URL: http://www.epix.net/~suspulib/

Susquehanna Depot Historical Society
P.O. Box 161
Susquehanna, PA 18847

Swedish Colonial Society
c/o Wallace Richter, Registrar
336 South Devon Avenue
Wayne, PA 19087
Tel: 610-688-1766
URL: http://libertynet.org/~gencap/scs.html

Tamaqua Historical Society
118 W. Broad Street
Tamaqua, PA 18252
Tel: 717-668-5722

Tioga County Historical Society
Robinson House/Rhoda Ladd Genealogy Library
120 Main Street
P.O. Box 724
Wellsboro, PA 16901
Tel: 717-724-6116
URL: http://www.rootsweb.com/~patioga/tchs.htm

Trappe Historical Society
201 Main Street
Trappe, PA 19426
Tel: 610-489-8883

Tri-County Heritage Society
8 Mill Road
Morgantown, PA 19543
Tel: 610-286-7477

Tulpehocken Settlement Historical Society
116 N. Front Street
P.O. Box 53
Womelsdorf, PA 19567
Tel: 610-589-2527

Tuscarora Township Historical Society
RD 2, Box 105-C
Laceyville, PA 18623
Tel: 717-869-2184

Ukrainian Fraternal Association
440 Wyoming Avenue
Scranton, PA 18503
Tel: 717-342-0937

Union City Historical Society/Museum
11 South Main Street
Union City, PA 16438
Tel: 814-438-7573

Union County Historical Society
103 S. Second Street
Lewisburg, PA 17837
Tel: 717-524-8666

University City Historical Society
40th and Woodland Avenue
Philadelphia, PA 19104
Tel: 215-387-3019

Valley Forge Historical Society
P.O. Box 122
Valley Forge, PA 19481
Tel: 610-783-0535
URL: http://www.libertynet.org/iha/valleyforge/

Venango County Historical Society
301 S. Park Street
Franklin, PA 16323
Tel: 814-437-2275

Victorian Vandergrift Museum and Historical Society
151 Lincoln Avenue
Vandergrift, PA 15690
Tel: 412-568-1990

Warren County Historical Society
210 Fourth Avenue
P.O. Box 427
Warren, PA 16365-0427
Tel: 814-723-1795

Washington County Historical Society
49 East Maiden Street
Washington, PA 15302
Tel: 412-225-6740

Wattsburg Area Historical Society
P.O. Box 240
Wattsburg, PA 16442
Tel: 814-739-2952

Wayne County Historical Society
810 Main Street
P.O. Box 446
Honesdale, PA 18431
Tel: 717-253-3240

Waynesboro Historical Society
138 W. Main Street
Waynesboro, PA 17268
Tel: 717-762-1747

West Whiteland Township Historical Commission
Whiteland Towne Center
Exton, PA 19341
Tel: 610-363-8091

Western Pennsylvania, Historical Society of
Pittsburgh Regional History Center
1212 Smallman Street
Pittsburgh, PA 15222
Tel: 412-681-5533
Fax: 412-681-3029

Westmoreland County Historical Society
951 Old Salem Road
Greensburg, PA 15601
Tel: 412-836-1800

Whitehall Historical Preservation Society
Mickley and Lenhart Roads
Whitehall, PA 18052
Tel: 610-776-7166

Wilkinsburg Historical Society
c/o Wilkinsburg Public Library
605 Ross Avenue
Pittsburgh, PA 15221
Tel: 412-244-2940

Wissahickon Valley Historical Society
Route 73 and School Road
Blue Bell, PA 19422
Tel: 215-646-6541

Wyoming County Historical Society
Harrison and Bridge Street
P.O. Box 309
Tunkhannock, PA 18657
Tel: 717-836-5303

Wyoming Historical & Geological Society
69 South Franklin Street
Wilkes-Barre, PA 18701
Tel: 717-822-1727

Yardley Historical Association
46 W. Afton Avenue
Yardley, PA 19067
Tel: 215-493-9883

York County, Historical Society of
250 East Market Street
York, PA 17403
Tel: 717-848-1587

Zelienople Historical Society
243 S. Main Street
Zelienople, PA 16063
Tel: 412-452-9457

LDS Family History Centers

Broomall Family History Center
721 Paxon Hollow Road
Broomall, PA 19008
Tel: 610-356-8507

Clarks Summit Family History Center
Leach Hill and Griffin Pond Roads
Clarks Summit, PA 18411
Tel: 717-587-5123

Doylestown Family History Center
Chapman and Ferry Roads
Doylestown, PA 18901
Tel: 215-348-0645

Erie Family History Center
1101 South Hill Road
Erie, PA 16505
Tel: 814-866-3611

Kane Family History Center
30 Chestnut Street
Kane, PA 16735
Tel: 814-837-9729

Knox Family History Center
Clarion Meetinghouse
Know, PA 16232
Tel: 814-797-1287

Lancaster Family History Center
1210 E. King Street
Lancaster, PA 17602
Tel: 717-295-1719

Philadelphia Family History Center
Broad & Wyoming Streets
Philadelphia, PA 19140
Tel: 215-329-3692

Pittsburgh Family History Center
46 School Street
Pittsburgh, PA 15220
Tel: 412-921-2115

Reading Family History Center
3344 Reading Crest Avenue
Reading, PA 19606
Tel: 610-929-0235

State College Family History Center
842 Whitehall Road
State College, PA 16802
Tel: 814-238-4560

York Family History Center
2100 Hollywood Drive
York, PA 17315
Tel: 717-854-9331

Archives/Libraries/Museums

Afro American Historical & Cultural Museum
7th and Arch Streets
Philadelphia, PA 19106
Tel: 215-574-0380
URL: http://www.fieldtrip.com/pa/55740380.htm

Allegheny Valley, Community Library of
415 E. 6th Avenue
Tarentum, PA 15084
Tel: 412-226-0770
URL: http://www.clpgh.org/ein/alvalley/

Altoona Area Public Library
1600 5th Avenue
Altoona, PA 16602-3621
Tel: 814-946-0417

American-Swedish Historical Museum
(in Franklin Delano Roosevelt Park)
1900 Patterson Avenue
Philadelphia, PA 19145
Tel: 215-389-1776
Email: ashm@libertynet.org
URL: http://www.libertynet.org/~ashm/

Annenberg Research Institute
420 Walnut Street
Philadelphia, PA 19106
Tel: 215-238-1290
Fax: 215-238-1540
URL: http://libertynet.org/~gencap/ari.html

Archives of the Moravian Church
41 W. Locust Street
Bethlehem, PA 18018
Tel: 610-866-3255

Armstrong County Historical Museum & Genealogical Society
300 North McKean Street
Kittanning, PA 16201-1345
Tel: 412-548-5707

Athenaeum of Philadelphia
219 S. Sixth Street
Philadelphia, PA 19106
Tel: 215-925-2688
Fax: 215-925-3755
Email: athena@libertynet.org
URL: http://www.libertynet.org/~athena/

Balch Institute for Ethnic Studies
18 South 7th Street
Philadelphia, PA 19106-3794
Tel: 215-925-8090
Email: BALCHLIB@HSLC.ORG
URL: http://www.libertynet.org/~balch/

Bedford County Pioneers Historical Society/Library
242 E. John Street
Bedford, PA 15522-1750
URL: http://www.rootsweb.com/~pabedfor/plibrary.html

Berks County, Historical Society of
Library and Museum
940 Centre Avenue
Reading, PA 19601
Tel: 610-375-4375
URL: http://www.berksweb.com/histsoc.html

Bloomsburg Public Library
225 Market Street
Bloomsburg, PA 17815
Tel: 717-451-0883
URL: http://www.bafn.org/library/bloom.htm

Bloomsburg University
Harvey A. Andruss Library
400 E. Second Street
Bloomsburg, PA 17815
Tel/TDD: 717-389-4204
Fax: 717-389-3895
URL: http://www.bloomu.edu/library/pages/library.html

Bradford County Historical Society/Museum
21 Main Street
Towanda, PA 18848-1803
Tel: 717-265-2240
URL: http://www.rootsweb.com/~sgrp/bchsmain.htm

Bucks County Historical Society
Spruance Library/Mercer Museum
84 S. Pine Street
Doylestown, PA 18901-4999
Tel: 215-345-0210
Fax: 215-230-0823
Email: bchs@philadelphia.libertynet.org
URL: http://www.libertynet.org/~bchs/Spruance.html

Buhl/Henderson Community Library
11 N. Sharpsville Avenue
Sharon, PA 16146-2107
Tel: 412-981-4360

Butler Area Public Library
Weir Genealogy Room
218 N. McKean Street
Butler, PA 16001-4911
Tel: 412-287-1715
URL: http://www.butlercounty.com/comminfo/libraries/butapl/library.htm

Cambria County Library
248 Main Street
Johnstown, PA 15901-1677
Tel: 814-536-5131

Carnegie Free Library
Beaver County Research Center
1301 Seventh Avenue
Beaver Falls, PA 15010
Tel: 412-846-4340
Fax: 412-846-0370

Carnegie Library of Pittsburgh
Pennsylvania Department
4400 Forbes Avenue
Pittsburgh, PA 15213
Tel: 412-622-3114
Email: padept@alphaclp.clpgh.org
URL: http://www.clpgh.org/clp/Pennsylvania/

Centre County Library/Historical Museum
203 N. Allegheny Street
Bellefonte, PA 16823-1601
Tel: 814-355-1516

Chester County Archives and Records Service
601 Westtown Road
West Chester, PA 19382-4527
Tel: 610-344-6760
URL: http://www.chesco.com/~cchs/chesco_archives.html

Citizens Library
55 South College Street
Washington, PA 15301
Tel: 412-222-2400

Civil War Library and Museum
1805 Pine Street
Philadelphia, PA 19103
Tel: 215-735-8196
URL: http://www.libertynet.org/~cwlm/

Coyle Free Library
102 N. Main Street
Chambersburg, PA 17201
Tel: 717-263-1054

Cumberland County Historical Society
Hamilton Library
21 North Pitt Street
Carlisle, PA 17013
Tel: 717-249-7610
URL: http://www1.trib.com/CUMBERLINK/cumb/hist.groups.html

Darby Free Library
History Room
1001 Main Street
P.O. Box 164
Darby, PA 19023-0164
Tel: 610-586-7310
Fax: 610-586-2781
Email: DARBYLIB@HSLC.ORG
URL: http://www.libertynet.org/~delcolib/da.html

David Library of the American Revolution
1201 River Road
P.O. Box 748
Washington Crossing, PA 18977
Tel: 215-493-6776
Fax: 215-493-9276
Email: dlar@libertynet.org
URL: http://www.libertynet.org/~dlar/dlar.html

Easton Area Public Library
6th and Church Streets
Easton, PA 18042
Tel: 610-258-2917

Erie County Public Library/Blasco Library
160 East Front Street
Erie, PA 16509
Tel: 814-451-6900
814-451-6927 (Heritage Room)
Fax: 814-451-6907
Email: erielib@velocity.com
URL: http://www.ecls.lib.pa.us/family.html

Eva K. Bowlby Public Library
311 N. West Street
Waynesburg, PA 15370-1238
Tel: 412-627-9776

Evangelical & Reformed Church, Historical Society of Archives
555 West James Street
Lancaster, PA 17603
Tel: 717-393-0654 ext. 27

Ford City Public Library
1136 4th Avenue
Fort City, PA 16226-1202
Tel: 412-763-3591

Franklin Public Library
Pennsylvania Room
421 12th Street
Franklin, PA 16323-1205
Tel: 814-432-5062

German Society of Pennsylvania
611 Spring Garden Street
Philadelphia, PA 19123
Tel: 215-627-2332
215-627-4365 (Library)
Fax: 215-627-5297
URL: http://libertynet.org/~gencap/germanpa.html

Germantown Historical Society
5501 Germantown Avenue (Market Square)
Philadelphia, PA 19144-2291
Tel: 215-844-0514 (Museum)
215-844-8428 (Library/Archives)
URL: http://libertynet.org/~gencap/germantown.html

Grand Army of the Republic War Museum/Ruan House Library
4278 Griscom Street
Philadelphia, PA 19124-3954
Tel: 215-289-6484
Email: GARMUSLIB@aol.com
URL: http://suvcw.org/garmus.htm

Green Free Library
134 Main Street
Wellsboro, PA 16901-1489
Tel: 717-724-4876

Greene County Historical Society/Library & Museum
RR 2
P.O. Box 127
Waynesburg, PA 15370
Tel: 412-627-3204
URL: http://www.greenepa.net/~museum/

Hoenstine Rental Library
414 Montgomery
P.O. Box 208
Hollidaysburg, PA 16648
Tel: 814-695-0632
URL: http://ourworld.compuserve.com/homepages/LLewis/hoenstin.htm

Holocaust Center of Greater Pittsburgh
242 McKee Place
Pittsburgh, PA 15213
Tel: 412-682-7111

James V. Brown Library
19 East 4th Street
Williamsport, PA 17701
Tel: 717-326-0536
URL: http://www.jvbrown.edu/jvblib.html

Juniata Mennonite Historical Center
HCR 63
Richfield, PA 17086
Tel: 717-694-3211

Lancaster County Historical Society/Library and Museum
230 North President Avenue
Lancaster, PA 17603
Tel: 717-392-4633
Fax: 717-293-2739
Email: lchs@ptd.net (Research requests)
lchs@juno.com (Information)
URL: http://lanclio.org/

Lancaster County Library
125 North Duke Street
Lancaster, PA 17602
Tel: 717-394-2651

Lancaster County Records and Archives Service
Old Courthouse
50 North Duke Street, Ground Floor
P.O. Box 3450
Lancaster, PA 17602
Tel: 717-299-8318

Lebanon Community Library
125 N. Seventh Street
Lebanon, PA 17046-5000
Tel: 717-273-7624

Library Company of Philadelphia
1314 Locust Street
Philadelphia, PA 19107
Tel: 215-546-3181
URL: http://libertynet.org/~gencap/licophil.html

Martinsburg Community Library
201 South Walnut Street
Martinsburg, PA 16662
Tel: 814-793-3335

Mechanicsburg Area Public Library
51 W. Simpson Street
Mechanicsburg, PA 17055-6323
Tel: 717-766-0171

Media/Upper Providence Free Library
Upper Providence Room
Front and Jackson Streets
Media, PA 19063
Tel: 610-566-1918
Email: medialib@hslc.org
URL: http://www.geocities.com/~delawarecounty/Library/

Mennonite Family History Library
10 W. Main Street
Elverson, PA 19520-0171
Tel: 610-286-0258
Fax: 610-286-6860
URL: http://feefhs.org/men/frg-mfh.html

Mennonite Historians of Eastern Pennsylvania
Mennonite Heritage Center
565 Yoder Road
P.O. Box 82
Harleysville, PA 19438
Tel: 215-256-3020
Fax: 215-256-3023
Email: mennhist@pond.com
URL: http://www.pond.com/~mennhist/

Mercer Area Library
145 N. Pitt Street
Mercer, PA 16137-1206
Tel: 412-662-4233

Methodist Historical Center
326 New Street
Philadelphia, PA 19106

Military Order of the Loyal Legion of the United States
1805 Pine Street
Philadelphia, PA 19103
Tel: 215-546-2425
Email: YJNW42A@prodigy.com
URL: http://suvcw.org/mollus.htm

Monroe County Public Library
913 Main Street
Stroudsburg, PA 18360
Tel: 717-421-0800

Montgomery County Archives
1880 Markley Street
Norristown, PA 19401
Tel: 610-278-3441

Montgomery County, Historical Society of Library and Genealogy Study Group
1654 DeKalb Street
Norristown, PA 19401
Tel: 610-272-0297
URL: http://libertynet.org/~gencap/montcopa.html

Montgomery County/Norristown Public Library
1001 Powell Street
Norristown, PA 19401
Tel: 610-278-5100

Montgomery Public Library
1 South Main Street
Montgomery, PA 17751
Tel: 717-547-6212

Mount Lebanon Public Library
16 Castle Shannon Boulevard
Pittsburgh, PA 15228-2252
Tel: 412-531-1912

Myerstown Community Library
199 N. College Street
Myerstown, PA 17067
Tel: 717-866-2800

National Museum of American Jewish History
55 North 5th Street
Philadelphia, PA 19123
Tel: 215-923-3811

New Castle Public Library
207 East North Street
New Castle, PA 16101
Tel: 412-658-6659

Northland Public Library
300 Cumberland Road
Pittsburgh, PA 15237

Oil City Library
2 Central Avenue
Oil City, PA 16301-2795
Tel: 814-678-3072

Osterhout Free Public Library
71 South Franklin Street
Wilkes-Barre, PA 18701-1287
Tel: 717-823-0156

Pennsylvania German Cultural Heritage Center
Kutztown University
Weisenberger Alumni Center
Kutztown, PA 19530
Tel: 610-683-1330
Email: pgchc@kutztown.edu
URL: http://www.kutztown.edu/community/pgchc/

Pennsylvania, Historical Society of
Library & Museum (Closed 11/27/97 - 4/13/98)
1300 Locust Street
Philadelphia, PA 19107
Tel: 215-732-6201
Fax: 215-732-2680
Email: hsppr@aol.com
URL: http://www.libertynet.org/~pahist/

Pennsylvania, State Library of
Main Reading Room
Forum Building, Room 102
Walnut Street and Commonwealth Avenue
P.O. Box 1601
Harrisburg, PA 17105
Tel: 717-787-4440
717-783-5950 (Reference)
Fax: 717-783-2070
TTY: 717-772-2863
Email: Geschwindt@shrsys.hslc.org
URL: http://www.cas.psu.edu/docs/pde/LIBSTATE.HTML

Pennsylvania State University
W313 Pattee Library
Historical Collection and Labor Archives
State Park, PA 16802
Tel: 814-863-2505
URL: http://www.libraries.psu.edu/crsweb/speccol/spcoll.htm

Philadelphia Archdiocesan Historical Research Center
100 E. Wynnewood Road
Wynnewood, PA 19096-3001
Tel: 610-667-2125
URL: http://www.archdiocese-phl.org/ch/archives.html

Philadelphia City Archives
401 North Broad Street, Suite 942
Philadelphia, PA 19108
Tel: 215-686-1580
URL: http://libertynet.org/~gencap/philcity.html

Philadelphia, Free Library of
Central Library
Social Science and History Department
1901 Vine Street
Philadelphia, PA 19103
Tel: 215-686-5322
URL: http://www.library.phila.gov/central/ssh/

Philadelphia Maritime Museum
321 Chestnut Street
Philadelphia, PA 19106
Tel: 215-925-5439

Pioneer Historical Society of Bedford County/Library
242 E. John Street
Bedford, PA 15522
Tel: 814-623-2011

Polish American Cultural Center
308 Walnut Street
Philadelphia, PA 19106
Tel: 215-922-1700

Pottsville Free Public Library
Reference Department
16 North Third Street
Pottsville, PA 17901-2905
Tel: 717-622-8880
Fax: 717-622-2157
Email: potlib@pottsville.infi.net
or pot@iu29.schiu.k12.pa.us
URL: http://www.pottsville.com/library/genie.htm

Priestly-Forsythe Library
100 King Street
Northumberland, PA 17857

Punxsutawney Area Historical & Genealogical Society
Bennis House Museum
401 West Mahoning Street
P.O. Box 286
Punxsutawney, PA 15767
Tel: 814-938-2555
814-938-7221
Email: mweimer@penn.com
URL: http://users.penn.com/~mweimer/historcl.html

Reading Public Library
100 South 5th
Reading, PA 19607
Tel: 610-478-6350

Ross Library
232 W. Main Street
Lock Haven, PA 17745-1241
Tel: 717-748-3321

St. Charles Borromeo Seminary
Ryan Memorial Library
1000 E. Wynnewood
Overbrook, PA 19096
Tel: 610-667-3394
Fax: 610-664-7913
URL: http://libertynet.org/~gencap/borromeo.html

Schwenkfelder Theological and Historical Library
1 Seminary Street
Pennsburg, PA 18073
Tel: 215-679-3103

Sewickley Public Library
500 Thorn Street
Sewickley, PA 15143-1533
Tel: 412-741-6920

Shippensburg Historical Society/Library
52 W. King Street
Shippensburg, PA 17257
Tel: 717-532-6727

Susquehanna County Free Library
2 Monument Square
Montrose, PA 18801
Tel: 717-278-1881
Email: suspulib@epix.net
URL: http://www.epix.net/~suspulib/

Temple University
Paley Library/Special Collections
13th and Berks Streets
Philadelphia, PA 19122
Tel: 215-787-8230
215-787-8211 (Hours)
Fax: 215-204-5201
URL: http://www.library.temple.edu/LIBCOLLS/

Union City Historical Society/Museum
11 South Main Street
Union City, PA 16438
Tel: 814-438-7573

U.S. Army Military History Institute
22 Ashburn Drive, Carlisle Barracks
Carlisle, PA 17013
Tel: 717-245-3611
Email: MHI-SC@carlisle-emh2.army.mil (Special Collections)
MHI-AR@carlisle-emh2.army.mil (Archives Collection)
MHI-HR@carlisle-emh2.army.mil (Historical Reference)
URL: http://carlisle-www.army.mil/usamhi/

University of Pennsylvania
Van Pelt Library
3420 Walnut Street
Philadelphia, PA 19104-6206
Tel: 215-898-7088
215-898-7554/5
Email: librefer@pobox.upenn.edu
URL: http://www.library.upenn.edu/vanpelt/collections/collections.html

University of Pittsburgh
Hillman Library
Pittsburgh, PA 15213
Tel: 412-648-7700
412-648-8981 (Archives)
URL: http://www.pitt.edu/~hilmlib/

Upper Darby Township/Sellers Memorial Free Public Library
76 South State Road
Upper Darby, PA 19082-1999
Tel: 610-789-4440

Warren Library Association
205 Market Street
Warren, PA 16365
Tel: 814-723-4650

West Chester University
Frances Harvey Green Library
University Avenue and High Street
West Chester, PA 19380

Tel: 610-436-3383
URL: http://www.wcupa.edu/library.fhg/

Wilkinsburg Public Library
605 Ross Avenue
Pittsburgh, PA 15221
Tel: 412-244-2940

NEWSPAPER REPOSITORIES

Pennsylvania State Library
Main Reading Room
Forum Building, Room 120
P.O. Box 1601
Harrisburg, PA 17105
Tel: 717-783-5968
Email: ali@unixl.stlib.state.pa.us
URL: http://www.cas.psu.edu/docs/pde/LIBCOLL.HTML

VITAL RECORDS

Philadelphia City Archives
401 N. Broad Street, Suite 942
Philadelphia, PA 19108
Tel: 215-686-1580
URL: http://libertynet.org/~gencap/philcity.html
Philadelphia 1860-1915

Pittsburgh Registrar of Wills
City/County Building
Pittsburgh, PA 15219
Pittsburgh 1870-1905

State Department of Health
Division of Vital Statistics
101 S. Mercer Street
P.O. Box 1528
New Castle, PA 16103
Tel: 412-656-3100
Birth and Death 1906-present

PENNSYLVANIA ON THE WEB

Free Library of Philadelphia-Genealogy Pathfinder
http://www.library.phila.gov/central/ssh/waltgen/
geneal1.htm

Kraig Ruckel's Palatine and Pennsylvania-Dutch Genealogy
http://www.geocities.com/Heartland/3955

Palatines to America-Online Immigrant Ancestor Registry Index
http://genealogy.org/~palam/ia_index.htm

Pennsylvania GenWeb Project
http://libertyweb.org/~gencap/pacounties.html

RHODE ISLAND

ARCHIVES, STATE & NATIONAL

National Archives—New England Region
380 Trapelo Road
Waltham, MA 02154-8104
Tel: 617-647-8100
Fax: 617-647-8460
Email: archives@waltham.nara.gov
URL: http://www.nara.gov/nara/regional/01nsbgil.html

Rhode Island State Archives
337 Westminster Street
Providence, RI 02903
Tel: 401-277-2353
Fax: 401-277-3199
URL: http://archives.state.ri.us/
gopher://archives.state.ri.us/

GENEALOGICAL SOCIETIES

American-French Genealogical Society
(Library at the First Universalist Church
78 Earle Street
Woonsocket, RI 02895)
P.O. Box 2113
Pawtucket, RI 02861
Tel/Fax: 401-765-6141
Email: afgs@ids.net
URL: http://users.ids.net/~afgs/afgshome.html

Italian Genealogy Society of America
P.O. Box 8571
Cranston, RI 02920-8571

New England Historical and Genealogical Society (NEHGS)
101 Newbury Street
Boston, MA 02116-3007
Tel: 617-836-5740
888-AT-NEHGS (Membership & Education)
888-BY-NEHGS (Sales)
888-90-NEHGS (Library Circulation)
Fax: 617-536-7307
Email: nehgs@nehgs.org
URL: http://www.nehgs.org/

Newport Genealogical Society
160 Bristol Ferry Road
Portsmouth, RI 02871
Tel: 401-847-1576

Rhode Island Families Association
P.O. Box 1414
Ashburn, RI 20146-1414
Email: rigr@erols.com
URL: http://www.erols.com/rigr/

Rhode Island Genealogical Society
507 Clarks Row
Bristol, RI 02809-1581

Rhode Island Mayflower Descendants
128 Massasoit
Warwick, RI 02888

Rhode Island Genealogical Society
P.O. Box 433
Greenville, RI 02828

Society of Mayflower Descendants
35 Hodsell Street
Cranston, RI 02910
Tel: 401-467-7594

Sons of the American Revolution, Rhode Island Society
P.O. Box 137
East Greenwich, RI 02818

HISTORICAL SOCIETIES

Block Island Historical Society
Old Town Road
Block Island, RI 02807
Tel: 401-466-2481

Bristol Historical and Preservation Society/ Library & Museum
48 Court Street
Bristol, RI 02809
Tel: 401-253-7223
401-253-5705

Charlestown Historical Society
P.O. Box 100
Charlestown, RI 02813-0100
Tel: 401-364-7507
URL: http://www.charlestown.com/ri/historicalsociety/index.htm

Coventry Historical Society
P.O. Box 401
Coventry, RI 02816

Cranston Historical Society
Sprague Mansion
1351 Cranston Street
Cranston, RI 02920
Tel: 401-944-9226
Email: RCarosi@aol.com
URL: http://www.geocities.com/Heartland/4678/Sprague.html

Jamestown Historical Society
Naragansett Avenue
Jamestown, RI 02835
Tel: 401-423-0784

Little Compton Historical Society
Wilbor House
548 West Main Road (Route 77)
P.O. Box 577
Little Compton, RI 02837
Tel: 401-635-4035

Middletown Historical Society
Paradise Avenue
Newport, RI 02840
Tel: 401-849-1870

New England Historical and Genealogical Society (NEHGS)
101 Newbury Street
Boston, MA 02116-3007
Tel: 617-836-5740
888-AT-NEHGS (Membership & Education)
888-BY-NEHGS (Sales)
888-90-NEHGS (Library Circulation)
Fax: 617-536-7307
Email: nehgs@nehgs.org
URL: http://www.nehgs.org/

Newport Historical Society
82 Touro Street
Newport, RI 02840
Tel: 401-846-0813

Rhode Island Black Heritage Society
46 Aborn Street
Providence, RI 02903

Rhode Island Historical Preservation and Heritage Commission
150 Benefit Street
Providence, RI 02903
Tel: 401-277-2678
Fax: 401-277-2968
TDD: 401-277-3700
URL: http://www.state.ri.us/stdept/sd50.htm

Rhode Island Historical Society/Library
110 Benevolent Street
Providence, RI 02906
Tel: 401-331-8575

Rhode Island Jewish Historical Association
130 Sessions Street
Providence, RI 02906
Tel: 401-331-1360

Westerly Historical Society
P.O. Box 91
Westerly, RI 02891
URL: http://www.watchhill.com/historicalsociety/index.html

LDS Family History Center

Warwick Family History Center
1000 Narragansett Pkwy.
Warwick, RI 02888
Tel: 401-463-8150

Archives/Libraries/Museums

American-French Genealogical Society/Library
c/o First Universalist Church
78 Earle Street
Woonsocket, RI 02895
Mail:
P.O. Box 2113
Pawtucket, RI 02861
Tel/Fax: 401-765-6141
Email: afgs@ids.net
URL: http://users.ids.net/~afgs/afgshome.html

Barrington Public Library
281 Country Road
Barrington, RI 02806
Tel: 401-247-1920
URL: http://www.ultranet.com/~bpl/

Bristol Historical and Preservation Society/ Library & Museum
48 Court Street
Bristol, RI 02809
Tel: 401-253-7223
401-253-5705

Brown University
Jay Hay Library
Providence, RI 02912
Tel: 401-863-2167
URL: http://www.brown.edu/Facilities/John_Carter_Brown_Library/

Brown University
John Carter Brown Library
20 Prospect Street
Providence, RI 02912
Tel: 401-863-2725
URL: http://www.brown.edu/Facilities/John_Carter_Brown_Library/

Coventry Public Library
1672 Flat River Road
Coventry, RI 02816
Tel: 401-822-9100
401-822-9105 (Reference)
Fax: 401-822-9133
Email: debbi@seq.clan.lib.ri.us
URL: http://seq.clan.lib.ri.us/cov/index.htm

Diocese of Providence
1 Cathedral Square
Providence, RI 02903
Tel: 401-278-4546

East Greenwich Free Library
82 Pierce Street
East Greenwich, RI 02818
Tel: 401-844-9510
Fax: 401-844-3790
URL: http://www.ultranet.com/~egrlib/

Jamestown Philomenian Library
Local History Collection
26 North Road
Jamestown, RI 02835
Tel: 401-423-7280
Fax: 401-423-7281
URL: http://www.wsii.com/rhodeisl/users/jlibrary/

Langworthy Public Library
24 Spring Street
P.O. Box 478
Hope Valley, RI 02832
Tel: 401-539-2851

Lincoln Public Library
145 Old River Road
Lincoln, RI 02865
Tel: 401-333-2421/2
Fax: 401-333-4154
Email: linpub@perseus.ultranet.com
URL: http://www.ultranet.com/~linpub/

New England Historical and Genealogical Society (NEHGS)
101 Newbury Street
Boston, MA 02116-3007
Tel: 617-836-5740
888-AT-NEHGS (Membership & Education)
888-BY-NEHGS (Sales)
888-90-NEHGS (Library Circulation)
Fax: 617-536-7307
Email: nehgs@nehgs.org
URL: http://www.nehgs.org/

Newport Historical Society/Library
82 Touro Street
Newport, RI 02840
Tel: 401-846-0813

Newport Public Library
Aquidneck Park
300 Spring Street
Newport, RI 02840
Tel: 401-847-8720

Providence City Archives
City Hall
25 Dorrance Street
Providence, RI 02903
Tel: 401-421-7740

Providence College
Phillips Memorial Library
River Avenue or Eaton Street
Providence, RI 02918
Tel: 401-865-2242
URL: http://www.providence.edu/pml/pmlhp1.htm

Providence Public Library
225 Washington Street
Providence, RI 02903
Tel: 401-455-8000
401-455-8005 (Reference)
Fax: 401-455-8080
TDD: 401-455-8089

Rhode Island Historical Society/Library
110 Benevolent Street
Providence, RI 02906
Tel: 401-331-8575

Rhode Island State Library
Rhode Island State House, Room 208
337 Westminster Street
Providence, RI 02903
Tel: 401-277-2473
401-277-2353
URL: http://www.sec.state.ri.us/library/web.htm

Supreme Court Judicial Records Center
One Hill Street
Pawtucket, RI 02860
Tel: 401-377-3249
Some early Court and Naturalization Records

United States Naval War College/Library
Code 1E3
686 Cushing Road
Newport, RI 02841-1207
Tel: 401-841-1435
401-841-3397
401-841-4345 (Government Documents)
Email: LIBREF@USNWC.EDU
URL: http://users.ids.net/~nwcird/

University of Rhode Island
Library/Special Collections
Kingstown, RI 02881
Tel: 401-874-4632
401-874-2594
Fax: 401-874-4608
Email: dcm@uriacc.uri.edu
klogan@uriacc.uri.edu
URL: http://www.library.uri.edu/Web-Files/Library_Services/Special_Collections/INHOM.HTM

Warwick Public Library
Greene Collection
600 Sandy Lane
Warwick, RI 02886
Tel: 401-739-5440
Fax: 401-732-2055
TDD: 401-739-3689
Email: warwickpl@ids.net
URL: http://users.ids.net/warwickpl/home.htm

West Warwick Public Library
1043 Main Street
West Warwick, RI 02893
Tel: 401-828-3750
Fax: 401-828-8493
TDD: 401-828-4730
Email: rickpe@dsl.rhilinet.gov
URL: http://www.ultranet.com/~wwpublib/

Westerly Public Library
38 Broad Street
P.O. Box 356
Westerly, RI 02891
Tel: 401-596-2877
Fax: 401-596-5600

Newspaper Repositories

Rhode Island Historical Society/Library
110 Benevolent Street
Providence, RI 02906
Tel: 401-331-0448
Email: madeleinetn@dfl.rhilinet.gov

Vital Records

State of Rhode Island, Dept. of Health
Division of Vital Records
Cannon Building, Room 101
75 Davis Street
Providence, RI 02908
Tel: 401-277-2811/2

Rhode Island on the Web

Rhode Island Cemeteries Database Home Page
http://members.tripod.com/~debyns/cemetery.html

Rhode Island Genealogy Page
http://users.ids.net/~jcraig/ri_gen.htm

Rhode Island GenWeb Project
http://www.rootsweb.com/~rigenweb/

SOUTH CAROLINA

ARCHIVES, STATE & NATIONAL

National Archives—Southeast Region
1557 St. Joseph Avenue
East Point, GA 30344-2593
Tel: 404-763-7477
Fax: 404-763-7033
Email: archives@atlanta.nara.gov
URL: http://www.nara.gov/nara/regional/04nsgil.html

South Carolina Department of Archives and History
1430 Senate Street
P.O. Box 11669, Capitol Station
Columbia, SC 29211-1669
Tel: 803-734-8577
803-834-8596
Fax: 803-734-8820
Email: sox@history.scdah.sc.edu
URL: http://www.scdah.sc.edu/homepage.htm

GENEALOGICAL SOCIETIES

Aiken-Barnwell Chapter SCGS
P.O. Box 415
Aiken, SC 29802
Email: lhutto@home.ifx.net
URL: http://www.ifx.net/~lhutto/page2.html

Anderson Chapter SCGS
P.O. Box 5743
Anderson, SC 29623

Augusta Genealogical Society/Library
1109 Broad Street
P.O. Box 3743
Augusta, GA 30914-3743
Tel: 706-722-4073
URL: http://interoz.com/ags/index.htm

Beaufort Chapter SCGS
P.O. Box 37
Ridgeland, SC 29936

Catawba-Wateree Chapter SCGS
c/o Camden Archives and Museum
1314 Broad Street
Camden, SC 29020
URL: http://members.aol.com/SCSunset/index.html

Charleston Chapter SCGS
P.O. Box 20266
Charleston, SC 29413

Chester District Genealogical Society
P.O. Box 336
Richburg, SC 29729

Columbia Chapter SCGS
P.O. Box 11353
Columbia, SC 29211

Dutch Fork Chapter SCGS
P.O. Box 481
Chapin, SC 29036

Fairfield Chapter SCGS
P.O. Box 696
Winnsboro, SC 29180

Georgetown Chapter SCGS
P.O. Box 218
Georgetown, SC 29442

Greenville Chapter SCGS
P.O. Box 16236
Greenville, SC 29606

Hilton Head Chapter SCGS
P.O. Box 5492
Hilton Head, SC 29928

Huguenot Society of South Carolina/Library
138 Logan Street
Charleston, SC 29401
Tel: 803-723-3235

Laurens District Chapter SCGS
P.O. Box 1217
Laurens, SC 29360

Lexington County Genealogical Association
P.O. Box 1442
Lexington, SC 29072

Old 96 District Chapter SCGS
P.O. Box 3468
Greenwood, SC 29648

Old Darlington District Chapter SCGS
Old Train Depot
114 S. Fourth Street
P.O. Box 175
Hartsville, SC 29551-0175
URL: http://members.aol.com/reneebb/oddc.htm

Old Edgefield District Chapter SCGS/Archives
104 Court House Square
P.O. Box 468
Edgefield, SC 29824

Old Newberry District Chapter SCGS
P.O. Box 154
Newberry, SC 29108

Old Pendleton District Chapter SCGS
1255 Corinth Road
Seneca, SC 29678
URL: http://home.aol.com/Oldp2

Old St. Bartholomew Chapter SCGS
125 Wade Hampton Avenue
Walterboro, SC 29488

Orangeburgh German-Swiss Genealogical Society
P.O. Box 974
Orangeburg, SC 29116-0974
Email: jeffries@netside.com
URL: http://www.netside.com/~genealogy/orangeburgh.htm

Pee Dee Chapter SCGS
P.O. Box 1428
Marion, SC 29571

Pinckney District Chapter SCGS
385 Spring Street
P.O. Box 5281
Spartanburg, SC 29301

Savannah River Valley Genealogical Society
c/o Hart County Library
Benson Street
Hartwell, GA 30643

Sumter Chapter SCGS
P.O. Box 2543
Sumter, SC 29150

Sumter County Genealogical Society
Sumter County Museum/Archives
219 W. Liberty Street
Sumter, SC 29150
Tel: 803-773-9144

HISTORICAL SOCIETIES

Bluffton Historical Preservation Society
P.O. Box 742
Bluffton, SC 29910

(Beaufort) Historic Beaufort Foundation
801 Bay Street
Beaufort, SC 29902
Tel: 803-524-6334

(Brattonsville) Historic Brattonsville
1444 Brattonsville Road
McConnells, SC 29726
Tel: 803-684-2327

(Camden) Historic Camden
South Broad Street
Camden, SC 29020
Tel: 803-432-9841

Central Heritage Society
416 Church Street
Central, SC 29630
Tel: 864-639-2156

Charleston Library Society
164 King Street
Charleston, SC 29401
Tel: 803-723-9912

Chester County Historical Society/Museum
107 McAliley Street
Chester, SC 29706-1741
Tel: 803-385-2330

Confederation of Local Historical Societies
South Carolina Dept. of Archives & History
1430 Senate Street
Columbia, SC 29211
Tel: 803-734-8595
Email: hornsby@history.scdah.sc.edu
URL: http://www.scdah.sc.edu/historg.htm

Edisto Island Historic Preservation Society
2343 Highway 174
Edisto Island, SC 29438
Tel: 803-869-1954

Georgetown County Historical Commission
Front Street
P.O. Box 902
Georgetown, SC 29440
Tel: 803-546-7423

Greenville Historical Society
107 Broadus Avenue
Greenville, SC 29601
Tel: 864-233-4103

Horry County Historical Society
P.O. Box 2025
Conway, SC 29526
URL: http://www.webgroup.com/~hchs/

Jewish Historical Society of South Carolina
c/o David Cohen
College of Charleston
66 George Street
Charleston, SC 29424-0001
Email: efolley@scsn.net
URL: http://www.scsn.net/users/efolley/jhssc/jhssc-home.html

Kershaw County Historical Society
811 Fair Street
P.O. Box 501
Camden, SC 29020
Tel: 803-425-1123
Email: jim@compuzone.net
URL: http://www.historic.com/kchs/

Pendleton District Historical Society
125 E. Queen Street
Pendleton, SC 29670
Tel: 864-646-3782

Piedmont Historical Society
P.O. Box 8096
Spartanburg, SC 29305

Richland County Historic Preservation Commission
1616 Blanding Street
Columbia, SC 29201
Tel: 803-252-1770

Saluda County Historical Society
Law Range Street
Saluda, SC 29138
Tel: 864-445-8550

South Carolina Historical Society/Library
100 Meeting Street
P.O. Box 5401
Spartanburg, SC 29304
Tel: 803-723-3225
Fax: 803-723-8584
URL: http://www.historic.com/schs/index.html

Spartanburg Historical Association
Regional Museum of Spartanburg County
501 Otis Boulevard
Spartanburg, SC 29302
Tel: 864-596-3501
URL: http://www.spartanarts.org/history/index.html

Union County Historical Foundation
(Museum located above American Federal Bank)
P.O. Drawer 220
Union, SC 29379

University South Caroliniana Library Society
South Caroliniana Library
University of South Carolina
Columbia, SC 29208
URL: http://www.sc.edu/library/socar/uscs/index.html

York County, Historical Center of
212 E. Jefferson Street
York, SC 29745
Tel: 803-684-7262

LDS Family History Centers

Charleston Family History Center
1519 Sam Rittenberg Blvd.
P.O. Box 20296
Charleston, SC 29407
Tel: 803-766-6017

Columbia Family History Center
4440 Fort Jackson Blvd.
Columbia, SC 29209
Tel: 803-782-7141

Florence Family History Center
600 Maynard
Florence, SC 29505
Tel: 803-665-0433

Greer Family History Center
1301 Boiling Springs Road
Greer, SC 29650
Tel: 803-627-0553

Archives/Libraries/Museums

Abbeville/Greenwood Regional Library
106 North Main Street
Greenwood, SC 29646-2240
Tel: 864-941-4650
Fax: 864-941-4651
URL: http://192.147.157.51:8000/hytelnet/USA49.html

Aiken County Historical Museum
433 Newberry Street, SW
Aidken, SC 29801
Tel: 803-642-2015
URL: http://www.scescape.com/aikenhistoricalmuseum/

Alexander Salley Archives
Middleton at Bull Street
Orangeburg, SC 29115

Avery Research Center for African American History & Culture
College of Charleston
125 Bull Street
Charleston, SC 29401
Tel: 803-727-2009
Fax: 803-727-2017
URL: http://www.cofc.edu/library/avery/avery.html

Calhoun County Museum
303 Butler Street
St. Matthews, SC 29135
Tel: 803-874-3964
Fax: 803-874-1242
Email: ccm@scsn.net

Camden Archives and Museum
1314 Broad Street
Camden, SC 29020-3535
Tel: 803-425-6050
Email: chamber@camden-sc.org/
URL: http://www.camden-sc.org/Museum.html

Charleston City Archives
701 E. Bay Street, Suite 348
Charleston, SC 29401
Tel: 803-724-7301

Charleston County Library
South Carolina Room
68 Calhoun Street
Mail:
P.O. Box 22391
Charleston, SC 29413
Tel: 803-723-1165
803-727-6720 (Voice)
Fax: 803-722-0429
URL: http://edisto.awod.com/ccl/

Charleston Diocesan Archives
119 Broad Street
P.O. Box 818
Charleston, SC 29402

Charleston Register of Mesne Conveyance
2 Courthouse Square
Charleston, SC 29401
Tel: 803-723-6780

Cherokee County Public Library
300 E. Rutledge Street
Gaffney, SC 29340
Tel: 864-487-2711
Fax: 864-487-2752

Citadel
Daniel Library
171 Moultrie Street
Charleston, SC 29409
Tel: 803-953-2569 (Reference)
Fax: 803-953-5190
Email: reichardtk@citadel.edu
URL: http://www.citadel.edu/citadel/otherserv/library/index.htm

Francis Marion University
James A. Rogers Library-Arundel Room
Florence, SC 29501-0547
Tel: 803-661-1300
URL: http://vax.fmarion.edu/marion/

Greenville County Library
Stow South Carolina Historical Room
300 College Street
Greenville, SC 29601
Tel: 864-242-5000
URL: http://gcl.greenville.lib.sc.us/index.htm

Laurens County Library
1017 West Main Street
Laurens, SC 29360
Tel: 864-984-0596
Fax: 864-984-0598

Old Edgefield District Chapter SCGS/Archives
104 Court House Square
P.O. Box 468
Edgefield, SC 29824

Orangeburg County Public Library
510 Louis Street, NE
Orangeburg, SC 29115

Richland County Public Library/Main Library
Local History Room
1431 Assembly Street
Columbia, SC 29201
Tel: 803-799-7084
URL: http://www.richland.lib.sc.us/index.html

Rock Hill Public Library
138 E. Black Street
P.O. Box 10032
Rock Hill, SC 29731-0032
Tel: 803-324-7624

South Carolina State Library
1500 Senate Street
P.O. Box 11469
Columbia, SC 29211
Tel: 803-734-8666
Fax: 803-734-8676
URL: http://www.state.sc.us/scsl/

Spartanburg Public Library
151 N. Church Street
Spartanburg, SC 29306
Tel: 864-596-3505
Fax: 864-596-3518

Sumter County Genealogical Society
Sumter County Museum/Archives
219 W. Liberty Street
Sumter, SC 29150
Tel: 803-773-9144

University of South Carolina
South Caroliniana Library
720 College Street
Columbia, SC 29208
Tel: 803-777-3131/2
Email: cuthrellb@tcl.sc.edu
URL: http://www.sc.edu/library/socar/index.html

NEWSPAPER REPOSITORIES

Charleston County Library
South Carolina Room
68 Calhoun Street
Mail:
P.O. Box 22391
Charleston, SC 29413
Tel: 803-723-1165
803-727-6720 (Voice)
Fax: 803-722-0429
URL: http://edisto.awod.com/ccl/

South Carolina Department of Archives and History
1430 Senate Street
P.O. Box 11669, Capitol Station
Columbia, SC 29211-1669
Tel: 803-734-8577
803-834-8596
Fax: 803-734-8820
Email: sox@history.scdah.sc.edu
URL: http://www.scdah.sc.edu/homepage.htm

University of South Carolina
South Caroliniana Library
720 College Street
Columbia, SC 29208
Tel: 803-777-3131/2
Email: cuthrellb@tcl.sc.edu
URL: http://www.sc.edu/library/socar/books.html#newspapers

VITAL RECORDS

South Carolina Department of Archives and History
1430 Senate Street
P.O. Box 11669, Capitol Station
Columbia, SC 29211-1669
Tel: 803-734-8577
803-834-8596
Fax: 803-734-8820
Email: sox@history.scdah.sc.edu
URL: http://www.scdah.sc.edu/homepage.htm
(Death starting 1915-50 years ago)

South Carolina Department of Health and Environment Control
Bureau of Vital Statistics
J. Marion Sims Building
2600 Bull Street
Columbia, SC 29201-1797
Tel: 803-734-4830
(All Birth and Marriage, Death last 50 years)

SOUTH CAROLINA ON THE WEB

**Charleston County Library/
South Carolina Room Home Page**
http://edisto.awod.com/ccl/scr.htm

Civil War @ Charleston
http://www.awod.com/gallery/

Confederate Corner (Kershaw and Lancaster Counties)
http://members.aol.com/GreySky285/confederate.html

Genealogical Research at the South Carolina Archives
http://www.scdah.sc.edu/genealre.htm

Roots and Branches-Genealogy from the Carolinas
http://www.qni.com/~rayfield/

South Carolina GenWeb Project
http:// www.geocities.com/Heartland/Hills/3837

South Carolina Information
http://www.sciway.net/

South Carolina Information-Genealogy
http://www.sciway.net/hist/special/genealogy.html

Travellers Southern Families
http://genealogy.traveller.com/genealogy/

SOUTH DAKOTA

ARCHIVES, STATE & NATIONAL

National Archives—Central Plains Region
2312 East Bannister Road
Kansas City, MO 64131-3011
Tel: 816-926-6272
Fax: 816-926-6982
Email: archives@kansascity.nara.gov
URL: http://www.nara.gov/nara/regional/-6nsgil.html

National Archives—Rocky Mountain Region
Denver Federal Center, Building 48
P.O. Box 25307
Denver, CO 80225-0307
Tel: 303-236-0817
Fax: 303-236-9354
Email: archives@denver.nara.gov
URL: http://www.nara.gov/nara/regional/08nsgil.html

South Dakota State Archives
Cultural Heritage Center
900 Governors Drive
Pierre, SD 57501-2217
Tel: 605-773-3804
Fax: 605-773-6041
Email: archref@chc.state.sd.us
URL: http://www.state.sd.us/state/executive/deca/cultural/library.htm

GENEALOGICAL SOCIETIES

Aberdeen Area Genealogical Society (SDGS)
P.O. Box 493
Aberdeen, SD 57402-0493

Bennett County Genealogical Society (SDGS)
P.O. Box 483
Allen, SD 57714

Brookings Area Genealogical Society (SDGS)
524 Fourth Street
Brookings, SD 57006

Czech Heritage Preservation Society
P.O. Box 3
Tabor, SD 57063

East River Genealogical Forum (SDGS)
RR 2, Box 148
Wolsey, SD 57384

Family Tree Society (SDGS)
P.O. Box 202
Winner, SD 57580

Heritage Club-Platte (SDGS)
Route 2, Box 128
Platte, SD 57369

Hyde County Historical and Genealogical Society (SDGS)
P.O. Box 392
Highmore, SD 57345

Lake County Genealogical Society
c/o Karl Mundt Library @ Dakota State University
Madison, SD 57042

Lyman-Brule Genealogical Society (SDGS)
P.O. Box 555
Chamberlain, SD 57325

Mitchell Area Genealogical Society (SDGS)
620 N. Edmunds
Mitchell, SD 57301

Moody County Genealogical Society (SDGS)
501 W. First Avenue
Flandreau, SD 57028-1003

Murdo Genealogical Society (SDGS)
P.O. Box 441
Murdo, SD 57559

North Central South Dakota Genealogical Society (SDGS)
178 Southshore Drive
Mina, SD 57462-3000
URL: http://www.geocities.com/Heartland/3194/ncgs.htm

Pierre-Ft. Pierre Genealogical Society (SDGS)
P.O. Box 925
Pierre, SD 57501

Rapid City Society for Genealogical Research, Inc. (SDGS)
(Library at Rapid City Public Library-
See Archives/Libraries/Museums)
P.O. Box 1495
Rapid City, SD 57709

Sioux Valley Genealogical Society (SDGS)
Siouxland Heritage Museum
200 West 6th Street
Sioux Falls, SD 57104-6001
Tel: 605-367-4210
Fax: 605-367-6004

South Dakota Genealogical Organization of Lyman Descendants (SDGOLD)
P.O. Box 145
Oacoma, SD 57365
Tel: 605-734-6338
URL: http://tool-box.com/rc/owa/freeweb.page?id+1034773

South Dakota Genealogical Society
P.O. Box 1101
Pierre, SD 57501

Tri-State Genealogical Society (SDGS)
c/o Belle Fourche Public Library
905 5th Street
Belle Fourche, SD 57717-1705

Watertown Genealogical Society (SDGS)
611 NE B Avenue
Watertown, SD 57201

Yankton Genealogical Society (SDGS)
1803 Douglas Avenue
Yankton, SD 57078

Historical Societies

Bennett County Historical Society
c/o Diana Nelson
HWC #1, Box 5
Martin, SD 57551

Brookings County Historical Society/Museum
Samara Avenue
Volga, SD 57071
Tel: 605-627-9215

Brookings Historic Preservation Commission
311 Third Avenue
Box 270, City Hall
Brookings, SD 57006
Tel: http://www.sdstate.edu/~wbhp/http/historic.html

Brown County Historical Society
Dacotah Prairie Museum
21 S. Main
Aberdeen, SD 57401
Tel: 605-626-7117
Fax: 605-626-4010

Brule County Historical Society
P.O. Box 47
Kimball, SD 57355

Chamberlain Area Historical Preservation Association, Inc (CAHPA)
115 West Lawler
Chamberlain, SD 57325
Tel/Fax: 605-734-6542
Email: barbara@wcenet.com
URL: http://www.geocities.com/Heartland/Hills/5089/

Codington County Historical Society
Kampeska Heritage Museum
27 First Avenue, SE
Watertown, SD 57201
Tel: 605-886-7335

Czech Heritage Preservation Society
P.O. Box 3
Tabor, SD 57063

Deuel County Historical Society/Museum
P.O. Box 233
Brandt, SD 57218-0233
Tel: 605-876-2201
605-876-2641

Douglas County Historical Society
710 Braddock
Armour, SD 57313
Tel: 605-724-2115

Fall River County Historical Society
Old Schoolhouse
300 N. Chicago St.
Hot Springs, SD 57747-1657
Tel: 605-745-5147

Garretson Area Historical Society
609 Main Avenue
Garretson, SD 57030
Tel: 605-594-6694

Gregory County Historical Society
P.O. Box 376
Burke, SD 57523
Tel: 605-775-2641

High Plains Heritage Society/Center Museum
825 Heritage Drive
P.O. Box 524h
Spearfish, SD 57783
Tel: 605-642-9378
Fax: 605-642-8463
URL: http://www.state.sd.us/state/executive/tourism/adds/highpla.htm

Hurley Historical Society
P.O. Box 302
Hurley, SD 57036
Tel: 605-238-5725

Hyde County Historical and Genealogical Society (SDGS)
P.O. Box 392
Highmore, SD 57345

Keystone Area Historical Society
410 3rd Street
Keystone, SD 57751
Tel: 605-666-4494

Lyman County Historical Museum
911 E. 9th Street
Presho, SD 57568
Tel: 605-895-9446

Menno Historical Society
150 Poplar
Menno, SD 57045
Tel: 605-387-2867

Minnehaha County Historical Society
Siouxland Heritage Museum
200 W. 6th Street
Sioux Falls, SD 57104-6001
Tel: 605-367-4210
Fax: 605-367-6004

Old Stanley County Historical Society
410 W. Main
P.O. Box 698
Fort Pierre, SD 57532
Tel: 605-223-2757

Potter County Historical Society
P.O. Box 1
Gettysburg, SD 57442
Tel: 605-765-5691

Prairie Historical Society
Prairie Village
P.O. Box 256
Madison, SD 57042
Tel: 605-256-3644

Society of Black Hills Pioneers
c/o Adams Memorial Museum
54 Sherman Street
Deadwood, SD 57732-1364
Tel: 605-578-1714

South Dakota State Historical Society
Cultural Heritage Center
900 Governors Drive
Pierre, SD 57501-2217
Tel: 605-773-3458
Fax: 605-773-6041
Email: jeffm@chc.state.sd.us
URL: http://www.state.sd.us/state/executive/deca/cultural/sdshs.htm

Tripp County Historical Society
East Highway 18
Winner, SD 57580
Tel: 605-842-0704

Union County Historical Society
124 E. Main Street
P.O. Box 552
Elk Point, SD 57025
Tel: 605-356-2445

Yankton County Historical Society
Dakota Territorial Museum
610 Summit Street
P.O. Box 1033
Yankton, SD 57078-1033
Tel: 605-665-3898

LDS Family History Centers

Gettysburg Family History Center
530 South Mannston
Gettysburg, SD 57442
Tel: 605-765-9270

Pierre Family History Center
508 North Jefferson
Pierre, SD 57501

Rapid City Family History Center
2822 Canyon Lake Drive
Rapid City, SD 57702
Tel: 605-343-8656

Rosebud Family History Center
Highway #7 West
Rosebud, SD 57570
Tel: 605-747-2818

Sioux Falls Family History Center
3900 South Fairhall Avenue
Sioux Falls, SD 57106
Tel: 605-361-1070

Archives/Libraries/Museums

Adams Memorial Museum
54 Sherman Street
Deadwood, SD 57732-1364
Tel: 605-578-1714
URL: http://www.blackhills.com/museum/index.html

Alexander Mitchell Public Library
Heritage Room, LL
519 South Kline Street
Aberdeen, SD 57401
Tel: 605-626-7097

American Indian Culture Research Center
P.O. Box 98
Marvin, SD 57251-0098
Tel: 605-432-5528
Fax: 605-432-4754
Email: indian@daknet.com
URL: http://www.daknet.com/~indian/dakota.html

Augustana College
Center for Western Studies
2001 S. Summit Avenue
Sioux Falls, SD 57197
Tel: 605-336-4007
Email: hthomps@inst.augi.edu
URL: http://inst.augie.edu/~asmith/ctr_w_st.html

Belle Fourche/Northwest Regional Public Library
905 5th Street
Belle Fourche, SD 57717-1705
Tel: 605-892-4407

Black Hills Mining Museum
323 W. Main Street
P.O. Box 694
Lead, SD 57754-1604
Tel: 605-584-1605
URL: http://www.mining-museum.blackhills.com/

Brookings Public Library
515 Third Street
Brookings, SD 57006
Tel: 605-692-9407
Fax: 605-692-9386
URL: http://www.sdstate.edu/~wbcg/http/library/library.html

Buechel Memorial Lakota Museum
St. Francis Mission
350 S. Oak Street
P.O. Box 499
St. Francis, SD 57572
Tel: 605-747-2745
Fax: 605-747-5057

Dacotah Prairie Museum
21 S. Main
Aberdeen, SD 57401
Tel: 605-626-7117
Fax: 605-626-4010

Deadwood Public Library
435 Williams Street
Deadwood, SD 57732-1113
Tel: 605-578-2821
Fax: 605-578-2170
Email: tdavis@sdln.net
URL: http://www.sdln.net/libs/dwd/Text/WebPages/WebHome.htm

Eureka Pioneer Museum
RR 1, Box 154
Eureka, SD 57437
Tel: 605-284-2711

Grace Balloch Memorial Library
Spearfish Municipal Service Center
South Dakota History Room
625 Fifth Street
Spearfish, SD 57783
Tel: 605-642-1330
URL: http://www.sdln.net/libs/spf/

High Plains Heritage Society/Center Museum
825 Heritage Drive
P.O. Box 524h
Spearfish, SD 57783
Tel: 605-642-9378
Fax: 605-642-8463
URL: http://www.state.sd.us/state/executive/tourism/adds/highpla.htm

Huron Public Library
521 Dakota Avenue, S.
Huron, SD 57350
Tel: 605-352-3778

Kampeska Heritage Museum
27 First Avenue, SE
Watertown, SD 57201
Tel: 605-886-7335

North American Baptists Archives
1605 Euclid Avenue
Sioux Falls, SD 57105
Tel: 605-336-6588

Rapid City Public Library
610 Quincy Street
Rapid City, SD 57701
Tel: 605-394-4171
URL: http://www.sdln.net/libs/rcp/

Rawlins Municipal Library
1000 E. Church Street
Pierre, SD 57501
Tel: 605-773-7421
Fax: 605-773-7423
URL: http://www.dakotariver.com/rawlins/index.htm

Scotland Heritage Chapel & Museum
811 6th Street
Scotland, SD 57059
Tel: 605-583-2978

Sioux Falls Public Library
201 North Main Avenue
Sioux Falls, SD 57102
Tel: 605-367-7081
URL: http://www.siouxland.lib.sd.us/

Siouxland Heritage Museum
200 W. 6th Street
Sioux Falls, SD 57104-6001
Tel: 605-367-4210
Fax: 605-367-6004

Smith-Zimmerman Museum
Dakota State University Campus
221 NE Eighth Street
Madison, SD 57042
Tel: 605-256-5308
URL: http://www.triton.dsu.edu/szmuseum/

South Dakota State Agricultural Heritage Museum
South Dakota State University
P.O. Box 2207C
Brookings, SD 57007-0999
Tel: 605-688-6226
Fax: 605-688-6303
Email: agmuseum@mg.sdstate.edu
URL: http://www.sdstate.edu/~wahm/

South Dakota State Historical Society
Cultural Heritage Center
900 Governors Drive
Pierre, SD 57501-2217
Tel: 605-773-3458
Fax: 605-773-6041
Email: jeffm@chc.state.sd.us
URL: http://www.state.sd.us/state/executive/deca/cultural/sdshs.htm

South Dakota State Library
Mercedes MacKay Memorial Building
800 Governors Drive
Pierre, SD 57501-2294
Tel: 605-773-3131
800-423-6665
Fax: 605-773-4950
Email: refrequest@stlib.state.sd.us
URL: http://www.state.sd.us/state/executive/deca/st_lib/st_lib.htm

South Dakota State University
Hilton M. Briggs Library
Box 2115
Brookings, SD 57007
Tel: 605-688-5106
Fax: 605-688-6133
URL: http://www.sdstate.edu/whbl/http/geninfo/geninfo.html

University of South Dakota
I.D. Weeks Library
Vermillion, SD 57069
Tel: 605-677-5305
605-677-5450 (Special Collections)
605-677-5629 (Government Documents)
URL: http://www.usd.edu/library/

Verendrye Museum/Archives
115 Deadwood Street
Fort Pierre, SD 57532
URL: http://www.iw.net/users/fpdc/vmuseum.htm

Vermillion Public Library
18 Church Street
Vermillion, SD 57069
Tel: 605-677-7060
URL: http://www.usd.edu/vpl/

Newspaper Repositories

South Dakota State Historical Society/Archives
South Dakota Newspaper Project
Cultural Heritage Center
900 Governor Drive
Pierre, SD 57501
Tel: 605-773-4370
URL: http://www.state.sd.us/state/executive/deca/cultural/newspap.htm

Vital Records

Vital Records, Department of Health
445 E. Capitol
Pierre, SD 57501-3185
Tel: 605-773-4961
Fax: 605-773-5683
Email: kathim@doh.state.sd.us
URL: http://www.state.sd.us/state/executive/doh/vital.htm

South Dakota on the Web

Homestead Records Information Page
http://members.aol.com/gkrell/homestead/home.html

Native American—SD GenWeb Project
http://www.geocities.com/Heartland/Plains/8430/index.htm

South Dakota GenWeb Project
http://www.geocities.com/Heartland/3194/index.html

TENNESSEE

ARCHIVES, STATE & NATIONAL

National Archives—Southeast Region
1557 St. Joseph Avenue
East Point, GA 30344-2593
Tel: 404-763-7477
Fax: 404-763-7033
Email: archives@atlanta.nara.gov
URL: http://www.nara.gov/nara/regional/04nsgil.html

Tennessee State Library and Archives
State Library and Archives Building
403 Seventh Avenue, North
Nashville, TN 37243-0312
Tel: 615-741-2764
615-741-2541
Email: reference@mail.state.tn.us
URL: http://www.state.tn.us/sos/statelib/tslahome.htm

GENEALOGICAL SOCIETIES

African American Historical & Genealogical Society (AAHGS)
Tennessee Chapter
P.O. Box 17684
Nashville, TN 37217

Blount County Genealogical & Historical Society
P.O. Box 4986
Maryville, TN 37802-4986

Delta Genealogical Society
c/o Rossville Public Library
504 McFarland Avenue
Rossville, GA 30741

Fentress County Genealogical Society
P.O. Box 178
Jamestown, TN 38556

First Families of Tennessee
c/o East Tennessee Historical Society
P.O. Box 1629
Knoxville, TN 37901-1629
Tel: 423-544-5732
Fax: 423-544-4319
URL: http://www.usit.net/tngenweb/ethisctr/1stfamtn.htm

Greene County Genealogical Society
P.O. Box 1903
Greenville, TN 37744-1903
Hamblen County Genealogical Society
P.O. Box 1213
Morristown, TN 37816-1213

Hancock County Historical & Genealogical Society
P.O. Box 277
Sneedville, TN 37869

Hawkins County Genealogical & Historical Society
P.O. Box 429
Rogersville, TN 37857

Jefferson County Genealogical Society
P.O. Box 267
Jefferson City, TN 37760

Jonesborough Genealogical Society
P.O. Box 314
Jonesborough, TN 37659

Lincoln County Genealogical Society
1508 West Washington Street
Fayetteville, TN 37334

McNairy County Genealogical Society
P.O. Box 1023
Selmer, TN 38375

Mid-West Tennessee Genealogical Society
P.O. Box 3343, Murray Station
Jackson, TN 38303-0343
URL: http://erc.jscc.cc.tn.us/jfn/libjmc/Genealogical.html

Middle Tennessee Genealogical Society
P.O. Box 190625
Nashville, TN 37219-0625

Morgan County Genealogical & Historical Society
Route 2, Box 992
Wartburg, TN 37887

Obion County Genealogical Society
P.O. Box 241
Union City, TN 38261

Pellissippi Genealogical & Historical Society
c/o Clinton Public Library
118 South Hicks
Clinton, TN 37716
Tel: 615-457-5400

Roane County Genealogical Society
P.O. Box 297
Kingston, TN 37763-0297

Signal Mountain Genealogical Society
103 Florida Avenue
Signal Mountain, TN 37377

Tennessee Genealogical Society/Library
9114 Davies Plantation Road
P.O. Box 247
Brunswick, TN 38014-0247
Tel: 901-381-1447
URL: http://www.memphismemphis.com/genealogy/tngen/

Upper Cumberland Genealogical Association
P.O. Box 575
Cookeville, TN 38503-0575
Email: clark@blomand.net
URL: http://www.jagunet.com/~mbar/ucga.htm

Watauga Association of Genealogists/Upper East Tennessee
P.O. Box 117
Johnson City, TN 37605-0117

Weakley County Genealogical Society
P.O. Box 92
Martin, TN 38237

HISTORICAL SOCIETIES

African American Historical & Genealogical Society (AAHGS)
Tennessee Chapter
P.O. Box 17684
Nashville, TN 37217

Bedford County Historical Society
624 South Brittain Street
Shelbyville, TN 37160

Blount County Genealogical & Historical Society
P.O. Box 4986
Maryville, TN 37802-4986

Bradley County Historical Society
c/o Cleveland Public Library
History Branch
795 Church Street, NE
Cleveland, TN 37311

Campbell County Historical Society
109 Crestview Drive
LaFollette, TN 37766

Chester County Historical Society
P.O. Box 721
Henderson, TN 38340-0721
URL: http://erc.jscc.cc.tn.us/jfn/libjmc/Chester.html

Claiborne County Historical Society
P.O. Box 32
Tazewell, TN 37879

Coffee County Historical Society
Coffee County Courthouse
101 W. Fort Street
Manchester, TN 37355
Tel: 615-728-0145
Email: jlewis@cafes.com
pswan@edge.net
jphilps@edge.net
URL: http://www.cafes.net/jlewis/pubs.htm

East Tennessee Historical Society
(Library at East Tennessee Historical Center-See Libraries below)
600 Market Street (Museum)
P.O. Box 1629
Knoxville, TN 37901-1629
Tel: 423-544-5732
Fax: 423-544-4319
URL: http://www.usit.net/tngenweb/eths.htm

Franklin County Historical Society
P.O. Box 130
Winchester, TN 37398

Giles County Historical Society
P.O. Box 693
Pulaski, TN 38478

Greene County Chapter, East Tennessee Historical Association
c/o Harry Roberts
105 Monument Avenue
Greeneville, TN 37743

Hancock County Historical & Genealogical Society
P.O. Box 277
Sneedville, TN 37869

Hardin County Historical Society
P.O. Box 1012
Savannah, TN 38372
URL: http://www.centuryinter.net/nacent/bs/history.htm

Hawkins County Genealogical & Historical Society
P.O. Box 429
Rogersville, TN 37857

Haywood County Historical Society/Museum
127 N. Grand Avenue
Brownsville, TN 38012
URL: http://erc.jscc.cc.tn.us/jfn/libjmc/Haywood.html

Loudon County Heritage Association
P.O. Box 466
Loudon, TN 37774

Macon County Historical Society
c/o Macon County Public Library
294 Chaffin Road
Lafayette, TN 37083
Tel: 615-666-6030

Marshall County Historical Society
224 Third Avenue, North
Lewisburg, TN 37091

Maury County Historical Society
P.O. Box 147
Columbia, TN 38401

Morgan County Genealogical & Historical Society
Route 2, Box 992
Wartburg, TN 37887

Old James County Historical Society
P.O. Box 203
Ooltewah, TN 37363

Oliver Springs Historical Society
Oliver Springs Southern Railway Depot
610 Walker Avenue
Oliver Springs, TN 37840
Mail:
OSHS
Internet Inquiry Service
Union Planters Building
727 Main Street
Oliver Springs, TN 37840
Tel: 423-435-1711
URL: http://www.public.usit.net/nwcs/

Pellissippi Genealogical & Historical Society
c/o Clinton Public Library
118 South Hicks
Clinton, TN 37716
Tel: 615-457-5400

Smoky Mountain Historical Society
P.O. Box 5078
Sevierville, TN 37864
Email: smhs@SmokyKin.com
URL: http://www.smokykin.com/smhs/

Tennessee Folklore Society
P.O. Box 529
Murfreesboro, TN 37133
Tel: 615-898-2576
Fax: 615-898-5098

Union County Historical Society
P.O. Box 95
Maynardville, TN 37807

Van Buren County Historical Society
P.O. Box 126
Spencer, TN 38585

Washington County Historical Association
P.O. Box 205
Jonesborough, TN 37659

Wayne County Historical Society
P.O. Box 866
Waynesboro, TN 38450

LDS Family History Centers

Bartlett Family History Center
4195 Kirby-Whitten Road
Bartlett, TN 38134
Tel: 901-388-9974

Chattanooga Family History Center
1019 North Moore Road
Chattanooga, TN 37412
Tel: 423-892-7632

Cordova Family History Center
8150 Walnut Grove Road
Cordova, TN 38018
Tel: 901-754-2545

Franklin Family History Center
1100 Grey Fox Road
Franklin, TN 37069
Tel: 615-794-4251

Kingsport Family History Center
100 Cannongate Road
Kingsport, TN 37660
Tel: 423-245-2321

Knoxville Family History Center
400 Kendall Road
Knoxville, TN 37919
Tel: 423-693-8252

Madison Family History Center
107 Twin Hill Drive
Madison, TN 37115
Tel: 615-859-6926

McMinnville Family History Center
183 Underwood Road
McMinnville, TN 37110
Tel: 615-473-1053

Archives/Libraries/Museums

Appalachian State University
Carol Grotnes Belk Library, 2nd Floor
W.L. Eury Appalachian Collection
Boone, NC 28608
Tel: 704-262-4041
Fax: 704-262-2553
Email: hayfj@appstate.edu
URL: http://www1.appstate.edu/dept/library/appcoll/history.html

Appalachian Studies Association
Regional Research Institute
West Virginia University
Morgantown, WV 26506
Tel: 304-558-0220 ext. 35

Art Circle Public Library
306 E. First Street
Crossville, TN 38555
Tel: 615-484-6790
Fax: 615-484-2350
URL: http://www.midtenn.net/~jhouston/index.html

Blount County Library
301 McGhee Street
Maryville, TN 37801
Tel: 423-982-0981

Carroll County Library
159 W. Main Street
Huntingdon, TN 38344
Tel: 901-986-1919
901-986-3991
Fax: 901-986-3585

Center for Appalachian Studies and Services
East Tennessee State University (ETSU)
Johnson City, TN 37614
Tel: 423-439-5348
Fax: 423-439-6340
URL: http://www.etsu-tn.edu/ARCHAPP/pracass.htm

Chattanooga/Hamilton County Bicentennial Library
Genealogy & Local History Department
1001 Broad Street
Chattanooga, TN 37402
Tel: 423-757-5310
423-757-5316

Clarksville Montgomery County Museum
200 S. 2nd Street
Clarksville, TN 37040-3400
Tel: 615-648-5780

Cleveland Public Library
History Branch
795 Church Street, NE
Cleveland, TN 37311
Tel: 615-472-2164
Email: cpl@chattanooga.net
URL: http://www.chattanooga.net/cpl/hb_index

Clinton Public Library
118 South Hicks
Clinton, TN 37716
Tel: 615-457-5400

Dandridge Memorial/Jefferson County Public Library
P.O. Box 339
Dandridge, TN 37725
Tel: 423-397-9758

East Tennessee Historical Center
314 Clinch Avenue
Knoxville, TN 37902-1610
Tel: 423-544-5739
URL: http://www.usit.net/tngenweb/ethisctr/ethisctr.htm
(Home to McClung Historical Collection, East Tennessee Historical Society, Sons of the American Revolution, and Knox County Archives)

East Tennessee State University
Sherrod Library
Archives of Appalachia and Special Collections
Johnson City, TN 37614
Tel: 423-929-6990
URL: http://www.etsu-tn.edu/ARCHAPP/

Fayetteville/Lincoln County Public Library
400 Division Street
Fayetteville, TN 37334
Tel: 615-433-3286

Greenville/Greene County Library
Tennessee Room
210 N. Main Street
Greeneville, TN 37745
Tel: 423-638-5034
Fax: 423-638-3841
Email: alp7@tricon.net
URL: http://ggc.library.net/

H.B. Stamps Memorial Library
407 E. Main Street
Rogersville, TN 37857
Tel: 423-272-8710

Hardin County Library
1013 Main Street
Savannah, TN 38372

Highland Rim Regional Library Center
2118 E. Main Street
Murfreesboro, TN 37130-4043
Tel: 615-893-3380

Jackson/Madison County Public Library
Tennessee Room
433 East Lafayette
Jackson, TN 38301
Tel: 901-425-8600
URL: http://erc.jscc.cc.tn.us/jfn/libjmc/

Jonesborough History Museum
117 Boone Street
Jonesborough, TN 37659
Tel: 423-753-1015

Magness Memorial Library
118 W. Main Street
McMinnville, TN 37110
Tel: 615-473-2428

Maury County Public Library
211 W. 8th Street
Columbia, TN 38402
Tel: 615-388-6332
Fax: 615-388-6337

Memphis/Shelby County Public Library and Information Center
History and Travel Department
1850 Peabody
Memphis, TN 38104
Tel: 901-725-8821
URL: http://www.memphislibrary.lib.tn.us/infohub/htdrafts.htm

Memphis/Shelby County Public Library
Cossitt Branch
33 South Front Street
Memphis, TN 38103
Tel: 901-526-1712
URL: http://www.memphislibrary.lib.tn.us/infohub/br1.htm

Morristown/Hamblen Library
417 West Main Street
Morristown, TN 37814
Tel: 423-586-6410

Mount Pleasant Public Library
200 Hay Long Avenue
P.O. Box 71
Mount Pleasant, TN 38474
Tel: 615-379-3752

Museum of Appalachia
2819 Andersonville Highway
Clinton, TN 37716
Tel: 423-494-7680

Nashville/Davidson County Public Library
225 8th Avenue, N.
Nashville, TN 37203
Tel: 615-862-5760

Rossville Public Library
504 McFarland Avenue
Rossville, GA 30741
Tel: 706-866-1368
Fax: 706-858-0251
Email: rossvill@voyageronline.net
URL: http://www.walker.public.lib.ga.us/branches/rossvill.xtm

Tennessee Genealogical Society/Library
9114 Davies Plantation Road
P.O. Box 247
Brunswick, TN 38014-0247
Tel: 901-381-1447
URL: http://www.memphismemphis.com/genealogy/tngen/

Tennessee State Library and Archives
State Library and Archives Building
403 Seventh Avenue, North
Nashville, TN 37243-0312
Tel: 615-741-2764
615-741-2541
Email: reference@mail.state.tn.us
URL: http://www.state.tn.us/sos/statelib/tslahome.htm

University of Memphis (Memphis State)
Brister Library, Special Collections
Mississippi Valley Collection
Memphis, TN 38104
Tel: 901-678-2210

University of Tennessee/Knoxville Library
Special Collections/Manuscripts
Knoxville, TN 37996
URL (Manuscripts):
http://toltec.lib.utk.edu/~speccoll/
URL (Library Guides): http://www.lib.utk.edu/collect/library_guides

Vanderbilt University
Jean and Alexander Heard Library
Special Collections and University Archives
419 21st Avenue, S.
Nashville, TN 37240
Tel: 615-322-2807
Email: harwell@library.vanderbilt.edu
URL: http://www.library.vanderbilt.edu/speccol/schome.html

Williamson County Public Library
Genealogy Room
611 West Main Street
Franklin, TN 37064
Tel: 615-794-3156
615-795-3105

NEWSPAPER REPOSITORIES

Tennessee State Library and Archives
State Library and Archives Building
403 Seventh Avenue, North
Nashville, TN 37243-0312
Tel: 615-741-2764
615-741-2541
Email: reference@mail.state.tn.us
URL: http://www.state.tn.us/sos/statelib/pubsvs/tn-obits.htm

University of Tennessee/Knoxville Library
Special Collections/Manuscripts
Knoxville, TN 37996
Tel: 423-974-4480
Email: jlloyd@utk.edu
URL: http://toltec.lib.utk.edu/~speccoll/newspaper/tnphome.html

Vital Records

Tennessee State Library and Archives
State Library and Archives Building
403 Seventh Avenue, North
Nashville, TN 37243-0312
Tel: 615-741-2764
615-741-2541
Email: reference@mail.state.tn.us
URL: http://www.state.tn.us/sos/statelib/tslahome.htm
Births for Nashville (1881-1908), Chattanooga (1879-1908), and Knoxville (1881-1908)
Deaths for Memphis (1848-1908), Nashville (1874-1908), Knoxville (1881-1908), and Chattanooga (1872-1908)
Births and Deaths (1908-1912)

Tennessee Vital Records
Central Services Building, 1st Floor
421 Fifth Avenue, North
Nashville, TN 37247-0450
Tel: 615-741-1763
Fax: 615-741-9860
To order by phone with charge card:
Tel: 615-741-0778
Fax: 615-726-2559
URL: http://www.state.tn.us/health/bir/vr0.html
Births (1914-Present) and Deaths (1914-50 Years ago)
No Birth or Death Records were recorded for the year 1913.

Tennessee on the Web

8th Tennessee Cavalry, CSA
http://www.jagunet.com/~mbar/8tncav.htm

American Civil War Page
http://funnelweb.utcc.utk.edu/~hoemann/warweb.html

Introduction to Tennessee Land History
http://www.ultranet.com/~deeds/tenn.htm

Smoky Mountain Ancestral Quest
http://www.smokykin.com/

Tennessee GenWeb Project
http://www.usit.net/tngenweb/index.html

Tennessee State Library and Archives
Historical & Genealogical Information
URL: http://www.state.tn.us/sos/statelib/pubsvs/intro.htm

Tennessee State Library and Archives
Online Index to Acts of Tennessee 1796-1830 by Name
http://www.state.tn.us/sos/statelib/pubsvs/actintro.htm

Texas

Archives, State & National

National Archives—Southeast Region
1557 St. Joseph Avenue
East Point, GA 30344-2593
Tel: 404-763-7477
Fax: 404-763-7033
Email: archives@atlanta.nara.gov
URL: http://www.nara.gov/nara/regional/04nsgil.html

Texas State Library and Archives Commission
Lorenzo de Zavala State Archives and Library Building
1201 Brazos Street
P.O. Box 12927
Austin, TX 78711
Tel: 512-463-5455
512-463-5463 (Genealogy Collection, Room 110)
Email: geninfo@tsl.state.tx.us
URL: http://www.tsl.state.tx.us/lobby/genfirst.htm

Genealogical Societies

Amarillo Genealogical Society
413 East Fourth Street
Amarillo, TX 79189
Tel: 806-378-3054

Ancestor Club
P.O. Box 157
Anahuac, TX 77514

Anderson County Genealogical Society
c/o Palestine Public Library
1101 North Cedar
Palestine, TX 75801
Email: bonniew@e-tex.com
URL: http://www.e-tex.com/personal/bonniew/acgs/acgs2.htm

Arlington Genealogical Society
101 East Abram Street
Arlington, TX 76010
Tel: 817-277-6026

Athens Genealogical Organization
121 South Prairieville Street
Athens, TX 75751
Tel: 903-675-2694

Austin Genealogical Society
P.O. Box 1507
Autsin, TX 78767-1507
Email: 70461.2144@compuserve.com
URL: http://www.main.org/ags/

Baytown Genealogical Society
P.O. Box 2486
Baytown, TX 77522
Tel: 713-479-3244

Big Spring, Genealogical Society of
810 East 12th Street
Big Spring, TX 79720
Tel: 915-267-7236

Big Thicket Genealogical Club
P.O. Box 1260
Kountze, TX 77625

Brazos Genealogical Association
P.O. Box 5493
Bryan, TX 77805
Email: holt@cy-net.net
URL: http://www2.cy-net.net/~bga/

Brazosport Genealogical Society
P.O. Box 813
Lake Jackson, TX 77566
Email: dpugh@brazosport.cc.tx.us
URL: http://gator1.brazosport.cc.tx.us/~gensoc/

Burkburnett Genealogical Society
215 East Fourth Street
Burkburnett, TX 76354
Tel: 817-569-2991

Burnet County Genealogical Society
100 East Washington Street
Burnet, TX 78611
Tel: 512-756-2328

Caldwell County Genealogical and Historical Society
215 South Pecan Avenue
Luling, TX 78648
Tel: 830-875-9466
Email: ccg&hsoc@bcsnet.net
URL: http://www.rootsweb.com/~txcaldwe/socpage.htm

Calhoun County Genealogical Society
P.O. Box 1150
Port Lavaca, TX 77979
Tel: 512-552-2588

Camp County Genealogical Society
P.O. Box 1083
Pittsburg, TX 75686

Cass County Genealogical Society
P.O. Box 880, Dept. CCW
Atlanta, TX 75551-0880
Tel: 903-796-6750

Central Texas Genealogical Society
c/o Waco-McLennan County Library
1717 Austin Avenue
Waco, TX 76701
Tel: 817-750-5945
URL: http://www.aisi.net/GenWeb/McLennanCo/

Chaparral Genealogical Society/Library
310 N. Live Oak
P.O. Box 606
Tomball, TX 77375
Tel: 713-255-9081

Cherokee County Genealogical Society
P.O. Box 1332
Jacksonville, TX 75766
Tel: 903-586-9067
Email: gordonbe@e-tex.com
URL: http://www.e-tex.com/personal/gordonbe/Texas GenWeb Cherokee County.htm

Childress Genealogical Society
117 Avenue B, NE
Childress, TX 79201

Clayton Library Friends
P.O. Box 271078
Houston, TX 77277

Coastal Bend Genealogical Society
P.O. Box 2711
Corpus Christi, TX 78403

Collin County Genealogical Society
P.O. Box 865052
Plano, TX 75086-5052
Tel: 214-596-3567
Email: Traceroots@aol.com
URL: http://www.starbase21.com/PSGenealogy/

Comal County Genealogy Society
P.O. Box 310583
New Braunfels, TX 78130
Tel: 210-629-1900

Coryell County Genealogical Society
811 Main Street
Gatesville, TX 76528
Tel: 817-865-5367

Cottle County Genealogical Society
P.O. Box 1005
Paducah, TX 79248

Cross Timbers Genealogical Society
P.O. Box 197
Gainesville, TX 76240

Cypress Basin Genealogical Society
P.O. Box 403
Mount Pleasant, TX 75455

Dallas County East Genealogical Society
7637 Mary Dan Drive
Dallas, TX 75217

Dallas Genealogical Society
P.O. Box 12648
Dallas, TX 75225-0648
URL: http://www.chrysalis.org/dgs/

Daughters of the Republic of Texas/Library and Museum
Alamo Plaza
P.O. Box 1401
San Antonio, TX 78295-1401
Tel: 210-225-1071
Fax: 210-212-8514
Email: drtl@salsa.net
URL: http://www.drtl.org/~drtl/

Deaf Smith County Genealogical Society
211 East Fourth Street
Hereford, TX 79045

Denison Library Genealogical Society
300 West Gandy
Denison, TX 75020
Tel: 903-465-9447

Denton County Genealogical Society
P.O. Box 23322, TWU Station
Denton, TX 76204

Donley County Genealogical Society
P.O. Box 116
Clarendon, TX 79226

East Bell County Genealogical Society
3219 Meadow Oaks Drive
Temple, TX 76502
Tel: 817-778-2073

East Texas Genealogical Society
P.O. Box 6967
Tyler, TX 75711
Tel: 903-759-4075
Email: jettiel@ballistic.com

El Paso Genealogical Society
c/o El Paso Public Library
501 North Mesa Street
El Paso, TX 79901
Tel: 915-543-5474
Email: patrussb@juno.com
URL: http://rgfn.epcc.edu/users/az289/

Ellis County Genealogical Society
P.O. Box 479
Waxahachie, TX 75168

Erath County, Cross Timbers Genealogical Society
c/o Stephensville Public Library
174 North Columbia
Stephenville, TX 76401
Tel: 817-965-5665

Fannin County Genealogical Society
605 Agnew
Bonham, TX 75418

Fort Belknap Genealogical Association
Murray Route
Graham, TX 76046

Fort Bend County Genealogical Society
P.O. Box 274
Richmond, TX 77406-0274
Tel: 713-341-2608

Fort Brown Genealogical Society
608 East Adams
Brownsville, TX 78520
Tel: 512-542-4824

Fort Worth Genealogical Society (FWGS)
P.O. Box 9767
Fort Worth, TX 76147
Tel: 817-457-3330
Email: joegrant@flash.net
URL: http://www.chrysalis.org/business/fwgen/

Freestone County Genealogical Society
P.O. Box 14
Fairfield, TX 75840
Tel: 903-389-2292

Gainesville Genealogical Group
Cooke County College
Gainesville, TX 76240

Galveston Genealogical Society
P.O. Box 461882
Garland, TX 75046

Garland Genealogical Society
P.O. Box 461882
Garland, TX 75046
Email: ljdolby@airmail.net
URL: http://www.geocities.com/TheTropics/1926/society.html

Gilmer Genealogical Society
West Pine Street
Gilmer, TX 75644

Grand Prairie Genealogical Society
P.O. Box 532026
Grand Prairie, TX 75053

Grayson County Genealogical Society
421 North Travis
Sherman, TX 75090
Tel: 903-892-7240

Gregg County Genealogical Society
P.O. Box 2985
Longview, TX 75606-2985
URL: http://www.chrysalis.org/dgs/gcgs.htm

Guadalupe County Genealogical Society
707 East College Street
Sequin, TX 78155
Tel: 512-379-1531

Gulf Coast Ancestry Researchers
P.O. Box 16
Wallisville, TX 77597

Hamilton County Genealogical Society
209 W. Henry
Hamilton, TX 76531
Tel: 817-386-4566
Email: hcgs@htcomp.net
URL: http://207.17.189.3/hcgs/

Hardin County Genealogical Society
335 Santa Fe
Silsbee, TX 77656

Harris County Genealogical Society
P.O. Box 391
Pasadena, TX 77501

Harrison County Genealogical Society
P.O. Box 597
Marshall, TX 75671
URL: http://www.rootsweb.com/~txharris/hcgensoc.htm

Haskell County Genealogical Society
300 North Avenue E
Haskell, TX 79521

Hays County Genealogical Society
P.O. Box 1837
San Marcos, TX 78666

Heart of Texas Genealogical Society
P.O. Box 1837
Rochelle, TX 76872

Hemphill County Genealogical Society
Route 2
Canadian, TX 79014

Hi-Plains Genealogical Society
c/o Unger Memorial Library
825 Austin Street
Plainview, TX 79072-7235
Tel: 806-296-1148
URL: http://www.texasonline.net/schools/unger/geneal.htm

Hill Country Genealogical Society
HC 7, Box 52
Llano, TX 78643

Hill County Genealogical Society
412 East Franklin
Hillsboro, TX 76645
Tel: 817-694-5483

Hispanic Genealogical Society
P.O. Box 231271
Houston, TX 77223-1271
URL: http://www.brokersys.com/~joguerra/jose.html

Hood County Genealogical Society
P.O. Box 1623
Granbury, TX 76048
Email: granbury@emcee.com
URL: http://www.genealogy.org/~granbury/

Hopkins County Genealogical Society
212 Main Street
P.O. Box 624
Sulphur Springs, TX 75483
Tel: 903-885-8523

Houston Area Genealogical Forum
Genealogical Record, Editor
P.O. Box 271466
Houston, TX 77277-1466
Tel: 713-827-4440
URL: http://pobox.com/~hgf/
or http://web.wt.net/~hgforum/

Humble Genealogical Society
P.O. Box 2723
Humble, TX 77338

Hunt County Genealogical Society
P.O Box 398
Greenville, TX 75403
Tel: 903-886-8690

Hutchinson County Genealogical Society
625 Weatherly Street
Borger, TX 79007

Johnson County Genealogical Society
P.O. Box 1256
Cleburne, TX 76033
URL: http://www.htcomp.net/jcgs/soc/soc.htm

Kaufman County Genealogical Society
P.O. Box 337
Terrell, TX 75160
Tel: 214-524-5605

Kendall County Genealogical Society
P.O. Box 623
Boerne, TX 78006

Kent County Genealogical Society
P.O. Box 6
Jayton, TX 79528

Kerrville, Genealogical Society of
505 Water Street
Kerrville, TX 78028
Tel: 210-257-8422

Kingsland Genealogical Society
P.O. Box 952
Kingsland, TX 78639
URL: http://www.rootsweb.com/~txkinggs/

Lamar County Genealogical Society
Paris Junior College Campus-Jess B. Alford Center
2400 Clarksville Street
PJC Box 187
Paris, TX 75460
Tel: 903-784-9448
Email: betsym@stargate.1starnet.com
URL: http://gen.1starnet.com/lamargen.htm

Lamesa Area Genealogical Society
P.O. Box 1264
Lamesa, TX 79331

Lancaster Genealogical Society
220 Main Street
Lancaster, TX 75146

Lee County Genealogical Society
177 South Mason
Giddings, TX 78942

Leon County Genealogical Society
Old Courthouse
P.O. Box 500
Centerville, TX 75833

Limestone County Genealogical Society
350 Rust Street
P.O. Box 1437
Mexia, TX 76667
Tel: 817-562-3231

Llano Estacado Genealogical Society
1313 West Ninth Street
Littlefield, TX 79339

Los Bexarenos Genealogical Society
P.O. Box 1935
San Antonio, TX 78297
Tel: 210-822-1526

Lower Gulf Coast Genealogical and Historical Society
Email: dsk@phoenix.net
URL: http://www.phoenix.net/~dsk/genealogy.html

Lufkin Genealogical Society
P.O. Box 150631
Lufkin, TX 75915

Madison County Genealogical Society
P.O. Box 26
Madisonville, TX 77864

Marion County Genealogical Society
P.O. Box 224
Jefferson, TX 75657-0224

Matagorda County Genealogical Society
P.O. Box 264
Bay City, TX 77404
Tel: 409-245-6931

McAllen Genealogical Society
601 N. Main Street
P.O. Box 4714
McAllen, TX 78502
Tel: 512-686-5669

Mesquite Historical and Genealogical Society
P.O. Box 850165
Mesquite, TX 75185-0165
Tel: 972-216-6229
Email: DStuart101@aol.com
URL: http://members.aol.com/dstuart101/mesquite/page1.htm

Mid-Cities Genealogical Society
P.O. Box 407
Bedford, TX 76095

Midland Genealogical Society
301 W. Missouri
P.O. Box 1191
Midland, TX 79702
Tel: 915-688-8991

Milam County Genealogical Society
c/o Lucy Hill Patterson Library
201 Ackerman Street
Rockdale, TX 76567
Email: 73203-360@compuserve.com
URL: http://www.clever.net/westok.net/mcgstex/

Montgomery County Genealogical and Historical Society
P.O. Box 867
Conroe, TX 77305-0867
URL: http://mcia.com/gsociety.htm

Nacogdoches County Genealogical Society
P.O. Box 4634, SAF Station
Nacogdoches, TX 75962
URL: http://users.aol.com/pphill235/ngs/ngshome.html

Navarro County Genealogical Society
P.O. Box 2278
Corsicana, TX 75151
Tel: 903-654-4810

New Boston Genealogical Society
P.O. Box 104
New Boston, TX 75570
Tel: 903-628-3467

North Collin County Genealogical Society
c/o McKinney Memorial Public Library
220 North Kentucky Street
McKinney, TX 75069
Tel: 972-542-4461
Fax: 972-542-1344
URL: http://www.psyberlink.net/~kcole/nccgs.htm

North Texas Genealogical Association
P.O. Box 4602
Wichita Falls, TX 76308
Email: fmaier@wf.net
URL: http://www.wf.net/~fmaier/

Northeast Texas, Genealogical Society of
Paris Junior College Campus-Jess B. Alford Center
2400 Clarksville Street
PJC Box 187
Paris, TX 75460
Tel: 903-784-9448

Pacer-Hunt County Genealogical Society
P.O. Box 2306
Quinlan, TX 75474

Pampa Genealogical Society
430 North Summer Street
Pampa, TX 79065

Parker County Genealogical Society
1214 Charles Street
Weatherford, TX 76086
Tel: 817-594-2767

Pecan Valley Genealogical Society
600 Carnegie Blvd.
Brownwood, TX 76801

Permian Basin Genealogical Society
321 West Fifth Street
Odessa, TX 79761
Tel: 915-332-0634

Piney Woods Pioneer Genealogical Society
Route 1, Box 405
Kountze, TX 77625

Porciones Genealogical Society
P.O. Box 392
Edinburg, TX 78540

Randolph Area Genealogical Society
P.O. Box 2134
Universal City, TX 78148
Tel: 210-659-7881

Red River County Genealogical Society
P.O. Box 516
Clarksville, TX 75426
Tel: 903-427-3991

Rockwall County Genealogical Society
P.O. Box 471
Rockwall, TX 75087

Root Seekers Genealogical Society
c/o Tri County Library
P.O. Box 1770
Mabank, TX 75147-1770
Tel: 903-451-2213

Rusk County Genealogical Society
P.O. Box 1314
Henderson, TX 75653

San Angelo Genealogical and Historical Society
P.O. Box 3453
San Angelo, TX 76902
URL: http://www.rootsweb.com/~saghs/index.htm

San Antonio Genealogical Society
P.O. Box 17461
San Antonio, TX 78217

San Marcos/Hays County Genealogy Society
P.O. Box 503
San Marcos, TX 78667

South Plains Genealogical Society
P.O. Box 6607
Lubbock, TX 79493

South Texas Genealogical Society
P.O. Box 768
Gonzales, TX 78269

South East Texas Genealogical and Historical Society
c/o Tyrell Historical Library
P.O. Box 3827
Beaumont, TX 77704
URL: http://members.aol.com/RootsLady/setghs/setghs.htm

Southwest Genealogical Society
1300 San Pedro Avenue
San Antonio, TX 78212

Southwest Texas Genealogical Society
P.O. Box 295
Uvalde, TX 78802

Stephens County Genealogical Society
P.O. Box 350
Breckenridge, TX 76424
Tel: 817-559-8471

Texarkana USA Genealogy Society
P.O. Box 2323
Texarkana, TX 75504

Texas State Genealogical Society
P.O. Box 110842
Carrollton, TX 75011

Texas City Ancestry Searchers
P.O. Box 3301
Texas City, TX 77592
Tel: 409-935-5343

Timpson Genealogical Society
P.O. Box 726
Timpson, TX 75975
Tel: 409-254-3344

Tip O'Texas Genealogical Society
c/o Harlingen Public Library
410 76 Drive
Harlingen, TX 78550
Tel: 210-430-6650

Tri-County Genealogical Society
P.O. Box 107
Leonard, TX 75452
Tel: 903-587-2246

TX-OK Panhandle Genealogical Society
Fifth and Ash
Perryton, TX 79070
Tel: 806-435-5801

Upton County Genealogical Society
P.O. Box 6
Rankin, TX 79778

Van Alstyne Genealogical Society
c/o Van Alstyne Public Library
P.O. Box 629
Van Alstyne, TX 75495
URL: http://home.texoma.net/~vanalstynepl/gen1.html

Van Zandt County Genealogical Society
P.O. Box 716
Canton, TX 75103-0716
Tel: 903-567-5012
Email: mp-zurawicz@csu.edu
URL: http://www.rootsweb.com/~txvzcgs/vzgs.htm

Victoria County Genealogical Society
302 North Main Street
Victoria, TX 77901
Email: buttram@icsi.net
URL: http://www.viptx.net/vcgs/vcgs.html

Walker County Genealogical Society
P.O. Box 1295
Huntsville, TX 77342-1295
Email: jdickenson@myriad.net
URL: http://personalwebs.myriad.net/jdickenson/wcgen.htm

Winters High School, Genealogical Society of
P.O. Box 125
Winters, TX 79567

Wood County Genealogical Society
P.O. Box 832
Quitman, TX 75783
Email: markreid@ballistic.com
URL: http://www.rootsweb.com/~txwood/wcgs/

HISTORICAL SOCIETIES

Bastrop County Historical Society
702 Main Street
P.O. Box 279
Bastrop, TX 78602
Tel: 512-321-6177

Beaumont Heritage Society
2985 French Road
Beaumont, TX 77706
Tel: 409-898-0348

Brazoria County Historical Society/Museum
Courthouse Square
100 East Cedar
Angleton, TX 77515
Tel: 409-849-5711 ext. 1208
Email:bchm@bchm.org
URL: http://www.tgn.net/~bchm/Genealogy/gene.html

Caldwell County Genealogical and Historical Society
215 South Pecan Avenue
Luling, TX 78648
Tel: 830-875-9466
Email:
URL: http://www.rootsweb.com/~txcaldwe/socpage.htm

Carson County Historical Survey Committee
Carson County Square House Museum
Highway 207
P.O. Box 276
Panhandle, TX 79068
Tel: 806-537-3524

Collin County Historical Society/Museum
Old Post Office
105 Chestnut
McKinney, TX 75069
Tel: 972-542-9457
URL: http://fohnix.metronet.com/~wayner/cchs/

Crockett County Historical Society/Museum
404 11th Street
Ozona, TX 76943
Tel: 915-392-2837

Dallas County Heritage Society
1717 Gano Street
Dallas, TX 75215
Tel: 214-421-5141

Dallas Historical Society
Hall of State, Fair Park
G.B. Dealey Library
P.O. Box 150038
Dallas, TX 75315
Tel: 214-421-4500
Fax: 214-421-7500
URL: http://www.startext.net/interact/dhs.htm

Dallas Jewish Historical Society
7900 Northaven Road
Dallas, TX 75230
Tel: 214-739-2737 ext. 261
Email: dvjcc@onramp.net
URL: http://dvjcc.ncc.com/dvjcc/DJHS.html

Denton County, Historical Society of
P.O. Box 50503
Denton, TX 76206-0503
Tel: 817-387-0995
Email: Mcochran@iglobal.net
URL: http://www.iglobal.net/mayhouse/dentonhistory-page.html

East Texas Historical Association
P.O. Box 6223, SFA Station
Nacogdoches, TX 75962
Tel: 409-468-2407
Fax: 409-468-2190
Email: AMcDonald@sfasu.edu
URL: http://www.libarts.sfasu.edu/ETHA.html

Edgewood Historical Society
103 E. Elm Street
Edgewood, TX 75117-2519
Tel: 903-896-1940

German-Texan Heritage Society
507 East 10th Street
P.O. Box 684171
Austin, TX 78768-4171
Tel: 512-482-0927

Gillespie County Historical Society
309 W. Main Street
Fredericksburg, TX 78624-3711
Tel: 210-997-2835

Gonzales Historical Society/Archives and Records Center
P.O. Box 114
Gonzales, TX 78629
Tel: 830-672-7970
Email: barney1@connecti.com
URL: http://www.connecti.com/~leehuff/index.htm

Henderson County Historical Society
217 N. Prairieville St.
P.O. Box 943
Athens, TX 75751
Tel: 903-677-3611

Jefferson Historical Society/Museum
223 Austin
Jefferson, TX 75657
Tel: 903-665-2775

Llano Estacado Heritage Society
1900 W. 8th Street
Plainview, TX 79072
Tel: 806-296-9599

Lower Gulf Coast Genealogical and Historical Society
Email: dsk@phoenix.net
URL: http://www.phoenix.net/~dsk/genealogy.html

Mesquite Historical and Genealogical Society
P.O. Box 850165
Mesquite, TX 75185-0165
Tel: 972-216-6229
Email: DStuart101@aol.com
URL: http://members.aol.com/dstuart101/mesquite/page1.htm

Montgomery County Genealogical and Historical Society
P.O. Box 867
Conroe, TX 77305-0867
URL: http://mcia.com/gsociety.htm

Newton County Historical Commission, Genealogy Division
P.O. Box 1383
Newton, TX 75966
Email: newton@jas.net (Subject=Genealogy)
URL: http://www.jas.net/~newton/

Panhandle-Plains Historical Museum
West Texas A & M University
2401 4th Avenue
WTAMU Box 967
Canyon, TX 79015
Tel: 806-656-2244
Fax: 806-656-2250
Email: museum@wtamu.edu
URL: http://www.wtamu.edu/museum/

Peters Colony Historical Society of Dallas County, Texas
P.O. Box 110846
Carrollton, TX 75011

San Angelo Genealogical and Historical Society
P.O. Box 3453
San Angelo, TX 76902
URL: http://www.rootsweb.com/~saghs/index.htm

Smithville Heritage Society
602 Main Street
Smithville, TX 78957
Tel: 512-237-4545

Somervell County Historical Society/Library
P.O. Box 669
Glen Rose, TX 76043

South East Texas Genealogical and Historical Society
c/o Tyrell Historical Library
P.O. Box 3827
Beaumont, TX 77704
URL: http://members.aol.com/RootsLady/setghs/setghs.htm

Southwest Railroad Historical Society
Age of Steam Railroad Museum
Fair Park
P.O. Box 153259
Dallas, TX 75315
Tel: 214-428-0101
Email: railroad@arlington.net
URL: http://www.startext.net/homes/railroad/

Taylor Historical Commission
Tel: 915-691-1894
URL: http://www.abilene.com/taylorhist/

Texas Historical Commission
P.O. Box 12276
Austin, TX 78711-2276
Tel: 512-463-6100
Fax: 512-475-4872
Email: thc@nueces.thc.state.tx.us
URL: http://www.thc.state.tx.us/

Texas Military Historical Society
P.O. Box 2383
Bellaire, TX 77402-2383
Email: tog@io.com
URL: http://www.io.com/~tog/tmhs.html

Texas State Historical Association
2306 Sid Richardson Hall
University Station
Austin, TX 78712
Tel: 512-471-1525
Fax: 512-471-1551
Email: rtyler@mail.utexas.edu
URL: http://www.dla.utexas.edu/texhist/

Texas Wendish Heritage Society/Museum and Research Library
Route 2, Box 155
Giddings, TX 78942
Tel: 409-366-2441
URL: http://www.geocities.com/Heartland/Plains/1860/index.html

Texian Heritage Society
15742 Fitzhugh Road
Austin, TX 78736
Tel: 512-264-2355
Email: cmyates@ix.netcom.com
URL: http://pw2.netcom.com/~cmyates/ths.html

Weimar Heritage Society/Museum
125 E. Main Street
Weimar, TX 78962
Tel: 409-725-8203

LDS FAMILY HISTORY CENTERS

Atlanta Family History Center
1806 S. Boggie Street
Atlanta, TX 75551
Tel: 903-796-5376

Austin Family History Center
1000 East Rutherford Lane
Austin, TX 78753
Tel: 512-837-3626

Clayton Library
Center for Genealogical Research
5300 Caroline
Houston, TX 77004-6896
Tel: 713-524-0101
URL: http://sparc.hpl.lib.tx.us/hpl/clayton.html

Dallas Family History Center
10701 Lake Highlands Drive
Dallas, TX 75218
Tel: 214-349-0730

Denton Family History Center
1801 Malone
Denton, TX 76201
Tel: 817-387-3065

Duncanville Family History Center
1019 Big Stone Gap
Duncanville, TX 75137
Tel: 214-709-0066

El Paso Family History Center
3651 Douglas
El Paso, TX 79903

Fort Worth Family History Center
5001 Altamesa Blvd.
Fort Worth, TX 76133
Tel: 817-292-8393

Friendswood Family History Center
505 Deseret
Friendswood, TX 77544
Tel: 281-996-9346

Georgetown Family History Center
218 Serenada Drive
Georgetown, TX 78628
Tel: 512-863-5927

Houston Family History Center
1802 Gunwale Road
Houston, TX 77062
Tel: 409-488-7747

Hurst Family History Center
4401 NE Loop 820
Hurst, TX 76053
Tel: 817-284-4472

Katy Family History Center
1928 Drexel
Katy, TX 77493
Tel: 2814-391-7689

Lubbock Family History Center
3211 58th Street
Lubbock, TX 79413
Tel: 806-792-5040

Lufkin Family History Center
606 Bending Oak
Lufkin, TX 75904
Tel: 409-637-7750

Manvel Family History Center
2700 Lehi Lane
Manvel, TX 77578
Tel: 409-331-5577

Pasadena Family History Center
4202 Yellowstone
Pasadena, TX 77504

Plano Family History Center
1700 Roundrock
Plano, TX 75075
Tel: 214-867-6479

San Antonio Family History Center
2103 St. Cloud
San Antonio, TX 78228
Tel: 210-736-2940

San Marcos Family History Center
120 Suncrest
San Marcos, TX 78666
Tel: 512-353-8672

Spring Family History Center
16535 Kleinwood
Spring, TX 77379
Tel: 281-251-5931

Texarkana Family History Center
3701 Moores Lane
Texarkana, TX 75503
Tel: 903-831-5225

Tyler Family History Center
1617 Shiloh Road
Tyler, TX 75703-2437
Tel: 903-509-8322

ARCHIVES/LIBRARIES/MUSEUMS

Abilene Public Library
202 Cedar Street
Abilene, TX 79601
Tel: 915-677-2474

Amarillo Public Library
413 East 4th Avenue
P.O. Box 2171
Amarillo, TX 79189-2171
Tel: 806-378-3054
Email: Marykay@hlc.actx.edu
URL: http://plutonium-erl.actx.edu/hlc/aplc.html

Angelo State University
Porter Henderson Library
West Texas Collection
P.O. Box 11013, ASU Station
San Angelo, TX 76909
Tel: 915-942-2164
Email: Suzanne.Campbell@angelo.edu
URL: http://www.angelo.edu/admn/library/westtx/westtx.htm

Arlington Public Library
101 East Abram
Arlington, TX 76010
Tel: 817-459-6901

Atlanta Public Library
Genealogy Section
101 W. Hiram Street
Atlanta, TX 75551
Tel: 903-796-2112
903-796-3434

Austin History Center
810 Guadalupe
Austin, TX 78701
Tel: 512-499-7480

Austin Public Library
800 Guadalupe
Austin, TX 78701
Tel: 512-499-7300

Bastrop Public Library
1100 Church Street
Bastrop, TX 78602
Tel: 512-321-5441
URL: http://www.main.org/library/bastlib.html

Bay City Public Library
1100 Seventh Street
Bay City, TX 77414
Tel: 409-245-6931

Beaumont Public Library
801 Pearl Street
P.O. Box 3827
Beaumont, TX 77704
Tel: 409-838-6606

Belton City Library
301 East 1st Avenue
Belton, TX 76513
Tel: 817-939-1161

Blanco/James A. and Evelyn Williams Memorial Library
310 Pecan Street
P.O. Box 489
Blanco, TX 78606
Tel: 210-833-4280
URL: http://www.texanet.net/bli/

Brazoria Branch Genealogical Library
620 South Brooks
Brazoria, TX 77422
Tel: 409-798-2372

Brazoria County Historical Society/Museum
Courthouse Square
100 East Cedar
Angleton, TX 77515
Tel: 409-849-5711 ext. 1208
Email:bchm@bchm.org
URL: http://www.tgn.net/~bchm/Genealogy/gene.html

Brownwood Public Library
600 Carnegie Street
Brownwood, TX 76801-7038
Tel: 915-646-0155

Bryan Public Library
201 East 26th Street
Bryan, TX 77803
Tel: 409-361-3715

Cameron Public Library
304 E. Third Street
Cameron, TX 76520
Tel: 817-697-2401

Carrollton Public Library
2001 Jackson Road
Carrollton, TX 75006-1743
Tel: 972-466-3353
972-466-3360
Fax: 972-466-3394
URL: http://isadore.tsl.state.tx.us/.www/netls.dir/netdial.htm

Catholic Archives of Texas
1600 Congress Avenue
Austin, TX 78801
Tel: 512-476-4888 ext. 48
Email: cat@onr.com

Catholic Museum Archives Building
2200 N. Spring Street
Amarillo, TX 79107
Tel: 806-381-9866

Center for Studies in Texas History
University of Texas/Austin
Austin, TX 78712
Email: rtyler@mail.utexas.edu
URL: http://www.dla.utexas.edu/texhist/

Chambers County Library
P.O. Box 520
Anahuac, TX 77514
Tel: 409-267-8261

Chaparral Genealogical Society/Library
310 N. Live Oak
P.O. Box 606
Tomball, TX 77375
Tel: 713-255-9081

Clayton Library
Center for Genealogical Research
5300 Caroline
Houston, TX 77004-6896
Tel: 713-524-0101
URL: http://sparc.hpl.lib.tx.us/hpl/clayton.html

Cleburne Public Library
302 West Henderson
P.O. Box 657
Cleburne, TX 76033-0657
Tel: 817-645-0934

Corpus Christi Public Library
805 Comanche
Corpus Christi, TX 78401
Tel: 512-880-7000
Email: library@ci.corpus-christi.tx.us
URL: http://www.ci.corpus-christi.tx.us/main.htm

Corsicana Public Library
100 North 12th Street
Corsicana, TX 75110
Tel: 903-654-4810

Crockett/John H. Wooters Public Library
708 E. Goliad Avenue
P.O. Box 1226
Crockett, TX 75835
Tel: 409-544-3089

Dallas Historical Society
Hall of State, Fair Park
G.B. Dealey Library
P.O. Box 150038
Dallas, TX 75315
Tel: 214-421-4500
Fax: 214-421-7500
URL: http://www.startext.net/interact/dhs.htm

Dallas Public Library/J. Erik Jonsson Branch
Genealogy Section
1515 Young Street
Dallas, TX 75201
Tel: 214-670-1400
Fax: 214-670-7839
URL: http://central4.lib.ci.dallas.tx.us/

Daughters of the Republic of Texas/Library and Museum
Alamo Plaza
P.O. Box 1401
San Antonio, TX 78295-1401
Tel: 210-225-1071
Fax: 210-212-8514
Email: drtl@salsa.net
URL: http://www.drtl.org/~drtl/

Deer Park Public Library
3009 Center Street
Deer Park, TX 77536-5063
Tel: 281-478-7208

Denison Library Genealogical Society
300 West Gandy
Denison, TX 75020
Tel: 903-465-9447
903-465-1797
Fax: 903-465-1130
URL: http://www.barr.org/denison.htm

Denton Public Library/Emily Fowler Central Library
502 Oakland Street
Denton, TX 76201
Tel: 817-566-8558
URL: http://www.iglobal.net/denton/library/index.html

Duncanville Public Library
103 East Wheatland
Duncanville, TX 75116
Tel: 972-780-5050

Ector County Library
321 W. 5th Street
Odessa, TX 79761-5024
Tel: 915-333-9633

El Paso Public Library
501 North Oregon Street
El Paso, TX 79901
Tel: 915-543-5440
915-543-5413

El Progreso Memorial Library
129 West Nopal
Uvalde, TX 78801
Tel: 210-278-2017

Euless Public Library
201 North Ector Drive
Euless, TX 76039
Tel: 817-685-1480

Fort Bend County/George Memorial Library
1001 Golfview Drive
Richmond, TX 77469
Tel: 281-342-4455
URL: http://www.fortbend.lib.tx.us/dept.html

Fort Worth Public Library
300 Taylor Street
Fort Worth, TX 76102
Tel: 817-871-7700
817-871-7740 (Genealogy)
URL: http://198.215.16.7:443/fortworth/fwpl/

Gatesville Public Library
805 Main
Gatesville, TX 76528
Tel: 817-865-5367

Gibbs Memorial Library
305 East Rusk
Mexia, TX 76667
Email: Gibbs.Library@mexia.com
URL: http://www.mexia.com/_gibbs/gen.htm

Gladys Harrington Public Library
1501 18th Street
Plano, TX 75074
Tel: 972-461-7175
URL: http://www.ci.plano.tx.us/library/harlib.htm
http://www.ci.plano.tx.us/library/genealogy.htm

Gonzales Historical Society/Archives and Records Center
P.O. Box 114
Gonzales, TX 78629
Tel: 830-672-7970
Email: barney1@connecti.com
URL: http://www.connecti.com/~leehuff/index.htm

Grand Prairie Memorial Library
901 Conover
Grand Prairie, TX 75051-1521
Tel: 972-264-1571

Grapevine Public Library
1201 S. Main Street
Grapevine, TX 76051-5545
Tel: 817-481-0341

Harlingen Public Library
504 East Tyler Avenue
Harlingen, TX 78550
Tel: 512-427-8841

Harrison County Historical Museum and Research Library
Old Courthouse Square
Marshall, TX 78501
URL: http://www.rootsweb.com/~txharris/hcmuseum.htm

Hillsboro City Library
118 South Waco Street
Hillsboro, TX 76645
Tel: 817-582-7385

Hood County Library
222 North Travis
Granbury, TX 76048
Tel: 817-573-3569

Houston Public Library/Metropolitan Research Center
500 McKinney Street
Houston, TX 77002
URL: http://sparc.hpl.lib.tx.us/

Huntsville Public Library
Genealogy/Texana/Local History Room
1216 14th Street
Huntsville, TX 77340
Tel: 409-291-5472

Irving Public Library
801 W. Irving Blvd.
P.O. Box 152288
Irving, TX 75015-2288
Tel: 972-721-2628
972-721-2606
Fax: 972-259-1171
URL: http://www.irving.lib.tx.us/

Kemp Public Library
1300 Lamar
Wichita Falls, TX 76301
Tel: 817-761-8800
Fax: 817-767-1058

Kurth Memorial Library
101 Cotton Square
Lufkin, TX 75901
Tel: 409-634-7617

Laredo Public Library
1120 San Bernardo Avenue
Laredo, TX 78040
Tel: 512-722-2435

Longview Public Library
222 West Cotton Street
Longview, TX 75601
Tel: 903-237-1350

Lubbock City/County Library
1306 9th Street
Lubbock, TX 79401
Tel: 806-767-2826
Fax: 806-747-4636

Lucy Hill Patterson Memorial Library
201 Ackerman Street
Rockdale, TX 76567
Tel: 512-446-3410
Fax: 512-446-5597
Email: ROCKDALE@ONR.COM
URL: http://www.main.org/patlib/patlib.htm

Luling Public Library
215 S. Pecan Avenue
Luling, TX 78648
Tel: 210-875-2813

McKinney Memorial Public Library
220 North Kentucky Street
McKinney, TX 75069
Tel: 972-542-4461
Fax: 972-542-1344

McMurry College Library
Scarborough Library of Genealogy
History and Biography of the South and Southwest
McMurry Station
Abilene, TX 79605
URL: http://www.alc.org/www/mcm/mcm_library.html

Mesquite Public Library
300 Grubb Drive
Mesquite, TX 75149
Tel: 972-216-6220
972-216-6229 (Genealogy)
Fax: 972-216-6740
URL: http://www.computek.net/mesqlib/

Montgomery County Library
104 I-45 North
P.O. Box 867
Conroe, TX 77301
Tel: 409-539-7814
409-788-8363 (Genealogy)
Fax: 409-788-8398
URL: http://mcia.com/library.htm
http://mcia.com/gene.htm

Moody Texas Ranger Library
P.O. Box 2570
Waco, TX 76702
Tel: 817-750-5986
Fax: 817-750-8629

Moore Memorial Library
1701 9th Avenue North
Texas City, TX 77590
Tel: 409-643-5979

Mount Pleasant Municipal Library
213 North Madison
Mount Pleasant, TX 75455
Tel: 903-572-2705
903-575-4180
Fax: 903-577-8000
Email: mppublib@stargate.1stargate.com
URL: http://www2.1stargate.com/mppublib/

New Boston Public Library
127 North Ellis
New Boston, TX 75570
Tel: 903-628-5414

Nicholson Memorial Library
625 Austin Street
Garland, TX 75040
Tel: 972-205-2544
972-205-2502 (Reference)
Fax: 972-205-2523
URL: http://library.usask.ca/hytelnet/usa/usa48.html

Palestine Public Library
Special Collections
1101 North Cedar
Palestine, TX 75801
Tel: 903-729-4121
URL: http://www.e-tex.com/personal/bonniew/acgs/gen.htm

Paris Junior College
A.M. Aikin Regional Archives
2400 Clarksville Street
Paris, TX 75460
URL: http://gen.1starnet.com/lamargen.htm

Paris Junior College
Mike Rheudasil Learning Center
2400 Clarksville Street
Paris, TX 75460
URL: http://gen.1starnet.com/lamargen.htm

Pilot Point Community Library
324 S. Washington Street
P.O. Box 969
Pilot Point, TX 76258
Tel: 817-686-5004

Port Arthur Public Library
3601 Cultural Center Drive
Port Arthur, TX 77642
Tel: 409-985-8838

Quitman Library
202 East Goode Street
P.O. Box 77
Quitman, TX 75783-0077
Tel: 903-763-4191

Richardson Public Library
900 Civic Center
Richardson, TX 75080-5298
Tel: 972-238-4000
Fax: 972-952-0870
URL: http://www.cor.net/library/

Rosenberg Library
2310 Sealy Street
Galveston, TX 77550
Tel: 409-763-6410
Fax: 409-763-0275

Round Rock Public Library
216 East Main Street
Round Rock, TX 78664
Tel: 512-218-7000
Fax: 512-218-7061
Email: dale@round-rock.tx.us
lindab@round-rock.tx.us
URL: http://www.ci.round-rock.tx.us/library/library.html

San Antonio Central Library/Central Library
Texana/Genealogy Department
600 Soledad
San Antonio, TX 78205
Tel: 210-207-2500
Email: libwebadmin@ci.sat.tx.us
URL: http://www.ci.sat.tx.us/sapl/html/saplgen.html

San Antonio Public Library
203 South St. Mary's Street
San Antonio, TX 78205

San Augustine Public Library
413 East Columbia
San Augustine, TX 75972
Tel: 409-275-5367

Scurry County Library
1916 23rd Street
Snyder, TX 79549
Tel: 915-573-5572

Sherman Public Library
421 N. Travis
Sherman, TX 75090-5975
Tel: 903-892-7240
Fax: 903-892-7101
URL: http://www.barr.org/sherman.htm

Somervell County Historical Society/Library
P.O. Box 669
Glen Rose, TX 76043

Southern Methodist University
Clements Center for Southwest Studies
356 Dallas Hall
P.O. Box 750176
Dallas, TX 75275-0176
Tel: 214-768-3684
Fax: 214-768-4129
Email: swcenter@mail.smu.edu
URL: http://www.smu.edu/~swcenter/

Stephen F. Austin State University
Center for East Texas Studies
Ferguson Building 340
P.O. Box 6134, SFA Station
Nacogdoches, TX 75962
Tel: 409-468-1392
Fax: 409-468-2190
Email: CETS@SFASU
URL: http://www.cets.sfasu.edu/ETRC/Index.html

Stephen F. Austin State University
Ralph W. Steen Library
Box 13055, SFA Station
Nacogdoches, TX 75962-3055
Tel: 409-468-4100
Email: vrigby@sfalib.sfasu.edu
URL: http://libweb.sfasu.edu/etrc/etrcbro.htm

Temple Public Library
101 North Main Street
Temple, TX 76501
Tel: 817-770-5555/6

Texarkana Public Library
600 W. Third Street
Texarkana, TX 75501
Tel: 903-794-2149
Fax: 903-794-2139
URL: http://darkstar.swsc.k12.ar.us/~sholmes/

Texas State General Land Office
Archives and Records Division
Stephen F. Austin Building
1700 North Congress Avenue
Austin, TX 78701
Tel: 512-463-5277
512-463-5388 (For Genealogy Group Presentations)
URL: http://www.glo.state.tx.us/central/arc/index.html

Texas State Library and Archives Commission
Lorenzo de Zavala State Archives and Library Building
1201 Brazos Street
P.O. Box 12927
Austin, TX 78711
Tel: 512-463-5455
512-463-5463 (Genealogy Collection, Room 110)
Email: geninfo@tsl.state.tx.us
URL: http://www.tsl.state.tx.us/lobby/genfirst.htm

Texas Wendish Heritage Society/Museum and Research Library
Route 2, Box 155
Giddings, TX 78942
Tel: 409-366-2441
URL: http://www.geocities.com/Heartland/Plains/1860/index.html

Tom Burnett Memorial Library
400 West Alameda
Iowa Park, TX 76367
Tel: 817-592-4981

Tyler Public Library
Genealogy and Local History Dept.
201 S. College
Tyler, TX 75702
Tel: 214-593-7323

Tyrell Public Library
695 Pearl Street
P.O. Box 3827
Beaumont, TX 77704
Tel: 409-833-2759
URL: http://www.rootsweb.com/~txjeffer/library.htm

Unger Memorial Library
Local History and Genealogy Section
825 Austin Street
Plainview, TX 79072-7235
Tel: 806-296-1148
Email: johnsigwald@texasonline.net
URL: http://www.texasonline.net/schools/unger/INDEX.HTM

University of Texas/Austin
The Center for American History
Eugene C. Barker Texas History Collections
Sid Richardson Hall, Unit 2
Austin, TX 78712
URL: http://www.lib.utexas.edu/Libs/CAH/

University of Texas/Austin
Perry Castaneda Library
Austin, TX 78712
Tel: 512-495-4250
URL: http://www.lib.utexas.edu/

University of Texas/El Paso (UTEP)
C.L. Sonnichsen Special Collections Dept.
El Paso, TX 79968
Tel: 915-747-5683
Fax: 915-747-5345
URL: http://www.utep.edu/~library/

Van Alstyne Public Library
117 N. Waco
P.O. Box 629
Van Alstyne TX 75495
Tel: 903-482-5991
URL: http://home.texoma.net/~vanalstynepl/

Van Zandt County Library of Genealogy and Local History
Van Zandt County Courthouse, Annex Building
Canton, TX 75103
Tel: 903-567-5012

Waco/McLennan County Library
1717 Austin Avenue
Waco, TX 76701
Tel: 817-754-4694

Walworth Harrison Public Library
Genealogy Room
3716 Lee Street
Greenville, TX 75401
Tel: 903-457-2992

Weatherford Public Library
1214 Charles Street
Weatherford, TX 76086
Tel: 817-594-2767

Weimar Heritage Society/Museum
125 E. Main Street
Weimar, TX 78962
Tel: 409-725-8203

West Texas A & M University
Panhandle-Plains Historical Museum
2401 4th Avenue
WTAMU Box 967
Canyon, TX 79015
Tel: 806-656-2244
Fax: 806-656-2250
Email: museum@wtamu.edu
URL: http://www.wtamu.edu/museum/

Western Texas College
Learning Resource Center
Snyder, TX 79549

Whitesboro Public Library
308 W. Main Street
Whitesboro, TX 76273
Tel: 903-564-5432
Fax: 903-564-6886

Newspaper Repositories

Texas State Library and Archives Commission
Lorenzo de Zavala State Archives and Library Building
1201 Brazos Street
P.O. Box 12927
Austin, TX 78711
Tel: 512-463-5455
512-463-5463 (Genealogy Collection, Room 110)
Email: geninfo@tsl.state.tx.us
URL: http://www.tsl.state.tx.us/lobby/ref/news.htm

University of Texas/Austin
The Center for American History
Eugene C. Barker Texas History Collections
Sid Richardson Hall, Unit 2
Austin, TX 78712
URL: http://www.lib.utexas.edu/Libs/PCL/refserv/per_micro/cah/

Vital Records

Department of Health, Bureau of Vital Statistics
1100 W. 49th Street
P.O. Box 12040
Austin, TX 78711-2040
Tel: 512-458-7111
512-458-4751
Email: register@stats.tdh.state.tx.us
URL: http://www.tdh.state.tx.us/bvs/t_bvs.htm

Texas on the Web

Brazoria County Historical Museum—Old 300 Genealogical Database
http://www.tgn.net/~bchm/Genealogy/gene.html

Brazos Genealogical Association—Links to Sites with Searchable Databases
http://www2.cy-net.net/bga/stlinks/us_south.html

Index to Confederate Pensions
http://www.tsl.state.tx.us/lobby/cpi/introcpi.htm

Texas Adjutant General Service Records 1836-1935
http://www.tsl.state.tx.us/lobby/genfirst.htm

Texas GenWeb Project
http://www.chrysalis.org/dgs/txgenweb.htm

Welcome to Family History—Family History Radio Show and The Family Historian magazine
http://www.ridethewave.com/familyhistory/

UTAH

ARCHIVES, STATE & NATIONAL

National Archives—Rocky Mountain Region
Denver Federal Center, Building 48
P.O. Box 25307
Denver, CO 80225-0307
Tel: 303-236-0817
Fax: 303-236-9354
Email: archives@denver.nara.gov
URL: http://www.nara.gov/nara/regional/08nsgil.html

Utah State Archives
Archives Building
P.O. Box 141021
Salt Lake City, UT 84114-1021
Tel: 801-538-3013 (Research Room)
Fax: 801-538-3354
Email: research@state.ut.us
URL: http://www.archives.state.ut.us/

GENEALOGICAL SOCIETIES

Cuban Genealogical Society
P.O. Box 2650
Salt Lake City, UT 84110-2650

Genealogical Society of Utah
35 North West Temple
Salt Lake City, UT 84150
URL: http://www.itd.nps.gov/cwss/gsu.html

St. George Genealogy Club
P.O. Box 184
St. George, UT 84770

Utah Blue Chips (Utah Computer Society)
P.O. Box 510811
Salt Lake City, UT 84151
Tel: 801-281-8339
BBS: 801-281-8770
Email: sysop@ucs.org (BBS)
URL: http://www.ucs.org/

Utah Genealogical Associatson
P.O. Box 1144
Salt Lake City, UT 84110
Tel: 888-INFO-UGA (Toll-free)
URL: http://www.infouga.org/

Utah Valley PAF Users Group
c/o Jay P. Markham, Pres.
490 East 600 South
Orem, UT 84058
Tel: 801-224-1167
URL: http://www.genealogy.org/~ovpafug/

Utah Valley PC Users Group
P.O. Box 1834
Provo, UT 84603
Email: uvpcug@xmission.com
URL: http://www.xmission.com/~uvpcug/

HISTORICAL SOCIETIES

Cache Valley Historical Society
Logan, UT 84321
Tel: 801-752-2169
801-752-5797

Daughters of the Utah Pioneers
Pioneer Memorial Museum
300 North Main
Salt Lake City, UT 84103
Tel: 801-538-1050
URL: http://eddy.media.utah.edu/medsol/UCME/d/DAUGHTERSUTPIO.html

Sons of the Utah Pioneers
3301 East 2920 South
Salt Lake City, UT 84109-4260
Email: editor@uvol.com
URL: http://www.uvol.com/sup/

Utah State Historical Society/Library
300 Rio Grande
Salt Lake City, UT 84101
Tel: 801-533-3500
801-533-3501 (Hours, Information)
Fax: 801-533-3502
TDD: 801-533-3503
Email: ushs@history.state.ut.us
cehistry.ushs@email.state.ut.us
URL: http://www.ce.ex.state.ut.us/history/

LDS FAMILY HISTORY CENTERS

Altamont Family History Center
Main Street
Altamont, UT 84001
Tel: 801-454-3422

American Fork Family History Center
381 South 300 East
American Fork, UT 84003
Tel: 801-763-2014

American Fork Family History Center
835 North 860 East
American Fork, UT 84003
Tel: 801-763-2093

Beaver Family History Center
1380 East 200 North
Beaver, UT 84713
Tel: 801-438-5262

Blanding Family History Center
200 South Main
Blanding, UT 84511
Tel: 801-678-2728

Bluffdale Family History Center
2742 West 14400 South
Bluffdale, UT 84512
Tel: 801-254-8127

Bountiful Family History Center
200 North 200 West
Bountiful, UT 84010
Tel: 801-299-4177

Brigham City Family History Center
10 South 4th East
Brigham City, UT 84302
Tel: 801-723-5995

Castle Dale Family History Center
33 East Main Street
Castle Dale, UT 84513
Tel: 801-381-2899

Cedar City Family History Center
155 East 400 South
Cedar City, UT 84720
Tel: 801-586-2296

Delta Family History Center
52 North 100 West
Delta, UT 84624
Tel: 801-864-3312

Draper Family History Center
13366 South 1300 East
Draper, UT 84020
Tel: 801-576-2821

Duchesne Family History Center
901 North 500 East
Duchesne, UT 84021
Tel: 801-738-5371

Enterprise Family History Center
88 South Center
Enterprise, UT 84725
Tel: 801-878-2520

Escalante Family History Center
80 South Center Street
Escalante, UT 84726
Tel: 801-826-4217

Eureka Family History Center
Main Street
Eureka, UT 84628

Farmington Family History Center
272 North Main Street
Farmington, UT 84025
Tel: 801-451-1905

Farmington Family History Center
695 South 200 East
Farmington, UT 84025
Tel: 801-451-1981

Farmington Family History Center
900 Compton Road
Farmington, UT 84025
Tel: 801-451-1945

Ferron Family History Center
35 West 200 North
Ferron, UT 84523
Tel: 801-384-3288

Fillmore Family History Center
21 South 300 West
Fillmore, UT 84631
Tel: 801-743-6614 ext. 114

Goshen Family History Center
70 South Center
Goshen, UT 84633
Tel: 801-667-3232

Helper Family History Center
150 Ridgeway Street
Helper, UT 84526
Tel: 801-472-3798

Huntington Family History Center
11 East 200 North
Huntington, UT 84528
Tel: 801-687-9090

Hurricane Family History Center
37 South 200 West
Hurricane, UT 84737
Tel: 801-635-2174

Hyrum Family History Center
245 North Apple Drive
Hyrum, UT 84319
Tel: 801-245-4551

Kanab Family History Center
202 East 100 North
Kanab, UT 84741
Tel: 801-644-5973

Kaysville Family History Center
201 South 600 East
Kaysville, UT 84037
Tel: 801-543-2845

Kaysville Family History Center
900 South Main Street
Kaysville, UT 84037
Tel: 801-543-2869

Kearns Family History Center
4660 West 5015 South
Kearns, UT 84118
Tel: 801-964-7371

Kearns Family History Center
5823 South 4800 West
Kearns, UT 84118
Tel: 801-964-7470

Kearns Family History Center
6175 Borax Avenue
Kearns, UT 84118

Laketown Family History Center
115 South 100 East
Laketown, UT 84038
Tel: 801-946-3262

Layton Family History Center
1589 East Gentile
Layton, UT 84040
Tel: 801-543-2908

Lehi Family History Center
200 North Center Street
Lehi, UT 84043
Tel: 801-768-3054

Lindon Family History Center
1050 East 100 North
Lindon, UT 84042
Tel: 801-785-7586

Loa Family History Center
14 South 100 West
Loa, UT 84747
Tel: 801-836-2322

Logan Family History Center
125 East 500 North
Logan, UT 84321
Tel: 801-755-5552

Logan Family History Center
50 North Main
Logan, UT 84321
Tel: 801-755-5594

Magna Family History Center
3151 South 7700 West
Magna, UT 84044
Tel: 801-252-2539

Magna Family History Center
8181 West 3320 South
Magna, UT 84044
Tel: 801-252-2530

Manti Family History Center
86 East 500 North
Manti, UT 84642
Tel: 801-835-8888

Mapleton Family History Center
1215 North 1000 West
Mapleton, UT 84664
Tel: 801-489-2999

Marion Family History Center
3038 North Highway 189
Provo, UT 84604
Tel: 801-783-2921

Midvale Family History Center
7155 South 540 East
Midvale, UT 84047
Tel: 801-562-8085

Midway Family History Center
160 West Main Street
Midway, UT 84049
Tel: 801-654-2760

Moab Family History Center
701 Locus Lane
Moab, UT 84532
Tel: 801-259-5563

Monticello Family History Center
347 North 2nd West
Monticello, UT 84535
Tel: 801-587-2139

Morgan Family History Center
93 North State Street
Morgan, UT 84050
Tel: 801-829-6261

Moroni Family History Center
300 North Center Street
Moroni, UT 84646
Tel: 801-436-8497

Mount Pleasant Family History Center
295 South State
Mount Pleasant, UT 84647

Murray Family History Center
4220 South 420 East
Murray, UT 84107
Tel: 801-264-4052

Murray Family History Center
5735 South Fashion Blvd.
Murray, UT 84107
Tel: 801-264-4145

Murray Family History Center
5750 South Nena Way
Murray, UT 84107
Tel: 801-264-4120

Murray Family History Center
6180 Glenoaks
Murray, UT 84107
Tel: 801-264-4137

Nephi Family History Center
351 North 100 West
Nephi, UT 84648
Tel: 801-623-1378

Ogden Family History Center
539 24th Street
Ogden, UT 84401
Tel: 801-626-1132

Orem Family History Center
1260 South 400 West
Orem, UT 84058
Tel: 801-222-0449

Orem Family History Center
195 West 300 South
Orem, UT 84058
Tel: 801-222-0399

Orem Family History Center
450 South 100 West
Orem, UT 84058
Tel: 801-222-0497

Orem Family History Center
546 North 500 West
Orem, UT 84057
Tel: 801-222-0529

Orem Family History Center
84 East 700 North
Orem, UT 84057
Tel: 801-222-0319

Panguitch Family History Center
290 East Center Street
Panguitch, UT 84759
Tel: 801-676-2201

Park City Family History Center
2300 Monitor Drive
Park City, UT 84060
Tel: 801-649-0725

Parowan Family History Center
87 West Center Street
Parowan, UT 84761
Tel: 801-477-8077

Payson Family History Center
590 South Main
Payson, UT 84651
Tel: 801-465-1349

Pleasant Grove Family History Center
1176 North 730 East
Pleasant Grove, UT 84062
Tel: 801-785-7570

Pleasant Grove Family History Center
800 North 100 West
Pleasant Grove, UT 84062
Tel: 801-785-0980

Price Family History Center
85 East 400 North
Price, UT 84501
Tel: 801-637-2071

Provo Family History Center
1402 South 570 West
Provo, UT 84601
Tel: 801-370-6849

Provo Family History Center
1915 North Canyon Road
Provo, UT 84604

Provo Family History Center
4000 North Timpview Avenue
Provo, UT 84604
Tel: 801-222-0567

Provo Family History Center
4300 North Canyon Road
Provo, UT 84604
Tel: 801-222-3108

Provo Family History Center
600 West 300 South
Provo, UT 84601
Tel: 801-370-6830

Provo Family History Center
667 North 600 East
Provo, UT 84606
Tel: 801-370-6713

Provo Family History Center
85 South 900 East
Provo, UT 84606
Tel: 801-370-6674

Provo Family History Center
(See Brigham Young University under
Libraries/Archives/Museums)

Richfield Family History Center
175 West Center
Richfield, UT 84701
Tel: 801-896-8057

Roosevelt Family History Center
290 West 300 North
Roosevelt, UT 84066
Tel: 801-722-9213

Salt Lake City Family History Center
1320 South Wasatch Drive
Salt Lake City, UT 84108

Salt Lake City Family History Center
1400 South 1900 East
Salt Lake City, UT 84108
Tel: 801-584-3142

Salt Lake City Family History Center
1750 East Spring Lane
Salt Lake City, UT 84117

Salt Lake City Family History Center
2675 East 4430 South
Salt Lake City, UT 84124

Salt Lake City Family History Center
Sons of Utah Pioneers Building
3301 East 2920 South
Salt Lake City, UT 84109
Tel: 801-468-5823

Salt Lake City Family History Center
4366 South 1500 East
Salt Lake City, UT 84124
Tel: 801-273-3862

Salt Lake City Family History Center
4630 South Lanark Road
Salt Lake City, UT 84124
Tel: 801-273-3815

Salt Lake City Family History Center
4917 Viewmont Street
Salt Lake City, UT 84117
Tel: 801-273-3784

Salt Lake City Family History Center
680 Second Avenue
Salt Lake City, UT 84103
Tel: 801-578-6661

Salt Lake City Family History Center
732 South 800 East
Salt Lake City, UT 84102
Tel: 801-578-6719

Salt Lake City Family History Center
760 North 1200 West
Salt Lake City, UT 84116
Tel: 801-578-6769

Salt Lake City Family History Library
(See Libraries/Archives/Museums)

Sandy Family History Library
10945 South 1700 East
Sandy, UT 84092
Tel: 801-576-2891

Sandy Family History Library
11350 South 1000 East
Sandy, UT 84094
Tel: 801-576-2949

Sandy Family History Library
1265 East 11000 South
Sandy, UT 84094
Tel: 801-576-2971

Sandy Family History Library
1440 East Raddon Drive
Sandy, UT 84092
Tel: 801-576-2834

Sandy Family History Library
1535 East Creek Road
Sandy, UT 84093
Tel: 801-944-2094

Sandy Family History Library
2126 East 10000 South
Sandy, UT 84092
Tel: 801-944-2131

Sandy Family History Library
630 East 10375 South
Sandy, UT 84070
Tel: 801-576-2953

Sandy Family History Library
8170 Short Hills Drive
Salt Lake City, UT 84121-5854
Tel: 801-944-2075

Sandy Family History Library
9636 South 1700 East
Sandy, UT 84092
Tel: 801-576-2991

Santaquin Family History Library
90 South 200 East
Santaquin, UT 84655

South Jordan Family History Library
9894 South 2700 West
South Jordan, UT 84095
Tel: 801-253-7008

Spanish Fork Family History Library
420 North Main Street
Spanish Fork, UT 84660
Tel: 801-798-5535

Springville Family History Library
415 South 200 East
Springville, UT 84663
Tel: 801-489-2956

St. George Family History Library
410 South 200 East
St. George, UT 84770
Tel: 801-673-4591

Syracuse Family History Library
1700 South 2000 West
Syracuse, UT 84075
Tel: 801-774-2183

Tooele Family History Library
1025 Southwest Drive
Tooele, UT 84074
Tel: 801-882-7514

Tremonton Family History Library
131 East 1500 South
Garland, UT 84312
Tel: 801-257-7015

Tropic Family History Library
100 West Center Street
Tropic, UT 84776
Tel: 801-679-8693

Vernal Family History Library
1186 South 500 East
Vernal, UT 84078
Tel: 801-789-3618

Wellington Family History Library
935 East Main Street
Wellington, UT 84542
Tel: 801-637-6717

Wendover Family History Library
269 B Street
Wendover, UT 84083
Tel: 801-665-2220

West Jordan Family History Library
5208 Cyclamen Way
West Jordan, UT 84084
Tel: 801-964-7455

West Jordan Family History Library
5360 West 7000 South
West Jordan, UT 84084
Tel: 801-964-7482

West Jordan Family History Library
7350 South 3200 West
West Jordan, UT 84084
Tel: 801-562-8285

West Valley City Family History Library
3280 South 4440 West
West Valley City, UT 84120
Tel: 801-964-7490

West Valley City Family History Library
3737 South 5600 West
West Valley City, UT 84120
Tel: 801-964-3012

West Valley City Family History Library
3900 South 4000 West
West Valley City, UT 84120
Tel: 801-964-7465

West Valley City Family History Library
4251 South 4800 West
West Valley City, UT 84120
Tel: 801-964-7250

West Valley City Family History Library
4505 South 3420 West
West Valley City, UT 84119
Tel: 801-964-3009

West Valley City Family History Library
7035 West 3605 South
West Valley City, UT 84084
Tel: 801-252-2560

ARCHIVES/LIBRARIES/MUSEUMS

American Genealogical Lending Library
P.O. Box 244
Bountiful, UT 84011
Tel: 801-298-5358
800-760-AGLL
Fax: 801-298-5468
URL: http://www.agll.com/

Brigham City Library
26 East Forest
Brigham City, UT 84302-2198
Tel: 801-723-5891
801-723-5850
Fax: 801-723-2813
Email: susan@peachy.bcpl.lib.ut.us
URL: http://www.state.lib.us/pubs/pldirect/bxbrighm.htm

Brigham Young University (BYU)
Harold B. Lee Library
Utah Valley Regional Family History Center, 4th Floor
Provo, UT 84602
Tel: 801-378-6200 (Family History Center)
801-378-2926 (Library Information)
URL: http://www.lib.byu.edu/

Cedar City Public Library
136 W. Center Street
Cedar City, UT 84720-2597
Tel: 901-586-6661
URL: http://www.state.lib.us/pubs/pldirect/ircedar.htm

Church of Jesus Christ of Latter-Day Saints
Historical Department
50 East North Temple
Salt Lake City, UT 84150

Everton's Genealogical Library
3223 South Main Street
P.O. Box 368
Nibley, UT 84323-0368
URL: http://www.everton.com/

Family History Library
Church of Jesus Christ of Latter-Day Saints
35 North West Temple
Salt Lake City, UT 84150
Tel: 801-240-2331
Some Unofficial Sites:
URL: http://bobcat.etsu.edu/ftpdir/genealogy/LDStext/ut-08456.txt
http://www.genealogy.org/~uvpafug/fhlslc.html
http://www.aros.net/~drwaff/slcfhl.htm
http://http.tamu.edu:8000/~mbg5500/genealogy/lds_gen_info.html

Logan Public Library
Archives
255 North Main
Logan, UT 84321
Tel: 801-750-9870
Fax: 801-753-5026
Email: precord@inter.state.lib.ut.us
URL: http://www.logan.lib.ut.us/

Manti Public Library
2 South Main Street
Manti, UT 84642-1349
Tel: 801-835-2201
URL: http://www.state.lib.us/pubs/pldirect/spmanti.htm

Ogden/Weber County Public Library
Special Collections
2464 Jefferson Avenue
Ogden, UT 84401-2488
Tel: 801-627-6913
Fax: 801-399-8519
URL: http://www.weberpl.lib.ut.us/

Orem Public Library
58 N. State Street
Orem, UT 84057
Tel: 801-224-7050

Provo City Library
425 W. Center Street
Provo, UT 84601
Tel: 801-379-6650
URL: http://lmc.einet.net/hytelnet/us759.html

Springville Public Library
50 South Main
Springville, UT 84663-1358
Tel: 801-489-2720
801-489-2721
Email: lcathera@inter.state.lib.ut.us
javerett@inter.state.lib.ut.us
URL: http://www.state.lib.us/pubs/pldirect/utsprvil.htm

Southern Utah University Library
Special Collections
351 Center Street, Garden Level
Cedar City, UT 84720
Tel: 801-586-7933
801-586-7945 (Special Collections)
Fax: 801-865-8152
Email: nickerson@suu.edu
clegg@suu.edu
URL: http://www.li.suu.edu/library/lispcoll.htm

University of Utah
Marriott Library
Special Collections, 5th Floor
1400 East 200 South
Salt Lake City, UT 84112
Email: gthompso@alexandria.lib.utah.edu
URL: http://www.lib.utah.edu/

Utah State Historical Society/Library
300 Rio Grande
Salt Lake City, UT 84101
Tel: 801-533-3500
801-533-3501 (Hours, Information)
Fax: 801-533-3502
TDD: 801-533-3503
Email: ushs@history.state.ut.us
cehistry.ushs@email.state.ut.us
URL: http://www.ce.ex.state.ut.us/history/

Utah State University
Merrill Library
Special Collections and Archives, 1st Floor
Logan, UT 84322
Tel: 801-797-2663
Email: annbut@library.lib.usu.edu
URL: http://www.usu.edu/~specol/index.html

Utah Valley State College (UVSC)
Library/Sparks Special Collection Room
800 West 1200 South
Orem, UT 84058
Tel: 801-222-8265
801-222-8173
URL: http://www.uvsc.edu/studsvc/library/

Newspaper Repositories

Family History Library
Church of Jesus Christ of Latter-Day Saints
35 North West Temple
Salt Lake City, UT 84150
Tel: 801-240-2331
Some Unofficial Sites:
URL: http://bobcat.etsu.edu/ftpdir/genealogy/LDStext/ut-08456.txt
http://www.genealogy.org/~uvpafug/fhlslc.html
http://www.aros.net/~drwaff/slcfhl.htm
http://http.tamu.edu:8000/~mbg5500/genealogy/lds_gen_info.html

University of Utah
Marriott Library
Serials Department
1400 East 200 South
Salt Lake City, UT 84112
Email: ystroup@alexandria.lib.utah.edu
URL: http://www.lib.utah.edu/instruction/newsletter/summer95/speccoll.html

Utah State Library
2150 South 300 West
Salt Lake City, UT 84115
Tel: 801-468-6777
801-466-5888
URL: http://www.state.lib.ut.us/www.htm

Utah State University
Merrill Library
Special Collections and Archives, 1st Floor
Logan, UT 84322
Tel: 801-797-2663
Email: annbut@library.lib.usu.edu
URL: http://www.usu.edu/~specol/index.html

Vital Records

Utah Bureau of Vital Records
288 North 1460 West
Salt Lake City, UT 84114-2855
Tel: 801-538-6105
Email: hlvr.vrequest@state.ut.us
URL: http://www.archives.state.ut.us/

Utah State Archives
Archives Building
P.O. Box 141021
Salt Lake City, UT 84114-1021
Tel: 801-538-3013 (Research Room)
Fax: 801-538-3354
Email: research@state.ut.us
URL: http://www.archives.state.ut.us/
Births and Deaths 1898-1905

Utah on the Web

BYU Genealogy WWW Server
http://reled.byu.edu/jsblab/genealog.htm

Pioneer-Utah's Online Electronic Library
http://pioneer.uen.org/

Utah GenWeb Project
http://www.lofthouse.com/USA/Utah/index.html

Utah History Encyclopedia
http://www.media.utah.edu/medsol/UCME/UHEindex.html

Utah Pioneer Sesquicentennial Celebration-Coordinating Council
http://www.ce.ex.state.ut.us/history/sesqui/

Utah Travel and Adventures
http://www.utah.com/

Utah Valley PAF Users Group
http://www.genealogy.org/~ovpafug/

VERMONT

ARCHIVES, STATE & NATIONAL

National Archives—New England Region
380 Trapelo Road
Waltham, MA 02154-8104
Tel: 617-647-8100
Fax: 617-647-8460
Email: archives@waltham.nara.gov
URL: http://www.nara.gov/nara/regional/01nsbgil.html

Vermont State Archives
Location at Redstone:
26 Terrace Street
Montpelier, VT
Mail:
109 State Street
Montpelier, VT 05609-1101
Tel: 802-828-2308
Email: gsanford@sec.state.vt.us
URL: http://www.sec.state.vt.us/archives/guide/archdex.htm

GENEALOGICAL SOCIETIES

Genealogical Society of Vermont
P.O. Box 1553
St. Albans, VT 05478-1006
Email: 76165.3613@compuserve.com
URL: http://ourworld.compuserve.com/homepages/induni_n_J/

New England Historical and Genealogical Society (NEHGS)
101 Newbury Street
Boston, MA 02116-3007
Tel: 617-836-5740
888-AT-NEHGS (Membership & Education)
888-BY-NEHGS (Sales)
888-90-NEHGS (Library Circulation)
Fax: 617-536-7307
Email: nehgs@nehgs.org
URL: http://www.nehgs.org/

Vermont French-Canadian Genealogical Society Library:
St. John's Club
9 Central Avenue
Burlington, VT
Mail:
P.O. Box 65128
Burlington, VT 05406-5128
Email: vtfcgs@aol.com
URL: http://members.aol.com/vtfcgs/genealogy/index.html

HISTORICAL SOCIETIES

Barnet Historical Society
Goodwillie House
Barnet Center, VT
Mail:
RR 1, Box 241
Barnet, VT 05821
Tel: 802-633-2611
802-633-2563

Bellows Falls Historical Society
6 Chase Park
Bellows Falls, VT 05051
Tel: 802-463-3706

Bethel Historical Society
Church Street
Bethel, VT 05032
Tel: 802-234-9413

Bradford Historical Society
Academy Building
Main Street
P.O. Box 301
Bradford, VT 05033
Tel: 802-222-9026

Braintree Historical Society
RFD 1, Thayer Brook Road
Randolph, VT 05060
Tel: 802-728-9291

Brattleboro Historical Society
230 Main Street, 3rd Floor
P.O. Box 6392
Brattleboro, VT 05302

Bridport Historical Society/Museum
Route 22-A
Mail:
RR 1, Box 656
Bridport, VT 05734
Tel: 802-758-2654

Bristol Historical Society/Museum
Howden Hall Community Center
Main Street
Bristol, VT 05443
Tel: 802-453-6029

Brookfield Historical Society
Marvin Newton House
Ridge Road
P.O. Box 405
Brookfield, VT 05036
Tel: 802-276-3959

Cabot Historical Society/Museum
Main Street
Cabot, VT
Mail:
RFD, Lower Cabot
Marshfield, VT 05658
Tel: 802-563-2558

Canaan Historical Society
c/o Alice Ward Library
Village Green, VT
Mail:
P.O. Box 134
Canaan, VT 05903
Tel: 802-266-7135
802-266-7766

Castleton Historical Society/Museum
Main Street
P.O. Box 219
Castleton, VT 05735
Tel: 802-468-5523

Cavendish Historical Society/Museum
RFD 1, Box 171
Cavendish, VT 05142
Tel: 802-484-7498

Charleston Historical Society
RR 1, Box 840
West Charleston, VT 05872
Tel: 802-895-4329

Chelsea Historical Society
Main Street
P.O. Box 206
Chelsea, VT 05038
Tel: 802-685-4860

Chester Historical Society
Main Street
Chester, VT 05143
Tel: 802-875-3767
802-875-2497

Chittenden County Historical Society
P.O. Box 1576
Burlington, VT 05402
Tel: 802-864-4716

Concord Historical Society/Museum
Concord Town Hall
Concord, VT
Mail:
HCR 60, Box 40
North Concord, VT 05858
Tel: 802-695-2288

Crystal Lake Falls Historical Association
The Pierce House
Water Street
P.O. Box 253
Barton, VT 05822
Tel: 802-525-6251
802-525-3583

Danville Historical Society/Archives
Pope Memorial Library
The Green
P.O. Box 260
Danville, VT 05828
Tel: 802-684-2256

Derby Historical Society
P.O. Box 357
Derby, VT 05829
Tel: 802-766-5324

Dorset Historical Society/Museum
P.O. Box 52
Dorset, VT 05251
Tel: 802-867-4450

Enosburgh Historical Society
Main Street
P.O. Box 98
Enosburgh Falls, VT 05450
Tel: 802-933-2102
802-933-4708

Essex Community Historical Society
Routes 15 and 128
Mail:
3 Browns River Road
Essex Junction, VT 05452
Tel: 802-878-6486

Fairlee Historical Society
Fairlee Town Hall
P.O. Box 95
Fairlee, VT 05045
Tel: 802-333-4363
802-333-9727

Georgia Historical Society/Museum
Georgia Center, VT
Mail:
RD 3
St. Albans, VT 05478
Tel: 802-524-3318

Glover Historical Society
Municipal Building, 2nd Floor
Glover, VT 05839
Tel: 802-525-6227 (Town Clerk)

Goodrich Memorial Library
70 Main Street
Newport, VT 05855
Tel: 802-334-7902

Grafton Historical Society/Museum
Main Street
P.O. Box 202
Grafton, VT 05146
Tel: 802-843-2305

Greensboro Historical Society/Museum
RR 1, Box 1290
Greensboro, VT 05841

Guilford Historical Society
RR 2, Box 18A
Brattleboro, VT 05301
Tel: 802-257-7306
802-254-9557

Halifax Historical Society
RR 4, Box 531
Brattleboro, VT 05301
Tel: 802-368-7490

Hartford Historical Society
15 Bridge Street
P.O. Box 547
Hartford, VT 05047
Tel: 802-295-9353
802-295-6382

Holland Historical Society
RD 1, Box 37, Derby Line
Holland, VT 05830
Tel: 802-895-4440

Huntington Historical Society
Lower Village
P.O. Box 147
Huntington, VT 05462
Tel: 802-434-4350

Island Pond Historical Society
Canadian Natl. Railway Station
P.O. Box 408
Island Pond, VT 05846
Tel: 802-482-3923

Isle La Motte Historical Society
1830 Schoolhouse
Isle La Motte, VT 05463
Tel: 802-928-3422

Jericho Historical Society
Old Red Mill, Route 15
P.O. Box 35
Jericho, VT 05465
Tel: 802-899-3225
URL: http://www.vermontcrafts.com/members/JericSoc322.html

Lincoln Historical Society
Quaker Street
Lincoln, VT
Mail:
RD 1, Box 60
Bristol, VT 05443
Tel/Fax: 802-453-3628

Londonderry Historical Society
RR 1, Box 41
South Londonderry, VT 05155
Tel: 802-824-5268

Manchester Historical Society
P.O. Box 363
Manchester, VT 05254
Tel: 802-362-3747

Marlboro Historical Society/Museum
P.O. Box 131
Marlboro, VT 05344
Tel: 802-254-9152

Middletown Springs Historical Society
The Green
P.O. Box 1001
Middletown Springs, VT 05757
Tel: 802-235-2376

Missisquoi Valley Historical Society/Museum
East Main Street
North Troy, VT 05859
Tel: 802-988-2677

Montgomery Historical Society/Museum
Route 118
Montgomery, VT 05470
Tel: 802-326-4404

Morristown Historical Society
P.O. Box 1299
Morrisville, VT 05661
Tel: 802-888-7617
802-888-5605

New England Historical and Genealogical Society (NEHGS)
101 Newbury Street
Boston, MA 02116-3007
Tel: 617-836-5740
888-AT-NEHGS (Membership & Education)
888-BY-NEHGS (Sales)
888-90-NEHGS (Library Circulation)
Fax: 617-536-7307
Email: nehgs@nehgs.org
URL: http://www.nehgs.org/

Norwich Historical Society
Church Street
P.O. Box 284
Norwich, VT 05055
Tel: 802-649-2711

Orleans County Historical Society/Museum and Library
Old Stone House Museum
Brownington, VT
Mail:
RFD 1, Box 500
Orleans, VT 05860
Tel: 802-754-2022
URL: http://homepages.together.net/~osh/

Peacham Historical Association
HCR 30, Box 12
Peacham, VT 05862
Tel: 802-592-3571

Pittsford Historical Society/Museum
Eaton Hall, Route 7
P.O. Box 423
Pittsford, VT 05763
Tel: 802-483-6623

Poultney Historical Society
RFD 1, Box 177
Poultney, VT 05764
Tel: 802-287-5268

Putney Historical Society
Town Hall
P.O. Box 233
Putney, VT 05346
Tel: 802-387-5862

Randolph Historical Society/Museum
P.O. Box 15
Randolph Center, VT 05060
Tel: 82-728-5398

Reading Historical Society/Museum
Reading, VT 05062
Tel: 802-484-7271

Readsboro Historical Society
Main Street
Mail:
RR 1, Box 277
Readsboro, VT 05350
Tel: 802-423-5394

Rochester Historical Society
Town Library
Rochester, VT 05767
Tel: 802-767-4453

Royalton Historical Society/Museum
RR 1, Box 89D
Royalton, VT 05068
Tel: 802-763-8567

Rutland Historical Society
96 Center Street
Rutland, VT 05701
Tel: 802-775-2006

St. Albans Historical Society/Museum
Church Street
P.O. Box 722
St. Albans, VT 05478
Tel: 802-527-7933

Saxtons River Historical Society/Museum
P.O. Box 18
Saxtons River, VT 05154
Tel: 802-869-2657
802-869-2328

Shaftsbury Historical Society
Baptist Meeting House, Route 7-A
P.O. Box 401
Shaftsbury, VT 05262

Shoreham Historical Society
Route 22-A
Shoreham, VT 05770
Tel: 802-897-2600

Springfield Art and Historical Society
Miller Art Center
9 Elm Street
P.O. Box 313
Springfield, VT 05156
Tel: 802-885-2451

Stannard Historical Society
9 Willey Road
Greensboro Bend, VT 05842
Tel: 802-533-2317

Stowe Historical Society
Akeley Memorial Building/Stowe History Room
Main Street
Stowe, VT 05672
Tel: 802-252-6133

Thetford Historical Society/Museum
P.O. Box 33
Thetford, VT 05074
Tel: 802-785-2430
802-333-4613

UVM Historic Preservation Program
Wheeler House
442 Main Street
Burlington, VT 05405
Tel: 802-656-3180
Email: histpres@zoo.uvm.edu
URL: http://www.uvm.edu/~histpres/index.html

Vermont Historical Society
Pavilion Office Building
109 State Street
Montpelier, VT 05602
Tel: 802-828-2291
Email: vhs@vhs.state.vt.us
or vt_his_soc@dol.state.vt.us
URL: http://www.state.vt.us/vhs/

Vermont Old Cemetery Association
c/o Charles Marchant
P.O. Box 132
Townshend, VT 05353
Tel: 802-660-8581
802-899-4640
URL: http://sageunix.uvm.edu/~rresnik/doc/voc.htm

Vernon Historians
RR 1, Box 196, Pond Road
Vernon, VT 05354
Tel: 802-254-8015

Wallingford Historical Society
P.O. Box 327
Wallingford, VT 05773
Tel: 802-446-2336

Waterbury Historical Society/Museum
28 North Main Street
Waterbury, VT 05676
Tel: 802-244-7036

Weathersfield Historical Society/Museum
Reverend Dan Foster House
Whed Center Road
Perkinsville, VT 05151
Tel: 802-263-5230
802-263-5361
802-263-9462
Fax: 802-263-9263

West Windsor Historical Society
Route 44
P.O. Box 12
Brownsville, VT 05037
Tel: 802-484-7474

Westminster Historical Society
Town Hall, Route 5
P.O. Box 2
Westminster, VT 05158
Tel: 802-387-5778

Whitingham Historical Society
P.O. Box 125
Jacksonville, VT 05342

Williamstown Historical Society
Main Street
Mail:
RFD 1, Box 812
Williamstown, VT 05679
Tel: 802-433-5475

Williston Historical Society
688 Williston Road
P.O. Box 995
Williston, VT 05495
Tel: 802-878-3048

Windham County, Historical Society of
Route 30
P.O. Box 246
Newfane, VT 05345
Tel: 802-365-4148

Winooski Historical Society
73 East Allen Street (Location)
21 Park Street (Mail)
Winooski, VT 05404
Tel: 802-655-3561

Woodstock Historical Society
26 Elm Street
Woodstock, VT 05091
Tel: 802-457-1822
URL: http://www.uvm.edu/~histpres/vtiana/woodstockhs.html

LDS FAMILY HISTORY CENTER

Berlin Family History Center
Hershey Road
Berlin, VT 05641
Tel: 802-229-0898

ARCHIVES/LIBRARIES/MUSEUMS

Aldrich Public Library
Vermont Room
6 Washington Street
Barre, VT 05641
Tel: 802-476-7550
802-476-5118
Email: barre@dol.state.vt.us
URL: http://www.uvm.edu/~histpres/vtiana/aldrich.html

Bennington Museum/Genealogical Library
West Main Street
Bennington, VT 05201
Tel: 802-447-1571
Fax: 802-447-8305
URL: http://www.neinfo.net/New_England/Vermont/Bennington/attractions/Bennington_Museum/index.htp
or http://www.bennington.com/museum/gene.html
or http://www.uvm.edu/~histpres/vtiana/benningtonmuseum.html

Bixby Memorial Library
258 Main Street
Vergennes, VT 05491
Tel: 802-877-2211
URL: http://www.uvm.edu/~histpres/vtiana/bixby.html

Brooks Memorial Library
Vermontiana Collection
224 Main Street
Brattleboro, VT 05301
Tel: 802-254-5290
Fax: 802-254-2309
Email: brattlib@brooks.lib.vt.us
URL: http://www.state.vt.us/libraries/b733/brookslibrary/

Castleton State College
Calvin Coolidge Library
Seminary Street
Castleton, VT 05735
Tel: 802-468-5611 ext. 257
Fax: 802-468-2421
URL: http://sparrow.csc.vsc.edu/library/menupage.htm

Danville Historical Society/Archives
Pope Memorial Library
The Green
P.O. Box 260
Danville, VT 05828
Tel: 802-684-2256

Fletcher Free Library
235 College Street
Burlington, VT 05401
Tel: 802-863-3403
802-865-7217 (Reference)
Fax: 802-865-7227
URL: http://www.uvm.edu/~histpres/vtiana/fletcher.html

Georgia Historical Society/Museum
Georgia Center, VT
Mail:
RD 3
St. Albans, VT 05478
Tel: 802-524-3318

Glover Historical Society
Municipal Building, 2nd Floor
Glover, VT 05839
Tel: 802-525-6227 (Town Clerk)

Goodrich Memorial Library
70 Main Street
Newport, VT 05855
Tel: 802-334-7902

Greensboro Historical Society/Museum
RR 1, Box 1290
Greensboro, VT 05841

Ilsley Public Library
Main Street
Middlebury, VT 05753
Tel: 802-388-4095
Fax: 802-388-4367
Email: ilsley_midd@dol.state.vt.us
URL: http://www.uvm.edu/~histpres/vtiana/ilsley.html

Lyndon State College
Samuel Read Hall Library
Northeast Kingdom Room
Lyndonville, VT 05851
Tel: 802-626-9371 ext. 147
URL: http://www.lsc.vsc.edu/SERVICES/
ACASER/LIBRARY.HTM

Martha Canfield Memorial Free Library
The Russell Vermontiana Collection
Main Street, Route 7A
P.O. Box 267
Arlington, VT 05250
Tel: 802-375-6153
URL: http://www.uvm.edu/~histpres/vtiana/arlington.html

Middlebury College
Starr Library
Meredith Wing, Level 4
Vermont Collection
Middlebury, VT 05753
Tel: 802-388-3711
Fax: 802-388-3467
Email: raum@myriad.middlebury.edu
URL: http://www.middlebury.edu/~lib/index.html

Milton Museum
Main Street
P.O. Box 2
Milton, VT 05468

New England Historical and Genealogical Society (NEHGS)
101 Newbury Street
Boston, MA 02116-3007
Tel: 617-836-5740
888-AT-NEHGS (Membership & Education)
888-BY-NEHGS (Sales)
888-90-NEHGS (Library Circulation)
Fax: 617-536-7307
Email: nehgs@nehgs.org
URL: http://www.nehgs.org/

Norman Williams Public Library
10 S. Park Street
Woodstock, VT 05091
Tel: 802-457-2295
Email: http://www.uvm.edu/~histpres/vtiana
/nwilliams.html

Orleans County Historical Society/Museum and Library
Old Stone House Museum
Brownington, VT
Mail:
RFD 1, Box 500
Orleans, VT 05860
Tel: 802-754-2022
URL: http://homepages.together.net/~osh/

Peacham Historical Association
HCR 30, Box 12
Peacham, VT 05862
Tel: 802-592-3571

Pittsford Historical Society/Museum
Eaton Hall, Route 7
P.O. Box 423
Pittsford, VT 05763
Tel: 802-483-6623

Rockingham Free Public Library/Museum
65 Westminster Street
Bellows Falls, VT 05101
Tel: 802-463-4270
URL: http://www.uvm.edu/~histpres/vtiana/rockingham.html

Rutland Free Library
10 Court Street
Rutland, VT 05701
Tel: 802-773-1860
URL: http://www.uvm.edu/~histpres/vtiana/rutland.html

St. Albans Free Library
Vermont Room
11 Maiden Land
St. Albans, VT 05478
Tel: 802-524-1507
Fax: 802-524-1514
Email: stalbans@dol.state.vt.us
URL: http://homepages.together.net/~shell/library.htm

St. Johnsbury Athenaeum
30 Main Street
St. Johnsbury, VT 05819-2289
Tel: 802-748-8291
URL: http://www.uvm.edu/~histpres/vtiana/stj.html

Saxtons River Historical Society/Museum
P.O. Box 18
Saxtons River, VT 05154
Tel: 802-869-2657
802-869-2328

Sheldon Museum
1 Park Street
Middlebury, VT 05753
Tel: 802-388-2117
Email: sheldon_mus@myriad.middlebury.edu
URL: http://www.vtweb.com/vermontweathervane/96.8august/history.html

University of Vermont
Bailey/Howe Library
Special Collections
Burlington, VT 05405
Tel: 802-656-2138
Fax: 802-656-4038
URL: http://sageunix.uvm.edu/~sc/

Vermont Department of Libraries
Reference and Law Services
109 State Street
Montpelier, VT 05609
Tel: 802-828-3261
Fax: 802-828-2199
URL: http://dol.state.vt.us/
or http://www.uvm.edu/~histpres/vtiana/vtlib.html

Vermont Folklife Center
2 Court Street
P.O. Box 442
Middlebury, VT 05753
Tel: 802-388-4964
Fax: 802-388-1844
Email: obrian@midd.cc.middlebury.edu
URL: http://www.uvm.edu/~histpres/vtiana/vtfolk.html

Newspaper Repositories

University of Vermont
Bailey/Howe Library
Special Collections
Burlington, VT 05405
Tel: 802-656-2138
Fax: 802-656-4038
Email: cgallagh@uvmvm.uvm.edu
URL: http://sageunix.uvm.edu/~sc/

Vermont Department of Libraries
Reference and Law Services
109 State Street
Montpelier, VT 05609
Tel: 802-828-3261
Fax: 802-828-2199
URL: http://dol.state.vt.us/
or http://www.uvm.edu/~histpres/vtiana/vtlib.html

Vital Records

Vermont General Services Center
Public Records Division
Route 2, Drawer 33
Middlesex, VT 05633-7601
Tel: 802-828-3288
802-828-2794 (Public Records)
802-828-3286 (Reference/Research Center)
Fax: 802-828-3710
URL: http://www.cit.state.vt.us/gsd/pubrec.htm

Vermont on the Web

Middlebury College, Starr Library-Vermont Genealogy Page
http://www.middlebury.edu/library/genealogy.html

UVM Historic Preservation Program
http://www.uvm.edu/~histpres/index.html

Vermont GenWeb Project
http://www.erols.com/tledoux/vtgenweb.htm

Vermont Historical Society
URL: http://www.state.vt.us/vhs/

VIRGINIA

ARCHIVES, STATE & NATIONAL

National Archives—Mid Atlantic Region
Ninth and Market Streets
Philadelphia, PA 19107-4292
Tel: 215-597-3000
Fax: 215-597-2303
Email: archives@philarch.nara.gov
URL: http://www.nara.gov/nara/regional/03nsgil.html

Library of Virginia, Archives Division
800 E. Broad Street
Richmond, VA 23219
Tel: 804-692-3888
Fax: 804-692-3556
URL: http://leo.vsla.edu/archives/genie.html

GENEALOGICAL SOCIETIES

Afro-American Historical and Genealogical Society/Hampton Roads
(AAHGS)
P.O. Box 2448
Newport News, VA 23609-2448

Alleghany Highlands Genealogical Society
c/o Virginia Smith, Pres.
605 Dolly Ann Drive
Covington, VA 24426

Allegheny Regional Family History Society (ARFHS)
P.O. Box 1804
Elkins, WV 26241
Tel: 304-636-1958
304-636-1959
URL: http://www.swcp.com/~dhickman/arfhs.html

Caroline County Genealogical Society
P.O. Box 9
Bowling Green, VA 22427

Central Virginia Genealogical Association
P.O. Box 5583
Charlottesville, VA 22905-5583
Email: cvga@avenue.gen.va.us
URL: http://monticello.avenue.gen.va.us/Community/Agencies/CVGA/

Fairfax Genealogical Society
P.O. Box 2290
Merrifield, VA 22116

Genealogical Research Institute of Virginia
P.O. Box 29178
Richmond, VA 23242

Genealogy and History of the Eastern Shore (GHOTES)
Email: bgcox@ix.netcom.com
URL: http://www.esva.net/ghotes/

Germanna Colonies in Virginia, Memorial Foundation of the
P.O. Box 693
Culpeper, VA 22701
Tel: 540-825-1496
Fax: 540-825-6572
Email: germanna@summit.net
URL: http://www.summit.net/GERMANNA/

Holston Territory Genealogical Society
P.O. Box 433
Bristol, VA 24203

Jewish Genealogical Society of Tidewater
Jewish Community Center
7300 Newport Avenue
Norfolk, VA 23505

Lee County Historical & Genealogical Society
P.O. Box 231
Jonesville, VA 24263

Loudoun County Genealogy Club
P.O. Box 254
Leesburg, VA 22075

Lower DelMarVa Genealogical Society
P.O. Box 3602
Salisbury, MD 21802-3602
Tel: 410-742-3501
410-546-0314
URL: http://bay.intercom.net/ldgs/index.html

National Genealogical Society/Library
4527 Seventeenth Street, North
Arlington, VA 22207-2363
Tel: 703-525-0050
703-841-9065 (Library)
Fax: 703-525-0052
Email: 76702.2417@compuserve.com
Library Email: ngslibe@wizard.net
URL: http://www.genealogy.org/~ngs/

Norfolk Genealogical Society
P.O. Box 12813, Thomas Corner Station
Norfolk, VA 23502

Page County, Genealogical Society of
5651 Mill Creek Road
Luray, VA 22835
Email: takelley@erols.com
URL: http://www.rootsweb.com/~vagspc/pcgs.html

Portsmouth Genealogical Society
601 Court Street
Portsmouth, VA 23704

Prince William County Genealogical Society
P.O. Box 2019
Manassas, VA 22110-0812

Rockbridge Area Genealogical Society (RAGS)
P.O. Box 75
Rockbridge Baths, VA 24473
Email: reddog@rockbridge.net (RAGS in Subject field)
URL: http://www.angelfire.com/va/rockbridge/index.html

Southwestern Virginia Genealogical Society
P.O. Box 12485
Roanoke, VA 24026

Tidewater Genealogical Society
P.O. Box 7650
Hampton, VA 23666

Virginia Beach Genealogical Society
P.O. Box 62901
Virginia Beach, VA 23466-2901

Virginia Genealogical Society
P.O. Box 7469
Richmond, VA 23221
URL: http://www6.pilot.infi.net/~cwt/vbgs.html

VA-NC Piedmont Genealogical Society
P.O. Box 2272
Danville, VA 24541
Tel: 804-799-5195 ext. 4
Email: vancsoc@juno.com
URL: http://www.ci.danville.va.us/libry/lib8b.htm

HISTORICAL SOCIETIES

Afro-American Historical and Genealogical Society/Hampton Roads
(AAHGS)
P.O. Box 2448
Newport News, VA 23609-2448

Albemarle County Historical Society
200 Second Street, NE
Charlottesville, VA 22902-5245
Tel: 804-296-1492
Fax: 804-296-4576
URL: http://monticello.avenue.gen.va.us/go/ACHS/

Amelia County Historical Society/Library
P.O. Box 113
Amelia, VA 23002
Tel: 804-561-3180

Arlington Historical Society/Museum
1805 S. Arlington Ridge Road
Arlington, VA 22202-1628
Tel: 703-892-4204

Association for the Preservation of Virginia Antiquities
204 W. Franklin Street
Richmond, VA 23220
Tel: 804-648-1889
Email: apva@apva.org
URL: http://www.apva.org/

Augusta County Historical Society
P.O. Box 686
Staunton, VA 24401

Avoca Museums and Historical Society
1514 Main Street
Altavista, VA 24517-1132
Tel: 804-369-1076

Bath County Historical Society
P.O. Box 212
Warm Springs, VA 24484

Bedford Historical Society
P.O. Box 602
Bedford, VA 24523

Botetourt County Historical Society, Inc.
Courthouse Square
P.O. Box 468
Fincastle, VA 24090
Tel: 540-473-3713
Email: ehonts@aol.com
URL: http://truth.idbsu.edu/bhs/bhs.html

Catholic Historical Society/Museum
624 N. Jefferson Street
Roanoke, VA 24016-1402
Tel: 540-982-0152

Chesterfield Historical Society
11001 Iron Bridge Road
P.O. Box 40
Chesterfield, VA 23832
Tel: 804-748-1026
Fax: 804-748-3032
URL: http://leo.vsla.edu/reposit/sites/chsv.html

Claiborne County Historical Society
Route 1, Box 589
Jonesville, VA 24263

Clark County Historical Association/Museum and Archives
Old County Courthouse, North Wing
P.O. Box 306
Berryville, VA 22611
Tel: 540-955-2600
URL: http://leo.vsla.edu/reposit/sites/ccha.html

Culpeper Historical Society
P.O. Box 785
Culpeper, VA 22701

Cumberland County Historical Society
P.O. Box 88
Cumberland, VA 23040

Eastern Shore of Virginia Historical Society/Museum
Kerr Place
69 Market Street
P.O. Box 193
Onancock, VA 23417
Tel: 757-787-8012
URL: http://leo.vsla.edu/reposit/sites/esvhs.html

Essex County Historical Society
Route 3, Box 498
Tappahannock, VA 22560
URL: http://www.iocc.com/~swright/esxsoc.html

Fairfax County, Historical Society of
P.O. Box 415
Fairfax, VA 22030
Tel: 703-246-2123

Fauquier Historical Society
Court House Square and Ashby Street
Warrenton, VA 22186
Tel: 540-347-5525

Fort Eustis Historical and Archaelogical Association
P.O. Box 4408
Fort Eustis, VA 23604

Germanna Colonies in Virginia, Memorial Foundation of the
P.O. Box 693
Culpeper, VA 22701
Tel: 540-825-1496
Fax: 540-825-6572
Email: germanna@summit.net
URL: http://www.summit.net/GERMANNA/

Giles County Historical Society
208 N. Main Street
P.O. Box 404
Pearisburg, VA 24134
Tel: 540-921-1050

Goochland County Historical Society
P.O. Box 602
Goochland, VA 23063
Tel: 804-556-3966
Fax: 804-556-4617
URL: http://leo.vsla.edu/reposit/sites/gchs.html

Grayson County Historical Society
Route 1, Box 293
Elk Creek, VA 24326

Greene County Historical Society
P.O. Box 185
Stanardsville, VA 22973

Gum Springs Historical Society
8100 Fordson Road
Alexandria, VA 22306
Tel: 703-799-1198
URL: http://www.lke-comply.com/fcmn/htm/gshs/gshs.htm

Hanover County Historical Society
P.O. Box 91
Hanover, VA 23069

Harrisonburg-Rockingham Historical Society
Shenandoah Valley Folk Art and Heritage Center
Bowman Road and High Street
P.O. Box 716
Dayton, VA 22821
Tel/Fax: 540-879-2616
URL: http://www.marketplace.staunton.va.us/valyhst/hrhs.html

King and Queen County Historical Society
"Canterbury"
Route 1, Box 18
Walkerton, VA 23177
URL: http://www.iocc.com/~swright/k&qsoc.html

King George County Historical Society
P.O. Box 424
King George, VA 22485

Lee County Historical & Genealogical Society
P.O. Box 231
Jonesville, VA 24263

Louisa County Historical Society/Library, Archives and Museum
Old Jail (next to courthouse)
Main Street
P.O. Box 1172
Louisa, VA 23093
URL: http://monticello.avenue.gen.va.us/Library/JMRL/Louisa/historical.html

Martinsville-Henry County Historical Society
P.O. Box Drawer 432
Martinsville, VA 24114

Mathews County Historical Society, Inc.
P.O. Box 855
Mathews, VA 23109

New River Historical Society
P.O. Box 373
Newbern, VA 24126

Norfolk County Historical Society
c/o Chesapeake Public Library
300 Cedar Road
Chesapeake, VA 23320

Northern Neck of Virginia Historical Society
Westmoreland County Museum
Courthouse Square
P.O. Box 716
Montross, VA 22520
Tel: 804-493-8440
URL: http://www.iocc.com/~swright/lansoc.html

Northumberland County Historical Society
Heathsville, VA 22473
Tel: 804-580-8581

Nottoway County Historical Association
RFD 1, Box 56
Crewe, VA 23930

Orange County Historical Society/Library and Archives
130 Caroline Street
Orange, VA 22960-1533
Tel: 540-672-5366
URL: http://206.107.180.50/tel16/orange/orange.htm

Patrick County Historical Society/Museum
Blue Ridge Street
P.O. Box 1045
Stuart, VA 24171
Tel: 540-694-2840
URL: http://leo.vsla.edu/reposit/sites/pchm.html

Pittsylvania Historical Society
P.O. Box 1206
Chatham, VA 24531

Rappahannock Historical Society/Library
P.O. Box 261
Washington, VA 22747-0261
Tel: 540-675-1163
URL: http://leo.vsla.edu/reposit/sites/rhs.html

Roanoke Valley Historical Society
One Market Square, SE
P.O. Box 1904
Roanoke, VA 24008
Tel: 540-342-5770
Fax: 540-224-1238
URL: http://leo.vsla.edu/reposit/sites/rvhs.html

Rockbridge Historical Society
101 E. Washington Street
Lexington, VA 24450
Tel: 540-464-1058
URL: http://leo.vsla.edu/reposit/sites/rohs.html

Rockingham County Historical Society
301 South Main Street
Harrisonburg, VA 22801

Salem Historical Society
801 E. Main Street
P.O. Box 201
Salem, VA 24153
Tel: 540-389-6760

Sergeant Kirkland's Historical Society/Museum
912 Lafayette Blvd.
Fredericksburg, VA 22401-5617
Tel: 540-899-5565

Shenandoah County Historical Society
c/o Shenandoah County Library
Stoney Creek Blvd
Route 1, Box 1-B
Edinburg, VA 22824
Tel: 540-984-8200

Smyth County Historical Society
P.O. Box 574
Marion, VA 24354

Tazewell County Historical Society
100 E. Main Street
P.O. Box 916
Tazewell, VA 24651-0916
Tel: 540-988-4069
URL: http://www.cc.utah.edu/~pdp7277/taze-soc.html

Virginia Historical Society
428 North Boulevard
P.O. Box 7311
Richmond, VA 23221-0311
Tel: 804-358-4901
804-342-9658 (Membership)
Email: kelly_winters@vahistorical.org
URL: http://www.vahistorical.org

Washington County, Historical Society of
P.O. Box 484
Abingdon, VA 24210

Winchester-Frederick County Historical Society
c/o Handley Library
100 W. Piccadilly Street
Winchester, VA 22601

LDS Family History Centers

Annandale Family History Center
3900 Howard Street
Annandale, VA 22003
Tel: 703-256-5518

Bassett Family History Center
Route 57 A
Stanleytown, VA 24055
Tel: 540-629-7613

Centreville Family History Center
14150 Upper Ridge Drive
Centreville, VA 22020
Tel: 703-830-5343

Charlottesville Family History Center
Hydraulic Road
Charlottesville, VA 22901
Tel: 804-973-9856

Chesapeake Family History Center
412 Scarborough Drive
Chesapeake, VA 23320
Tel: 804-482-8600

Dale City Family History Center
3000 Dale Blvd.
Dale City, VA 22193
Tel: 703-670-5977

Falls Church Family History Center
2034 Great Falls Street
Falls Church, VA 22043
Tel: 703-532-9019

Fredericksburg Family History Center
1710 Bragg Road
Fredericksburg, VA 22407
Tel: 540-786-5641

Gloucester Family History Center
8381 George Washington Hwy.
Gloucester, VA 23061
Tel: 804-693-5095

Hamilton Family History Center
Old Route 7 and Reid Street
Hamilton, VA 22068
Tel: 703-338-9526

Harrisonburg Family History Center
210 South Avenue
Harrisonburg, VA 22801
Tel: 540-433-2945

Midlothian Family History Center
4601 N. Bailey Bridge Road
Midlothian, VA 23112
Tel: 804-763-4318

Newport News Family History Center
901 Denhigh Blvd.
Newport News, VA 23608
Tel: 757-874-2335

Oakton Family History Center
2719 Hunter Mill Road
Oakton, VA 22124
Tel: 703-281-1836

Pembroke Family History Center
Route 460
Pembroke, VA 24136
Tel: 703-626-7264

Richmond Family History Center
5600 Monument Avenue
Richmond, VA 23226
Tel: 804-288-8134

Salem Family History Center
6311 Wayburn Drive
Salem, VA 24153
Tel: 540-562-2052

Virginia Beach Family History Center
4760 Princess Anne Road
Virginia Beach, VA 23462
Tel: 757-467-3302

Waynesboro Family History Center
2825 Jefferson Lane
Waynesboro, VA 22980
Tel: 540-942-1036

Winchester Family History Center
Apple Pie Ridge
Winchester, VA 22603
Tel: 540-722-6055

ARCHIVES/LIBRARIES/MUSEUMS

Albemarle County Historical Society
200 Second Street, NE
Charlottesville, VA 22902-5245
Tel: 804-296-1492
Fax: 804-296-4576
URL: http://monticello.avenue.gen.va.us/go/ACHS/

Alexandria Black History Resource Center
638 N. Alfred Street
Alexandria, VA 22314-1823
Tel: 703-838-4356
URL: http://ci.alexandria.va.us/libraries_museums/bhrc.html

Alexandria Library
Lloyd House
220 Washington Street
Alexandria, VA 22314
Tel: 703-838-4577
Fax: 703-706-3912
URL: http://www.alexandria.lib.va.us/lloyd.html

Allen E. Roberts Masonic Library and Museum
4115 Nine Mile Road
Richmond, VA 23223-4926
Tel: 804-222-3110
Fax: 804-222-4253
URL: http://leo.vsla.edu/reposit/sites/aerml.html

Amelia County Historical Society/Library
P.O. Box 113
Amelia, VA 23002
Tel: 804-561-3180

Amherst County Public Library
803 Main Street
Amherst, VA 24521
Tel: 804-946-9388
Fax: 804-946-9348
Email: lwilkins@leo.vsla.edu
URL: http://leo.vsla.edu/reposit/sites/acpl.html

Arlington Central Public Library
1015 North Quincy Street
Arlington, VA 22201-4603
Tel: 703-358-5959

Bassett Branch Library
3964 Fairystone Park Highway
Bassett, VA 24055
Mail:
Route 7, Box 250
Bassett, VA 24055
Tel: 540-629-2426
540-629-9191
Fax: 540-629-9840
URL: http://leo.vsla.edu/reposit/sites/bbl.html

Blue Ridge Regional Library
310 East Church Street
P.O. Box 5264
Martinsville, VA 24112
Tel: 540-632-7125

Bridgewater College
Alexander Mack Memorial Library
East College Street
Bridgewater, VA 22812
Tel: 540-828-2501 ext. 510
Fax: 540-828-5482
Email: rgreenaw@bridgewater.edu
URL: http://www.bridgewater.edu/departments/library/library.html

Bristol Public Library
701 Goode Street
Bristol, VA 24201
Tel: 540-669-9444
Fax: 540-669-5593
URL: http://leo.vsla.edu/reposit/sites/bpl.html

Buchanan County Public Library
Poe Town Road
Route 2, Box 3
Grundy, VA 24614
Tel: 540-935-6581
Fax: 540-935-6292
Email: bcpl@mtinter.net
URL: http://www.mtinter.net/bcpl/
or http://leo.vsla.edu/reposit/sites/bcpl.html

Central Rappahannock Regional Library
1201 Caroline Street
Fredericksburg, VA 22401
Tel: 540-372-1160
540-371-1144
Fax: 540-373-9411
540-371-7965
URL: http://leo.vsla.edu/reposit/sites/crrl.html

Charles Taylor Arts Center
4205 Victoria Blvd.
Hampton, VA 23669
Tel: 757-727-1051
Fax: 757-727-1152
URL: http://leo.vsla.edu/reposit/sites/ctac.html

Chesapeake Public Library
William McGhee Wallace Memorial Room
298 Cedar Road
Chesapeake, VA 23320
Tel: 757-382-6461
Fax: 757-436-8301
URL: http://leo.vsla.edu/reposit/sites/cpl.html

Chesterfield Historical Society
11001 Iron Bridge Road
P.O. Box 40
Chesterfield, VA 23832
Tel: 804-748-1026
Fax: 804-748-3032
URL: http://leo.vsla.edu/reposit/sites/chsv.html

Clark County Historical Association/Museum and Archives
Old County Courthouse, North Wing
P.O. Box 306
Berryville, VA 22611
Tel: 540-955-2600
URL: http://leo.vsla.edu/reposit/sites/ccha.html

College of William and Mary
Earl Gregg Swem Library
Williamsburg, VA 23187-8794
Tel: 757-221-3067
Fax: 757-221-2635
Email: web@mail.swem.wm.edu
URL: http://swem.wm.edu/

Culpeper Town and County Library
105 E. Main
Culpeper, VA 22701
Tel: 540-825-8691
Fax: 540-825-8691
URL: http://leo.vsla.edu/reposit/sites/ctcl.html

Danville Public Library
511 Patton Street
Danville, VA 24541
Tel: 804-799-5195
Email: cmo@ci.danville.va.us
URL: http://www.ci.danville.va.us/libry/lib8.htm

Eastern Mennonite University
Menno Simons Historical Library/Archives
1200 Park Road
Harrisonburg, VA 22801
Tel: 540-432-4177
540-432-4170
540-432-4169
Fax: 540-432-4977
Email: lehmanjo@emu.edu
bowmanlb@emu.edu
URL: http://www.emu.edu/units/library/histlib.htm

Eastern Shore of Virginia Historical Society/Museum
Kerr Place
69 Market Street
P.O. Box 193
Onancock, VA 23417
Tel: 757-787-8012
URL: http://leo.vsla.edu/reposit/sites/esvhs.html

Eastern Shore Public Library
P.O. Box 360
Accomac, VA 23301
Tel: 757-787-3400

Essex Public Library
Highway 17
Tappahannock, VA 22560
Tel: 804-443-4945
Fax: 804-443-6444
URL: http://leo.vsla.edu/reposit/sites/epl.html

Fairfax County Regional Library
Virginia Room
3915 Chain Bridge Road
Fairfax, VA 22030
Tel: 703-246-2123
Fax: 703-385-6977
703-385-1911
Email: wwwlib@co.fairfax.va.us
URL: http://www.co.fairfax.va.us/library/virginia/va_room.htm

Fluvanna County Library
P.O. Box 548
Fork Union, VA 23055
Tel/Fax: 804-842-2230
URL: http://leo.vsla.edu/reposit/sites/fcl.html

Franklin County Public Library
Local History Room
128 E. Court Street
Rocky Mount, VA 24151
Tel: 540-483-3098
Fax: 540-483-1568
Email: dbass@leo.vsla.edu
URL: http://leo.vsla.edu/reposit/sites/fcpl.html

Galax/Carroll Regional Library
608 W. Stuart Drive
Galax, VA 24333
Tel: 540-236-2042
Fax: 540-236-5153
Email: lbryant@leo.vsla.edu
URL: http://leo.vsla.edu/reposit/sites/gcrl.html

George Mason University
Fenwick Library-Special Collections
Fairfax, VA 22030-4444
Tel: 703-993-2220
Fax: 703-993-2229
Email: speccoll@osf1.gmu.edu
URL: http://www.gmu.edu/library/specialcollections/

Gunston Hall Plantation/Library and Archives
10709 Gunston Road
Mason Neck, VA 22079-3901
Tel: 703-550-9220
Fax: 703-550-9480
Email: abaker2@leo.vsla.edu
URL: http://leo.vsla.edu/reposit/sites/ghpl.html

Hampton Public Library
Virginiana Room
4207 Victoria Boulevard
Hampton, VA 23669
Tel: 757-727-1154
Fax: 757-727-1152
URL: http://www.whro.org/cl/hpl/

Handley Library
100 W. Piccadilly Street
Winchester, VA 22601
Tel: 540-662-9041
Fax: 540-722-4769
Email: handley@shentel.net
URL: http://leo.vsla.edu/reposit/sites/hrl.html

Heritage Library
P.O. Box 8
Providence Forge, VA 23140
Tel: 804-966-2480
Fax: 804-966-5982
URL: http://leo.vsla.edu/reposit/sites/hl.html

Historic Crab Orchard Museum
US 19/460
Mail:
Route 1, Box 194
Tazewell, VA 24651
Tel: 540-988-6755
Fax: 540-988-9400
URL: http://leo.vsla.edu/reposit/sites/hcom.html

Historic Fincastle, Inc.
James Early Cabin
121 E. Murray Street
P.O. Box 19
Fincastle, VA 24090
Tel: 540-473-3077
URL: http://leo.vsla.edu/reposit/sites/hfi.html

J. Robert Jamerson Memorial Library
106 Main Street
P.O. Box 789
Appomattox, VA 24522
Tel: 804-352-5340
Fax: 804-352-0933
URL: http://leo.vsla.edu/reposit/sites/jrj.html

James Madison University
Carrier Library-Special Collections
Harrisonburg, VA 22801
Tel: 540-568-3612
Fax: 540-568-3405
Email: bolgiace@jmu.edu
URL: http://www.jmu.edu/libliaison/sc/aboutsc.htm

James Monroe Museum and Memorial Library
908 Charles Street
Fredericksburg, VA 22401
Tel: 540-899-4559

Jefferson/Madison Regional Library
201 East Market Street
Charlottesville, VA 22903
Tel: 804-979-7151
Fax: 804-971-7035
Email: jmacdona@avenue.gen.va.us
URL: http://monticello.avenue.gen.va.us/Library/JMRL/

Jones Memorial Library
2311 Memorial Avenue
Lynchburg, VA 24501
Tel/Fax: 804-846-0501
URL: http://leo.vsla.edu/reposit/sites/jml.html

Kenmore Association Library
1201 Washington Avenue
Fredericksburg, VA 22401
Tel: 540-373-3381
Fax: 540-371-6066
URL: http://leo.vsla.edu/reposit/sites/kal.html

Kirn/Norfolk Public Library
301 East City Hall Avenue
Norfolk, VA 23510-1703
Tel: 757-664-7323

Library of Virginia
800 E. Broad Street
Richmond, VA 23219
Tel: 804-692-3500 (Main)
804-692-3777 (Library Reference)
804-692-3600 (Records Management)
Fax: 804-692-3556
804-692-3603 (Records Management)
URL: http://leo.vsla.edu/lva/lva.html

Louisa County Historical Society/Library, Archives and Museum
Old Jail (next to courthouse)
Main Street
P.O. Box 1172
Louisa, VA 23093
URL: http://monticello.avenue.gen.va.us/Library/JMRL/Louisa/historical.html

Madison County Library
402 N. Main Street
P.O. Box 243
Madison, VA 22727
Tel: 540-948-4720
Fax: 540-948-4919
URL: http://leo.vsla.edu/reposit/sites/mcl.html

Manassas Museum
9101 Prince William Street
P.O. Box 560
Manassas, VA 22110
Tel: 703-368-1873
Fax: 703-257-8406
URL: http://leo.vsla.edu/reposit/sites/mm.html

Mariners Museum/Library and Archives
100 Museum Drive
Newport News, VA 23606
Tel: 757-596-2222
Email: tmmlib@infi.net
URL: http://www.mariner.org/library.html

Mary Ball Washington Museum and Library
Route 3
P.O. Box 97
Lancaster, VA 22503-0097
Tel: 804-462-7280
URL: http://leo.vsla.edu/reposit/sites/mbwm.html

Montgomery/Floyd Regional Library
125 Sheltman Street
Christianburg, VA 24073
Tel: 540-382-6965
Fax: 540-382-6964
URL: http://www.montgomery-floyd.lib.va.us/

Montgomery Museum and Lewis Miller Regional Art Center
300 S. Pepper Street
P.O. Box 31
Christiansburg, VA 24073
Tel: 540-382-5644
URL: http://leo.vsla.edu/reposit/sites/mmlm.html

Museum of American Frontier Culture Library
1250 Richmond Road
P.O. Box 810
Staunton, VA 24402
Tel: 540-332-7850
Fax: 540-332-9989
URL: http://leo.vsla.edu/reposit/sites/mafc.html

National Genealogical Society/Library
4527 Seventeenth Street, North
Arlington, VA 22207-2363
Tel: 703-525-0050
703-841-9065 (Library)
Fax: 703-525-0052
Email: 76702.2417@compuserve.com
Library Email: ngslibe@wizard.net
URL: http://www.genealogy.org/~ngs/

Newport News Public Library
Martha Woodroof Hiden Virginiana Collection
110 Main Street
Newport News, VA 23601
Tel: 757-591-4858
Fax: 757-928-6866
757-591-4860
URL: http://leo.vsla.edu/reposit/sites/nnpl.html

Nottoway County Library
State Road 625
Nottoway, VA 23955
Tel: 804-645-9310
Fax: 804-645-8513
URL: http://leo.vsla.edu/reposit/sites/ncl.html

Orange County Historical Society/Library and Archives
130 Caroline Street
Orange, VA 22960-1533
Tel: 540-672-5366
URL: http://206.107.180.50/tel16/orange/orange.htm

Page Public Library
100 Zerkel Street
P.O. Box 734
Luray, VA 22835
Tel: 540-743-6867

Patrick County Historical Society/Museum
Blue Ridge Street
P.O. Box 1045
Stuart, VA 24171
Tel: 540-694-2840
URL: http://leo.vsla.edu/reposit/sites/pchm.html

Pearisburg Public Library
112 Tazewell Street
Pearisburg, VA 24134
Tel: 540-921-2556
Fax: 540-921-1708
URL: http://leo.vsla.edu/reposit/sites/pepl.html

Petersburg National Battlefield Library
P.O. Box 549
Petersburg, VA 23804
Tel: 804-732-6092
804-732-3531
Fax: 804-732-0835
URL: http://leo.vsla.edu/reposit/sites/pnbl.html

Petersburg Public Library/William R. McKenney Branch
137 South Sycamore Street
Petersburg, VA 23803
Tel: 804-733-2387

Portsmouth Public Library
601 Court Street
Portsmouth, VA 23704
Tel: 757-393-8501
757-393-8045/6
757-393-8975
Fax: 757-393-5107
URL: http://leo.vsla.edu/reposit/sites/popl.html

Prince William Public Library System/Bull Run Regional Library
Ruth Emmons Lloyd Information Center (RELIC)
8051 Aston Avenue
Manassas, VA 22110
Tel: 703-792-4540
Fax: 703-792-4520
URL: http://leo.vsla.edu/reposit/sites/pwpl.html

Radford Public Library
30 First Street
Radford, VA 24141
Tel: 540-731-3621
Fax: 540-731-4857
URL: http://fillmore-west.montgomery-floyd.lib.va.us/pub/compages/radpublib/index.html

Rappahannock Historical Society/Library
P.O. Box 261
Washington, VA 22747-0261
Tel: 540-675-1163
URL: http://leo.vsla.edu/reposit/sites/rhs.html

Roanoke City Public Library
Virginia Room
706 South Jefferson Street
Roanoke, VA 24016
Tel: 540-981-2475
Fax: 540-981-1781

Rockingham Public Library
45 Newman Avenue
Harrisonburg, VA 22801
Tel: 540-434-4475
Fax: 540-434-4382
URL: http://home.rica.net/rpl/

Shenandoah County Library
Stoney Creek Blvd
Route 1, Box 1-B
Edinburg, VA 22824
Tel: 540-984-8200

Shenandoah Valley Folk Art and Heritage Center
Genealogy Research Library
Bowman Road and High Street
P.O. Box 716
Dayton, VA 22821
Tel/Fax: 540-879-2616
540-879-2681 (Museum)
Email: blandsr@jmu.edu
URL: http://www.marketplace.staunton.va.us/valyhst/hrhs.html

Southside Regional Library
Washington Street
P.O. Box 10
Boydton, VA 23917
Tel: 804-738-6580
Fax: 804-738-6070
URL: http://leo.vsla.edu/reposit/sites/srl.html

Suffolk Public Library System
443 Washington Street
Suffolk, VA 23434
Tel: 757-934-7686
Fax: 757-539-7155
URL: http://leo.vsla.edu/reposit/sites/spls.html

Thomas Balch Library
208 West Market Street
Leesburg, VA 22075
Tel: 703-779-1328
Fax: 703-779-7363
URL: http://leo.vsla.edu/reposit/sites/tbl.html

Union Theological Seminary in Virginia/Library
3401 Brook Road
Richmond, VA 23227
Tel: 804-278-4310
Fax: 804-355-3919
URL: http://leo.vsla.edu/reposit/sites/uts.html

University of Virginia
Alderman Library
Charlottesville, VA 22903
Tel: 804-924-3021
Email: aldref@virginia.edu
URL: http://www.lib.virginia.edu/index.html

Virginia Beach Public Library
Local History Collection
4100 Virginia Beach Blvd.
Virginia Beach, VA 23452
Tel: 757-431-3071
757-431-3001 (Reference)
Fax: 757-431-3022
757-431-3018
URL: http://leo.vsla.edu/reposit/sites/vbpl.html

Virginia Commonwealth University (VCU)
James Branch Cabell Library
901 Park Avenue
Box 842033
Richmond, VA 23284-2033
Tel: 804-828-1108
Fax: 804-828-0151
Email: bpittman@gems.vcu.edu
URL: http://exlibris.uls.vcu.edu/library/speccoll.html

Virginia Historical Society
428 North Boulevard
P.O. Box 7311
Richmond, VA 23221-0311
Tel: 804-358-4901
804-342-9658 (Membership)
Email: kelly_winters@vahistorical.org
URL: http://www.vahistorical.org

Virginia Military Institute Archives
Preston Library
Lexington, VA 24450
Tel: 540-464-7566
Fax: 540-464-7279
Email: jacobdb@vax.vmi.edu
URL: http://www.vmi.edu/~archtml/index.html

Virginia Polytechnic Institute and State University
Newman Library-Special Collections and Manuscripts
P.O. Box 90001
Blacksburg, VA 24062-9001
Tel: 540-231-6308
Fax: 540-231-3694
Email: gailmac@vt.edu
URL: http://schlar2.lib.vt.edu/spec/Spechp3.html

Walter Cecil Rawls Library/Museum
22511 Main Street
P.O. Box 310
Courtland, VA 23837
Tel: 757-653-2821
Fax: 757-653-9374
URL: http://leo.vsla.edu/reposit/sites/wcr.html

Washington and Lee University
James G. Leyburn Library
Special Collections
Lexington, VA 24450
Tel: 540-463-8649
540-463-8640
540-463-8663
Fax: 540-463-8640
Email: bbrown@wlu.edu
URL: http://www.wlu.edu/~library/leyburn/index.html

Waynesboro Public Library
600 South Wayne Avenue
Waynesboro, VA 22980
Tel: 540-942-6746
Fax: 540-942-6753
URL: http://leo.vsla.edu/reposit/sites/wpl.html

Wilderness Road Regional Museum
P.O. Box 373
Newbern, VA 24126
Tel: 540-674-4835
URL: http://leo.vsla.edu/reposit/sites/wrrm.html

Wytheville Community College
F.B. Kegley Library
Genealogical and Local History Collection
1000 E. Main Street
Wytheville, VA 24382
Tel: 540-223-4742/3
Fax: 540-223-4778
Email: WCROBEA@WC.CC.VA.US
URL: http://www.naxs.com/wcc/proud.htm

Newspaper Repositories

College of William and Mary
Earl Gregg Swem Library
Williamsburg, VA 23187-8794
Tel: 757-221-3067
Fax: 757-221-2635
Email: web@mail.swem.wm.edu
URL: http://swem.wm.edu/

Library of Virginia
800 E. Broad Street
Richmond, VA 23219
Tel: 804-692-3742t)
Tel: 804-692-3742
Email: esomay@leo.vsla.edu
URL: http://www.lib.virginia.edu/cataloging/vnp/home.html

University of Virginia
Alderman Library
Charlottesville, VA 22903
Tel: 804-924-3021
Email: aldref@virginia.edu
URL: http://www.lib.virginia.edu/index.html

Virginia Historical Society
428 North Boulevard
P.O. Box 7311
Richmond, VA 23221-0311
Tel: 804-358-4901
804-342-9658 (Membership)
Email: kelly_winters@vahistorical.org
URL: http://www.vahistorical.org

Newspapers in Virginia Database
URL: http://image.vtls.com/newspaper/

Virginia Newspaper Project
URL: http://www.lib.virginia.edu/cataloging/vnp/home.html

Vital Records

Library of Virginia
800 E. Broad Street
Richmond, VA 23219
Tel: 804-692-3500 (Main)
804-692-3777 (Library Reference)
804-692-3600 (Records Management)
Fax: 804-692-3556
804-692-3603 (Records Management)
URL: http://leo.vsla.edu/lva/lva.html
Births and Deaths 1853-1896.
Marriages before 1936.

Virginia Department of Health
Office of Vital Records
James Madison Building
P.O. Box 1000
Richmond, VA 23208
Tel: 804-786-6228 (Recorded Message)
804-786-6201
URL: http://www.vdh.state.va.us/misc/f_08.htm
http://www.vdh.state.va.us/misc/gene.htm (Genealogy Page)
Births and Deaths from 1913-present.
Marriages from 1936-present.

There was no law requiring registration of births and deaths between 1896 and 1912.

Virginia on the Web

Dayna's Southern Page
http://home.texoma.net/~mmcmullen/welcome.html

Genealogy and History of the Eastern Shore (GHOTES)
http://www.esva.net/ghotes/

Library of Virginia
http://leo.vsla.edu/

Library of Virginia, Archives Division
http://leo.vsla.edu/archives/genie.html

Library of Virginia, Digital Collection
http://image.vtls.com/

Melungeon Ancestry Research and Information Page
http://www.bright.net/~kat/melung.htm

Order of Descendants of Ancient Planters
http://tyner.simplenet.com/PLANTERS.HTM

Travellers Southern Families
http://genealogy.travellers.com/genealogy/southern.htm

Virginia Colonial Records Database Project
http://leo.vsla.edu/colonial/vcrp.html

Virginia Genealogy Home Page
http://www.wp.com/genealogy/

Virginia GenWeb Project
http://www.rootsweb.com/~vagenweb/

VIVA—Virtual Library of Virginia
http://www.viva.lib.va.us/

WASHINGTON

ARCHIVES, STATE & NATIONAL

National Archives—Pacific Northwest Region
6125 Sand Point Way, NE
Seattle, WA 98115
Tel: 206-526-6507
Fax: 206-526-4344
Email: archives@seattle.nara.gov
URL: http://www.nara.gov/nara/regional/10nsgil.html

Washington State Archives
1120 Washington Street, SE
P.O. Box 40238
Olympia, WA 98504-0238
Tel: 360-753-5485 (Administration)
360-586-1492 (Research)
URL: http://www.wa.gov/sec/archives/main.htm

Washington State Regional Archives
URL: http://www.wa.gov/sec/archives/branches.htm

Central Regional Branch
Central Washington University
Bledsow-Washington Archives Building
MS 7547
Ellensburg, WA 98926-7547
Tel: 509-963-2136
Fax: 509-963-1753
(Benton, Chelan, Douglas, Franklin, Grant, Kittitas, Klickitat, Okanogan, and Yakima Counties)

Eastern Regional Branch
Eastern Washington University
MS-84, TAW Room 211
Cheney, WA 99004-2423
Tel: 509-359-6900
Fax: 509-359-2476
(Adams, Asotin, Columbia, Ferry, Garfield, Lincoln, Pend Oreille, Spokane, Stevens, Walla Walla, and Whitman Counties)

Northwest Regional Branch
Western Washington University
Goltz-Murray Archives Building
Bellingham, WA 98225-9123
Tel: 360-650-3125
Fax: 360-650-3323
(Clallam, Island, Jefferson, San Juan, Skagit, Snohomish, and Whatcom Counties)

Puget Sound Regional Branch
P.O. Box 68286
Seattle, WA 98168-0286
Tel: 206-439-3785
Fax: 206-439-3708
(King, Kitsap and Pierce Counties)

Southwest Regional Branch
1120 Washington Street, SE
P.O. Box 40238
Olympia, WA 98504-0238
Tel: 360-753-1684
Fax: 360-664-8814
(Clark, Cowlitz, Grays Harbor, Lewis, Mason, Pacific, Skamania, Thurston, and Wahkiakum Counties)

GENEALOGICAL SOCIETIES

Camwood Genealogical Group
c/o Stanwood Library
9701 271st Street NW
Stanwood, WA 98292
Tel: 206-629-3132

Chelan Valley Genealogical Society
P.O. Box Y
Chelan, WA 98816

Clallam County Genealogical Society
223 E. 4th Street
Port Angeles, WA 98362-3098

Clark County Genealogical Society
Clark County Historical Museum
1511 Main Street
P.O. Box 2728
Vancouver, WA 98668-2728
Email: katschke@worldaccessnet.com
URL: http://www.worldaccess.com/NonProfitOrganizations/ccgs/

Columbia County Genealogical and Historical Society
P.O. Box 74
Dayton, WA 99328-0074

Douglas County Genealogical Society
P.O. Box 580
Waterville, WA 98858-0580

Eastern Washington Genealogical Society
P.O. Box 1826
Spokane, WA 99210-1826
Email: deacon70@juno.com
URL: http://www.onlinepub.net/ewgs/

Eastside Genealogical Society
P.O. Box 374
Bellevue, WA 98009-0374
URL: http://www.kcls.org/brl/bellcoll.html#genealogy

Fiske Genealogical Foundation/Library
1644 43rd Avenue E
Seattle, WA 98122-3222
Tel: 206-328-2716

Forks Genealogical Society
c/o Forks Memorial Library
Forks, WA 98331

Germans from Russia Heritage Society
Puget Sound Chapter
c/o Vi Sieler, Sec.
17956 W. Spring Lake Drive SE
Renton, WA 98058
Tel: 425-432-5627
URL: http://www.teleport.com/nonprofit/grhs/pugetsnd.html

Grant County Genealogical Society
Ephrata Public Library
45 Alder Street, NW
Ephrata, WA 98823

Grays Harbor Genealogical Society
P.O. Box 867
Cosmopolis, WA 98537-0867

Jefferson County Genealogical Society
210 Madison Street
Port Townsend, WA 98368

Kitsap County Genealogical Society
4305 Lakeview Drive, SE
Port Orchard, WA 98366

Kittitas County Genealogical Society/Library
413 N. Maine, Suite I
P.O. Box 1342
Ellensburg, WA 98926

Lewis County Genealogical Society
P.O. Box 782
Chehalis, WA 98532

Lower Columbia Genealogical Society
P.O. Box 472
Longview, WA 98632-0472

Mason County Genealogical Society
P.O. Box 1535
Shelon, WA 98584-1535

North Beach Genealogical Society
P.O. Box 2007
Ocean Shores, WA 98569

North Central Washington Genealogical Society
P.O. Box 5280
Wenatchee, WA 98807-5280

Northeast Washington Genealogical Society
c/o Colville Public Library
195 South Oak
Colville, WA 99114

Northern Kittitas County Genealogical Society
P.O. Box 535
Cle Elum, WA 98922

Okanogan County Genealogical Society
Route 1, Box 323
Omak, WA 98841-0323

Olympia Genealogical Society
P.O. Box 1313
Olympia, WA 98507-1313
Email: gmccoy@thurston.com

Pacific County Genealogical Society
P.O. Box 843
Ocean Park, WA 98640-0843

Pierce County, Genealogical Society of
P.O. Box 98634
Tacoma, WA 98498-0634

Puget Sound Genealogical Society
Givens Community Center
1026 Sidney Avenue, Suite 110
Port Orchard, WA 98366
Tel: 360-874-8813
Email: macdonalda@wvin.com
URL: http://www.rootsweb.com/~wapsgs/homepage.htm

Seattle Genealogical Society/Library
8511 15th Avenue, NE
P.O. Box 75388
Seattle, WA 98507

Skagit Valley Genealogical Society
P.O. Box 715
Conway, WA 98238-0715

Sky Valley Genealogical Society
912 First Street
Salem, WA 98294

Sno-Isle Genealogical Society
P.O. Box 63
Edmonds, WA 98020-0063

South King County Genealogical Society
P.O. Box 3174
Kent, WA 98032-3174

Stillaguamish Valley Genealogical Society/Library
20325 71st Avenue, NE
P.O. Box 34
Arlington, WA 98223-0034

Sumner Genealogical Group
c/o Sumner Public Library
1116 Fryar Avenue
Sumner, WA 98390
Tel: 206-863-0441

Tacoma-Pierce County Genealogical Society
P.O. Box 1952
Tacoma, WA 98401-1952
Tel: 253-572-6650
URL: http://www.rootsweb.com/~watpcgs/tpcgs.htm

Tonasket Genealogical Society
P.O. Box 84
Tonasket, WA 98855

Tri-City Genealogical Society
P.O. Box 1410
Richland, WA 98352-1410

Twin Rivers Genealogical Society
P.O. Box 386
Lewiston, WA 83501-2824

Walla Walla Valley Genealogical Society
P.O. Box 115
Walla Walla, WA 99362-0115

Washington State Genealogical Society
P.O. Box 1422
Olympia, WA 98507-1422
Email: gmccoy@thurston.com
URL: http://www.thurston.com/~rmccoy/wsgshome.htm

Wenatchee Area Genealogical Society
P.O. Box 5280
Wenatchee, WA 98807-5280

Whatcom Genealogical Society
P.O. Box 1493
Bellingham, WA 98227-1493

Whidbey Island Genealogical Searchers
P.O. Box 627
Oak Harbor, WA 98277-0627

Whitman County Genealogical Society
P.O. Box 393
Pullman, WA 99163-0393
Tel: 509-332-2386
509-334-1732
URL: http://www.wsu.edu:8080/~mbsimon/wcgs/index.html

Willapa Harbor Genealogical Society
507 Duryea
Raymond, WA 98577

Yakima Valley Genealogical Society
North Third Street and East B (First Christian Church)
P.O. Box 445
Yakima, WA 98907-0445
Tel: 509-248-1328
Email: fl635@nwinfo.net
URL: http://www.rootsweb.com/~wayvgs/

Historical Societies

Adams County Historical Society/Museum
Phillips Building
P.O. Box 188
Lind, WA 99341
Tel: 509-677-3393

Anderson Island Historical Society
9306 Otso Point Road
Anderson Island, WA 98303
Tel: 206-884-2135

Bainbridge Island Historical Society/Museum
7650 NE High School Road
P.O. Box 11653
Bainbridge Island, WA 98110-2621
Tel: 206-842-2773

Benton County Historical Society/Museum
Prosser City Park
7th and Paterson
P.O. Box 591
Prosser, WA 99350
Tel: 509-786-3842

Black Diamond Historical Society/Museum
32627 Railroad Avenue
P.O. Box 232
Black Diamond, WA 98010-9762
Tel: 360-886-2142

Camas-Washougal Historical Society/Museum
16th and Front
P.O. Box 204
Washougal, WA 98671
Tel: 360-835-2725

Chelan County Historical Society/Museum
600 Cottage Avenue
P.O. Box 22
Cashmere, WA 98815-1602
Tel: 509-782-3230

Clallum Historical Society/Museum
223 E. 4th Street
Port Angeles, WA 98362-3025
Tel: 360-452-7831

Cle Elum Historical Society/Museum
221 E. 1st Street
P.O. Box 43
Cle Elum, WA 98922-1103
Tel: 509-674-5702

Daughters of the Pioneers Association
Pioneer Hall
4526 119th SE
Bellevue, WA 98006
Tel: 206-746-6305

East Benton County Historical Society/Museum
205 Keewaydin Drive
Kennewick, WA 99336-0602
Tel: 509-582-7704
Email: ebchs@tcfn.org
URL: http://www.owt.com/ebchs/ebchs/

Eastern Washington State Historical Society
2316 W. 1st Avenue
Spokane, WA 99204-1006
Tel: 509-456-3931

Edmonds-South Snohomish County Historical Society
118 5th Avenue, N.
Edmonds, WA 98020-3145
Tel: 206-774-0900

Fort Vancouver Historical Society
Clark County Historical Museum
1511 Main Street
Vancouver, WA 98660
URL: http://www.teleport.com/~gcermak/clarkcohistory/

Fox Island Historical Society/Museum
1017 9th Avenue
P.O. Box 242
Fox Island, WA 98333
Tel: 206-549-2461
206-549-2239

Franklin County Historical Society/Museum
305 N. 4th Avenue
Pasco, WA 99301-5324
Tel: 509-547-3714
URL: http://www.tricity.wsu.edu/~pkeller/tc/museums/FranklinCo.html

Gig Harbor Peninsula Historical Society
3510 Rosedale Street
P.O. Box 744
Gig Harbor, WA 98335
Tel: 206-858-6722

Island County Historical Society
902 NW Alexander
P.O. Box 305
Coupeville, WA 98239
Tel: 360-678-3310

Issaquah Historical Society
154 SE Andrews Street
Issaquah, WA 98027
Tel: 206-392-3500

Jefferson County Historical Society/Museum
McCurdy Research Library
210 Madison Street
Port Townsend, WA 98368
Tel: 360-385-1003
URL: http://www.rumford.com/jcmuseumhome.html

Lake Chelan Historical Society
204 Woodin Avenue
P.O. Box 1948
Chelan, WA 98816
Tel: 509-682-5644

Lewis County Historical Society
599 NW Front Way
Chehalis, WA 98532
Tel: 360-748-0831

Lopez Island Historical Society/Museum
P.O. Box 361
Lopez Island, WA 98261
Tel: 360-468-2049

Maple Valley Historical Society
P.O. Box 123
Maple Valley, WA 98038

Mason County Historical Society
Old Library Building
5th Street and Railroad Avenue
P.O. Box 1366
Shelton, WA 98584
Tel: 360-426-1020

Mukilteo Historical Society
304 Lincoln Avenue
Mukilteo, WA 98275
Tel: 425-355-2144

Okanogan Historical Society
1410 2nd Avenue North
P.O. Box 1299
Okanogan, WA 98840
Tel: 509-422-4272

Pacific County Historical Society
1008 W. Robert Bush Drive
South Bend, WA 98586
Tel: 360-875-5224

Pend Oreille County Historical Society
402 S. Washington Avenue
P.O. Box 1409
Newport, WA 99156
Tel: 509-447-5388

Puget Sound Maritime Historical Society
(Collection at Museum of History and Industry and Univ. of WA)
P.O. Box 9731
Seattle, WA 98109-9731
Tel: 206-324-1126
206-938-2397
Email: maritime@psmaritime.org
URL: http://www.psmaritime.org/

Puget Sound Railway Historical Association
P.O. Box 459
Snoqualmie, WA 98065-0459
Tel: 425-888-0373

Renton County Historical Society/Museum
235 Mill Avenue, South
Renton, WA 98055
Tel: 206-255-2330

San Juan Historical Society/Museum
405 Price
Friday Harbor, WA 98250
Tel: 360-378-3949

Seattle-King County Historical Society
Museum of History and Industry
2700 24th East
Seattle, WA 98112
Tel: 206-324-1126

Skagit County Historical Museum
501 S. 4th
P.O. Box 818
La Conner, WA 98257

Snohomish County Historical Association
Heritage Center, Museum and Library
2817 Rockefeller Avenue
P.O. Box 5203
Everett, WA 98206
Tel: 425-259-2022

Snoqualmie Valley Historical Society/Museum
320 N. Bend Blvd. North
North Bend, WA 98045
Tel: 425-888-3200

Spanaway Historical Society
812 176th Street East
Spanaway, WA 98387
Tel: 253-536-6655

Stanwood Area Historical Society
P.O. Box 69
Stanwood, WA 98292
Tel: 360-629-3352

Stevens County Historical Society
700 N. Wynne Street
Colville, WA 99114
Tel: 509-684-5968

Swedish Finn Historical Society
6512 23rd Avenue, NW, #301
Seattle, WA 98117
Tel: 206-706-0738

Tacoma Historical Society
3712 S. Cedar Street, #101
P.O. Box 1865
Tacoma, WA 98401
Tel: 253-472-3738
Email: ths@powerscourt.com
URL: http://www.powerscourt.com/ths/

Wahkiakum County Historical Society/Museum
65 River Street
P.O. Box 541
Cathlamet, WA 98612
Tel: 360-795-3954

Washington State Historical Society
Research Center
315 North Stadium Way
Tacoma, WA 98403
Tel: 253-272-WSHS
888-BE-THERE (Toll-Free)
253-798-5914 (Research Center)
Email: jmartin@wshs.wa.gov (Membership)
lweber@wshs.wa.gov (Research Library Appointments)
URL: http://www.wshs.org/

Washington State Railroads Historical Society
P.O. Box 552
Pasco, WA 99301
Email: jimbowe@gte.net
URL: http://home1.gte.net/jimbowe/WSRHS1.htm

White River Valley Historical Society
918 H Street, SE
Auburn, WA 98002
Tel: 253-939-2783

Whitman County Historical Society
623 N. Perkins Avenue
P.O. Box 67
Colfax, WA 99111
Email: jillwhel@wsu.edu
URL: http://www.wsu.edu:8080/~kemeyer/wchs.html

Yakima Valley Museum and Historical Association
2105 Tieton Drive
Yakima, WA 98902
Tel: 509-248-0747
URL: http://www.wolfenet.com/~museum/

LDS Family History Centers

Auburn Family History Center
625 M Street, NE
Auburn, WA 98002
Tel: 253-735-2009

Bellevue Family History Center
10605 NE 20th Street
Bellevue, WA 98004
Tel: 425-454-2690

Bellingham Family History Center
2925 James Street
Bellingham, WA 98225
Tel: 360-738-1849

Bremerton Family History Center
2225 North Perry Avenue
Bremerton, WA 98310
Tel: 206-479-9370

Bremerton Family History Center
9256 Nels Nelson NW
Bremerton, WA 98311
Tel: 360-698-5552

Chehalis Family History Center
2195 Jackson Highway
Chehalis, WA 98532
Tel: 360-748-1516

Ellensburg Family History Center
1700 Brick Road
Ellensburg, WA 98926
Tel: 509-925-5192

Elma Family History Center
702 East Main
Elma, WA 98541
Tel: 360-482-5982

Ephrata Family History Center
1301 Division East
Ephrata, WA 98823
Tel: 509-754-4762

Everett Family History Center
9509 19th Avenue SE
Everett, WA 98208
Tel: 425-337-0457

Federal Way Family History Center
34815 Weyerhauser Way South
Federal Way, WA 98001
Tel: 253-874-3803

Kirkland Family History Center
Juanita Drive NE
Kirkland, WA 98034
Tel: 425-821-8781

Lake Stevens Family History Center
10120 Chapel Hill Road
Lake Stevens, WA 98258
Tel: 360-334-0754

Longview Family History Center
1731 30th Avenue
Longview, WA 98632
Tel: 360-577-8234

Moses Lake Family History Center
1515 South Division
Moses Lake, WA 98837
Tel: 509-765-8711

Mount Vernon Family History Center
1700 Hazel Street
Mount Vernon, WA 98273
Tel: 360-424-7723

Mountlake Terrace Family History Center
22015 48th Avenue West
Mountlake Terrace, WA 98043
Tel: 425-776-6678

North Bend Family History Center
527 Mt. Si Blvd.
North Bend, WA 98045
Tel: 425-888-1098

Olympia Family History Center
1116 Yew
Olympia, WA 98506
Tel: 360-705-4176

Omak Family History Center
Engh Road
Omak, WA 98841
Tel: 509-826-4802

Othello Family History Center
12th and Rainier
Othello, WA 99344
Tel: 509-488-6412

Port Angeles Family History Center
Monroe Road
Port Angeles, WA 98362
Tel: 360-452-1521

Puyallup Family History Center
13420 94th Avenue East
Puyallup, WA 98373
Tel: 253-840-1673

Quincy Family History Center
1102 2nd Avenue SE
Quincy, WA 98848
Tel: 509-787-2521

Richland Family History Center
1314 Goethals
Richland, WA 99352
Tel: 509-946-6637

Seattle Family History Center
5701 Eighth NE
Seattle, WA 98108
Tel: 206-522-1233

Seattle Family History Center
14020 SW Ambaum Blvd
Seattle, WA 98166
Tel: 206-243-4028

Spokane Family History Center
10405 West Melville Road
Spokane, WA 99210
Tel: 509-455-9735

Spokane Family History Center
1717 East 30th Avenue
Spokane, WA 99203
Tel: 509-455-7164

Spokane Family History Center
401 West Regina
Spokane, WA 99218
Tel: 509-466-4633

Spokane Family History Center
East 13608 40th
Spokane, WA
Tel: 509-926-0551

Sumner Family History Center
512 Valley Avenue
Sumner, WA 98390
Tel: 253-863-3383

Tacoma Family History Center
5941 South 12th
Tacoma, WA 98465
Tel: 253-564-1103

Vancouver Family History Center
11101 NE 119th Street
Vancouver, WA 98662
Tel: 360-253-4701

Vancouver Family History Center
18300 NE 18th Street
Vancouver, WA 98684
Tel: 360-896-5567

Vancouver Family History Center
2223 NW 99th
Vancouver, WA 98665
Tel: 360-573-7881

Walla Walla Family History Center
1821 South 2nd Street
Walla Walla, WA 99362
Tel: 509-529-9211

Wenatchee Family History Center
667 Tenth NE
Wenatchee, WA 98802
Tel: 509-884-1836

Yakima Family History Center
1006 South 16th Avenue
Yakima, WA 98902
Tel: 509-452-3626

ARCHIVES/LIBRARIES/MUSEUMS

Anacortes Museum/Research Library
1305 8th Street
Anacortes, WA 98221-1833
Tel: 360-293-1915
URL: http://www.library.anacortes.wa.us/museum/ahmhom.htm

Auburn Public Library
808 9th Street, SE
Auburn, WA 98002
Tel: 253-931-3018

Bellingham Public Library
210 Central Street
P.O. Box 1197
Bellingham, WA 98225
URL: http://www.city-govt.ci.bellingham.wa.us//bplhome.htm

Bellevue Regional Library
Special Collections
1111 110th Avenue, NE
Bellevue, WA 98004
Tel: 425-450-1765
URL: http://www.kcls.org/brl/brlpage.html

Burlington Public Library
900 E. Fairhaven Street
Burlington, WA 98233
Tel: 360-755-0760
Email: burlpl@sos.net
URL: http://www.sos.net/home/burlpl/bplib.htm

Clark County Museum
1511 Main
Vancouver, WA 98668
Tel: 360-695-4681

Colville Public Library
195 South Oak Street
Colville, WA 99114
Tel: 509-684-6620

Dupont Historical Museum
207 Barksdale Avenue
P.O. Box 173
Dupont, WA 98327
Tel: 206-964-2399
206-964-8121

East Benton County Historical Society/Museum
205 Keewaydin Drive
Kennewick, WA 99336-0602
Tel: 509-582-7704
Email: ebchs@tcfn.org
URL: http://www.owt.com/ebchs/ebchs/

Ellensburg Public Library
209 N. Ruby Street
Ellensburg, WA 98926
Tel: 509-962-7250

Ephrata Public Library
45 Alder Street, NW
Ephrata, WA 98823

Everett Public Library
Northwest Room
2702 Hoyt Avenue
Everett, WA 98201
Tel: 425-259-8020
Email: cameronj@wln.com
URL: http://www.walib.spl.org/everett/

Fiske Genealogical Foundation/Library
1644 43rd Avenue E
Seattle, WA 98122-3222
Tel: 206-328-2716

Forks Memorial Library
171 N. Forks Avenue
P.O. Box 1817
Forks, WA 98331
Tel: 360-374-6402

Forks Timber Museum
1421 S. Forks Avenue
Forks, WA 98331
Tel: 360-374-9663

Fort Vancouver Regional Library
1007 East Mill Plain Blvd.
Vancouver, WA 98663
Tel: 503-289-1336
URL: http://www.fvrl.org/

Grant County Historical Museum
742 Basin Street, NW
P.O. Box 1141
Ephrata, WA 98823
Tel: 509-754-3334

Heritage Quest Genealogy Research Library
220 Bridge Street, SW
P.O. Box 1119
Orting, WA 98360
Tel: 360-893-2799
Email: HQRLibrary@aol.com

Highline Community College Library
Special Collections
2400 S. 240th Street
Des Moines, WA 98198-9800
Tel: 206-878-3710 ext. 3232 (Reference Desk)
Email: tpollard@hcc.ctc.edu
URL: http://www.highline.ctc.edu/library/home.htm

Hudson's Bay Company Archives
Provincial Archives of Manitoba
200 Vaughan Street
Winnipeg, Manitoba R3C 1T5
Tel: 204-945-4949
Fax: 204-948-3236
Email: hbca@chc.gov.mb.ca
URL: http://www.gov.mb.ca/chc/archives/hbca/index.html

Jefferson County Historical Society/Museum
McCurdy Research Library
210 Madison Street
Port Townsend, WA 98368
Tel: 360-385-1003
URL: http://www.rumford.com/jcmuseumhome.html

King County Law Library
W621 King County Courthouse
516 3rd Avenue
Seattle, WA 98104
Tel: 206-296-0940
Fax: 206-205-0513
URL: http://www.nwlaw.com/kcll/

Kitsap Regional Library/Poulsbo Branch
700 NE Lincoln Road
Poulsbo, WA 98370
Tel: 253-779-2915
URL: http://www.kitsap.lib.wa.us/branches/poulsbo/pltext.html

Kittitas County Genealogical Society/Library
413 N. Maine, Suite I
P.O. Box 1342
Ellensburg, WA 98926

Kittitas County Museum
114 E. Third Avenue
P.O. Box 265
Ellensburg, WA 98926
Tel: 509-925-3778

Makah Cultural and Research Center
P.O. Box 160
Neah Bay, WA 98357
Tel: 360-645-2711

Marymoor Museum
6046 W. Lake Sammamish Parkway, NE
P.O. Box 162
Redmond, WA 98073
Tel: 425-885-3684

Mid-Columbia Library
405 South Dayton
Kennewick, WA 99336
Tel: 509-586-3156
Email: sue@mcl.lib.wa.us
URL: http://www.wln.com/~refnet/index.html

Mount Vernon City Library
315 Snoqualmie Street
Mount Vernon, WA 98273
Tel: 206-336-6209
Email: lib@sos.net
URL: http://www.mount-vernon.wa.us/

Museum of History and Industry
Maritime Library
2700 24th Avenue, East
Seattle, WA 98112
Tel: 206-324-1126
Fax: 206-324-1346
Email: gizmo@historymuse-nw.org
URL: http://www.historymuse-nw.org/

Neill Public Library
North 210 Grand Avenue
Pullman, WA 99163
Tel: 509-334-4555 (Weekdays)
509-334-3595 (Evenings and Weekends)
Fax: 509-334-6051
URL: http://www.neill-lib.org/

Nordic Heritage Museum
3014 NW 67th Street
Seattle, WA 98117
Tel: 206-789-5707
Fax: 206-789-3271
URL: http://www.ohwy.com/wa/n/nordichm.htm

North Central Washington Museum
127 S. Mission Street
Wenatchee, WA 98801
Tel: 509-664-3340

Northwest Seaport Maritime Heritage Center
1002 Valley Street
Seattle, WA 98109-4332
Tel: 206-447-9800

Olympia Timberland Library
313 8th Avenue
Olympia, WA 98501-1307
Tel: 360-352-0595
URL: http://timber20.timberland.lib.wa.us/trlinfo.htm

Orcas Island Historical Museum
P.O. Box 134
Eastsound, WA 98245
Tel: 360-376-4849

Pacific Lutheran University
Robert A.L. Mortvedt Library
Tacoma, WA 98447
Tel: 253-535-7586
URL: http://www.plu.edu/libr/services.html
Scandinavian Immigrant Experience Collection
URL: http://www.plu.edu/libr/siec.html
Archives
URL: http://www.plu.edu/libr/archives

Richland Public Library
955 Northlake Drive
Richland, WA 99352
Tel: 509-943-7454
URL: http://www.richland.lib.wa.us/

Seattle Genealogical Society/Library
8511 15th Avenue, NE
P.O. Box 75388
Seattle, WA 98507

Seattle Pacific University Library
3307 Third Avenue West
Seattle, WA 98119-1997
Tel: 206-281-2982
URL: http://www.spu.edu/depts/library/

Seattle Public Library
Humanities Department
1000 4th Avenue
Seattle, WA 98104
Tel: 206-386-4625
206-386-4640
URL: http://www.spl.lib.wa.us/contents.html

Seattle Public Schools Archives and Records Management Center
Frank B. Cooper Elementary School, Room 20
5950 Delridge Way, SW, AB-345
Seattle, WA 98106
Tel: 206-281-6564
Fax: 206-281-6466
Email: etoews@is.ssd.k12.wa.us
URL: http://sea.css.ssd.k12.wa.us/archives/welcome.htm

Seattle University
Lemieux Library
900 Broadway
Seattle, WA 98122
Tel: 206-296-6228 (Hours)
206-296-6230 (Reference)
Email: libref@seattleu.edu
URL: http://www.seattleu.edu/lemlib/llhomepg.htm

Shoreline Historical Museum
749 N. 175th Street
Seattle, WA 98133
Tel: 206-542-7111

Snohomish County Historical Association
Heritage Center, Museum and Library
2817 Rockefeller Avenue
P.O. Box 5203
Everett, WA 98206
Tel: 425-259-2022

Spokane Public Library
Genealogy Room
906 West Main Avenue
Spokane, WA 99201
Tel: 509-626-5300
URL: http://splnet.spokpl.lib.wa.us/

Stanwood Library
9701 271st Street, NW
P.O. Box 247
Stanwood, WA 98292
Tel: 206-629-3132

Steilacoom Historical Museum
112 Main Street
Steilacoom, WA 98388
Tel: 253-584-4133

Steilacoom Tribal Cultural Center/Museum
1515 Lafayette Street
Steilacoom, WA 98388
Tel: 253-584-6308

Stillaguamish Valley Genealogical Society/Library
20325 71st Avenue, NE
P.O. Box 34
Arlington, WA 98223-0034

Stillaguamish Valley Pioneer Museum
20722 67th Avenue, NE
Arlington, WA 98223
Tel: 360-435-7289
URL: http://www.ohwy.com/wa/s/stillvpm.htm

Suquamish Museum
Port Madison Indian Reservation
15383 Sandy Hook Road
Suquamish, WA 98392
Tel: 360-598-3311 ext. 422
URL: http://www.oz.net/seattle/arts_ent/museums/suquamish.html

Tacoma Public Library
Northwest Room
1102 S. Tacoma Way
Tacoma, WA 98402
Tel: 253-591-5666
Fax: 253-627-1693
Email: webfoot@tpl.lib.wa.us
URL: http://www.tpl.lib.wa.us/

Toppenish Museum
1 S. Elm Street
Toppenish, WA 98948
Tel: 509-865-4510

University of Puget Sound
Collins Memorial Library/Archives
1500 North Warner
Tacoma, WA 98416
Tel: 253-756-3100
Fax: 253-756-3500
URL: http://www.ups.edu/library/services/archives/intro.htm

University of Washington
Suzzallo Library
Special Collections
Box 352900
Seattle, WA 98199
Tel: 206-543-0140 (Hours)
206-543-0242 (Information)
URL: http://www.lib.washington.edu/libinfo/libunits/suzzalo/stacks/

Washington State Historical Society
Heritage Research Center
315 North Stadium Way
Tacoma, WA 98403
Tel: 253-272-WSHS
888-BE-THERE (Toll-Free)
253-798-5914 (Research Center)
Email: jmartin@wshs.wa.gov (Membership)
plarkins@wshs.wa.gov (Education)
URL: http://www.wshs.org/

Washington State Library
Library Building on the Capitol Campus
415 15th Avenue, SW
P.O. Box 42460
Olympia, WA 98504-2460
Tel: 360-753-3087 (Information)
360-753-4024 (Washington History and Current Events)
Fax: 360-753-2475
360-753-7575
Email: gpalmer@statelib.wa.gov
URL: http://www.wa.gov/wsl/

Washington State University
Holland Library
Manuscripts, Archives, and Special Collections
Pullman, WA 99164-5610
Tel: 509-335-MASC

Whatcom Museum Archives
Syre Education Center
201 Prospect Street
Mail:
121 Prospect Street
Bellingham, WA 98226
Tel: 360-676-6981
360-738-7397
Fax: 360-738-7409
URL: http://www.city-govt.ci.bellingham.wa.us/cobweb/museum/welcome.htm

Whitman County Library
102 S. Main Street
Colfax. WA 99111
Tel: 509-397-4366

Yakima Indian Nation Cultural Center
Highway 97
Toppenish, WA 98948
Tel: 509-865-2900
URL: http://www.yakima.net/yakima/tourist/indian.htm

Newspaper Repositories

Washington State Library
Library Building on the Capitol Campus
415 15th Avenue, SW
P.O. Box 42460
Olympia, WA 98504-2460
Tel: 360-753-4024 (Washington History and Current Events)
Fax: 360-753-2475
360-753-7575
Email: gpalmer@statelib.wa.gov
URL: http://www.wa.gov/wsl/ervlib.htm#Sharing

Vital Records

Department of Health
Center for Health Statistics
P.O. Box 9709
Olympia, WA 98507-9709
Tel: 360-753-5936
360-753-4379 (Order by Phone)
Fax: 360-753-2586 (Order by Fax)
URL: http://www.doh.wa.gov/Topics/chs-cert.html

Washington on the Web

East Benton County Historical Society/1910 Benton County Census
URL: http://www.owt.com/ebchs/ebchs/census.htm

Puget Sound Maritime Historical Society/Kitsap County Indexes
http://www.psmaritime.org/

Tacoma-Pierce County Genealogical Society
URL: http://www.rootsweb.com/~watpcgs/tpcgs.htm

Tacoma Public Library's Northwest History Databases
URL: http://www.tpl.lib.wa.us/nwr/nwdata.htm

Washington State Genealogical Society
http://www.thurston.com/~rmccoy/wsgshome.htm

Washington GenWeb Project
http://www.rootsweb.com/~wagenweb/

WEST VIRGINIA

ARCHIVES, STATE & NATIONAL

National Archives—Mid Atlantic Region
Ninth and Market Streets
Philadelphia, PA 19107-4292
Tel: 215-597-3000
Fax: 215-597-2303
Email: archives@philarch.nara.gov
URL: http://www.nara.gov/nara/regional/03nsgil.html

West Virginia State Archives and History Library
West Virginia Division of Culture and History
Cultural Center, Capitol Complex
1900 Kanawha Boulevard, East
Charleston, WV 25305-0300
Tel: 304-558-0230
Fax: 304-558-2779
URL: http://www.wvlc.wvnet.edu/history/wvsamenu.html

GENEALOGICAL SOCIETIES

Allegheny Regional Family History Society (ARFHS)
P.O. Box 1804
Elkins, WV 26241
Tel: 304-636-1958
304-636-1959
URL: http://www.swcp.com/~dhickman/arfhs.html

Boone County Genealogical Society
P.O. Box 306
Madison, WV 25130

Braxton County Genealogical Society
Elk River Route, Box 32
Gassaway, WV 26624

Brooke County Genealogical Society
P.O. Box 144
Beech Bottom, WV 26030-0144
URL: http://209.41.90.162/bcg/

Calhoun County Historical and Genealogical Society
Board of Education Plaza
High Street
P.O. Box 242
Grantsville, WV 26147
Tel: 304-354-7614

Daughters of American Pioneers, Centennial Chapter
2334 Broad Street
Parkersburg, WV 26101

Fayette and Raleigh Counties, Genealogical Society of
P.O. Box 68
Oak Hill, WV 25901-0068

Hacker's Creek Pioneer Descendants
Central West Virginia Genealogy and History Library
Route 1, Box 238
Jane Lew, WV 26378
Tel: 304-269-7091
Fax: 304-269-4430
Email: hcpd.lewisco@westvirginia.com
URL: http://www.rootsweb.com/~hcpd/

Harrison County Genealogical Society
P.O. Box 387
Clarksburg, WV 26301

Kanawha Valley Genealogical Society/Library
P.O. Box 8555
South Charleston, WV 25303

KYOWVA Genealogical Society
Keenan House (Library)
232 Main Street
Guyandotte, WV
Mail:
P.O. Box 1254
Huntington, WV 25715

Lincoln County Genealogical Society
7999 Lynn Avenue
Hamlin, WV 25523
URL: http://fly.hiwaay.net/~jjadkins/lcwv/LCGS.html

Logan County Genealogical Society
Southern West Virginia Community College Library
P.O. Box 1959
Logan, WV 25601

Marion County Genealogical Club
c/o Marion County Library, Genealogy Room
321 Monroe Street
Fairmont, WV 26554
Tel: 304-366-1210/1
URL: http://members.harborcom.net/~rfalin/wv/society/mcgci.html

Mineral County Genealogical/Historical Society
107 Orchard Street
Keyser, WV 26726

Mining Your History Foundation
P.O. Box 6923
Charleston, WV 25362-0923
Tel: 304-525-5720
Email: hcpd.lewisco@westvirginia.com
URL: http://www.rootsweb.com/~myhf/

Mingo County Genealogical Society
P.O. Box 2581
Williamson, WV 25661
URL: http://www.rootsweb.com/~wvmingo/mingogs.htm

Morgan County Historical and Genealogical Society
P.O. Box 52
Berkeley Springs, WV 25411

Nicholas County Historical and Genealogical Society
P.O. Box 443
Summersville, WV 26651
Tel: 304-872-1696
304-872-2478
URL: http://svis.org/shirley/Nicholas.htm

Taylor County Historical and Genealogical Society
P.O. Box 522
Grafton, WV 26354
Tel: 304-265-5015

Tri-State Genealogical and Historical Society
P.O. Box 454
Newell, WV 26050

West Augusta Historical and Genealogical Society
2515 Tenth Avenue
Parkersburg, WV 26101-5829

West Virginia Genealogical Society/Library
5238 Elk River Road, N.
P.O. Box 249
Elkview, WV 25071

Wetzel County Genealogical Society, Inc.
P.O. Box 464
New Martinsville, WV 26155-0464

Wheeling Area Genealogical Society
2237 Marshall Avenue
Wheeling, WV 26003
URL: http://www.hostville.com/wags/

Wyoming County Genealogical Society
P.O. Box 1186
Pineville, WV 24874-1186
Tel: 304-732-8394
304-294-6108
304-732-9472
URL: http://members.aol.com/jlcooke/gensoc.htm

HISTORICAL SOCIETIES

Barbour County Historical Society
146 N. Main
Philippi, WV 26416
Tel: 304-457-4846
304-457-3349

Berkeley County Historical Society
Belle Boyd House
126 East Race Street
P.O. Box 1624
Martinsburg, WV 25401
Tel: 304-267-4713

Braxton County Historical Society
Route 1, Box 14
Exchange, WV 26619
Tel: 304-765-2415

Brooke County Historical Society/Library
10th and Main
Mail:
1200 Pleasant Avenue
Wellsburg, WV 26070

Buffalo Historical Society
P.O. Box 144
Buffalo, WV 25033
Tel: 304-937-2241

Cabell-Wayne County Historical Society
P.O. Box 9412
Huntington, WV 25704

Calhoun County Historical and Genealogical Society
Board of Education Plaza
High Street
P.O. Box 242
Grantsville, WV 26147
Tel: 304-354-7614

Clay County Landmarks Commission and Historical Society
P.O. Box 523
Clay, WV 25043

Doddridge County Historical Society
P.O. Box 23
West Union, WV 26456

Elk/Blue Creek Historical Society
P.O. Box 649
Elkview, WV 25071

Fayette County Historical Society
P.O. Box 463
Ansted, WV 25812-0463
Tel: 304-469-9505

Gilmer County Historical Society
c/o Kyle Emerson
214 Walnut Street
Glenville, WV 26351
Tel: 304-462-5620

Grant County Historical Society
P.O. Box 665
Petersburg, WV 26847
Tel: 304-257-1444

Greenbrier Historical Society/Library
North House Museum
301 West Washington Street
Lewisburg, WV 24901

Tel: 304-645-3398
Email: ghs@access.mountain.net
URL: http://web.mountain.net/~ghs/ghs.html

Hampshire County Historical Society
170 East Birch Lane
Rommney, WV 26757
Tel: 304-822-3185 (Hampshire County Public Library)

Hancock County Historical Society of West Virginia
c/o Frank D. Bowman, Pres.
3669 Main Street
Weirton, WV 26062
Tel: 304-748-4829

Hardy County Historical Society
P.O. Box 644
Moorefield, WV 26836

Harpers Ferry Historical Association
Harpers Ferry National Historic Park
Shenandoah Street
P.O. Box 197
Harpers Ferry, WV 25425
Tel: 304-535-6881
800-821-5206
Email: hfha@intrepid.net
URL: http://www.nps.gov/hafe/hf_shop.htm

Harrison County Historical Society
Stealy Goff Vance House
123 West Main Street
P.O. Box 2074
Clarksburg, WV 26302-2074
Tel: 304-842-3073

Helvetia, Historical Society of
General Delivery
Helvetia, WV 26224

Historic Shepherdstown Commission/Museum
Entler Hotel, Room 200
P.O. Box 1786
Shepherdstown, WV 25443
Tel: 304-876-0910

Jackson County Historical Society
P.O. Box 22
Ripley, WV 25271
Tel: 304-372-2541

Jefferson County Historical Society
P.O. Box 485
Charles Town, WV 25414

Lewis County Historical Society
252 Main Avenue
Weston, WV 26452

Kanawha Valley Historical and Preservation Society
P.O. Box 2283
Charlestown, WV 25328

Marion County Historical Society
P.O. Box 1636
Fairmont, WV 26555-1636

Marshall County Historical Society
P.O. Box 267
Moundsville, WV 26041

Mason City Historical Society
6 Brown Street
Mason, WV 25260

Mason Historical Society
P.O. Box 125
Hartford, WV 25247

McDowell Historical Society
P.O. Box 369
War, WV 24892
Tel: 304-875-2841

Mercer County Historical Society, Inc.
P.O. Box 5012
Princeton, WV 24740
Tel: 304-425-2697
304-487-5026

Mineral County Genealogical/Historical Society
107 Orchard Street
Keyser, WV 26726

Mingo County Historical Society
10 Collier Street
Kermit, WV 25674
Tel: 304-393-3370

Monongalia Historical Society
P.O. Box 127
Morgantown, WV 26505

Monroe County Historical Society
P.O. Box 465
Union, WV 24983

Morgan County Historical and Genealogical Society
P.O. Box 52
Berkeley Springs, WV 25411

Mountain State Railroad and Logging Historical Association
P.O. Box 89
Cass, WV 24927

National Railway Historical Society
Collis P. Huntington Chapter
1429 Chestnut Street
Kenova, WV 25530
Tel: 304-453-1641
URL: http://www.serve.com/cphrrhs/

Nicholas County Historical and Genealogical Society
P.O. Box 443
Summersville, WV 26651
Tel: 304-872-1696
304-872-2478
URL: http://svis.org/shirley/Nicholas.htm

Pendleton County Historical Society
Main Street
P.O. Box 383
Franklin, WV 26807
Tel: 304-358-7366

Pleasants County Historical Society/Museum
Jim Spence Community Building
Pleasants County Park
605 Cherry Street
Mail:
P.O. Box 335
Saint Marys, WV 26170
Tel: 304-684-7621

Pocahontas County Historical Society/Archives
810 Second Avenue
Marlinton, WV 24954
Tel: 304-799-6659 (Summer)
304-799-4973 (Year Round)

Preston County Historical Society
300 W. State Avenue
Terra Alta, WV 26764
Tel: 304-329-1468

Raleigh County Historical Society
Wildwood House
Beckley, WV
Mail:
P.O. Box 897
Skelton, WV 25919-0897

Randolph County Historical Society/Library
P.O. Box 1164
Elkins, WV 26241
Tel: 304-636-0841
304-636-1958/9

Ritchie County Historical Society
200 South Church Street
Harrisville, WV 26362
Tel: 304-643-2738

Roane County Historical Society
P.O. Box 161
Spencer, WV 25276

Saint Albans Historical Society
2745 Lincoln Avenue
Saint Albans, WV
Mail:
919 Lee Street
Saint Albans, WV 25177
Tel: 304-727-5972

Summers County Historical Society
P.O. Box 1335
Hinton, WV 25951
Tel: 304-466-0794

Taylor County Historical and Genealogical Society
P.O. Box 522
Grafton, WV 26354
Tel: 304-265-5015

Tri-State Genealogical and Historical Society
P.O. Box 454
Newell, WV 26050

Tucker County Historical Society
Town Building
P.O. Box 13
Hambleton, WV 26269
Tel: 304-478-2916

Tyler County Heritage and Historical Society
P.O. Box 317
Middlebourne, WV 26149
Tel: 304-758-4288

Upper Vandalia Historical Society
P.O. Box 517
Poca, WV 25159

Upshur County Historical Society
History Center
81 West Main Street
P.O. Box 2082
Buckhannon, WV 26201
Tel: 304-472-2738
URL: http://www.msys.net/uchs/

Webster County Historical Society
P.O. Box 1012
Summersville, WV 26651

West Augusta Historical and Genealogical Society
2515 Tenth Avenue
Parkersburg, WV 26101-5829

West Virginia and Regional History Association
West Virginia University Libraries
Colson Hall, WVU
P.O. Box 6464
Morgantown, WV 26506-6464
Tel: 304-293-3536

West Virginia Baptist Historical Society
Conference Center
Route 2, Box 304
Ripley, WV 25271

West Virginia Historical Society
P.O. Box 5220
Charleston, WV 25305-0300
Tel: 304-348-2277
304-348-0230
URL: http://www.wvlc.wvnet.edu/history/wvhssoc.html

Wheeling Area Historical Society
63 Oakland Avenue
Wheeling, WV 26003

Wood County Historical and Preservation Society, Inc.
c/o Jeff Little, Pres.
1212 Washington Avenue
Parkersburg, WV 26101

LDS Family History Centers

Charleston Family History Center
2007 McClure Parkway
Charleston, WV 25312
Tel: 304-984-9333

Fairmont Family History Center
Route 73N
Fairmont, WV 26554
Tel: 304-363-0116

Huntington Family History Center
5640 Shawnee Drive
Huntington, WV 25705
Tel: 304-736-0250

Archives/Libraries/Museums

Alderson-Braddus College
Pickett Library
College Hill
Philippi, WV 26416
Tel: 304-457-1700 ext. 306
304-457-6229
Fax: 304-457-6239
URL: http://ab.edu/ab/catalog/facilities.html

Beckley Exhibition Coal Mine
Drawer AJ
Beckley, WV 25802

Bethany College
T.W. Phillips Library
Alexander Campbell Archives
Bethany, WV 26032
Tel: 304-829-7325
Fax: 304-829-7333
URL: http://info.bethany.wvnet.edu/Resources/Library/*Index.html

Boone-Madison Public Library
375 Main Street
Madison, WV 25130
Tel/Fax: 304-369-4675

Brooke County Historical Society/Library
10th and Main
Mail:
1200 Pleasant Avenue
Wellsburg, WV 26070

Brooke County Public Library
945 Main Street
Wellsburg, WV 26070
Tel/Fax: 304-757-1551

Burnsville Public Library
Kanawha Street
Burnsville, WV 26335
Tel/Fax: 304-853-2338

Cabell County Public Library/Huntington Branch
455 Ninth Street Plaza
Huntington, WV 25701
Tel: 304-523-9451
Fax: 304-522-4721

Central West Virginia Genealogy and History Library
Hacker's Creek Pioneer Descendants
Route 1, Box 238
Jane Lew, WV 26378
Tel: 304-269-7091
Fax: 304-269-4430
Email: hcpd.lewisco@westvirginia.com
URL: http://www.rootsweb.com/~hcpd/

Clarksburg-Harrison Public Library
West Virginia Collections
404 West Pike Street
Clarksburg, WV 26301
Tel: 304-624-6512 ext. 21

Davis and Elkins College
Booth Library
100 Campus Drive
Elkins, WV 26241
Tel: 304-636-1900
Fax: 304-636-0650
URL: http://www.dne.wvnet.edu/PROGS/LIBRARY.HTM

Doddridge County Public Library
117 Court Street
West Union, WV 26458
Tel/Fax: 304-873-1941

Dora B. Woodyard Memorial Library
P.O. Box 340
Elizabeth, WV 26143
Tel/Fax: 304-275-4295

Elkins/Randolph County Public Library
416 Davis Avenue
Elkins, WV 26241
Tel/Fax: 304-636-1121

Fairmont State College
Ruth Ann Musick Library
Fairmont, WV 26554-2491
Tel: 304-367-4123
Fax: 304-366-4870
URL: http://129.71.46.56/

Family Research Library and Archives
Wilma Myers
805 State Street
Gassaway, WV 26624

Fort New Salem
Salem-Teikyo University
Salem, WV 26426
Tel: 304-782-8245
304-782-5323
URL: http://stulib.salem-teikyo.wvnet.edu/www/fort_menu_3796.html

Gassaway Public Library
100 Birch Street
Gassaway, WV 26624
Tel/Fax: 304-364-8292

Gilmer County Public Library
214 Walnut Street
Glenville, WV 26351
Tel/Fax: 304-462-8444

Greenbrier Historical Society/Library
North House Museum
301 West Washington Street
Lewisburg, WV 24901
Tel: 304-645-3398
Email: ghs@access.mountain.net
URL: http://web.mountain.net/~ghs/ghs.html

Hamlin/Lincoln County Public Library
Genealogical Research Room
8146 Court Avenue
Hamlin, WV 25523-1434
Tel: 304-824-5481

Hampshire County Historical Society
170 East Birch Lane
Rommney, WV 26757
Tel: 304-822-3185 (Hampshire County Public Library)

Hampshire County Public Library
153 West Main Street
Romney, WV 26757
Tel: 304-822-3185
Fax: 304-822-3955

Hardy County Public Library
102 North Main Street
Moorefield, WV 26836
Tel: 304-538-6560
Fax: 304-538-2639

Harpers Ferry National Historical Park
P.O. Box 65
Harpers Ferry, WV 25425
Tel: 304-535-6020
304-535-6441

Harrison County Historical Society
Stealy Goff Vance House
123 West Main Street
P.O. Box 2074
Clarksburg, WV 26302-2074
Tel: 304-842-3073

Henderson Hall
Henderson Hall Historic District
Route 2, Box 103
Williamstown, WV 26187
Tel: 304-375-2129
304-295-4772

Hinton Railroad Museum
217 7th Avenue
Hinton, WV 25951
Tel: 307-466-1433

Kanawha Valley Genealogical Society/Library
P.O. Box 8555
South Charleston, WV 25303

Kanawha County Public Library
123 Capitol Street
Charlestown, WV 25301
Tel: 304-343-4646

KYOWVA Genealogical Society
Keenan House (Library)
232 Main Street
Guyandotte, WV
Mail:
P.O. Box 1254
Huntington, WV 25715

Lee Cabin Museum
Lost River State Park
Route 2, Box 24
Mathias, WV 26812

Marion County Library
Genealogy Room
321 Monroe Street
Fairmont, WV 26554
Tel: 304-366-1210/1

Marshall University
James E. Morrow Library
Special Collections Department-West Virginia Collection
Huntington, WV 25755
Tel: 304-696-2343
304-696-2320
URL: http://www.marshall.edu/speccoll/wvcoll.html

Martinsburg-Berkeley County Public Library
Public Square
101 West King Street
Martinsburg, WV 25401
Tel: 304-267-8933
Fax: 307-267-9720

Mary H. Weir Public Library
3442 Main Street
Weirton, WV 26062-4590
Tel: 304-797-8510

Mason City Public Library
8 Brown Street
P.O. Box 609
Mason City, WV 25260
Tel: 304-773-5580

Mason County Public Library
6th and Viand Street
Point Pleasant, WV 25550
Tel: 304-675-2913
Fax: 304-675-2943

Miracle Valley City/County Public Library
700 Fifth Street
Moundsville, WV 26041
Tel: 304-845-6911
Fax: 304-845-6912

Monroe County Public Library
Route 219
P.O. Box 558
Union, WV 24983
Tel: 304-772-3038
Fax: 304-772-4052

Moomau Public Library
One North Main Street
Petersburg, WV 26847
Tel/Fax: 304-257-4122

Morgantown Public Library
West Virginia Collection and Archives
373 Spruce Street
Morgantown, WV 26505
Tel: 304-291-7425
Fax: 304-291-7437

Ohio County Public Library
52 16th Street
Wheeling, WV 26003

Old Charles Town Library
200 East Washington Street
Charles Town, WV 25414
Tel: 304-725-2208

Parkersburg and Wood County Public Library
3100 Emerson Avenue
Parkersburg, WV 26104
Tel: 304-485-6564
Fax: 304-485-6580

Pendleton County Public Library
P.O. Box 519
Franklin, WV 26807
Tel: 304-358-2515

Philippi Public Library
102 South Main Street
Philippi, WV 26416
Tel: 304-457-3495

Pleasants County Historical Society/Museum
Jim Spence Community Building
Pleasants County Park
605 Cherry Street
Mail:
P.O. Box 335
Saint Marys, WV 26170
Tel: 304-684-7621

Pleasants County Public Library
101 Lafayette Street
St. Marys, WV 26170-1025
Tel/Fax: 304-684-7494

Pocahontas County Historical Society/Archives
810 Second Avenue
Marlinton, WV 24954
Tel: 304-799-6659 (Summer)
304-799-4973 (Year Round)

Pricketts Fort Memorial Foundation
Pricketts Fort State Park
Route 3
Fairmont, WV 26554
Tel: 304-363-3030

Putnam County Library
4219 State Route 34
Hurricane, WV 25526
Tel: 304-757-7308
Fax: 304-757-7307

Quinwood Public Library
P.O. Box 157
Quinwood, WV 25981
Tel/Fax: 304-438-6741

Randolph County Historical Society/Library
P.O. Box 1164
Elkins, WV 26241
Tel: 304-636-0841
304-636-1958/9

Ritchie County Public Library
130 N. Court Street
Harrisville, WV 26362
Tel/Fax: 304-643-2717

Roane County Public Library
Parking Plaza
Spencer, WV 25276
Tel/Fax: 304-927-1130

Shepherdstown Public Library
P.O. Box 278
Shepherdstown, WV 25443
Tel: 304-876-2783

Summers County Public Library
201 Temple Street
Hinton, WV 25951
Tel: 304-466-4490
Fax: 304-466-5260

Sutton Public Library
General Delivery
Sutton, WV 26601
Tel: 304-765-7224

Taylor County Public Library
200 Beech Street
Grafton, WV 26354
Tel/Fax: 304-265-5015

Upshur County Public Library
RR 6, Box 480
Buckhannon, WV 26201
Tel: 304-472-5475

West Huntington Public Library
428 W. 14th Street
Huntington, WV 25704
Tel: 304-523-5426

West Virginia Baptist Historical Society
Conference Center
Route 2, Box 304
Ripley, WV 25271

West Virginia Genealogical Society/Library
5238 Elk River Road, N.
P.O. Box 249
Elkview, WV 25071

West Virginia State Archives and History Library
West Virginia Division of Culture and History
Cultural Center, Capitol Complex
1900 Kanawha Boulevard, East
Charleston, WV 25305-0300
Tel: 304-558-0230
Fax: 304-558-2779
URL: http://www.wvlc.wvnet.edu/history/wvsamenu.html

West Virginia State Farm Museum
Route 1, Box 479
Point Pleasant, WV 25550
Tel: 304-675-5737

West Virginia University Library
Special Collections
Colson Hall, WVU
P.O. Box 6464
Morgantown, WV 26506-6464
Tel: 304-293-3536/7
Fax: 304-293-6638
URL: http://www.wvu.edu/~library/collect.htm

Williamson Public Library
Court House Annex
Williamson, WV 25661
Tel/Fax: 304-235-2402

Wyoming County Public Library
Castle Rock Avenue
P.O. Box 130
Pineville, WV 24874
Tel: 307-732-6228

Newspaper Repositories

West Virginia State Archives and History Library
West Virginia Division of Culture and History
Cultural Center, Capitol Complex
1900 Kanawha Boulevard, East
Charleston, WV 25305-0300
Tel: 304-558-0230
Fax: 304-558-2779
URL: http://www.wvlc.wvnet.edu/history/wvsamenu.html

West Virginia University Library
Special Collections
Colson Hall, WVU
P.O. Box 6464
Morgantown, WV 26506-6464
Tel: 304-293-3536
Fax: 304-293-6638
Email: hforbes@wvu.edu
URL: http://www.wvu.edu/~library/wvarhc.htm

VITAL RECORDS

Division of Health, Vital Registration
Capitol Complex
Building 3, Room 516
Charleston, WV 25305
Tel: 304-558-2931

WEST VIRGINIA ON THE WEB

Civil War in West Virginia
http://www.wvlc.wvnet.edu/history/cwmenu.html

Don Norman's West Virginia Family Histories
http://www.everton.com/norman/norman.don/norman.htm

West Virginia GenWeb Project
http://members.harborcom.net/~rfalin/wv/

West Virginia Historical Resources Guide-Marshall University
http://www.marshall.edu/speccoll/rg-title.html

West Virginia Histories Homepage (A Bibliography)
http://www.clearlight.com/~wvhh/

West Virginia Infomine
http://www.wvlc.wvnet.edu/

West Virginia Military Research from the WV GenWeb
http://members.harborcom.net/~rfalin/military/index.html

West Virginia State Archives Civil War Medals Homepage
http://www.wvlc.wvnet.edu/history/medals.html

West Virginia State Archives Genealogy Surname Exchange
http://www.wvlc.wvnet.edu/history/surintro.html

West Virginia State Archives History Databases
http://www.wvlc.wvnet.edu/history/historyw.html

WISCONSIN

ARCHIVES, STATE & NATIONAL

National Archives—Great Lakes Region
7358 Pulaski Road
Chicago, IL 60629
Tel: 773-581-7816
Fax: 773-353-1294
Email: archives@chicago.nara.gov
URL: http://www.nara.gov/nara/regional/05nsgil.htm

State Historical Society of Wisconsin/Archives Division
816 State Street
Madison, WI 53706
Tel: 608-264-6460
Email: Paul.Hedges@ccmail.adp.wisc.edu
URL: http://www.wisc.edu/shs-archives/

Area Research Centers
URL: http://www.wisc.edu/shs-archives/arcnet/index.html
For individual homepages with more information on each Area Research Center, see the section on Archives/Libraries/Museums

Madeline Island Historical Museum
P.O. Box 9
La Pointe, WI 54850
Tel: 715-747-2415
URL: http://www.wisc.edu/shs-archives/arcnet/madislan.html
(Original Materials for Ashland, Bayfield, and Iron Counties—See Vaughn Public Library for Microfilm)

Superior Public Library
1530 Tower Avenue
Superior, WI 54880
Tel: 715-394-8860
URL: http://www.wisc.edu/shs-archives/arcnet/superior.html
(Douglas County)

University of Wisconsin/Eau Claire
William D. McIntyre Library
Special Collections Department
Eau Claire, WI 54702-5010
Tel: 715-836-2739
URL: http://www.wisc.edu/shs-archives/arcnet/eauclair.html
(Buffalo, Chippewa, Clark, Eau Claire, Price, Rusk, Sawyer, and Taylor Counties)

University of Wisconsin/Green Bay
Cofrin Library, 7th Floor
2420 Nicolet Drive
Green Bay, WI 54311-7001
Tel: 414-465-2539
URL: http://www.wisc.edu/shs-archives/arcnet/greenbay.html
(Brown, Calumet, Door, Florence, Kewaunee, Manitowoc, Marinette, Menominee, Oconto, Outagamie, and Shawano Counties)

University of Wisconsin/La Crosse
Murphy Library Resource Center
La Crosse, WI 54601
Tel: 608-785-8511
URL: http://www.wisc.edu/shs-archives/arcnet/lacrosse.html
(Jackson, La Crosse, Monroe, Trempealeau, and Vernon Counties)

University of Wisconsin/Milwaukee
Golda Meir Library, Room W250
Milwaukee Urban Archives
P.O. Box 604
Milwaukee, WI 53201-0604
Tel: 414-229-5402
URL: http://www.wisc.edu/shs-archives/arcnet/milwauke.html
(Milwaukee, Ozaukee, Sheboygan, Washington, and Waukesha Counties)

University of Wisconsin/Oshkosh
Forrest R. Polk Library
800 Algoma Boulevard
Oshkosh, WI 54901
Tel: 414-424-0828
414-424-3347
URL: http://www.wisc.edu/shs-archives/arcnet/oshkosh.html
(Dodge, Fond du Lac, Green Lake, Marquette, and Winnebago Counties)

University of Wisconsin/Parkside
D276 Wyllie Library Learning Center
University Archives and Area Research Center
900 Wood Road
Kenosha, WI 53141-2000
Tel: 414-595-2411
URL: http://www.wisc.edu/shs-archives/arcnet/parkside.html
(Racine and Kenosha Counties)

University of Wisconsin/Platteville
Elton S. Karrmann Library
Southwest Wisconsin Room
Platteville, WI 53818-3099
Tel: 608-342-1719
URL: http://www.wisc.edu/shs-archives/arcnet/plattvil.html
(Crawford, Grant, Green, Iowa, Lafayette, and Richland Counties)

University of Wisconsin/River Falls
Chalmer Davee Library
120 Cascade Avenue
River Falls, WI 54022
Tel: 715-425-3567
URL: http://www.wisc.edu/shs-archives/arcnet/riverfls.html
(Burnett, Polk, St. Croix, Pierce, and Washburn Counties)

University of Wisconsin/Stevens Point
Learning Resources Center
Stevens Point, WI 54481
Tel: 715-346-2586
URL: http://www.wisc.edu/shs-archives/arcnet/stevens.html
(Adams, Forest, Juneau, Langlade, Lincoln, Marathon, Oneida, Portage, Vilas, Waupaca, Waushara, and Wood Counties)

University of Wisconsin/Stout
Library Learning Center
Menomonie, WI 54751
Tel: 715-232-2300
URL: http://www.wisc.edu/shs-archives/arcnet/stout.html
(Barron, Dunn, and Pepin Counties)

University of Wisconsin/Whitewater
Harold Anderson Library
800 West Main Street
Whitewater, WI 53190
Tel: 414-472-5520
URL: http://www.wisc.edu/shs-archives/arcnet/whitewtr.html
(Jefferson, Rock, and Walworth Counties)

Vaughn Public Library
502 West Main Street
Ashland, WI 54806
Tel: 715-682-7060
(Microfilmed Materials for Ashland, Bayfield, and Iron Counties-See Madeline Island for Original Material)

GENEALOGICAL SOCIETIES

Bay Area Genealogical Society
P.O. Box 283
Green Bay, WI 54305

Bayfield County Genealogical Society
c/o Carol Jones Wilson
Route 1, Box 139
Mason, WI 54856

Chippewa County Genealogical Society
c/o Anne Adams Keller
1427 Hilltop Blvd.
Chippewa Falls, WI 54729

Daughters of the American Revolution, Wisconsin State Society
URL: http://www.execpc.com/~drg/wisdar.html

Dunn County Genealogical Society
P.O. Box 633
Menomonie, WI 54751

Eau Claire, Genealogical Research Society of
c/o Chippewa Valley Museum
Carson Park Drive
P.O. Box 1204
Eau Claire, WI 54702
Tel: 715-834-7871

Fond du Lac County Genealogical Society
c/o Spillman Library
719 Wisconsin Avenue
North Fond du Lac, WI 54935

Forest County Historical and Genealogical Society/Museum
105 West Jackson Street
Crandon, WI 54520
Tel: 715-478-5900

Fox Valley Genealogical Society
P.O. Box 1592
Appleton, WI 54913-1592

French-Canadian/Acadian Genealogical of Wisconsin
c/o Beverly Louisiana Belle
4527 South Oakwood Terrace
New Berlin, WI 53151

German Interest Group of Southern Wisconsin
P.O. Box 2185
Janesville, WI 53547-2185
Tel: 608-757-2777
URL: http://feefhs.org/ger/gigsw/frggigsw.html

Grant County Genealogical Society
c/o Karen Reese, Pres.
P.O. Box 281
Dickeyville, WI 53808-0281
Email: reese@mwci.net
URL: http://www.rootsweb.com/~wigrant/gcgensoc.htm

Hartford Genealogical Society
c/o Hartford Public Library
109 North Main Street
Hartford, WI 53027

Heart O' Wisconsin Genealogical Society
c/o MacMillan Memorial Library
490 East Grand Avenue
Wisconsin Rapids, WI 54494

Jackson County Footprints (Genealogy Club)
W11770 County Road P
Black River Falls, WI 54615-5926

Kenosha County Genealogical Society
c/o Lois R. Stein
4902 52nd Street
Kenosha, WI 53142

Lafayette County Genealogical Workshop
P.O. Box 443
Shullsburg, WI 53586

LaCrosse Area Genealogical Society
P.O. Box 1782
LaCrosse, WI 54601

Manitowoc County Genealogical Society
P.O. Box 345
Manitowoc, WI 54220

Marathon County Genealogical Society
P.O. Box 1518
Wausau, WI 54402-1518

Marshfield Area Genealogy Group
P.O. Box 337
Marshfield, WI 54449

Milwaukee County Genealogical Society
P.O. Box 27326
Milwaukee, WI 53227

Milwaukee PAF Users Group (MPAFUG)
P.O. Box 268
Muskego, WI 53150
Email: akoes24194@aol.com
URL: http://www.execpc.com/~bheck/mpafug.html

Monroe, Juneau, Jackson County Wisconsin Genealogy Workshop
c/o Carolyn Habelman, Pres.
Route 3, Box 253
Black River Falls, WI 54615

Northern Wisconsin Genealogists
P.O. Box 321
Shawano, WI 54166

Northwoods Genealogical Society
P.O. Box 1132
Rhinelander, WI 54501

Oconomowoc Genealogical Club of Waukesha County
c/o Alice B. Palmer
733 East Sherman Avenue
Oconomowoc, WI 53066

Polish Genealogical Society of Wisconsin
P.O. Box 37476
Milwaukee, WI 53237

Pomeranian Society of Freistadt
(Pommerscher Verein Freistadt Rundschreiben)
P.O. Box 204
Germantown, WI 53022

Plymouth Genealogical Society
c/o Plymouth Public Library
317 East Main
Plymouth, WI 53073

Rock County Genealogical Society
c/o Rock County Historical Society
10 S. High Street
P.O. Box 711
Janesville, WI 53547
Tel: 608-756-4509
URL: http://als.lib.wi.us/firstcall/l80te903.htm

Saint Croix Valley Genealogical Society
P.O. Box 396
River Falls, WI 54022

Sheboygan County Genealogical Society
518 Water Street
Sheboygan Falls, WI 53085

Sons of the American Revolution, Wisconsin State Society
URL: http://www.execpc.com/~drg/srwi.html

Stevens Point Area Genealogical Society
c/o Portage County Library
1001 Main Street
Stevens Point, WI 54481-2860

Twin Ports Genealogical Society
P.O. Box 16895
Duluth, MN 55816-0895

Walworth County Genealogical Society
P.O. Box 159
Delavan, WI 53115-0159

Washburn County Genealogical Society
P.O. Box 366
Shell Lake, WI 54871

Watertown Genealogical Society
P.O. Box 91
Watertown, WI 53094-0091

Waukesha County Genealogical Society
P.O. Box 1541
Waukesha, WI 53187-1541

White Pine Genealogical Society
P.O. Box 512
Marienette, WI 54143

Winnebagoland Genealogical Society
c/o Oshkosh Public Library
106 Washington Avenue
Oshkosh, WI 54901-4985

Wisconsin Jewish Genealogical Society
c/o Penny Deshur
9280 North Fairway Drive
Milwaukee, WI 53217

Wisconsin State Genealogical Society
2109 20th Avenue
Monroe, WI 53566

Historical Societies

Ashland County Historical Society
Genealogy Department
P.O. Box 433
Ashland, WI 54806

Bayfield Heritage Association
117 S. 1st
Bayfield, WI 54814
Tel: 715-779-5958

Beloit Historical Society/Library
845 Hackett Street
Beloit, WI 53511
Tel: 608-365-7835
URL: http://als.lib.wi.us/firstcall/l80te8kx.htm

Berlin Historical Society
111 South Adams Avenue
Berlin, WI 54923
Tel: 414-361-4343

Burlington Historical Society/Museum
232 N. Perkins Blvd.
Burlington, WI 53105
Tel: 414-767-2884

Chippewa County Historical Society
123 Allen Street
Chippewa Falls, WI 54729
Tel: 715-723-4399

Clark County Historical Society
215 E. 5th Street
Neillsville, WI 54456-1942

Cliff High Historical Society
N7526 Lower Cliff Road
Sherwood, WI 54169-9703
Tel: 414-989-1636

Dartford Historical Society
501 Mill Street
Green Lake, WI 54941
Tel: 414-294-6194

Dodge County Historical Society
105 Park Avenue
Beaver Dam, WI 53916
Tel: 414-887-1266

Dunn County Historical Society
1820 Wakanda Street
Menomonie, WI 54751
Tel: 715-232-8685
Email: dchs@discover-net.net
URL: http://discover-net.net/~dchs/

Fennimore Railroad Historical Society/Museum
610 Lincoln Avenue
Fennimore, WI 53809
Tel: 608-822-6144

Fond du Lac County Historical Society
P.O. Box 1284
Fond du Lac, WI 54935

Forest County Historical and Genealogical Society/Museum
105 West Jackson Street
Crandon, WI 54520
Tel: 715-478-5900

Headwaters Historical Society
P.O. Box 2011
Eagle River, WI 54521

Iron County Historical Society/Museum
303 Iron Street
Hurley, WI 54534
Tel: 715-561-2244

Jackson County Historical Society
13 South 1st Street
Black River Falls, WI 54615

Kenosha County Historical Society/Museum
6300 3rd Avenue
Kenosha, WI 53143
Tel: 414-654-5770

LaCrosse County Historical Society
Swarthout and Riverside Museum
112 9th Street
LaCrosse, WI 54601
Tel: 608-782-1980

Madeline Island Historical Preservation Association
P.O. Box 250
LaPointe, WI 54850

Manitowoc County Historical Society
736 Revere Drive
P.O. Box 574
Manitowoc, WI 54221
Tel: 414-684-5110
414-684-4445
URL: http://www.excel.net/business/l_veris/p_crest.htm

Marathon County Historical Society/Museum and Library
403 McIndoe Street
Wausau, WI 54401
Tel: 715-848-6143

Mazomanie Historical Society/Museum
118 Brodhead Street
Mazomanie, WI 53560
Tel: 608-795-2992

Menomonee Falls Historical Society
P.O. Box 91
Menomonee Falls, WI 53051

Mercer Historical Society
Mercer, WI 54547
Tel: 715-476-9191

Middleton Area Historical Society
7410 Hubbard Avenue
Middleton, WI 53562
Tel: 608-836-7614

Milwaukee County Historical Society
910 North Old World Third Street
Milwaukee, WI 53203
Tel: 414-273-8288
URL: http://www.mcfls.org/LCOMM/ml.htm

Milton Historical Society
P.O. Box 245
Milton, WI 53563
Tel: 608-868-7772
URL: http://als.lib.wi.us/firstcall/l80tedht.htm

Neenah Historical Society
336 Main Street
Neenah, WI 54956
Tel: 414-729-0244

New Glarus Historical Society
612 7th Avenue
New Glarus, WI 53574
Tel: 608-527-2317

North Wood County Historical Society
212 W. 3rd Street
Marshfield, WI 54449
Tel: 715-387-3322

Oak Creek Historical Society
P.O. Box 243
Oak Creek, WI 53154
Email: larryr3670@aol.com
URL: http://members.aol.com/larryr3670/CC_HISTR/Ochsocie.htm

Oconomowoc Historical Society/Museum
103 W. Jefferson Street
Oconomowoc, WI 53066

Oconto County Historical Society
917 Park Avenue
Oconto, WI 54153
Tel: 414-834-6206

Omro Area Historical Society
144 E. Main Street
Omro, WI 54963
Tel: 414-685-6123

Ozaukee County Historical Society
P.O. Box 206
Cedarburg, WI 53012
URL: http://www.msoe.edu/~reyer/pioneer/

Pewaukee Area Historical Society
206 E. Wisconsin Avenue
Pewaukee, WI 53072
Tel: 414-691-0233

Pierce County Historical Association
414 E. Main Street
Ellsworth, WI 54011
Tel: 715-273-6611

Porter County Historical Society
1475 Water Street
Stevens Point, WI 54481
Tel: 715-344-4423

Racine County Historical Society and Museum
Local History and Genealogical Library
701 S. Main Street
P.O. Box 1527
Racine, WI 53401
Tel: 414-636-3926

Rhinelander Historical Society/Museum
9 S. Pelham Street
Rhinelander, WI 54501
Tel: 715-369-3833

Rivers Two Historical Society
1622 Jefferson Street
Two Rivers, WI 54241
Tel: 414-793-2490

Rock County Historical Society/Museum and Library
10 S. High Street
P.O. Box 8096
Janesville, WI 53545
Tel: 608-756-4509
URL: http://als.lib.wi.us/firstcall/l80te83c.htm

St. Croix County Historical Society
1004 3rd Street
Hudson, WI 54016
Tel: 715-386-2654

Sauk County Historical Society/Museum
531 Fourth Avenue
P.O. Box 651
Baraboo, WI 53913
Tel: 608-356-1001
URL: http://www.saukcounty.com/schs.htm

Seventh Day Baptist Historical Society
P.O. Box 1678
Janesville, WI 53547

Stanley Area Historical Society
228 Helgerson
Stanley, WI 54768
Tel: 715-644-5880
URL: http://timbertrails.com/sahsm1.htm

State Historical Society of Wisconsin
816 State Street
Madison, WI 53706
Tel: 608-264-6534
608-264-6535 (Reference)
608-264-6525 (Government Publications Reference)
URL: http://www.shsw.wisc.edu/

Wauwatosa Historical Society
7406 Hillcrest Drive
Milwaukee, WI 53213
Tel: 414-774-8672

Webster House Historical Society
9 E. Rockwell Street
Elkhorn, WI 53121
Tel: 414-723-4248

Winnebago County Historical/Archaelogical Society
Morgan House
234 Church Street
Oshkosh, WI 54901
Tel: 414-235-3091
414-232-0200

Winneconne Historical Society
611 W. Main Street
Winneconne, WI 54986
Tel: 414-582-4132

Wisconsin Black Historical Society
2620 W. Center Street
Milwaukee, WI 53206
Tel: 414-372-7677

Wisconsin Marine Historical Society
814 W. Wisconsin Avenue
Milwaukee, WI 53233-2385
Tel: 414-286-3074
Email: wmhs@execpc.com
URL: http://www.execpc.com/~wmhs/

Wisconsin State Old Cemetery Society
9955 West St. Martens Road
Franklin, WI 53132

LDS Family History Centers

Appleton Family History Center
425 West Park Ridge Avenue
Appleton, WI 54911
Tel: 414-733-5358

Eau Claire Family History Center
3335 Stein Blvd.
Eau Claire, WI 54701
Tel: 715-834-8271

Hales Corner Family History Center
9600 West Grange Avenue
Hales Corner, WI 53130
Tel: 414-425-4182

Kenosha Family History Center
1444 30th Avenue
Kenosha, WI 53144
Tel: 414-552-8887

Madison Family History Center
1711 University Avenue
Madison, WI 53705
Tel: 608-238-4844
Email: halhovorka@aol.com
URL: http://www.cae.wisc.edu/~porterb/lds/fam_hist.html

Shawano Family History Center
910 East Lingler Avenue
Shawano, WI 54166
Tel: 715-526-2946

Wausau Family History Center
5405 Rib Mountain Drive
Wausau, WI 54401
Tel: 715-359-7171

Archives/Libraries/Museums

Appleton Public Library
225 N. Oneida Street
Appleton, WI 54911
Tel/TDD: 414-832-6173
Fax: 414-832-6182
Email: bkelly@apl.org
URL: http://apl.org/

Beaver Dam Community Library
311 South Spring Street
Beaver Dam, WI 53916
Tel: 920-887-4631
Fax: 920-887-4633
Email: bdlib@peoples.net
or bdlib@centuryinter.net
URL: http://www.peoples.net/~bdlib/

Beloit Historical Society/Library
845 Hackett Street
Beloit, WI 53511
Tel: 608-365-7835
URL: http://als.lib.wi.us/firstcall/l80te8kx.htm

Beloit Public Library
409 Pleasant Street
Beloit, WI 53511
Tel: 608-364-2905
Fax: 608-364-2907
URL: http://als.lib.wi.us/BPL/

Brown County Library
Local History and Genealogy Dept.
515 Pine Street
Green Bay, WI 54301
Tel: 414-448-4400
URL: http://www.dct.com/org/bcl/

Chippewa Falls Public Library
105 W. Central Street
Chippewa Falls, WI 54729
Tel: 715-723-1146
Fax: 715-720-6922

Chippewa Valley Museum
Carson Park Drive
P.O. Box 1204
Eau Claire, WI 54702
Tel: 715-834-7871
URL: http://timbertrails.com/cvm1.htm

Cudahy Public Library
4665 South Packard Avenue
Cudahy, WI 53110
Tel: 414-769-2244
Fax: 414-769-2252

Darlington Public Library
525 N. Main Street
Darlington, WI 53530-0312
Tel/Fax: 608-776-4171

Door County Library
107 S. 4th Avenue
Sturgeon Bay, WI 54235-2203
Tel: 715-695-3601
Fax: 715-695-3510

Fond du Lac Public Library
32 Sheboygan Street
Fond du Lac, WI 54935
Tel: 414-929-7085
Fax: 414-929-7082

Hartford Public Library
115 North Main Street
Hartford, WI 53027
Tel: 414-673-8240
Fax: 414-673-8300
URL: http://www.mcfls.org/LCOMM/ml.htm

Hartland Public Library
110 E. Park Avenue
P.O. Box 18
Hartland, WI 53029
Tel: 414-367-3350
Fax: 414-367-2251
URL: http://www.mcfls.org/LCOMM/ml.htm

Kenosha Public Library
7979 38th Avenue
Kenosha, WI 53142
Tel: 414-942-3721
Fax: 414-942-3727

LaCrosse Public Library
Archives and Local History
800 Main Street
LaCrosse, WI 54601
Tel: 608-789-7100
Fax: 608-789-7106

Madeline Island Historical Museum
P.O. Box 9
La Pointe, WI 54850
Tel: 715-747-2415

Madison Public Library
201 W. Mifflin Street
Madison, WI 53703
Tel: 608-267-1184
608-266-4338
608-266-6300
URL: http://elink.scls.lib.wi.us/madison/index2.html

Manitowoc County Historical Society
736 Revere Drive
P.O. Box 574
Manitowoc, WI 54221
Tel: 414-684-5110
414-684-4445
URL: http://www.excel.net/business/l_veris/p_crest.htm

Marathon County Historical Society/Museum and Library
403 McIndoe Street
Wausau, WI 54401
Tel: 715-848-6143

Marathon County Public Library
300 First Street
Wausau, WI 54401
Tel: 715-848-1017
715-847-5530
URL: http://www.co.marathon.wi.us/library/index.html

Maude Shunk Public Library
W156 N8446 Pilgrim Road
Menomonee Falls, WI 53051
Tel: 414-255-8390
Fax:414-255-8408

McMillan Memorial Library
490 East Grand Avenue
Wisconsin Rapids, WI 54494
Tel: 715-423-1040
Fax: 715-423-2665
TDD: 715-423-5138
Email: mcmweb@scls.lib.wi.us
URL: http://elink.scls.lib.wi.us/mcmillan/

Milwaukee County Historical Society
910 North Old World Third Street
Milwaukee, WI 53203
Tel: 414-273-8288
URL: http://www.mcfls.org/LCOMM/ml.htm

Milwaukee Public Library
814 West Wisconsin Avenue
Milwaukee, WI 53233
Tel: 414-286-3000
Fax: 414-286-2137
URL: http://www.mcfls.org/LCOMM/ml/htm

Monroe County Local History Room/Research Library
200 W. Main Street
P.O. Box 419
Sparta, WI 54656
Tel: 609-269-8680
Fax: 609-269-8921

Neenah Public Library
240 E. Wisconsin Avenue
Neenah, WI 54956
Tel: 414-751-4722
URL: http://www.focol.org/~npl/

North Fond du Lac Village Public Library
719 Wisconsin Avenue
North Fond Du Lac, WI 54935

Northland College
Dexter Library Area Research Center
1411 Ellis Avenue
Ashland, WI 54806

Oconomowoc Public Library
200 South Street
Oconomowoc, WI 53066
Tel: 414-569-2193
Fax: 414-569-2176

Oshkosh Public Library
106 Washington Avenue
Oshkosh, WI 54901
Tel: 414-236-5200
414-236-5226 (Genealogy and Local History)
URL: http://axp.winnefox.org/www/opl/

Oshkosh Public Museum Library
1331 Algoma Blvd.
Oshkosh, WI 54901
Tel: 414-424-4732
Fax: 414-424-4738

Plymouth Public Library
130 Division
Plymouth, WI 53073
Tel: 414-892-4416

Portage County Library
1001 Main Street
Stevens Point, WI 54481

Racine County Historical Society and Museum
Local History and Genealogical Library
701 S. Main Street
P.O. Box 1527
Racine, WI 53401
Tel: 414-636-3926

Racine Public Library
75 Seventh Street
Racine, WI 53403
Tel: 414-636-9248
Fax: 414-636-9260

Sheboygan County Historical Research Center
518 Water Street
Sheboygan Falls, WI 53085
Tel: 414-467-4667

State Historical Society of Wisconsin/Library Division
816 State Street
Madison, WI 53706
Tel: 608-264-6534
608-264-6535 (Reference)
608-264-6525 (Government Publications Reference)
URL: http://www.wisc.edu/shs-library/

Superior Public Library
1530 Tower Avenue
Superior, WI 54880
Tel: 715-394-8860

University of Wisconsin/Eau Claire
William D. McIntyre Library
Special Collections Department
Local History Collection
Eau Claire, WI 54702-5010
Tel: 715-836-3873
Email: lynchld@uwec.edu
URL: http://www.uwec.edu/Admin/Library/speccoll.html

University of Wisconsin/Green Bay
Cofrin Library, 7th Floor
2420 Nicolet Drive
Green Bay, WI 54311-7001
Tel: 414-465-2539
URL: http://www.uwgb.edu/~library/index.html

University of Wisconsin/La Crosse
Murphy Library Resource Center
Special Collections
1631 Pine Street
La Crosse, WI 54601
Tel: 608-785-8505
Fax: 608-785-8639
URL: http://www.uwlax.edu/MurphyLibrary.html

University of Wisconsin/Milwaukee
Golda Meir Library, Room W250
Milwaukee Urban Archives
P.O. Box 604
Milwaukee, WI 53201-0604
Tel: 414-229-5402
URL: http://www.uwm.edu/Library/arch/

University of Wisconsin/Oshkosh
Forrest R. Polk Library
800 Algoma Boulevard
Oshkosh, WI 54901
Tel: 414-424-0828
414-424-3347
URL: http://www.uwosh.edu/home_pages/departments/llr/

University of Wisconsin/Parkside
D276 Wyllie Library Learning Center
University Archives and Area Research Center
900 Wood Road
Kenosha, WI 53141-2000
Tel: 414-595-2411

University of Wisconsin/Platteville
Elton S. Karrmann Library
Southwest Wisconsin Room
Platteville, WI 53818-3099
Tel: 608-342-1719
URL: http://vms.www.uwplatt.edu/~library/

University of Wisconsin/River Falls
Chalmer Davee Library
120 Cascade Avenue
River Falls, WI 54022
Tel: 715-425-3567
URL: http://www.uwrf.edu/library/welcome.html

University of Wisconsin/Stevens Point
Learning Resources Center
Nelis R. Kampenga University Archives
Stevens Point, WI 54481
Tel: 715-346-2586
URL: http://www.uwsp.edu/acaddept/library/depts/archives/archives.htm

University of Wisconsin/Stout
Library Learning Center
Menomonie, WI 54751
Tel: 715-232-2300
URL: http://www.uwstout.edu/lib/libhome.html

University of Wisconsin/Whitewater
Harold Anderson Library
800 West Main Street
Whitewater, WI 53190
Tel: 414-472-5520
URL: http://www.uww.edu/Library/archicol.html

Vaughn Public Library
502 West Main Street
Ashland, WI 54806
Tel: 715-682-7060

Vesterheim Genealogical Center and Naeseth Library
415 W. Main Street
Madison, WI 53703-3116
Fax: 608-258-6842
Email: vesterheim@juno.com
URL: http://fjordinfo.vestdata.no/offentleg/sffarkiv/sffutvgc.htm

Waukesha Public Library
321 Wisconsin Avenue
Waukesha, WI 53186
Tel: 414-524-3682
Fax: 414-524-3677
URL: http://www.mcfls.org/LCOMM/ml/htm

Wauwatosa Public Library
7635 W. North Avenue
Wauwatosa, WI 53213
Tel: 414-471-8484
Fax: 414-479-8984
Email: tosa@mcfls.org
URL: http://www.execpc.com/~tpublib/

Whitefish Bay Public Library
5420 N. Marlborough Drive
Whitefish Bay, WI 53217
Tel: 414-964-4380
Fax: 414-964-5733
URL: http://www.mcfls.org/LCOMM/ml/htm

Wisconsin Marine Historical Society
814 W. Wisconsin Avenue
Milwaukee, WI 53233-2385
Tel: 414-286-3074
Email: wmhs@execpc.com
URL: http://www.execpc.com/~wmhs/

Newspaper Repositories

State Historical Society of Wisconsin
816 State Street
Madison, WI 53706
Tel: 608-264-6598
Email: james.danky@ccmail.adp.wisc.edu
URL: http://www.wisc.edu/shs~library/collect.html

Vital Records

Wisconsin State Department of Health and Family Services
Vital Records
One West Wilson
P.O. Box 309
Madison, WI 53701-0309
Tel: 608-266-1371
URL: http://www.dhfs.state.wi.us/Programs/Records/vitlindex.htm

Wisconsin on the Web

Wisconsin GenWeb Project
http://www.tc.umn.edu/nlhome/m125/thar0018/wi/

Wisconsin Land Records—Interactive Search
http://searches.rootsweb.com/cgi-bin/wisconsin/wisconsin.pl

WYOMING

ARCHIVES, STATE & NATIONAL

National Archives-Rocky Mountain Region
Denver Federal Center, Building 48
P.O. Box 25307
Denver, CO 80225-0307
Tel: 303-236-0817
Fax: 303-236-9354
Email: archives@denver.nara.gov
URL: http://www.nara.gov/nara/regional/08nsgil.html

Wyoming State Archives and Historical Department
Division of Archives
State Office Building, Lower Level
6101 Yellowstone Road
Cheyenne, WY 82002
Tel: 307-777-7826
Fax: 307-777-7826
URL: http://commerce.state.wy.us/CR/Archives/

GENEALOGICAL SOCIETIES

Albany County Genealogical Society
P.O. Box 6163
Laramie, WY 82070

Cheyenne Genealogical Society
c/o Laramie County Library
2800 Central Avenue
Cheyenne, WY 82001

Converse County Genealogical Society
c/o Raylee Blankenbaker
119 North 9th Street
Douglas, WY 82633

Fremont County Genealogical Society
c/o Riverton Branch Library
1330 West Park Avenue
Riverton, WY 82501

Laramie Peekers Genealogy Society of Platte County
c/o Cindy Anderson
1108 21st Street
Wheatland, WY 82201

Natrona County Genealogical Society
P.O. Box 9244
Casper, WY 82601

Park County Genealogy Society
P.O. Box 3056
Cody, WY 82414

Powell Valley Genealogical Club
P.O. Box 184
Powell, WY 82435

Sheridan Genealogical Society, Inc.
c/o Sheridan County/Fulmer Public Library
Wyoming Room
335 West Alger Street
Sheridan, WY 82801

Sublette County Genealogy Society
P.O. Box 1186
Pindale, WY 82941

HISTORICAL SOCIETIES

Albany County Historical Society
Email: amyml@uwyo.edu
URL: http://www.uwyo.edu/ahc/achs/index.html

Fort Phil Kearney/Bozeman Trail Associaton
P.O. Box 5013
Sheridan, WY 82801

Lincoln County Historical Society
Kemmerer, WY 83101

State Historic Preservation Office
6101 Yellowstone Road, 2nd Floor
Cheyenne, WY 82002
Tel: 307-777-7697
Fax: 307-777-6421
URL: http://commerce.state.wy.us/cr/SHPO/

Union Pacific Historical Society
P.O. Box 4006
Cheyenne, WY 82003
URL: http://www.uphs.org/uphs.html

Wyoming State Historical Society
1740H184 Dell Range Road
Cheyenne, WY 82009

LDS FAMILY HISTORY CENTERS

Afton Family History Center
365 Jefferson Avenue
Afton, WY 83110
Tel: 307-886-3905

Casper Family History Center
3931 West 45th
Casper, WY 82604
Tel: 307-234-3326

Cheyenne Family History Center
Laramie County Library
2800 Central Avenue
Cheyenne, WY 82001
Tel: 307-634-3561
Fax: 307-634-2082
TDD: 307-634-0105
URL: http://www.wsl.state.wy.us/wyld/libraries/larm/

Cody Family History Center
1407 Heart Mountain Street
Cody, WY 82414
Tel: 307-587-3427

Diamondville Family History Center
512 McGovern Avenue
Diamondville, WY 83116
Tel: 307-877-6821

Evanston Family History Center
1224 Morse Lee Street
Evanston, WY 82930
Tel: 307-789-2648

Gilettte Family History Center
1500 O'Hara
Gillette, WY 82716
Tel: 307-686-9177

Green River Family History Center
220 Shoshone Avenue
Green River, WY 82935
Tel: 307-875-3972

Jackson Hole Family History Center
420 East Broadway
Jackson, WY 83001
Tel: 307-733-6337

Laramie Family History Center
1219 Grand Avenue
Laramie, WY 82070
Tel: 307-745-3234

Lovell Family History Center
50 West Main
Lovell, WY 82431
Tel: 307-548-2963

Lyman Family History Center
Highway 410
(/2 mile north of Urie Interchange)
Lyman, WY 82937
Tel: 307-786-4559

Rawlins Family History Center
117 West Kendrick Street
Rawlins, WY 82301
Tel: 307-324-5459

Riverton Family History Center
North 4th West and Elizabeth Drive
Riverton, WY 82501
Tel: 307-856-5290

Rock Springs Family History Center
2055 Edgar Street
Rock Springs, WY 82901
Tel: 307-362-8062

Sheridan Family History Center
2051 Colonial Drive
Sheridan, WY 82801
Tel: 307-672-8611

Worland Family History Center
434 North Sagebrush Drive
Worland, WY 82401
Tel: 307-347-8958

ARCHIVES/LIBRARIES/MUSEUMS

Albany Public Library
310 S. 8th Street
Laramie, WY 82070-3969
Tel: 307-721-2580
Email: ssimpson@will.state.wy.us
URL: http://www-wsl.state.wy.us/wyld/libraries/alby/

Buffalo Bill Historical Center
Harold McCracken Research Library
720 Sheridan Avenue
Cody, WY 82414
Tel: 307-587-4771
Email: hmrl@wave.park.wy.us
URL: http://www.truewest.com/BBHC/index.htm

Casper College
Goodstein Foundation Library
Special Collections
125 College Drive
Casper, WY 82601
Tel: 307-268-2680
Fax: 307-268-2682
Email: cspcbibman@wyld.state.wy.us
URL: http://www.cc.whech.edu/library/sc.htm

Goshen County Public Library
2001 East A Street
Torrington, WY 82240
Tel: 307-532-3411

Laramie County Library
2800 Central Avenue
Cheyenne, WY 82001
Tel: 307-634-3561
Fax: 307-634-2082
TDD: 307-634-0105
URL: http://www.wsl.state.wy.us/wyld/libraries/larm/

Laramie Plains Museum
603 Ivinson Avenue
Laramie, WY 82070
Tel: 307-742-4448

National Historic Trails Interpretive Center
(Still in the planning stages)
500 N. Center Street
Casper, WY 82601
Tel: 307-265-8030
URL: http://w3.trib.com/~rlund/NHTIC.html

National U.S. Marshals Museum
Wyoming Territorial Prison and Old West Park
975 Snowy Range Road
Laramie, WY 82070
Tel: 800-845-2287
307-745-6161
Fax: 307-745-8620
Email: prison@lariat.org
URL: http://www2.wyoprisonpark.org/OldWest/WTPMarshals.html

Park County Library
1057 Sheridan Avenue
Cody, WY 82414
Tel: 307-587-6204

Platte County Public Library
Wyoming Room
904 9th Street
Wheatland, WY 82201
Tel: 307-322-2689
307-322-2783
Fax: 307-322-3540
URL: http://www-wsl.state.wy.us/wyld/libraries/plat/

Riverton Branch Library
1330 West Park Avenue
Riverton, WY 82501
Tel: 307-856-3556

Riverton Museum/Research Library
700 E. Park Avenue
Riverton, WY 82501
Tel: 307-856-2665
Email: ljost@wyoming.com
URL: http://www.wyoming.com/~RIVERTON/musintro.htm

Rock River Museum
131 Avenue C
Rock River, WY 82058
Tel: 307-378-2386

Sheridan County/Fulmer Public Library
Wyoming Room
335 West Alger Street
Sheridan, WY 82801
Tel: 307-674-8585
Fax: 307-674-7374
URL: http://www-wsl.state.wy.us/wyld/libraries/sher/

Sweetwater County Historical Museum
County Courthouse, Ground Floor
80 West Flaming Gorge Way
Green River, WY 82935
Tel: 307-872-6435
URL: http://www.wwcc.cc.wy.us/community/sweetwater/museum/index.html
or http://monhome.sw2.k12.wy.us/projects/museum.html

Teton County Historical Center
1005 Mercell Avenue
P.O. Box 1005
Jackson, WY 83001
Tel: 307-733-9605

Teton County Library
320 S. King
P.O. Box 1629
Jackson, WY 83001
Tel: 307-733-2164
URL: http://www-wsl.state.wy.us/wyld/libraries/tetn/

Uinta County Library
701 Main Street
Evanston, WY 82930
Tel: 307-789-2770

University of Wyoming
American Heritage Center
Centennial Complex
2221 Willett Drive
P.O. Box 3924
Laramie, WY 82070
Tel: 307-766-4114
307-766-2570
Fax: 307-766-5511
URL: http://www.uwyo.edu/ahc/ahcinfo.htm

Western Wyoming Community College Library
2500 College Drive
Rock Springs, WY 82902-0428
Tel: 307-382-1700
Fax: 307-382-7665
URL: http://www.wwcc.cc.wy.us/college/library/

Wyoming State Library
Division of the Department of Administration and Information
Supreme Court and State Library Building
2301 Capitol Avenue
Cheyenne, WY 82002-0060
Tel: 307-777-7281
Fax: 307-777-6289
URL: http://www.wsl.state.wy.us/

Yellowstone National Park Museum
P.O. Box 168
Yellowstone National Park, WY 82190
Tel: 307-344-2262
URL: http://www.cr.nps.gov/csd/collections/yell.html

Newspaper Repositories

University of Wyoming Library
P.O. Box 3334, University Station
Laramie, WY 82071
Tel: 307-766-3224
Email: ftacij@uwyo.edu
URL: http://www.uwyo.edu/lib/coemf.htm#wyonews

Vital Records

Division of Health and Medical Services
Vital Records
Hathaway Building
Cheyenne, WY 82002
Tel: 307-777-7591
Fax: 307-635-4103
URL: http://wdhfs.state.wy.us/vital_records/DEFAULT.HTM

Wyoming on the Web

Oregon/California Trails Association (OCTA)
http://bobcat.etsu.edu/octa/octahome.htm

Oregon/California Trails Association (OCTA)/Wyoming Chapter
http://w3.trib.com/~rlund/treks.html

Stannary of Wyoming
http://plains.uwyo.edu/~lcurtis/index.htm

Wyoming GenWeb Project
http://www.dsenter.com/wyoming/